A HISTORY OF ENGLISH LITERATURE

Volume IV

(In Four Volumes)

by

Chen Jia

The Commercial Press

1988 · Beijing

YĪNG GUÓ WÉN XUÉ SHǏ

英 国 文 学 史

第 四 册

陈 嘉 著

商 务 印 书 馆 出 版
（北京王府井大街 36 号）
新华书店北京发行所发行
北京第二新华印刷厂印刷
ISBN 7-100-00195-1/G·61

1986 年 2 月第 1 版	开本 850×1168 1/32
1988 年 2 月北京第 2 次印刷	字数 530 千
印数 9,600 册	印张 17 ⁵/₈

定价: 2.85 元

Contents

Chapter IX
ENGLISH LITERATURE OF EARLY TWENTIETH CENTURY

i

Chapter Nine

ENGLISH LITERATURE OF EARLY TWENTIETH CENTURY

SECTION I INTRODUCTION

a. Historical Background: Political and Social.

While the two Jubilees celebrating respectively the 50th and the 60th anniversary of Queen Victoria's reign in 1887 and 1897 testified to the height of political and military power for the British Empire, the Boer War of 1899-1902, between the British colonialists in South Africa and the two independent republics of Dutch settlers, the Orange Free State and the Transvaal Republic, marked the precipitant decline in Britain's prestige and prosperity. The bankruptcy of British rural economy beginning from the 1870s grew more acute in the early years of the 20th century, and England was no longer the most important workshop of the world by 1900, being surpassed or equalled by her rival powers the U.S.A. and Germany in many fields of industrial output. In the meantime, finance capital rose to great prominence and much surplus capital owned by the British financial oligarchy was exported as loans and investments to British colonies and to foreign countries instead of being used to replenish the backward machinery in Britain's domestic factories and plants. Three large-scale strikes in the years 1911-1914, by more than 200,000 railwaymen and three million coalminers and over 80,000 transport workers in London, came with the formation of the Labour Party and the spread of the theories of socialism among the British workers. On the European scene the newly emerged imperial powers Germany and Italy clamoured for more colonies, and the triple alliance of Germany, Austria and Italy was formed with their cry for the redivision of the world, while the triple entente lining up England and France with Russia was negotiated in opposition to the Central European powers. The First World War finally broke out in 1914, leading to four years of intense trench warfare in Western Europe and to widespread fighting in colonies and semi-colonies in Africa and Asia.

Britain emerged from World War I in 1918 as a victor, yet she was very much impoverished and weakened. The establishment of the Irish Free State in 1922 and the granting of Dominion status to Canada, Australia, New Zealand and South Africa one after another shook the foundations of the British Empire,while the United States began to dominate the world economically, politically and militarily in Britain's place. On the domestic scene, Britain's rural economy grew worse and her industrial equipment became old-fashioned and lagged behind that of the U.S.A. and Germany and even Japan, and large-scale unemployment and general economic depression resulted. The U.S.S.R. emerged in 1917 and the joint efforts of Britain and a dozen other capitalist countries to intervene militarily and politically and to stifle the newborn socialist state ended in failure. Though the general strike of 1926 lasted only a few days, yet in 1929 the great economic depression started in the U.S. and spread quickly to the whole capitalist world in Western Europe, and in 1931 a coalition of the so-called Nationalist Government was formed to meet the financial crisis threatening Britain.

In the Twenties fascism began in Italy under Mussolini and the Italian invasion of Abyssinia was condemned but nothing was done about it. In the early Thirties the rise of Hitler in Germany posed a major threat to all Western Europe as the "Anschluss" of Austria and the occupation first of the Sudetenland and then of the whole of Czechoslovakia showed clearly the Nazis' ambitions for world conquest. Chamberlain had to resign with the failure of his conciliation program, while the Civil War in Spain that provided the testing ground for the conflict between republicanism and fascism resulted in victory for Franco who had the support of Hitler and Mussolini. Preparations for war led to the building of the Maginot Line and the Siegfried Line of defence respectively by France

2

and Germany. The talks between the British and French Governments with the Soviet Union broke off and Japan allied herself with Germany and Italy to form the Axis. The Second World War became inevitable and the Nazi invasion of Poland in 1939 triggered off the world-wide conflagration.

The great political, economic and military upheavals in the first four decades that ushered in two big wars of world proportions naturally had their strong and indelible impact upon the general culture in Europe and upon the literary scene in Britain.

b. General Cultural Background

The rapid development of science and technology in the last years of the 19th century and the early decades of the 20th led on the one hand to great gains in material wealth and large-scale agricultural and industrial production, but on the other hand it resulted in world-wide economic depression and mass unemployment and particularly wholesale massacre and destruction brought about by World War I. Much skepticism and disillusionment spread among the whole post-World-War-I generation and Oswald Spengler's book "The Decline of the West" voiced the common sentiments of distrust in the modern Western civilization while in the field of literature T.S. Eliot's "The Waste Land" in both title and content echoed the despair and despondency prevalent among the intellectuals in the two decades following 1918. Many educated people turned to conservatism, to traditional Christian religion, to Catholicism, some even to Oswald Mosley's fascist camp, while many others, attracted to Marxism and to the Soviet regime now firmly entrenched in Russia under Lenin and Stalin, turned to the Left, to socialism and communism, with not a few going to Spain to join the International Brigade fighting for republicanism there against Franco. The 1930s, sometimes known as the Red Decade, ended abruptly with the signing of the Non-Aggression Pact between Hitler and Stalin in 1939, on the eve of World War II.

The influence of the theory of evolution advanced by Charles

Darwin in the mid-19th century spread far and wide, and the orthodox Christian belief in God and the Creation of the World was gradually replaced either by complete atheism or by faith in all sorts of myths of Oriental or Occidental origin. In the field of psychology, the influence of Carl Jung and especially of Sigmund Freud, the Austrian physician with his theory of the subconscious mind and dreams, which effected a drastic change in one's understanding of human consciousness in connection with human conduct, was both broad and penetrating to many British authors of the 20th century, particularly those of the 1920s like Joyce and Virginia Woolf with their "stream-of-consciousness" method in prose fiction.

Following the Education Act of 1870 that first rendered elementary education compulsory and universal, the steadily growing rate of literacy among the masses of people not only created in 20th-century Britain a very large public of vastly varying literary standards and personal tastes, but also produced more writers from the ranks of the labouring people and a greater number of literary works depicting the life of the oppressed and exploited multitude. The fight for equality of women with men, which manifested itself early in 1882 with the passage in British Parliament of the Married Women's Property Act, was followed by the admission of women to the British universities and then by the winning of women's suffrage first in 1918 and fully in 1928.

c. English Poetry: 1900-1940

The first four decades of the twentieth century was a great period for English poetry. At the turn of the century there were the imperialist songs of Rudyard Kipling and the pessimistic poems of A. E. Housman. In the first two decades of the new century Thomas Hardy who had been one of the major novelists in the late Victorian age became a distinguished poet with his numerous volumes of verse that dilated more or less on the same themes of chance and irony in human existence that had prevailed in his works of prose fiction. W. B. Yeats who had begun his poetic career in the

1890s by following the French symbolists and Arthur Symons' aestheticism turned to old Irish myths for inspiration and wrote not only poems but also many verse dramas as he plunged into his self-imposed task of managing and producing plays for the Irish Abbey Theatre in Dublin. The two poet laureates Robert Bridges and John Masefield both produced some few poems of note, but Bridges' major contribution to English poetry lies in his introduction to the world in 1922 of the posthumous poems of Gerard Manly Hopkins whose too fervent religious faith forbade him the publication of his verse in his own lifetime. Hopkins thus curiously resembles Emily Dickinson of America in being a poet of the 19th century whose influence was only felt in the early twentieth, and Hopkins was popular with a number of English poets of the 1920s and 1930s not only for his intense interest in nature and his search for spiritual guerdon in religion, but also for his innovations in verse, with his "sprung rhythm" and alliterative devices. But the numerous poets who wrote and lived and enjoyed minor fame in the first thirty years of the twentieth century were usually known as "Georgian Poets" (more with disapprobation than esteem) and war poets (some of them were also regarded as among the Georgian Poets), and a few were of the school of Imagism. The Georgian Poets were not limited to those whose poems appeared in the five successive anthologies published by Edward March under the title of "Georgian Poetry", nor did they all write verse that contained the characteristics of tameness, imprecision and overornamentation. Some few of them, like Walter de la Mare and W.H. Davies, could occasionally rise to classic succinctness. The war poets were generally of two groups; a few of them (Rupert Brooke, Julian Grenfell, etc.) sang hymns of patriotism glorifying the heroic sacrifices of war for national defence, while a larger number (Siegfried Sassoon, Wilfrid Owen, Isaac Rosenberg, etc.) detailed the miseries of trench warfare and condemned the barbarity and cruelty of mass massacre. Imagism flourished more in the United States than in England, coming as a sort of reaction to Georgianism by emphasizing hardness, clearness and conciseness and boasting chiefly of the anthology "Des Imagistes" (1914) and "Some Imagist Poets" edited by Ezra Pound and prefaced by Richard Aldington, and of T.E. Hulme as the theorist of the movement. But all these were but minor poets attaining each to his or her own degree of excellence, though their formidable total output calls for our attention and careful anthologizing.

Even in the 1910s a new star has risen in English poetry, T. S. Eliot, who came from the United States but settled down in England, and whose eventual naturalization and profession of Anglo-Catholicism turned him into an English poet. Though on account of his great fame he was claimed by many also as an American poet, yet what he wrote about was chiefly of England and his influence was certainly greater in Britain than on the other side of the Atlantic. From his early mild satires on high society in England in his "Prufrock" volume, he sank deep into post-war pessimism in "The Waste Land", though in the latter poem there were already unmistakable signs of his turning to religion for solace. His last poems, especially "The Four Quartets", showed definitely his religious and philosophic bent, though his last efforts at verse drama, written and staged after World War II, demonstrated his great skill in blending with expert care religious themes and comic stage effects, in definite departure from his earlier and soberer "Murder in the Cathedral". Otherwise, Eliot also was an important literary critic. In the meantime, the other giant writing poetry in the English language, W.B. Yeats, turned gradually from Irish mythology and ancient Irish legends to modern political Ireland (in "Easter, 1916", etc.) and finally to the world of art which he specified as the proper haven for the aged (in "Sailing for Byzantium" and "Byzantium"), but he always kept his aristocratic pose and went in for old castles and occultism.

In the 1930s a group of outstanding poets headed for the Left in their protest against the fascism springing up on the Continent, headed by W.H. Auden and flanked by two Irishmen, Louis MacNeice and Cecil Day Lewis, and by Stephen Spender who once briefly joined the British Communist Party and went to Spain on the Republican side in the Civil War. However, after the outbreak of World War II in 1939, they lost their radical political enthusiasm and went their several ways. Auden remained a poet of importance though he became naturalized as an American and his later verse dealt almost entirely with American reality, so that he went in the reverse direction of T.S. Eliot and became more an American than a British poet.

Another poet of note who had a long career lasting from the twenties to the sixties was the Scottish singer of humble origins and radical inclinations, Hugh McDiarmid (pseudonym of Christopher Murray Grieve). He wrote much of his verse in Scots dialect and some in English, and in his three "Hymns to Lenin" and his poems on Glasgow and Edinburgh, and especially in his early masterpiece "A Drunk Man Looks at the Thistle", he showed his eulogy of socialism and his condemnation of capitalist Edinburgh and Glasgow, and above all, his patriotism toward Scotland and the Scottish people. His long years of stay in a remote island north of Scotland cultivated his love of wild nature and his philosophical mood toward simple natural objects and simple people living far away from civilization. Another Scottish poet of minor importance who had the same humble family background as McDiarmid is Edwin Muir whose disillusionment with modern Western civilization such as he witnessed in Glasgow led him back in his poetry to simple country life close to nature and to ancient myths and religious beliefs.

One of the poets of World War I whose remembered war poems are those written long afterwards and who is known now chiefly for his poems on romantic love and on certain philosophical and ironical topics, is Robert Graves. In contrast to Graves' long literary career of several decades, Dylan Thomas of Wales led a short, meteoric existence as he flourished from the mid-Thirties to the early Fifties with his poems dealing chiefly with his experience in boyhood and youth. He had a lyrical gift and was known for the strange violence of his imagery and for the alliteration and internal rhyming which he learned from Gerard Manly Hopkins.

In the first half of the 20th century, there were a few other minor poets in England who deserve our passing mention here. The most important of the three Sitwells, Edith Sitwell, exerted considerable influence in reacting against the sentimentality of literary "Georgianism" in her serialised anthology of poetry, entitled "Wheels" (1916—1921), displayed her exaggerated rhythmic and metaphorical effects in her volumes of "Facade" and "The Sleeping Beauty" in the 1920s, mimicked the breakdown of Western material civilization in "Gold Coast Customs" in 1929, and ended up in the 1940s with her aristocratic pose of a prophetic commentator after she joined Roman Catholicism. Then there was D.H. Lawrence who was chiefly a novelist yet who turned out a number of brilliant poems many of which had to do with the plant and animal world and the poet's sympathy for it but a few of which dealt with his keen observation of human existence in such poem as "Piano" and "How Beastly the Bourgeois Is."

The great figures in English poetry in the early decades of the 20th century were then, Thomas Hardy and W.B. Yeats in the early years, and T.S. Eliot flourished from the 1920s to the 1940s, with Yeats sharing the honours and W.B. Auden and Hugh McDiarmid making their important contributions. The host of minor poets were legion, and as they vied with one another in distinction and merit in some special way or other, they enriched the field of poetry in the modern period at least to compete on equal terms with the Victorian Age.

d. English Drama: 1900—1940

After the flowering of English comedy in the last decades of the 19th century, which boasted of the brilliant comedies of Oscar Wilde, Arthur Wing Pinero and Henry Arthur Jones, George Bernard Shaw started his long dramatic career of nearly half a century with his "Unpleasant Plays" which included two powerful pieces "Widowers' Houses" (1892) and "Mrs. Warren's Profession" (1892) trumpeting their indictment of terrible economic exploitation through landlordism and prostitution. Though both plays were banned after a few performances, they remained Shaw's most radical dramas as he followed in the path of Ibsenism with these problem plays. The series that followed, the "Pleasant Plays", including chiefly "Arms and the Man" and "Candida", contained much more diluted satire. "Major Barbara" was the only piece of the playwright's later dramas that touched on the theme of economic exploitation but the clever ending of awry humour took the edge off the reprimand of the gunpowder king that was noticeably suggested at the beginning. Shaw's growing popularity that came with his many striking plays through the first four decades of the new century, from "John Bull's Other Island" (comment on the English exploitation of Ireland) to "Man and Superman" (the life-force theory), from "Pygmalion" (on the wonders of speech changes upon a Cockney flower-girl) to "Back to Methuselah" (a fantasy from 4004 B. C. through the 1920s all the way to 21920 A.D.) and from "St. Joan" (on Jeanne d'Arc) to "The Apple Cart" (on modern British politics), showed the clever dramatist to be a consistent master of wit and paradoxes but his influence waned with the passage of time.

At about the same time as Shaw, John Galsworthy and James Matthew Barrie also flourished with their dramas. Galsworthy was better known as a novelist but his realistic plays on legal problems and on industrial strikes ("The Silver Box", 1906; "Strife", 1910) brought him great fame as he showed much sympathy for the industrial workers, ordinary clerks and domestic servants who suffered under the unjust laws and low wages of the time. Barrie, on the other hand, excelled in fantasy, starting his successful career with "Peter Pan" about "the boy who wouldn't grow up",(1904) and reaching his height of fame with "The Admirable Crichton" (1902) and "What Every Woman Knows" (1908), both filled with humour and common sense. But Barrie's popularity ended with the First World War and he was all but forgotten after the 1930s.

In Ireland the founding of the Abbey Theatre in Dublin in 1904 brought much lustre to a whole series of Irish playwrights including W.B. Yeats, Lady Gregory, Lennox Robinson, St. John Ervine, and Sean O'Casey but especially starring John Millington Synge whose "Riders to the Sea" (1904), "The Playboy of the Western World" (1907) and the unfinished "Deirdre of the Sorrows" (published in 1910), attained to heights of lyric comedy or depths of ironic tragedy. Yeats and Lady Gregory, as the earlier participants of the Irish Literary Renaissance, introduced Irish myths and folk legends with much adroitness while Sean O'Casey's early plays "Juno and the Paycock" (1924) and "The Plough and the Stars" (1926), took us to the miseries of the Irish lower classes in Dublin during their fight for national independence.

In the meantime, in the London theatres, Harley Granville-Barker as actor-dramatist-producer distinguished himself with his brand new problem-plays, especially "The Voysey Inheritance" (1905) and "The Madras House" (1910), as he also was a producer of modern dramas of Continental dramatists Ibsen, Maeterlinck and Hauptmann as well as a critic of Shakespearean drama ("Prefaces to Shakespeare", 1927—1947). Granville-Barker's plays are often formless in plot but they usually achieve skilful characterization and brilliant dialogue. In contrast to Granville-Barker's plays of artistic finesse, there were the popular comedies of W. Somerset Maugham who followed the tradition of comedies of manners of the Restoration and the eighteenth century by providing cleverly-manipulated situations and witty dialogue, but the themes were generally conventional and insignificant and except in one or two of his later comedies (e.g. "The Circle") the characters were tame and not well drawn. He too flourished as a dramatist chiefly in the first twenty years of the century.

A passing mention should be made of William Archer as a famous dramatic critic who was known for his efforts in introducing Ibsen to the English audience and at popularizing Shaw and whose services as a dramatist historian and critic were outstanding in the early decades of the 20th century.

Provincial drama in England flourished in Birmingham and Manchester chiefly in the years before 1920. In the Gaiety Theatre in Manchester there were memorable performances of "Hindle Wakes" (1912) by Stanley Houghton and "Hobson's Choice" (1916) by Harold Brighouse, whereas in Birmingham Repertory Theatre there were "Abraham Lincoln" (1918) and "Birdin Hand" (1918) by its manager John Drinkwater, "The Farmer's Wife" (1924) by Eden Phillpotts that won the record run of 1300 performances, and the successful romantic love drama about the Brownings, "The Barretts of Wimpole Street" (1930) by Rudolf Besier.

In the 1920s and 1930s, a rival to W. Somerset Maugham in the field of popular comedies of witty dialogue and ingenious situations was Noel Coward (1899—1973) who won great theatrical successes with "The Vortex" (1923), "Hay Fever" (1925), "Private Lives" (1930) and "Design for Living" (1933) in amorous comedies but who also distinguished himself in other genres such as the operatta ("Bitter Sweet", 1929), the chronicle-pageant ("Cavalcade", 1931) and the farce ("Blithe Spirit", 1941) and showed his versatile talent in acting, singing and composing of songs besides playwriting. However, like Maugham's comedies, Coward's light dramas of sophistication and amorality appealed only to the decadent fashionable society of the inter-war years and they failed to achieve true and lasting artistic excellence.

A Scottish medical doctor and director of the Scottish National Theatre Society as well as founder of Glasgow Citizen's Theatre, James Bridie (pseudonym of Osborne Henry Mavor, 1888—1951), wrote in the 1930s and 1940s some forty plays which included chiefly biblical themes in modern dress and a few of which scored stage successes. His best known play "Tobias and the Angel" (1930) tells a fantastic tale set in ancient times in the Middle East and involving the outwitting of a demon with a charm and the actual disguise of Archangel Raphael as a Porter, while another supernatural drama, "Mr. Bolfry" (1943), unfolds the hair-raising story of a conjuration of the devil who appears as Mr. Bolfry and whose umbrella that has been left behind him "gets up and walks by itself out of the room" in the morning following the dreadful nightmare of all present at a minister's manse in the Scottish Highlands. A third play of note is "The Anatomist" (1930) which was based on an actual Burke and Hare murder case in Edinburgh in 1928, and here an atmosphere of horror and mystery is well blended with the everyday scenes of lectures on the anatomy of human bodies and of practice in surgical dissection. Bridie's strong sense of the theatre was the saving grace that in these better plays of his mends the flaws in his technical craftsmanship and gains credence from the audience for his apparently unbelievable stories of supernatural presence.

A minor novelist in his own right, Christopher Isherwood (1904—) collaborated in the 1930s with W.H. Auden in the writing of three plays, among which the tragedy "The Ascent of H6" (1937) is the better known and deals with the struggle for far-away colonial possessions between two imperialist nations that ends in destruction of an expeditionary mountain party by an avalanche. Another playwright who flourished in the 1930s and 1940s was Christopher Fry (pseudonym of Christopher Harris,1907—),whose plays in verse and prose deal frequently with medieval, religious themes. His early one-acter, "The Boy with a Cart" (produced in 1937 and published in 1939), deals with a local saint who eventually builds a church with miraculous aid. But he is chiefly known for his verse comedy "The Lady's Not for Burning" (performed in 1948, published in 1949). The year is supposed to be near 1400 A.D., and the story starts with a discharged soldier Thomas Mendip who accuses himself of murder, and with a woman Jennet Jourdemayne who is accused of being a witch for having turned into a dog a poor trader of rags and bones. As the Mayor decides to burn Jennet but hesitates to hang Mendip, the poor trader Matthew Skipp appears, neither murdered by Mendip nor turned into a dog by Jennet. So Jennet is set free and Mendip leaves the town with her. The play is further enriched by a comic underplot involving the two sons of the mayor's sister and the mayor's clerk and a girl loved by all three of the young men. The eloquent verse was highly praised and the comedy was a prolonged success on the stage.

T.S. Eliot, the great poet, was possibly the most outstanding playwright after Shaw and Galsworthy and the Irish dramatists of the Abbey Theatre. Following his early attempts in drama, that included "Sweeney Agonistes" (subtitled "Fragments of an Aristophanic Melodrama", 1932) and "The Rock" (a religious pageant-play, 1934), he wrote for the Canterbury Festival in 1935 an important religious play in verse, "Murder in the Cathedral", in which he celebrated the martyrdom of St. Thomas à Becket by combining the chorus and the myth element of classical Greek tragedy with the use of allegory in the medieval Morality Play. Then in the two decades of 1939—1959, Eliot displayed his great religious enthusiasm and his acquired dramatic talent in a series of four verse plays on contemporary themes that demonstrated both his deep Christian convictions of sin and expiation and his adroit mastery of the theatre: "The Family Reunion" (1939), "The Cocktail Party" (1949), "The Confidential Clerk" (1953) and "The Elder Statesman" (1959). The solemn and versatile poet became in his later plays also the earnest but successful dramatist.

e. English Prose Fiction: 1900—1940

In the early years of the twentieth century, prior to World War I, there were five well-known novelists vying with one another in England. There was the outstanding figure Joseph Conrad who was born in Poland and did not start learning the English language till eighteen years of age but who published his great novels "Lord Jim" in 1900, "Heart of Darkness' in 1902 and "Nostromo" in 1904, each dealing with the hero's intense mental conflicts over some moral problem set against a remote colonial background and containing subtle undertones indicting colonialism. There was on the other extreme, among the apologists of imperialism and colonialism, the Indian-born Rudyard Kipling who began with journalism and poetry and short stories in the last years of the 19th century wrote at least one important novel, "Kim" (1901), which tells of the titular boy-hero's multi-coloured experience as he served the British Secret Service in India under cover of travelling into the Indian hills with a Tibetan lama. Though the book gives a rather faithful and vivid account of the various strata of Indian life, it preaches flagrantly one of the insidious ways by which the British rulers dominated the Indian sub-continent. Then in between there were the three native-born-and-brought-up writers John Galsworthy, Arnold Bennett and H.G. Wells. Galsworthy with his Harrow and Oxford background was the spokesman of the English upper class who in his novels and dramas (especially in his two trilogies on the Forsytes, "The Forsyte Saga" and "A Modern Comedy") described truthfully the propertied class in late Victorian and Edwardian society, and whose first important novel "The Man of Property" (1906) that established his fame contained with some satirical thrusts on the aristocratic and business world of London which were however somewhat diluted by his humour and sympathy. Arnold Bennett came of a shopkeeper's family in the Midlands pottery towns and wrote chiefly of the tame lower-middle-class life in the provinces in the prosaic, naturalistic vein, but his gift in lifting the major figures, Constance and Sophia Baines in "The Old Wives' Tale" (1908) and Henry and Viola Earlforward in "Riceyman Steps" (1923), from their humdrum existence into "round characters" (Bennett's own word) of flesh and blood, with all their subtle inner workings of mind traced step by step as the few events in the tales are unfolded, cannot fail to win distinction for the novels as masterful records of "little men" and their vicissitudes of life in Edwardian and early Georgian England. H.G. Wells emerged from even humbler origins than Bennett and became one of the earliest science-fiction writers and an author of radical social novels. With the rapid progress in science and technology Wells' science fiction, like "The First Man in the Moon" (1901), dates terribly, but his social novels: "Kipps" (about a "little man" and his accidentally-won fortunes, published

1905), "Tono-Bungay" (about a poor boy turned scientist and his uncle selling fake patent medicine, 1909), "Ann Veronica" (about an emancipated woman and a defiant suffragist of the 1900s, 1909) and "The History of Mr. Polly" (about the adventures and misadventures of a young bankrupt shopkeeper, published 1910), though they were past records of the Edwardian era, yet contained some mild social satire on the struggle of the lower-class individuals for upward mobility in England in the 1900s.

Of these five novelists, Conrad is the only one who has survived the test of time and now still is regarded as a first-rate writer of 20th-century prose fiction. But in pre-war England these five novelists and their major works dominated the field of prose fiction though the three last novels of Henry James which appeared contemporaneously in the first years of the new century "The Wings of Dove" (1902), "The Ambassadors" (1903) and "The Golden Bowl" (1904), and which were so vastly different in theme as well as in plot and prose style, earned much greater fame after World War II with their intricate descriptions of the doings of the idly rich but cultured circles of England and America, and with their subtle psychological analysis and artful literary exuberance they took the fancy of post-war reading public.

In the second decade of the 20th century, there were a number of newcomers onto the scene. Some of them were simply popular writers of fiction, like Hugh Walpole (1884—1940) who first won his popularity with his story of two schoolmasters in a private boarding school ("Mr. Perrin and Mr. Traill", 1911) and P.G. Wodehouse (1881—1975) who became extremely well known in the English-speaking world with his series of humorous novels of absurdly farcical situations round about the wealthy aristocrat Bertie Wooster and his inimitable butler Jeeves (in the series beginning with "My Man Jeeves" in 1919). There was the sadly ignored Dorothy Richardson (1873—1959) who first brought the stream-of-consciousness method into English fiction with her "Painted Roofs" (1915) which became the first of a series of thirteen linked novels eventually collected under the title of "Pilgrimage" (1938). There were the two short-lived brilliant short story writers H.H. Munro (1870—1916), born in Burma, and known under his pseudonym "Saki", and Katherine Mansfield (pseudonym of Kathleen Mansfield Beauchamp, 1888—1923), from New Zealand. "Saki" wrote a few novels of some importance ("The Unbearable Bassington" in 1912, a bitter satire on the shallow, pleasure-seeking upper-class men and women), but his short stories ("Reginald", 1904; "The Chronicles of Clovis", 1911; and "Beasts and Superbeasts", 1914) were famed for the humour, epigrammatic wit and penetrating satire in them. Katherine Mansfield was a much greater figure than Saki; she was one of the best writers of short stories in the English language. Her first book of stories, "In a German Pension", was based largely on the experience of her childhood and early youth in New Zealand, but her two best-known collections, "Bliss" (1920) and "The Garden Party" (1922), contained most of her subtle psychological studies of super sensitive characters that are carefully portrayed often with only a few significant touches.

There was also the appearance of a true working-class novel by a housepainter Robert Tressell (pseudonym of Robert Noolan, 1868—1911) whose "The Ragged Trousered Philanthropists" was first published in an abridged form in 1914 to serve as an important document of indictment of economic exploitation that led to terrible miseries for the workers and their families.

There were also three novelists of outstanding significance: Ford Madox Ford (1873—1939), W. Somerset Maugham (1874—1965) and E.M. Forster (1879—1970). Ford Madox Ford (who wrote under the name of Ford Madox Hueffer up to 1921) collaborated with Conrad in the novel "The Inheritors" in 1901, and then wrote his Tudor Trilogy (beginning with "The Fifth Queen", 1905) that dealt with the story of Katherine Howard, and first distinguished himself with "The Good Soldier" (1915) in which Ford tried, like Conrad, to experiment with the technique of oblique reportage, by making the protagonist of the novel, John Dowell, also its narrator, to take the place of the traditional role of the omniscient author. But Ford's most notable work was generally supposed to be the sequence of war novels, the tetralogy ("Parade's End") centering on Christopher Tietjens, son of a Yorkshire landowner and containing "Some Do Not" (1924), "No More Parades" (1925), "A Man Could Stand Up" (1926) and "Last Post" (1928). The whole series covers the period from 1910 to the post-war world and the story is narrated backwards and forwards, with numerous flashbacks to break up chronological sequence, and with external events interlaced with inner meditation and agitation. Ford's novels have been increasingly appreciated since the Second World War. Maugham who began his literary career by being a very successful playwright in the 1900s produced in the 1910s two of his great novels "Of Human Bondage" (1915) which was semi-autobiographical and "The Moon and Sixpence" (1919) which was somewhat based on the life of the famous French painter Paul Gauguin. Another important novel of his, "Cakes and Ale", came in 1930. Forster, reputed to be one of the Bloomsbury Group of intellectuals in the post-1918 period, wrote from 1905 to 1910 his four early novels ("Where Angels Feared to Tread", 1905; "The Longest Journey", 1907; "A Room with a View", 1908, and "Howards End" 1910) to censure middle-class respectability and snobbery and to advocate human sympathy and mutual understanding, but whose last and most important novel, "A Passage to India", a powerful exposé of racial discrimination in British colonial rule in India, did not appear till 1924.

In the 1910s, two of the great novelists of "Modernism", D.H. Lawrence (1885—1930) and James Joyce (1882—1941) wrote their first important semi-autobiographical works, "Sons and Lovers" (1913) and "A Portrait of the Artist as a Young Man" (1916) respectively, to be followed by their masterpieces "The Rainbow" (1915) and "Women in Love" (1921) and "Ulysses" (1922) and "Finneganns Wake" (1939).

The 1920s were marked by the most mature works of the three

"Modernist" novelists D.H. Lawrence (with his "Women in Love'"), James Joyce (with his "Ulysses") and Virginia Woolf (with her Mrs. Dalloway", 1925, and "To the Lighthouse", 1927), and by Forster's masterpiece "A Passage to India", Katherine Mansfield's best short stories as well as Aldous Huxley's height of achievement, "Point Counter Point" (1928), a powerful, all-round exposé of the decadent aristocrats and intellectuals of post-war England.

A few minor novelists of the 1920s should be briefly mentioned here in passing. There was Richard Aldington (1892—1962) who, besides being an active participant as a poet in the Imagist movement in the 1910s, also produced a most typical war novel, "Death of a Hero" (1929), with its bitter denunciation of the folly and destructiveness of the imperialist war of 1914—1918.

Rose Macaulay (1881—1958) won her popularity with "Potterism" (1920) in which through the portrayal of the chief characters Mr. Potter the press magnate and Mrs. Potter the none-too-successful novelist the author satirized the folly and stupidity as well as the greed and the hypocrisy and many other foibles in the post-war society. "Told by an Idiot" (1923) is a stronger satire on a Victorian parson as he shifts his belief successively from the Anglican Church to Roman Catholicism, and to Dissent, to Agnosticism, to Christian socialism, and so on, from the year 1879 to 1923. The author stands by as a sceptic while the observations of the clergyman's changes by his wife and his six children are sardonically recorded. Macaulay also wrote a historical novel of a sort, "They Were Defeated", supposedly to tell the story of the 17th-century poet Robert Herrick, a country vicar who wrote famous love lyrics.

David Garnett (1892—1981), son of the well-known critic, Edward Garnett, was chiefly known for his first novel, "Lady into Fox" (1922), a short fantasy novel that tells of a woman living in Oxfordshire in 1880 suddenly turned into a small bright red vixen that gradually acquired animal habits, disappeared and reappeared with five cubs, and was finally killed by hunters and hounds, while the husband remained faithful and loving to the woman after her transformation and even to the cubs.

T.F. Powys (1875—1953), the most outstanding of the three Powys brothers that included J.C. Powys (more a literary critic and lecturer than a novelist, 1872—1963) and Llewellyn Powys (more a writer of travel sketches and essays than a novelist 1884—1939), wrote chiefly in the 1920s about rural life in Dorset where he led a secluded existence almost all the time, but he has been remembered since chiefly for his novel "Mr. Weston's Good Wine" (1927) in which God himself appears in a village on a November evening as a travelling wine merchant selling "Good Wine" and "Dark Wine" and accompanied by his angelic assistant Michael and which told of various villagers as well as the unbelieving village pastor and his daughter Tamar. This was obviously a specimen of escapist fiction though the sins and foibles of many village people are described with ironic humour.

The 1930s, sometimes known as the Red Decade on account of the popular swing of many intellectuals toward the Left, contained a few novels on working-class life by two working-class writers in Scotland and Wales. There was in Scotland Lewis Grassic Gibbon (pseudonym of James Leslie Mitchell, 1901—1935) who was born and brought up in rural Aberdeenshire and Kincardineshire and who wrote a trilogy of novels, "A Scots Quair"(1946), consisting of "Sunset Song" (1932), "Cloud Howe" (1933) and "Gray Granite" (1934) and dealing with Scottish life of three generations of a family of peasants and workers first in a village, then in a provincial town and finally in an industrial city. There was a Welsh minor-novelist Lewis Jones (1897—1939) who wrote two novels on the active struggle between the miners and the mine-owners: "Cwmardy" (1937) and "We Live: The Story of a Welsh Mining Valley" (1939).

Joyce and Virginia Woolf continued to turn out their novels in the 1930s while Maugham and Aldous Huxley wrote well into 1940s, but their best works had already appeared in the 1920s. Now, in the fourth decade of the present century a host of new novelists emerged. Wyndham Lewis (1884—1957) began publishing prose fiction on Bohemian life in Paris in 1918 ("Tarr") but he reached maturity with his "Apes of God" (1930) in which he ridiculed the artists' circles of the 1920s. Joyce Cary (1888—1957), born in Ireland and educated at Oxford, spent long years holding jobs in Nigeria and started writing African novels in the 1930s, achieving success in 1939 with "Mister Johnson" which was about a Nigerian clerk engaged in all sorts of adventures but finally condemned to death for robbery and murder. Cary continued to write two trilogies in the 1940s and 1950s, and the most significant of the six novels, "The Horse's Mouth"(1944), narrates in first person singular the story of a visionary artist Gully Jimson who has no care for money or morality and leads a wretched life of many misadventures but who is a great comic figure consumed by his lifelong passion for his eccentric paintings. Ivy Compton-Burnett (1892—1969), a novelist of upper-class life in country houses in late Victorian and Edwardian periods, started writing in the 1920s ("Pastors and Masters", 1925; "Brothers and Sisters", 1929) and continuing through the 1930s ("Men and Wives", 1931; "More Women than Men", 1933; "A House and its Head", 1935; "Daughters and Sons", 1937; "A Family and a Fortune", 1939) and 1940s ("Parents and Children", 1941; "Elders and Betters", 1944; "Manservant and Maidservant", 1947) all the way down to the 1950s ("Darkness and Day", 1951; "Mother and Son", 1955; "A Father and His Fate", 1957). Her novels have often been compared with her best-liked author Jane Austen's in that they deal chiefly with human relationships, or rather relationships between different members of a family, and out of the moral preoccupations shared by Austen and Compton-Burnett there is much underlying satire beneath the many conversations filled with humour and sprinkled over with wit. Like Austen, her limited personal experience in life necessarily narrows down her scope of narration, but unlike Austen, down below the surface respectability of the characters, Compton-Burnett's fiction reflects more serious crimes of murder, incest and forgery that are more peculiar to the modern world. Leopold Hamilton Myers (1881—1944) is known chiefly for his tetralogy (published together as "The Near and the Far" in 1943 but appearing separately as "The Near and the Far", 1929; "Prince Jali", 1931; "Rajah Amar", 1935; "The Pool of Vishnu", 1940), with its setting in India in the 16th century, under the rule of Emperor Akbar. Instead of treating the whole as a historical novel, Myers described the political intrigues in India of far away and long ago with the object of making them reflect the perplexing issues of the modern West, but this was not always successfully managed and so Myers' fiction has since been much neglected.

Elizabeth Bowen (1899—1973), born in Dublin of Welsh extraction, began her career as novelist and short story writer in the 1920s ("The Hotel", 1927, and "The Last September", 1929, both novels dealing with children as major characters), but it was in the 1930s, with her novels "The House in Paris" (1935) and especially "The Death of the Heart" (1938), that Bowen attained to maturity in her special field of fiction, i.e., on the miseries of the adolescents. "The Death of the Heart" gave a detailed account of Portia Quayne's life from her orphaned girlhood to her wandering existence of unbefriended youth, as the author poured out her sympathy for the poor, ridiculed and deluded girl tossed from her uncongenial step-brother and his wife to the shallow, flirtatious person who rejects her after pretending to be in love with her.

Another minor novelist who flourished chiefly in the 1930s but who is now much forgotten (though he kept on writing popular fiction till 1950s and 1960s) was A.J. Cronin. He was born in Scotland, studied and practiced medicine in the 1910s and 1920s, then abandoned his medical career for literature and distinguished himself particularly with two of his early novels, "The Stars Look Down" (1935) and "The Citadel" (1936), the first dealing sympathetically with the Scottish miners in their struggle against their capitalist bosses and the second having to do with the experience of a medical doctor who was faced with a lifelong conflict of whether medical science should be used to serve humanity or simply to secure personal profit in wealth and reputation. "The Citadel" once achieved great popularity with the general reading public.

There were in the late 1920s and early 1930s a number of writers who in their disillusionment and dissatisfaction with the drift of material civilization in the West turned to religion for their spiritual comfort, and some of them joined Catholicism. T.S. Eliot joined the Anglican Church which he chose to call "Anglo-Catholic", while two younger writers, Evelyn Waugh (1903—1966) and Graham Greene (1904—   ) joined the Roman Catholic Church, Waugh in 1927 and Greene in 1930. Both of them won fame as important novelists, and many of their novels fell under the influence of their religious faith. Waugh's two early novels, "Decline and Fall" (1928) and "Vile Bodies" (1930),were satires on the high society in London, but his later fiction, like "Brideshead Revisited", while still exposing the lives of sin and debauchery led by members of a Catholic family, revealed nevertheless their strong, recurrent religious fervour which became a sort of dominant obsession with them. In the case of Graham Greene, his novels are mostly concerned with the adventures of Catholic believers some of whom may even commit terrible crimes of murder and gangsterism (e.g. "Brighton Rock", 1938) while others would even risk their lives in order to do what a devout Catholic should do (e.g. "The Power and the Glory", 1940).

Then there was the unusual case of a writer George Orwell (1903—1950), who first turned to the Left and wrote about his experience of living among the poor and the unemployed workers in the industrial areas of the West (e.g. "Down and Out in Paris and London", 1933; "The Road to Wigan Pier", 1937) and even joined the Spanish Civil War on the republican side, but his later disillusionment made him change into an anti-communist writer, when he wrote "Animal Farm" (1945) and "Nineteen Eighty-Four" (1949), both being fierce attacks on the Soviet Union and specially on Stalin.

J.B. Priestley (1894—) has been known as a popular novelist as well as a playwright. His best known novel, "The Good Companions", tells a vivacious tale of three odd characters, an elderly carpenter dismissed from his job, a young teacher of music, also discharged from school, and an oldish spinster left alone with some little money, meeting a company of travelling theatrical troupe, and of their vicissitudes of successes and failures on the road. The substance is thin, but the story is most entertaining and the narrative style is intriguing. It is somewhat Dickensonian in that it is filled with humour and occasionally it leads to uproarious laughter. Another novel, less popular, was entitled "Angel Pavement", which deals with the humdrum life of a number of employees in a small business concern in London and with the appearance of an unexpected adventurer who for some time averts the financial ruin of the company but whose unscrupulous behaviour is finally exposed with his sudden disappearance. The innocent lower-middle-class people in London are here described with much sympathy.

Finally, a few words should be said about the rise of the detective story as a popular branch of prose fiction in the 20th century. At the turn of the century Sir Conan Doyle (1859 — 1930) first flourished with his Sherlock Holmes stories. But the new genre gained its momentum in the 1920s and 1930s, with the many inventive murder mysteries of Agatha Christie (1890—1975) and of Dorothy Sayers (1893—1957).

The above is a general picture of English prose fiction in the years 1900—1940. Some few of the more prominent novelists and their works will be discussed more in detail.

The march of prose fiction proceeded during and after the Second World War, and the novelists flourishing after 1940 are not touched upon in this historical survey, as it is obvious they yet have to stand the test of time.

f. English Prose (Essays and Biographies): 1900—1940

English essays of the light and informal type flourished mainly in the early decades of the 20th century. They followed more or less the tradition of familiar essays of early 19th century, such as those written by Lamb and Hazlitt and De Quincey, and also by Leigh Hunt and Walter Savage Landor. They were not essays on literary criticism or for moral edification or practical information or for other serious purposes, but they were written essentially to provide entertainment, and so humour was the dominant factor, accompanied by an abundance of witty and ironic remarks, and whatever satire that might occasionally lurk behind the clever and paradoxical and cynical observations was generally very light and airy and even hardly noticeable.

The most outstanding and the wittiest of these essayists was Max Beerbohm (1872—1956) who had been associated with Arthur Symons and Aubrey Beardsley and the "Yellow Book" of the 1890s and who in the sixty years of his career (from 1896 to 1956) as a brilliant essayist launched his ironic parodies and satirical comments on men and manners in his urbane and felicitous style ("Yet Again", 1909; "And Even Now", 1921; "Things New and Old", 1923; "Zuleika Dobson", 1911; "A Christmas Garland", 1912, etc.). Beerbohm was also a caricaturist with his satirical drawings, ("Caricatures of Twenty-Five Gentlemen", 1896; "Observations", 1925), and worked together with Bernard Shaw as a dramatic critic for the "Saturday Review" (1898—1910), his articles in which magazine were later selected and revised under the title of "Around Theatres" (1924, 1953). His parodies of contemporary authors in "A Christmas Garland" included such well-known writers as Bernard Shaw, George Meredith, George Moore, Henry James, Hardy, Conrad, Wells, Bennett, Galsworthy, Kipling, and other essayists Chesterton, Belloc, A.C. Benson, Frank Harris, and Edmund Gosse.

G.K. Chesterton (1874—1936) and Hilaire Belloc (1870—1953), two close friends who were both Catholics and poets as well as essayists (Chesterton's "Tremendous Trifles", 1909; "The Uses of Diversity", 1920; "Generally Speaking", 1928; "As I Was Saying", 1936; and Belloc's "On Nothing", 1908; "On Everything", 1909; "On Anything", 1910; "On Something", 1910) have generally been mentioned together in literary histories (Shaw once called them "The Chester-belloc"). However, Chesterton was better known because he was also a novelist ("The Man Who Was Thursday", 1908 and his "Father Brown" detective stories evolving round a Roman Catholic priest detective) and a biographer (including his biographies on Browning, Dickens, Shaw, Thackeray, Cobbett, Stevenson, Chaucer, St. Francis of Assisi and St. Thomas Aquinas), and because he voiced his strong political views both against Toryism and Imperialism (as represented by Kipling) and against "socialism" (as represented by Shaw and Wells).

Another important essayist of early 20th century was E.V. Lucas (1868—1938) who as a biographer and disciple of Charles Lamb was partly responsible for the revival of interest in the familiar essay as a literary genre. His volumes of essays include: "Fireside and Sunshine" (1906), "Character and Comedy" (1907), "Loiterer's Harvest" (1913), "Adventures and Enthusiasms" (1920), "Events and Embroideries" (1926) and "Adventures and Misgivings" (1938). Mentioned together with Lucas was Robert Lynd (1879—1949) who came from Belfast, Ireland and whose essays were also very definitely in the tradition of Charles Lamb, full of humour and sentiment ("The Pleasures of Ignorance", 1921; "I Tremble to Think", 1936; "Life's Little Oddities", 1941).

Familiar essays waned after the 1920s, and what came nearest to them were the two volumes of "The Common Reader" (1925 and 1932) by Virginia Woolf which were actually critical works though written in the easy-going and conversational style of the light essays.

Many biographies were written in the earlier half of the twentieth century, but mention needs to be made here only of Lytton Strachey (1880—1932) who belonged to the Bloomsbury Group and whose two brilliant biographies, "Eminent Victorians" (1918) and "Queen Victoria" (1921) started a new fashion for the writing of biographies which was followed on the European Continent by Emil Ludwig (1881—1948) in Germany with his "Napoleon" (1927), "Bismarck" (1927) and "Goethe" (1928) and by Andre Maurois (1885—1967) in France with his "Ariel: The Life of Shelley" (1924). 'Eminent Victorians" which has generally been considered superior to "Queen Victoria" contained several very brilliant biographical essays on outstanding figures in the Victorian age, such as General Gordon, Florence Nightingale, Cardinal Manning and Dr. Thomas Arnold, and in these essays Strachey tried to consider a biographer an artist who must choose and rearrange the events in the life of the person described instead of merely accumulating details of biographical facts as was usually done in the past. And this was his new approach that made Strachey's works popular and started the new tradition of inserting human elements into biography. Actually, writing in this way necessarily pulls the heroic figures of history down from their pedestals by making them appear more like ordinary human beings and at the same time relieves the readers from the dull monotony of year-by-year accounts of minute details such as were generally given in formal biographies.

SECTION II ENGLISH POETRY: 1900—1920

a. Four Minor Poets at the Turn of the Century: Robert Bridges, John Masefield, Rudyard Kipling, A.E. Housman.

There were many English poets of some distinction who flourished in the first two decades of the 20th century. Before taking up Thomas Hardy and W.B. Yeats as well as the three groups of "Georgian Poets", the war poets and the imagist poets, four minor poets of the period deserve brief discussion: Rudyard Kipling (1865—1936) and A.E. Housman (1859—1936) who started writing verse before 1900, and then the two poet-laureates Robert Bridges (1844—1930) and John Masefield (1878—1967) who were both known and remembered chiefly for a few short lyrics which were written at the turn of the century.

Bridges was born of a prosperous landed family and educated at Eton and Oxford. He received training in medicine and beginning from 1874 he actually practised as a physician for several years. However, he retired from the medical profession on account of poor health, travelled in Europe and the Middle East and started publishing five volumes of "Shorter Poems" before 1893. These were followed by more ambitious poems such as two sequences of sonnets, two masques, and eight plays and in 1913 he was appointed Poet Laureate. In 1918 he made his important contribution to poetry by being instrumental in the first and posthumous publication of the poems of his friend Gerard Manly Hopkins. In his old age he published a philosophical poem of over 4000 lines, "The Testament of Beauty" (1929), elaborating on the testimony of Beauty that God is Love and experimenting with his loose unrhymed Alexandrines which are measured by the number of syllables rather than by accentuation. His finest lyrics of his earlier years were deservedly popular and were often anthologized (e.g. "Nightingales", "London Snow", "A Passer-by"). The first nine lines of "London Snow" are especially admirable specimens of leisurely and carefully drawn descriptions of snowfall in his experimental verse of loose metres:

> "When men were all asleep the snow came flying,
> In large white flakes falling on the city brown,
> Stealthily and perpetually settling and loosely lying,
> Hushing the latest traffic of the drowsy town;
> Deadening, muffling, stifling its murmurs failing;
> Lazily and incessantly floating down and down.
> Silently sifting and veiling road, roof and railing;
> Hiding difference, making unevenness even,
> Into angles and crevices softly drifting and sailing."

Here the influence of Gerard Manly Hopkins is distinctly visible, in the occasional alliterative effects and in the irregular number of syllables in regular accentual lines, but the more important achievement of the poem is the rich, highly ornamented descriptive sketch that reveals Bridges' aesthetic impression of the snow storm as it fell.

John Masefield had an early wish for experience at sea and was from his youth apprenticed on ships and sailed to distant parts of the world. He took various odd jobs abroad, including serving as a bar attendant and working in a carpet factory. In 1897 he returned to England and started the career of a writer, first contributing light essays and articles to London periodicals and the "Manchester Guardian". His first collection of poems, "Salt-Water Ballads", came out in 1902, to be followed by "Ballads and Poems" (1910) and narrative poems such as "The Everlasting Mercy" (1911), "Dauber" (1913) and "Reynard the Fox" (1919), all of which won differing degrees of popularity. Especially "The Everlasting Mercy", which deals with a drunken poacher turning from his debaucheries in pubs and with women to religious conversion to Christianity, created quite a sensation with the public upon its first appearance, though it only contains a goodly number of explosive lines of near-blasphemous speech curiously mixed with religious fervour that are rather effective both artistically and metrically, such as:

"I drank, I fought, I poached, I whored,
I did despite unto the Lord."

Masefield also dabbled in dramas and novels, but his lasting fame rests almost solely on his earlier poetry having to do with nautical life. "Cargoes" and "Sea Fever" are two of his better known pieces, of which the last stanza from the latter is particularly celebrated, with the long anapaest line and the true zest for vagrant life on the seas:

"I must down to the seas again to the vagrant gipsy life,
To the gull's way and the whale's way where the wind's like a whetted knife;
And all I ask is a merry yarn from a laughing fellow-rover,
And a quiet sleep and a sweet dream when the long trick's over."

A poet better known and more influential than either Bridges or Masefield was Rudyard Kipling whose novels and stories and poems belonged mostly to the last years of the 19th century though he wrote his most widely read novel "Kim" in 1901 (to be dealt with later) and he lived on till 1936. He began his successful poetic career with his "Departmental Ditties" as early as 1886, but it was not till the publication of "Barrack-Room Ballads" (1890, 1892) that he really attained to maturity as a poet. He was often regarded and denounced as the poet of British imperialism which was most clearly visible in the poem "Recessional", a hymn he wrote in celebration of Queen Victoria's Diamond Jubilee in 1897. Here, writing in the solemn tones of a religious hymn to be sung at a church service, the poet of imperialism recounts the past glories of the vast empire and then, asking for the help of God, warns against any possible forgetfulness of what he calls imperial duties, "Lest we forget — lest we forget!"

"God of our fathers, known of old —
Lord of our far-flung battle-line —
Beneath whose awful hand we hold
Domination over palm and pine —
Lord God of Hosts, be with us yet
Lest we forget — lest we forget!"

In "The White Man's Burden" Kipling crystalized his propaganda for colonialism with the high-sounding theory of the White colonialists not extending their colonial rule for their own interests but rather to bring civilization to the natives who are barbarous and unable to govern themselves. In his well-known poem "The Ballad of East and West" he somewhat disguised the imperialist relationship between the East and the West or between the British imperialists and the colonial people by refuting the saying that "East is east, west is west, and never the twain shall meet", and substituted it with another myth that there is only the difference between the strong and the weak. But the real upshot of the story told in the "Ballad" is the strong man of the East eventually becoming the willing servant of the strong man of the West after they meet and find out about each other's strength.

Kipling not only sang about the justice as well as the glories of imperialism and colonialism, but as a true defender of imperialist interests he even showed his worries about the possible decline of colonialism and warned the ruling class to take care and guard well their imperial interests. So in a poem like "Mary Gloster", the strong, iron-handed old pirate of a father is described as a true hero who warns his weak son against growing soft and infirm in a parasitic existence. Of course many of his poems were written from the point of view of the rank and file in the British army stationed in India as they voiced their personal thoughts and feelings. In "Danny Deever", it is about the common soldiers' feelings of dread in watching the hanging of their fellow combatant, Danny Deever. In "Mandalay", it is about a demobbed soldier yearning for the East and his Burma girl there. But these impassioned expressions of rollicking balladry and cockneyed accents showing at once the poet's admiring and patronizing attitude toward these private soldiers serving in the Orient are the chief reasons for the great charm and popularity of Kipling's verse, such as:

"But that's all shove be'ind me — long ago an' far away,
An' there ain't no 'buses runnin' from the Bank to Mandalay;
An' I'm learnin' 'ere in London what the ten-year soldiers
   tells:
"If you've 'eard the East a 'callin', you won't never 'eed
   naught else',"
         (from "Mandalay")

and:

"What makes the rear-rank breathe so 'ard?' said Files-on-
  Parade.
'It's bitter cold, it's bitter cold,' " the Colour-Sergeant said.
'What makes that front-rank man fall down?' said Files-
  on-Parade.
'A touch o' sun, a touch o' sun', the Colour-Sergeant said,
  They are hangin' Danny Deever, they are marchin' of
  'im round,
  They 'ave 'alted Danny Deever by 'is coffin on the
  ground;

30

An' 'e'll swing in 'arf a minute for a sneakin' shootin'
hound—
O they've hangin' Danny Deever in the mornin'!"

A. E. Housman (Alfred Edward Housman) went to Oxford but
failed in his final examination in 1881, and in 1882 he had to serve
as a civil servant in the Patent Office in London. In the meantime
he spent all his leisure time in classical studies until he became
famous as a classical scholar, and in 1892 he was appointed Professor of Latin, first at London University(1892—1911)and then at
Cambridge (1911—1936). He was recognized as one of the greatest
English classicists and gained his high reputation as an unchallenged
editor and critic of Latin poets Manilius, Juvenal and Lucan, with
his meticulous attention to minute texual problems. His first book
of verse, "A Shropshire Lad" appeared in 1896 and won almost
instantaneous acclaim. But his next slim volume, "Last Poems",
came many years later, in 1922, to be followed by "More
Poems", published shortly after his death in 1936 by his brother
Laurence Housman, himself a poet and also a playwright, and
containing poems generally inferior to those in the two earlier volumes.

Housman's total poetic output was small, yet he exerted immense popularity and much influence both during his lifetime and
afterwards. His solitary, secluded and apparently unhappy life
had its stamps on his poetry which was full of pessimism and
cynicism, accentuating on the brevity of life and the general sadness of human existence. Occasionally he seemed to touch on the
"Gather Ye Rosebuds" theme, but his enjoyment of the present
was almost invariably dampened by his melancholic temperament.
In "When I Was One-and-twenty", the last two lines of the second
stanza serving as an answer to the last two lines of the first stanza
show clearly Housman's ironic comment on human disillusionment that comes all too quickly with the fleeting of time even in
one's youth:

"When I was one-and-twenty,

No use to talk to me."
And then:
> "And I am two-and-twenty,
> And oh, 'tis true, 'tis true."

And this idea of fleeting youth naturally leads to the thoughts of death. So in the short poem of only two stanzas "With Rue My Heart Is Laden", the author laments his boy-and-girlfriends of the past who were now dead and buried:

> "With rue my heart is laden
> For golden friends I had,
> For many a rose-lipped maiden
> And many a lightfoot lad.

> By brooks too broad for leaping
> The lightfoot boys are laid;
> The rose-lipped girls are sleeping
> In fields where roses fade."

The extreme simplicity and conciseness with which these lamentations are conveyed added much to the sadness of the poet.

The poet also wrote about soldiers dying in war:

> "Far and near and low and louder
> On the roads of earth go by,
> Dear to friends and food for powder,
> soldiers marching, all to die."

This is his indictment of imperialist wars.

But death is not the only foe of human beings. There are many woes attending those who are alive. Housman even wished to be "drunk forever" in order to rid himself of the sufferings he had to endure when sober.

> "Could man be drunk forever
> With liquor, love, or fights,
> Lief should I rouse at morning
> And lief lie down of nights.
> But men at whiles are sober

> And think by fits and starts,
> And if they think, they fasten
> Their hands upon their hearts."

On the other hand, for those who find pleasure in living, the life span of a normal person is all too short, and especially youth goes almost unnoticeably and so even a man of seventy does not have much time to enjoy himself. So in "Loveliest of Trees", the poet speaks for a lover of nature:

> "Now, of my threescore years and ten,
> Twenty will not come again,
> And take from seventy springs a score,
> It only leaves me fifty more.
> And since to look at things in bloom
> Fifty springs are little room,
> About the woodlands I will go
> To see the cherry hung with snow."

Housman was under the influence of ancient Greek and Latin lyric poetry and also of the traditional ballads, and his classical scholarship taught him to strive always for succinctness and lucidity in his verse. He deserves best to be remembered of the group of four minor English poets at the turn of the century.

b. Gerard Manly Hopkins

Gerard Manly Hopkins (1844—1889) plays a strange role in the historical development of English poetry. Similar to Emily Dickinson in American poetry, Hopkins lived and wrote in late 19th century but his poems were not published till well into the 20th century, and though his sentiments were essentially Victorian, the influence of his verse upon the British poets were nevertheless considerable in the 1920s and 1930s.

Born of a very religious High-Anglican family of considerable means, Hopkins studied classics at Oxford and fell much under the influence of the Oxford Movement which meant chiefly the revival of ritualistic and dogmatic Christianity within the Anglican Church

under the leadership of John Henry Newman. Then, after New-
man eventually embraced Catholicism, Hopkins also joined the
Roman Church in 1866 and was ordained as a Jesuit priest in 1877.
In 1884 he was also appointed Professor of Classics at University
College, Dublin.

Hopkins was also interested in painting and music, but was
particularly attracted to poetry. However, for some time he felt
it difficult to reconcile his duties of a religious profession with his
career of a poet, and he even burned his poems finished prior to his
conversion to the Society of Jesus and he only picked up the
writing of poetry once again in and after 1875. But he refused to
have his poetry published during his lifetime, and so the first
edition of his poems did not come out till 1918 with the help of
his close friend Robert Bridges who became poet laureate in
1913.

Hopkins' poetry all has to do with his thoughts and sentiments toward the Christian religion. His best known poems either
reveal his fervent belief in the Christian God or unfold his poignant
feelings in intense spiritual conflict between implicit faith and latent
skepticism typical of many intellectuals of the Victorian age. Perhaps the most admirable of his poems for the general reader of
today are those dealing with the poet's wonder at the world of nature which he believed to be the handiwork of his God. His
best known and often anthologized sonnets such as "Spring",
"God's Grandeur", "The Starlight Night", "The Windhover"
and "Pied Beauty", are very beautiful hymns addressed to
nature, whether the specific reference be to the Spring season, to
sunset and dawn, to the stars, to a falcon or to the multicoloured
plant and animal world (e.g. "Dappled Things"), and we find in
them the poet's child-like wonder and adoration that eventually
and inevitably leads to his worship of God who is somehow responsible for all these beautiful objects of the natural world. The
pictures of nature or natural objects in the poems are generally
very subtly and intricately woven, and Hopkins' fervent belief in

the Christian God is ever present with all its warmth and intoxication. And there is often a strange sort of lyricism in some of his haunting lines of imperishable beauty, such as the first eight lines in the sonnet entitled "Spring":

Nothing is so beautiful as Spring —
　　　When weeds, in wheels, shoot long and lovely and lush;
　　　　　Thrush's eggs look little low heavens, and thrush
　　　Through the echoing timber does so rinse and wring
　　　The ear, it strikes like lightnings to hear him sing;
　　　　　The glassy peartree leaves and blooms, they brush
　　　　　The descending blue; that blue is all in a rush
　　　With richness; the racing lambs too have fair their fling.

or the first eight lines in the sonnet entitled "The Starlight Light":

Look at the stars! look, look up at the skies!
　　　look at all the fire-folk sitting in the air!
　　　The bright boroughs, the circle-citadels there!
Down in dim woods the diamond delves! the elves' eyes!
The grey lawns cold were gold, where quickgold lies!
　　　Wind-beat whitebeam! airy abeles set on a flare!
　　　Flake-doves sent floating forth at a farmyard scare! —
Ah well! it is all a purchase, all is a prize.

Or the first four lines of another sonnet "Hurrahing in Harvest":

Summer ends now; now, barbarous in beauty, the stooks rise
Around; up above, what wind-walks! what lovely behaviour
Of silk-sack clouds! has wilder, wilful-wavier
Meal-drift moulded ever and melted across skies?

And there are many such enchanting lines in Hopkins' verse that celebrate the poet's wonder at the world of nature not unsimilar on the one hand to early Middle English nature lyrics like "Sumer is icumen in" and on the other echoing Keats' "Ode on Autumn", but this wonder at earthly beauty in Hopkins' case invariably leads to his thoughts of Christian God and fills his heart with devotion, as we find in the last sextet of one of his most famous lyrics "God's Grandeur":

> And for all this, nature is never spent;
> There lives the dearest freshness deep down things;
> And though the last lights off the black West went ·
> Oh, morning, at the brown brink eastward, springs—
> Because the Holy Ghost over the bent
> World broods with warm breast and with ah! bright
> wings.

Hopkins was an important innovator of rhythmic verse who experimented with patterns of alliteration, with internal rhymes and with varieties of assonance and he especially developed his theory of "Sprung rhythm". These peculiar characteristics of verse may be seen in the sonnet "The Windhover" which he thought to be his best poem and of which the first eight lines give a vivid description of the windhover, a sparrow-hawk or kestrel that can hover in the wind, even head-on:

> "I caught this morning morning's minion, king—
> dom of daylight's dauphin, dapple-dawn-drawn Falcon,
> in his riding
> Of the rolling level underneath him steady air, and
> striding
> High there, how he rung upon the rein of a wimpling wing
> In his ecstasy! then off, off forth on swing,
> As a skate's heel sweeps smooth on a bow-bend: the hurl
> and gliding
> Rebuffed the big wind. My heart in hiding
> Stirred for a bird, — the achieve of, the mastery of the
> thing!"

As usual, here the poet attributes the beauty of the bird to God, but his innovation of this unusual rhythmic effect of the poem is worth our attention if not our admiration. Of course, in these experiments although Hopkins tried to go back to the Anglo-Saxon and Middle English poetry for inspiration, he was actually very much under the influence of Keats and the PreRaphaelites. However, as his poetry first saw light in the 20th century, many British poets of the Post-World-War-I period supposed him to have derived from the Metaphysical tradition of Donne and showed their allegiance to him in their modernist verse.

Perhaps the most interesting of Hopkins' poems to us are those that reveal the religious poet's inner conflict between inherent faith and intruding doubt. "Thou art indeed just, Lord" is possibly his most effective poem of this category in which he raised a very simple but very difficult question:

"Why do sinners' ways prosper? and why must
Disappointment all I endeavour end?"
Here the poet lays bare his heart before his God (and actually before all his readers), and though in starting he seems to have anticipated the question by affirming "Thou art indeed just, Lord", yet skepticism persists as he rejoins with:

"Oh, the sots and thralls of lust
Do in spare hours more thrive than I that spend,
Sir, life upon thy cause."
and also:

"birds built, but not I build;"
and in the end all he can do is to implore for God's help in a general and mysterious way,

"O thou lord of life, send my roots rain."
This is a most striking poem in the sense that it unfolds unreservedly the innermost spiritual crisis of an extremely devout follower of the Catholic Church in very direct yet also slightly elaborate language through a highly rationalized train of thought. This is very typical of an intellectual turned fervent religious man not only in the Victorian age but at any time and in any place.

Yet another very interesting piece of an earlier day is also worth our attention: "Heaven-Haven", a short poem that in eight simple lines delineates the complete innocence of a nun taking the veil:

> I have desired to go
> Where springs not fail,
> To fields where flies no sharp and sided hail
> And a few lilies blow.
>
> And I have asked to go
> Where no storms come,
> Where the green swell is in the havens dumb,
> And out of the swing of the sea.

Here is a vivid picture of the never-never land of a young innocent nun's dream exquisitely told in simple words so totally different from the usual run of over-ornamented, over-worked verse of Hopkins. Though this quite impossible dream is conceived by the poet to be something that may only occur to a newly initiated nun and so is not to be taken too seriously, yet there were and perhaps still are some very few such novices in certain religious institutions who do actually entertain such beautiful, vain hopes too good to be realizable. Certainly the extreme simplicity of thought and language here is an admirable literary feat comparable to an other-worldly poem like "The Blessed Damozel" by Dante Gabriel Rossetti.

We must not overlook Gerard Manly Hopkins' innovations in verse rhythm and lyricism, nor should we belittle the high tribute paid him by 20th-century poets like W.H. Auden, Stephen Spender, C. Day Lewis and Dylan Thomas as they acknowledged their indebtedness to him.

c. Thomas Hardy

Thomas Hardy's poetry was generally considered of some importance in his lifetime, though in the first half of the present century it was rated as much below his prose fiction in literary excellence. But his poetic reputation has risen in recent years and now he is often regarded as a major English poet, and his more than 900 poems of no great length are almost as great works of art as his many great novels of late 19th century. His only long work in verse,

The Dynasts, which was his "Iliad of Europe from 1789 to 1815", has however been somewhat neglected, partly because this unperformable verse-drama is a bit diffuse and modelled somewhat after the closet dramas of Byron and Shelley, especially in its resemblance to "Prometheus Unbound".

Hardy's short pieces contained in eight volumes were published in a long stretch of 30 years, between 1898 and 1928, while quite a number of poems in the earliest book "Wessex Poems" were obviously written when he was busily engaged in the writing of his novels. This great poetic output dealt with a variety of themes, ranging from impersonal narratives to highly personal emotional pieces, from philosophical speculations to comments on local or international events, and the poet indulges in many different experiments in metre and language, in ballad metre and short-lined verse, in simple rhymes and in occasional alliteration, sometimes in spontaneous language and sometimes in well-chosen diction and even archaic words. But in each poem one gets the feeling that the poet works on it with care and deliberation, never casually or haphazardly though sometimes a bit artificially.

Hardy's poems of political and social content are comparatively few. "Drummer Hodge" was a dirge for a Wessex soldier who was killed in the Boer War (1899—1902) and was buried in the strange distant land of South Africa. "Channel Firing", written in April 1914, was a record of English warships' gunnery practice in the English Channel a few months previous to the First World War, but the narrator of the poem was supposed to be a corpse conversing with other ghosts and commenting on modern warfare as worse than battles in earlier history. One stanza of the poem may be regarded as a comment on all modern wars and all preparations for war:

> "All nations striving strong to make
> Red war yet redder. Mad as hatters
> They do no more for Christ' sake
> Than you who are helpless in such matters."

Then, in "There Was a Great Calm" with a subtitle "On the Sign-ing of the Armistice, November 11, 1918," Hardy quietly records the changes brought about by the armistice, showing the wonder of all the people at the battlefront and in the rear at the sudden end of hostilities but revealing the poet's comment on the unrea-sonableness of war in the last line of the first as well as the last stanza of the poem, where "The Pensive Spirit of Pity Whispered, 'Why'?"

The answer to this "why" is a bitter one:

> "Foes distraught
>
> Pierced the thinned peoples in a brute-like blindness,"

while the propaganda that war was fought to make the world a better one to live in is also answered bluntly;

> "old hopes that earth was bettering slowly
>
> Were dead and damned."

The trench warfare of World War I was dubbed

> "the four years' dance
>
> of Death in the now familiar flats of France"

and the armistice is ironically summed up in the last stanza:

> "Calm fell. From heaven distilled a clemency;
>
> There was peace on earth, and silence in the sky;
>
> Some could, some could not, shake off misery
>
> The sinister spirit sneered: "It had to be."

This reveals again Hardy's idea of fate in human history.

But Hardy's most scintillating comment on war appears in the well-known poem "In Time of 'The Breaking of Nations' ". Here, as World War I was raging, in 1915, Hardy mentioned the simplest actions of ordinary people, a man plowing his field and lovers "come whispering by" as more important because more last-ing than world-wide strife:

> "War's annals will fade into night
>
> Ere their story die."

Human history and important events are subjects for Hardy's verse. He wrote on "The Roman Road", and while remembering the

Roman helmed legionaries who first walked on the Roman Road, he contrasted "its days of Now and Then" and reminisced fondly of his mother guiding "his infant steps", "When/ We walked that ancient thoroughfare,/ The Roman Road." Shortly after the sinking of the famous luxury liner the Titanic in 1912, Hardy wrote "The Convergence of the Twain" (with the subtitle "Lines on the Loss of the 'Titanic'"), and pointed out significantly that it was "The Immanent Will that stirs and urges everything" that made the ship collide with an iceberg. Less importantly, when the poet once witnessed a partial eclipse of the moon, he wrote a sonnet that ended with a philosophical question on human misery and greatness:

"Is such the stellar gauge of earthly show,
Nation at war with nation, brains that teem,
Heroes, and women fairer than the skies?"

Another occasional poem "Lausanne", was written upon his visit to Gibbon's old garden, to commemorate "the 110th anniversary of the completion of the Decline and Fall at the same hour and place" (the subtitle of the poem). Here the poet visualized with great admiration the great historian as the latter finished his great work on Roman history, and deplored the lack of such great minds as worthy of Milton's praise for writers of truth in "Areopagitica". In "The Schreckhorn" written after the death of Leslie Stephen, Hardy recalls his climb up this high peak in the Swiss Alps once with the great essayist and mountain-climber and speaks of his friend affectionately and with admiration. These few examples of Hardy's occasional poetry may illustrate the philosophic bent of the ageing poet who was a skeptic and a pessimist of calm and resignation.

Hardy's great gift of story-telling reveals itself in a number of narrative poems of no great length, in ballad style if not in ballad metre. "A Trampwoman's Tragedy", obviously based on some incident that happened in the 1820s, tells of a tramp-woman who flirted with another travel-companion John in order to tease her lover, but the latter took it in earnest and stabbed and killed John and was later hanged for murder. While the way the story was told and the metre and rhyme resembled very much those of the popular ballads, the mood of pessimism mixed with irony makes one recall Hardy's earlier novels where chance played such an important part in leading to human tragedy. "The Rash Bride" is another tragic love story. Here, John going to serenade a sweet young widow finds her just married to another man Giles Swetman the day before and faints away, and when Giles scolds her for jilting John, she rushes out and drowns herself in the well. The dismal description of her burial at the end of the poem adds to the sadness of the tale. Another example of a ballad-like poem is "Midnight on the Great Western", in which is described a journeying boy travelling all alone in the third class seat on the railway, and the question is raised but not answered as to "to what he was going, or whence he came". This sympathetic attitude toward the lorn boy is almost Wordsworthian, but the ending is typically Hardy's as the poet refers to the "world unknown" for the journeying boy as "this region of sin that you find you in" and vainly hopes for him "a sphere" far above "our rude realm". Yet another ballad-like poem is "The Phantom Horsewoman" in which a queer man sees a vision all the time of "a ghost girl-rider" until he withers away while "Time touches her not". Hardy did not normally believe in the supernaturals but this is a kind of legend common to old ballads.

Hardy wrote many poems of autobiographical content, and among them there were a goodly number in memory of his first wife Emma who died in 1912 and whom he remembered poignantly for their earlier love and later alienation.

In "A Broken Appointment" Hardy blamed her for a broken appointment in the past, he deplored:

"You love not me,
And love alone can lend you loyalty,
I know and knew it."

though he admitted that she once did console him:

"Once you, a woman, came
To soothe a time-worn man; even though it be

You love not me?"
In "The Going", he lamented their recent alienation as he rem-
inisced the past "While Life unrolled us its very best":
"Why, then, latterly did we not speak,
Did we not think of those days long dead,
And ere your vanishing strive to seek
That time's renewal? We might have said,
'In this bright spring weather
We'll visit together
Those places that once we visited'"
Then, after her death he wrote a whole group of poems in 1912—
13 to commemorate her, prefixed with an epigraph from Virgil's
"Aeneid", "Veteris vestigia flammae" (meaning "relics of the old
flame"). Among them, in "I Found Her Out There", he recalled
his visiting her in her native Cornwall in 1870 when they were
both happy and young, and bewailed her being laid to rest in
1912. A year later, in "The Voice", the poet seems to hear her
voice once again and visualized his meeting with her at one time
in the past:
"Let me view you, then,
Standing as when I drew near to the town
Where you would wait for me: yes, as I knew you then,
Even to the original air, blue gown!"
Similarly, in "After a Journey", Hardy again seemed "to view a
voiceless ghost", who brought him back to their "olden haunts",
the waterfall and "the cave just under", "forty years ago", and
as he reminisced he blamed her for their later alienation:
"What have you now found to say of our past—
Scanned across the dark space wherein I have lacked you?
Summer gave us sweets, but autumn wrought division?
Things were not lastly as firstly well
With us twain, you tell?
But all's closed now, despite Time's division."
The most poignant poem of the lot was "The Walk", in which he

showed his missing her in his walks, in simple language:

> "You did not walk with me
> Of late to the hilltop tree
> By the gated ways
> As in earlier days."

Many lines are quoted here from the numerous poems Hardy wrote after his first wife's death, because quite a few of these were among his finest poems in which his true mixed feelings of happiness and regret in his relations with her are expressed very sincerely and in plain, beautiful language.

Hardy never approved of the onrush of modern civilization; he never had real hopes for the future. In one of his early poems, written before December 31, 1900, "The Darkling Thrush", the poet was bidding farewell to the old century and welcoming in the new. He was standing at one gate to watch "all mankind" going back to "their household fires", but

> "The ancient pulse of germ and birth
> Was shrunken hard and dry,
> And every spirit upon earth
> Seemed fervourless as I."

The only joyous note was the "full-hearted evensong" of "an aged thrush, frail, gaunt, and small," and the poem ends on a note of pessimism and irony:

> "So little cause for carolings
> Of such ecstatic sound
> Was written on terrestial things
> Afar or nigh around,"

and if the thrush knew of "some blessed Hope", the poet was unaware of it.

Hardy wrote much on human sufferings and philosophized on them. In "The Subalterns", the various forces, "the leaden sky", "the North", Sickness and Death, that brought misery of all kinds to human beings all made excuses for their malevolence by declaring themselves only the subalterns or junior officers of

some evil Will ruling the universe. Similarly, in "Let Me Enjoy",
the first stanza runs:

"Let me enjoy the earth no less
Because the all-enacting Might
That fashioned forth its loveliness
Had other aims than my delight."

Much more important and representative of Hardy's philosophy
of malign chance controlling the human world is the short poem
"Hap". There is certainly much bitterness expressed here in the
irony of human existence:

How arrives it joy lies slain
And why unblooms the best hope ever sown?
Crass casualty obstructs the sun and rain,
And dicing Time for gladness casts a moan ....
These purblind Doomsters had as readily strown
Blisses about my pilgrimage as pain."

In "The Impercipient", which he composed after attending
a cathedral service, he declared with some regret that he could not
join in the Christian faith with many others.

Many of Hardy's best poems deal with his reminiscences of
the past as an old man. In "Neutral Tones", the remembrance of
a scene of souring love is compared to neutral tones of wood engraving, as the natural phenomena around the lovers are colourless
("the sun was white", the few fallen leaves from an ash tree "were
grey") and

"The smile on your mouth was the deadest thing
Alive enough to have strength to die;
And a girl of bitterness swept thereby
Like an ominous bird a-wing."

"Wessex Heights" records Hardy's feelings for his old
native place where he always called Wessex in his stories and
novels, contrasting it favourably with the towns, and yearns for
the liberty he used to have there and the woman he used to love.
The group of three poems entitled "In Tenebris" (meaning "In

Darkness") all points to the past. The first of the group deals with the poet's memory of my bereavement-pain. The first three stanzas here are among the best, sad but stoical lines written by the pessimist poet:

> Wintertime nighs;
> But my bereavement-pain
> It cannot bring again:
> Twice no one dies.
>
> Flower-petals flee;
> But since it once hath been,
> No more that severing scene
> Can harrow me.
>
> Bird faint in dread;
> I shall not lose old strength
> In the lone frost's black length:
> Strength long since fled.

The short and terse expressions (e.g. "Twice no one dies.", "Flower-petals flee") and well-weighed and purposely archaic words (e.g. "nighs", "hath been", "The lone frost's black length") are most effective here in voicing the poet's despondency on the one hand and his courageous endurance on the other. In the third poem of "In Tenebris", Hardy recalled some of the innocent, happy moments in the past and rather wished that then

> "I well might have passed and the ending have come—
> ...
> Ere I had learnt that the world was a welter of futile doing."

Hardy was always keenly aware of the passage of time. In "Where the Picnic Was", he recalled the scene of a certain picnic in the past, and comparing his visit to the same place now, he lamented that while "We four came" then, "two have wandered far" "where no picnics are" and "one—has shut her eyes." In "The House of Hospitalities", the poet called to mind his former gatherings with his friends here in the house of hospitalities, but

> "Time has tired me since we met here

When the folk now dead were young,
Since the viands were outset here
And quaint songs sung."

...

"Now no Christmas brings in neighbours
And the New Year comes unlit;
Where we sang the mole now labours,
And spiders knit."

Hardy's most pungent comment on the passage of time that stamped him as a thoroughgoing pessimist is a short poem entitled "Going and Staying", which runs thus:

"The mooing sun-shape on the spray,
The sparkles where the brook was flowing,
Pink faces, plightings, moonlit May, —
These were the things we wished would stay;
But they are going.
"Seasons of blankness as of snow,
The silent bleed of a world decaying,
The moan of multitudes in woe, —
These were the things we wished would go;
But they were staying."

Here, the good things mentioned in the first stanza are mostly about nature, while the undesirable things singled out in the second stanza include the miseries of human society such as Hardy witnessed, "a world decaying" and "the moan of multitudes". This significantly shows Hardy's attitude toward the society he lived in, and in a sense serves as a plea for his pessimism.

As many of Hardy's poems were written in his old age, he not infrequently revealed his melancholy thoughts of an old man. In "I Look at My Glass" Hardy bewails the decrease of physical strength in his old age without any diminution in his heart throbbings. In "Heredity", Hardy as a disbeliever in eternal human existence in the soul follows rather the theory of heredity based somewhat on Darwinism by emphasizing the family face as the eternal thing in man:

> "I am the family face;
> Flesh perishes, I live on."

In "He Never Expected Much", which was written on his eighty-sixth birthday, Hardy pretended to have heard since his childhood from the mysterious voice of World that the latter did not promise him overmuch, "just neutral-tinted haps and such", and the poet said World had kept faith with him. In other words, Hardy considered his life as consisting of "neutral-tinted haps", but the most significant part of the poem lies in World's supposed estimate of the different attitudes of human beings toward it.

> "Many have loved me desperately,
> Many with smooth serenity,
> While some have shown contempt of me
> Till they dropped underground."

This is perhaps a much rosier picture of the existing human society by the pessimist poet who in his old age had become respected by the world and therefore rather reconciled to it.

"Afterwards" contained the aged poet's imaginings of what people would say of him after his death. Here the references are only to what happens in the world of nature: the green leaves of May, the alighting of a hawk upon the thorn at dusk, the hedgehog travelling over the lawn in nocturnal blackness, the full-starred heavens in winter, and the evening knell amid the breeze; and the recurring comment that he used to notice all these things makes one wonder whether he was merely suggesting his closeness to nature, to plants and animals and stars or he was actually indicating his abhorrence or at least aversion to human society. There was however a definite note of resignation throughout the poem, as befitting an old man who struggled hard in his youth but who gained recognition and comfort in his ripe age. The bitterness he used to have was now gone, but his pessimism remained in its exhausted state. "Afterwards" is a much eulogized and frequently anthologized poem, but it is a work of a writer of strong social conscience whose fire was dying out.

What Hardy wrote was generally considered traditional poetry — traditional particularly in his use of rhyme and metre and also in his normal treatment of daily life. He was most untraditional, especially for a poet in the first quarter of the 20th century, in being a heathen or agnostic, who openly declared his disbelief in orthodox Christianity, especially in the theory of the Fall of Man which was such a deeply-rooted belief among English and all Western intellectual world through the centuries and which such important 20th-century poets as T.S. Eliot and W.H. Auden in their later life so fervently believed in. It was certainly a courageous thing, even for Hardy as a post-Darwinian to announce to the world in the year 1898, in a poem written at a Cathedral service:

"That with this bright believing band
I have no claim to be,
That faith by which my comrades stand
Seem fantasies to me."

The epigram taken from Gloucester's speech in "King Lear" and prefixed to "Tess of the D'Urbervilles":

"As flies to wanton boys, are we to the gods,
They kill us for their sport."

is so heathen in spirit, that the dominant idea of chance or fate determining human affairs rules out the thought of original sin entirely and hearkens all the way back to the author's belief in the irony of fate such as we witnessed in his first collection of stories significantly entitled "Life's Little Ironies". This emphasis on irony was sometimes even abhorrently and at the same time facetiously expressed, as in "Ah, Are You Digging On My Grave?" where not her former lover or her nearest dearest kin or her enemy but a little dog was digging the dead woman's grave in order to bury a bone there. The bitterness Hardy felt toward the tragic as well as the comic ironies in his world of chance or "hap" was certainly the most dominant thing in his mind and so was everywhere present in his fiction and verse.

However, alongside of his consistent pessimism, Hardy was a stoic and at the same time had his "joie de vivre". In an elegiac mood Hardy wrote "Shut Out that Moon" which begins:

"Close up the casement, draw the blind,
      Shut out that stealing moon,
She wears too much the guise she wore
      Before our lutes were strewn
With years-deep dust, and names we read
      On a white stone were hewn."

and ends:

"Too fragrant was Life's early bloom
      Too tart the fruit it brought."

The suggestion that life may be cruel to you, yet you should endure it, is inherent in this bitterly wrought poem.

Yet Hardy in his younger days especially enjoyed drinking and dancing and love. So in "Great Things", he recalled:

"Sweet cider is a great thing,
      A great thing to me."
"The dance it is a great thing,
      A great thing to me"
"Love is, yea, a great thing,
      A great thing to me."

And he summed up in the last stanza:

"Joy-jaunts, impassioned flings,
      Love, and its ecstasy,
Will always have been great things,
      Great things to me!"

Though Hardy spent a long stretch of his life in London, he was ever fond of country life and always described with gusto the simple landscape in the countryside or the suburbs. So in his "Snow in the Suburbs" written in 1915, a vivid scene of a big snowstorm is drawn, and the effect of snow on the trees and pavements, and on a sparrow and a cat, is quietly and very meticulously given, but not a word touching human beings. This is again evidence that especially as he grew older he fell himself closer to nature and more sick of human society, so that in his descriptions of the natural world he did not want to refer to the human part in it.

Hardy was a lyricist, though his verse was never so smooth or mellifluous. He adopted the ballad metre quite often and in his early verse he frequently wrote short lines, with echoes of Skelton, though occasionally he wrote very long lines (e.g. "Afterwards", "The Rash Bride"). He almost always employed rhymes which seemed to come easy with him, almost effortless. He usually made careful choice of words that prevented the easy flow of his verse, but once in a while he used very simple language and achieved delightful Skeltonic rhythm, as in "I Need Not Go", "I Found Her Out There" and "In Tenebris, I". "I Need Not Go" ended with:

> "New cares may claim me
> New love inflame us,
> She will not blame me,
> But suffer it so".

And "In Tenebris, I" contained such lines as "Twice no one dies" and "Flower petals flee".

Some critics suggest that there was something "modernist" in Hardy's poetry, this is true particularly in his adoption of the ballad metre and Skeltonian lines and in his meticulous choice of words and expressions (including archaic ones) that makes him resemble Auden in some ways. What truly distinguishes him from the other important poets of the 20th century (including T. S. Eliot, Yeats and Auden) is his open rejection of Christian faith or any belief in magic or spiritualism. Though there was an outburst against Victorian orthodoxy in the 1890s, with Pater and Wilde and Symons, yet Christianity had always kept its sustained sway, even among intellectuals, and as the decline of Britain's political and military supremacy and the ravages of the World War I in the first quarter of the new century drove a number of poets to Anglicanism (e.g. T.S. Eliot) or Catholicism and to mysticism and spiritualism (e.g. Yeats), Hardy's outspoken attitude of skepticism or disbelief was at least partly of the "modern" temper, even though it was unhappily accompanied ever with pessimism. Yet this pessimism was in no uncertain terms a sort of protest, albeit an ineffectual one, against the social and political status quo in England of the poet's day.

Hardy's place as a major English poet in the first three decades of the twentieth century can stand any challenge, and his poetry served as an important link between the great Victorian poets and Eliot and Yeats of the modernist tradition.

d. Georgian Poets and Poetry of World War I and Imagism in England

From 1912 to 1922, five anthologies of English verse entitled "Georgian Poetry" were edited by Edward Marsh and were issued from the Poetry Bookshop in London. The term "Georgian Poets" became well-known and it generally referred to those poets who published their poems in these anthologies and whose poetry showed the characteristics of the very early years of the reign of George V (1910—1936) when England enjoyed quiet prosperity previous to the First World War. They were popular poets and some of them wrote excellent and memorable poetry, though nowadays Georgianism is much depreciated. Some of these poets wrote consistently but many of them later outgrew their Georgianism.

Among the more important poets of this group was Walter de la Mare.

Walter de la Mare (1873—1956) was a voluminous writer of poetry and fiction and even of drama who belonged rather to the 19th century than to the 20th, chiefly on account of his romantic temper in poetry, so that he has been sometimes called "the belated last poet of the romantic tradition". Especially in the few poems that brought him fame he distinguished himself with the infusion of magic and mystery in the atmosphere of his poetry that reminded one of Coleridge and Keats. In one of his best known poems "The Listeners" we are introduced into the magic land in

which a Traveller knocked several times "on the moonlit door"
and, receiving no response except from "a host of phantari listeners" "in the lone house", he shouted in the silence:

> "Tell them I came, and no one answered,
>   That I kept my word."

This episode that seemed to take place out of time and space
and to exist for only a few brief moments hearkened back to "The
Rime of the Ancient Mariner" and "The Eve of St. Agnes". Equally
shrouded in mystery is a poem like "All That's Past", another
simple lyric tracing back to the undated past, in which the first
stanza out of three contains such strange charm that it sounded
a jarring note in the age of modernist poetry which fell under the
influence of the Metaphysical Poetry of the 17th century. The brief
lines challenge interpretation or analysis:

> "Very old are the woods,
>   And the buds that break
> Out of the brier's boughs,
>   When March winds wake,
> So old with their beauty are —
>   Oh, no man knows
> Through what wild centuries
>   Roves back the rose." (from "All That's Past")

It is a pity there are not many poems by de la Mare that are
comparable to the two discussed above.

Another well-known figure among the Georgian Poets was
W. H. Davies (1871—1940) who led a tramp's life, lost one of his
legs in a railway accident and wrote hundreds of brief and simple
nature lyrics. His poetry belonged almost all to quiet traditionalism,
and many of them didn't have any distinction. Occasionally, even
rarely, do we come across a few lines that are somewhat striking
and expressive of the poet's genuine thoughts, as for instance in
a poem entitled "Leisure", the first 2-line stanza reads:

> "What is this life if, full of care,
>   We have no time to stand and stare."

Ralph Hodgson who led a long life (1871—1962) of reticence, and lived partly in America, was largely forgotten after his "Georgian Poetry" days. Some few thought-provoking poems are still preserved in anthologies today. "The Hammers" contained such lines as:

"And I listened, and I heard
Hammers beating, night and day,
In the palaces newly-reared,
Beating it to dust and clay:
Other hammers, muffled hammers,
Silent hammers of decay."

Or in "The House Across the Way", we find the poet philosophizing:

"And the wind blew under the carpet
And it said, or it seemed to say:
'Truly, all men must go a-ghosting
And no man knows his day!
And the leaves stared in at the window
Like people at a play."

John Drinkwater (1882—1937) was possibly the most representative of the so-called "Georgian poets" at their worst. He wrote on very conventional themes in traditional verse form, and had little to distinguish himself with. However, there was a quiet and contemplative dignity in a short poem like "Reciprocity", in which he tried to meditate on common natural phenomena like meadows and stars and trees:

"I do not think that skies and meadows are
Moral, or that the fixture of a star
Comes of a quiet spirit, or that trees
Have wisdom in their windless silences.
Yet these are things invested in my mood
With constancy, and peace, and fortitude;
That in my troubled season I can cry
Upon the wide composure of the sky,

　　　　And envy fields, and wish that I might be
　　　　As little daunted as a star or tree."
Of course Drinkwater was otherwise known as manager of Birmingham Repertory Theatre in 1913 and as playwright of a number of chronicle dramas, including chiefly "Abraham Lincoln" (1918) which brought him popular success.

James Elroy Flecker (1884—1915) spent a number of years in the Near East, working in the consular service at Constantinople, Smyrna and Beirut, and wrote many colourful and mellifluous poems in lush language about stories in the Orient. Of the few poems still remembered are "The Golden Road to Samarkand" and "The Old Ships". From the former poem, memorable lines may be found in the speech of a merchant:
　　　　"We travel not for trafficking alone:
　　　　By hotter winds our fiery hearts are fanned
　　　For lost of knowing what should not be known
　　　　We make the Golden Journey to Samarkand."
The latter poem begins with:
　　　　"I have seen old ships sail like swans asleep
　　　　Beyond the village which men still call Tyre,
　　　　With leaden age o'ercargoed, dipping deep
　　　　For Famagusta and the hidden sun
　　　　That rings black Cyprus with a lake of fire."
The exotic picture of old ships of far away and long ago that provided attractions for the readers of the early decades of the present century has lost its charm for us today.

Laurence Binyon (1893—1943) who worked for many long years in the British Museum may be considered a Georgian though he was also a war poet who wrote not only about World War I, but also about the blitz of World War II. His masterpiece for which he is now chiefly remembered is the poem entitled "For the Fallen" (1914), which is a poem of patriotism that mourns the war dead "with proud thanksgiving" but which is celebrated for the following lines:

"They shall grow not old, as we that are left grow old:
Age shall not weary them, nor the years condemn.
At the going down of the sun and in the morning
We will remember them."

The first two lines make us recall the famous dirge in Shakespeare's "Cymbeline", which begins with "Fear no more the heat of the sun".

Binyon's "The Burning of the Leaves" (1942), written twenty-eight years later in connection with the Second World War, laments the destruction brought about by the blitz but expresses his faith in the eventual restoration of London's former glory:

"They will come again; the leaf and the flower, to arise
From squalor of rottenness into the old splendour,
And magical scents to a wondering memory bring,
The same glory, to shine upon different eyes.
Earth cares for her own ruins, not for ours.
Nothing is certain, only the certain spring."

The poem ends thus on a philosophic note.

Harold Monro (1879—1932) founded the famous Poetry Book-shop in the Bloomsbury area which was responsible for the publication of "Georgian Poetry" edited by Edward Marsh. In "Living" he contemplates on life and death and naively but very sincerely asks the unanswerable question:

"How shall I reconcile the two conditions:
Living, and yet — to die?"

Edmund Blunden (1896—1974) was both a Georgian poet who wrote nature poetry and a poet of World War I. He went to Christ's Hospital and Oxford before he took part in the battles of the Somme, Ypres and Passchendaele in 1916—1918. His later life was spent in teaching English literature at Tokyo, Hongkong and Oxford. Though his early pastoral pieces resembled somewhat the poems of W.H. Davies on the country scene, yet his quiet, contemplative and nostalgic lyrics like "Forefathers" and "Almswoman" showed his genuine affection and admiration for simple, old labouring folk rather than for mere descriptions of natural beauty ("The Pike", "The Midnight Skaters"). His chief record of his experience on the Western Front, "Undertones of War" (1928), was written chiefly in prose but interpersed with short poems. In this book and in other poems on the war he generally avoided descriptions of physical horror and outrage, but often very quietly and indirectly but unmistakably he condemned the barbarity and the terrible destruction caused by war, as when he talked of the "sack of potatoes spouting blood" and of the "pair of boots still containing someone's feet", and in the second stanza in a poem entitled "Report on Experience", he referred subtly to the great damage brought about by war:

> "I have seen a green country, useful to the race,
> Knocked silly with guns and mines, its villages vanished,
> Even the last rat and last kestrel banished —"

Blunden was a war poet with a difference.

Lascelles Abercrombie (1881—1938) and Wilfrid Wilson Gibson (1878—1962) were both Georgian poets in that some of their poems appeared in the first volume of "Georgian Poetry" (1911—12) under Edward Marsh's editorship. Abercrombie, like Bottomley, tried to write poetic drama but with little success, and was also a critic with his own theory of poetry. He was Professor of English Literature in the University of Leeds (1922—29) and in the University of London (1929—35), but his short poems, at their best, contained colourful imagery and smooth versification but were lacking in intellectual or emotional depth, as in a love poem "All Last Night" which opens with the following stanza:

> "All last night I had quiet
> In a fragrant dream and warm:
> She had become my Sabbath,
> And round my neck, her arm."

W. W. Gibson devoted his whole life to poetry. One distinguishing feature of much of his verse was to provide a voice for the "inarticulate poor", as in the narrative poem "Money" he told with much sympathy how a miner who was a victim of a pit accident left four pounds, seventeen shillings and fivepence for his widow and how she starved herself to death with the sum of money tied round her neck. Also in a short 8-line poem "Henry Turnbull" was described very succinctly and matter-of-factly the poor man Henry who died shortly after he had his drink, and his whole property consisting of "two greasy pennies" was used by his undertaker to keep his eyelids shut, "And so he lies with tuppence change till Doomsday on his eyes". He also wrote about trench warfare in World War I. In a poem entitled "Breakfast" was vividly pictured a soldier shot dead in the trenches by simply raising his head to curse and bet with his fellow:

> "I bet a rasher to a loaf of bread
> That Hall United would beat Halifax....
> Ginger raised his head
> And cursed, and took the bet, and dropped back dead."

None of these Georgian poets given above have become known as great poets, but some of them in a few pieces of their output produced delightful and memorable verse worthy of mention in the historical development of 20th-century English poetry.

English Poetry of the First World War

During and after the First World War there were a host of war poets in England. Among them the most memorable and indeed the most romantic figure was unquestionably Rupert Brooke (1887—1915) whose sonnet of old-fashioned patriotism "The Soldier" was celebrated for the inimitable lines in it of:

> "If I should die, think only this of me,
> That there's some corner of a foreign field
> That is forever England."

But this romanticizing of one of the most cruel wars in human history, the First World War, was a rare exception, though Brooke was much praised at the time for his patriotism and he has since been remembered chiefly for this one poem, which was the final

58

one of his five war sonnets. The ironic thing was that Brooke was at one time a socialist, joined the Fabians, and was a representative figure of social and cultural protest against Victorianism.

Wilfrid Owen (1893—1918) was possibly the most important of the war poets. He went to the University of London and then taught school and spent some time in France before he enlisted in 1915 and was sent to the Somme battles in 1917. He was wounded and invalided and then convalesced in Scotland and England, then was sent back to France and was killed in battle in early November, 1918, a week before the Armistice. Before the war he was planning to become a clergyman and he wrote on the miseries of poor people, as in a poem entitled "Miners" in which the poet seeing the coal in his hearth thinks with pity for the

> "poor lads
> Lost in the ground,"

and for the

> "moans down there
> Of boys that slept wry sleep, and men
> Writhing for air."

But Owen was chiefly known as a war poet who not only painted harrowing pictures of the dead and the wounded in the war, but also made sarcastic suggestions and ironical comments on the mental agonies of dying soldiers in trench warfare. "Greater Love" begins pathetically with:

> "Red lips are not so red
> As the stained stones kissed by the English dead"

and then the poet ironically considers this kissing as "greater love" than the wooing of lovers. In "Anthem for Doomed Youth", the firing of guns and rifles are mockingly regarded as substitutes for prayers and knells for numerous dead soldiers "who die as cattle" in fighting:

> "What passing-bells for these who die as cattle?
> Only the monstrous anger of the guns.
> Only the stuttering rifles' rapid rattle

Can patter out their hasty orisons."

In "Insensibility", the poet opens sarcastically:

"Happy are men who yet before they are killed
Can let their veins run cold."

These and similar lines all show so strikingly the bitterness that the poet must have felt so very keenly as he watched his fellow-soldiers die slowly before him. Even more bitingly, Owen in describing a gas attack denounced patriotic propaganda for war in "Dulce at Decorum Est" the title of which was taken from an ode by Horace, where the completed line: "Dulce at decorum est pro patria mori" means "Sweet and honourable it is to die for one's country". Here, after describing the violent death of a soldier who was not quick enough in putting on his gas mask during the attack ("the white eyes writhing in his face", "the blood / Come gargling from the froth-corrupted lungs"), the poet declared with mounting bitterness:

"My friend, you would not tell with such high zeal
To children ardent for some desperate glory,
The old Lie: Dulce at decorum est
Pro patria mori."

The most pathetic and harrowing piece of all Owen's war poems is "Strange Meeting" in which the brief exchange between the dying enemy and the nearly dead soldier who escaped reaches its climax in the last four and half lines:

"I am the enemy you killed, my friend.
I knew you in this dark, for so you frowned
Yesterday through me as you jabbed and killed,
I parried; but my hands were loath and cold.
Let us sleep now ..."

The tragic tone is also highlighted earlier in the first exchange of words between the two soldiers:

" 'Strange friend,' I said, 'here is no cause to mourn'.
'None,' said the other, 'save the undone years,
The hopelessness. Whatever hope is yours,

Was my life also.'"

This seeming sentimentality (actually it's true pathos) leads to the poet's summing-up of his main idea in his war poetry:

"The pity of war, the pity was distilled."

Indeed in the "Preface" which before his untimely death the poet sketched out for his future publication of poetry, he announced the same thought:

"This book is not about heroes. English poetry is not yet fit to speak of them.

...

Above all I am not concerned with Poetry.
My subject is war, and the pity of war.
The Poetry is in the Pity."

Owen's poetry is also known for his experiments (i.e. imperfect or half rhymes), which he employed to relieve monotony and to create a feeling of "remoteness, darkness, emptiness, shock". While this device was rather extensively used, it was present all the way through the poem "Strange Meeting" (e.g. "escaped" and "scooped", "groined" and "groaned", "bestirred" and "stared", etc.). This had its influence upon later poets, especially upon Auden and C. Day Lewis.

Edward Thomas (1878—1917) was born in London of Welsh parents and was educated at St. Paul's School and at Oxford. He married early and lived under financial pressures as he worked as a free lance prose writer about nature and country life and wrote biographical studies of Swinburne and Maeterlinck. He did not turn to poetry till after he met and was encouraged by the American poet Robert Frost when the latter came to England in 1913. His early poems appeared in an anthology in 1915 under the pseudonym of Edward Eastaway. He enlisted in 1915 when he was already thirty-eight and could have easily stayed out of the war, but he was sent to the front and was killed in action at Arras in France in April, 1917.

Thomas was first of all a nature poet. He had great affection for country life, and most of his best poems showed his fondness of and his philosophical observations on birds ("The Owl") and plants ("Swedes", "Tall Nettles", "Old Man") and other natural phenomena like the moon ("Liberty"), the clouds ("The Clouds That Are So Light"), the brooks ("The Brooks") and snow ("Snow", "Thaw"). "The Owl" is particularly well known and often anthologized and is typical of his melancholy and his sympathy for the soldiers and the poor. The last stanza sums up his poignant thoughts:

"And salted was my food, and my repose,
Salted and sobered, too, by the bird's voice
Speaking for all who lay under the stars,
Soldiers and poor, unable to rejoice."

The last two lines reveal the poet's attitude toward the war.

In the poem entitled "Liberty", the first dozen lines enchantingly indicate the poet's meditative strain as he links himself with the moonlight in front of him:

"The last light has gone out of the world, except
This moonlight lying on the grass like frost
Beyond the brink of the tall elm's shadow.
It is as if everything else had slept
Many an age, unforgotten and lost —
The men that were, the things done, long ago,
All I have thought; and but the moon and I
Live yet and here stand idle over a grave
Where all is buried. Both have liberty
To dream what we could do if we were free
To do something we had desired long,
The moon and I."

This seemingly intimate talk with the moon resembled much we may find in ancient Chinese poetry. But the philosophical ending definitely reflected the thoughts of a Western poet:

"And yet I, still am half in love with pain,
With what is imperfect, with both tears and mirth,

With things that have an end, with life and earth,
And this moon that leaves me dark within the door."
The first line is a distant echo of Keats.

Thomas' poetic musings on nature were often connected with his obsessions on the quick passage of time ("The Brook", "The Sun Used to Shine", "February Afternoon"). In "February Afternoon", the poet noted how the birds and plants remained the same as a thousand years went by:

"Men heard this roar of parleying starlings, saw
A thousand years ago even as now,
Black rooks with white gulls following the plough."

and:

"Time swims before me, making as a day
A thousand years, while the broad ploughland oak
Roars mill-like and men strike and bear the stroke
of war as ever, audacious or resigned,
And God still sits aloft in the array
That we have wrought him, stone-deaf and stone-
blind."

This thought of natural objects remaining essentially the same while a long lapse of time raced by resembled again many an old Chinese poem recalling the ancient times, without the accompanying lamentations on the brevity of human existence in the Chinese texts. However, Thomas did bewail the drying up of emotions that he used to experience in his younger days. In "Tears", he recalled two former occasions when he would have shed tears, and then stated dryly "It seems I have no tears left."

Though the bulk of Edward Thomas's poetry did not have to do directly with the First World War in which he was once wounded and finally killed, he did produce some very memorable pieces about the ravages of war. The best known of them is "Adlestrop", which indirectly reflected the many soldiers who died in the war, so that when the express train stopped at Adlestrop by chance, there was complete desolation at the station:

"It was late June,
The steam hissed. Someone cleared his throat.
No one left and no one came
On the bare platform. What I saw
Was Adlestrop — only the name."

And only trees and birds appeared on the scene, no human beings.

"In Memoriam (Easter, 1915)", a short poem of four lines, was yet a succinct record of the sad recollection at Eastertide of those men killed at battle who would never come back to gather flowers with their sweethearts. In "Lights Out", the stoical note of wandering thoughts of a man ready to die in battle is given in simple words of classical finish:

"There is not any book
Or face of dearest look
That I would not turn from now
To go into the unknown
I must enter, and leave, alone,
I know not how."

Occasionally Thomas also wrote on the theme of love, as in "No One So Much As You". There is a delicate touch of tenderness and a lingering sense of regret in such lines as:

"None ever was so fair
As I thought you:
Not a word can I bear
Spoken against you"

and:

"My eyes scarce dare meet you
Lest they should prove
I but respond to you
And do not love."

Edward Thomas was a first-rate lyricist, and he showed his great gift in using simple and carefully chosen words to express rather obliquely but effectively his poignant thoughts in the short lines he usually wrote in.

Isaac Rosenberg (1890—1918) also died in battle in France just a few months before Armistice. He was born in Bristol in 1890 of a humble Anglo-Jewish family and they moved to London in 1897. He learned engraving at the age of fourteen and then studied art at the Slade School of Art in 1911—14. He sold some of his pictures and published poems as early as 1912. On account of his weak lungs he went to South Africa in 1914—15, but upon his return to England he enlisted and in 1918 he was killed in action.

His early poems on love and other subjects showed the influence of Donne, but his fame rested on his war poems which often contained realistic sketches of trench warfare. Perhaps the most anthologized piece, "Break of Day in the Trenches", deals chiefly with the poet's musings on seeing a rat leaping over his hand in the trenches. Rosenberg's thoughts on the "cosmopolitan sympathies" of the rat who would touch a German soldier's hand just as it did his English hand, and his speculations on the rat's inward grin and its sight of "the shrieking iron and flame" are queer ideas for a soldier in battle and bear close though ludicrous resemblance to Donne's poem on the flea that had bitten him and his mistress (in "The Flea").

Equally playful was "Louse Hunting", which described how the sleepy soldiers in the trenches were roused by a louse and how they sprang up "to hunt the verminous brood" of lice. Other poems showed the more sombre mental state of the soldiers. "Returning, We Hear the Larks" was another very effective war poem in which were described the ambiguous feelings of the soldiers hearing the singing of the larks, "strange joy" amid the "sinister threat" of death. The last stanza of the short poem gave a good description of the mixed emotions of the trench fighters:

> "Death could drop from the dark
> As easily as song —
> But song only dropped,

Like a blind man's dreams on the sand
    By dangerous tides;
    Like a girl's dark hair, for she dreams no ruin lies there,
    Or her kisses where a serpent hides."
"Dead Man's Dump" was even somberer, with its vivid, lucid picture of dead soldiers on the battlefield. Here is a harrowing vision of wheeled vehicles of war running over the sprawling dead:
    "The wheeled lurched over sprawled dead
    But pained them not, though their bones crunched,
    Their shut mouths made no moan.
    They lie there huddled, friend and foeman,
    Man born of man, and born of woman,
    And shells go crying over them
    From night till night and now."
A still more horrid picture of a soldier who just died was painted in a later stanza:
    "A man's brains splattered on
    A stretcher-bearer's face;
    His shook shoulder slipped their load,
    But when they bent to look again
    The drowning soul was sunk too deep
    For human tenderness."
Then further down the poem was given a sketch of a soldier "not long dead":
    "Here is one not long dead;
    His dark hearing caught our far wheels,
    And the choked soul stretched weak hands
    To reach the living word the far wheels said,
    The blood-dazed intelligence beating for light,
    Crying through the suspense of far torturing wheels
    Swift for the end to break
    Or the wheels to break,
    Cried as the tide of the world broke over his sight."
Rosenberg was one of the best known of the war poets, chiefly for

his realistic representation of the horrors of World War I that took so many lives with its trench shelling and gas poisoning.

Julian Grenfell (1888—1915), yet another poet who fell in the war, was more akin to Rupert Brooke than to the others, on account of his glorification of war and his readiness to take up a soldier's duty. However, he was a much less important figure than Brooke, though he earned his fame immediately after his death in April 1915, when "The Times" published his verses, "Into Battle", for which he was chiefly known.

Ivor Gurney (1890—1937) did not die in battle, but his sufferings at the front were partly responsible for his mental collapse in 1922 and from then on he was confined in an asylum until his death fifteen years later. He had an aptitude for music early in life and went to the Royal College of Music in 1911 and then again in 1919, shortly after the war. He was first known as a composer, and only later as a poet. He enlisted in 1914, was sent to France in 1915, and was wounded in 1916. He returned to the front in 1917 and suffering from a poison-gas attack, he returned to England and was invalided in one mental hospital after another, until 1918.

Ivor Gurney put down in his poems many minute details of the life of soldiers marching to battle and staying in the trenches and expressed his dulled feelings of pain and ennui at trench life as well as his ever-present yearnings for home on the Severn. In "Toward Lillers" and "Canadians", he described his weariness at marching on behind the lines and near the front, his fording the Death Valley "up to the thighs in chill mud", his sight of the tiny aeroplanes that encircle "high over the two ditches of heartsick men", and his impressions of "a company of Canadians" relieved by him and his fellow-soldiers, with their "faces infinitely grimed in". Greater horrors were represented in "The Silent One", in which a heart-rending description was given of one soldier who died on the barbed wire and was still hanging there, and then a brief exchange of words, accompanied by "bullets whizzing", was reported of soldiers crawling through a hole in the barbed wire. On the other hand, the thoughts of home were uppermost in "Crucifix Corner" and "December 30th", as the poet and his fellow-soldiers reminisced of their home scenes upon the approach of Christmas and New Year's Eve. There was much bitterness as the poet concluded "Crucifix Corner" with:

"Forgotten, forgotten the hard time's true clothing,
And stars were happy to see Man make Fate plaything."

while near the end in "December 30th", sadness prevailed, with the poet bewailing to his dear one back home, about the death of many of his friends and the mental torture he himself was in:

"Men I have known fine, are dead in France, in exile,
One of my friends is dumb, other friends dead also,
And I that loved you, past am in torture's spite
Cursing the hour that bore me, pain that bred all
My greater longings; Love only to you, the last-year
date."

Though most of these poems were prosy because they dealt with practical details at the front, some few pieces were more lyrical. "To His Love" was the sad dirge of a girl back home lamenting her lover who died far away from the Severn:

"He's gone, all our plans
Are useless indeed.
We'll walk no more on Cotswold
Where the sheep feed
Quietly and take no heed."

A much more outstanding figure among the war poets of World War I was Siegfried Sassoon (1886—1967) who was possibly the most disillusioned of them all as far as the war was concerned and who protested so strongly in public that he was sent to Craiglockhart Hospital for shell-shocked officers near Edinburgh, though it was reported that he fought bravely at the front and won the Military Cross for bravery. Later, when the authorities refused to court-martial him for his declaration of pacifism, he returned to the front and was promoted and again wounded. His volume of bitter anti-war poems; "Counterattack" (1918), issued before the end of the war, was the first published expression of the horrors of World War I by one who fought in it. He survived the war and kept on writing poetry, and he also wrote an autobiographical trilogy in prose. The first of these, which was fictional, was "The Complete Memoirs of George Sherston" (1928, 1930, 1936), and included "Memoirs of a Fox-Hunting Man" (1928), "Memoirs of an Infantry Officer" (1930) and "Sherston's Progress" (1936), while the second factual trilogy included "The Old Century" (1938), "The Weald of Youth" (1942) and "Siegfried's Journey 1916—1920" (1945). Both trilogies had to do with the poet's personal experience in war.

Though Sassoon wrote on all kinds of themes in his long career as a poet, it is his war poetry that particularly deserves attention. His most frequently anthologized poem, "Attack", describes very minutely the horrors of war at the front and reflects the soldiers' intense desire for the war to stop. The short poem begins with the "spouts of drifting smoke that shroud / The menacing scarred slope", then the tanks and the barbed wire are described, then bombs and guns are mentioned and the reaction of soldiers to them, and finally the soldiers (obviously the author's) vehement call to stop the war. The final half-line: "O Jesus, make it stop", speaks volumes of the common soldier's wish or prayer or curse for the cruel imperialist war to come to an end as quickly as possible. In "Wirers", we have a detailed account of the squad of wirers going out of the trenches to repair the barbed-wire fence. A most ironic touch revealing the eager desire of soldiers to leave the front is to be found in a short poem "Stand-to: Good Friday Morning". Here the cryptic remarks on the background and the impatient, foul language that follows are most effective in conveying the poet's anti-war sentiments:

"Dawn was misty; the skies were still;
Larks were singing, discordant, shrill:

They seemed happy; but I felt ill.
Deep in water I splashed my way
Up the trench to our bogged front line,
Rain had fallen the whole damned night.
O Jesus, send me a wound today,
And I'll believe in Your bread and wine,
And get my bloody old sins washed white;"

Especially in the last three lines where the speaker would rather be wounded and leave the front than remain, we can feel his strong disgust with the war.

A few words must be said here about David Jones (1895—1974) who was born of a Welsh father and an English mother, who was trained as an artist, and who was the author of "In Parenthesis", an important document on World War I. He joined the army in 1915 and participated and was wounded in the Battle of the Somme in 1917, but he returned to the front later and served as a private soldier until the end of the war. He resumed his art studies in 1919 and became an illustrator, engraver and water colourist. He was converted to Roman Catholicism in 1921. In 1929 he started writing "In Parenthesis" which was published in 1937 and for a later edition of which T.S. Eliot wrote a preface to point out Jones' "affinity" with James Joyce, Ezra Pound and Eliot himself. In 1952 appeared Jones' later work, "The Anathemata" which was an obscure but powerful long religious poem.

"In Parenthesis", a long work of 40,000 words, was a strange mixture of prose and free verse in seven parts that dealt with the activities of members of a British infantry unit from its period of training in England in December 1915 to its participation in the terrible Somme offensive of July, 1916. The author was an eyewitness and participant of the incidents recorded here, and his companions of war described consisted of "mostly Londoners with an admixture of Welshmen", in the author's own words. He tried to link up his and his companions' experience in modern warfare with "the battles of long ago", with the soldiers of ancient myths and legends, and so here the records of World War I are curiously blended with references to events in English and Welsh history and literature and this hinders our straight-forward reading and leads to confusion in our comprehension of the work. "In Parenthesis" is so called, according to the author in his preface, partly because it was written "in a kind of space between" his other activities and partly because to him and his companions as "amateur soldiers" "The war itself was a parenthesis". While the earlier of the seven parts of "In Parenthesis" dealt with the preparations for war, in England and then in France behind the lines, the last part described the actual experience of war in the Richebourg sector of the Western Front, and gave a very vivid picture of trench warfare in World War I, particularly of the Battle of the Somme in 1916 with its extremely heavy casualty lists. The work was begun as a piece of reminiscences more than ten years after the war, in 1929, and was not published till 1937, almost on the eve of another world debacle. The interest in ancient myths in creative writing, particularly in poetry, was growing since the first decade of the 20th century, so here Jones made scattered references to the Arthurian legend, and devoted his concentrated attention to "Y Gododdin", a 6th-century Welsh epic, that described the raid of 300 Welshmen upon an English kingdom and the subsequent destruction of this raiding group. However, the important thing about "In Parenthesis" is the rather detailed account of the soldiers behind the lines and at battle, though it is always somewhat mixed up with incidents and persons in ancient legends. The book is certainly a queer document on war, recollected in tranquillity and philosophized by a Catholic writer long years after his actual experience in the battlefield.

The Imagist Poetry in Britain in the 1910s

Imagism as a movement in modern poetry was an Anglo-American venture, though as far as actual practitioners of this school of poetry are concerned, the movement was more American than British, for not only one of its founders was Ezra Pound, essentially an American poet in spite of his long sojourns in Europe and his great influence on English poets and poetry in the 1910s and early 1920s, but Hilda Doolittle, an American poet wedded to Richard Aldington of England, was possibly the most important imagist poet on either side of the Atlantic and another American poet Amy Lowell wrote many poems based on the theory of imagism and so distinguished herself in that field that Ezra Pound once even spoke of "Amygism" on account of her great enthusiasm for the movement. Of course, in England there was T. E. Hulme (1883—1917), who together with Pound was quite a spokesman for the movement, as he advocated discipline and precision in presentation and objected to emotional indulgence and to verbiage. After Hulme's death at the Western Front in 1917, Herbert Read edited and published his essays "Speculations" (1924) at the appendix to which were included five Imagist fragments among his poetry. Then there were F. S. Flint (1885—1960) and Richard Aldington (1892—1962) who were active advocators and supporters of imagism and who contributed to the anthology "Des Imagistes" (1914) edited by Ezra Pound and to "Some Imagist Poets" (1915). To the latter Aldington wrote a preface in which he defined the principles of the Imagist movement as: To use the language of common speech ... to employ always the exact word ... To create new rhythms ... To present an image ... poetry should render particulars exactly and not deal in vague generalities ... To produce poetry that is hard and clear ..., concentration is of the very essence of poetry." Ezra Pound has sometimes been considered as the founder of the movement because it is said that he invented the term "Imagiste" in an appendix to his "Ripostes" (1912) and that he also gave a definition of an image: "An 'Image' is that which presents an intellectual and emotional complex in an instant of time." Aldington also published, together with his wife Hilda Doolittle, a volume of verse entitled "Images, Old and New" (1915), although he is better known for his war novel, "Death of a Hero" (1929) and a later novel "All Men Are

Enemies" (1933). F.S. Flint came from a poor family and once worked as a barber's lather boy, but he studied hard and later entered the Civil Service. For some time he was prominent as a poet in the Imagist movement and published volumes of poetry: "In the Net of Stars" (1909), "Cadences" (1915) and "Otherworld" (1920).

Imagism as a movement was short-lived. It flourished chiefly in the 1910s, but the influence was widely felt for a time, not only in the poems of Ezra Pound but also in the early verse of T. S. Eliot.

e. William Butler Yeats.

One of the great names in English poetry in the first four decades of the 20th century is that of an Irishman, William Butler Yeats (1865—1939). Yeats was born in Dublin of a Protestant painter's family. He went to school in London and in Dublin and then he entered the Dublin School of Art but soon left it to devote himself to poetry. His first poems were published in the Dublin University Review in 1885, and in 1887 he went to London where he got acquainted with William Morris and Oscar Wilde and began to work on an edition of William Blake. In 1889 appeared his book "The Wanderings of Oisin" and in 1891 he became one of the founders of the Rhymers' Club and fell under the influence of the Pre-Raphaelites and of Spenser and Shelley. He had fallen in love with Maud Gonne for whom he wrote a verse play "The Countess Cathleen" which appeared in 1892. In 1894 he visited Paris and was introduced to modern French poetry, especially the Symbolists, by his friend the poet-critic Arthur Symons. In 1896 he met Lady Augusta Gregory and John Millington Synge, and he got to know not only the great stories of the heroic age of Irish history but also Gaelic poetry through translations. In 1899 he published another volume of lyrics, "The Wind Among the Reeds".

In 1904 Yeats became President of the Irish National Dramatic Society and, together with Lady Gregory and with the financial help of Miss A.E.F. Horniman, he founded the Abbey Theatre in Dublin. After that, for a number of years Yeats was busily involved in the management of the theatre, and from 1904 to the end of his life in 1939 he wrote more than twenty plays, mostly in verse, and had many of them staged in the Abbey Theatre. In the meantime he kept on writing poetry until his eight-volume "Collected Works" was published in 1908. In 1911 Yeats went on an American tour with the Abbey troupe and began his friendship with Ezra Pound who introduced to him the Japanese Noh plays and started him on to the writing of plays for dancers.

The Easter Rising of 1916 in Dublin which a number of his friends including Maud Gonne participated had its strong effect upon the poet who not only wrote a poem on the event but also referred to the revolutionary activities in Ireland in a number of his later writings. However, he never had much enthusiasm for revolutionary work himself but stood aloof with his aristocratic pose. In 1917 Yeats bought an old Norman tower at Ballylee in Galway, on the west coast of Ireland, and had it repaired and then moved in to live there following his marriage in the same year. In 1922 he was appointed a senator of the new Irish Free State and in 1923 he was awarded the Nobel Prize for literature. He kept on publishing his poems: "The Green Helmet and Other Poems" in 1910, "Responsibilities" in 1914, "The Wild Swan at Coole" in 1917, "Later Poems" in 1922, "The Tower" in 1928 and "The Winding Stair" in 1929; while his autobiographical work in prose, "The Trembling of the Veil" appeared in 1922 and "A Vision" in 1925 and 1937, this last being an attempt to work out his symbolic "system" of personality and history for "a fuller realization" of himself as an artist. At this last stage he was more and more under the influence of occultism and much of his poetry was very complicated and obscure.

Yeats had a very long poetic career, stretching from his early works in the 1880s and 1890s to the 1930s. He also distinguished himself as a playwright, particularly of verse drama, and devoted much of his energy to the founding and the management of the

Dublin Abbey Theatre as the core of the Irish Literary Renaissance. But his fame rested chiefly on his poetry, and T.S. Eliot considered him to be the greatest English-speaking poet of his age.

Aside from his poetic dramas, Yeats wrote mostly shorter poems and lyrics. His early lyrics, written in the 1890s when he was very much influenced by the aestheticism of the Pre-Raphalites and symbolism from France, have been admired for several generations for their memorable lines of great beauty, such as we find in the middle stanza of "The Lake Isle of Innisfree":

> And I shall have some peace there, for peace comes drop-
> ping slow,
> Dropping from the veils of the morning to where the
> cricket sings;
> There midnight's all a glimmer, and noon a purple glow,
> And evening full of the linnet's wings."

or in the first stanza of a later poem "The Wild Swans at Coole":

> "The trees are in their autumn beauty,
> The woodland paths are dry,
> Under the October twilight the water
> Mirrors a still sky;
> Upon the brimming water among the stones
> Are nine and fifty swans.

These poems and others including "When You Are Old", "The Rose of the World" and "The Man Who Dreamed of Faeryland", were definitely composed in the romantic tradition of Spenser and Shelley, with vague suggestions of mysticism of the earlier William Blake.

Yeats' hopeless but passionate love for the beautiful actress Maud Gonne was responsible for a number of his memorable love lyrics: "Adam's Curse", "No Second Troy", "The Cold Heaven", etc. The first five lines in "No Second Troy" are especially poignant with emotion as the poet tries to persuade himself not to blame Maud Gonne for her participation in revolutionary activities:

"Why should I blame her that she filled my days
With misery, or that she would of late
Have taught to ignorant men most violent ways,
Or hurled the little streets upon the great,
Had they but courage equal to desire?"
As the short poem winds up with:
"Why, what could she have done, being what she is?
Was there another Troy for her to burn?"
Here the whole argument sounds very much like the curious blending of the rational with the emotional aspects of love in the metaphysical poetry of John Donne. Written in 1910, a poem like this marked Yeats' departure from the aestheticism of the early period of his verse and pointed to the poet's inclination toward modernist poetry such as was adopted in the 1910s and 1920s by T.S. Eliot.

Yeats' attitude toward the Nationalist Movement in Ireland went through several different stages. Beginning from the late 1880s he got interested in the Irish national tradition, going back to ancient Gaelic poetry and the folk legends and myths of long ago, and from the early 1890s he started to write many verse plays based on the old Irish legends and myths, about Cuchulain and his wife and mistresses, about the tragic story of Deirdre, about Cathleen Ni Houlihan, about the Countess Cathleen and about other folk tales. Most of these plays were staged in the Abbey Theatre the founding of which was prompted by Yeats' desire to revive ancient Irish literature. But by 1913 the poet was apparently disillusioned with the state of Irish national movement for independence from Britain, so in the poem "September 1913" the question was asked:
"Was it for this the wild geese spread
The gray wing upon every tide;
For this that all that blood was shed,
For this Edward Fitzgerald died,
And Robert Emmet and Wolfe Tone,

All that delirium of the brave?"
and the answer was a sad one:
"But let them be, they're dead and gone,
They're with O'Leary in the grave."

However, when the Irish nationalists launched a heroic revolt against the British government on Easter Sunday of 1916 and
a week of street fighting followed, Yeats was once more stirred
up, and in the poem "Easter 1916", he celebrated the Easter Rising in which many participants were his personal friends.   Here
Yeats began by recounting his familiarity with these friends before the Rising, and then noted the change coming over them with
their fight for national independence:

"All changed, changed utterly:
A terrible beauty is born."

He goes on to describe one after another those friends who joined
in the Rising and to mark the change in each of them. He admired them for their united efforts in proclaiming   an Irish Republic:

"Hearts with one purpose alone
Through summer and winter seem
Enchanted to a stone
To trouble the living stream."

And then he bewailed the sacrifice that came with the failure of
the Rising:

"Too long a sacrifice
Can make a stone of the heart.
O when may it suffice?
That is Heaven's part, our part
To murmur name upon name,
As a mother names her child
When sleep at last has come
On limbs that had run wild.
What is it but nightfall?
No, no, not night but death.

Was it needless death after all?
......
We know their dream; enough
To know they dreamed and are dead;
And what if excess of love
Bewildered them till they died?
I write it out in a verse —
MacDonagh and MacBride
And Connolly and Pearse
Now and in time to be,
Wherever green is worn,
Are changed, changed utterly:
A terrible beauty is born."

Though the poem was written in an intimate personal vein because the poet was expressing his feelings not only toward the Rising but also toward his friends and acquaintances, his national pride and patriotic sentiments were unquestionably there. Of course, Yeats with his strong aristocratic inclinations never thought much of the mass actions even for the national cause, as in his two later poems on two of the women who joined in the Rising ("On a Political Prisoner" and "In Memory of Eva Gore-Booth and Con Markiewicz") he referred to revolutionary activities they participated in with much contempt. In "On a Political Prisoner", as Yeats showed his sympathy for Countess Markiewicz who served a sentence in prison for her part in the Rising, he deprecatingly spoke of her participation in the Nationalist Movement:

"before her mind
Became a bitter, an abstract thing,
Her thought some popular enmity:
Blind and leader of the blind
Drinking the foul ditch where they lie?"

These lines certainly jar with the beautiful lyricism that preceded and follows after them:

"She that but little patience knew,

From childhood on, had now so much
A grey gull lost its fear and flew
Down to her cell and there alit,
And there endured her fingers' touch
And from her fingers ate its bit."

And then, comparing her to "any rock-bred, sea-borne bird":

"Sea-borne, or balanced on the air
When first it sprang out of the nest
Upon some lofty rock to stare
Upon the cloudy canopy,
While under its storm-beaten breast
Cried out the hollows of the sea."

Similarly, "In Memory of Eva Gore-Booth and Con Markiewicz" gives us a charming picture of these two women who were Yeats' friends and who took part in the Easter Rising, but again the poet refers disapprovingly to their part in revolutionary politics:

"The older is condemned to death,
Pardoned, drags out lonely years
Conspiring among the ignorant.
I know not what the younger dreams —
Some vague Utopia — and she seems,
When withered old and skeleton-gaunt,
An image of such politics."

Otherwise the poem contains some very charming, meditative lines such as:

The innocent and the beautiful
Have no enemy but time;
Arise and bid me strike a match
And strike another till time catch:
Should the conflagration climb
Run till all the sages know."

In his old age Yeats felt bitterly the loss of youth and so wanted to turn away from the sensual world of growth and change and to go and stay in the realm of art which is eternal and timeless. These

sentiments were recorded emphatically in his two companion poems
"Sailing to Byzantium" (1928) and "Byzantium" (1933), Byzantium
being modern Istanbul and the former capital of Eastern Christianity from the 6th to the 15th century and a place where Yeats expressed his wish (in "The Vision") to go and where in the 6th century
"religious, aesthetic and practical life were one". In "Sailing to
Byzantium" Yeats declares that Ireland or the sensual world of nature "is no country for old men" because there

> "Caught in that sensual music all neglect
> Monuments of unageing intellect".

So the poet wants to leave and go to Byzantium:

> "And therefore I have sailed the seas and come
> To the holy city of Byzantium."

And then,

> "Once out of nature I shall never take
> My bodily form from any natural thing,
> But such a form as Grecian goldsmiths make
> Of hammered gold and gold enamelling
> To keep a drowsy Emperor awake;
> Or set upon a golden bough to sing
> To lords and ladies of Byzantium
> Of what is past, or passing, or to come."

Here we see Yeats, like Keats, indulging in a beautiful dream of eternal beauty in the world of art. In the later poem "Byzantium",
Yeats kept on with the same theme of the permanence of art placed
in contrast with the changing world of human sensual existence:

> "A starlit or a moonlit dome disdains
> All that man is,
> All mere complexities,
> The fury and the mire of human veins."

But Byzantium in this second poem was developed into a symbol
of a mummy that is "superhuman" and that is mysteriously "death-
in-life and life-in-death". Here Yeats began to indulge in his
obscure, occultist vision of Byzantium as a world of changelessness

and purity far above

> "Common bird or petal
> And all complexities of mire or blood."

In his poems written in the last decade of his life Yeats frequently touched upon the contrast between the young and the old, between sensual and intellectual life, between transitory physical vigour and permanent wisdom of art. A short poem of eight lines, "After Long Silences", sums up succinctly this theme:

> "Speech after long silence; it is right,
> All other lovers being estranged or dead,
> Unfriendly lamplight hid under its shade,
> The curtains drawn upon unfriendly night,
> That we descant and yet again descant
> Upon the supreme theme of Art and Song:
> Bodily decrepitude is wisdom; young
> We loved each other and were ignorant."

A number of poems describing enchanting pictures or colourful works of art were written by Yeats in his old age. "Leda and the Swan", written possibly with Michelangelo's painting of the rape of Leda by Zeus in mind, touches upon Helen and Clytemnaestra as the fruit of the union, with much power:

> "A shudder in the loins engenders there
> The broken wall, the burning roof and tower
> And Agamemnon dead."

In "Long-Legged Fly", three stanzas describe three vivid scenes of three well-known historical and legendary figures: Julius Caesar planning for his campaign in his tent, Helen of Troy training herself in her adolescence, and Michelangelo on the scaffold painting the first Adam in the Sistine Chapel. More thought-provoking was the poem "Lapis Lazuli", with the poet's comment on a piece of deep blue stone, "carved", according to Yeats himself, "by some Chinese sculptor into the semblance of a mountain with temple, trees, paths, and an ascetic and pupil about to climb the mountain." After commenting on the terrible threat of modern warfare ("Aeroplane and

Zeppelin will come out") and the link between the tragic and the gay
in Shakespearean tragedies of "Hamlet" and "Lear", the poet ends
up with an appreciative description of the Chinese piece of sculp-
ture:

> "Every discoloration of the stone,
> Every accidental crack or dent,
> Seems a watercourse or an avalanche,
> Or lofty slope where it still snows
> Though doubtless plum or cherry branch
> Sweetness the little halfway house
> These Chinamen climb towards, and I
> Delight to imagine them seated there;
> There, on the mountain and the sky,
> On all the tragic scene they stare.
> One asks for mournful melodies;
> Accomplished fingers begin to play.
> Their eyes mid many wrinkles, their eyes,
> Their ancient, glittering eyes, are gay."

In "Under Ben Bulben", a poem in Yeats' last volume which he ends
with an epitaph for himself, the poet again pointed out the high mission of art:

> "Poet and sculptor, do the work,
> Nor let the modish painter shirk
> What his great forefathers did,
> Bring the soul of man to God."

Then he wrote rhapsodically about 15th-century Italian art:

> "Quattrocento put in paint
> On backgrounds of a God or Saint
> Gardens where a soul's at ease;
> Where everything that meets the eye,
> Flowers and grass and cloudless sky,
> Resemble forms that are or seem
> When sleepers wake and yet still dream,
> With only bed and bedstead there,

That heavens had opened."

Then in his unique way he called on the Irish poets to sing about the peasants and the aristocracy:

"Sing the peasantry, and then
Hard-riding country gentlemen,
The holiness of monks, and after
Porter-drinkers' randy laughter;
Sing the lords and ladies gay
That were beaten into the clay
Through seven heroic centuries;
Cast your mind on other days
That we in coming days may be
Still the indomitable Irishry."

Here we may see clearly Yeats' aristocratic bent and his lingering affection for the past of Ireland. The poem ends with the poet's self-phrased epitaph:

"Cast a cold eye
On life, on death.
Horseman, pass by!"

Yeats was first of all a poet, and only secondarily a playwright. However, he not only was one of the founders of the Irish Literary Theatre in 1899 (together with Edward Martyn and George Moore the novelist) and much more importantly of the Abbey Theatre in Dublin in 1904 (together with Lady Gregory) but he also wrote no less than 20 plays (chiefly one-acters) in a stretch of 48 years (from 1892—1939). With his firm convictions in the revival of ancient Irish myths and legends as the mainstay of the Irish literary renaissance for which he and Lady Gregory worked with enthusiasm throughout their lives, Yeats used chiefly Irish legendary material as the story threads in his plays. His first play or five scenes in verse, "The Countess Cathleen" (1892), which was part of the programme for the first performance of the Irish Literary Theatre in Dublin in 1899, tells of the mythical Countess Cathleen who showed her great charity to the poor Irish people by selling to two demons disguised as merchants her own soul in order to give relief to the starving crowd in a season of great drought and famine when her own wealth ran out. Here the weird atmosphere of mystery and terror and the simple unadorned verse of smooth lyricism show the unmistakable influence of Pre-Raphaelitism and especially of the poetry of Dante Gabriel Rossetti. The Countess Cathleen's simple words of her selfless love for her people certainly express the young poet's idealistic portrait of an altruistic aristocrat:

> "From this day for ever
> I'll have no joy or sorrow of my own."

And her parting speech just before her death:

> "Bend down your faces, Oona and Aleel:
> I gaze upon them as the swallow gazes
> Upon the nest under the eave, before
> She wanders the loud waters. Do not weep
> Too great a while, for there is many a candle
> On the High Altar, though one fall. Aleel,
> Who sang about the dancers of the woods,
> That know not the hard burden of the world
> Having but breath in their kind bodies, farewell!
> And farewell, Oona, you who played with me,
> And bore me in your arms about the house
> When I was but a child, and therefore happy,
> Therefore happy, even like those that dance,
> The storm is in my hair, and I must go."

Yeats' early verse plays, based on the Irish folk tales and written at the turn of the century (1894—1904) are perhaps better known than his later dramas. "The Land of Heart's Desire" has its setting in a fairyland at a remote time in the past. A newly-wed woman absorbed in ancient lore about fairies and the fairyland, Mary Bruin, is hopelessly enchanted by a faery child, and dies upon the latter's promise of the land of her heart's desire, in spite of the exhortation of the aged Father Hart and the power of the Crucifix as well as the persuasions of her husband and his parents. The poet seems here to suggest the irresistible charms of the fairyland in lines of great lyrical beauty:

"Until she came into the Land of Faery,
Where nobody gets old and godly and grave,
Where nobody gets old and crafty and wise,
Where nobody gets old and bitter of tongue."

and:

"Where beauty has no ebb, decay no flood,
But joy is wisdom, time an endless song."

"The King's Threshold" tells of an old poet named Seanchan who intends to starve himself to death at the king's threshold in order to protest against the indignities he has suffered at the court and who is only appeased at last by the king's offer of his crown. Yeats is obviously attempting to show the great authority of the poet over the king who stands for material power. "The Pot of Broth" is a farce that relates how a tramp tricks a country couple out of their food.

A more serious play of patriotism is "Cathleen Ni Hoolihan" in which a poor old woman calling herself "Cathleen the daughter of Hoolihan" comes into the Gillane household and Michael the young man of the family leaves his betrothed and follows her voice to join the French ships coming to the aid of Ireland. The call to her service uttered by the old woman asks for sacrifice from patriotic young men to fight for their own country, in its haunting rhythm of lyrical stoicism:

"It is a hard service they take that help me. Many that are red-cheeked now will be pale-cheeked; many that have been free to walk the hills and the bogs and the rushes will be sent to walk hard streets in far countries; ...

They shall be remembered for ever,
They shall be alive for ever,
They shall be speaking for ever,
The people shall hear them for ever."

Yeats wrote several plays about Cuchulain, a heroic legendary warrior who singlehandedly defended his country Ireland against invaders. In "On Baile's Strand" (1904) Cuchulain vowing allegiance to Conchubar the king of Ulster kills a youth in combat who turns out to be his own son by the warrior queen Aoife. In "The Death of Cuchulain",Cuchulain is finally killed by Aoife, after his mistress Eithne Inguba brings a message for him from his wife Emer. In "The Only Jealousy of Emer" (1919) the conflict is shown between Emer and Eithne Inguba before the ghost of Cuchulain who is washed ashore by the waves. In "The Green Helmet", after a fight for the green helmet, it is given to Cuchulain.

But true tragedy is only to be found in "Deirdre" (1907) where Yeats sings of the most colourful and most pathetic love story in all Irish legends, that of Deirdre and her lover Naoise, both of whom were treacherously betrayed by the tyrannical old king Conchubar. When the two lovers discover that they have been cheated by Conchubar, Deirdre utters one of the most lyrical speeches in reminiscing her first night together with Naoise in the woods and in bidding him her last farewell:

"Do you remember that first night in the woods
We lay all night on leaves, and looking up,
When the first grey of the dawn awoke the birds,
Saw leaves above us? You thought that I still slept,
And bending down to kiss me on the eyes,
Found they were open. Bend and kiss me now,
For it may be the last before our death.
And when that's over, we'll be different,
Imperishable things, a cloud and a fire
And I know nothing but this body, nothing
But that old vehement, bewildering kiss."

Yeats wrote a number of other memorable plays. There are two modernized versions of two of Sophocles' plays about King Oedipus and Oedipus at Colonnus. There are two plays about Jesus Christ: "Calvary" (1920) that contains one dialogue between Christ and Lazarus and another between Christ and Judas, and "The

Resurrection" (1931) which is about Christ's meeting with three worshippers of Dionysus, the Hebrew, the Syrian and the Greek. There is "The Words upon the Window-Pane" (1934) in which through the agency of Mrs. Henderson the medium, the voices of Swift and his two women Stella and Vanessa are summoned to a spiritualist séance. Then there is also "The Cat and the Moon" (1926) which shows a blind man carrying a lame man and gives their different answers to a question by the musician and which may have inspired the writing of the well-known play "Waiting for Godot" by Samuel Beckett.

All in all, Yeats' plays are known for their invocation of the fairyland atmosphere and of the supernatural of far away and long ago in Irish legends and folklore, while many of his verse dramas are celebrated for the beautiful passages of lyrical poetry to be found in them. Their importance also lies in the part they played as one of the mainstays in the Irish literary theatre, particularly at the Abbey Theatre in Dublin.

SECTION III ENGLISH DRAMA: 1900—1930

a. George Bernard Shaw

George Bernard Shaw (1856—1950) was born in Dublin, Ireland, of English parentage. His father was a small official who habitually got drunk and whose means was not enough to provide for the family. His mother had a good voice and helped out in family finance by giving music lessons. As a boy, Shaw did not distinguish himself at school, but was much interested in literature, music and art. It was beyond his family means to send him to a university, and so when he left school for good at 14, he was put into a job as clerk and later as cashier in a land-agent's office in Dublin. Engaged in the collecting of rents, he had to go every week to the squalid Dublin tenements and mixed with the masses of poor people and this experience enabled him to sympathize with the miseries of the poor and provided material for his first play, "The Widowers' Houses". Also, all the years of his childhood and early youth he spent in Ireland made Shaw understand the sufferings of the Irish people under the oppression of the English ruling classes, and left in him vivid impressions of the hard lot of the Irish which he was later to introduce into some of his plays, particularly in "John Bull's Other Island". Then his family broke up and his mother went to London to sing in concerts there and to give music lessons. In 1876, at the age of 20, Shaw resigned from his job and also went to London.

His first three years in London he spent chiefly in the libraries, picking up an education for himself and only doing odd jobs for small earnings. In 1879 he started to write novels. From 1879 to 1883 he wrote a total of five novels and he had a hard time getting them published, and the first to be published was the last of the five novels, "The Unsocial Socialist", in 1884. The first novel of the series, "Immaturity", a story about a clerk, was not published till 1930, while the other three, "The Irrational Knot" (about a poor musician), "Love Among the Artists" (about an electrical engineer) and "Cashel Byron's Profession" (about a world-famous prizefighter marrying a priggishly refined lady of property), appeared in serials in the magazines of "Our Corner" and "Today", respectively in 1885—87, 1885—88 and 1885—86. All these novels have one thing in common, the portrayal of one principal character who is detached from his surroundings and who is conscious of a distance of superiority between himself and others. This aloofness and feeling of superiority, which were to last throughout the author's life and were responsible for his love of paradoxes and witty remarks and for his striving for the unusual and unconventional, very naturally attracted him to the Fabians who placed their hopes for the world in the intellectual and intelligent few. Of these five novels, the most important is "The Unsocial Socialist", which was written after the author had attended socialist meetings and read Marx's "Capital". The hero of the novel, Sidney Trefusis, son of a cotton manufacturer, is shown at the opening of the book as having discovered the origin of his wealth and of that of all his class. And with this knowledge the hero of the novel wishes to break every tie that binds him with his class and he starts by leaving his wife whom he loves and going to a hermit's cave in the country and living there as a labourer. He decides to devote his energies and money to assisting the organization of the workers, to unite them in "a vast international association" with socialism as its aim. Then his wife dies and he returns to his former environment and begins to attack the men and women of his own class from within, as one of themselves. He also engages himself in "working out a scheme" for the reorganization of industry. But at the close of the story the hero marries a girl who has not the least interest in problems of capitalism and socialism, and he proposes to interfere no more "with the slowly grinding mill of Evolution!" And this ultimate belief in evolution as against revolution for the hero shows definitely Shaw's inclination already then toward Fabianism.

In 1882 Shaw happened to attend a speech by Henry George, author of "Progress and Poverty" who advocated the nationalization of land as a solution to the social problems of the time, and this made a deep impression on Shaw and he began to take interest in social theories. Then, shortly after this, Shaw attended a public meeting of Hyndman's Democratic Federation and there he was told of Marx. So he went to the British Museum Reading Room and there read Marx's 'Capital' in a French translation. Then, in 1884, he joined the Fabian Society shortly after its founding and in 1885 he was elected a member of its Executive Committee. The Fabian influence was obvious in many of Shaw's plays.

Over a period of thirteen years (1885—1898) Shaw was engaged chiefly in a journalistic career, serving as critic of art, music and drama for different newspapers and magazines. As a critic he was strongly against "Art for Art's Sake", and as a dramatic critic he levelled his attack on the plays with well-constructed plots but very meagre contents which then filled the theatres, and he fought for the staging of social dramas of Ibsen's. He delivered a number of lectures on "The Doll's House", "Ghosts", and Ibsen's other plays, and in 1891 published his critical essay "The Quintessence of Ibsenism." He also wrote other critical essays, including chiefly "The Sanity of Art" (1895) and "The Perfect Wagnerite" (1898). Shaw also delivered many lectures on socialism during this period.

Shaw's dramatic career began in 1892, with the appearance of his first play, "Widowers' Houses", on the London stage. This is the first of the three "Unpleasant Plays" which include also "The Philanderer" (1893) and "Mrs. Warren's Profession" (1893), and which will be dealt with more fully later. These were followed by four "Pleasant Plays", including "Arms and the Man" (1894), "Candida" (1895), "The Man of Destiny" (1897), and "You Never Can Tell" (1898). In "Arms and the Man" and "The Man of Destiny" Shaw tries to shatter the romantic halo that was thrown around war heroes and military heroism, while in "Candida" the romantic veil is torn off the confident clergyman, the great preacher, the orator of wonderful eloquence who does not even have enough time to speak to all the organizations that invite him to speak. "You Never Can Tell", the weakest of the four, touches on the problem of the disintegration of a bourgeois family. Then, the third series of Shaw's plays, appearing near the close of the 19th century under the title of "Three Plays for Puritans", include "The Devil's Disciple" (1897), "Captain Brassbound's Conversion" (1897) and "Caesar and Cleopatra" (1898). In the preface to these three plays Shaw explains the title of "Plays for Puritans" and attacked the English theatres of the time which were then run on purely business basis and in which vulgar dramas on meaningless erotic themes were produced to cater to the low tastes of the bourgeois audiences. Shaw considers it necessary for "Puritans" of his age to stop the production of such vulgar plays as did the Puritans of the 17th century. In the plays "The Devil's Disciple" and "Caesar and Cleopatra" Shaw turns to history but still keeps an eye always on contemporary society. So the figures at the time of the American Revolution in 1777 in the first play and Caesar and Cleopatra of ancient Roman history in the second are both given the feelings and speeches and actions of modern men and women. In "Captain Brassbound's Conversion" Shaw touches on the colonial problem by having the scene placed in colonial Morocco. All three plays show the dramatist's attack on British imperialism and his severe criticism of the oppression and hypocrisy of the British bourgeoisie.

In 1898 Shaw got married to an Irish millionairess who was also a Fabian, and after the marriage Shaw went to no more street meetings and to few socialist lectures outside of the Fabian circle.

In 1903 came a well-known play of Shaw's, "Man and Superman", which has as its sub-title "A Comedy and a Philosophy" and to which is appendixed a collection of aphorisms and paradoxes on social themes, "The Revolutionist's Handbook and Pocket Companion." Here Shaw dropped his attacks on capitalism and his preaching of socialism but embarked on the biological theory of the mysterious "Life Force". He rejected Darwinism and followed the teachings of Lamarck and pointed out that this "Life Force" was responsible for all growth in the natural world and was the explanation of the relationship between man and woman. So in three of the acts of the play, the 1st, 2nd and 4th acts, which are separable from the third act and are the only parts for actual staging, the story tells particularly of the love and marriage of the hero and the heroine and Shaw tries to explain that the woman is more an instrument of the Life Force and therefore takes the active part in love and marriage so as to fulfill the human duties of procreation, and that man usually tries to run away from Life Force so as to be able to develop his potentialities in art and other activities in life. The third act is set apart by itself, in which the hero, running away from the heroine and the Life Force, falls asleep on the way and dreams of being in hell and conversing with the Devil. This act, though also containing an explanation of the Life Force and a sort of parody of the controversies in the socialist movement of the 1880s, nevertheless touches on criticisms on the bourgeois civilization, and there are satiric remarks against militarism and the use of modern technology for the purpose of destruction.

"Man and Superman" was followed by "John Bull's Other Is-land" (1904), which was written for, but rejected by W. B. Yeats' Irish National Theatre. It is Shaw's most powerful attack on Eng-lish imperialism, because he was himself an Irishman and his know-ledge of the miseries of the Irish people gathered in his younger days made him hate the terrible oppression and exploitation of the Irish by the English ruling classes for so many centuries. The story is about an Englishman, Tom Broadbent, who, with the help of his Irish partner in civil engineering, a dreamy Irish idealist turned real-ist, Larry Doyle, works out a scheme for a land syndicate, which tries to lend more money to the small farmers than the latter can pay the interest and then to foreclose the mortgages and take posses-sion of the land. Broadbent also gets himself adopted as Parlia-mentary candidate for Rosscullen on the platform of Home Rule for Ireland. In the play all the tricks used by the English imperial-ists for the attainment of their ends are exposed via the actions and speeches of the hero Broadbent.

"Major Barbara" (1905) is perhaps the most powerful of Shaw's plays written between the Boer War of 1899—1902 and the be-ginning of the First World War in 1914. It is significant for its search-ing analysis of the capitalist society and for its sharp criticism on the hypocrisy and the Mammonism of the capitalists and will be dis-cussed in detail later.

The plays written after "Major Barbara" and before the begin-ning of the First World War show a definite decline in the sharpness of social criticism. So, in "Getting Married" (1908), "Misalliance" (1910) and "Fanny's First Play" (1910), is discussed chiefly the prob-lem of family and marriage, though once in "Misalliance" the is-sue of capitalism and socialism is touched upon.

Then in "The Doctor's Dilemma" (1911) there is the satire on doctors, journalists and art critics and on the place of science in bour-geois society. In "The Dark Lady of the Sonnets" (1919) the theme is that of the necessity of the creation of a national theatre in England, plus Shaw's attempt to show Shakespeare as not a born dramatic and poetic genius but rather an indefatigable artist who takes down every poetic phrase and dramatic situation in his notebooks and later turns them to use in his plays. In "Androcles and the Lion" (1912—13) Shaw makes use of the old story of a run-away slave being made to confront a lion in the circus in ancient Rome and writes a satire on the early Christian martyrs and on Christian religion.

Of the group of plays written before 1914, "Pygmalion" is better known, and was a great theatrical success. At the beginning of the play the external difference is pointed out between the language of the rich and the well-educated and that of the common people of the streets and we are told that "correct speech" has been considered by the upper classes as the mark of culture. Then a linguist makes an experiment by taking in a flower girl from the streets who speaks the simple, uncultured language with a vulgar cockney accent, and after six months of training in "correct speech" the vulgar girl becomes as cultured as any aristocratic woman and is considered so by all the men and women of the so-called "high" society of culture. So here Shaw ridicules the worthless dolls of the London "Society" and satirizes the fashionable schools for noble ladies which take such pains to give "culture" to aristocratic women. But there is another point of significance in the play. The linguist only gives the flower girl the external coat of "culture" by training her in "correct speech", but the girl turns out to be a really "cultured" person, much more "cultured" than many aristocratic women who only have the pose of "culture". At the end of the play when the girl leaves his house, she indicates that the professor by treating her like a "cultured" woman has awakened in her the real culture she has been born with. With this Shaw undoubtedly tries to show that the simple people have the real culture in them which the noble ladies do not have. Therefore the linguist is compared to the "Pygmalion" in ancient Greek mythology, a famous sculptor who creates a beautiful statue of a woman and then falls in love with her when she is turned into a real woman of flesh and blood by the Goddess of Love. However, by showing the heroine at the close of the drama as a real "Lady" stitching genteelly at her needle work and carefully pronouncing all her correct vowels, Shaw defeats his own purpose in trying to exalt the simple girl above the duchesses and baronesses who are "cultured" only in their exteriors.

During the years of the First World War, Shaw was a pacifist. At the end of 1914 he wrote a pamphlet, "Commonsense about the War", in which he showed his support of the war but pointed out the responsibility of the English policy for the outbreak of the hostilities. He pointed out that the enemy of humanity is not Germany nor England, but capitalists and imperialists, and that if German imperialists seem worse than their English counterparts, it is because the latter are more consummate masters of hypocrisy. He even said:

"No doubt the heroic remedy ... is that both armies should shoot their officers and go home to gather in their harvests in the villages and make revolutions in the towns."

Then, when the Great October Socialist Revolution came, Shaw was among the first representatives of the advanced Western European intelligentsia to greet it with enthusiasm. At a stormy meeting of the Fabian Society he arose abruptly to make his statement, "We are socialists. The Russian side is our side."

During the war years he wrote a number of short plays which were later collected and published under the title of "Playlets of the War" (1919). These include: "O'Flaherty, V.C.", in which is shown the futility of heroism in the unjust war; "Augustus Does His Bit", a true farce presenting the false patriotism of the British bourgeoisie; "The Inca of Perusalem", a satire on German militarism, and "Ammajanska, the Bolshevik Empress", a discussion on the question of revolutionary methods of struggle against militarism.

"Heartbreak House", begun in 1913 but not published till 1919 is one of Shaw's more important works. It has as its sub-title "A Fantasia in the Russian Manner on English Themes", and in its preface Shaw acknowledges his indebtedness to the great Russian writer Chekhov. Disillusioned after the war, Shaw in this play attempts to comprehend the deepest contradictions of the modern time.

"Back to Methuselah" (1921) is an ambitious attempt with five parts, equivalent to five plays, and the time of the action extends from the time of Adam and Eve to the year 31920 A.D. Here Shaw believes that the chief obstacle for man to achieve a life of reason is the shortness of his earthly existence, and that it is necessary for man to live at least to 300 years of age, comparable to the long-lived Methuselah, before he can accumulate enough experience and wisdom to live a really rational and happy life. In the fifth and last part of the long work, as mankind is shown to have reached their utmost limit in development, in the year 31920, the physiological functions of man are by then reduced to the minimum and the mental faculties are raised to the highest pitch of development. Shaw the Fabian who believes in the superman of high intellect here tries again to utter his faith. The play also contains scenes where the world of politics at the time of the First World War is satirically presented, and Lloyd George and Asquith, two prominent English politicians, are ridiculed under fictitious names as typical representatives in bourgeois politics.

"Back to Methuselah" was followed by "St. Joan" (1923) which is one of Shaw's most popular and most successful plays on the stage. The story is that of Jeanne d'Arc who led the French people to drive out the invading English troops but who was finally betrayed and tried and executed by the English invaders. In the first three of the six scenes of the play we see the surge of a popular rising, with Joan at its head, winning over the waverers and carrying them along with it, sweeping aside all those who say that France can never be liberated, infecting the court and the king with its own enthusiasm, inspiring the army and making straight for the enemy's gun in the confidence of victory. But soon Shaw's faith in individualism turns the conflict into one between individuals, and Joan is no longer shown as a leader of the people but merely as an individual fighting against her betrayers and her enemies. Then in the Epilogue to the play Joan becomes a lonely saint and the whole atmosphere becomes one of religious mysticism. However, there are passages in the play in which confidence in the common people makes Joan a truly great figure, and the great conflict between the people and their rulers gives significance to the play, somewhat in spite of the author's intentions.

In 1929, a world-wide economic depression set in, and Shaw began to turn again to political themes and voiced his sharp criticism on the current political events in the Western world. He wrote "The Apple Cart" (1929), a satire on Western parliamentary system that deals with a cabinet crisis and with the attempt of American imperialism to swallow up Britain. Here we see again Shaw's wit and sarcasm, manifested in the form of paradoxes.

In 1932, Shaw wrote "Too True to be Good". As the title of the play indicates, Shaw means here to speak the bitter truth rather than sugared falsehoods. The entire society is shown to be full of lies and those who wish to live an upright life strive in vain for the true path out of the contradictions of the society. Both the old and the young generations of the intelligentsia have lost their ideals and illusions as a result of the war. There is a definite note of despair in the words and views of many of the characters in the play. Shaw seems himself to see the inevitable doom of the British Empire in the loss of hope among the intellectuals of the day.

The Fabian view that only intellectuals and not the workers can carry out the task of socialism is very vividly illustrated in the play "On the Rocks" (1933), where the leader of the workers' party rejects the plan for socialist reforms in England but the supporters of the plan are shown to be rather the representatives of the ruling class. Of course Shaw was rather alluding to the betrayal of the working class by the leaders of the British Labour Party like MacDonald, as indeed in this play there are also other topical allusions to events of the day such as the Fascist police and unemployed workers.

In the comedies that followed, in "The Simpleton of the Unexpected Isle" (1934), "The Millionairess" (1936), "Geneva" (1938)
and "In Good King Charles's Golden Days" (1939), Shaw continued
with his criticism on the bourgeois society and with his paradoxes, but his satires grew weaker and more ineffectual with time.

During the Second World War Shaw published a book entitled
"Political What's What" (1944) in which are summed up all his observations on social life and on the progress of science and culture.
Here once again Shaw showed his negative attitude toward capitalism
but declared that he remained a supporter for the gradual change
in social system. Although in this book there are to be found examples of Shaw's confusion in his theories, yet it is obvious that Shaw
is deeply convinced of the necessity for the creation of socialist organizations in England and in the whole world.

Bernard Shaw consistently fought against the representatives
of decadent art, as he openly and frankly declared himself in favour
of the art of ideas. Once he said, "I am not an adherent to art for
art's sake. I will not even lift a finger to write artistic works in which
there is nothing but artistic quality." And this view is to be found
in his numerous critical writings.

Shaw died in 1950, in his 94th year. A brilliant dramatist and
publicist, Shaw played an important role in the literature of his age.
He had his limitations of a Fabian, as he himself knew of this and
said once that he had "long been laughed at in Russia as 'a good
man fallen among Fabians'". But these limitations should not
over-shadow the great contributions he made to literature.

Possibly Shaw's three most powerful dramas are two plays from
his earliest days, "Widowers' Houses" and "Mrs. Warren's Profession", and "Major Barbara" from his middle period, for these
three Shaw's brilliant satires were aimed at the capitalist system itself and not simply at some of the vices or foibles of the bourgeois
society, as he tried to point out the terrible crime of economic exploitation as the foundation of all other social evils including polit-

ical oppression and all other kinds of tyranny.

"Widowers' Houses", the very first of all Shaw's plays which only had a run of two days before it was stifled by the press and the audience, was based on the author's early experience as a rent-collector and the theme is the intense exploitation via the renting of houses in the slums. A young aristocrat and medical student, Harry Trench, becomes engaged to Blanche Sartorius, daughter of a rich slum-landlord of London, but when he finds out from the rent-collector Lickcheese the disgraceful source of his future father-in-law's income, he insists that Blanche refuses to take any of her old man's money after their marriage and that they can live on his own small income of 700 pounds. Soon enough, however, he learns to his great horror that his own money is also derived somehow from Sartorius' slums via a mortgage, and he surrenders finally and he even willingly participates in a new and more heartless scheme of making still more money with those slums, when Lickcheese, now independent and wealthy, comes to suggest to Sartorius to make certain repairs on the slums in order to get a bigger amount of compensation by the time these slums are pulled down to make way for a new street running into the Strand.

The chief object of attack in this play is therefore the prevalence of economic exploitation in the bourgeois world, so that Trench who only has a comparatively small income of 700 pounds also lives on exploitation, and in fact, there's exploitation not only in the investments of money in factories or banks or commerce or as exported capital for foreign lands, but even in houses, particularly houses in slum districts that pay high returns, higher even than from big mansions. So, as Shaw himself writes in the Preface to the play, "In 'Widowers Houses' I have shown middle-class respectability and younger son gentility fattening on the poverty of the slum as flies fatten on filth." Here Shaw tries to drive home his point of the ruthlessness of exploitation in capitalist society. So Lickcheese the rent-collector tells the unbelieving Trench: "Look at that bag of money on the table. Hardly a penny of that but there was a hungry child crying for the bread it should have bought." And Lickcheese proceeds to reveal how these "tenement houses, let from week to week by the room or half-room-aye, or quarter-room" and "calculated on the cubic foot of space" pay higher rents than a mansion in the most fashionable district in London, and also how three women have been hurt on a staircase because it was not mended. A third object of attack in the play is the hypocrisy of the dignified-looking exploiters. Sartorius to all appearances is a prosperous business man who takes good care of his extravagant daughter and is ready to look after her and her husband upon their marriage, and only when this practical landlord of the slums laughs at the sentimental views of his would-be son-in-law Harry Trench and declares emphatically that a business man should never be influenced by moral considerations, do we see Shaw tearing the veil of hypocrisy off the ruling class of exploiters. And then Lickcheese's proposal to Sartorius to speedily repair his slums in Robbins Row in order to obtain greater compensations because he has filched the government secret that a street will be built through this lot further adds to the terrible picture of all the dirtiest means of money-making possible in bourgeois society. And Trench who at first seems to have moral compunctions against dirty exploitation succumbs eventually and even is willing to join in the new venture proposed by Lickcheese and approved of by Sartorius. This also shows how great the temptation is for dirtying one's hand in making money in the capitalist world and also how a man from the parasitic class of small exploiters such as Trench very naturally joins forces with other and bigger exploiters.

After "The Philanderer" which is supposed to be a sort of a satire on what was then popularly known as the Ibsenite new woman but which is actually a diversion between two serious dramas, came "Mrs. Warren's Profession" which was banned as immoral by the censors but which was considered by the dramatist himself as "much my best play" and should be ranked among the greatest of Shaw's plays, because the social satire here is the sharpest and the bitterest.

The titular heroine of the drama Mrs. Warren comes from a very poor family and after working for some time as waitress and bar-maid becomes a prostitute and then is part-owner and manager of a chain of prostitution houses in different capitals of Central Europe. The play opens as she comes back from abroad to visit her daughter Vivie who has been brought up as a girl of a well-to-do family and given a good education. Mrs. Warren comes with two of her friends, one of whom is a partner of hers in the business of running brothels, an old, dissolute aristocrat, Sir George Crofts. He tries to make love to Vivie, and is rejected by her after she finds out about the real nature of her mother's so-called business. Disillusioned and unable to live on her mother's income any longer, Vivie goes to work in London. Such is the central thread of story in the play. A minor thread is Vivie's relationship with a neighbour boy Frank Gardner whose father, a solemn clergyman, happens to be an old lover of Mrs. Warren's, and whose attempt to make love to Vivie is called a halt to by Crofts' ill-intentioned revelation to the two of them of their half-brother-and-half-sister relationship. But this secondary plot only serves to expose the promiscuous lives of seemingly dignified and even religious persons in the bourgeois society and to add to the complexity of plot and character-drawing. The important conflict in the drama is that between Vivie who is clever and well-educated but does not know much of the world and the terrible bourgeois world represented first by Crofts and also by her own mother.

The theme of the play is the use of prostitution houses for purposes of exploitation in the capitalist society. In order to point out emphatically the prevalence of exploitation everywhere and via the dirtiest possible means in the so-called civilized world, Shaw shocks his audience by showing how poor but good-looking women not only sell their good looks and their very bodies to maintain their existence and are exploited by factory owners and restaurant and bar proprietors while working for them, but also, what is far more terrible, how prostitution houses are used as a means and a safe one too for investment and money-making, even by such respectable aristocrats like Sir George Crofts. Here we see the resemblance between this play and "Widowers' Houses" in that both hit at the very heart of capitalism as a social system according to which economic exploitation is a legitimate thing to be adopted everywhere and even via the lowest and dirtiest means. And Crofts, like Sartorius, is thoroughly unashamed of playing such dirty tricks to get high premiums as he answers Vivie's challenge with blatant self-righteousness even: "Why the devil shouldn't I invest my money that way? I take the interest on my capital like other people. I hope you don't think I dirty my own hands with the work." Here Shaw strikes at the very foundation of the capitalist society where it is a matter of course for one to take the interest on one's capital, and let the devil care by which dirty means. And also the hypocrisy of bourgeois respectability is satirized for it is also the common thing with all investors of capital to take the interest on one's capital but without dirtying one's own hand in the work. Crofts further voices Shaw's exposé of the prevalence of exploitation in the capitalist society by telling Vivie that all the most respectable and honourable persons in the English bourgeois society, including the Duke of Belgravia, the Archbishop of Canterbury and Crofts' own brother the M. P., all get their money via the dirtiest ways of exploitation, and that, therefore, "if you're going to pick and choose your acquaintances on moral principles, you'd better clear out of this country, unless you want to cut yourself out of all decent society."

In "Mrs. Warren's Profession", therefore, Shaw proceeds from attacking one of the abuses in the capitalist world to the condemnation of the entire bourgeois society, the whole capitalist system, by pointing out how commonly and with what dirtiest means capitalist exploitation is normally carried on. And at the same time Shaw exposes the extreme hypocrisy in that society for at the back of the respectability and moral dignity and nobility of character and all that sort of gibberish uttered all the time by the ruling classes to cover themselves with honour and glory, there are the dirtiest and the cruelest ways of exploitation with which they make their money and live their grand, civilized lives but which lead to untold miseries for millions of poor down-trodden people. In this sense this play is the fiercest of all Shaw's attacks on capitalism, more vivid and effective than "Widowers' Houses" because the chief characters, Mrs. Warren, Vivie and Crofts here are fuller portraits than Sartorius, Lickcheese and Trench in the earlier drama.

While there are only exploiters among the major figures in "Widowers' Houses", there is at least the semblance of a positive character in Vivie in the later play. But even Vivie who seems to uphold her idealistic views against not only Crofts but also her mother and to find a way out of the dirty mess of capitalist exploitation by going to live on her "honest work", does not really find her way out (though Shaw obviously intends that she does), for first of all it is impossible for any one individual to break thoroughly with the society unless one goes in for revolution to overthrow that society, and then, after all, Vivie's "honest work" at "actuarial calculations and conveyancing" at Honoria Fraser's chambers in Chancery Lane is no "honest work" actually but rather "dirtying one's own hands" in slaving for the capitalists who are the ones to need such calculations for their dirtiest practices of exploitation, while her other seemingly innocuous intentions of doing "some law" and "with one eye on the Stock Exchange" (in her speech with "dear old Praedie" in Act I) would mean even more direct participation in the evil doings of the ruling classes in their oppression as well as exploitation of the poor millions. So Shaw's dream of a positive character and of a correct path out of the labyrinth of capitalist society is no more than an idle dream of a reformist.

One other serious shortcoming in the drama needs to be pointed out. The choice of Mrs. Warren as the protagonist in the drama is unfortunate, for her dubious position of being at first one of the oppressed and exploited and later becoming herself one of the exploiters brings unsurmountable confusion to the theme of the drama and the result is that the author seems to have drawn a line between Mrs. Warren and Crofts, intending for the audience to condemn Crofts but sympathize with Mrs. Warren, while actually Mrs. Warren may deserve one's sympathy in her early stage of suffering under exploitation but she certainly cannot be pardoned for becoming an exploiter herself of other girls.

"Major Barbara" again touches on the fundamental issue of capitalism, although here again Shaw's Fabianism comes to the fore. The story evolves chiefly round the titular heroine Major Barbara, her father and her fiancé. Andrew Undershaft, the girl's father, is the "cannon king", a big manufacturer and merchant of ammunition. Barbara is a "major" in the Salvation Army and sincerely wishes to save the souls as well as the bodies of the poor people, and Cusins her fiancé, a professor, shares her wish to help improve the conditions of the poor workers. The conflict here is chiefly that between Undershaft on the one hand and his daughter Barbara and her fiancé Cusins on the other, and Undershaft wins the first battle by buying over the organization of the Salvation Army with his money and that of the Whisky King, Bodger. Barbara quits the Salvation Army but finally her fiancé inherits Undershaft's property and she goes to work in the factory for the saving of the poor workers' souls. From the development of the story Undershaft seems to be the hero and the well-meaning Barbara and Cusins seem to submit, but Shaw rather suggests here that to fight successfully against capitalism one must have "power" and that Cusins means to gain the needed "power" by securing inheritance to the huge property of Undershaft's. But that of course is an illusion, it is Fabianism, especially since here again the workers are shown to be quite unable to fight the battle themselves, and such bourgeois intellectuals as Barbara and Cusins are needed to fight the battle for them. And the ending of the play is almost a sort of compromise with capitalism, when Barbara and Cusins go in together to the cannon foundry to work.

But "Major Barbara" is still a great satire on the capitalist society. In what Undershaft does and says are revealed the outstanding characteristics of capitalism and capitalists. First of all, we can see that tricks are played by the capitalists in order to prevent a revolution. Undershaft spends a large sum of money to buy over the Salvation Army because this religious institution is considered useful in feeding the poor workers with bread and with salvation and thus pacifying the workers and diverting them from revolutionary activities. Another trick employed by Undershaft is to create an aristocracy among the workers in his foundry, so that the only ambition of these workers is to rise in the social scale, to join the Primrose League and shake hands with a duchess, and not to get involved in overthrowing the capitalist system. Here we find the two most commonly used methods with which the capitalists all over the world try to lead the workers away from any thought of revolution, and here they are vividly presented in the play.

Undershaft also represents the capitalists in his religion of money, his cash worship. He manufactures weapons of war for the purpose of profit and for nothing else, so he declares that he sells arms "to all men who offer an honest price for them, without respect of persons or principles, to Royalist and Republican, to Communist and Capitalist, to Protestant and to Catholics, to burglar and policeman, to black man and white man and yellow man, to all sorts and conditions, all nationalities, all faiths, all follies, all causes and all crimes." And like Sartorius and Crofts he too says he is "unashamed" of doing all this, he is never troubled by moral considerations or conscience, because cash only is the all-important thing with him. And with this cash he has great power, so much so that he and the other big capitalists are actually the rulers of the whole world, with all governments under their control and all the politicians as their personal servants and puppets in their hands. So he impresses his son with his show of contempt for the government cabinets and parliaments in the whole capitalist world;

"The government of your country! I am the government of your country: I and Lazarus. Do you suppose that you and half a dozen amateurs like you, sitting in a row in that foolish gabble shop, can govern Undershaft and Lazarus? No, my friend: you will do what pays us. You will make war when it suits us, and keep peace when it doesn't. You will find out that trade requires certain measures when we have decided on those measures. When I want anything to keep my dividends up, you will discover that my want is national need. When other people want something to keep my dividends down, you call out the police and the military. And in return you shall have the support and applause of my newspapers, and the delight of imagining that you are a great statesman."

All this is a realistic picture not only of the first decade of the 20th century when the play was staged and published, but also of the decades before and the decades after, so long as monopoly capitalism holds its sway in Britain and in all other bourgeois nations. The big capitalists, the monopolists, have controlled the capitalist governments everywhere, though on the surface there are different political parties and different prime ministers and presidents and parliaments who are invested with power to rule. And when the war comes, armament industrialists and merchants, capitalists and monopolists, actually sell their products to all and everybody who are ready to pay for the weapons of war, to both sides of the belligerents, to the enemies of their own countries even, and this we find in the First World War and in the Second World War and in many other small and local wars in different parts of the globe through all the decades of the 20th century.

So in the character of Undershaft are exposed the essential characteristics of the capitalists in their shameless actions to make money and to gain power, and this exposé is presented with all the bitterness of satire. This is Shaw's contribution in this play. But while on the one hand Undershaft shamelessly declares in all frankness his entirely unscrupulous ways for making money, on the other hand he also used underhand means to undermine the workers' movements by creating an aristocracy among the workers and by supporting and buying over such seemingly harmless and even spiritual institutions as the Salvation Army. So there is at once frankness and hypocrisy, used to suit the needs for direct gains of money and for indirect gains of money by first spending huge sums of money. But beyond this sharp satire on capitalism and its dirty tricks and its shameless actions, Shaw seems to get confused and can only suggest a certain sort of compromise to defeat capitalism by some vague and indirect means or other in the dim and uncertain future. Yet, in spite of this serious limitation, "Major Barbara" is a courageous indictment of monopoly capitalism.

Different from the three plays of Shaw's as analyzed above, "The Apple Cart" ushers in, as it were, a new type of drama for the Irish playwright, the satirical comedy on contemporary politics, of which he was to write a goodly number in the last stage of his dramatic career. Written in the year (1929) of the landslide of economic depression which swept through the whole of the capitalist world, "The Apple Cart" dealt a powerful blow at the tottering political structure of bourgeois England by attacking chiefly the pseudo-democratic parliamentarianism in England and exposing the treachery of the Labour Party and also hinting at the dependence of the English bourgeois nation on American monopolists and imperialists.

The seemingly nonsensical "Prologue", which contains nothing but the irrelevant but very exciting dialogue between King Magnus and his mistress "Pompilia", is actually a sharp satirical thrust not only at the moral degeneracy of the king or the ruling clique but also at the complicated situation of all sorts of dirty tricks and intrigues employed in the struggle for power among the different political cliques and individuals in bourgeois England. The main body of the play contains two parts. In Act I a cabinet crisis is described through which the party in power (resembling the Labour Party government in England in the 1920's) tries to force the English king to do whatever they ask him to do, but the king refuses to do so by threatening to retire from the throne in favour of his son and then to compete with the party in question in a government election campaign in the capacity of a mere citizen. This frightens the party in power for they know too well that they have long lost the support of the people, and so a compromise is reached, with both sides promising not to trespass on each other. But actually it is not the question of a struggle between the party in power and the king, for the real power to rule rests with the big monopoly capitalists represented in the play by "The Breakages, Limited" which, according to one of the characters, can interfere in almost every enterprise where there is money interest to be gained and against which it is impossible to gainsay. Shaw explains this intention of his in the Preface to the play: "The conflict is not really one between royalty and democracy, but between both and plutocracy. The plutocrats first use democracy as pretext and openly shatter the king's power with violence, and now buy up and swallow up democracy. Money talks, money prints, money broadcasts, money reigns, and kings and Labour leaders alike have to register its decrees;and even,by a staggering paradox, to finance its enterprises and guarantee its profits! "

In this play we may see Shaw's disillusionment in the Labour Party, as he shows here in the person of Mrs. Boanerges, a Labour member of the Cabinet, how these Labourites disguising themselves as workers and pretending to be serving the interests of the working class are actually no more than adroit old foxes tenaciously holding on to their warm snug jobs and receiving a fair share of the government pie without even the moral compunction of having deceived the workers. And all the other politicians besides the Labourites are shown to be just as eager above everything else to struggle for their own personal interests, and an extremely ugly picture is painted here by the playwright, especially in the ridiculous appearances of the women ministers in the cabinet.

In Act II the especially significant thing is the revelation first of the growing economic dependence of England upon the imperialist United States of America after the First World War and then of the threat of American imperialism to swallow up Britain eco-

nomically and politically and also culturally. Here the American ambassador Vanhattan goes to see King Magnus of England and announces that the American government suggests the return of America
to the British Empire. The king collapses upon hearing the news
for he considers this "the end of England" and declares his intention
to fight for national independence to the last drop of his blood, but
Vanhattan answers flatly that that is impossible for the American
government would use the fleet of the League of Nations to block-
ade England and would also launch a boycott and "the two thousand million dollars a year would stop". And Vanhattan goes to
point out how Americanized England has already become: "we
find here everything we are accustomed to; our industrial products,
our books, our plays, our spirits, our Christian Science churches, our
osteopaths, our movies and talkies. But it is a small parcel and say
our goods and our ideas." And this satire on the subordination of
England to America is not only true of England in the post-First-
World-War period but is equally applicable to England of today.

"The Apple Cart" may be a topical play in the sense that it refers particularly to the England of the late 1920s and to the Labour
Party and to the other political phenomena of that day, but it has
its lasting significance for, so far as the bourgeois parliamentarian
system still operates and the English government remains dependent
upon American monopolists the satire in this drama will continue
to have its pungent, critical effect.

Shaw has written so many plays and most of them have attained
to such a high level of artistic achievement that it is difficult to say
which are the best of his works, or which are the most representative, but even with a none-too-careful analysis of four of his better
dramas as we have done with "Widowers' Houses", "Mrs. Warren's Profession", "Major Barbara" and "The Apple Cart", we may
see quite clearly that Shaw was a most courageous satirist on capitalism and imperialism and that with his brilliant character-portrayal and scintillating dialogue he succeeded in making use of the drama
as an effective weapon to attack not alone the various social evils in

the bourgeois world but also the very foundations of monopoly capitalism, though he fell unfortunately under the influence of Fabian reformism.

b. James Matthew Barrie (1860—1937)

Barrie was born in Scotland in a handloom weaver's family. After studying at home under his mother's instructions, he went to Dumfries Academy and then Edinburgh University, where he graduated in 1882. He started writing early, at first journalistic articles and reviews, for the "Nottingham Journal" in 1883—84, and then for the London newspapers in 1885. In 1888 he wrote his first successful book, "Auld Licht Idylls", a collection of sketches of Scottish life. He followed up with other works, until in 1891, when he began his series of sentimental writings, including "The Little Minister" (1891), "Margaret Ogilvy (1895) which was written to his memories of his mother, and "Sentimental Tommy" (1896) and its sequel "Tommy and Grizel" (1900). Barrie first wrote about Peter Pan in stories which came out as "Peter and Wendy" (1902).

But even in the 1890s Barrie already tried his hand in playwriting, first in minor pieces like "Ibsen's Ghost" (1891), "Walker, London" (1892), "The Professor's Love Story" (1892), and the dramatized version of "The Little Minister (1897), but it was in the first decade of the 20th century that he won his fame as a dramatist, with "Quality Street"(produced 1902),"The Admirable Crichton" (staged 1902), "Peter Pan" (produced 1904) and "What Every Woman Knows" (produced 1908). These were followed in the next decade by other full length plays "Dear Brutus" (produced 1917) and "Mary Rose" (1920) and a large number of one-acters: notably "The Twelve-Pound Look" (1910), "Rosalind" (1912), "The Will" (1913), "The Old Lady Shows Her Medels" (1917) and "Shall We Join the Ladies?" (1921). In the early decades of the 20th century, almost till the beginning of World War II, Barrie's fame as a playwright ranked with many critics and audiences as almost only next to G.B. Shaw in popularity and in merit, as his important plays were almost all written in the first twenty years of the century.

Barrie did not have a successful family life, he was married and then divorced. In 1919 he became Rector of St. Andrews University in Scotland, in 1930—37 was Rector of Edinburgh University.

Though Barrie's name as dramatist suffered so much after his death that for decades now he has hardly been mentioned as a playwright of any prominence in the English-speaking world, he has yet been remembered as the author of "Peter Pan", of the titular hero of the play known as "the boy who wouldn't grow up."

The eclipse of Barrie's glory in British drama has been only too natural, when we take into account the low popular enthusiasm for romantic fantasy and particularly for sentimental whimsicality among the reading public and the theatrical audiences in the West since the Second World War. However, in a historical survey of British drama in the first 40 years of the 20th century we have to give Barrie his proper place in his time and especially to provide reasonable estimates of his more important plays.

"Peter Pan" is certainly the best known and the longest remembered of Barrie's works, in fact nowadays if one thinks of Barrie as a dramatist of some stature at all, one invariably identifies him as the author of "Peter Pan", much as Lewis Carroll makes one instantly recall his "Alice in Wonderland". There is no doubt some resemblance between "Peter Pan" and "Alice in Wonderland", though Carroll's book is much more of a children's classic than Barrie's Play.

"Peter Pan" begins in a little top room of a flat where Mr. and Mrs. Darling and their three children Wendy, John and Michael live, with the dog Nana as the nurse and another very small maid Liza. Act I is first about their doings in the nursery where before the three children go to sleep, they are washed by Nana who however offends Mr. Darling and is chained up and taken below. Then unguarded by Nana, the nursery is invaded by Peter Pan who has run away from home on the day of his birth and who now enters flying through the window and is accompanied by a very small fairy Tinker Bell. Peter looks for his shadow that was clipped by Nana during his first trip to the room, finds it but cannot stick it on to his body, and Wendy waking up tries to sew it on to him. Soon all three children wake up and Peter take them flying out of the window to the Never Land. The middle three acts of the play as well as Act V, Scene I, are devoted to Peter's and the three children's adventures in the Never Land, including their experience with the pirates and their leader Captain Hook, the Red Indians who try to guard the children against the pirates, a small house built for Wendy and their "home under the Ground", the crocodile as the archenemy of Captain Hook, the mermaid's lagoon, and the pirate ship. Finally Peter agrees to take the three children back to the Darling parents and they fly into the nursery through the window as Mrs. Darling has been waiting night after night for their return and Mr. Darling is doing his penance in the kennel that belongs to Nana. Mrs. Darling offers to adopt Peter but he as the boy who does not wish to grow up leaves and goes on living with the fairies and the other lost boys "who fall out of their prams when the nurse is looking the other way." Mrs. Darling promises to let Wendy go to him for a week each year to help with spring cleaning.

Though the details given are mostly conventional such as the pirates and the Indians, the fairies and the barking dog that keeps the spirits away, and the villainous Captain Jas Hook and the crocodile, yet the idea is new — that this Peter Pan is a boy who would not grow up, or according to Peter's own version: "I ran away the day I was born ... Because I heard father and mother talking of what I was to be when I became a man. I want always to be a little boy and to have fun; so I ran away to Kensington Gardens and lived a long time among the fairies." I suppose some boys may have such a thought, certainly very few of them would take it seriously but the idea is more of an adult's yearning for the prolongation of his (or her) lost boyhood (or girlbood), as indeed the author with much nostalgia declared in his "Dedication" of the play ("To the Five") his indebtedness to his boyhood companions for their happy memories of the past. There is no question that it is this nostalgia of every grown-up reader for his or her childhood fun that endears the play to so many people and establishes the great popularity of the story both in Barrie's day and later. However, with the exception of Peter Pan and possibly also of Wendy, there are no striking character portrayals and the really interesting episode in the plot is the scene of the Darlings in the nursery in Act I rather than those seemingly fantastic story threads in the Never Land involving the pirates and the Indians in their impossible settings.

Another full-length play involving the supernaturals is "Mary Rose" where the heroine disappears and reappears twice in an island among the Hebrides, "The Island that Likes to be Visited", and then finally appears in the guise of a ghost in the old house in the third and last act of the play. Here, from the very first act the atmosphere of fantasy predominates — first Harry the sailor from Australia is forbidden to enter into the back room and then is warned of a ghost by a shivering old woman Mrs. Otery and then the slowly-folded story of Mary Rose's mysterious disappearance on a remote small island in the Outer Hebrides and of her strange reappearance twenty days later. And the weird, well-nigh unbelievable tale is anticipated in the quotation by old man Morland to his aged wife in Act I of Hamlet's speech to Horatio: "There are more things in heaven and earth than are dreamt of in your philosophy." The supernatural element becomes more striking toward the end of Act II when Mary Rose hears whisperings calling her and then after a struggle passes out of the view of her husband Simon and the boatman Cameron, right on the stage this time while in Act I, the story of her disappearance is only narrated to Simon by her parents. Then in Act III, twenty-five years later, when Simon just came back from a long voyage to the old house to visit his wife's aged parents, a telegram came from Cameron the erstwhile boatman of the Hebrides to tell them that they just found Mary Rose on the island and that Cameron now a bearded clergyman was coming with her.

Then is revealed the strange fact that Mary Rose appears completely unchanged from what she was twenty-five years ago while her
parents and husband and the old boatman Cameron have all changed
almost beyond recognition. The awkward moment when Mary
Rose refuses to acknowledge the passage of time and goes into the
inner room to look for her baby Harry is ingeniously cut short by
the author with the darkening of the stage, and when the lights come
back the scene is shifted back to the beginning of Act I when Harry
is talking to Mrs. Otery about the ghost in the house, and she is
now informing him of the death of the old man and his wife, the
drowning of Simon in the war and the death also of Mary Rose.
After Mrs. Otery shivers talking about the ghost and leaves Harry alone, Mary Rose appears as the ghost, but she cannot recognize
Harry even with his several efforts to lead her on, and finally she
leaves him upon the call of "celestial music."

Though we have little use for ghost stories of any kind, though
in "Mary Rose" Barrie seemed to lack the excuse available in "Peter Pan" for the introduction of the supernatural as a nursery tale
to satisfy the fancy of the children for the fantastic, yet the tale is
at least very intriguingly told and the other-worldly atmosphere on
"The Island that Likes to Be Visited" (as Cameron describes it: "It
was not always here, so they are saying. Then one day it was here.")
pervading almost the entire second act is also superbly managed,
not to speak of the adroit management of the plot throughout.
Barrie at least shows himself a consummate master of the theatre
in creating such masterful scenes of make-believe that almost make
the audience willingly suspend their disbelief.

J.M. Barrie's plays are often known for the thesis each of them
is meant to advance. "Dear Brutus", the most obvious but the
least significant of these dramas, is made to illustrate what Shakespeare tried to point out in "Julius Caesar" when Cassius speaks
to Brutus:

"The fault, dear Brutus, is not in our stars,
But in our selves, that we are underlings."

Barrie in this play tries to prove that certain chance incidents in the people's lives do not shape their futures for them, and that even if people were given their "second chances" in life they would generally drift in the same or similar direction as they did the first time. So, a number of the characters in the play "Dear Brutus" went out into a wood on a midsummer eve and there began their lives once again, with the result that they made practically the same kind of mess of their lives as in real life. There are of course several very comic scenes in the course of their "second chances" in life, but the play contains nothing much else to recommend it.

The two most striking plays by Barrie are "The Admirable Crichton" and "What Every Woman Knows", particularly the former. An old aristocrat Lord Loam is supposed to have advanced ideas on social equality, so once every month he and his daughters and relatives would entertain "on an equal footing" the many servants in the household at tea, to the embarrassment not only of his daughters but also of the servants themselves, some of whom insist that they rank higher than the others. Here we have the author's satire on what happens in an earl's house in Mayfair where all the fashionable aristocrats have their homes. The earl's three idle daughters who are so much waited upon by their three maids, and the idiosyncratic Lord Loam with his "radical views" of social equality and his emptyheadedness and his hopeless attempt at making his monthly speech, while the three other young men who are later to marry the three daughters are all dreadfully inept dandies in their different ways: The Honourable Ernest Woolney with his ridiculous "flair" for epigrams, the Reverend John Treherne who is only good for cricket and nothing else, and young Lord Brocklehurst who depends on his mother to do everything for him. And the only person who seems to be able to do any serious thinking is Crichton the butler who even in Act I reveals his philosophy of "Whatever is natural is right." And the first act anticipates the household's adventures on the yacht.

Then in Act II, the yacht is shipwrecked and everybody is lost upon a desert island in the Pacific. The plight of the aristocratic family is described and Crichton begins to show his superior skill in adapting himself to the new environment. By Act III, the family is already somewhat comfortably settled on the island two years after their arrival, and Crichton is now lord of the isle, the governor, whose favour is courted by everyone and who now designates the earl's eldest daughter Mary as his betrothed instead of Tweeny. But at the end of the act, a ship is sighted at sea, and with the electric appliances set up by Crichton on the island they are able to signal to the ship which now lands and is ready to take them all back to England, and a sudden change comes over Crichton who again starts to address Lady Mary as "my lady". The fourth and last act brings us back to Mayfair, and everything returns to what it was before the disastrous sea adventure, and Crichton becomes once again the irreproachable butler though Lady Mary has her qualms about leaving him to go back to young Lord Brocklehurst.

This is a situation piece, in which the change in situation changes everything, and Crichton is dubbed "admirable" because he can adapt himself to whatever situation he may be in. In Act I he was a staunch conservative, as he launches forth in his justification of "division into classes" in "civilized society":

"The divisions into classes, my lord, are not artificial. They are the natural outcome of a civilized society. There must always be a master and servants in all civilized communities, for it is natural",

and he even speaks in favour of an aristocratic household:

"I am the son of a butler and a lady's maid — perhaps the happiest of all combinations; and to me the most beautiful thing in the world is a haughty, aristocratic English house with every one kept in his place. Though I were equal to your ladyship [addressing Lady Mary], where would be the pleasure to me? It would be counterbalanced by the pain of feeling that Thomas and John [1st and 2nd footman respectively, who are much lower than Crichton the butler] were equal to me."

But even then, when Catherine queries him "if we were to return to Nature", he also has his apt answer to it that anticipates his later attitude and actions:

"If we did, my lady, the first thing we should do would be to elect a head. Circumstances might alter cases; the same person might not be master; the same persons might not be servants. I can't say as to that, not should we have the deciding of it. Nature would decide for us."

And so when they were cast upon the desert island, Crichton acts differently but really holds the same view:

"My lady, I disbelieved in equality at home because it was against nature, and for that same reason I as utterly disbelieve in it on an island. ... There must always, my lady, be one to command and others to obey."

And then toward the end of Act III, when the ship arrives to take them all back to England, Crichton declares firmly:

"It means that our life on the island has come to a natural end."

And finally, when Lady Brocklehurst tries to find out from Crichton what actually happened to the Loam family on the island, Crichton makes an ambiguous answer but to the purpose:

"I think I may say there was as little equality there as elsewhere."

Of course, the play has to end with Crichton giving notice of his wish to leave the household: "I had not told you, my lord, but as soon as your lordship is suitably settled, I wish to leave service."

It is quite obvious that Barrie's essentially conservative temper, here as elsewhere, upholds the English social status quo while he may be uttering his mild satires on the English aristocratic society almost all the way through the play. This is especially pronounced at the end of "The Admirable Crichton", in the last exchange of conversation between Lady Mary and Crichton:

Lady Mary: You are the best man among us.

Crichton:	On an island, my lady, perhaps; but in England, no.
Lady Mary:	Then there is something wrong with England.
Crichton:	My lady, not even from you can I listen to a word against England.

Here, in this apparent expression of patriotism and of humour, Barrie very highly yet very definitely shows us where he stands!

But this play is meant above all to be a comedy, with comic situations sprinkled all over and an abundance of humour as well as occasional thrusts of epigrammatic wit, so even if there are in it certain serious ideas that the author seems to try to get across to the audience, they are certainly not to be taken too seriously. What is more, Barrie is very definitely against social equality, and though he seems sometimes to disapprove of the idleness and uselessness and vanity and hypocrisy of the members of the aristocracy, he thinks also with much contempt of all the servants in the Loam household except Crichton who is able but who favours inequality. However, the exposé of the hypocrisy of the Loam household in Act IV when they pretend they did much for themselves on the island is unmistakable, even if it is much diluted with the ever-present humour that arises out of the ambiguities in their conversation and the ironic situation created by Lady Brocklehurst's insistent though foiled attempts to find out the truth about the happenings on the island. Then there is the outright farcical incident of Ernest being punished on the island with a bucket of cold water on his head whenever he utters an epigram, though his epigrams are really not brilliant nor witty when compared with those in the comedies of manners of the Restoration and of Sheridan and Wilde.

"The Admirable Crichton" has been and will be commended by audiences and readers alike for the clever management of the theme and the central situation, for the many comic scenes and for the delightful humour that creeps up in situation as well as in dialogue, yet its chief saving grace is the numerous satirical hits, often quite unintended by the author as they may be, on the vacuity and general ineptitude of the English aristocracy of Barrie's day.

"What Every Woman Knows" is again a play constructed on a situation and on an idea — the idea here being the oldfashioned one of what an intelligent middle-class woman knows (or should know) how to humour her husband, whereas the odd situation is that of a poor youth caught as a burglar stealing into a family library to read books and then contracted to marry the plain-faced girl of the family in return for a timely loan of 300 pounds. However, this is also a dramatic study of a brilliant heroine whose superior intelligence more than makes up for her homely appearance. Maggie Wylie's self knowledge that her plainness would hardly get her a husband agrees to her father's and brother's plan to bind her in marriage to the poor but ambitious John Shand. But when Shand wins his seat at parliament on the eve of their wedding she has the courage to free him from his obligation to marry her, and then later when he falls into love with a noble lady, she again shows her willingness to leave him and let him be united to the other woman. But her secret — i.e. what every woman knows — is to help him polish up his speeches so that he can achieve success in politics, and so, once he doesn't have her help, his speeches fall to pieces. This shows her cleverness, but the whole theme is built on the foundations of the social acknowledgement of man's superiority over woman, so that the really clever woman can only secretly lend assistance to her husband who is supposed to have risen to popularity by his own efforts. Of course this play was produced in 1908, about a decade before English women gained their suffrage rights. But still, this further confirms Barrie's conservative stand in social problems.

"What Every Woman Knows" is, however, a great play in that there are several wonderful situations and numerous humorous touches that have made it a great success on the stage, and above all, we find one very colourful character portrait in Margaret Wylie, later Margaret Shand.

The first play by Barrie that started him on the road to success in drama was "Quality Street" (produced 1902). Staged a year after Queen Victoria's death, this play was very definitely "Victorian", particularly in its reflections of Victorian morality and Victorian sentiment (or sentimentality).

The story is supposed to take place during the decade of the Napoleonic Wars, first in 1805 and then shortly after the Battle of Waterloo in 1815. The Misses Susan and Phoebe Throssel live in Quality Street in a small country town, Susan being a respected and self-respecting old maid of the genteel society there while "Phoebe of the Ringlets" is still in her marriageable age and is expecting momentarily a certain army surgeon Valentine Brown to call and propose to her. The atmosphere in the blue and white room of the Misses Throssel is that of suffocating Victoria respectability where the old spinsters are thoroughly shocked upon hearing a younger sister read aloud from an "Indelicate" romance about a lover gathering his girl in his arms and raining hot, burning kisses on her eyes and mouth, and where the English army joins in fighting only "for King and Country" and "an English soldier never sacks nor loots" in captured towns. But Valentine Brown comes not to ask for Phoebe's hand but to tell her he has just enlisted in the army and is leaving the next day, and so another old maid is hopelessly added to the genteel society in Quality Street. And what is sadder, the Throssels have lost almost all their money through unwise investment of it as suggested by Valentine Brown, and so the two sisters have to make their living by opening a little school in their blue and white room, "for genteel children only, of course." Then ten years later, just as Miss Susan and Miss Phoebe are ending their last lesson for the school term, amid the martial music celebrating the victory at the Battle of Waterloo reappears Captain Valentine Brown who has returned with the loss of his left hand and who is shocked to find the former "Phoebe of the Ringlets" now an aged schoolmistress twenty years older than she was. So Phoebe puts on once again her ringlets and disguises herself as her niece Miss Livvy and she is taken to ball after ball by Valentine Brown. As she wins success there at the dances, she gradually becomes detected by Valentine Brown, and finally he comes to ask for the hand not of the young and pretty but imaginary Miss Livvy but of Phoebe the schoolmistress whom he has always loved. The fourth and last act is almost farcical but a brilliant *coup de théâtre* when Valentine pretends to take the non-existent Livvy away with him in his coach and then comes back to propose to Phoebe. But this is a typically satisfactory ending for Victorian genteelness and Victorian sentimentality.

"Quality Street" is another situation drama: the story hinges upon the change in situation, from a girl of ringlets with her youth and charm to a worn-out elderly schoolmistress of ten years later, and the use of disguise (as Sophia pretends to be her niece Livvy) also works a shift in situation for Captain Valentine Brown. And these changes in situation lead on the one hand to pathos and sentimentality and on the other to dramatic irony and humour.

There is unquestionably some satire on the genteel society, especially in Act I, although the reproach is much diluted with the abundance of humour; in fact the author with his inborn conservatism seems here to try to justify to a certain extent the Victorian moral code while he very definitely considers the insistence on strict morals to be going much too far.

'Quality Street' is not a great play from the artistic point of view, but it provides a most effective vehicle for the stage, and it shows Barrie as a gifted playwright with his mastery of dramatic technique.

A few words need be said on Barrie's one-act plays. "The Twelve Pound Look" is certainly the most celebrated of his many one-acters. This play contains penetrating satire, rare for Barrie, on the vacuity and vain-glory of a wealthy middle class citizen of London who apes and aspires to join gentility. The man in question, Harry Simms, who believes in the religion of success and who is to be made a knight in a few days is now rehearsing with his wife the whole morning the ceremony of the dubbing. Then the typist Kate appears from the Flora Type-writing Agency who has been asked to type answers to hundreds of letters and telegrams congratulating the awaited conferring of knighthood to the master of the house. She is very efficient and knows all about what she is to say in the letters, to the admiration of Mrs. Simms who is soon to be Lady Simms. Then when Harry Simms reappears and confronts Kate, he is dumbfounded and dismisses his wife at once. Kate turns out to be Harry's first wife who left him fourteen years ago because she couldn't endure him and after she had earned her first twelve pounds to pay for the type-writing machine. In their ensuing conversation she mentions his "hardness", his "coarseness", his "contempt for the weak", his "want of ideals", his "ignoble views of women", but particularly his "success" that made it finally impossible for her to remain his wife, and so he is only worth twelve pounds to her for with that sum to buy a typewriter she can make her own livelihood and be free of him. This dampens his spirit considerably, and then comes the last straw when Mrs. Simms the second wife reappears and is interested not only in the typist as "a capable woman" with "a very contented face" but also in the price of the typewriting machine.

This is again a situation piece, as the situation of the runaway wife returning to confront the prospering would-be knight Harry leads to irony and humour, and inevitably to satire. The play is very adroitly managed technically and is effective both on the stage and for reading. It is certainly a brilliant gem of light satire and good theatre, though such a situation is too clearly an artificially-contrived one and therefore suffers from improbability. Other brilliant one-acters of Barrie's include "Rosalind", "The Will", "The Old Lady Shows Her Medals" and "Shall We Join the Ladies?"

c. Granville-Barker and Drama at Manchester and Birmingham
    Aside from George Bernard Shaw, John Galsworthy, J. M. Barrie and writers for the Irish Abbey Theatre such as W. B. Yeats, Lady Gregory, J. M. Synge, Sean O'Casey, etc., other dramatists of some importance and influence in the first quarter of the 20th

century include Harley Granville-Barker and the dramatists for the Gaiety Theatre at Manchester and for the Birmingham Repertory Theatre.

Harley Granville-Barker (1877—1946) was dramatist, actor, director, producer and critic, all connected with the theatre. Born in London in an estate agent's family, he received his stage training at the age of 13 at a theatre school, and at 15 he appeared on the London stage at the Comedy Theatre with Sarah Thorne's theatrical Company. Later he joined Ben Greet's Shakespeare Company and in 1906 he married Lillah McCarthy of that company who played many of the leading roles at the Court Theatre where he was manager after 1904 and where he presented the plays of Continental dramatists Ibsen, Maurice Maeterlinck and Gerhart Hauptmann and also of English and Irish writers G.B. Shaw, John Galsworthy, W. B. Yeats, John Masefield, as well as Gilbert Murray's English verse translations of Greek classics of Euripedes, Sophocles and Aeschylus. In fact, it was through his productions that Shaw's plays first won their fame in the theatre. From the beginning, Barker cared more for dignified theatrical companies and their activities than for the purely professional drama of West End theatres in London, and as early as 1900 he was play-producer at the experimental Stage Society where his first play "The Marrying of Ann Leete" was performed. He was not only a good friend of Shaw's, but also of the well-known dramatic critic and playwright William Archer (1856—1924) with whom he collaborated in an article "Scheme and Estimates for a National Theatre" (1904). His career as producer also included his Shakespeare productions of "The Winter's Tale", "Twelfth Night" and "A Midsummer Night's Dream" at the Savoy Theatre in 1912—14,when these Shakespearean plays were produced with continuous action on an open stage and with scrupulous attention to the text and to the speaking of verse. His three important plays, "The Voysey Inheritance" (1905), "Waste"(1907)and "The Madras House"(1910)were all performed in the first decade of the 20th century. But following his second marriage in 1918, he was estranged from many of his former associates in the theatrical world and he gave up his career not only as actor and director but also as producer, and merely wrote critical works on Shakespeare's plays and adapted certain plays from the Spanish of Martinez Sierra and of the brothers Joaquin and Serafin Alvarez Quintero. Only two plays were written by himself in the 1920s ("The Secret Life" and "His Majesty" in 1923 and 1928 respectively), neither of them with any significance, but the ponderous work of his later years consisted chiefly of five volumes of "Prefaces to Shakespeare" (published 1927, 1930, 1937, 1945, 1947), which gave him distinction as a Shakespearean scholar and critic. During World War I he served with the Red Cross. After the war he was president of the British Drama League and then settled down for some years in Paris, serving as Director of the British Institute of the University of Paris in 1937—39. Early in World War II he went to Spain (1940) and then to the U. S., working for the British Information Services and giving lectures at Harvard University. He returned to Paris in 1946 and died in the same year.

"The Voysey Inheritance" deals with the illegal practices carried on in the office of solicitors Voysey & Son in the Lincoln's Inn, London, and with the consequences of the misappropriation of the securities, trust funds and other properties of their clients for speculation purposes. The father dies and his son Edward inherits the precarious business, with some speculative investments bringing in good dividends and others sustaining heavy capital losses. Yet he has to carry on, on the one hand reducing the deficit in some cases while on the other managing to ward off the threat of blackmail from the chief clerk in the firm. Then the crisis comes when his chief client insists on withdrawing his securities but half of the money has been lost in speculation. Eventually Edward and the woman who has agreed to marry him try hard and work out a way to save the firm from ruin and Edward from imprisonment.

"The Voysey Inheritance" was in a sense a problem play. Performed in 1905, it was still very much under the influence of Ib-

sen and more directly of the early plays of Shaw. It also was somewhat under the sway of naturalism that reigned supreme on the European Continent in the last years of the 19th century. Here is presented the conflict between legal fraud and moral qualms. But
the distinguishing feature of the play is the vivid portrayal of the
major characters especially of Edward Voysey, whose inner conflict
and external behaviour are both fully drawn.

"Waste" was also a powerful drama, ending in the suicide of
a politician. The title is suggestive of the tragic significance of the
principal figure in the drama. The play only had one private performance, as no license was allowed by the censor for its public production, possibly because the story contains abortion and death resulting from it.

"The Madras House" tells a loosely constructed story, with
Philip Madras the young proprietor of the wealthy drapery firm
the Madras House as the major figure and the central link. Act I
gives a detailed picture of what happens on a Sunday in the household of the Huxtables, with Mr. Huxtable the not-too-well-educa-
ted but fairly well-off proprietor of the drapery establishment of
Roberts and Huxtables and his wife Mrs. Huxtable the proud and
domineering mistress of good breeding and their six spinster-daugh-
ters aged between thirty-nine and twenty-six as the main figures in
the scene, plus three intruders Mrs. Amelia Madras, the deserted
wife of Constantine, Philip Madras her son, and Major Hippisly
Thomas who is Philip's friend and the London manager of Mr.
Eustace State an American millionaire businessman. There is the
reference here to Mr. State's plan for the purchase of the Madras
House as well as Roberts and Huxtables and to the impending
arrival in London of Mr. Constantine Madras who has been away
for many years and has embraced Mohammedanism, but the portrayals of the Huxtables figure large in the greater part of the act.

Act II shifts to Philip Madras's office and waiting room in the
Madras House where Philip is chiefly concerned with the accusation of illicit love between a clever and attractive shop-girl Miss

Yates and Third Man in the hosiery Mr. Brigstock, by the housekeeper at Peckham Miss Chancellor, and then with the terrible fuss and counter-accusation against Miss Chancellor by Mrs. Brigstock, over the obvious pregnancy of Miss Yates who refuses to name the unborn baby's father. Philip the humane employer tries to pacify all four people involved, but to little avail. Then there follow short scenes between Philip and his wife Jessica the refined, charming lady of virtue and intelligence and between Philip and Major Thomas, and we are acquainted with the none-too-natural relations between the young Madras couple and with the somewhat unnatural intimacy between Thomas and Jessica.

Act III takes place in the rotunda or the round-domed hall of the Madras House where a conference is held to discuss the sale of the Madras House and Roberts and Huxtables by their owners to a wealthy American business man and is participated by Philip Madras, Mr. Huxtable, Mr. State the American and his manager Major Thomas and also Constantine Madras the retired owner of the Madras House. But first there is a sort of fashion-show manoeuvred by the manager of the establishment Mr. Windlesham to impress upon the would-be purchaser of the firm Mr. State, and costume models *numero un* to *numero dix* appear in turn with their modish latest-fashion-costumes from Paris on. When the parade of the costume models is over, Constantine throws a bombshell by declaring himself to be a Mohammedan living in southern Arabia and revealing his attitude toward women and uttering his comments on the costume models as well as on the six spinster daughters of the Huxtable household. And a quarrel seems to hang in the air between Constantine and Mr. Huxtable the injured Amelia's brother. Then the business deal for the sale of the two drapery firms is very swiftly settled with a gesture of generosity on Constantine's part. And the act ends with the threatened storm of Mr. Huxtable toward Constantine calmed down and with a little pleasantry indulged in by Philip in his brief remarks with Major Thomas about Jessica.

Act IV has to do entirely with the Madras family, or rather with the strained relations between old Mrs. Madras and Jessica, between Constantine and his deserted wife, between Constantine and Philip, and finally between Philip and Jessica. Constantine is identified as the man responsible for Miss Yates' pregnancy, and he is leaving for his home in the East, while Philip denying inheritance from Constantine and refusing the offer of directorship from Mr. State needs to reduce his expenses at home and to readjust his relations with Jessica. The final episode of tête-à-tête between Philip and Jessica to which "there is no end" according to the dramatist, sounds like a bit of a comedy of manners, or a high comedy but really it isn't — it's just a unique bit of the dramatist's fun.

The four acts are described here in great detail chiefly to show the naturalistic bent of the play. Though Philip Madras appears in all four acts of the play, he does not really dominate in any of them, nor is the story chiefly concerned with the development of his character or career. Roughly speaking, the first act is chiefly about the Huxtables, the second act about the goings-on in the Madras House, the third about the sale of the House, and the fourth about the two generations of the Madras family. The chief incident — the sale of the Madras House — takes up less than five minutes at the conference table or less than one-tenth of the 3rd act. It is quite obvious, therefore, that the author means here to demonstrate "a slice of life" theory of drama that was prevalent on the Continental stage in the last lap of the 19th century and the beginning of the 20th, for here interesting details — such as the depiction of the six spinsterish Misses Huxtable in Act I, Philip Madras' patient attempts to resolve the scandals involving Miss Yates, Mr. and Mrs. Brigstock and Miss Chancellor in Act II, and the pass-in-review of the Parisian-fashion costume models, *numero un* to *numero dix* in Act III — are all fully represented with nothing left out, and these extraneous details are given here not to further the plot nor to add to the portrayal of characters, but simply for their own sake.

However in a sense "The Madras House" may be classed among

the "problem plays" in that all through the play the problem of woman in society is either directly discussed or indirectly referred to or hinted at and many different types of women are given: first the fundamental difference between the women in Western society and in the East (in Southern Arabia), or rather in Christendom and in the Mohammedan world, and then within the Christian world different women like Miss Yates, Mrs. Brighouse and Miss Chancellor (for all their different traits they all belong to the lower society) and the more wealthy ones including the Huxtable girls on the one hand and Jessica on the other (or Mrs. Huxtable on the one hand and Mrs. Amelia Madras on the other). And of course there are different attitudes held by different men toward women — by Constantine and Huxtable and Mr. State of the old school and Major Thomas and Philip Madras among the younger set, not forgetting the unique Mr. Windlesham the manager of the Madras House who herds the costume models around for show. Aside from the mention of monogamy in connection with Constantine's harem and that of polyandry by Philip in his casual remarks with Major Thomas, the most engrossing episode on the woman question is the apparently interminable discussion on "the modern woman" in the Western World between Philip and Jessica at the very end of the drama. Of course the dialogue between the couple here is "of ships and shoes", i.e., from "civilization" at "White Chapel High Street" to proper education for Mildred their little daughter, yet their talk is centred on what one thinks about the women of different kinds and different social stations, beginning from Miss Yates and the "six thin girls" in the Huxtable household to Jessica herself, with her subscriptions to London Symphony Concerts, with her "Persian carpet on the floor" and "Last Supper by Ghirlandajo, over the mentelpiece", with her "aristocracy of good feeling and good taste", with her "Honour and Dignity and Purity", with her beauty and her virtue, with her "culture" and her "civilization". This last topic is most interesting because it deals with the apparent uselessness of intelligent and charming and cultural women of the upper / classes in

England (who are really comparable in a way to the women in a Mohammedan harem though the author didn't choose to make the comparison). It is very likely that Granville-Barker in this play purposely dealt with the woman question as the drama was written in the heyday of the woman's suffrage movement, before the suffrage rights were won in 1919.

An experienced man in the theatre, Granville-Barker excelled in the writing of brilliant dialogue which not only can be quite serious and witty at the same time(as in the conversation between Philip and Major Thomas and also between Philip and Jessica), but also cynical and ironical (as in the speeches of Constantine declaring his faith in Mohammedanism and in all that goes with it). What is more, in "Madras House", the dramatist has succeeded in producing several well-moulded character creations. There are Mr. Huxtable and Mrs. Huxtable, both adhering to strict moral codes of Victorianism but the former ever betraying his lack of education and his weakness of character (especially in front of an imperturbable person like Constantine Madras)while the latter acts in a domineering way toward everybody and has pretensions to refinement of high society. There is Constantine Madras the Mohammedan who is not only a libertine in theory and in practice, even in his old age, but who is a dare-devil in his speech and in his criticisms of hypocrisy in Christian society. Then there is someone who falls halfway between Constantine and Philip, Major Thomas the "Mean Sensual Man",easily tempted by attractive women intellectual and otherwise, but ever afraid of them and trying to escape from them. But the most carefully chiselled figure is Philip Madras who is the hero in the play if there ever is one. Philip is in a way the author's ideal, being an idealist ready to give up "seven hundred a year and a directorship" offered by Mr. State but rather eager to stand for the County Council because "It's a muddled country" and he wants to go "self-sacrificing" and "to do dull, hard work over drains and disinfectants" for the poor people he sees all the time "at a London Street". And he tries to persuade Jessica in the first place "to teach

Mildred[their daughter]to "look out of the window at the life outside" and then for herself to "pay for free womanhood", to be one of the "common woman" among "common men". Of course the author knows as the hero Philip himself knows, that this self-sacrifice on his part won't really help matters, and so he leaves the tête-à-tête between Philip and Jessica unended — up in the air, so to speak — at the very end of the play, though the dramatist seems to hint that at least there is momentary happiness for the intellectual couple who have the best will in the world.

Of English drama in the first quarter of the 20th century mention should be made briefly of the theatrical activities in the two provincial centres of Manchester and Birmingham. In Manchester the Gaiety Theatre which like the Irish Abbey Theatre was also subsidized by Miss A.E.F. Horniman, in 1908, became the home of a theatrical company that up till 1917 put on a number of plays by Stanley Houghton (1881—1913), Harold Brighouse (1882—1958) and Allan Monkhouse (1858—1936). These dramatists were grouped together as the Manchester School.

Stanley Houghton, the leading member of the Lancashire playwrights, was chiefly known for his "Hindle Wakes" (1912), which was closely related to the movement for the emancipation of women then going on in England. The story is about an escapade of Alan Jeffcote the son of a wealthy cottonmill owner and Fanny Hawthorne an ordinary weaver and the daughter of an employee at the mill. According to conventional morality the two youngsters should be married and the parents of both families insist on it, though the boy has first to break off his engagement to another woman Beatrice. Then the surprise ending comes with the rebellious Fanny declaring her refusal to marry Alan to preserve the appearance of virtue, and announcing her determination to leave her home and live alone on her wages as a weaver. Performed in 1912, 11 years after the death of Queen Victoria, the play showed the clean break from the strait-laced moral code of Victorianism and was a timely piece as a sort of declaration of independence for the new woman.

Harold Brighouse wrote chiefly one-act plays, but he achieved his distinction in "Hobson's Choice", a full-length play, that also had more or less to do with the movement for the emancipation of women. Hobson, a provincial boot-maker and a widower, tyrannizes over his three unmarried daughters,until his eldest daughter and capable house-keeper and shop-manager Maggie sets up her own shop with a men-tally-retarded yet an extremely skilful bootmaker as her husband and master-craftsman and takes away all the boot-making business from the old man. In the end, with the help of her younger sister's fiancé, Maggie succeeds in dividing up much of her father's property and now the only choice for him is to become a sleeping partner in their shared boot-making firm.

Both "Hindle Wakes" and "Hobson's Choice" are lively come-dies with much irony and humour and both deal with the social prob-lems of the day, — in one case with conventional morality and in the other with family tyranny, but both connected with the social posi-tion of women. The problem plays under the influence of Ibsen and partly of Shaw still had their sway in the early years of the century, prior to World War I.

Another provincial theatre, the Birmingham Repertory Thea-tre, also flourished for some time after its founding in 1913, John Drinkwater was its first manager and one of its leading dramatists, with "Abraham Lincoln" as the most successful of his several plays on historical personages.

d. The Irish Abbey Theatre, Lady Gregory, Synge

In the first half of the 20th century, especially in the years before the First World War,drama written in the English language flourish-ed in Ireland, particularly in Dublin. Previously, in 1899, W.B. Yeats, Edward Martyn, George Moore and others had founded in Dublin the Irish Literary Theatre as the first practical outcome of the move-ment towards an Irish literary renaissance, but only by 1904, after the acquisition of the Abbey Theatre by Miss A. E. F. Horniman, did the

Irish players have a regular theatre of their own to put on plays by Irish playwrights based on Irish mythology and legends and also on contemporary Irish life. Yeats and Lady Gregory played the leading roles in promoting the native Irish drama presented by the native Irish company of actors and actresses, which even went to England and America on extensive tours and won international fame. The more important plays staged in the early decades of the century include, besides the celebrated one-acters by Yeats and Lady Gregory, chiefly the plays by J. M. Synge and Sean O'Casey. Lennox Robinson and St. John Ervine also contributed their plays for production at the Abbey Theatre and served for some time as manager there (Robinson in 1910—23 and Ervine in 1915). The Abbey Theatre survived long after the establishment of the Irish Free State and then the Irish Republic, and even after it was partially destroyed by fire in 1951, its work continued with aid from the Eire government.

Wife to a former colonial governor, Lady Gregory (1850—1932) wrote many plays, full-length dramas as well as short ones, for the Abbey Theatre, but she has chiefly been known for some of her earliest one-acters. "The Rising of the Moon" is certainly the best deserving to be praised as a patriotic play for the Irish Nationalist as the hero not only escapes from death but wins a policeman's sympathy, too, though the author points out in a note that some extreme Nationalists were offended at the performance for having the policeman shown "in too favourable a light". Several other plays show merely the dramatist's sense of humour: "Spreading the news" tells the simple tale of a blatant lie spread quickly even before the very persons who are directly involved in the false news; "Hyacinth Halvey" shows that the exaggerated report of "exemplary character" about a man coming to a new environment may make it rather uncomfortable for him; "The Gaol Gate" reveals the sad plight of a woman visiting her innocent son in a jail and finding him to have been hanged the day before; and "The Workhouse Ward" pictures two aged men in the workhouse bickering endlessly with each other and yet refusing to be parted when given the chance. Although none of these short pieces attains to any high achievement as comedy, yet the rustic humour and the native feeling of simple fun and wit won recognition both from stage audiences and in play-reading.

John Millington Synge (1871—1909) was born near Dublin and in his boyhood was under the influence of his Protestant evangelical mother. In 1892 he was awarded the Harmony and Counterpoint Scholarship of the Royal Irish Academy of Music and graduated from Trinity College in Dublin. He went to Germany and Italy and then spent his time mainly in Paris, giving up his religious belief and his ambition in a musical career and turning to the study of French classical drama. In 1899, he met W. B. Yeats in Paris and under the latter's advice he returned to Ireland and spent some years on the Aran Islands off the coast of Ireland. His life among the peasants there enabled him to pick up the Irish folk tales as well as the colloquial speech which were to inspire him to the writing of a total of five plays staged in his lifetime (1903—1909) and of the unfinished "Deirdre of the Sorrows" published posthumously in 1910. Though his plays were not well received by the audiences at the time, and "The Playboy of the Western World" even provoked a week of nightly riots in the theatre, yet they led to a big revival of Irish drama at the Abbey Theatre and made Synge first among the playwrights who made the Abbey Theatre and the Irish players famous in the years before World War I.

Synge wrote altogether six plays. Of his three short plays, "Riders to the Sea" is justly famous. An old Irish woman who lived with her family in a fisherman's cottage on an island off the west coast of Ireland has lost her husband and four of her six sons at sea and is now faced with the reported drowning of another son Michael. Then her last remaining son Bartlet, against her wishes and those of her two daughters Cathleen and Nora, is going by boat to a horse fair with a red mare and a grey pony. Cathleen and Nora examine a shirt and a stocking taken from a drowned man washed ashore and identify them as belonging to Michael. Then the mother Maurya returns and laments that she has seen Michael riding on the grey pony with his fine clothes and new shoes. Soon enough several old women come into the cottage crossing themselves and "keening", followed by a group of men carrying the dead body of Bartlet on a plank who had been knocked over into the sea by the grey pony and washed out to a great surf on the white rocks. There are passages of great poetry in Maurya's keening:

> "They are all gone now, and there isn't anything more the sea can do to me ... I've no call now to be up crying and praying when the wind breaks from the south, and you can hear the surf is in the east, and the surf is in the west, making a great stir with the two noises, and they hitting one on the other. I'll have no call now to be going down and getting Holy Water in the dark night after Sambain, and I won't care what way the sea is when the other women will be keening."

Toward the end of the one-acter, she says, "They're all together this time, and the end is come," and then after praying to God to have mercy on the souls of all her sons, on her own soul, "and on the soul of every one is left living in the world," she adds:

> "Michael has a clean burial in the far north, by the grace of the Almighty God. Bartley will have a fine coffin out of the white boards, and a deep grave surely. What more can we want than that? No man at all can be living forever, and we must be satisfied."

Her stoicism here after all her sufferings and her resignation to fate obviously wins the approval of Synge the playwright, as they represent faithfully the attitude of helplessness of the Irish peasants in face of hardships.

"The Shadows of the Glen" tells the story of an aged Irish farmer who pretends to be dead and then rises to chastise his wife ready to be married to a young "herd", and of the tramp who eventually leaves the cottage with the wife driven out by her husband. There is plenty of humour in the old man's pretense to be dead and especially in his drinking with his wife's young lover after her departure with the tramp.

"The Tinker's Wedding" contains in its two acts a bitter satire on the village priests of Ireland who try to squeeze as much money as they can out of the very poor people far away from civilization. A man and a woman, both tinkers, are trying to get the village priest to marry them in the Christian fashion, but the priest is not satisfied with the gold coin of ten shillings they offer him for the service, and finally the two tinkers are roused to anger and they beat the priest up badly. There is the old woman, the young tinker Michael's mother, who serves as comic relief in the play by drinking and begging for pennies to buy drinks with.Here we have yet another picture of the grimness of life in out-of-the-way corners of rural Ireland.

The three full-length plays by Synge show much greater depths than to be found in the three shorter pieces. "The Well of the Saints", with its setting at "some lonely mountainous district in the east of Ireland one or more centuries ago", relates how two blind old beggars, man and wife, Martin and Mary Doul, suddenly gained their sight from being administered holy water from the well of the saints, by the wandering friar of a saint walking by,how each of them discovered to their mutual horror the ugliness of his or her spouse, and how when they later lost their sight again, they felt comforted and happy and did not wish to be cured their blindness once again. There is something very highly philosophical behind this apparently impossible story which again pictures the miseries of the poor and ignorant people in remote parts of Ireland with their superstitious beliefs and their simple ways of life.

Synge is chiefly known for his fantastic folk drama "The Playboy of the Western World" which is again placed "near a village, on a wild coast of Mayo". Michael James Flaherty, a village public-house owner on the coast of Mayo, is going to a funeral wake somewhere and leaving behind him his daughter Margaret (called Pegeen Mike). Her cousin, a young farmer named Shawn Reogh whom she intends to marry, comes on a visit but is afraid of a certain Father Reilly for keeping her company for the night. Suddenly a weary, dirty and very much frightened young man by the name of Chris Mahon enters and wishes to stay safe there after he reveals his identity as a murderer of his old father for forcing him to marry a wealthy widow twice his age. He is instantly taken for a hero by Pegeen and other girls and a Widow Quin who herself once inadvertently hit her husband and was indirectly responsible for his death. But the following morning his father, Old Mahon, appears surprisingly at the cottage, have been stunned by Chris' blow but not killed, and when the son returns from winning his honours at the village sports he is knocked down first by the father and then in their ensuing fight outside the young man again deals the old man an apparently fatal blow. This time Chris is no longer regarded as hero but is pinioned by the village people as murderer. Unexpectedly Old Mahon revives again and creeps back into the room to take his son's part against the village accusers, and Pegeen rebuffs her cousin Shawn's offer to wed her by lamenting over Chris: "Oh, my grief, I've lost him surely. I've lost the only playboy of the western world."

While it is difficult for us normally to appreciate a play in which the apparent murderer of one's own father should be made first a hero upon report and then a criminal upon actual sight of the deed, even in a wild setting amid out-of-the-way people far away from "civilization", it is interesting to note Synge's own defence of his plays as set forth in his "Preface" to "The Tinker's Wedding":

> "The drama is made serious — in the Freud sense of the word — not by the degree in which it is taken up with problems that are serious in themselves, but by the degree in which it gives the nourishment, not very easy to define, on which our imaginations live."

He adds that we go to the theatre

> "As we go to a dinner where the food we need is taken with pleasure and excitement,"

and he objects to the problem plays such as those of Ibsen but points out that

> "Of the things which nourish the imagination humour is one of the most needful, and it is dangerous to limit or destroy it."

It is certainly fascinating and highly stimulating to come across characters so typical of Irish peasantry in a setting so fantastic and so remote from the madding crowd, that reported murder very naturally loses its social significance but becomes strangely romantic,and it suits one's wild fancy to see the old father so easily reconciled to his son in spite of the harsh words and the terrible blows exchanged between them. And the wry humour arising out of these quaint events against a sombre background can only add to the charm of the simple life and simple ways of thinking peculiar to the Irish peasantry living in almost complete seclusion from the outside world. However, these plays by Synge, including this striking comedy that contains the mock-heroic "playboy of the western world", show unmistakable signs of decadence in the modern bourgeois-aristocratic world at a time when disillusionment in the unsatisfactory social reality of 20th-century Europe led the playwright to seek his escape in an idealized peasantry of patriarchalism. It is vain for the amoral dramatist to imagine the total absence of moral values in whatever the rustic people might do in the far away and the long ago.

The truly great drama by Synge is however his unfinished tragedy "Deirdre of the Sorrows" which is based on the age-old legend of the young lovers Deirdre and Naisi meeting their fate at the hands of the treacherous old king Conchubor. The plot here follows closely the old story thread according to which Deirdre and her lover Naisi cleverly ran away from Conchubor's clutches and had seven years of happiness in the wood in Alban, and then the two returned to Emain Macha where they fell into the trap set for them by Conchubor and where Naisi and his two brothers were killed by Conchubor and Deirdre killed herself. But Sygne changed the motivation for Deirdre to go back to Emain Macha by suggesting that she was afraid her love with Naisi should wither as they grew old. Deirdre is made in the play to lament not only the brevity of human existence, but also the brevity of youth and of love: "The dawn and evening are a little while, the winter and summer pass quickly, and what way would you and I, Naisi, have joy forever?" And then: "There's no place to stay always ...."

It's a long time we've had, pressing the lips together, going up and down, resting in our arms, Naisi, waking with the smell of June in the tops of the grasses, and listening to the birds in the branches that are highest .... It's a long time we've had, but the end has come, surely."

And she asks:

"And isn't it a better thing to be following on to a near death, than to be bending the head down, and dragging with the feet, and seeing one day a blight showing upon love where it is sweet and tender?" And Naisi has to agree finally: "You're right, maybe. It should be a poor thing to see great lovers and they sleepy and old."

Here Synge touches on the tragic theme that has its universal significance, and the tragic deaths of Deirdre and Naisi and his two brothers are thus dignified endings comparable to those in ancient Greek tragedies, as Deirdre declares just before she kills herself:

"I have put away sorrow like a shoe that is worn out and muddy, for it is I have had a life that will be envied by great companies .... It is not a small thing to be rid of grey hairs, and the loosening of the teeth .... It was the choice of lives we had in the clear woods, and in the grave we're safe, surely." And again similar to the Greek tragedies, the idea of fate hanging over human lives is here also with Deirdre, when she first asks of Naisi upon their first meeting: "Do many know what is foretold, that Deirdre will be the ruin of the Sons of Usna, and have a little grave by herself, and a story will be told forever?" And then she declares to him in prediction:

"It's for that maybe I'm called Deirdre, the girl of many sorrows ... for it's a sweet life you and I could have, Naisi .... It should be a sweet thing to have what is best and richest, if it's for a short space only."

Though there are many passages in Synge's other dramas that read like great poetry, truly beautiful poetic flights are only to be found in this his last play as he following in the steps of Yeats and AE took up the famed legendary tragedy of Deirdre.

In spite of his short career, Synge was nevertheless the most prominent of the Irish playwrights who contributed to the Abbey Theatre in Dublin.

e. Sean O'Casey

Sean O'Casey was born in 1884 of a poor Irish family in Dublin, Ireland. His father died when he was only three years old and his mother had to take care of a big family. All through his childhood he suffered from poverty and misery. While yet a boy he suffered from a serious eye-ailment which almost brought him blindness. When he was 14, he started to work, and he passed through the varied experience of being an apprentice at a commercial firm., and of working on the railway, at the dockyard, in an iron-monger's shop and with a carpenter. These years of a labourer's life with all its attendant miseries steeled him and made him realize the injustice of the capitalist society. And the Irish environment in which he was brought up had its specially deep impression on him of the threefold oppression the Irish people had to endure under the oppression of British colonial rule, of the Irish landlords and bourgeoisie and of the Catholic Church which served the ruling classes both foreign and domestic. O'Casey was an active worker in the workers' unions in Ireland and in 1913 he participated in the big tram-workers' and other workers' strike in Dublin which lasted for five months. Then in 1916 he again took an active part in the historically well-known Easter Rising when the Irish people rose against British imperialism in the middle of the first world war. The rising was suppressed after seven days' fighting and O'Casey was arrested and barely escaped death.

In the meantime O'Casey started to write. After his novel "The Story of the Citizen Army" which appeared in 1919, he turned to drama,and in the 1920s he wrote a series of plays, "The Shadow of a Gunman" (1923), "Juno and the Paycock" (1924), "The Plough and the Stars" (1926) and "The Silver Tassie" (1929). Of these the first three were produced in the National Irish Theatre, the Abbey Theatre in Dublin, produced there not without a stiff fight put up by the author, while "The Silver Tassie" was absolutely forbidden and was later shown in a London theatre. O'Casey followed a totally different path from that of the literary men and women of the "Irish Renaissance" movement, many of whom, including Yeats, Synge, and Lady Gregory, were more interested in the revival of the primitive past and avoided contemporary politics and social problems. For all his respects for Yeats, O'Casey refused to work only for purely aesthetic perfection in his writings and fought this tendency of working only for aesthetic achievement. On the other hand, though O'Casey was at first rather attracted to the writings of James Joyce, particularly to the latter's highly elaborate style, he differed essentially from Joyce in dealing ever with the social conflicts and struggles of his day.

O'Casey's dramas of the 1930's all had to do with actual political struggle in Ireland: "The Shadow of a Gunman", "Juno and the Paycock", "The Plough and the Stars" and "The Silver Tassie" dealt respectively with the conflict between the Irish citizen army and the British colonial troops in 1920, the civil strife between the Irish republican army and the left-wing Sinn Fein group in 1922—23, the Easter Rising of 1916, and the World War of 1914—18. Disillusionment over the Irish politicians' betrayal of national interests in their compromise with British imperialism made O'Casey leave his native country and to settle in England in 1926.

The 1930s and the early 1940s marked a period of further flowering of O'Casey's multi-sided genius. He continued to write plays: "Within the Gates" (1933), "Purple Dust" (1940), "The Star Turns Red" (1940), and "Red Roses for Me" (1943), but he also published a book of critical essays "The Flying Wasp" in 1937 and launched the first two of his volumes of autobiographical novels, "I Knock at the Door" (1939) and "Pictures in the Hallway" (1940). In the 1930s he also joined the Communist Party of Great Britain.

Beginning from the end of the Second World War, O'Casey's literary activities consisted chiefly in the completion of the series of six autobiographical novels (the last four being "Drums Under the Windows" (1946), "Inishfallen, Fare Thee Well" (1949), "Rose and Crown" (1952) and "Sunset and Evening Star" (1954), but he also turned out several plays: "Oak Leaves and Lavender" (1942), "Cock-a-Doodle Dandy" (1949) and "The Bishop's Bonfire" (1955), and a second book of critical essays, "The Green Crow" (1956).

O'Casey's dramas may be divided up into three periods: those in the 1920s, those in the years 1930—1945, and those after 1945.

"The Shadow of a Gunman" is a satire on the mock-heroism of a decadent poet named Devoran, against the background of guerilla fightings between the Irish citizen army and the British colonial force. Devoran who is mistaken for a gunman of the citizen army and is flattered and considered a hero, is actually the "shadow" of a gunman who in the minute of danger shows his cowardice and real worthlessness. The real gunman, Maguire, appears only in one scene and is then killed by the enemy. The real figure of prominence in the play is Minnie Powell, a common working gril who loves Devoran as a national-liberating hero and who sacrifices her own life in order to rescue him from danger.

"Juno and the Paycock", with the civil war of 1927—33 as background, tells of the family of a poor unemployed worker in the slums of Dublin. The major story thread evolves round the rumour that the family is about to receive a huge inheritance; the drama begins with the rising hope of the family, continues with the preparations for a celebration and the borrowing of money for the purpose and ends with the rumour turning out to be untrue and the family sinking into greater distress than ever. There is much humour and irony as well as pathos, but the real significance of the play lies in the superb portrayals of the four major figures that reveal the intense social and political struggle in the war-torn Ireland. The father Jack Boyle, nicknamed the Paycock because he is idle and vain like a peacock, is unemployed and gets drunk all the time but he is ever boastful and vainly hopeful. The mother Juno is a capable woman who has to do everything to support the family and to bear all the hardships that befall any of its members. The daughter Mary Boyle is vain and hopes to live a life of comfort and luxury but she finds herself pregnant and deserted by her lover. The son Johnny Boyle joins the left-wing Sinn Fein group in their fight against the government, but he betrays one of his comrades and is shot to death by a gunman in revenge. The chief defect of the drama is the note of despair hanging over the whole action while the real heroes of the Irish civil war only move behind the scenes. However, the pictures of the miseries of a poor family of an unemployed worker and the vivid portraits of the traitor Johnny and the vain girl Mary and the good-for-nothing worker Jack Boyle not only led to the success of this play on the stage but established O'Casey's fame as one of the foremost Irish dramatists in the 20th century.

"In "The Plough and the Stars" are portrayed the republican patriots of Ireland who took part in the Dublin Rising of 1916. The hero of the play Clithroe thinks nothing of personal danger in his fight for the liberty of Ireland and he abandons his beloved wife Nora in order to join in the uprising. These patriots carry the tri-coloured banner of Ireland and the standard of the Citizens' Army on which are drawn the plough and the stars. The rising is routed by the police, and Clithroe dies, while his wife loses her senses out of grief over his death. Here with great force O'Casey represents the revolutionary spirit of the people, and in the narration of the barricade-fighting we can see the heroic figures of Irish patriots fighting for the liberty of their native land. In contrast to these patriots is painted the pseudo-patriotism of liberal-bourgeois chatterers whose empty talk and real indifference to the welfare of their country are depicted with a subtle note of censure.

In "The Plough and the Stars" the revolutionary activities are pushed more to the foreground than in O'Casey's earlier dramas, and Clithroe the revolutionary figure becomes the major character whose actions dominate the story and whose courageous death fitly symbolizes the central tragedy in the play, the failure of the Rising. And there is much study of the inner contradictions of the hero before he finally decides to take leave of his fond wife Nora and to plunge into the Rising. The death by a stray shot of Bessie the old neighbour woman who has come to take care of the distraught Nora after Clithroe's death, in the last act of the play, adds to the tragic effect.

"Silver Tassie" is the weakest of O'Casey's four plays of the 1920s. Though here, through the story of Harry Heegan the football hero being maimed for life in World War I, the playwright launches his attack on the imperialist war which makes brutal sacrifice of innocent soldiers cheated into enlisting for the so-called honour of the country but which brings profit to many war profiteers, yet the desertion of the maimed Harry and the blinded Teddie by their girls Jassie and Susie seems to overshadow the curse of the imperialist war in the final scene of the play.

O'Casey wrote four plays in the decade and a half before the end of the Second World War. "Within the Gates" is a fantastic play of sheer symbolism. The four scenes of the play are placed in the morning, noon, evening and night of the four seasons of spring, summer, autumn and winter, all "within the gates" of a park. A number of unnamed characters, each representing a type, move about in an atmosphere of oppressiveness that seems to suggest that the whole world has gone awry, but the complicated allegorical significance of the play is hard to catch.

"Purple Dust" is a play satirizing the wealthy English bourgeoisie who consider themselves the defenders of traditional Irish culture of the remote past. The story here is about two rich English gentlemen, Basil Stokes and Cyril Poges, buying an old Tudor-Elizabethan mansion in the Irish countryside, bringing their mistresses, two Irish women, with them to the mansion. They try to restore the place to its ancient grandeur but finally get themselves stranded in the building with flood water raging into the house. In contrast with these stupid and ridiculous members of the English bourgeoisie are portrayed in the play three Irish workmen and their foreman O'Killigain, with much zest for life and a strong feeling of personal dignity as well as a keen sense of humour. With his intense hatred for the English ruling classes in Ireland O'Casey here tries to thoroughly expose the ridiculous side of the English bourgeoisie as well as the disintegration of the traditional grandeur of the British Empire, but the story is a bit too fantastic and the situations are often quite impossible.

"The Star Turns Red", dedicated by the author "To the Men and Women Who Fought Through the Great Dublin Lockout in Nineteen Hundred and Thirteen", deals with the theme of the conflict between the workers who are led by the Communists and the Fascist organization, the Saffron Shirts, who are supported by the Purple Priest and the Lord Mayor,with the Brown Priest inclining to the side of the workers and the several Union leaders indifferent to the conflict and ready to betray the workers. In Act I the conflict is symbolized in that between two brothers Jack (a Communist) and Kian (a Fascist) in the home of "the Old Man" and "the Old Woman". Jack goes to attend a strikers' demonstration, after refusing to go with his sweetheart Julia (daughter of a neighbour Michael and also a Communist) to a dance. The Lord Mayor and the Purple Priest urge the Old Man to persuade Jack to leave the ranks of the Communists, as Kian also comes with several members of the Fascist Saffron Shirts to warn Jack. Julia, in an attempt to shield Jack, slaps the leader of the Saffron Shirts across his face and she is ordered to be taken away and whipped. Michael, Julia's father and also a worker and a Communist, comes to protest against their whipping of his daughter and attempts to strike the leader, but Kian shoots him and he dies. In the second act, the leaders of the General Workers' Union who have grown indifferent to the workers' interests and to their strike and now want to discard the strike-leader Red Jim,who is patterned after Jim Larkin, the great leader of the famous dockers' strike in Dublin in 1913. The third act deals with the funeral of Michael and a clear portrayal of Red Jim and of the Purple Priest is given. Then in the fourth and last act as the Christmas Carol of "Silent Night" is followed by the playing of the "Internationale" in the distance, sirens and pistol shots are heard to announce the outbreak of violence between the strikers and the police, and soon Red Jim and the Red Guards enter and use the residence of the Lord Mayor as a fortress. Jack is reported killed in the street fighting but the Purple Priest and Kian come with a flag of truce. Kian is struck with sorrow over his brother Jack's death and deserts the Saffron Shirts. The Purple Priest fails to persuade Red Jim to lay down his arms and to ask the Brown Priest to leave the workers' side, and the latter goes away amidst the curses of the Red Guards and the workers. Then the play ends with the Red Star rising and glowing brighter and brighter as all the Communists, workers, soldiers and sailors join in the loud singing of the "Internationale".

Here we find the successful portrayal of a great leader of the workers in Red Jim while the fascists, the Saffron Shirts and their running dogs the Purple Priest, the Lord Mayor, the treacherous Union leaders, as well as Joybell the Catholic flag-wagger are thoroughly satirized and depicted as sharply grotesque figures.

"Red Rose for Me" quite possibly refers again to the Dublin Transport Union Strike of 1913. In the first act, the hero Ayamonn Breydon, a young worker, scholar and poet, is living with his mother in a two-roomed house in the Dublin slums. He is trying to memorize a passage from Shakespeare in order to take part in a performance for workers' relief and he refuses to leave the workers' union despite his sweetheart Sheila's persuasion. Many visitors come to his lodging, including a landlord of houses Brennan, a strong Irish nationalist Roery O'Salacaun, a mocker of sacred things Mullcanny, and three superstitious Catholic neighbour women Eeada, Dympna and Finnoola, and here we have a realistic picture of the Irish population in the slums. In the second act Ayamonn gradually discards his illusion of a peaceful solution for the conflict between the capitalists and the workers. While the capitalists refuse to raise the workers' wages and even plan to break up the strikers' meeting with armed force, Ayamonn decides to plunge into battle, accepting the request of the railwaymen to speak at their meeting and rejecting the rector's warning. When Sheila urges him to desert the strike and to try to get a better job for himself, he scolds her and breaks with her. The third act takes place in a Dublin street beside a bridge that crosses the river Liffey. There is vividly portrayed the abject poverty and sufferings of the slum-dwellers, including the three superstitious women

Eeada, Dympna and Finnoola who sell cakes and apples and violets. These men and women, all worn-out and hungry and many of them homeless and unemployed, were sitting and lounging against a gloomy grey sky, and then Ayamonn comes and tries to talk them out of the gloom and urge them to keep in step with the workers' strike and to build with their own hands a new and bright city out of the mean and wretched Dublin. Then the scene in the street suddenly brightens and the setting sun sheds its crimson hues upon the wretched slum-dwellers and makes their bodies and faces all aglow, and the people as well as the dreary skyline of the city seem to be completely transformed and these poor people seem to take on a new vigour. Traces of their hunger and fatigue disappear, their backs are straightened and their faces light up with beauty, and they sing a song with pride and exaltation, to build a brave city free from hunger and hardship, from things that are ugly and common and mean. But soon afterwards the sun sets and the momentary transformation is past, and the backs of these people are bent down again and their eyes grow dull, and in the distance may be heard the tramp of marching soldiers obviously sent to prevent the meeting of the workers and to stop their strike. The fourth act opens on the grounds of the Protestant church of St. Burnupus. The Rector of the church is kind and sympathetic to Ayamonn and the strikers, but the figure of Inspector Finglas of the Mounted Police is there to threaten with armed suppression of the strikers. The Rector and Sheila try to dissuade Ayamonn from going to speak at the workers' meeting but the latter refuses to listen and goes. Soon a bugle-call sounding a charge is heard, followed by the sound of galloping horses and then several volleys of rifle-fire, and the next minute the death of Ayamonn is reported, with abullet-hole in his chest. Then a few hours later Ayamonn's dead body is carried into the church and Sheila comes and lays a bunch of crimson roses on the body's breast, while a song of "Red Roses for Me" is sung by one of the characters at the very end of the play.

The dramatist has succeeded in presenting a rather comprehensive picture of the Irish people in the Dublin slums and in portraying a hero in Ayamonn who develops steadily from an undetermined and peace-minded participant in the workers' movement to a strong, well-seasoned supporter of the strikers in their fight against the ruling classes. Ayamonn dies, but eventual victory of the workers and the wretched poor people of Ireland is suggested in the symbolic scene in Act III of the wretched slum-dwellers suddenly lit up in bright colours by the setting sun. And there is much beautiful poetry in the play.

The three plays written by O'Casey after the Second World War clearly mark a decline in the playwright's dramatic career. "Oak Leaves and Lavender",written immediately after the end of the Second World War, is frankly a war play, with many details of the war introduced such as blackout curtains, air-raid wardens, official regulations, conservative programs, etc. The story deals chiefly with the activities of two air-men when they are on leave and after they die in battle, and one of them, Drishogue O'Morrigun, is a Communist. "Cocka-Doodle Dandy" is a fantastic play in which the whole atmosphere is pervaded with superstition centering around a cock. Obviously the playwright means here to satirize the superstition among the wealthy, lustful men as well as the despotic sway of the priest in rural Ireland. "The Bishop's Bonfire" is a satire on rural Ireland with its bishops and canons and counts and councillors and the havoc they wrought on the Irish people. For the coming of the great bishop, the erstwhile Bill Mullarkey who was born in the very town he is now returning, the whole town is filled with the flapping of flags, paper flowers and white candles, and the councillor Count Reiligan is having his house painted and decorated to welcome the bishop with the new carpet, the new statue, the new desk, the new chair, the new gilded looking glass, together with hot water bottle and a rug and choice wine. Then at the end of the play a big blazing bonfire is to be seen flaming high for the welcome of the bishop. The figures of the Councillor Count Reiligan and Canon (later Monsignor) Burren dominating over the others are depicted to represent the two-fold oppression of priesthood and bourgeois-aristocracy tyrannizing over the Irish people, while a number of the down-trodden are shown in the drama, including the two daughters of the Count who in their different ways have to stifle their love longings and joy of living, the girls' lovers Manus and Daniel who spurn the oppressive atmosphere in rural Ireland and leave for foreign shores, as well as the curate Father Boherce a low official in the church and the old Cedger Sleehaun who is dismissed from service because he voices freely his criticisms on Catholic priesthood and on the ways of the bourgeois world. But there is rebellion in the air as Daniel and Manus leave and the canon (now Monsignor) has to stoop and coax one of the masons to peel the spuds and pluck the plovers for the bishop. The final tragic death of the pious daughter of the count Foorawn, shot by her lover Manus when he was caught by her in the act of stealing money from the safe, is merely a coup de theatre that brings the play to its climax of death in the house, in sharp contrast with the cheers and the blazing bonfire outside to welcome the bishop thither. Here is devastating satire on the goings-on in backward, priest-ridden rural Ireland.

The many plays of O'Casey, from his "Shadow of a Gunman" and "Juno and the Paycock" and "The Plough and the Stars" of the 1920's through "The Star Turns Red" and "Red Roses for Me" of the 1940's, to "The Bishop's Bonfire" of the middle 1950's, we find a glorious train of plays with enthusiasm for revolutionary struggle and satire on the feudal-bourgeois, Catholic society of Ireland and England.

O'Casey wrote a series of six autobiographical novels between 1939 and 1954. They are: "I Knock at the Door" (1939), "Pictures in the Hallway" (1942), "Drums Under the Windows" (1945), "Inishfallen, Fare Thee Well" (1949), "Rose and Crown" (1952) and "Sunset and Evening Star" (1954). These six volumes cover the whole of Johnny Casside's or the author's life, from his birth and early childhood to 1954, and his long life is reviewed in these books in indissoluble contact with the liberation struggle of his people and with the social and political developments in Ireland and England from the last years of the 19th century to the middle decades of the 20th. The literary form chosen for the purpose — the autobiographical novel

— enables the author to give a broad, realistic picture of historical events, including stirring descriptions of mass actions, portraits of political and literary figures, and chapters that generalize and sum up whole periods in the history of Ireland and of England.

"I Knock at the Door", the first of the six volumes, tells the story of Johnny Casside's (i.e., Sean O'Casey's) boyhood up to the age of twelve, a story of years of hunger and pain cushioned by his mother's love, a story of Ireland's agony in her battle to be free. The book opens with the birth of the hero, Johnny Casside, the youngest of seven children of a poor Protestant family in the Dublin slums. When he was five, he had ailments on his eyes and he almost went blind, and his mother took him to a doctor for treatment and they were told he had to undergo a long period of cure. Then his father fell off a ladder and broke his spine and after a time died. The burial of his father is vividly described, with satirical touches on the clergyman who officiated at the burial. Then follows a sketch of his two eldest brothers Michael and Tom working as clerks at the telegraph and post offices respectively and of his elder sister Ellen, the teacher of an infants' school, expecting to be married to a bugler. Then Tom and Michael joined the army and Ellen married the bugler, and they went away, and the mother was left alone with her two youngest children, both sons, Archie and Johnny. Then we are told, after a few episodes of Johnny's innocent boyish pastimes, how a Protestant clergyman, the Reverend Mr. Hunter, told the boy's mother to send him to school, how Johnny was cruelly beaten up by the schoolmaster, how his eyes grew bad again and he had to go once again to the hospital for treatment, how he had to go to Sunday School and church upon Mr. Hunter's peremptory orders and was treated badly there by the Sunday School teacher on account of his poverty, how he went back to school again and was severely beaten by old schoolmaster Slogan for the offence of certain other boys, how in his uncontrollable passion of hate he struck at Slogan's bald, old head with a heavy ebony ruler and then ran away home, how Mr. Hunter came and asked the boy's mother to punish the child for the crime and how she refused to obey the clergyman, how with his eyes in bandages he imagined the military review in Dublin in celebration of Queen Victoria's birthday, how he went with his mother to buy their weekly supply of meagre food and how he stole a lump of bacon and an egg when a drunkard upset food-trays in a baker's shop, how he and his mother went on a tram to witness the celebrations of Queen Victoria's jubilee and how they witnessed instead a fight between the students of Trinity College and the crowd and later between the crowd and the police, and how finally his sister Ellen brought him a book of grammar and he began to study in earnest and "knocked at the door" of life. Through the whole length of the narration there is the atmosphere of the poor Irish people suffering under the two-fold oppression of the English rulers and the native bourgeoisie.

And the personal events of the boy Johnny Casside are narrated frequently with references to political events of the Irish nation in the background. So the birth of the hero in the first chapter of the book is accompanied by the description of the parade of soldiers in Dublin in celebration of the Queen's birthday, and then when the boy's mother is taking him to see an eye doctor, they pass by the Irish patriot Parnell who is being cheered by the people. Then in another chapter, the conductor of a tram commenting sarcastically on "The Vice-Regal Ball with all the gulls o' Dublin gawkin' at the notabilities flockin' in to a fine feed an' a gay night in Dublin Castle", hums a patriotic song:

"Oh, black's your heart, Clan Oliver, and colder than the clay!
Oh, high's your head, Clan Sassenach, since Sarsfield's gone away!
It's little love you bear us, for sake of long ago.
But hold your hand, for Ireland still can strike a deadly blow."

Also, the Dublin Castle Ball is described in verse form with bitter satire, and then the hero's two elder brothers Michael and Tom are shown to have joined the army to fight for the Queen, and his sister Ellen in marrying the bugler is described as uttering her thoughts of loyalty to the English rulers. How many among the Irish were deceived by the propaganda of the English rulers into willing submission is fully explained here, and the English policy of arousing enmity between the Protestants and Catholics in Ireland and of glorifying the imperial conquests of Britain abroad is also censured. Then there is the scene of the review of the troops, on Queen Victoria's birthday, as visualized in the mind's eye of the little boy here, and definite sarcasm is revealed in the review ending in rain, though the paraders sang,

"The twenty-fourth of May, the Queen's birthday,
We'll let it rain tomorrow, but it mustn't rain today!"

Then toward the end of the book we have another scene on the celebration of something about Queen Victoria described with much sarcasm. And amid this celebration the conductor of a tram sang in a low voice a song about the Irish patriot of long ago, Wolfe Tone, a Protestant who went over to France nearly a hundred years ago and brought back a great fleet to help the Irish fight the English invaders. And then also amidst the celebration a crowd of people, defying the college students for singing "God Save the Queen!" , raised the national flag, the green flag, of Ireland and sang a song against the "English tyrant". And the crowd surged forward, broke the line of policemen barring their way, and attacked the college boys with fists and sticks, driving them back, back toward the college gates. But then the mounted police came and drove the crowd away.

But these scenes of struggle between the Irish patriots and the English rulers and their running dogs serves only as the background to the story, though occasionally it emerges and occupies the centre of the stage in the narrative. The main thread of the story is concerned with the description of the hero's boyhood experience. Half-starved and half-blind, he has to face all the different kinds of sufferings and different forms of oppression and tyranny. And the courageous fight the boy puts up against these different forms of oppression and tyranny as well as the equally courageous fight put up by the various Irish patriots in the story against English tyranny (from Parnell and Wolfe Tone to the conductor of a tram and a common crowd in Dublin) illustrate well O'Casey's ever-present thought of the two-fold oppression the Irish people had to endure and his conviction in. eventual victory over this twofold oppresion.

In this autobiographical novel the figures of the boy Johnny and his mother stand out as vivid characters fully portrayed: the boy's courage and pertinacity and the mother's patience and strength are well illustrated with many details, some of which are quite sad and even pathetic while others achieve sometimes subtle humour and sometimes open laughter. The artistic qualities of this book as a novel stand above the later five volumes, with the unity of its story and the vividness of its character-portrayal.

"Pictures in the Hallway" is a direct continuation of "I Knock at the Door" in narrating the adolescent days of Johnny Casside, with much space given to the description of the conflict between the worker and the capitalist. Here the hero Johnny Casside is shown to be a rebel who would rather starve than submit.

The third novel, "Drums Under the Windows", has as its theme the great class battles of the Irish workers in which O'Casey took an active part. The book describes the famous strikes and mass demonstrations of 1913 (regarded by Lenin as "A turning point in the history of the labour movement and of socialism in Ireland"), the colourful figure of Comrade Larkin(the Secretary of the Irish Transport Workers' Union whom Lenin called"a talented leader" and "a man of seething Irish energy") and the Easter Rising of 1916, all these being based on the author's personal knowledge. Especially interesting and significant is a chapter in the book, entitled "Prometheus Hibernica", in which Jim Larkin's powerful speeches to the masses are vividly recalled by O'Casey. The Easter Rising is also described very realistically, including its failure and the mistakes made by the Irish liberation movement as well as the losses resulting from these mistakes. Especially impressive is the scene of the author, Sean as a young man living in a period of imperialist terror and bourgeois-nationalist demagogy, "reading, reading the new catechism of the

'Communist Manifesto' with its great commandment: Workers of all lands, unite! And in all the shouting and the tumult and the misery around, he heard the roll of new drums, the blowing of new bugles, and the sound of millions of men marching."

The fourth volume of the series, "Inishfallen, Fare Thee Well" tells of O'Casey's final break with the Irish bourgeois-nationalist movement, and in it the author writes much about the different members of his family and of the great poverty and oppression that ruined them all. His sister was a talented musician; his brother Michael had the makings of an artist, and another brother, Archie, longed to be a building engineer. But their talents were crushed, as O'Casey puts it, by the "spiritual pastors and masters." Particularly vivid is the image of the author's mother, mentioned in all the first four volumes, but particularly clearly portrayed in this the fourth book. Here we find her having survived all her children except Sean and having lived in poverty all her long life. She is described as an "indomitable woman", and in this volume she dies, and the scene of her death is particularly memorable, as her surviving son, Sean, drapes her coffin with a Red Flag.

The first four volumes of the autobiographical novels deal with the life of the hero Johnny Casside in Ireland, as the boy grows and becomes a worker and then, after great trials and miseries of life, gradually turns into a militant fighter. Then with his final break with the bourgeois rulers in Ireland he goes to settle down in England, and the last two of the autobiographical novels have to do with his life chiefly in England.

The fifth book, "Rose and Crown", deals with the hero's adventures in England (and in America) in the late 1920's and the early 1930's, against the historical background of the General Strike of 1926 and the national economic crisis in England in 1931. Here, though the personal events of the hero, about his first advent in London and his first dramatic adventure in a London theatre, about his poverty and his determination not to write plays to cater to bourgeois tastes, about his meetings and conversations with Shaw, H. G. Wells and W.B. Yeats, and about his trip to America for the opening there of his play "Within the Gates", still form prominent episodes in the book, the political events assume preponderate proportions in this volume as the betrayal of the Labour Party and the notorious figures of Ramsay MacDonald, Philip Snowden and J. H. Thomas, who played infamous traitors' roles in the General Strike and in the national crisis, are vividly described and bitterly satirized, and Stanley Baldwin the Conservative Prime Minister is depicted in a most sarcastic scene. On the personal side, Sean's own trip to America is described to show the contrast between the rich and the poor in the richest bourgeois country in the world.

The sixth and last volume of the autobiographical novels, "Sunset and Evening Star", deals with Sean O'Casey's adventures from the late 1930's till after the Second World War. The major historical events which sometimes forge into the foreground of the narrative include the British policy of conciliation adopted by Chamberlain toward fascist Germany and the outbreak of the Second World War, the power of the Red Army, the German invasions of Denmark, Norway, Holland and Belgium, the debacle at Dunkirk and the French defeat, then the "Battle of Britain", then the vicious American propaganda in the post-war years of the necessity of setting up American military basis in Europe, the cold war and the threat of atom war. In this volume the writer's personal life retreats to a less observable corner, leaving only his experience of hiding in underground dugouts during the German bombing raid in the war and his associations with friends and acquaintances, especially with Shaw, while a lot of space is given to the Second World War. There are hilariously satirical scenes about Hitler and Chamberlain, especially the imagined scene of Chamberlain's visit to conciliate Hitler, and then there are also scenes of light irony showing Mosley the English fascist and his Black Shirts and describing the Nazi army stopped in their Polish invasion by the Red Army at the River Bug. The episodes exposing the postwar American propaganda of cold war and the threat of atom war are also filled with devastating sarcasm, with a happy blending of frank satire and subtle humour O'Casey is a great master of. The passages concerning his personal experience are highlighted with his admirable comment on G. B. Shaw and with his own declaration of optimism as he reaches the ripe old age of "sunset and evening star".

The six autobiographical novels of O'Casey's, taken together, make up a monumental work of great biography plus fiction, telling the life and adventures of the author's more than seventy years of existence against the kaleidoscopic historical background of great social, political and military struggle from the 1880's down to the 1950's. And the language used, sometimes simple and sometimes ornate, sometimes colloquial and at other times poetic, but always appropriate and effective, adds greatly to the beauty of these volumes. Though some of O'Casey's plays may have achieved true excellence, these autobiographical novels in the bunch seem to outweigh even his best plays of his earlier literary career.

SECTION IV ENGLISH PROSE FICTION: 1900—1920

a. Joseph Conrad (1857—1924)

Joseph Conrad was a pen-name for his novels. His original name was Teodor Josef Konrad Korzeniowaki. He was born in the Soviet Ukraine, of Polish parents, both of whom belonged to the Polish landed gentry. His father was a poet and a patriot and was involved in the Polish insurrection against Russian rule in 1863, and for that the family was exiled to northern Russia where the hardships and the rigorous climate were partly responsible for the mother's death. In 1869 young Conrad went with his father to Cracow, a city in Southern Poland, then under Russian rule, and there he first went to school. His father died soon after, and his uncle Thaddeus assumed responsibility for the child for almost a quarter of a century afterwards. The novelist in his boyhood yearned to become a sailor, and finally in 1874 he left for Marseilles and joined a French merchant navy first to Martinique, then again to other islands in the West Indies in 1875 and 1876, as apprentice and as steward respectively on some French vessel. On one of the voyages the ship sailed along the coast of Venezuela where he got his information later used in his important novel "Nostromo", and in another voyage he met a Corsican sailor named Dominic Cervoni who became the model for several major characters in Conrad's novels. Between voyages Conrad spent much of his time in artistic circles in Marseilles and probably took part in some unfortunate smuggling and gun-running adventure in support of Don Carlos VII, a claimant to the Spanish throne. The future novelist also got involved with a Spanish girl at about this time and for her sake he probably participated in a duel, and he also ruined himself financially in a gambling venture at Monte Carlo. Then in 1878 he first signed up as a deckhand on a British freighter, bound for Constantinople from Marseilles, and later in the year he first landed in England. Beginning from 1878 he served for 16 years in the British merchant navy, rising to Second Mate in 1850, to First Mate in 1884, and passing the Board of Trade examination for a Master Mariner's Certificate (i.e., as Captain of a ship) in 1886, shortly after he became a naturalized British subject earlier in the year. His novels 'Youth" and "The Nigger of the 'Narcissus'" were based on his experience on the "Palestine" freighter bound for Bangkok in 1883 and on the "Narcissus" from Bombay to Dunkirk in 1883—1884, respectively. His voyage as first mate to Samerang, Java in 1887 gave him material for his novel "Typhoon", while his five to six voyages among the islands of the Southeastern Asian Archipelago provided him with background knowledge for the adventures and the locale for "Lord Jim", "Almayer's Folly" and "An Outcast of the Islands". He started to write novels in his London lodgings between voyages in 1889, but in 1890—1891 he fulfilled his long-felt desire to visit the Congo as captain of a Belgian company's river steamer. This extremely arduous adventure which included a 36-days' journey of 200 miles by caravan track up the river Congo, supplied him with story material for his most impressive "Heart of Darkness', but also permanently undermined his health. His numerous voyages enabled him to visit the East Indies and Australia and India many times, but by 1894 his sea career was practically over though he did not finally abandon any expectation of returning to the merchant service till 1898.

His first novel "Almayer's Folly" appeared in 1895, and he married in 1896 a woman who was not his mental equal but who took good care of him till his death. He settled down in London and wrote novel after novel but real popularity did not come to him till 1913, eighteen years after his first published novel, when "Chance" brought him extremely favourable reviews and a big sale both in England and in the United States. Before that time his family finance was often in straitened circumstances, though he had made many friends among the well-known British and American writers of the day, including Galsworthy, Henry James, Stephen Crane, H. G. Wells, Arnold Bennett, Virginia Woolf and Bertrand Russell, most of whom considered him as a novelist of exceptional genius.

Though the raw material for most of his novels was gathered in the last quarters of the 19th century and a number of them were written or at least begun in the 1890's, only three of the full-length novels ("Almayer's Folly", "An Outcast of the Islands" and "The Nigger of the 'Narcissus'"), as well as one collection of short tales ("Tales of Unrest"), were published between 1895—1898, while his first great novel "Lord Jim" appeared in 1900, followed by a dozen completed novels and several collections of short stories between 1902 and 1923, so that he was truly a 20th-century novelist. His case was a striking example of one who hardly knew any English until he was 21 but who later became a well-known novelist in English and developed his own style in the adopted language. In the last decade of his life he was already widely known, but in the sixty years since his death his fame has gone up steadily and, with his marked influence upon William Faulkner, Graham Greene and Andre Malraux, he ranks now among the most important of English noveliests of the 20th century.

"Almayer's Folly", Conrad's first published novel (1895), deals with the adventures of Karpar Almayer and his daughter Nina and her lover, a rajah's son from Bali, with the setting placed in a trading station in Borneo, then part of Dutch colony in the East Indies. There are rich and vivid descriptions of the river and forest and of a new house built by the hero and called ironically "Almayer's Folly". This first novel established Conrad's fame as a master of exotic scenes and romantic atmosphere.

Conrad's first novel of true importance is "The Nigger of the 'Narcissus'" in which the author turned from the superficially colourful Malaya subjects to a much deeper and more intense concern with life and death. Here the domineering figure is a gigantic Negro named James Wait who is haunted by the Spirit of Death upon his first appearance in the novel when he goes sick with a terrific cough almost at the very beginning of the voyage, and whose presence ever as a dying man continues to haunt the "Narcissus" and the whole crew on board, amidst an elemental storm that almost sinks the ship. All the other persons on the ship, from the Captain and the chief mate, and the oldest seaman Singleton, down to the religious cook and the new hand and seditious Cockney named Donkin, are all at once repelled and attracted to Wait, who as the only black man among the White people inspires sympathy from the whole crew yet who is blamed by all as responsible for the misadventures of the voyage. Although the novel continues with stirring episodes of the terrific gale and near-disaster of the ship as well as the threat of mutiny set on by Donkin, the most arresting theme is the mysterious fate of the Negro seaman who hardly ever emerges from his bunk but around whom evolves all the other characters and all the main incidents in the tale. As Conrad announces in the Preface to the novel, he obviously tries in the story to illustrate his theory that "speaks to our capacity for delight and wonder, to the sense of mystery surrounding our lives; to our sense of pity, and beauty, and pain; to the latent feeling of fellowship with all creation — and to the subtle but invincible conviction of solidarity that knits together the loneliness of innumerable hearts, to the solidarity in dreams, in joy, in sorrow, in aspirations, in illusions, in hope, in fear, which binds men to each other, which binds together all humanity — the dead to the living and the living to the unborn." To these words Conrad adds:"All art ... appeals primarily to the senses, and the artistic aim when expressing itself in written words must also make its appeal through the senses, if its high desire is to reach the secret spring of responsive emotions."

In "The Nigger of the 'Narcissus'", Conrad also first experimented with telling the tale not directly by himself as author, but through some one who is also an eye-witness of the tale told. In this novel the story is told by an omniscient shipmate on the "Narcissus" who serves the double capacity of narrator and of participant in the action. This seemed to add depth and complexity to Conrad's aim at seeking the truth in a work of prose fiction, and he later further developed this device by introducing a regular narrator Marlowe in four of his tales: "Youth, "Heart of Darkness", "Lord Jim" and "Chance".

One of Conrad's most colourful and most effectively told tales is "Lord Jim", considered by some as his greatest novel. Though Jim is the central figure throughout, the novel falls naturally into two parts, the first part dealing with the hero's adventures on the steamship "Patna" until its miscarriage while the second and more eventful half tells of Jim's vicissitudes at Patusan (somewhere in the East Indies). The first climactic moment comes near the end of the first part when the "Patna" that was carrying some 800 pilgrims from an Eastern part for Mecca the Mohammedan holyland struck some submerged object and appeared to be sinking. The deserter of a captain and his engineers as well as the other White men on the ship were aware of the danger and they were going to escape in the seven life-boats, leaving the pilgrims to the mercy of the waves. Jim jumped into one of the life-boats on the spur of the moment as he and the captain and the engineers abandoned the "Patna". However, they learned not long after that the "Patna" did not sink but was towed to Aden by a French gunboat, and they were then charged at the Court of Inquiry for "abandoning in the moment of danger the lives and property confided to their charge" as officers on the ship, and the captain and Jim were thereupon deprived of their certificates as master and mate. To Jim who was ever proud of his honour, this was an insurmountable blow to his personal dignity and integrity, especially when each time his sympathetic friend Captain Marlowe secured some new job in the coastal area, report of his bad name ever haunted him and made it impossible for him to stay on. Finally Marlowe gets Jim appointed agent and manager of a remote trading-post at Patusan far up a tropical river. There Jim quickly won favours from an elderly chief Doramin and became an intimate friend and companion of the latter's warrior son Dain Waris, earning from the people there the honoured title of Tuan Jim which meant Lord Jim. Jim took to wife the stepdaughter of the former manager of the trading post, a West Malayan Portuguese named Cornelius, and called her Jewel. Then a pirate known as Gentleman Brown came secretly to Patusan with his men and started to bring havoc to the colony. Cornelius betrayed Jim and the Patusans by telling the piratical gang a secret path and Brown killed Dain Waris. Jim felt very sad over the tragedy of his friend and unarmed he went to Doramin to plead his own innocence, but the latter shot him dead.

In "Lord Jim" Conrad obviously was immersed in his idea of blending the moral with the aesthetic considerations in the portrayal of the central character. Lord Jim is described as an idealist, an almost hopelessly romantic idealist, who feels his great and continual remorse over the cowardly and dishonoured role he played when deserting his duty as a seaman he jumped into the lifeboat to save his own skin, and who tries hard thereafter to atone for the great blot on his honour until he meets his death somewhat heroically for some criminal act he has no share in. To Conrad moral integrity is the highest trait of heroism and so Lord Jim's failure to live up to it is the most terrible blemish in his character and only his moral courage in facing death at the end can restore him to dignity and honour. And only moral uprightness can give high aesthetic values to any character and to any work of art. Conrad here followed the traditional view of laying unduly great emphasis on the personal integrity of an individual as the decisive factor, while overlooking the all-important interrelationship between the individuals and the society they live in. Actually, no matter what the captain or the mate of a merchant vessel does or fails to do, no matter what the manager of a trading station in a remote colony in the Orient may strive for honour or moral integrity, all these persons are willy-nilly the servants or instruments of European colonialism doing their honourable or dishonourable bit for the oppression or exploitation of the colonial peoples. But of course a man who was born and bred to his aristocratic temper such as Conrad was could not be aware of this. So it was only too natural for the novelist to try to consider Lord Jim as a heroic figure with his lifelong strivings after personal honour and moral integrity. While Jim's ignominious conduct to save his own life at the cost of dereliction of duty is vividly described to show the terrific inner conflict within the man, the chain of events that lead first to his success in redeeming himself by gaining confidence and good will from the natives and their chief and the chief's son and finally to his readiness to face death with calmness and courage is narrated with a great tour de force that brings much aesthetic pleasure to the readers. At least "Lord Jim" is a powerful novel that is also a great work of art.

It was in the last years of his sea career that Conrad went to the Congo and gathered the necessary raw material with which to write his most harrowing work of fiction — "Heart of Darkness" — which is certainly also his greatest story that unrelentingly condemns the imperialism and colonialism that swallow up almost the whole continent of Africa.

The story begins with Marlowe telling his friends about his visit to the Congo in Central Africa in order to take over the post of a captain of a river-steamer who had been killed by one of the natives there. He had for quite some time wanted to go to that river though he knew it to be "a place of darkness" and so he was happy to be appointed to this job. He went to sign the contract at a trading society at Brussels and then boarded a French steamer to go to the mouth of the big Congo river where the seat of the government was. Thirty miles up the river on a small steamer he was shown by the Swedish captain the trading station of the Company. There he witnessed the horrible sight of "the grove of death", "the gloomy circle of some Inferno", of many "black shadows of disease and starvation", who were working and dying. He met a welldressed white man who was the Company's chief accountant, who told him first about the ivory gathered there and then about a Mr. Kurtz, a first-class agent, "a very remarkable person", "at present in charge of a trading post ... in the true ivory country." Next he left the station with "a caravan of sixty men, for a two hundred mile tramp." On the way he met many mysterious Negroes "armed with all kinds of fearful weapons" and a white man who said that he came there "to make money". Fifteen days later, he came in sight of the big Congo river again and arrived at the Central Station where he met the general manager and saw the sunken steamer that he was to command. The manager spoke again of Mr. Kurtz who was ill, and said the repair for the wretched ship in the river would take three months. There Marlowe also met another white man who was a young aristocratic first-class agent and a brickmaker and who also spoke of Mr. Kurtz as "the chief of the Inner Station", as "a prodigy", as "an emissary of pity, and science, and progress," a "universal genius". "Yes. Today he is chief of the best station, next year he will be assistant manager, two years more and he will be General Manager."

Then we get a picture of this most primeval part of the earth when Marlowe finally started on his journey on the newly-repaired steamer: "Going up that river was like travelling back to the earliest beginnings of the world, when vegetation rioted on the earth and the big trees were kings. An empty stream, a great silence, an impenetrable forest. The air was warm, thick, heavy, sluggish.

There was no joy in the brilliance of sunshine. The long stretches of the waterway ran on, deserted, into the gloom of overshadowed distances. On silvery sandbanks hippos and alligators sunned themselves side by side. The broadening waters flowed through a mob of wooded islands; you lost your way on that river as you would in a desert, and butted all day long against shoals, trying to find the channel, till you thought yourself bewitched and cut off forever from everything you had known once — somewhere — far away — in another existence perhaps." The steamer seemed to be crawling toward Kurtz as Marlowe and those on board "penetrated deeper and deeper into the heart of darkness".

On their way up the river they met with all sorts of strange adventures, all of them somehow linked up with Kurtz. About eight miles from Kurtz's station, there was "a glimpse of the towering multitude of trees, of the immense matted jungle", and there came "a very loud cry" and then a "tumultuous and mournful uproar". The pilgrims on the steamer were all open-mouthed and "darting scared glances, with Winchesters at 'ready' in their hands", and they whispered to one another, "Will they attack? .... We will all be butchered in the fog". But there was the thick fog and if the black savages on the bank of the river should try to reach the steamer in their canoes, they would get lost. But later the fog lifted when they sailed to about a mile and a half below Kurtz's station, and arrows from the shore came flying at the steamer and "naked breasts, arms, legs, glaring eyes" could be made out from the bush on the river-bank very near the ship. The pilgrims on the steamer opened their gun-fire into the bush but it was of no avail, while the black helmsman died of a sharp spear-thrust that caught him just below the ribs. However, as soon as Marlowe started to pull at the line of the steam-whistle in the steamer, and jerked out screech after screech, instantly the tumult of angry and warlike yells were checked and the shower of arrows stopped.

All this time there were frequent references to Mr. Kurtz and to the possibility that Kurtz was also dead, and always with high reverence to "the gifted Kurtz", and Marlowe paused in his tale-telling to give an account of Kurtz — that he had been educated partly in England, that his mother was half-English and his father was half-French, that he had written a report to the International Society for the Suppression of Savage Customs, that he had the power to charm or frighten rudimentary souls into an aggravated witch dance in his honour.

Then finally they saw in the distance Kurtz's station and upon landing they met a young Russian the son of an arch-priest, who was a staunch admirer of Kurtz and who told him how Kurtz went to the tribesmen "with thunder and lightning" and "could be very terrible" in his expeditions for ivory. This Russian adventurer and trader in ivory also showed Marlowe the terrible rows of black heads of the dead natives stuck on the posts of a fence of Kurtz's station, and explained how the chiefs of the tribes would crawl to show their respects to Kurtz. Then appeared Kurtz, sick in a stretcher carried by a group of black natives, followed by pilgrims carrying his weapons of guns and a rifle and a revolver, as well as his correspondence of torn envelopes and open letters. Then came "a wild and gorgeous apparition of a woman", "draped in striped and fringed clothes", with "brass leggings to the knees", "brass wire gauntlets to the elbow", and "innumerable necklaces of glassbeads on her neck," and then she disappeared. The manager and the Russian both behaved obsequiously to Kurtz, and deplored the fact that Kurtz was very sick though they declared that "Mr. Kurtz had done more harm than good to the Company" and that Kurtz's "method is unsound".

Then at night Marlowe went on shore from the steamer and came face to face with Mr. Kurtz and entered into a queer sort of conversation with him. Kurtz was carried onto the steamer, but a wild mass of human bodies including the black woman shouted on the bank of the river and Marlowe pulled the string of the whistle which sent all the people on shore away.

Then "the brown current ran swiftly out of the heart of darkness", as the steamer sailed down the Congo river, with Kurtz on it dying and raving about "my intended, my station, my career, my ideas." Then the engines broke down and the steamer had to stop for repairs at the head of an island, and one evening Marlowe heard Kurtz say, "I am lying here in the dark waiting for death" and he saw "on that ivory face the expression of sombre pride, of ruthless power, of craven terror, of an intense and hopeless despair." And just before Kurtz died, he cried in a whisper at some image, at some vision — he cried out twice, a cry that was no more than a breath: "The horror! The horror!" Shortly after came the announcement from a black boy: "Mistah Kurtz — he dead."

The story was wound up by Marlowe with his comment on Kurtz, with his meetings with a man from the Company and with one of Kurtz's cousins, and finally with his visit to Kurtz's "intended".

"Heart of Darkness" means many things to Conrad. Near the beginning of the story Marlowe and his friends were watching the scene on the Thames River just a little below London, when Marlowe said suddenly: "And this also ...has been one of the dark places of the earth". He was referring to London in the first century B. C. when the Romans under Julius Caesar first came to England. Obviously Conrad here compared the London (and England) of 55 B. C. as they appeared to the then more civilized Romans, with what the Congo of 1890 seemed to Conrad and other Europeans of the time. So, after Marlowe got to the Congo and made a 200-mile tramp into the heart of Central Africa and then sailed on the repaired steamer further up the river, and particularly when he and his crew came near Kurtz's trading station, there was the significant mention of the heart of darkness. "We penetrated deeper and deeper into the heart of darkness." Later, when Marlowe had to sum up the popular legend up the Congo River about Kurtz's "ability to talk" or his "gift of expression", he spoke almost rhapsodically of "the bewildering, the illuminating, the most exalted and the most contemptible, the pulsating stream of light, or the deceitful flow from the heart of an impenetrable darkness". And then when finally

Marlowe and his crew were leaving the Congo on the steamer with the dying Kurtz on board, there was another meaningful observation on their departure from the heart of darkness:"The brown current ran swiftly out of the heart of darkness, bearing us down towards the sea with twice the speed of our upward progress." Then, just before Kurtz's death, Marlowe described Kurtz's physical as well as mental state with the phrase of "impenetrable darkness": "His was an impenetrable darkness. I looked at him as you peer down at a man who is lying at the bottom of a precipice where the sun never shines," and Kurtz himself also comments on his dying moments as "I am lying here in the dark waiting for death." Finally as the whole story told by Marlowe comes to an end, and as the author made a symbolic reference to the black clouds and an overcast sky and the general mood pervading Marlowe and his friends at the moment as leading to "the heart of ... darkness", "the offing was barred by a black bank of clouds, and the tranquil waterway leading to the uttermost ends of the earth flowed sombre under an overcast sky — seemed to lead into the heart of an immense darkness."

From all the above cited passages it is quite obvious that by the heart of darkness Conrad first of all referred to the primitive and barbarous world of the Congo, but he must have also in mind the barbarous and cruel ways by which the imperialist, colonialist rulers of the West imposed upon the primitive superstitious black natives of Central Africa, especially the unspeakable acts of murder and highhanded oppression and exploitation that were perpetuated by the servants of the Belgian King Leopold II such as Kurtz. In this respect Conrad whose long sea career enabled him to have an extensive view and knowledge of colonialism and imperialism in Africa and Asia and Latin America in the late 19th and early 20th century was best suited to utter his indictment of the bestial and inhuman role played by the ruthless perpetrators of economic plunder and to shatter the colourful sham of "white man's burden" as advanced by imperialist lackeys like Rudyard Kipling. The brilliant portrayal of Kurtz was a masterly stroke of satire and humour. Kurtz who earned his fame as "a first-class agent", a "universal genius", "a remarkable person", "an emissary of pity, and science, and progress", "chief of the best station", "that man" who could "make rain and fine weather," "a gifted creature", "one of the immortals", was actually a man who killed many natives and had their heads drying on the stakes under his own windows and yet made all the natives adore them and obey him and crawl to him to show their respect. What is more, he was one who could raid the country "with thunder and lightning" in his repeated expeditions for ivory and yet could write an eloquent report for the International Society for the Suppression of Savage Customs in which he declared that the Whites must approach the savages "with the might of a deity" and "exert a power for good practically unbounded" and then he ended by calling on the Whites to "exterminate all the brutes". In fact, while eulogistic epithets one after another are showered upon the man, his real personality of an evil-doer is touched upon here and there as the story proceeds: "He had taken a high seat amongst the devils of the land," "He had the power to charm frightened rudimentary souls into an aggravated witch-dance in his honour," "Mr. Kurtz's methods had ruined the district," "Mr. Kurtz lacked restraint in the gratification of his various lusts," and "Mr. Kurtz has done more harm than good to the Company," and even his idolizer the young Russian agent's eulogy of him that "this man has enlarged my mind" has an ironic ring in it. Conrad also showed his great skill at narration by the use of innumerable suggestions of Kurtz as a remarkable man before this first-class agent finally appeared in the story: the suspense created by the many references to Kurtz leads the reader to such heights of curiosity and eagerness to meet this man of mystery that upon the sick man's actual appearance on the scene the satirical effect is overwhelming. On the one hand so many natives attended on him with so much respect, while on the other there was his insatiable greed for ivory and there were his in numerable acts of savagery that culminated in the rows of heads "black, dried, sunken with closed eyelids" that hung on the stakes outside his windows for "ornamentation". And then the last moments of the dying man were pictured to provide an incongruous anticlimax for the ambitious colonialist trader vanquished by severe illness and approaching death. Though even during his last struggle to keep himself alive, he still boasted: "I had immense plans" and "I was on the threshold of great things", he still talked of "My intended, my station, my career, my ideas" and in his ravings he even "desired to have kings meet him at railway stations on his return from some ghastly nowhere, where he intended to accomplish great things." Then finally there appeared "on that ivory face the expression of sombre pride, of ruthless power, of crown error —- of an intense and hopeless despair" as he uttered his final cry "in a whisper at some image, at some vision"; the dubious, ambiguous words of "The horror! The horror!" A subtle analysis and a powerful indictment we have here of this most admirable and most remarkable lackey of imperialism and colonialism. However, Conrad partly mars this superb effect of his firm stand against colonial oppression and exploitation, in the last part of the story when the author tried to show his "loyalty to Kurtz" and to reaffirm Kurtz as "a remarkable man" by declaring that the man's last cry of "The horror" showed his "candour", "conviction", "wisdom", "truth" and "sincerity", and when the novelist described in great detail his visit to Kurtz's girl back in London who adored Kurtz beyond all description, and this episode evoked the reader's pity for Kurtz rather than abhorrence.

Taken all in all, "Heart of Darkness" is certainly the greatest of Conrad's stories that shows the author's great humanity and his unreserved horror at the crimes perpetrated by colonialists and imperialists all over the world, in spite of his aristocratic inclinations and his essential conservatism.

"Nostromo", agreed upon by most of Conrad's critics as his greatest novel, was set in the South American Republic of Costaguana, of which "the geographical base" the author in one of his letters to Edmund Gosse declared to be "mainly Venezuela; but there are bits of Mexico in it", and the city of the activities of the novel "Sulaco is intended for all South America in the seventh decade of the nineteenth century." In Sulaco there was the San Tomé silver mine which was a concession given by the government of Costaguana to an English family, the Goulds, and Charles Gould, supported by a millionaire European financier Halroyd, was the successful master of the mine. There was the Ocean Steam Navigation Company that took care of the transportation by sea of the mined silver and of which the superintendent was Captain Joseph Mitchell who had as foreman of his lighters or open loading barges one Italian sailor named Nostromo. There was a foreign colony in Solaco, including a medical man Dr. Monygham and the chief engineer of the railway Don Pépe and others.

Many revolutions led to many changes in the government of the country. Don Vincente Ribiera as president-dictator was supported by Don Jose Avellanos who had a beautiful daughter Antonia and who had a brilliant journalist under his protection, Martin Decoud, from Paris and in love with Antonia. Then a general under Ribiera, named Montero, started a rebellion, and Ribiera had to run for his life, with the invaluable assistance from Nostromo, but a ship under Colonel Sotillo who had surrendered to Montero came by sea to land in Sulaco whereas an army under Montero's brother Pedrito marched by land to the mining town. All the populace in Sulaco, including the foreign colony there headed by Charles Gould and his wife Emilia, were all uncertain of their fate. In the meantime the Goulds and Martin Decoud who had a vague idea of a counter-revolution agreed to load a large amount of silver belonging to the mine in the largest of the barges and to send it across the sea to a small port out of Costaguana territory, and Nostromo who had unquestioned bravery and incorruptibility was given this assignment to save the silver and was to be accompanied by Martin Decoud. But as they sailed into the gulf they first discovered a hide merchant Hirch hidden in the lighter, then they saw Sotello's steamer with his soldiers coming into the gulf, and they decided to go to the islets the Isabels nearby in order to hide there till the next day. But the barge encountered the steamer, Hirsch fell over and clung to and was taken up into the steamer, and the barge leaked and finally was run aground on the Great Isabel, the largest of the islets. Nostromo and Decoud buried the silver ingots in a cavity on the islet and Nostromo went back to Sulaco, leaving behind Decoud who, being well-known as a journalist and showing strong support to the Ribiera regime, would be killed if fallen into the hands of the Montero troops. Decoud committed suicide by drowning after suffering from intolerable solitude for many days on the Great Isabel, but Nostromo the symbol of incorruptibility was eventually tempted by his desire to keep to himself the silver concealed on the islet and known to no one else. Finally, after the Montero rebellion was quelled and Sulaco returned to the norm and the Goulds still owned the silver mine, Nostromo pretended to grow rich slowly by taking bit by bit the silver hidden on the Great Isabel where now a lighthouse was built and was taken care of by his friend and fellow Italian Giorgio Viola and his two daughters Linda and Giselle. Nostromo was supposed to be the fiancé to the elder Linda but he actually loved Giselle and often visited the latter at the islet very late at night. One night he went on a visit and was shot by Giorgio Viola who took him for an intruder coming to carry off one of his daughters. Mortally wounded, Nostromo asked to see Mrs. Gould to tell her about the secret hiding place of the silver, but she wished to hear no more of the lost treasure.

Though Conrad seems to describe with warmth and enthusiasm the mine owner Charles Gould and his wife Emilia Gould as well as the other members of the European colony there (including the physician of the mine, Dr. Monygham, the priest Father Corbelan, the chief engineer of the railway Don Pépe and also Don Jose Avellanos and his daughter Antonia and her lover Martin Decoud) and to approve of the loyalty of Captain Mitchell and Nostromo and Georgio Viola to the European ruling clique, yet Nostromo's doubts of his own folly in serving the Goulds and others who were very probably simply making use of him without having the least care for his safety and welfare suggest the awareness by even such a simple person as Nostromo of the European colonizers' attempt to exploit the common people. Especially significant are the cynical remarks uttered by Nostromo in his final conversation with Mrs. Gould before his death. Speaking of that night he went to save the silver for the Goulds, Nostromo said: "I wondered what would become of me, now I know. Death was to come upon me unawares. He went away! He betrayed me. And you think I have killed him! You are all alike, you fine people. The silver has killed me. It has held me. It holds me yet. Nobody knows where it is. But you are the wife of Don Carlos, who put it into my hands and said, 'Save it on your life!' And when I returned, and you all thought it was lost, what do I hear? 'It was nothing of importance. Let it go. Up, Nostromo, the faithful, and ride away to save us, for dear life!' " And when Mrs. Gould said; "I, too, have hated the idea of that silver from the bottom of my heart." Nostromo countered:

"Marvellous! — that one of you should hate the wealth that you know so well how to take from the hands of the poor. The world rests upon the poor, as old Giorgio says. You have been always good to the poor. But there is something accursed in wealth." Though here he admits Mrs. Gould to be "good to the poor", yet the words "the wealth that you know so well how to take from the poor" and "the world rests upon the poor", certainly show clearly Conrad's acknowledgment of the poor as producers of wealth and his insight into the state of exploitation that exists in the relationship between the wealthy ruling class and the poor working people. Then the cynicism of Martin Decoud who was born in the country and now was persuaded to stay on to become a journalist simply because of his love for a girl there named Antonia Avellanos makes him utter his patriotic sentiments against foreign or chiefly European robbery or exploitation. He speaks of the European traders and colonizers of centuries ago as "thieves" and "speculators" that include Drake and other "grave and reverend persons in England" and also big financiers of Europe and the United States and deplores the fact that "it has always been our (referring to his country and his fore-fathers in South America) fate to be ... robbed ... exploited!" These words may be from a young Spanish Creole journalist trained in Paris, yet the author's obvious admiration for the youth's brilliance suggests at least part-approval of Decoud's views unfolded here.

However, Conrad's chief concern seems to point to the impor-tance of "material interest" to every human being, that it applies not only to Ribiera and Montero and Charles Gould but even to Nostro-mo, with his emphasis on Nostromo who is known to everyone and for a long time as incorruptible. This misanthropic view is consistent with the novelist's pessimistic outlook on the whole world.

In "Nostromo" as in his other novels Conrad paid much atten-tion to the portrayal of characters, including even some minor char-acters. There is Charles Gould whose chief interest is in the silver mine, to the neglect of everything else and everybody, including his wife. There is Martin Decoud who prides himself on being extremely clever and who is very eloquent in his speeches and in his letters, but whose cleverness eventually leads to his death. There are Giorgio Viola and his wife Teresa, both simple souls with their deep affection for Nostromo. There is the contrastive study of the two Viola daugh-ters, Linda and Giselle. There is the strong and somewhat disinterest-ed attachment of Dr. Monygham for Mrs. Gould. But above all, there is the careful study of Nostromo who may seem to be too much of an idealized figure, yet the internal conflict of the man looms large not only between his desire to remain upright and incorruptible and his weakness for the silver thrown upon him by sheer fortune, but also between his open, affianced relation with Linda and his secret, devouring passion for Giselle. Besides, his loyalty to his superiors in social station is not entirely unquestioned and his de-votion to Teresa Viola on the one hand and to Mrs. Gould on the other is sometimes confused with his other personal and social considerations, occasionally of greater moment.

The plot in the novel is a bit loose, there being several parallel story threads running through the whole length of the work and intersecting one another at moments. The main thread is the political one, dealing chiefly with the rebellion of General Montero and his brother against the reigning president-dictator Ribiera and with its repercussions on the city of Sulaco and on the San Tomé silver mine owned by the Englishman Charles Gould. And the attempt of the Goulds and the other Europeans there to save the silver from falling into the hands of the Montero rebels and then the events following upon the removal of the metals on a lighterman all come as the logical sequence of the rebellion of the Montero brothers against Ribiera. But around the Goulds and their silver mine are many Europeans who are more or less attracted to live at Sulaco after the Goulds have brought prosperity to the port, and there are also the local people as well as imported workers working for or related to the Ocean Steam Navigation Company and the National Central Railway, especially the sailors on the lightermen headed by Captain Mitchell and next to him Nostromo and his friends the Violas. Another important story thread is that involving Nostromo and the two Viola sisters and their father, and to this thread the last third of the whole story is devoted and the final tragedy in the book emanates from the unhappy love relations. There is the minor thread of love interest between Martin Decoud and Antonia, and linked to that is Antonia's father Don José Avellanos' staunch support for the Ribiera regime and the journal "Porvenir" founded by Avellanos and edited by Decoud and siding indubitably with the Ribierists against Montero. Although many characters are depicted in the novel, the chief figures are Nostromo and Charles Gould and Martin Decoud, and aside from the political story of revolution or rebellion, the two love stories command our chief attention.

Here there is the absence of an extra narrator Marlowe, yet the novelist apparently wishes again to tell his story and describe his characters from more angles than one. This is particularly striking after Martin Decoud arrives on the scene, when not only a long letter by the young man to his sister in Paris takes up much space and gives a vivid account of the happenings immediately after the news of Montero's success in his rebellion but for several episodes before and after the above-said letter the viewpoint is consistently that of Decoud who serves for the nonce as narrator of the events. This actually adds to the vividness of the story.

"Nostromo" is a great novel because here as in "Heart of Darkness' Conrad touched upon the activities of European colonizers in distant parts of the world where the natives are ignorant and primitive and where the colonizers are exploiters of varying degrees. The novelist condemns not only the superstition in the Congo and the "revolutions" in Costaguana (i.e. South America), but also the Europeans who dwell there for their own profit. Perhaps the indictment on the colonizers is stronger in "Heart of Darkness" than in "Nostromo" and the novelist shows much greater sympathy toward the Goulds and other Europeans than toward Kurtz and the other agents in Belgian Congo, but the satire toward the exploiters in "Nostromo" is still there, though much subtler. Then of course, in "Nostromo" much attention is focussed on the mental conflict or rather spiritual crisis, within the "incorruptible" Nostromo, especially in the last part of the novel, though the Genoese sailor more than once tries to justify himself for keeping the silver to himself by disclaiming his loyalty to the European mine-owner. The psychological analysis of Nostromo is of much greater depth than Kurtz in "Heart of Darkness" and Jim in "Lord Jim", yet the portrayal of Kurtz contains greater art, on account of the greater complexity and subtler ambiguity in the obnoxiousness as well as the pitiableness of the ruthless colonizer who probably was not so wicked at the start of his disgraceful career. However, in all the three great stories of his, "Lord Jim", "Heart of Darkness" and "Nostromo", Conrad shows himself not only a great master of the art of fiction but also a careful analyzer of human consciousness who makes his appeal, according to Conrad in his preface to "The Nigger of the 'Narcissus'": "to our sense of pity, and beauty, and pain; to the latest feeling of fellowship with all creation — and to the subtle but invincible conviction of solidarity that knits together the loneliness of innumerable hearts, to the solidarity in dreams, in joy, in sorrow, in aspirations, in illusions, in hope, in fear, which binds men to each other, which binds together all humanity". In the three towering figures of Jim, Kurtz and Nostromo, we find in their innermost struggles their very different yet also very similar dreams, aspirations and illusions, joys and sorrows, hopes and fears that bind them and the readers together, in the common loneliness of all their hearts. Of course there is a tinge of the Christian ideas of morality, of conscience, of sin and atonement that creeps imperceptibly, almost inevitably, into the mental make-up of Jim and Nostromo, even of Kurtz, but the novelist's insight into any character as neither entirely good nor totally bad and his sympathy for general human weaknesses even when such weaknesses have already degenerated into downright criminal acts lead on the one hand to the creation of vivid and lifelike portraits of the major figures in his fiction and on the other distinguish Conrad as a great artist who has produced enduring works of art and "whose subtle and resistless power endows passing events with their true meaning, and creates the moral, the emotional atmosphere of the place and time." And "Nostromo" is a greater novel than either "Lord Jim" or "Heart of Darkness" if only in the sense that here there is besides the titular hero another colourful and many-sided character of curious magnitude in Martin Decoud who is torn between his love for his own "patrie" and his deep-rooted European affiliations, between his interest in Antonia and his broad interest in politics and in revolution, between his dilettantism and his journalistic profession, and who is caught in the political and military chaos and plunges into his self-sought tragedy.

Aside from "Lord Jim" and "Heart of Darkness" the narrator Marlowe appears in two other novels by Conrad, in the earlier "Youth" (1902) and in a much later work, "Chance" (1913). The story in "Youth" is a very close reproduction of Conrad's real experience on sea in his younger days, and here Marlowe is not only the narrator but also the hero present in the novel from beginning to end. The mythical "Judea" in "Youth" is easily identifiable to the "Palestine" on which the novelist sailed as second mate in 1881 on a routine trip from London to Newcastle-upon-Tyne for a cargo of coal and then to Bangkok, but bad fortune delayed the ship again and again, first by heavy winds and high seas and then for repairs upon the loss of sail and for leaks at several English ports for almost a whole year before it left Europe for the Orient, and then in the Indian Ocean there was first smoke that had to be quenched by pumping water into the vessel and later there was a big fire that led to a terrible explosion, until finally the officers and the seamen all had to abandon the ship and they rowed for many nights and days before they landed at Mintok on the island of Bangka, off the coast of Sumatra (not Bangkok as in the novel). The whole story is about the sailors on a ship and about their adventures on the seas and at the ports, and though Conrad made some necessary changes in the events, the voyage in the novel is essentially the same he experienced, and it is true that this is a "feat of memory", "a record of experience" and that the "experience, in its facts, in its inwardness and in its outward colouring, begins and ends in myself", as Conrad declares in "The Author's Note", written to be affixed to the 1917 edition of the novel, and it is also true to fact, as Conrad announces with Marlowe as his mouthpiece in the novel, "It was my skipper's first command."

However, Conrad chose to turn this prosaic and ill-fated voyage into a romantic adventure. Viewed as one of his earliest adventures on the distant seas, Conrad speaks again through Marlowe at the end of the novel, "And this is how I see the East ... for me all the East is contained in that vision of my youth", and again, "This was the East of the ancient navigators, so old, so mysterious, resplendent and sombre, living and unchanged, full of anger and promise." Even the burning of the "Judea" in the vast Indian Ocean was described with a romantic colouring by Marlowe:

"She burned furiously; mournful and imposing like a funeral pile kindled in the night, surrounded by the sea, watched over by the stars. A magnificent death had come like a grace, like a gift, like a reward to that old ship at the end of her laborious days. The surrender of her weary ghost to the keeping of stars and sea was stirring like the sight of a glorious triumph. The masts fell just before daybreak, and for a moment there was a burst and turmoil of sparks that seemed to fill with flying fire the night patient and watchful, the vast night lying silent upon the sea. At daylight she was only a charred shell, floating still under a cloud of smoke and bearing a glowing mass of coal within."

Here we can see the immense effort on Conrad's part to romanticize the ship which was anything but romantic, for the ship was ancient and on its protracted voyage, the captain and first mate were old, and the cargo of coal was dirty and also difficult to control. But Conrad was recollecting one of his earliest adventures (at 24) when he was 56, and the title "Youth" indicated all too clearly his fond remembrance of his youth and one of his earliest voyages.

"Chance", a later and generally speaking an inferior novel, was however the novel that first brought Conrad the pecuniary reward in its English and American editions and its serialization in the New York "Herald" and also his wide recognition as one of the masters of the novel, as a gifted and original writer, as a remarkable author, as a great architect of fiction.

"Chance" tells a very complicated story and is divisible into two main parts, the first about De Barrel in his younger days as a clerk to a dock company and then as an office worker in a West End bank who by improper means rose to great fortune but later became bankrupt as a prey of swindlers and was imprisoned, while the second part deals chiefly with the adventures of De Barrel's daughter Flora who was saved from suicide by a Mr. and Mrs. Fyne, and who then married Mrs. Fyne's brother Captain Roderick Anthony of a ship named "Fernsdale", and when the ship sank in a collision and Anthony as captain died with the vessel, Hora was rescued together with the ship's second mate Powell. And the two parts are linked by an episode about De Barrel emerging from prison and trying to poison Anthony but having to take the poison himself when his criminal attempt was found out by Powell. The story about the swindles in the financial circles in the earlier portion of the novel is obviously based on many notorious swindling cases known in the first decade of the 20th century in England and France and much publicized at the time in books and particularly in newspapers, but this must have been partly responsible for the popularity of the book when it appeared in serialized and then in book form. The episodes about Flora's childhood miseries under her cruel governess, her attempt at suicide after her father's financial crash, her friendship with the Fynes, her elopement with Captain Anthony, her father's death upon taking the poisonous drink meant for Anthony, and finally Anthony's death as the captain of the sunken ship and her rescue, are eventful and exciting and therefore also full of popular appeal. However, the external events in the novel may be colourful and intriguing, yet there is little psychological study of the major characters that frequently was the chief virtue of Conrad's great novels, for here De Barrel was no more than a representative figure of a swindler in modern life who was interested only in money schemes, whereas Flora may have endured much in the vicissitudes of her life, yet she is largely a plaything of chance or fate. The only significant feature in this novel lies in the narrative method employed, which with the use of a narrator and then with changes in the narrator tries to introduce different lights cast upon the characters' secret selves from different angles. In "Chance", Marlowe is still the chief narrator but he doesn't interfere in the story much, except perhaps when he saves Flora from suicide at the very edge of a precipice. Yet he is not the only narrator; in his narration there is introduced another narrator Mrs. Fyne who takes over for a time the story-telling, but soon enough she yields her place to a third narrator in Powell the second mate of the "Fernsdale", and then when Powell finishes his story Mrs. Fyne resumes her office of narrator, to be eventually replaced again by Marlowe, who winds up the entire story. So there are three narrators whose three narratives are enveloped one within another. Such shifts from the first narrator to the second and then to the third and finally back to the first necessarily bring about successive shifts in point of view and in emphasis, and this complicated narrative technique has been regarded by some critic as "some equivalent of the verbal stream of consciousness" which was to blossom a decade later in the novels of Virginia Woolf and James Joyce. At any rate, Conrad was apparently trying to use this new and extended device of narrators other than the author in order to add depth and variety to his story and to introduce impersonation into the portrayal of the characters.

"Typhoon" is the only novel by Conrad which directly deals with a ship sailing to a Chinese port with Chinese coolies on board. Written at about the same time as "Youth", "Typhoon" records Conrad's early experience sailing on the high seas and facing rough storms, and contains vivid descriptions of a typhoon that for thirty hours threatens to sink the ship "Nan-Shan" and forces the crew as well as the Chinese passengers to seek for safety in the dark alleyways and under hatchways in the lower deck to be rocked to and fro and from side to side of the ship. And set against the violence and terror of the sea is Captain MacWhirr, a rugged, simple-minded but resolute man who is brave enough to combat against all the savagery of wind and wave and who towers above all the other characters for his strong sense of honesty and justice. Here we have a hero who not only succeeds in braving the storm and finally bringing to the port of Fu-Chao the two hundred Chinese coolies safe and sound on their return voyage after years of working abroad but who pacifies the officers and crew on the way and settles the squabbles among the Chinese coolies by distributing equally the savings of their silver dollars upon arrival. Like "The Nigger of 'Narcissus" and "Youth", "Typhoon" is another typical novel of the sea that belongs to Conrad's early works of fiction when the romance and the adventures of tough voyages to remote parts of the world were still fresh and vivid in the author's memory.

Two other novels of Conrad's that do not deal with the sea but is fraught with political conflicts are "The Secret Agent" (1907) and

"Under Western Eyes" (1911), both of which have received more public attention in recent years. Both novels involve secret revolutionary activities and violence and contain intricate plots, but "The Secret Agent" is placed in England, chiefly in London, whereas "Under Western Eyes" has its setting in Czarist St. Petersburg and the Little Russia quarter in Geneva.

"The Secret Agent" is chiefly about Adolf Verloc, a double agent working for and against an international anarchist organization and about his wife Winnie, with the attempted bombing of Greenwich Observatory as one of the major events which was based on an actual historical fact on February 15, 1894, when Conrad was himself in London. A foreign diplomat Vladimir suggested to Verloc to blow up the Greenwich Observatory with one of his homemade bombs, and Verloc then concealing himself as keeper of a small stationery shop in Soho goes to carry out the task with the help of his wife's half-idiot younger brother Stevie, but Stevie stumbles in Greenwich Park and drops the bomb which blows him up in explosion. Winnie eventually finds out and stabs Verloc to death and then leaves with one of Verloc's companions Ossi for the Continent of Europe, but when Ossi finds out about the killing of Verloc by Winnie, he deserts her and she jumps into the English Channel from the steamer taking her across.

In a letter to Galsworthy about the story dealing with Verloc Conrad declared:

"I had no idea to consider Anarchism politically — or to treat it seriously in its philosophical aspect: as a manifestation of human nature in its discontent and imbecility."

But while he thus announces that he has "no social or philosophical intention", Conrad yet admits that his story may have some "moral significance". On the one hand it is possible that the novelist is interested in the possibility of Verloc's responsiblity for the half-idiot Stevie's death due to the explosion of the bomb, and also in Winnie's conduct in killing Verloc on her suspicion of his above-stated responsibility, while on the other hand the figure of the professor as one of the staunch Anarchists and Verloc's associates described in the novel may be a person of an inferior position and puny appearance yet he with his fingers ever holding a detonator for the bomb is a man of strong will to be feared, a revolutionary ascetic without libidinal ties, almost a maniac in his absolute devotion to his cause, and on a whole he seems to be the novelist's mouthpiece to voice his utter pessimism and despair, and to reveal his contempt for maniacal political activity such as he witnessed in London at the time.

"Under Western Eyes" tells the story mainly through the diary of one of the principal characters Razumov, who reveals the killing of a minister of state in Czarist Russia by his fellow student and a revolutionary named Haldin at St. Petersburg but who then confesses to a woman he loves, Natalie, and to a group of conspirators and is severely punished by the latter. There is much of psychological study especially of Razumov as the story progresses. At first, because he has no sympathy for Haldin and the latter's revolutionary beliefs he finds to his horror Haldin's hiding in his apartment after the assassination of the minister, but he agrees to go and ask Haldin's associate Ziemianitch to help Haldin get away. Then when he fails to awaken the drunken peasant Ziemianitch, he reports to the police the presence of Haldin who is then arrested, tried and hanged. When he is queried by the police who suspect him, he goes to Geneva to be with the revolutionary conspirators there. He is not suspected by them, and only a report from a revolutionary agent in St. Petersburg speaks of the betrayer of Haldin as Ziemianitch who has already been hanged. But Razumov meets Haldin's mother and his sister Natalie and becomes attached to the latter, and he eventually confesses to her his betrayal of her brother, and later also to the other conspirators. Then the conspirators beat him up, maim his ears, and throw him into the street where he is knocked down by a tramcar and is crippled as a result.

This rather labyrinthian plot suggests the strong moral conflict that must be going on all the time within Razumov following his betrayal of Haldin, and that apparently became Conrad's chief concern. Of course the story naturally had to do with Conrad's remembrances of his father Apollo Korzeniowski and his revolutionary activities for Poland against Russian rule, so that some biographers and critics of Conrad have even suggested Haldin as a prototypical Apollo Korzeniowski (and Conrad's mother Ewa as Natalie and even Natalie's mother Mrs. Haldin). But this autobiographical element is after all of little importance, what is much more significant is the irony and ambiguity in the portrayal of Razumov. Like the author, Razumov has no great enthusiasm for revolutionary beliefs and actions, yet he is willing to help the revolutionary Haldin go into hiding after assassination. He even goes into the trouble of visiting Ziemianitch the peasant to enlist the latter's assistance. Then when he betrays Haldin he is conscience-stricken, yet he tries his best to save himself from detention and lies to Haldin's conspirators in Geneva. He assumes an appearance of innocence before Haldin's mother and sister, and only after his close associations with the sister Natalie that he finally confesses his betrayal of Haldin. Then it is inevitable for him to confess also to Haldin's fellow revolutionaries and to get severely punished by them. Here again we find Conrad delving into the inner recesses of his major character's mind and investigating into human conduct and motivation.

Both "The Secret Agent" and "Under Western Eyes" deal with political themes involving secret revolutionary organizations and their revolutionary activities and are related in some ways to his memories of his father as a Polish patriot against Czarist Russian oppression of Poland, yet in neither novel does Conrad show his great enthusiasm for revolutionary people or revolutionary aspirations. As a writer Conrad quite consistently adopted an aristocratic stand.

"Victory" (1915), coming after "Chance" which brought Conrad wide recognition and material reward, was possibly his last important novel. The principal character in the novel, Axel Heyst (called "Berg" in an early manuscript), stands for the pessimism and despair of Conrad in old age. The locale is Indonesia. Morrison, owner and captain of a small trading vessel, is saved by Heyst when he lends him the use of the ship, and Heyst later becomes manager of the Tropical Belt Coal Company founded by Morrison. Morrison dies on a visit back in England, but a hotel-owner Schomberg in Sourabaya spreads the rumour that Heyst who now is in a remote island of Samburan has stolen from Morrison and then murdered him. Heyst also saves an English girl Lena who is persecuted by Schomberg while travelling the Indonesian islands with the Zangia-como's Ladies Orchestra, and he and Lena elope to his bungalow on the island of Samburan. A group of three criminals, a card-sharper Mr. Jones, his bodyguard Ricardo and the primitive-looking Pedro, are directed by Schomberg to get Heyst's hidden treasure in Samburan. Ricardo first murders Pedro, then Jones finding Ricardo together with Lena fires at them, wounding the bodyguard but killing the girl. Jones is drowned and Heyst kills himself in the fire that burns up the bungalow.

Heyst who at first follows his father's philosophy "to remain free from absurdities of existence" is nevertheless drawn into a life of many conflicts and much violence, far away in a remote corner of a deserted island in Indonesia. His friendship with Morrison in the early part of the novel and his love for Lena in the later portions provide the inner disturbances to disrupt his calm and detached view of life, and then the enmity of the hotel owner Schomberg and espe-cially the violent actions of murder and shooting perpetuated by the criminal trio of Jones, Ricardo and Pedro, inflict upon him the external intrusion that ends not alone his peace of mind but his very life and being. It is possible that this novel is in a sense the aged novelist's revelation of his own mood of gloom on the eve of the First World War.

"The Arrow of Gold" (1919), the last novel of note by Conrad and one completed after World War I, hearkens back to the nov-elist's years of early youth in Marseilles, France, as many of the events described here are directly based on the author's own expe-rience in those Marseilles days: the support of Don Carlos's claim to the Spanish throne, the gun-running and the duelling, as well as Conrad's Corsican friend Dominic Cervoni, but the chief significance of the book lies, I think, in Conrad's apparently first attempt here in the vivid portrayal of a woman character in Dona Rita.

Dona Rita de Lastada, a peasant girl and goat-herd from her native Basque country, is brought to Paris by a rich painter Henry Allègre and educated into a sophisticated woman of the world. After his death she inherits much of his fortune and becomes mistress to the Pretender Don Carlos de Bourbon and living in Marseilles she works as a devoted Carlist and meets Captain Blunt from North Carolina and Monsieur George who undertakes gun-running with his Corsican friend Dominic. After the political debacle Dona Rita rejects Blunt who woos her for her fortune as well as her childhood worshipper Ontega, and chooses to go with Monsieur George as her lover. But upon the report that Blunt slanders him George challenges Blunt to a duel, and he is badly wounded in the chest. Rita nurses him back to health, then suddenly vanishes out of his life when he no longer needs her services, only leaving to him her hairpin of a gold arrow with a jewelled shaft.

Exciting and engrossing may be parts of "The Arrow of Gold" (and of "Victory", for that matter) as story-telling or even as character-portraits, these later novels of Conrad's do not measure up to his great novels of the middle period, in which the author delved more deeply into the inner workings of the mind of Kurtz, Jim and Nostromo, even Decoud, and shattered the false apologies for European colonialism in Africa, South America and the Orient.

Conrad started to write fiction in earnest in the 1890s when his career on the sea gradually came to its end, but he did not distinguish himself till his first major novel "Lord Jim" was published in 1900, to be followed by some publications of ten novels and stories till he achieved financial success and popular recognition in 1913 with "Chance". Almost all his novels and stories are based on his personal experience, supplemented by his readings, so that he is not known for his inventive power as a novelist. In his lifetime his reputation chiefly lay in the romantic, exotic nature of his tales set in remote lands and seas, in the exciting episodes of his stories and his skill at engrossing narration, in his vivid creations of heroic and usually tragic figures. In the fluctuations of his literary fame since his death in 1924, he has often been praised for the "modernity" in his works of fiction, first of all in his absorbing interest in the innermost conflicts in human consciousness, in his penetrating portrayals of sharp mental contradictions of the major characters in his novels, in his outpouring sympathy for the conscience-stricken individuals of personal misdemeanors or public outrages, and in his extensive use of symbols and images.

However, coming from a family of landed gentry, Conrad always maintained his aristocratic attitude toward revolutionaries and revolutionary activities, although his father was a Polish patriot who was an active participant in a Polish insurrection against Russian rule. And living amidst unscrupulous capitalist intrigues and treacheries and political perplexities and economic crises that faced all of Europe in the turn of the century, he very naturally fell into a mood of despair and pessimism which mounted with the approach of the First World War. But his voyages to remote parts of the world enabled him to see broad humanity of all races and creeds, of different social stations and economic circumstances, with all their joys and sorrows and hopes and fears, and particularly with their miseries and disillusionments, their loneliness and their despairs, and his knowledge of imperial aggrandizements of colonial misrules made it possible for him to see the "heart of darkness" in the far-flung colonial possessions of European imperialist nations, to discern there on the one hand the primitive superstition and ignorance and poverty and miserable livelihood among the natives in remote Africa, South America and the East Indies but on the other the high-handed oppression and brutality and intense exploitation by the colonialists and their agents at the farthest trading stations. The indictment of colonial oppression and exploitation is the strongest in the vivid descriptions of Mr. Kurtz and other agents in

Belgian Congo, alongside the truthful pictures of the barbarism and helplessness of the African natives there, yet the accusations of the evils of colonialism are there also in "Nostromo" and "Lord Jim" and in most other novels with Malaya or Indonesia as the background, though often much subtler and in some cases barely noticeable. I suppose it is easier for a Pole to see more clearly and to record with less bias the "darkness" in colonial rule than for one who is a native of some European colonial nation, but the fact Conrad saw and recorded these social and political wrongs, albeit often indirectly, is certainly one of the most distinctive features that have earned for him the prominent place among the great novelists of early 20th century. Artistically, his careful psychological analysis of his major characters is undeniably an outstanding achievement, even though in a number of cases such an analysis is made chiefly out of moral considerations. The portraits of Kurtz, Jim and Nostromo are nevertheless most carefully etched and will long be remembered in the gallery of superb character-creations in European fiction.

b. Rudyard Kipling

Rudyard Kipling (1865—1933), the most prominent writer to defend British imperialism and colonialism, was born in India of an English civil servant's family, his father being the director of a museum in Lahore. When he was a boy, he was sent back to England to receive his education, and at eighteen he went back to India and became a journalist (from 1882 to 1892). As he was well acquainted with the life in India, he started to write about it in his stories and poems. Of his numerous writings, the better known works include: "Barrack-Room Ballads" (1892), "The Seven Seas" (1896) and "The Five Nations" (1903) among his volumes of poetry; "The Jungle Book" (1895) and "Just So Stories" (1902) among his stories for children; "Soldiers Three" (1889), "Life's Handicaps" (1891) and "Many Inventions" (1893) among his other stories; "Captain Courageous" (1897) and "Kim" (1901) among his novels. As most of these works appeared in the last years of the 19th century and his influence as an author also reached its heyday at that time, we may consider Kipling as essentially a writer of the 1880s and 1890s though he lived and wrote well into the 20th century. .

In the collections of short stories which first brought Kipling fame and which even later were often regarded as among his most important works, Kipling used his knowledge of Indian life to write about the British colonial officials and officers and soldiers there and their wives and children, with the result that on the one hand the colonial material appeared new and attractive to the British reading public at home while on the other hand the stories taken from real life and the claim to realism and the characters in them being mostly drawn from the lower strata of British residents in India assumed a curiously democratic colouring. In fact, in writing about the private lives of these minor British colonialists in India in these earlier stories of his, Kipling actually pointed out the various vices and foibles of these minor officials or officers and their wives, satirizing to a certain extent their spiritual inanition and loneliness and their petty interests and conflicts. Yet even though there were such satirical thrusts here and there, they were always rather mild rebuffs not unmixed with humour and they never touched upon the essential qualities in the lives of these colonialists or upon the social system which was actually responsible for the vices and foibles satirized. What is more, the reader is made to sympathize with those minor colonialists who seem to have been forced to lead their dull and tame lives in the outposts of empire away from "civilization" and who actually are shouldering the responsibility of building the ever-expanding empire in the distant lands, to the greater glory of the British nation. In this sense Kipling in his most ingenious way served as an out-and-out apologist of British imperialism and colonialism in the biggest and richest of British colonies, India.

In Kipling's short stories and in his novels there are frequently narrated the inner contradictions of the major characters, between their wish to realize their personal desires and ambitions and the necessity to be thoroughly disciplined and unconditionally obedient servants to imperial and colonial interests. And, true to his loyalty to imperialism, Kipling generally makes these major characters in his stories emerge from such contradictions as willing slaves to the higher interests of colonialism. This is most obvious in one of his best known collections of short stories, "Soldiers Three" and its sequels "Life's Handicaps" and "Many Inventions", in which the narratives about the three plain soldiers of the British colonial troops, one from Ireland, another from "Cockney" London and a third from Yorkshire, may tell of these rank-and-filers' strong personal desires for wealth and position and even of their occasional disorderly behaviour and grumblings about their own lot, yet all of them are described as always looking up to their commanding officers and being ready to die for the Queen and the Empire.

Especially significant is the theme in what has often been considered Kipling's best novel, "Kim". Here the novelist tells of the adventures of an orphaned son of a sergeant in an Irish regiment stationed in India, Kimball O'Hara. After spending his childhood more or less as a vagabond in Lahore and then meeting an old lama from Tibet, he begins to accompany the latter in his travels and becomes his most intimate companion. Then his father's fellow soldiers in the regiment find him and adopt him and send him to school, but he still keeps up his relations with the old lama and in his holidays resumes his wanderings with the old religious man. He is discovered by the colonel of the regiment to have aptitude for secret service and his knowledge of the Indian languages and customs and his relationship with the old lama all come in useful to him in his work of espionage on behalf of the British army and government in India. He ends with success in carrying out the secret service tasks assigned to him by the colonel. Here in the figure of Kim we may find Kipling's ideal among British colonialists: one who has lived long in the colony and mixed thoroughly with the natives there and known their speech and habits and customs and so can carry out most faithfully and satisfactorily the task that may be assigned to him by the British authorities in the colony for more thorough and more effective colonization. The apparent innocence of the boy also makes him an ideal person for secret service, and his relationship of long standing with the old lama helps also to make use of that superstitious man to serve the interests of the Empire. And the novel has been very successful and widely read because of the elaborate descriptions of the Indian scene with all the strange customs and habits of the natives there and because of the atmosphere of mystery surrounding not only the old lama but also the child Kim in their wanderings and strange adventures among strange people, though it needs to be pointed out that the figure of the old beggary lama is highly improbable and that many of the strange persons and incidents in the tale are pure inventions on the author's part to serve his imperialist outlook, created out of airy nothing and not based on actual observations of real life.

Not only in his narrations about the British colonialists in India but also in his descriptions of the Indians and their life either as background for the narrations or for their own sake, we find ever the intrusion of Kipling the author and his imperialist ideology. The miserable existence of the natives (e.g., as in his short stories "Little Tobra" and "The City of Dreadful Night"), their poverty and hunger and near-starvation, their dirtiness and their insanitation, their religious fanaticism and superstition and general ignorance, and their backwardness in almost every respect, are all portrayed with great vividness, not with an emphasis on the necessity of change for the better that would involve national liberation or at least social reforms, but with the aim to putting the blame on the Indians themselves as an inferior race who cannot do anything to better their existence and who become thus "the White Man's Burden" and depend on the British colonialists to alleviate their sufferings for them. Thus, in a story like "William the Conqueror", alongside of pictures of horror describing the starvation and death of whole villages in India in a year of famine, there are highlighted the activities of the British colonial officials organizing for famine relief, and the writer implicitly propagandizes on behalf of colonialism. Even when Kipling occasionally relates of the none-too-benevolent conduct of the colonialists toward the natives, as in the story of "Lispeth" where an Indian girl is loved but is later discarded by a Britisher in India, the author does show some sympathy for the wronged native (for Lispeth and others like her) but he also hastens to indicate that such conduct, regrettable as it may be, is after all quite natural and therefore not to be held up for heavy censure.

Kipling's attempt to create the myth of the "superiority" of the White Man over the natives becomes a downright distortion of truth in a story like "Wee Willie Winkle" where the six-year-old Willie, son of a British colonel, upon meeting a plundering group of Afgham armed mountaineers, acts the part of a youthful representative of the "master race" and by delivering a short but commanding speech successfully saves himself from danger and dishonour. In other stories, Kipling also tells of how the natives look up to European magistrates but have no sufficient respect for their own officials, and even of how a petty official of mixed Anglo-Indian blood has the courage to organize a force to put down a native rising simply because he remembers his responsibility to rule as a quarter-breed European. Sometimes, Kipling works in the interests of colonialism in a different way, by praising the old patriarchal India and throwing over it a romantic and poetic exterior, in contrast with the modern India which is struggling to do away with all that is old and backward, as if to suggest that the real India is the old mystical one and that that is what should be preserved while the modern European civilization is foreign and should not be introduced to take the place of the good old Indian ways.

The only works by Kipling that do not so offensively smell of imperialism and colonialism are his few collections of stories for children: "The Jungle Book", "The Second Jungle Book" and "Just So Stories". Here, though in his descriptions of stronger animals in the jungles swallowing up and dominating the weaker beasts the author quite unmistakably was trying to introduce the theory of social Darwinism by emphasizing the struggle for existence and the survival of the fittest (especially since the animals are described here to resemble human beings), yet at least the note of imperialist domination by brutal force is not so directly nor so strikingly present and in these stories there are the refreshing spirit of the world of nature, vivid pictures of wild nature and outdoor life, as well as delightful descriptions of courage and cleverness of different animals, and these are of sufficient interest to children as well as to the general reading public.

On the whole Kipling as the most talented writer in imperialist literature exerted his baneful influence in the last decades of the 19th and the early years of the 20th centuries, especially since he is a voluminous writer and writes well enough in verse as well as in prose.

c. John Galsworthy

John Galsworthy (1867—1935) came from an upper middle class family, his father being a prominent London lawyer. He was educated at Harrow and then at Oxford, travelled on the Continent of Europe and in other parts of the world, was trained to be a lawyer and in 1890 actually practised law. But soon he turned to literature though his knowledge of law continued to be useful in his writings. He did not publish anything till he was 30. His first works of fiction: "From the Four Winds" (1897), "Jocelyn" (1898) and "Villa Rubein" (1900), were published under the pseudonym of John Sinjohn. These novels were not remarkable as literary works, and it took Galsworthy some time and effort before he learned to master the literary craft. "The Island Pharisees", appearing in 1904, was his first novel to attract public attention, his first important social novel. In 1906 came "The Man of Property", and it gained for him wide recognition as a prominent novelist. This was followed by a number of other novels, including "The Country House" (1907), the story of an aristocratic family that lives in the modern fashion but still holds sacred certain old aristocratic traditions; "Fraternity"

(1909), a contrasting picture of the life of the well-to-do middle class and of the poor; and "The Freelands" (1915), a realistic presentation of class struggle in the English countryside. In all his works written before and up to the First World War, Galsworthy showed his critical attitude toward the contemporary society in England; he blamed the ruling classes for their inhumanity in leading their way of life and expressed his sympathy for the masses of people suffering under social injustice.

In 1920 Galsworthy took up the story thread of "The Man of Property" and wrote its two sequels, "In Chancery" (1920) and "To Let" (1921), and these three novels together, plus two "Interludes" entitled "Indian Summer of a Forsyte" and "Awakening", were published together as a trilogy under the title of "The Forsyte Saga". Then the story of the Forsyte family, from the 1880s to the time after the First World War, was continued in a second trilogy, "A Modern Comedy", which contained "The White Monkey" (1924), "The Silver Spoon" (1926) and "The Swan Song" (1928). In the last novel of this series we are brought to the close of the life of the most prominent character in the whole story, Soames Forsyte. During the last years of his life, Galsworthy completed a third trilogy entitled "End of the Chapter", which includes "Maid in Waiting" (1931), "Flowering Wilderness" (1932) and "Over the River" (1933), but in which the narrative is concerned chiefly with a rather distant relative of the Forsyte family. While these three trilogies are equally interesting as records of social history, yet the earliest group is more valuable because more realistic.

Galsworthy was also a dramatist and wrote more than twenty plays, including one-acters and full-length dramas. Of these plays the more important are "The Silver Box" (1909), "Strife" (1909), "Justice" (1910), "The Skin Game" (1920), "A Family Man" (1922) and "Loyalties" (1922). In several of these plays Galsworthy used his knowledge of English law to write dramatic satires. Later Galsworthy became the president of a writers' association known as the Pen Club, and in 1932 he received the Nobel Prize for literature. In his writings he was under the influence of the great French realists of the 19th century, Flaubert and Maupassant, and of the Russian classical realists, Tolstoy, Turgenev and Chekhov.

Of Galsworthy's novels, his two trilogies dealing with the Forsyte family as well as "The Island Pharisees" deserve more detailed consideration. The central figure of the novel "The Island Pharisees" is Richard Shelton, a young man belonging to the upper middle class. He meets with a Belgian, Ferran, who with his acute mind and keen observation has lost faith in all the values of the modern Western society. Ferran then brings down upon Shelton a whole cascade of judgments which make the latter turn thoughtful and look upon his habitual world in a new and different way. Shelton gets acquainted with the life of the poor, and before him appears a picture of glaring social inequality in the world. So he can no more find any moral justification for the privileged existence of the people of his own class. He becomes convinced of the stupidity and the narrow-mindedness of the upper middle class, and their meanness and hypocrisy and self-interest sicken him. And this new outlook makes him alter the plans of his life and break off with his fiancée, Antonia Dennant, a young aristocratic woman who cannot understand his new ideals. "The Island Pharisees" here refers to England and the "Pharisees" are the English bourgeoisie.

In one of the earlier scenes, in which Richard Shelton and his uncle Edmund Paramor discuss the terms of the marriage settlement to be drawn for the impending union between Shelton and his fiancée Antonia, we are given a vivid exposé of the predominance of practical money considerations in connection with a supposedly romantic love-match. The ridiculousness of the views of the idealistic husband-to-be, Shelton, placed before the seriously practical "common sense" of the seventy-year-old lawyer his uncle is presented here with much irony and sarcasm to show the contrast between the conventional bourgeois hypocrisy and the unconventional desire to be fair and honest. And here Galsworthy's legal knowledge was of help to him in making this penetrating satire on English laws which reflect the hypocrisy and self-righteousness in bourgeois conventions.

In the same novel, another bit of bitter satire is concerned with British imperialism in India. The hero Richard Shelton unexpectedly meets an old college-mate of his, Croker, who has just returned from India, and in their conversation about the plague and the famine in India Shelton shocks his friend by coming out frankly that the British imperialists fill their pockets with money in India while pretending they are bringing progress and civilization to the backward natives. This is a direct hit at the popular imperialist propaganda in the 1890s and before the First World War that was spread by men like Kipling about "the White Man's Burden." However, in spite of his censure of the hypocrisy of the English imperialists as Pharisees, Galsworthy has a world of sympathy for them nevertheless. So he makes his hero Shelton feel "sorry for the signs of trouble" on Croker's face and then smile uneasily and say, "Why shouldn't we fill our pockets? I only object to the humbug that we talk."

Though the two trilogies of "The Forsyte Saga" and "A Modern Comedy", containing six full-length novels and four short "interludes", form one continuous narrative of the history of the Forsyte family from the middle of the 1880s to the middle of the 1920s, different parts were written in different years and therefore they represented different stages in the author's spiritual growth and in his world outlook. The first of the novels, "The Man of Property", was written eight years before the beginning of the First World War and twelve and fourteen years respectively before the first of the four interludes ("The Indian Summer of a Forsyte") and the second of the novels ("In Chancery") and the social criticism in it is much sharper than in all the later parts of the two trilogies, which were all written after the conclusion of the War when the permanent crisis of British imperialism became more obvious and the author became more conservative and more eager to offer apologies for the declining Western society. However, even in these later novels Galsworthy's insistence on presenting the truth, unpleasant though it may be to him, enables him to maintain throughout a more or less objective picture of social reality and to make the whole of "The Forsyte Saga" and "A Modern Comedy" an epic of the decay and downfall of the capitalist British society.

The central figure in "The Man of Property", "the man of property", is Soames Forsyte, though many other Forsytes, including his father James and his five uncles and a number of his cousins, are also described. The Forsytes have one predominent trait in common, though more vividly represented in Soames, the trait of making the accumulation of wealth or property their chief aim in life. This trait of bourgeois consideration of everything, even of one's wife, in terms of one's property, is the central point of criticism which Galsworthy tries to level at the entire bourgeois class with Soames chosen to represent the whole tribe. This view is expressed directly through the mouth of young Jolyon Forsyte, one of Soames' cousins, who by turning an artist and marrying some one out of his own class is shown as a rebel to the conventional ways of the Forsytes. In the chapter significantly entitled "Diagnosis of a Forsyte", when Young Jolyon is asked by his father Old Jolyon to talk to Bosinney, an architect and the fiancé of Young Jolyon's daughter June, and to warn Bosinney against making love to Soames' wife Irene, Young Jolyon made this "diagnosis" or analysis of the predominant possessive instinct of the Forsytes. However, here the author shows at the same time his sympathy and even admiration for these Forsytes with their solid acquisitive instinct.

"The Man of Property" opens with the family gathering of all the Forsytes upon the occasion of the engagement of June Forsyte, grand-daughter of Old Jolyon (eldest of the six brothers of the older generation of Forsytes described in the narrative) and daughter of Young Jolyon, to Philip Bosinney, an architect who is interested in art and not in practical things in life and who is therefore the antithesis to the Forsytes. Here an opportunity is provided for a general introduction to the Forsyte family, to its origins and to its different members with different professions but the same bourgeois instinct. After this beginning, though there are still a few chapters employed for the description of the other Forsytes, the story centres itself on the Soames-Irene-Bosinney triangle. At the opening scene, Soames and Irene are introduced as being already married, though only recently, and as they appear on the betrothal of June Forsyte and Philip Bosinney, there is already the vague indication of Irene's unhappy union with Soames and the mutual attraction between Irene and Bosinney. Then Soames, in order to please Irene and to try to "possess" her the more thoroughly, asks the architect Bosinney to build a country house for them at Robin Hill, and this gives Bosinney and Irene more chances, and excuses, to see each other, and soon it becomes quite obvious that they are in love with each other and rumours arise. Irene and Bosinney find their common interest in art and they spend much time together and more money on the decoration of the house than was stipulated by Soames. Soames tries to have his revenge on Bosinney by suing him at the court for spending beyond the terms specified in the contract, and he wins the case. Irene on the other hand does not even care for appearances in her relations with Bosinney and antagonizes Soames by refusing to have anything to do with him. The final upshot of the story is Bosinney's death, being run over by a car in the London fog, and Irene's leaving her husband Soames. In treating of this story, Galsworthy is very definitely on the side of Irene and Bosinney, showing much sympathy for them as people outside the pale of the practical, money-making world of the Forsytes, and as rebels who share their common belief in art and beauty, but he also pities Soames for having married the wrong woman and for having entrusted the building of his house to the wrong architect, though he certainly blames Soames for being too practical, for extending his sense of property to the physical as well as spiritual possession of his wife, and for employing the dirty trick of revenge on his rival by suing the latter at the court. However, the author with his instinctive sympathy for the "under-dog" or the oppressed ones sides quite naturally and unmistakably with the rebel-pair. So Galsworthy's portrait of Soames in this first of the Forsyte novels is very different from his treatment of the same character in the later works where Soames, growing older and maturer, becomes more and more an object of sympathy rather than that of aversion to the novelist.

The second novel of the first trilogy, "In Chancery", continues the story of Irene and Soames following their separation and then divorce. Soames marries a beautiful young woman, Annette, of French parentage, twenty years his junior, in a loveless union and he has practically bought her. On the other hand, Irene marries Young Jolyon after the death of the latter's second wife the governess, and their relationship is based on their common artistic inclinations.

The third novel of the first trilogy, "To Let", deals with the new generation of the Forsytes. Soames' daughter by Annette, Fleur, and Irene's son by Young Jolyon, Jon, meet and fall in love with each other. This becomes known to their parents, and while Soames who dotes on Fleur is even ready to beg Irene to agree to the marriage of the two young people, Young Jolyon writes to him and objects strongly to the match. Irene declares that she would not interfere, yet she is also definitely against the union. Finally Jon runs away with his mother Irene to America, and Fleur gets married to a young aristocrat, Michael Mont, whom she does not love. Here the author describes Soames' great affection for the daughter which seems to make a new man out of the practical and almost inhuman "man of property". And here the author seems to have changed his attitude not only toward Soames but toward all the Forsytes, towards the bourgeoisie as a whole. The critical attitude has been replaced by one of sympathy and pity.

The second trilogy on the Forsyte story, "A Modern Comedy" deals with England of the years 1922—1926 and with Fleur as the heroine. In the first of the three novels, "The White Monkey", the story evolves chiefly round the triangle of Michael Mont and Fleur and Fleur's lover, the poet Wilfred Desert. Wilfred tells Michael to his face that he is in love with Fleur, and Michael tells Fleur to make her own choice. Fleur decides to remain with Michael, and Wilfred leaves England. The life of the new generation is described as vain and empty, symbolized by the picture of "The White Monkey" which Soames gives Fleur.

In the second novel of the second trilogy, "The Silver Spoon", Fleur gets involved in a petty quarrel with another woman, Marjorie Ferrar, and this develops into a society scandal, with many other persons taking sides on the two contending parties. Michael on his part is attracted to politics and this gives Galsworthy an opportunity to create a series of interesting satirical descriptions of bourgeois politics, including ironic thrusts at the British Labour Party which at one time gained control of the government but failed to introduce any real changes.

The last novel of the second trilogy, "Swan Song", opens with the description of the General Strike of 1926 which created terrific fright among all the Forsytes, or all the members of the British bourgeoisie. Galsworthy does not describe the workers during this strike, but he shows vividly here how the rich people at the time sensed the danger and started to defend their property and their way of life, how all sorts of volunteer corps were organized by them, including volunteer police, type-setters, engine-drivers, stokers and others, how even upper society women took part in this work of resisting the strikers. Fleur and other "society women" ran a restaurant for the strike-breakers and they themselves served there as waitresses. Then the strike was over, the threat of danger passed, and the Forsytes returned to their habitual way of life. Here, though Galsworthy intends to describe the important historical event of the strike in an objective way, he actually shows his sympathy for the ruling class in combatting the strikers. However, the realistic details concerning the persons in the story indicate quite clearly the great threat of the General Strike to the status quo in England.

During the time of the strike Fleur meets her former lover

Jon, son of Irene and Young Jolyon, who has returned with his wife to England to live. Fleur's former passion for him flares up anew, and she arranges a rendezvous with him at the place where they had their first meeting. Jon tells her that he is married and decided to make the final break with her. Fleur is in despair and plans her suicide. Then it happens that one night her father's house is on fire, as a result of a carelessly abandoned cigarette butt, and Soames goes to save his pictures which he has collected as a connoisseur. Just in time he saves Fleur as she is waiting beneath a big picture for it to fall on her. He snatches her away but receives the blow from the fall of the picture himself. So he saves his daughter from her attempt at suicide but dies of it himself. In this novel we see the completion of the transformation of the character of Soames. Here he becomes a representative of high moral stability, a man whose solidity of character contrasts with the effeminate disillusionment and weak-willedness of the younger generation. If at one time the pictures for him were only objects for speculation and money-making, now in risking his life to save these pictures from the fire because they are objects of art and beauty, he reveals his selfless love for beauty. So, while in his earlier work he places the bourgeois sense of property against artistic inclinations and beauty and considers the two as quite incompatible one with the other, Galsworthy in his last novel on Soames Forsyte reconciles the two in the person of Soames, the "man of property". And, to make Soames' character appear the more admirable, the more worthy of our sympathy, Galsworthy here shows Soames with the spirit of deep affection and self-sacrifice as the old man dies himself in order to save his daughter from death.

The broad canvas of the two trilogies is not only a realistic record of political and family life in modern England, but here Galsworthy has shown all too clearly the important historical change going on in England from the 1880's to the 1920's, the change which means the decline of the bourgeois society. And this is vividly presented through an interesting story and through the psychological study of the chief figures.

Of Galsworthy's many plays, "Strife" gives the most penetrating exposé of the social contradictions in English society of the time. The play deals with a strike in the Trenartha Tin Plate Works, situated somewhere on the borders of England and Wales. The workers start a strike to ask for better wages and improvement in their working conditions. A way of compromise is first suggested, but neither side would agree to it. John Anthony, the Chairman of the Company that owns the factory, is described as a typical capitalist who shows his great contempt for the workers and refuses to talk of concessions. On the other side, the leader of the strikers, David Roberts, hates the capitalists and also is strongly opposed to the compromise suggested. The meeting between the capitalists and the workers in the first act is a powerful scene in which the intense antagonism between the two conflicting classes in the capitalist world is vividly presented, and the clash described is extremely dramatic and realistic. The impasse that follows the negotiations lasts and the workers suffer from the strike. Vivid and sympathetic descriptions of the miseries of the strikers and their families are given, and the strike story is told from another angle when the daughter of John Anthony, the Chairman of the Board, is shown to pay a visit to the wife of Roberts the strike leader, hoping to bring about a compromise which consists of approximately the same terms as were suggested at the very beginning.

Galsworthy creates two powerful men from the two contending classes, and the struggle is presented in a number of scenes rather as a conflict between two individuals than between two classes. Herein lies both the strength and the weakness of the play, for on the one hand this makes the drama more intense in the fiery words thrown at each other by the two chief characters, but on the other hand the class struggle appears to be no more than the clash between two strong personalities, although the author emphasizes the social basis of the actions and words of the two men. The splendid scene of Roberts' speeches of defiance before the capitalists and of Anthony's wrathful answers to his challenges is a truthful representation of the direct conflict between the representatives of Capital and of Labour, particularly as the chief spokesman for the workers speaks out their grievances and their antagonism against the capitalists who are their oppressors, though the author apparently tries to show that Roberts is going possibly a bit too far in his accusations, yet what the leader of the strike says is the truth and well represents the workers' feelings toward the capitalists. When Anthony says, "There can be only one master", and Roberts answers, "Then, by Gad, it'll be us," the whole spirit of the workers' fight for socialism that was in the air in England in early 20th century is clearly voiced. Galsworthy is here merely representing the two sides of the argument in what he considers to be the objective way, and the great power in Roberts' speeches shows the author's sympathy for the workers' cause though not necessarily also his approval. The fact that the play begins with the suggestion of a compromise and ends with the eventual agreement on both sides to practically the same compromise suggests the author's view that the prolonged clash, leading to sufferings and pain on both sides, may be and can be and should best be avoided. Also, Galsworthy believes that there are humane persons among the bourgeoisie in contrast with the cruel, aggressive ones, just as there are moderate people and radical people among the workers, and he hopes that the "humane" capitalists and the "moderate" workers should and would gain supremacy and get together to find a peaceful solution to alleviate the miseries of the workers and at the same time to preserve intact the capitalist system. Therefore, the play ends in the defeat of the two extremists in the two camps, as the moderate elements in both parties bring about the reasonable compromise, with concessions on both sides. In this respect, Galsworthy's view is comparable to that of Elizabeth Gaskell in her novels.

Besides "Strife", two other plays of Galsworthy's are noteworthy, "The Silver Box" and "Justice". In "The Silver Box" the theme is that of social injustice with regard to the legal apparatus which serves the ruling class to oppress the poor. Both the poor man Jones and the rich man's son Jack Barthwick are guilty of the theft of a silver box, but Jones the unemployed is tried at the court and punished severely while Jack Barthwick with the influence of his father the M.P. is saved from disgrace. The life of luxury of the Barthwicks in their comfortable homes is vividly contrasted with the miserable living conditions of the poor and unemployed having to beg for money in the streets. Galsworthy here shows his great sympathy for the downtrodden and his antipathy for the all-too-apparent social inequality in England. In "Justice" the theme is again an attack on the English system of criminal law which always protects the ruling class and their private property and spells misery and even death for the poor. An upright young man of good reputation Falder forges a cheque in order to help a woman free herself from her terrible husband and to enable himself to run away with her to Australia, but the forgery is discovered and he is arrested and tried at the court. Galsworthy makes use of this trial scene, through the words of the lawyer and especially of the judge, to point out the fact in modern British society that the law and the law courts are instruments to protect the ruling class and their wealth and power. Falder suffers terribly much in his term in prison, spiritually as well as physically, and when he is on parole he fails to find work because of his loss of a good reputation, and then, when he has to resort once again to forgery, this time that of a letter of recommendations, he is arrested again and he commits suicide. Criminal law should be held responsible for the death of this man, Galsworthy obviously seems here to affirm this.

d. Herbert George Wells.

Herbert George Wells (1866—1946) was born of a poor family not far from London. His father and mother were at first gardener and servant-maid in a rich landlord's home, then they opened a small chinaware shop but it was quite a failure and the family depended chiefly upon the father's income as a professional cricketer. Then he broke his leg and the mother had to go back and become the landlord's housekeeper while young Herbert had to stop his schooling and was apprenticed to a draper. Then he took up different professions in turn, as an apprentice in a pharmacist's shop, as a postman, as a shop clerk, and then as a schoolteacher. He studied hard in his leisure hours and entered and graduated from the Normal School of Science, in South Kensington, a surburb of London, and taught there for some time. He got a scholarship and went to London University and studied under the well-known scientist Thomas Huxley. Then he started to write for the magazines (his contributions to which at the time were later collected under the title of "Select Conversations with an Uncle and Two Other Reminiscences", 1895) and his first two works, the novel "The Time Machine" and the collection of short stories "The Stolen Bacillus and Other Incidents" (both appearing in 1895) brought him fame and he gave up his scientific and teaching career and from then on devoted himself to literature.

Well's numerous works written in the long stretch of almost half a century may be conveniently divided into three periods: (1) from the 1890's to the First World War, (2) the First World War years and the early 1920's, (3) from the late 1920's to the early 1940s. His novels may be grouped in three distinct groups: (1) the novels of scientific fantasy, which appeared throughout his career but chiefly in the first and last periods of his writing, (2) the novels of social life appearing chiefly in the first period, and (3) the novels of discussion, and related to these are Well's books on history. Wells' distinction lies in his works of scientific fantasy which are not only numerous but also outstanding, though some few of his social novels are popular and deserve much attention.

H. G. Wells joined the Fabian Society in 1903, but in 1906 he criticized sharply Sidney and Beatrice Webb, two of the leading spirits among the Fabians, and in 1908 he withdrew his membership. Yet he said he was a socialist ever since his student days, adding that he was not a Marxist but a Rodbertusian socialist (a follower of Johann Karl Rodbertus, 1805—1875, a German economist). As he was born and brought up in an environment of misery, he was strongly aware of terrible social injustice and wanted to change the bourgeois society but he was opposed to the theory of class struggle and inclined to reformism, consistently failing to see the strength of the working class while vaguely believing in the ability of scientists and technologists to solve the social contradictions.

The First World War came and shocked Wells, and in his consuming desire for peace he turned for a time to the mysterious supernatural for help, and his spiritual crisis led him to depart from the materialism of a scientist to adopt the idealism of seeking for answers to social problems in the realm of religion (as in "God the Invisible King", 1917; "The Soul of a Bishop", 1917; "Joan and Peter", 1918; "The Undying Fire", 1919).

In 1920 Wells paid a visit to the Soviet Union, and in 1921 after his return he wrote a record of his impressions of the visit, "Russia in the Shadows", in which he showed his scepticism toward the glorious prospects of socialism in Russia, yet in which he revealed his admiration for the Communist Party in the Soviet Union and for Lenin, for their determination and great spiritual strength to bring about socialism and communism. And after his return from the Soviet Union he turned again to the writing of scientific fantasies.

In 1926 he witnessed the General Strike taking place in England and was much impressed by it. In his book "Meanwhile" (1927) he for the first time dealt with the workers' movement in his writings and showed the sympathy of a bourgeois intellectual for the strike. Here he also indicated his admiration for the British Communists who formed the backbone of the strike and who with their revolutionary enthusiasm and spirit of self-sacrifice were true fighters in the working class movement, although he still was here a steadfast follower of reformism and sceptical toward socialism and communism.

In 1934 Wells went to the Soviet Union for a second visit, and his well-known conversation with Stalin shows that Wells still stuck to his reformist views advancing his theory of the possibility of organizing economic planning in capitalist society and of thereby gradually transforming the capitalist system into socialism without the need of a social revolution.

The rise of fascism and the threat of a new war in the 1930s made Wells take his firm stand against German and Italian fascism and imperialist wars. This is shown especially in his works "The Shape of Things to Come", 1933; and "The Croquet Player", (1937). During the years of the Second World War Wells warmly supported the anti-fascist struggle of all the nations in the world.

Of the fantasies written in the early period of Wells' career, "The Time Machine", "The Island of Dr. Moreau" and "The Invisible Man" are the better known. "The Time Machine" describes a traveller making use of a specially designed machine to land on the earth at a future time extremely remote from the present day, in the year 802,701. At that time the human beings are described as divided into two distinct classes: on the one hand there are the Elois, the descendents of the modern bourgeoisie who live idle, parasitic lives of pleasure and luxury on the surface of the earth, while on the other hand there are the Morlocks, the offspring of the modern workers who look like beasts and live beneath the surface of the earth and work in the underground factories there. The Elois eat and live and do no work and so have become dwarfish, while the Morlocks live inhuman lives of perennial hard labour, they work for the Elois in the daytime but at night they emerge from under the earth and catch the Elois and eat them up. This terrible picture of the striking contrast between the life of the bourgeoisie and that of the poor workers was possibly intended as a bitter criticism of the present capitalist system with the existence of "two nations" in sharp contradiction with each other.

In "The Island of Dr. Moreau" a young biologist Edward Prendick drifted onto an island after shipwreck and there he discovered a brave scientist Dr. Moreau making a zoological experiment to transform animals into men through all sorts of operations. Then after the transformation these animals were made to cultivate human habits, such as walking on two legs instead of on all fours and wearing clothes and building simple houses and carrying heavy burdens and even teaching them to speak, with an operation on the vocal cord. But these animals with human forms and habits do not naturally or willingly conform to these habits, and so they have to be threatened into obedience by commandments which declare the enforcement of punishments for any violation and ask the question repeatedly: Aren't we human beings? and they are all extremely afraid of Dr. Moreau. Then there was sudden confusion and the animals were liberated from the threats and the punishments, but they very quickly reverted back to their barbarism and once more started to walk on all fours. This novel of sheer fantasy is possibly meant to be a satire on the predatory nature of the bourgeois society in which laws are needed to restrain the animalistic behaviour of the plunderers in the world.

In "The Invisible Man", perhaps the most popular of Wells' novels, a poor but talented scientist Griffin tried to discover an element by which he could make himself invisible to others. Under difficult conditions and much social pressure he worked with unusual creative genius and perseverance and finally succeeded in making his desired scientific discovery. Yet, in spite of his personal life of poverty and misery and his hatred for social injustice, his wonderful discovery did not make him happy. Under the vicious influence of the bourgeois society he fell into the cesspool of extreme individualism from which he could not extricate himself. Instead of using his remarkable discovery for the benefit of the people he wanted to become a sort of "superman" over and above the whole society, and the people began to be afraid of him and they gathered together to oppose him and he tried to hit back and degenerated into a murderer, but finally met with defeat and died. Here Wells tried to point out that technology which at the hands of the many should normally bring happiness to men might turn out to be harmful if it should fall into the hands of extremely selfish individuals. The earlier portions of the novel, however, also seem to indicate yet another view of the author that a scientist frequently has to fight against the opposition of the bourgeois society before he can achieve really important scientific discoveries or inventions, or in other words, that the bourgeois society is hostile to the development of science and technology. The novel is particularly successful because here Wells creates a vivid portrait of the scientist Griffin, showing his spiritual conflict as well as the realistic details of his everyday life. And the attack here on the Nietzschean superman theory of reaction is the more effective, with the vivid portrayal of Griffin who represents that theory.

Two of Wells' earlier scientific fantasies, "The War of the Worlds" and "The First Man in the Moon", seem to have greater significance today with the space flights already a reality, yet actually they are satires directed toward the dangers facing the bourgeois society of the contemporary world. In "The War of the Worlds" the men from the planet of Mars are shown to be invading the earth, ending in victory for the Martians and the complete destruction of human civilization on earth. Here the extremely cruel Martians with their barbarous annihilation of human beings after their triumph are compared with the European colonialists carrying out their almost complete annihilation of the natives in Tasmania within half a century, so that the barbarism of the Martians is simply a satire on the barbarism of imperialism and colonialism. Also, here the defeat of the human beings on earth by the Martians is attributed to the internecine wars and contradictions and disunity in the bourgeois world as well as the backwardness in science and technology there. The Martians, described as beings with simply a big head each and 60 tentacles and therefore extremely selfish and devoid of any reason or feelings, are naturally meant to satirize the idle race of the big bourgeoisie. Though "The First Men in the Moon" has lost much of its interest today following the actual landing of space-

men on the moon, yet the intended satire on bourgeois human society is unmistakable. Here Wells describes what the first group of
men landing on the moon find there. The inhabitants in the moon,
the Selenites, are said to be queer persons of abnormal appearance,
with one of them seeming to have only one extremely big tentacle-
like arm and a huge right fore-limb, another with a big thigh balanced on stilts, while a third with a long, outstretched nose resembling that of an elephant. Certain persons seem to be fit only to
do one kind of work, the carrier with big, solid feet, the docker with
only a back and hands while the gate-keeper has a fully-developed
right arm for closing the gate. The function of each person's head
is also different from that of another, some having only the power
of memory while others with strongly developed capacity for thinking and reasoning. When there is no work to be done on the moon,
the unemployed are doped into a state of sleep until it is once
again time for them to wake up and labour. The ruling class in the moon
consists of executives and specialists and scholars, with big heads
and under-developed muscles, so that they have to have all sorts of
attendants to wait on them and doing things for them. Through
the description we find an exaggerated picture of the division of
labour carried out to ridiculous lengths, and here we may perceive
Wells' satire on the idle rulers and hardworking labourers in the
bourgeois world as well as his retort to the reactionary theory of
Herbert Spencer that in human society, according to the natural
division of labour, the ruling class is the brain that directs while
the workers are the hands that should do all the work.

In other scientific fantasies of this early period of Wells' career there are: "When the Sleeper Wakes", a terrible picture of
the rule of the monopolists; "The Food of the Gods", a sort of
utopian vision of a more perfect race of men fed with a special kind
of food; "In the Days of the Comet", a fantastic story of the terrible bourgeois society transformed by the miracle of the comet
meeting the earth into the golden age, with the loss of selfishness
and individualism that prevent human beings from attaining hap-

piness and harmony.

In "The War in the Air" (1908) and "The World Set Free" (1914), written on the eve of the First World War, Wells showed his prophetic anticipation of the world conflict that employed highly destructive weapons. Both are actually anti-imperialist-war pamphlets.

Wells wrote a number of realistic novels on social life, mostly in the early period of his writing, before the First World War. These include: "The Wheels of Chance" (1896), "Love and Mr. Lewisham" (1900), "Kipps" (1905), "Ann Veronica" (1909), "Tono-Bungay" (1909) and "The History of Mr. Polly" (1910), and of these "Love and Mr. Lewisham" and "Kipps" and "Tono-Bungay" are better known. "Love and Mr. Lewisham" is based somewhat on the author's reminiscences of his own experience at the Normal School of Science, as he presents the contrast between the poverty and misery of the people right next to the school and the shining windows and bright clothes of the rich bourgeoisie living in great luxury two blocks away.

"Kipps" is a much more interesting novel. The central figure Kipps is a typical "little man" from the lower middle class. He is short-sighted in everything but tries to climb up with all his strength to the upper society. Yet the social world frightens him and he runs away from the brilliant circle to which he has been climbing and gets married to a servant-woman and becomes the owner of a small shop and quietly spends the rest of his life there. The realistic portrait of Kipps is vividly drawn and he becomes so typical of many tame and insignificant members of the lower middle class of modern England that his name has often been used in early 20th-century England to refer to such persons. The novel paints the drabness of the modern Western society and the colourless persons like Kipps as victims of that society.

"Tono-Bungay" is possibly the most effective of all Wells' novels on social life. The story is one of George Ponderevo and his nephew who make a large fortune selling a worthless patent medicine called Tono-Bungay, supposed to serve as a tonic. The secret of their success lies in the use of advertising and publicity in order to cheat the customers into buying the medicine, and also in the unscrupulous ways employed to compete with the other druggists and pharmacists. In other words, the most typical means of cheat and plunder is resorted to so that the poor tradesman Ponderevo rises to great wealth. But he meets with reverses when he becomes bolder and tries to take a hand in speculation. The enterprise fails as the harmful beverage gets involved in a law-case, and Ponderevo in running away from pursuit dies on the way. The novel is a thorough-going satire on the prevalent practice in cheating and fooling the people in order to gain wealth in the commercial world in modern England, and the character of Ponderevo as a vulgar, selfish and greedy commercial capitalist is well portrayed while a broad picture is given here of the dissolution of modern English society at the end of the 19th and the beginning of the 20th century.

During the years of the First World War, besides writing a number of novels acknowledging the existence of God and the necessity of religion, Wells also showed his disillusionment in the war. While in the earlier ones among the collection of his essays "The War That Will End War" (1914), Wells seemed to be some-what taken in by the propaganda of the British government which puts the blame of the war entirely on Germany and tries to justify the actions of England and France and America, gradually in the later essays of the collection he became aware of the profit gained by the capitalists from the war and therefore of the inglorious war objectives of the English ruling class. In the novel "Mr. Brittling Sees It Through" (1916), Wells declares his own attitude towards the war through the mouth of Mr. Brittling, cursing the disaster and havoc caused by the war and condemning militarism, although here in order to gain peace he turns to God for help.

After his visit to the Soviet Union Wells wrote no more idea-listic novels calling for God's help, but he turned once again to the writing of scientific fantasies. "Men Like Gods" (1921), a utopian novel describing a group of Englishmen arriving in an ideal world but not feeling at home there; and "The Dream" (1924), a utopian novel in reverse describing a man in the future ideal world (in the 40th century) dreaming of life in England in the 20th century and thereby satirizing the contemporary Western society.

In the years shortly after the First World War, Wells also wrote a number of books on history among which "The Outline of History" (1920) and "A Short History of the World" (1922) are better known, the first being an extremely widely read book by the general reading public of the time.

"Meanwhile" is one of Wells' discussion novels. There is no fantasy at all, but the plot is a very thin one while the characters in it indulge in much discussion. A group of Englishmen are described spending their summer in the French Riviera and discussing the fate of the decaying Western society, when the General Strike breaks out in England from May 4 to May 12, in 1926. And in a letter from one of the characters in the story, Mr. Rylands who has been an eyewitness of the strike, a complete survey of the strike is sympathetically given.

Also written in the late 1920's are two novels by Wells worth our attention: "The World of William Clissold" (1926) and "Mr. Blettsworthy on Rampol Island" (1928). "The World of William Clissold" is another discussion novel. It is supposed to be the biography of William Clissold, a man who is both a scholar and a capitalist, but actually it is a hotch-potch of discussions reflecting the views of the author himself on economics, politics, history, philosophy, ethics, religion and art, and most of the time Clissold the chief character speaks for Wells the author. Clissold is shown in the novel to be thoroughly dissatisfied with the contemporary bourgeois society: he considers merchants to be like robbers, bankers to be like blood-suckers, newspapers, broadcasts and motion pictures to have become instruments of capitalists for their propaganda and profit; he attacks chauvinism and especially monopoly capitalism. And he wants eagerly to change the world. All this is very well, and true. But Clissold suggests for all the progressive elements from every social stratum to join hands and take over the management of the world economy, and to educate all the people to work not for oneself but for the whole human race and thus to root out the social evils and crimes of the capitalist world. And he advocates what he calls "new liberalism" which is not only to ask for freedom in education, in commerce, in religious worship and in self-expression but also freedom from the excessive freedom demanded from the system of private ownership and freedom from the philosophy of individualism.

"Mr. Blettsworthy on Rampole Island" is another book of fantasy. A bourgeois intellectual Mr. Blettsworthy gets shipwrecked on a voyage and loses consciousness and in a dream he finds himself on Rampole Island meeting with the cannibalistic natives there and learning of the innumerable horrible ways of life of these primitive barbarians. Then he feels he is really in the streets of New York and the bewildering life around him confuses him and makes him seem to see the horrors on Rampole Island. Finally he returns to the "civilized" bourgeois world and to his great surprise many things he saw on Rampole Island actually happen also in the bourgeois environment. Here the satire on the predatory nature of the bourgeois world is told from an angle not unsimilar to that employed by the great 18th century English novelist Swift in his "Gulliver's Travels", just as Wells himself declared that in his scientific fantasies he was following in the example of Swift. The notorious murder case of Sacco and Vanzetti which took place in America in the 1920's is used here as the starting point for this novel in which the satire is particularly directed at the bourgeois society in America.

Several of Wells' last group of novels are strongly antifascist ("The Autocracy of Mr. Parham", 1930; "The Shape of Things to Come", 1933; "The Croquet Players", 1936; "You Can't Be Too Careful", 1941). In "The Autocracy of Mr. Parham", through the device of a dream Wells calls attention to the threat of fascism in England as well as on the European Continent, but he vainly hoped that a scientist may come to save the country from fascism and that enlightened capitalists would be hostile to fascism. In both "The Croquet Player" and "You Can't Be Too Careful" Wells warns that ordinary individuals among the middle classes in England may actually act as staunch supporters of fascism without themselves realizing it. In the former novel, a short-sighted but self-complacent croquet player wishes to place himself outside all struggle and so advocates non-interference in international affairs, including the conflict between the fascist and the republican forces in the Civil War in Spain in the 1930s, while the policy of non-interference adopted by the governments of a number of countries actually helped the German and Italian fascists in making Franco set up its dictatorial rule in Spain. In "You Can't Be Too Careful", the chief character Tewler, a Kippsian representative of the English middle class, with his lack of human feelings and his vulgar desire for business gains hates communism and tries to seek for salvation from fascism and chauvinism, but eventually he finds himself to have made a terrible mistake, for fascism brings about the Second World War and Hitler instead of striking at the Soviet Union turns his weapons of destruction against the Western powers. Soon Hitler and his Nazis are defeated but the author warns that fascism is not thereby exterminated but may rise again if we aren't careful.

"The Shape of Things to Come", written in the year Hitler rose to power in Germany, is a different sort of fantasy in which the author seems to predict the coming of the Second World War and its consequences. The book was extremely widely read at the time and then made into a movie and it exerted much influence. The story takes place in "Every Town" and the beginning of the war is placed in the year 1940 and the conflict is described as lasting 30 years. There is the vivid description of large-scale destruction of people and things, as a result of the use of all possible weapons of war, until the whole human civilization seems to face extinction and is only finally saved by a group of engineers on a remote island who with their invention of a special kind of narcotic throw the whole world into a state of anaesthesia and then have a national social organization all ready upon the re-awakening of all the people in the world. This fantasy contains a thorough-going condemnation of fascist war but the solution is again typical of Wells with his reformist views and his trust particularly placed upon the scientists and technical men to save the terrible bourgeois society from its doom.

Though Wells wrote a few discussion novels which are at least stimulating and also several novels of social life in which the bourgeois society is satirized through the realistic description of bourgeois individuals and their ridiculous and contemptible actions, his chief contribution to literature lies in the numerous scientific fantasies which he wrote with the aim of satirizing the ugly bourgeois social reality from different angles and of trying to suggest a remedy, a solution. He generally succeeds in producing the effect of satire which is sometimes devastating. He offers no proper solutions to terrible social problems, because he is afraid of the people, and fails to realize the strength in the masses but rather places his trust in the few intellectuals, scholars and scientists and technologists. In this respect his outlook resembles in one way that of Shaw's and in another that of Galsworthy.

e. Arnold Bennett

Arnold Bennett (1867—1931) was born in a lawyer's family and then studied at London University. After his graduation he served for a time as a clerk in his father's solicitor's office, but later he gave it up and in 1893 became assistant editor and then editor of the London periodical "Woman". Although his earliest writings appeared in the periodical "The Yellow Book", he did not follow the tradition of the aesthetic school of Symons and Beardsley in his later works. As a voluminous writer of different genres of fiction, drama, literary criticism, etc., Bennett is chiefly known as a novelist, and his chief works are "The Old Wives' Tale" (1908) and his Clayhanger trilogy ("Clayhanger", 1910; "Hilda Lessways",

1911; "These Twain", 1916; all three reprinted under one title, "The Clayhanger Family", 1925)and other novels and stories about the pottery centres of Five Towns ("Anna of the Five Towns", 1902; "Tales of the Five Towns", 1905; "The Grim Smile of the Five Towns", 1907). Since the middle decades of the 20th century, Bennett has also been known for his later novels, particularly "Riceyman Steps" (1923). Then he broadened the canvas of his story-telling, and wrote a political novel "Lord Raingo" (1926) which deals with the intrigues and interplays between Downing Street (the Prime Minister) and Westminster (the Houses of Parliament) through the portraits that suggest the wartime Prime Minister Lloyd George and his personal secretary and mistress and which was based on the author's experience at the Ministry of Information in 1938. His last novel, "Imperial Palace" was published in 1930, a year before his death. He also wrote dramas, and his collaborated effort with Edward Knoblock, "Milestones", which in three acts referring to three separate dates of 1860, 1885 and 1912 gives a historical view of the changes in beliefs as well as in *mores* of the three succeeding generations of the Rhead family with its enterprises in shipbuilding. "Milestones" was a successful play in 1912 amid repeated failures of Bennett's several other plays.

"Old Wives' Tale" is a long narrative of the lives of two sisters Constance and Sophia Baines, daughters of a draper of Bursley, one of the pottery centres known as the Five Towns, and it begins with their childhood and goes on through long years of disillusionment down to their old age and death. Constance, tamer and more sensible than her sister, married the chief assistant in the shop, Samuel Povey, and lives a dull and colourless life in Bursley, while Sophia, more flippant and ambitious, elopes with Gerald Scales, an unprincipled commercial traveller who has come into a fortune but who first marries her under compulsion and then carries her to Paris and finally deserts her. Sophia then has to struggle to live on in Paris, becomes the landlady of a boarding-house, lives through the siege of Paris by the Germans in 1870 and makes a lot of money during those days of excitement and finally returns to her home town and meets again her sister Constance, and the novel ends with the death of these two old wives. While many of the incidents in the novel as well as the actions and thoughts and feelings of many of the characters in it give objectively a picture of hypocrisy and deceit and cruelty and money-worship and a hundred other vices in the bourgeois society, whether in the Five Towns in England or in Paris in France, yet the author does not seem purposely to point out this ugly side of that society but he tells his tale in the aimless way of naturalism, and often the narration is oppressed with too many minute details of no importance at all, including very detailed descriptions of a kitchen or a parlour. At the end of the novel the writer seems to try to draw a conclusion about human life, but all the meaning about the life of either Constance or Sophia is simply the passage of time, from childhood to old age and death, and besides that no further meaning is to be found. Such is the result of Bennett's naturalism. In this sense, Virginia Woolf's criticism of Bennett as the chief of what she called the "Materialists" in English fiction is not without its grounds. However, if we examine the novel from the numerous realistic details contained in it, we may yet find sufficient criticism of the bourgeois society though it was never meant to be there by the novelist.

In "Clayhanger" the description of Clayhanger in his childhood working in the workshop where he has to endure hard labour way into the night is a more open condemnation of child labour and oppression, and then when he grows up and becomes despotic and thinks only of his purse, his son leaves him and he ruins his own life — here we may again see the vicious influence of the bourgeois society upon a man brought up in the oppressive atmosphere of hard labour and tyranny.

"Riceyman Steps" is a novel that contains only three chief characters, Henry Earlforward, Mrs. Violet Arb who later becomes Henry's wife and their general servant Elsie. Nothing spectacular happens, but the humdrum existence of the three is given in great detail, highlighted only by the wedding of the middle-aged couple, their eventual sickness and sudden death, and Elsie's advance from a charwoman to the status of a general servant and her adventures with her humble yet colourful lover Joe. Henry Earl-forward, an owner of a small secondhand bookstore, has the predominant character of a miser but is nevertheless very considerate and tactful, and his relations with the equally careful yet slightly more audacious-in-spending woman are described step by step. The timid approaches of the old bachelor and the widow in their courtship are masterfully depicted, and the small skirmishes on their wedding day and shortly after are meticulously pictured, replete with their mutual psychological reactions in the course of the seemingly unimportant yet actually significant little acts and words. Henry's repeated refusals to see a doctor and to go to the hospital, and then Violet's sudden illness and death and finally Henry's unwitnessed collapse are climactic episodes that wind up the story, but they are all results of their dominant personal traits of consistent miserliness in one case and of patient considerations in the other. The naturalistic emphasis on details described of the general environment and of the interplay of words and actions are here the same as in Bennett's earlier works of fiction, but there is perhaps more in the novel the expressions of latent thoughts and feelings of the major characters, and so the character-portrayal is here further rounded with psychological details on top of the materialistic ones.

Arnold Bennett is today more outdated as a novelist even than Wells and Galsworthy, because he followed more the traditional ways of narrative art of the 18th and 19th centuries and this accounted for the recent decline in his reputation as a prominent writer of fiction.

F. W. Somerset Maugham

William Somerset Maugham (1874—1965) was born in Paris when his father was a solicitor at the British Embassy there, and he received his early education in France. But both his mother and father died during his childhood, respectively when he was eight and ten years old, and he went to live in England under the rigorous care of his uncle an awesome clergyman. He led a rather unhappy life both in his uncle's home and at the King's School. He studied philosophy for a short period at Heidelberg University in Germany and there he first cultivated his lasting interest in drama and painting, but his early years in France and his extensive reading in French literature in his short childhood sojourn in southern France had much influence upon his literary taste and style. He refused to be ordained as a clergyman and took up the study of medicine and surgery. He was qualified as a doctor but never practiced medicine. He travelled extensively on the European Continent, particularly in Italy and Spain, then settled down for a number of years in Paris and moved among painters and writers there. All this acquaintance with foreign lands was largely responsible for his adoption of a writer's career, for the cosmopolitanism and broad perspective in his writings, and also for his employment of Paul Ganguin's life and career in his novel "The Moon and Sixpence".

Maugham started writing novels in the late 1890s, but his first novel based on his hospital experience of the miseries of the slum patients, "Liza of Lambeth" (1897), was completely neglected upon its appearance. In the first decade of the 20th century he turned to the writing of plays and quite unexpectedly popular success came to him as a playwright when in 1908 four of his plays ("Lady Frederick", "Jack Straw", "Mrs. Dot" and "The Explorer") ran successfully at the same time in the West End theatres in London (creating an almost unprecedented success story in London theatrical history) and were subsequently popular also on the American stage. From then on till the early thirties Maugham became an established dramatist and wrote upwards of altogether thirty plays, but he also took time off to write novels and short stories and other prose writings, especially his most important, semi-autobiographical novel, "Of Human Bondage" (1915).

Maugham travelled more extensively after the First World War, and much of his experience thus gained was told in his collections of short stories: "Ashenden, or The British Agent" (1928) which recorded his duties with the British Intelligent Service in Switzerland, France, Italy and Russia, in World War I; "On a Chinese Screen" (1922), records of his observations during his travels in China in the early twenties; "The Gentleman in the Parlour" (1930), a record of his journey from Rangoon to Haiphong, through Burma, Siam, Cambodia and Annam; and "The Trembling of a Leaf" (1921), stories about his adventures in the islands in the Pacific. Of his later writings, there were the two outstanding novels, "Cakes and Ale" (1930) and "The Moon and Sixpence" (1919), and his later comedies including "The Circle" (1921) and "Our Betters" (1923) and one of the better known of his later novels, "The Razor's Edge" (1943).

"Of Human Bondage", an admittedly autobiographical novel, is W. Somerset Maugham's most important work chiefly because the details are largely drawn from the author's own experience and are therefore especially vivid and realistic. One is fascinated particularly by the seemingly unvarnished episodes in the early life of Philip Carey the hero, both when the orphaned child goes to live with his very stern clergyman of an uncle and wins the true affections of his childless aunt, and when in King's School at Tercanbury he suffers at the hands of his schoolmates and of his teacher Mr. Watson partly on account of his deformity of a club foot and later also because of his unwillingness to go into the Church. In these episodes the reader cannot fail to be impressed by such authentic documents of a child's and a youth's joys and woes. Even later, when he spends a year in Germany and has his experience at the boarding-house and his first sexual adventure with an old spinster twice his age, when he returns to England and tries and fails to become a clerk in an accountant's office in London, and when he goes abroad again, this time to Paris to study painting and he encounters numerous incidents and people there, the truthfulness of the narration is no less impressive and delightful. However, as after Philip Carey gives up painting to take up medicine, particularly as soon as he meets and gets involved with Mildred Rogers, the novel loses its charms, especially in the repeated ruptures and resumptions of the two lovers' relations which get more and more tiring and monotonous as the hero fails to effect his final break with her. But the worst flaw in the novel comes at the end of the book when after finding no meaning in life the hero reconciles himself to the society by seeking for simple pleasures in loving a girl of great innocence and by adopting thus the return-to-nature "motif" which is hardly compatible with the twentieth-century world of sophistication. However, "Of Human Bondage" has the distinction of giving a series of attractive kaleidoscopic pictures of much of his own childhood and youth in inevitable disguise, and his nostalgia of days in the past led him sometimes to delightful scenes and at other times to sentimental reminiscences. But coming after the numerous theatrical successes in his drawing-room comedies of wit and repartee and published amidst the First World War (in 1915), the author must have written the novel in his moments of disillusionment when he tried to seek for relief from ennui by indulging in the recollections of certain outstanding memories of his past life and so there is perhaps here less of the cynicism that seems to pervade his other writings and more of the desire to escape from sordid reality and it is this last that accounts chiefly for his gratification at the simple pleasures with Sally Athelny which follow at the heels of his unpleasant experience with Mildred Rogers. The simplicity of style so pleasantly lucid and readable is particularly attractive in this "recherche du temps perdu".

Perhaps even more delightful and colourful is his book based on Paul Gauguin, "The Moon and Sixpence". Here Maugham tells the story in the first person singular, himself serving as a participant in the story as well as the narrator. The three parts of Charles Strickland's career, in London, in Paris, and in Tahiti are related by the author with himself as an eye-witness or as a researcher, in order to add to the vividness of the story.

In London Charles Strickland appears very seldom in person but he is known and described chiefly as the dull, uninteresting stockbroker husband of Mrs. Strickland, who is a vivacious lady interested in the arts and a friend to the author. Only the sudden disastrous disappearance of Strickland and its exasperating consequence upon his wife are given prominence in the narrative. Charles Strickland figures large in the author's numerous encounters with him in Paris, where he goes to fulfill his ruling passion of becoming a painter. The hero is as repulsive as ever, in fact even more so than before, but the author stresses above all the man's uncontrollable desire to paint, so that all other common pleasures in life seem unimportant to him and he becomes even extremely unreasonable in his dealings with others, including his wife and children, and his friends ready to help him. His wife and her sister and brother-in-law are convinced that he must have left his home with some woman, but actually he goes alone to Paris and lives in a garret. A fellow painter Dirk Stroeve tries his best to help Strickland, even has him brought to his own studio to be nursed by his own wife Blanche when Strickland is sick and seems to be dying, but as soon as he recovers, Strickland takes Blanche away from Dirk quite relentlessly. His paintings are never sold, in fact hardly vendable because no one would buys them, and Dirk is the only one to recognize a genius in Strickland. Then suddenly Strickland leaves for Marseilles and following a brief stay there as a down-and-outer he gets his job as common sailor on a ship and eventually arrives in Tahiti in the South Pacific. Only a quarter of the novel is devoted to the author's account of Charles Strickland in Tahiti, but that is certainly the most thrilling part of the tale, not so much because of the unusual events that happen to Strickland (Gauguin) there, as on account of the lugubrious descriptions and the exuberant language with which those events are told. Even the very locale of Tahiti gives Maugham an occasion for a rhapsodic sketch upon his first sight of the island:

"Tahiti is a lofty green island, with deep folds of a dark-er green, in which you divine silent valleys; there is mystery in their sombre depths, down which murmur and plash cool streams, and you feel that in those umbrageous places life from immemorial times has been led according to immemorial ways. Even here is something sad and terrible. But the impression is fleeting, and serves only to give a greater acuteness to the enjoyment of the moment .... For Tahiti is smiling and friendly; it is like a lovely woman graciously prodigal of her charm and beauty; and nothing can be more conciliatory than the entrance into the harbour at Papeete. The schooners moored to the quay are trim and neat, the little town along the bay is white and urbane, and the flamboyants, scarlet against the blue sky, flaunt their colour like a cry of passion. They are sensual with an unashamed violence that leaves you breathless. And the crowd that throngs the wharf as the steamer draws alongside is gay and debonair; it is a noisy, cheerful, gesticulating crowd. It is a sea of brown faces. You have an impression of coloured movement against the flaming blue of the sky. Everything is done with a great deal of bustle, the unloading of the baggage, the examination of the customs; and everyone seems to smile at you. It is very hot. The colour dazzles you."

The story of Strickland's sojourn at Tahiti is told in three installments by three narrators whom the author met several years after the painter's death. Mrs. Tiaré Johnson, fat, old proprietress of the Hotel de la Fleur, tells of how she found a wife for the poor, penniless but perverse Strickland shortly after his arrival in the South Pacific island, how a native girl named Ata took a fancy to the artist and he agreed to marry her, and how Strickland and Ata went to live happily in her little house some eight kilometres away from Papeete and soon they had a baby while the painter did nothing but paint. Then Capitaine Brunot, a middle-aged French settler on the neighbouring island of the Paumotus, described Strickland's place which he visited: "where Strickland lived had the beauty of the Garden of Eden ... a corner hidden away from all the world, with the blue sky overhead and the rich, luxuriant trees ... It was a feast of colour. And it was fragrant and cool. Words cannot describe that paradise." Finally an old French physician Dr. Coutras tells of the last days of Charles Strickland, of how he was asked to pay a visit to the painter, how he was shocked to find the latter stricken with leprosy, but still painting away at his own house, and how he several years later went there again and discovered the artist dead but the walls of the house completely covered by strange and elaborate paintings. The haunting description of the painted walls, given by Maugham via Dr. Coutras, is another masterly piece of prose composition :

> "From floor to ceiling the walls were covered with a strange and elaborate composition. It was indescribably wonderful and mysterious. It took his [i.e. Dr. Coutras'] breath away. It filled him with an emotion which he could not understand or analyse. He felt the awe and the delight which a man might feel who watched the beginning of a world. It was tremendous, sensual, passionate; and yet there was something horrible there, too, something which made him afraid. It was the work of a man who had delved into the hidden depths of nature and had discovered secrets which were beautiful and fearful too. It was the work of a man who knew things which it is unholy for men to know. There was something primeval there and terrible. It was not human. It brought to his mind vague recollections of black magic. It was beautiful and obscene."

And Dr. Coutras' remark on this sight, "Mon Dieu, this is genius", was too obviously also Maugham's comment.

Taken all in all, "The Moon and Sixpence" is a most unusual book, and I think the most striking novel by W. Somerset Maugham. The author here assembled together the many fragments that made up the man, Charles Strickland (alias Paul Gauguin), and tried to mould the convincing portrait of an artist who just had to be an artist and whose consuming passion was to express himself through his paintings. And Maugham succeeded in creating the towering figure of a man who was strange and repulsive but a genius, while the racy, conversational style of Maugham's admirable prose becomes here the fittest vehicle for which an engrossing tale told in a desultory way.

Another outstanding novel by Maugham is "Cakes and Ale". Here the chief figure is a representative of the spirit of hedonism Rosie Driffield, though it has commonly been supposed that Driffield and Alroy Kear were caricatures respectively of Thomas Hardy and Hugh Walpole. Actually whether the supposition is true or not is of little importance, because Rosie as the heroine is a most lively character-portrait whereas Driffield and Kear are but pale and insignificant figures in comparison.

The story of Rosie, like that of Charles Strickland in "The Moon and Sixpence", is also told in three installments — as she appeared in Blackstable, then in London and finally in New York City, with digressive episodes in between. Also comparable to the story of Gauguin the author in this novel is again an important participant and a ubiquitous eye-witness of almost all the major figures and events that evolve round the mijor character Rosie and of course also her husband Edward Driffield. In the Blackstable installment, the author was only a schoolboy of fifteen, but he used to know the Driffields well enough as he took bicycle rides with them and visited often their humble home in the neighbourhood, and he knew Rosie to have been a barmaid before her marriage to Edward Driffield, who was then a little known novelist. And Rosie was known even then to have a bad reputation of "carrying on with" men of all sorts and there were not only vivid scenes of much frolic and even debauchery in Driffield's home but mention was also made of Rosie's clandestine meeting at night with a married coal merchant George Kemp who was much older than herself. Then there was the news of sudden decamping of the Driffields from Blackstable where they left all their debts unpaid. The second installment of the story was about the Driffields' life in London as the author knew it when he was twenty and a medical student. Now Edward Driffield was literary editor of a weekly paper and his last book sold better, but Rosie was having a number of love affairs with their friends(including even the author himself) and Edward Driffield didn't seem to bother. Rosie even had an affair with a vulgar, rich, old Dutch Jew named Jack Kuyper who took her out night after night for some three weeks and then gave her an expensive gift of a fur cape worth two hundred and sixty pounds upon leaving her. Then the sudden news was told of Rosie having left her husband and run away with George Kemp the coal merchant who was said to have gone completely bankrupt and deserted his wife and sons. Later it was narrated that a registered mail of ten or twenty pounds for Rosie's mother had come from New York, apparently from Rosie. Finally, after a long episode about the visit of the author and his fellow-novelist Alroy Kear to the home of the now widowed second Mrs. Driffield, the third and last installment of the story begins with the author receiving upon a visit to New York a letter from "Rose Iggulden (formerly Driffield)". Then in the last chapter of the book, at the brief encounter between the author and Rosie at her apartment in Yonkers, near New York City, Rosie was described as a wealthy, seventy-year-old widow of George Iggulden (alias Kemp) who was as frank and as much in love with life as ever. But in the chapter just before this final one, as the second Mrs. Driffield and Alroy Kear and the author were together discussing Rosie, the author's comments on Rosie are most significant and seemed to be a sort of summing-up of Rosie's character:

> "She was a very nice woman. I never saw her in a bad
> temper. You only had to say you wanted something for
> her to give it to you, I never heard her say a disagreeable
> thing about any one. She had a heart of gold."

And:

"She was a very simple woman. Her instincts were healthy and ingenuous. She loved to make people happy." Whether these words are meant to produce a favourable impression of Rosie upon the reader is of less importance, for it only points to the author's amorality; what is more important is that in spite of her faults, of which promiscuity is naturally the foremost, Rosie Driffield is a brilliant portrait in Maugham's gallery of woman characters in his fictional works. And this distinguishes the book as an outstanding novel by Maugham.

Again, the numerous diversional episodes in between the three main installments, obviously purposely inserted by the author, are here even more interesting than similar digressional interludes in "The Moon and Sixpence", for they contain vivid portraits of such minor but eccentric figures as Alroy Kear, Mrs. Barton Trafford and the second Mrs. Driffield, as well as the important story thread of the writing of a biography for Edward Driffield which became the chief *raison d'être* of the descriptions of the Driffields and especially of Rosie. The racy language here is again very typical of Maugham, and the easy conversational tone throughout constitutes one of the principal charms of Maugham's prose style.

Of Maugham's later novels only "The Razor's Edge" was much praised after its publication, yet it definitely showed the decline of the author's powers as a novelist, though the story on the whole is entertaining enough and it is told with the usual lucidity and suppleness of the author's prose style. This is not a book about any major figure but tells the tale of an upper-class family of America's midwest, the Bradleys, that includes the mother Louisa, the daughter Isabel, her uncle Elliott Templeton, her boy friend Larry Darrell, her husband Gray Maturin and his father Henry. Actually, Larry is the hero whose portrait is most fully drawn, with Elliott Templeton and Isabel sharing the honours of the author's careful psychological analysis. Larry is not satisfied with leading an ordinary life of wealth and comfort but tries to make something out of life. He studies hard, works in a mine and at a farm, travels abroad as a sailor and even goes to India and lives in the Buddhist temples, and engages in religious and philosophical contemplation, but he finds it impossible to realize his ideal even after he has the experience of "being one with the Absolute", and he returns to the Western world. The book ends with Larry deciding vaguely to "go back to America" and live "with calmness, forebearance, compassion, selflessness and continence", while he declares that "the greatest ideal man can set before himself is self-perfection." Larry as the hero in the novel seems to suggest the mental state Maugham was in his old age. Like Larry he is thoroughly disillusioned with Western civilization and is somewhat attracted to Eastern philosophy and religion, but finally he has to settle down to a vague proposition of "self-perfection". And this is not untypical of many a Western intellectual of the 20th century who is trying hard to grope his way out of the morass of capitalism.

The other two characters, Elliott Templeton and Isabel Bradley, are typical figures in the bourgeois world. Elliott tries to amass wealth and then to ape the ways of the fashionable society, while Isabel gives up love for a life of material comfort but can be very ruthless toward any rival of hers in love. Both are conventional characters but very subtly portrayed figures and are made to serve as targets for the author's penetrating satire.

The story threads are loosely woven together and the narrative lacks unity and suspense. Especially unsatisfactory is the ending of the tale which seems to drift pointlessly. And the part of the novel in which Larry tells of his experience in India and practices his superhuman cure on Gray Maturin involves superstition that the author himself seems to believe in and even to endorse. Also Larry's narration of the Hindu theory of the transmigration of souls appears to suggest Maugham's own quasi-belief in its possibility, and Larry's vivid description of how, in his own words, "I felt as though I were suddenly released from my body and as pure spirit partook of a loveliness I had never conceived", also seems at least to indicate the author's unwillingness to deny Larry's mystical experience of his momentary "union with the Absolute". This faith in supernatural power in the middle decades of the 20th century is certainly a step backward, even for an aged Western intellectual who could find no way out of the modern materialist capitalist civilization.

Maugham also wrote many short stories and sketches. His book "On a Chinese Screen" may be written essentially by some one who had had little knowledge of the Chinese nation and who inherited somewhat the usual attitude of British colonialists toward the Oriental peoples, yet while he described some of the Chinese labouring people as rather ignorant and superstitious he showed them as generally possessed of strong personality and kind-hearted benevolence and he always manifested his sympathetic understanding of various types of the Chinese people high and low. On the other hand, he often disapproved of the highhandedness and arrogance of the Westerners resident in China.

An interesting collection of short stories by Maugham is entitled "The Trembling of a Leaf" which includes chiefly exotic stories dealing with what happens on the islands in the Pacific. One of the stories, "Miss Thompson", later renamed "Rain", tells of a fanatical Christian missionary's attempt to convert a prostitute Sadie Thompson which ends tragically with his succumbing finally to her sexual attractions. This story was later dramatized and became a great theatrical success, and then it was eventually filmed. The satire on religious fanaticism here is stronger than to be found in any other story by Maugham and the story remains one of his best.

Maugham was also a dramatist. His early plays, chiefly drawing-room comedies, followed the tradition of Restoration Comedies of Manners and that of Oscar Wilde and Henry Arthur Jones, and depended principally on striking dramatic situations and clever dialogue for their popular success on the stage. In his later dramas, particularly in such plays as "The Circle" and "Our Betters", there is more conscious effort on the playwright's part to satirize the fashionable society in England and America, though witty dialogue is still the main thing and the theme is almost sheer nonsense. "The Circle" deals with the theme of elopement: the circle is complete when the daughter-in-law elopes in the same way the mother did thirty years ago and the persuasions of the mother in question and of the latter's erstwhile lover and husband all fail at the last moment. Again the very artificial situation is here created, that of the elderly triangle of husband, wife and lover being invited by the daughter-in-law to the house to meet and talk amiably while the younger triangle of husband, wife and lover are engaged again in the same old problem of elopement. This most dramatic yet comic situation is expertly invented and managed by Maugham the master-craftman of the theatre, and the play is filled with subtle humour and bitter irony. Of course, a theme like this was very much restricted to the historical period in which it was unfolded, and so the play now loses interest for most readers and audiences alike. "Our Betters" is more definitely a satire on those wealthy American heiresses who in exchange for their money marry the lords and dukes and princes of European countries for their titles and most of whom lead frivolous and wild lives of parties, dinners and amours. Again climactic situations are introduced and witty dialogue is brought in wherever possible, and again the play is hollow in theme and is very much dated in the light of readers and audiences half a century later. However, Maugham in his later dramas was a much more serious writer than in his earlier plays which simply catered to the frivolous public of the day.

Somerset Maugham's reputation as a writer has waned much since his heyday in the first three decades of the present century. However, though his plays and short stories and sketches may be largely forgotten, three outstanding novels of his, "Of Human Bondage", "The Moon and Sixpence" and "Cakes and Ale" will continue to be remembered if not for the negligible social criticism latent in them, at least for the brilliant portrayals of such characters as Philip Carey, Charles Strickland and Rosie Driffield and for the extremely lucid and delightful prose style which makes these novels so easily readable.

g. D. H. Lawrence

David Herbert Lawrence (1885—1930) was born in the Midlands mining village of Eastwood, Nottinghamshire. His father was a coal-miner and his mother was a schoolteacher who was better educated and came to despise her coarse and often drunken husband. She had much influence upon Lawrence the novelist, to the extent that his love for her kept frustrating his relationships with girls, but it was through her efforts that Lawrence with the education received was able to escape from the mining world of his father.

Lawrence was somewhat sickly as a child and so instead of having close associations with other boys he knew well the mining town and the countryside and spent much time on books. He won a scholarship to Nottingham high school, then worked as a clerk and as an elementary school teacher (1902—06), and studied for two years at Nottingham University College where he obtained a teacher's certificate in 1908. His first published work was a group of his early poems in the "English Review" in 1909, and in 1910 appeared his early short story and then his first novel "The White Peacock". In the meantime he had been teaching school at Croydon, a southern suburb of London. It was in 1910 that he broke his engagement with Jessie Chambers (identified generally with Miriam in "Sons and Lovers"), became engaged to Louis Burrows, witnessed his mother's death and began the first version of "Sons and Lovers", which was published in 1913.

In 1912 his serious illness made him give up teaching and following his return to Eastwood he met and fell in love with Frieda von Rochthofen who was the German wife of a former professor of his named Weekley. He eloped with Frieda to Germany and then to Italy and they were married in 1914 when she was divorced by her husband. The threat of war brought them back to England in June, 1914, but Frieda's German origins and Lawrence's objection to the war gave them much trouble with the authorities. However, he kept on writing poetry, finished a play "The Widowing of Mrs. Holroyd" (only recently produced with success on the stage), began a novel called "The Lost Girl" (completed after the war), produced a number of short stories and took his first steps toward a novel which was called "The Sisters" but which was later split into "The Rainbow" (1915) and "Women in Love" (1921).

"The Rainbow" was banned and his strong reaction to this made him leave England as soon as the war was over. He and Frieda went to Italy in November 1919, then to Ceylon, Australia, New Zealand, the South Seas, the United States, Mexico, and then back to Italy and then finally the south of France. These wanderings led to the writing of many travel books: "Twilight in Italy" (1916), "Sea and Sardinia" (1921), "Mornings in Mexico" (1927) and "Etruscan Places" (1932). Between 1919 and 1930, the year of his death, Lawrence wrote more poetry, a number of short stories and novellas, and several novels: "Women in Love" (1921), "Aaron's Rod" (1922), "Kangaroo" (1923), "The Plumed Serpent" (1926), and "Lady Chatterley's Lover" (1928). He showed his indebtedness to Freud in his works written in reply to the Austrian physician and psychopathologist: "Psychoanalysis and the Unconscious" (1921) and "Fantasia of the Unconscious" (1922). He made his defense of "Lady Chatterley's Lover" first in "À Propos of Lady Chatterley's Lover" (at first entitled "My Skirmish with Jolly Roger") and then in a pamphlet "Pornography and Obscenity" (1929). His other prose writings of interest include: "Studies in Classic American Literature" (1923) and "Movements in European History" (1921). He died in the south of France in 1930, aged forty-four, of tuberculosis.

Lawrence is a poet of some importance. He wrote a quantity of verse and some few of his poems, particularly those on animals and plants, have their distinctive quality and are included in most anthologies. His poetry resembles his fiction in that there is in it ever something strange, something with the poet's strong emotions embedded in it, something reminding us ever of love and sex. Quite a number of his poems that touch on the plant world and the animal world ("Medlars and Sorb-Apples", "Figs", "Bavarian Genetians", "River Roses", "Cypresses", the "Tortoise Sequence", "Bat", "The Mosquito", "Humming Bird", "Mountain Lion" and "Snake", show his much enthusiasm for and his understanding of vegetable and animal life that suggest the influence possibly of Walt Whitman. Especially in "Snake" and "Bavarian Genetians" are revealed the poet's warm feelings of curiosity and affection that seem to draw the serpent and the blue-flowered plant close to him and place them on an equal footing with him. But in "Tortoise Shout" and "Figs" Lawrence's obsession with sex life in his novels emerge with the indulgent use of all the frank and sensual terms of sex. Perhaps most admirable of all his poems is "Piano" where the sight of a child sitting under the piano makes the author recall the "glamour" of his own childhood days and "weep like a child for the past". Standing quite apart from his other poems is one entitled "How Beastly the Bourgeois Is" in which Lawrence tears off the English gentleman's "eminently presentable" exterior and reveals the latter's true essence of "either a fool or a bully", "stale", "hollow" and "rather nasty".

But Lawrence is above all a writer of prose fiction. Of the many short stories he wrote, "The Prussian Officer" is an outstanding hit on German militarism, though the author seems to suggest that it is the frustration in sex satisfaction in the all-male military camp that is largely responsible for the officer's brutality and inhuman cruelty toward his orderly in the story. With his other stories there is the recurrent theme of love being distorted by the feeling of possessiveness or false romanticism, and there is frequently the author's suggestion of the need for a truly living relationship between a man and a woman if love is to be successful, a suggestion which comes up again in his more important novels.

His first important novel, "Sons and Lovers", is obviously strongly autobiographical. There is in it a rather realistic representation of mining life in the Midlands that the author was familiar with in his childhood and early manhood, but more significant is the resemblance of the strong bond of mother love between Mrs. Morel and Paul in the novel to the novelist's own mother's strong hold upon Lawrence, and the parallel stretches itself to Paul's early unsuccessful love affairs with Miriam (Jessie Chambers in Lawrence's real life) and Clara. The story of these four major figures in the novel is unfolded in the conventional way, but the relations of Paul with his mother and the two women he loves are depicted with particular care as the changes in their psychological and emotional reactions toward one another are traced analytically and in great detail. And what is truly significant, a man born of the working class and himself a small clerk is made the hero in the novel and Miriam is a farmer's daughter while Clara is a married woman estranged from her husband. Freud's influence is also quite obvious here, though Paul's inability to tear himself away from his mother which definitely suggests an illustration of "Oedipus Complex" seems rather to have been based on Lawrence's own experience. But at least we may find already in this early novel Lawrence's original and apparently idealistic view of love as a consuming passion that should link up soul with body in a true living union if it is to attain to real success.

Of Lawrence's novellas or short novels, "St. Mawr" has generally been considered the most important. The titular hero is a stallion of great beauty and indomitable spirit, but the story evolves around the two chief woman characters, mother and daughter, Mrs. Witt and Louise Carrington, both of whom serve more or less as the author's mouthpieces and yet have much life and spirit in them. Both women are wealthy Americans who have had all they seem to have wanted out of life: worldly comfort, moving about in aristocratic as well as artistic circles, much experience in conventional and exotic love and sex and marriage, but they both feel dissatisfied with life because they cannot find "the mystic new man" to come into their lives, and St. Mawr is only a symbol of the spirrited male so much desired. Here is given perhaps the most outspoken version of Lawrence's theory or faith in love and sex which seemed to him to be one of the most powerful things in human existence, yet the true significance of the novella lies first of all in the exposé, willy-nilly on the author's part, of the extreme decadence of aristocratic social life in England and throughout the West (witness the descriptions of Rico as an artist and of his circle of friends in the London Society), which inevitably leads those tired and disillusioned with such existence to desire to run away in desperation, even to the wild west in America. Then of course the psychological analysis of Mrs. Witt, Louise and Rico and even of their servants Lewis and Phoenix is superbly done, and the conversations and letters and private cogitations of these several characters are written in such delightful and mellifluous language as is rarely to be found in other works of Lawrence's.

The two great novels by Lawrence are "The Rainbow" and "Women in Love". The first is a family chronicle of the Brangwens stretching through three generations; while the second deals with the lives and loves of two Brangwen women, Ursula and Gudrun, of the third generation. "The Rainbow" opens with the marriage of Tom Brangwen, a hard-working, well-to-do farmer in Nottinghamshire, to a Polish widow Lydia Lensky who came with her small daughter Anna Lensky. There is a very vivid description of how Tom, at first not on good terms with Anna, gradually develops into full sympathy for the child. Then Tom's nephew, Will Brangwen, a lace-designer and a wood carver, falls in love and marries Anna. Will and Anna are very much in love at first but Anna later gets tired of their love and concentrates her attention on the bringing-up of her six children. Then the latter half of the book has to do almost entirely with Ursula, the eldest child of the six, whose adventures in life are traced from her girlhood up to her last year in college. Detailed accounts are given of her love affair with Anton Skrenbensky, a young army engineer and son of an exiled Polish Baron, of her brief Lesbian adventure with her class-mistress Winifred Inger during her last two terms at high school and of her miserable experience as an elementary school teacher of unruly children in the small town of Ilkeston. In all these episodes the inner workings in Ursula's mind are so vividly and minutely presented that they remind one of the great novels of psychological analysis such as Flaubert's "Madame Bovary" and the great Russian novels of Dostoevsky and even of Leo Tolstoy while the influence of Freud is also distinctly visible. Here the woman's dissatisfaction with the mere physical love of either the husband or the lover which represented Lawrence's recurrent view on love and sex and marriage is reflected through the depiction of the marital relations between Tom Brangwen and Lydia Lensky and between Will and Anna and through the narration of Ursula's love life in connection with Winifred Inger and especially with Anton Skrebensky. Ursula's final break with Anton is particularly suggestive, when she confides to her friend Dorothy, "Love — love — love — what does it mean — what does it amount to? So much personal gratification. It doesn't lead anywhere." And so the novel ends with the heroine watching the forming of a rainbow: "She saw in the rainbow the earth's new architecture, the old, brittle corruption of houses and factories away, the world built up in a living fabric of Truth, fitting to the over-arching heaven." But here again it is not the author's views but rather the emotional depth of a character like Ursula with her thoroughgoing disillusionment toward the deadening social environment of hers that makes the novel an outstanding artistic achievement. In the chapter entitled "The Man's World" Lawrence has given us a vivid picture of Ursula's experience of a school-teacher in the countryside for two years when out of her wish to be freed from the oppressive atmosphere at home and to gain the financial independence she had to endure the misery of facing the unruly children of her class on the one hand and of being ill-treated by the headmaster on the other. Here, rather in spite of himself the author succeeds particularly in showing the heroine's mental sufferings of a woman subjected to inferiority, in a man's world.

"Women in Love", the sequel, is a more powerful novel than "The Rainbow". The story here is concentrated on the love affairs of the two sisters Ursula and Gudrun, both of whom had appeared in the earlier novel and both are teachers in a local school in the Midland mining region. Ursula's relations with the school inspector Rupert Birkin end happily in marriage though their passion of love frequently leads to hatred, with Birkin bearing resemblance to Lawrence the author in his views on love and marriage, whereas the tempestuous passion between Gudrun who has studied art in London and Gerald Crich who is the eldest son and heir to a decrepit, dying colliery-owner develops suddenly after his father's death and then ends in tragedy during their holiday trip to the Tyrolean Mountains and their brief cohabitation there. The four major characters are portrayed very vividly and the conflicts between Gudrun and Gerald on the one hand and between Ursula and Rupert Birkin on the other are described in great detail and in striking contrast. Then there is given a rather complete picture of the Crich family, especially the father and Gerald's sisters Diana and Winifred, and transient though highly informative glimpses are provided of the bohemian life of the artists' circles in London and particularly of the somewhat tense atmosphere between the miners and the more wealthy inhabitants in the small mining town. Lawrence's humble family origin must have given him a very keen awareness of the social division into the rich and the poor, although he doesn't seem to show much sympathy for the underprivileged. The chief concern of the novelist in the book is very obviously to paint a few vivid portraits and narrate some exciting scenes in order to illustrate his striking views on love and sex and marriage. While in "The Rainbow" Lawrence also touches upon the relationship between two different generations (such as that between Tom Brangwen and his step-daughter Anna and especially that between Will Brangwen and his daughters Ursula and Gudrun), in "Women in Love" the theme seems to be simply the man-woman relationship of which two types are represented: the calmer, more deliberate search for an adequate love relationship (Ursula and Rupert Birkin) and the more impulsive and reckless plunge into the vortex of passion (Gudrun and Gerald Crich). Apparently the novelist seems to approve of the former type as the happy ending for the elder pair demonstrates, but in any case, the author seems to suggest that love is inextricably woven together with hate and that the inevitable struggle manifests itself in the numerous lovers' quarrels of great heat and bitterness. What is more, Birkin who serves somewhat as Lawrence's mouthpiece, pronounces his idea of love and marriage as "a pure balance of two single beings" which he compares with "two single equal stars balanced in conjunction", but he emphasizes that even in their ultimate intimacy the two lovers (or a married couple) should each have "freedom" or "a freedom together". At the end of the story Birkin while looking at the dead body of his good friend Gerald Crich declares to Ursula "his wish to have two kinds of love. "Having you, I can live all my life without anybody else, any other sheer intimacy. But to make it complete, really happy, I wanted eternal union with a man too: another kind of love." Whether this also represents Lawrence's view or not is unimportant as indeed the whole revelation of the novelist's views on love and marriage is of no real consequence to us. The true significance of "Women in Love" lies in Lawrence's thorough-going exploration into intimate human relationships against the deadening background and the sombre atmosphere of industrialized capitalist England in early 20th century, and the admirable artistic finish we find in the novel, in the choice of striking and meaningful scenes such as the buying and giving away of an old chair, the episode about the enraged rabbit and the slow death of the old mine-owner Crich, and more especially the psychological analyses of the major figures via their dialogues and their actions, and all this earns for the novel an enviable place in the historical development of the English novel between Hardy and Joyce.

Of Lawrence's four last novels, "Aaron's Rod" (1922), with a beginning resembling that in Bunyan's "The Pilgrim's Progress", deals with Aaron Sisson, a checkweighman and secretary to the Miners' Union for a colliery in Nottinghamshire, who gives up his job and deserts his wife and children to become a flautist in an orchestra in London, who later wanderes through Europe in search of himself and becomes the lover of an aristocratic woman in Italy but continues to feel attached to his wife, and whose flute which is his "rod" and symbolizes his capacity to grow and blossom is destroyed finally in an anarchist bomb explosion. Here the theme is on the surface that of the relations of man and woman in love and marriage, but actually Lawrence's message is to portray the hero in the novel (like the author himself) as one fleeing from Western civilization and attempting to save his soul from destruction. This novel was praised very highly by Lawrence's friend and critic John Middleton Murry whose review of the novel in his periodical "Nation and Athenaeum" reads:

"To read 'Aaron's Rod' is to drink of a fountain of life. ... 'Aaron's Rod' is the most important thing that has happened to English literature since the war. To my mind it is much more important than 'Ulysses'."

"Kangaroo", published in 1923 and based on Lawrencés visit to Australia in 1922, is ostensibly a novel on Australia, a country he seems to admire because it is so different from the "vulgar" and "materialist" Western Europe, but again it actually deals with Lawrence's own problems as is the case with all his other novels. However, Lawrence includes in the book detailed descriptions of the political activities in Sydney in 1922 of a right-wing secret army made up largely of ex-servicemen which he learned from some private source but which were unknown to the Australian authorities. This indicates Lawrence's adverse attitude toward fascism.

"The Plumed Serpent" (1925) has its setting in Mexico which he visited in 1923 and it deals chiefly with the primitive religious sect there worshipping the Aztec bird-serpent god Quetzalcoatl that symbolizes the fertilizing contact of earth and sky. Lawrence here shows his disgust for the passive submission to the leader and the violence and the mass hysteria involved, as the leader fails in his quest to free man's instinctual nature from the restrictions of self-consciousness. At the beginning of the book there is a detailed account of a bullfight in Mexico that Lawrence himself must have witnessed, and here the author voices his strong disapproval of the scene of brutality as the bull disembowells an old blindfolded horse.

"Lady Chatterley's Lover" (1928) has the author's familiar picture of the industrial relations in the mining area as the background but deals chiefly with Lady Chatterley's illicit love affair with her husband's game-keeper Oliver Mellors. Sir Clifford Chatterley, owner of coalpits and a big family land-estate, was wounded at war and paralyzed from the waist down. He is estranged from his wife Constance who has had an unsatisfactory affair with an Irish playwright and then is accidentally drawn to the gamekeeper Mellors living alone on the estate. Their physical contact develops into love and eventually she is expecting a child. Her husband has agreed to her having a child by another man but he refuses to divorce her because he thinks Mellors of working-class origin to be socially inferior for her to marry. Finally Constance and Mellors decide to go away together. There are in the novel very detailed accounts of love-making which go much beyond the objectionable passages in Lawrence's earlier novels, and so when the author succeeded in getting the novel published in a small private edition by a Florentine bookseller and publisher, a strong furor of condemnations and attacks rose even from Lawrence's own friends. Lawrence tried to defend himself. He even pleaded that he was attempting "to make the sex relation valid and precious, instead of shameful" and that the novel "is beautiful and tender and frail as the naked self is." But the consensus of public opinion has ever been strongly against the over-frank descriptions of "the sex relation" in the unexpurgated editions of the book, in spite of his repeated attempts to defend the novel in his essay entitled "Pornography and Obscenity" (1930) where he admitted to have written "harmless" obscene passages but disclaimed pornography to which he himself objected.

Lawrence was also a painter, and he devoted much time to painting in the last few years of his life. He painted biblical and other themes, and in many of them are to be found naked or half-naked bodies of men and women. Then in June, 1929, twenty-five paintings of his, fifteen oils and ten water-colours, were exhibited in Dorothy Warren's Gallery in London, but within a short time there was a police raid at the exhibition and thirteen of the twenty-five pictures were seized on the charge of obscenity by the London police court. The seized pictures were later returned to Lawrence with the latter's compromising that they would not be exhibited again in England.

Lawrence's two essays on psychoanalysis, "Psychoanalysis and the Unconscious" (1923) and "Fantasia of the Unconscious" (1923) are important in showing his attitude toward Freud and his indebtedness if any to the latter. In "Fantasia of the Unconscious", Lawrence objected to what he said was "the clue to the Freudian theory", that "A sexual motive is to be attributed to all human activity." He declared that though "we are bound to admit that into all human relationship, a large element of sex enters" ("We are thankful that Freud has insisted on this"), yet there is "something else, of even higher importance, and great dynamic power", that is, "the pure disinterested craving of the human male to make something wonderful, out of his own head and his own self, and his own faith and delight, which starts everything going". And the author points that: "That is, the essentially religious or creative motive is the first motive for all human activity. The sexual motive comes second. And there is a great conflict between the interests of the two, at all times." This quoted passage indicates all too clearly that Lawrence was indebted to a certain extent to Freud but only to a limited extent. Besides, in the other and earlier and shorter essay, "Psychoanalysis and the Unconscious", Lawrence further places psychoanalysis against morality: "Psychoanalysis is, under a therapeutic disguise, to do away entirely with the moral faculty in man". Because he considers that all Freud's Complexes, "caused by the inhibition of some so-called normal sex-impulse", can only be removed or cured by accepting them "as part of the normal sex-manifestation" though they are suppressed, and that all these inhibitions that lead to neurosis and insanity are wrong. But to adopt certain human conduct in order to cure these inhibitions of complexes that include incest-craving is obviously to go against the moral code in any human society. So Lawrence's acceptance of Freud's doctrine is a limited one. But Lawrence believes in the soul, in "the souls of the dead", and he prefaces this statement of his belief by saying "I am sorry to say" and "I am almost ashamed to say," in the Introduction to "Fantasia of the Unconscious". Therefore, these two essays are important for our better understanding of Lawrence.

D.H. Lawrence has often been considered to belong to the "modernist" school of writers in early 20th-century Britain, but he is very different from Yeats, T.S. Eliot and James Joyce, the three other great "Moderns", not only in the matter of experiments in new technique in writing, but more especially in the themes he dealt with (particularly in his novels and stories) and in the philosophical beliefs behind them. His father was a miner and his childhood and early youth were mostly spent in or near the mining districts, but he was more under the influence of his petty-bourgeois school-teacher of a mother, and eventually his thoughts and sentiments became more aristocratic than otherwise. He spoke highly of "aristocratic individualism": "It takes a great aristocrat to be capable of great tenderness and gentleness and unselfishness: the tenderness and gentleness of strength." (in Chapter Two of "Apocalypse") He had rather contempt for the working class, though he felt strongly against the bourgeois civilization of the West.

However, Lawrence was a rebel, not only against the materialism of the modern Western society, but also against conventional religion and morality. He was attracted to Australia and even to

America as the new world because he was fed up with the old European civilization and he was eager to go to the South Seas though he was rather disappointed when he actually visited Tahiti. He did not believe in orthodox Christianity nor in occultism of any sort, and he spoke slightingly of mysticism, but he believed in the existence of God rather unwaveringly. He cared little for the orthodox views toward sex morals, but he had his own moral code for love and marriage. He was one of the frankest writers on sex relations in fiction, but he defended his most objectionable descriptions even in "Lady Chatterley's Lover" by saying that his was "the truly moral and religious position". His excuse was that those passages accused of pornography contained simply obscene expressions which only represented the plain facts of life. On this controversy the important fact is that the majority of readers of his novels, particularly of "Lady Chatterley's Lover" and the majority of people who saw his objectionable paintings charged him with pornography as well as obscenity, and the verdict of the majority cannot be overlooked. Of course, the ban on the book has since been lifted in the West.

Lawrence did not deal much with social problems, but he seemed to concentrate in his fiction on human relationships, especially on those between a man and a woman in connection with the themes of love and marriage. But he usually exalted man above woman, though in his important novels and stories he took much effort in delineating the leading woman characters as well as man characters and he emphasized the need of the two lovers to be spiritual companions to each other as well as participants in physical love relationship. In "Women in Love", the hero Birkin even suggests that the spiritual and physical love between him and the heroine Ursula is not enough, but that a man besides a woman needs another man. This queer suggestion very possibly represents Lawrence's own view as Birkin is often supposed to stand for the author with his views. All this emanates obviously from Lawrence's stand of aristocratic individualism.

All in all, Lawrence was an idealist in his philosophical views of God and the soul, a rebel in his attitude toward the modern materialistic civilization of the West and toward conventional religion and morality, and an aristocratic individualist in his absorbing interest chiefly in the relationship of a man and a woman and in the themes of love and marriage, to the neglect of larger social issues. But Lawrence generally treated his themes in a more or less novel way, especially in "The Rainbow" and "Women in Love", and made very careful, detailed portraitures of his chief characters, particularly the heroes and heroines in his novels and stories. These artistic successes of his were largely responsible for his high standing as a novelist and story-teller, though the charges against him and the bans on his book, curiously enough, usually enhanced rather than diminished his fame. On the other hand, his great sympathy for the plants and animals brought charm to Lawrence's poetry and made him a poet of major importance. In spite of his short life, Lawrence was also a writer of numerous interesting and significant works of prose and criticism.

h. Robert Tressell and his "Ragged-Trousered Philanthropists"

Working-class literature in England, after its periods of flowering in the 1830's—1850's during the Chartist Movement and in the 1880's at the first wave of the socialist movement, had chiefly one book by one author to boast of (Robert Tressell's "The Ragged-Trousered Philanthropists") in the three decades from the 1890's to the 1910's. Then in the 1920's and the 1930's, we have, besides the first group of Marxist critics Ralph Fox and Christopher Caudwell there appeared drama and prose by Sean O'Casey and fiction by Lewis Jones. In the 1930's there were also a group of so-called "fellow-travellers" of communism, including such poets as W. H. Auden, Stephen Spender, C. Day Lewis and Louis MacNeice, all of whom later left the revolutionary path. In the 1940s and 1950s, there were a group of literary critics including T. A. Jackson, Alec West and Arnold Kettle, while O'Casey continued to write and he completed his monumental six-volume autobiographical fiction which contained both critical comments on English society and typical Irish humour.

Robert Tressell is the pseudonym of Robert Noonan, a house-painter and sign-writer. Probably born in 1869 or 1870 either in London or in Dublin, Tressell was of Irish extraction. His parents died when he was small and he became a worker when he was 14. After being forced to wander in different places in England as a result of unemployment, he went to South Africa in 1897 to work there as foreman of signwriters. He started his literary activities in Johannesburg by writing for some publications there. When the Boer War began, Tressell was on the side of the Boers and he took an active part in the organization of an Irish brigade, but he was expelled from Johannesburg. He returned to England and settled down in Hastings, a small town in southern England, in 1902, with his daughter. The ten years he spent as a worker in Hastings were the bitterest days of his life, and he was soon attracted to socialism. According to the reminiscences of his friends, he was particularly interested in Swift, Fielding and Dickens in his wide reading. In 1906 he joined the Social Democratic Federation and from then on he became an active propagandist of socialism, writing slogans and leaflets and distributing them himself. His lodging became a place of gathering where the socialists held their meetings, and he frequently gave lectures on economics and politics to his fellow workers. Tressell was also a wall painter and a follower of William Morris. He worked on the novel "The Ragged-Trousered Philanthropists" in 1905—1910 during his holidays and rest-hours after work, and even after he contracted tuberculosis in 1907 he kept on working in order to finish the book. He died of tuberculosis in early 1911. The book was kept by her daughter and through her efforts when she was a servant-girl in London, it was published in an abbreviated and altered form in 1914, being revised by a Fabian authoress Jessie Pope. Only two-thirds of the original book was preserved in this edition while the concluding chapters were omitted and an earlier passage, about the pessimistic thoughts of suicide once entertained by the socialist worker and hero of the novel, was lifted out of its original context and placed at the end of the book instead. In 1918 appeared a still shorter edition but it was widely circulated, especially among the workers. In 1955 came the new edition of the full text of the novel, published by Lawrence and Wishart, and faithfully based upon the original manuscript recently unearthed.

"The Ragged-Trousered Philanthropists" is an unusual novel as it tells the story of the lives and miseries of workers of all ages and of their families in the four seasons, from winter through spring, summer, autumn and back to winter. The book opens with the description of a group of housepainters at work, from the boy apprentice Bert White to the old Jack Lindon. Here the author deals with the workers' extremely meagre common meals, with the socialist worker Frank Owen lecturing to them about socialism, and with all of them, including the foreman Crass, showing their great fear for the manager of the Rushton firm, Hunter, nicknamed "Misery" or "Nimrod", who has slaved the greater part of his life for Rushton the capitalist and who is a terror to all the workers because he makes them work as hard as possible and dismisses them when they don't work hard enough. Then the story branches off into minor threads — about Bert White the boy apprentice being brutally treated, about the married worker Easton who is never able to make his both ends meet and therefore fails to get on with his wife Ruth, about Frank Owen ever conscious of social inequality in the capitalist society and always ready to help his fellow workers, about old Jack Lindon dismissed from work but having a big family to support, about the ageing Philpot eventually becoming the victim of an accident owing to the lack of necessary safety measures, about Harlow barely escaping injury while doing risky work without safety guarantee, about Sawkins working at under-pay willingly and Newman forced to work at under-pay, about the treacherous Slyme seducing his fellow-worker's wife, and about Barrington a rich man's son turned worker and socialist and preaching socialism and helping out fellow workers. Here a whole gallery of vivid portraits are painted of workers of different ages and types, woven rather neatly together with the passing of the four seasons. Besides these characters there are on the one hand the family members of these workers, including particularly Frank Owen's little son Frankie, the innocent fatherless grand-children of Jack Lindon, and Ruth the unfortunate wife of Easton's, and on the other hand the capitalists and their henchmen, including the dreadful enemy of the workers Hunter the manager and also the foreman Crass, and Rushton the terrible exploiter, and his fellow exploiters, Sweater the mayor, Didlum the house-furnishing capitalist, Grinder the monopolizer of the greengrocery trade, and Sir Graball D'Encloseland the Tory candidate for M.P., who competes against the Liberal Grinder at the election. All these exploiters and their assistants were well drawn, with plenty of satire as well as humour. But among all these characters Owen stands out as the symbol of an awakened worker just as Crass and Hunter represent the terrible tools of the capitalists.

The first half of the novel is all about the winter season when work was scarce and so the workers were all the time threatened with dismissal and unemployment, especially in the two chapters "The Reign of the Terror" and "The Slaughter". Then with the coming of April and May and June there was just a bit more work, but the workers had to work longer hours as the day was longer. But after September there were again mass dismissals. And the total impression of the gross social injustice in the relations between the workers and their employers leads to socialism as the only possible solution.

Even when the workers are lucky enough to keep their jobs for a time, their life is still a very miserable one, as they have to pay high rent and all sorts of taxes. Their wives and children are poorly fed and poorly clad and their weakened health leads to illnesses. Old workers who have worked hard all their lives are dismissed merely on account of their age and they, like Jack Lindon, have to end their lives in the workhouse. Young apprentices, like Bert White, are admitted as apprentices when their poor parents have to pay a huge sum of several pounds for the boys to learn the trade, but actually instead of being given much training, the youngsters are made to do much heavy manual work of the unskilled kind for several years without any pay at all.

However, the preaching of socialism by the socialist worker Owen and later also by Barrington, are usually lengthy, frequently dull.

A sub-topic in the novel is the corruption of the municipal government system in the town of Mugsborough, the locale of the story. All the members of the Municipal Council, called "brigands" by the author, and nicknamed "forty thieves", work together for their common benefit and cheat the workers into electing them and enabling them to reap illegal and legal profits out of the municipal funds which come from the taxes on all the tax-payers. The members of the Town Council, with the exception of one, Dr. Weakling, a physician, are all respectable citizens, including the Mayor Mr. Sweater, the managing director and principal shareholder of a large drapery business, Mr. Grinder, a monopoliser of the greengrocer trade, Mr. Didlum, the house-furnisher, and Mr. Rushton, the owner of Rushton and Co., Builders Decorators and General Contractors, the employer of all the house-painters in the story, but they pass resolutions and overrule the sole objections of Dr. Weakling, not for the good of the people but to increase their own personal gains at the expense of the tax-payers.

So, "The Ragged-Trousered Philanthropists" is a realistic novel that condemns capitalist exploitation by giving a vivid picture of workers suffering from terrible oppression and exploitation by their employers not only openly and directly but also by tricks and all sorts of underhand means. However, as a novel there are too many characters and too many scattered scenes to produce the desired effect upon the readers.

SECTION V ENGLISH POETRY: 1920—1940

a. Thomas Stearns Eliot (1888—1965)

T.S. Eliot was born in St. Louis, Missouri, son of a successful, cultivated businessman and grandson of a New England Uni-
tarian clergyman. He studied first at Smith Academy in St. Louis,
then went to Harvard for both his undergraduate and graduate studies (1906—10, 1911—14). He fell under the influence of Irving
Babbit who lectured against Romanticism and George Santayana
the philosopher and became interested in Elizabethan and Jacobean
literature (particularly Donne and Webster), the Italian Renaissance
(especially Dante) and Indian mystical philosophy of Buddhism.
In 1908 he came across Arthur Symons' "The Symbolist Movement
in Literature" and was fascinated by the poetry of Jules La-Forgue
and other recent French poets Mallarme and Verlaine. In 1910—11
he spent a year in Paris and studied the philosophy of Henri Bergson. In 1914 he went to Germany to study the philosophy at Mar-
burg, but the First World War broke out in September and he left
Germany to study Greek philosophy at Oxford in order to complete his doctoral dissertation for Harvard on the Oxford philosopher
F.H. Bradley.

In the meantime he had written poetry and in 1915 his first
major poem "The Love Song of J. Alfred Prufrock" (written in
1910—11) was first published in Chicago's "Poetry" magazine. He
married and turned to teaching at Highgate School, London, for a
living, and in 1917—25 he worked in the foreign department of
Lloyd's Bank. In 1917 he became assistant editor of an Avant Garde
magazine "The Egoist" and his first collection of poems "Prufrock
and Other Observations" appeared in the same year, to be followed
by two other collections, "Gerontion" in 1919 and "Poems" in
1920. In 1922 he also became editor of "The Criterion", an influential right-wing literary journal which continued till 1939. In these

years he was well acquainted with the élite intellectual circle known as the Bloomsbury Group. Then, in 1922, after his consultation with Ezra Pound who helped in trimming the poem, "The Waste Land" appeared,which was at first controversial but has since been generally regarded as Eliot's major effort at poetry. In 1925 appeared his "Poems 1909—1925"which included "The Hollow Men" and he became a director of the publishers Faber and Gwyer (later Faber and Faber).

In 1927 came an important turning point in Eliot's life: he became a British subject and joined the Anglican Church. From that time on there was greater solemnity and religious fervour in Eliot's poems: "Ash Wednesday" (1930), "Burnt Norton" (1936), "East Coker" (1940), "The Dry Salvages" (1941), and "Little Gidding" (1942), with the last four poems collected and republished as "Four Quartets" (1944).

Eliot's adventures in the field of drama almost all have to do with religious themes. He began with a fragment of an Aristophanic melodrama, "Sweeny Agonistes" (1931), first published under the title of "Wanna Go Home, Baby?" (1926—27) and a pageant play written in aid of a London Churches fund, "The Rock" (1934), of which only the Choruses were retained in his collected poems. Then appeared the best known of his verse-drama, "Murder in the Cathedral" (1935), written for the annual festival of Canterbury Cathedral and dealing with the murder of the Archbishop of Canterbury Thomas Becket in 1170 by Henry II. His later attempts at poetic drama were allegedly to achieve the combination of good popular entertainment with poetry of a high order that he admired in Elizabethan and Jacobean drama. "The Family Reunion" (1939) was more directly under the influence of ancient Greek tragedy. His three later plays, all popular successes and all social comedies, appeared in the 1950s. "The Cocktail Party" (1950) is a more forceful play on the Christian doctrine of sin and redemption, while "The Confidential Clerk" (1954) and "The Elder Statesman" (1959) also carried out Eliot's theory that verse drama should conform to natural speech-rhythms and not be consciously poetic.

Eliot has also been known as an important critic. His first two volumes of essays "The Sacred Wood" (1920) and "Homage to Dryden" (1924) contain two of his most notable critical essays: "Tradition and the Individual Talent" and "The Metaphysical Poets". After his conversion to the Church of England in 1927, he wrote another collection of essays "For Lancelot Andrewes" (1928), in the preface to which he made the since famous statement that he was "classicist in literature, royalist in politics, and Anglo-Catholic in religion". He veered further to the right in his later years when he showed his sympathy with the authoritarian views of Charles Maurras and the virtually fascist and Catholic French organization "Action Francaise" and he placed more and more emphasis on "order", "hierarchy" and racial homogeneity in his social thought. In 1934, in his lactures delivered at the University of Virginia which were later collected under "After Strange Gods", he expressed such ultra-right political and social opinions that he himself later suppressed them.

Eliot's first wife who was estranged from him even in the 1930s died in 1947 and he remarried in 1957 Valerie Fletcher who later was responsible for the publication of the uncut version of "The Waste Land" in 1971. Eliot's fame grew in the 1930s and 1940s in the English-speaking countries, and the widespread acceptance of him as a great poet and a great critic in post-World-War-II years could only be paralleled by that of Samuel Johnson in the 18th century.

In 1947 he received an honorary degree from Harvard University and in 1948 he was awarded the Order of Merit by the British Crown and received the Nobel Prize for Literature.

Eliot's poetry may be divided into two periods: the early period from 1915 to 1925, the later period from 1927 onward, 1927 being the year in which he became a British citizen and was received into the Church of England.

"The Love Song of J. Alfred Prufrock", the first poem of importance by Eliot, was one of the most memorable pieces because of its unflinching and undisguised satire on the genteel society. The condescending visit to the poor district with its cheap hotels and restaurants is contrasted, at the beginning of the poem, with the highly affected conversation carried on among women of fashion in their drawing-room (or even in their ball-rooms). Then the repeated utterances of "there will be time" further indicate the emptiness, the listlessness and the boredom of these men and women who have too much time on their hands:

> There will be time, there will be time
> To prepare a face to meet the faces that you meet;
> There will be time to murder and create,
> And time for the works and days of hands
> That lift and drop a question on your plate;
> Time for you and time for me,
> And time yet for a hundred indecisions,
> And for a hundred visions and revisions,
> Before the taking of a toast and tea.

Here the phrasings, like "to prepare a face to meet the faces", "to murder and create", "lift and drop a question on your plate", "time yet for a hundred indecisions" and "for a hundred visions and revisions/ Before the taking of a toast and tea", convey devastating satire on how the idle rich spend or squander their time. This is followed by a brief sketch of J. Alfred Prufrock, partly humorous and partly ironic:

> "with a bald spot in the middle of my hair"

and

> "But how his arms and legs are thin!"

and

> "My morning coat, my collar mounting firmly to the chin,
> My necktie rich and modest, but inserted by a simple pin"

and especially:

> "Do I dare
> Disturb the universe?"

The topic of boredom is next returned to, in the three subsequent passages beginning:

> For I have known them all already, known them all —
> Have known the evenings, mornings, afternoons,
> And I have known the eyes already, known them all —
> And I have known the arms already, known them all —

Here again the satire is all too plain, in such lines and phrases as

> I have measured out my life with coffee spoons,
> The eyes that fix you in a formulated phrase,
> When I am pinned and wriggling on the wall,

and

> Is it perfume from a dress
> That makes me so digress?

The speaker's wanderings in the slum quarters are again referred to: "narrow streets" and "lonely men in shirt-sleeves", but instead of showing the slightest sign of sympathy for the poor, the austere gentleman in the author rather turns to the possibility of his being reprimanded by the genteel society:

> I should have been a pair of ragged claws
> Scuttling across the floors of silent seas.

But boredom is the main theme that must be returned to again and again,

> And the afternoon, the evening, sleeps so peacefully!
> Smoothed by long fingers, ...

and nothing but the most ineffectual talk is the routine hardly to be broken:

> Should I, after tea and cakes and ices,
> Have the courage to force the moment to its crisis?

The gentleman's effort to summon up courage to say something of any importance is described ironically:

> But though I have wept and fasted, wept and prayed,
> Though I have seen my head (grown slightly bald) brought
> in upon a platter,

And the result is even more ironical, with the gentleman's courage slipping and his having to depart:

> I have seen the moment of my greatness flicker,
> And I have seen the eternal Footman hold my coat, and
>   snicker,
> And in short, I was afraid.

The timid speaker then proceeds to examine whether it is worthwhile to bring up the question that he failed to bring up, as the author purposely exaggerates the importance of that question:

> To have squeezed the universe into a ball
> To roll it toward some overwhelming question,
> To say: 'I am Lazarus, come from the dead,
> Come back to tell you all, I shall tell you all'—

and then anticipates the total indifference of the lady who hears the question:

> If one, settling a pillow by her head,
> Should say: "That is not what I meant at all.
> That is not it, at all.'

The poem ends on a note of sadness as the speaker shows himself keenly aware of his own insignificance:

> No! I am not Prince Hamlet, nor was meant to be;
> Am an attendant lord, one that will do
> To swell a progress, start a scene or two,
> Advise the prince; no doubt, an easy tool,
> ...
> Full of high sentence, but a bit obtuse;
> At times, indeed, almost ridiculous —
> Almost, at times, the Fool ....

Here no doubt we only get a peep at the polite society in the Western world, and the satire, though obvious and at times quite piercing, is after all only a superficial one. Yet vivid pictures are painted almost everywhere, with images "hard", "dry", clear and precise that show unmistakably the influence upon the poet at the time of the school of Imagists, with H.E. Hulme as its theorist and Ezra Pound as its popularizer. And the language used embellishes the theme and adds greatly to the significance of the poem as an effective piece of satire.

In a sense T.S. Eliot did what Wordsworth had done a century earlier in debunking "poetic diction" by introducing new, popular, "prosaic" (and in Eliot's case, also scientific) words and phrases into English verse. Outstanding examples of this new style are:

"When the evening is spread out against the sky
    Like a patient etherised upon a table;"
"I have measured out my life with coffee spoons;"
"To spit out all the butt-ends of my days and ways?"
"But as if a magic lantern threw the nerves in patterns
    on a screen:"
"Shall I part my hair behind? Do I dare to eat a peach?"
"The muttering retreats
Of restless nights in one-night cheap hotels
And sawdust restaurants with oyster shells:"
"Streets that follow like a tedious argument
Of insidious intent
To lead you to an overwhelming question."

But the most scintillating lines are:

"In the room the women come and go
    Talking of Michelangelo."

"The Love Song of J. Alfred Prufrock" may not be a great poem, but is a subtle and also none-too-subtle satire on the modern bluestockings and their gentleman admirers or companions, particularly because it is written in a superb, effectively ironic style. And Eliot's contribution to the modernization of language in English poetry must not be overlooked.

Of Eliot's poems written between "Prufrock" and "The Waste Land", "The Hippopotamus" is possibly the most significant chiefly on account of its curiously unrelenting satire on the Christian Church (curious if we consider Eliot's attitude toward the Church in the after-years). The Church is here compared to the hippopotamus: the hippo is weak because it is made of flesh and blood, but the True Church is firm and strong because it is based upon a rock; the hippo may not always attain its material ends, but the True Church doesn't have to do anything but is sure to get its dividends; some fruits are too high for the hippo to reach but the Church gets plenty of fruits from far and wide; the hippo sounds harsh at mating time but hymns sung to God always sound harmonious; the hippo hunts at night and sleeps in the daytime but the Church can gather wealth and rest at the same time because "God works in a mysterious way". The Christian Church, whether Catholic or Protestant or Eastern Orthodox, are all very wealthy and they don't have to do much to gather in the wealth. That's the main theme. But the satire here, as elsewhere in Eliot's poetry, lies chiefly in the poet's ingenious and apt choice of words and phrases: "can never fail", "need never stir" and especially "God works in a mysterious way", etc. It is certainly hard to imagine that Eliot who had written about the Church in this fashion here could later on have become a fervent believer in Anglo-Catholicism and could have written his later poetry in his reverently religious tenor. Of course, here in "The Hippopotamus" as also in "Mr. Eliot's Sunday Morning Service" Eliot was only attacking the commercialism of the church and not the church itself.

Of the other poems in the 1917 volume, "Portrait of a Lady" is a sort of companion piece to "Prufrock", for here the satire is aimed chiefly at a certain lady of the genteel society. The emphasis is laid more on the conjectured speeches of the lady and on the descriptions of the settings in which the supposed actions take place. The background for the first section of the poem is the concert which leads the lady and her "friend" to their first important friendly encounter; the scene for section two is in the same room but the time for this second memorable meeting of the lady and the youth is in the spring; then the third and last section deals with the parting, apparently for ever, of the two on one October night, and then with the young man's imaginings of the lady's death some time in the future. Again here the apt use of words and phrases and the subtle suggestions of gestures and postures are employed extensively for satire on the lady and the high society she belongs to, such as:

"An atmosphere of Juliet's tomb"
    "to hear the latest Pole
Transmit the Preludes, through his hair and fingertips."
"In a life composed of so much, so much of odds and
    ends,"
"Let us take the air, in a tobacco trance,
Admire the monuments,
Discuss the late events,
Correct our watches by the public clocks.
Then sit for half an hour and drink our bocks."
"Yet with these April sunsets, that somehow recall
My buried life, and Paris in the Spring,"
"I shall sit here, serving tea to friends."
"I mount the stairs and turn the handle of the door
And feel as if I had mounted on my hands and knees."
"My smile falls heavily among the bric-a-brac."
"I have been wondering frequently of late
(But our beginnings never know our ends!)
Why we have not developed into friends."
"We must leave it now to fate.
You will write, at any rate.
Perhaps it is not too late."

One feels however that there is more of nuance here in the moods expressed than in "Prufrock", and that there is just a bit — a very small bit, perhaps — of sympathy on the author's part for the lady in question than for Prufrock and his circle.

"Preludes", "Rhapsody on a Windy Bight" and "Morning at the Window" are a group of short poems describing in detail certain people and what happen to them on different hours of the day (and night), and here the poet deals more with common people, including labouring people, with "broken blinds and chimneypots", "the sawdust-trampled street", "early coffee-stands", "dinghy shades/ In a thousand furnished rooms", "the border of her dress/ Is torn and stained with sand", "a broken spring in a factory yard", "the cat ... devours a morsel of rancid butter", "the bed is open; the tooth-brush hangs on the wall","rattling breakfast plates in basement kitchens", and "tear from a passer-by with muddy skirts". There is however little depth in these poems, perhaps because the poet did not know the common people well enough.

Three other poems go together: "The Boston Evening Transcript," "Aunt Helen" and "Cousin Nancy". They are once again about the upper circles the poet was familiar with. So though the themes dealt with are of no great importance, here and there appear a few ironical touches typical of Eliot. So in "The Boston Evening Transcript", we find:

> I mount the steps and ring the bell, turning
> Wearily, as one would turn to nod good-bye to La
>   Rochefoucauld,
> If the street were time and he at the end of the street,"

And in "Aunt Helen" and "Cousin Nancy" respectively with:

> And the footman sat upon the dining-table
> Holding the second housemaid on his knees—
> Who had always been so careful while her mistress lived.

and a none-too-respectful reference to Arnold and Emerson:

> Upon the glazen shelves kept watch
> Matthew and Waldo, guardians of the faith,
> The army of unalterable law.

Elsewhere in these two poems may also be found trenchant lines such as:

> Now when she dies there was silence in heaven
> And silence at her end of the street.

and

> Miss Nancy Ellicott smoked
> And danced all the modern dances;
> And her aunts were not quite sure how they felt about it,
> But they knew that it was modern.

The wit and humour in these particular lines light up these otherwise insignificant verses and serve to satirize, albeit all too mildly, the ridiculousness, the pomposity and the foibles of the very rich and the not so very rich.

"Mr. Apollinax", "Conversation Galante" and "La Figlia Che Piange" (i.e. "The Girl Who Weeps") are portrait poems. Mr. Apollinax, or the son of Apollo, is depicted first as a man who laughs, and different impressions of his laughter are vividly given:

"His laughter tinkled among the teacups",

"He laughed like an irresponsible foetus."

"His laughter was submarine and profound
Like the old man of the sea's."

Then various comments are made on the man:

"He is a charming man", "He must be unbalanced", "There was something he said that I might have challenged." Then minor touches of humour accompany the main satire on Apollinax: in the last two lines of the poem, friends or observers of Apollinax are also alluded to in the typical Eliot fashion:

"Of dowager Mrs. Phlaccus, and Professor and Mrs. Cheetah

I remember a slice of lemon, and a bitten macaroon."

In each of the three stanzas of "Conversation Galante" is given first a speech of the man indulging in philosophical speculations, to be followed each time by a curt reply from the lady who seems to be totally uninterested in such "serious" talk which appears digressive to her. But the man is incorrigible. He is undeterred by such rather discourteous or dubious remarks of hers: "How you digress!" and "Does this refer to me?" as his words become even more abstract and he even ventures to call her "the eternal humorist" and "the eternal enemy of the absolute", by way of mild criticism, which eventually calls for her ambiguous yet obviously derogatory comment, "Are we then so serious?" The humour and irony and the suggestion of mild satire in this poem depend chiefly on the abstruse thought content of the man's speeches and on the abrupt, sarcastic volleys from the lady.

"La Figlia Che Piange" gives a picture of the weeping girl encountering and then departing from the object of her affection: the first stanza describes the beauty of the girl with pain in her heart, the second expresses the speaker's wish for the beauty to last and survive his parting from her, and the third and last passage recounts the girl's departure and its after-effect upon the speaker who is troubled a long time afterwards by his imagings of the loss of beauty. There is much lyricism in the poem, and the lingering sadness over beauty and pain is very subtly told in poignant verse.

Of the poems that appeared for the first time in the 1920 volume, "Gerontion" marks the growth of despair and disillusionment in the poet that eventually leads up to "The Waste Land". Gerontion, a little old man, who has little to boast of about his past exploits ("neither at the hot gates", "nor fought in the warm rain", "nor knee deep in the salt marsh, heaving a cutlass"), but has seen much of the world (people like Mr. Silvero, Hakagawa, Madame de Tornquist, Fraulein von Kulp, and knowledge of "whispering ambitions", "vanities", "unnatural vices" and "impudent crimes"), is now at the end of his tether ("I have lost my sight, smell, hearing, taste and touch"). His personal feeling of sadness over his impotence in every way ("I an old man,/ A dull head among windy spaces.") suggests the general mood of despair for all people and all things in the world. Written in 1920, shortly after World War I, Eliot here expressed his personal feeling of disillusionment as well as the general despondency of the people of Western Europe over the crisis of Western civilization.

"Whispers of Immortality" is a more significant poem in the 1920 volume, for here Eliot's evolved idea of finding immortality from thoughts of death, which he claims to have learned from John Donne the poet and John Webster the dramatist, both of the 17th century, is first expressed in its rudimentary form. The poem first states the views of Webster and Donne:

Webster was much possessed by death

> And saw the skull beneath the skin;

while in the case of Donne,

> He knew the anguish of the marrow
> The ague of the skeleton;
> No contact possible to flesh
> Allayed the fever of the bone.

Therefore Webster and Donne saw beyond the flesh, and tried to find immortality beyond the death of the body. But according to the modern view (which the poet obviously disapproves of) one only thinks of human life in terms of flesh, lowering actually the human beings to "animal kingdom" (thus Grishkin is compared to the Brazilian jaguar), and when the humans fail to find immortality in flesh, they try to indulge in "the Abstract Entities" or abstract conception of death which is actually no help at all:

> "But our lot crawls between dry ribs
> To keep our metaphysics warm."

So all we moderns get is only "whispers of immortality". It may not be a far-fetched thought to conclude that Eliot's dissatisfaction with these whispers of immortality and his approval of Donne's and Webster's far-fetching attempts to find immortality after death eventually led him to find spiritual comfort in religion and thus anticipated his acceptance of Anglo-Catholicism.

"Sweeney Among the Nightingales" is another poem of the period on the theme of death. Sweeney, conceived as a sort of the ape man, is threatened with death. The person in the Spanish cape and Rachel née Rabinovitch "are suspect, thought to be in league", the former trying to seduce Sweeney ("tries to sit on Sweeney's knees") while the latter "tears at the grapes with murderous paws". But it's the "silent man in mocha brown" and the host conversing with someone at the door who are apparently responsible for the murder which comes as the deserved punishment for lechery or improper conduct with women, and therefore the Agamemnon story is brought in at the end of the poem. Here the thoughts of death linked with sex already seem to take shape in Eliot's mind, as we are to find such thoughts developed more fully in "The Waste Land" and the poet's later poems. Likewise, much symbolism and myth are here freely introduced, as we are to witness such style in his later poems.

"The Waste Land" has generally been accepted as Eliot's most important single poem. The first thing that needs to be said about "The Waste Land" is that in Eliot's view the waste land stands for Western Europe, or for Western civilization as a whole. In this sense Eliot's view falls into line with that of many other literary men, thinkers, philosophers, historians and other intellectuals in Western Europe in the 1920s, that is, in the period immediately or shortly after the First World War. "The Decline of the West" (1927), a well-known book by the German writer Oswald Spengler, is a representative work of those years in which the intellectuals in the West began to doubt whether the modern Western civilization that brought about rapid industrial development and great material progress as well as money worship and moral degradation was actually bringing to the human beings physical and spiritual blessing or rather large-scale destruction and slaughter in the world-wide war and spiritual and cultural degeneration. Therefore in "The Waste Land" Eliot aimed above all else at a search for regeneration for the human race, and in this sense the poem has its undeniable significance in its negation of the bourgeois status quo in Western Europe and in its quest for change. But Eliot was all through his life an anti-socialist, anti-communist, who only had horrors and fears for the socialist revolution that took place in Russia under Lenin, and so, instead of trying to find his solution for the terrible status quo of his time in revolution and socialism or at least in some change in social system, he rather turned to ancient myths and to religion. That is his aristocratic limitation which he phrased very aptly for himself: "classicist in literature, royalist in politics, and Anglo-Catholic in religion".

In the general note affixed to his publication of "The Waste Land" in book form in 1922, Eliot stated very definitely: "Not only the title, but the plan and a good deal of the incidental symbolism of the poem were suggested by Miss Jessie L. Weston's book on the Grail legend: *From Ritual to Romance.* He also acknowledged his indebtedness to a work of anthropology, Sir James Fraser's "The Golden Bough" (especially the two volumes "Adonis, Attis, Osiris"), in which Fraser deals with ancient vegetation myths and fertility ceremonies. Miss Weston links the ancient fertility myths with the Christian legend of the Holy Grail. So, according to an archetypal fertility myth, the death, infirmity or impotence of the Fisher King brought drought and desolation to the land and also the failure of the power to reproduce living things, both men and beasts, but this symbolic Waste Land can be revived, according to the Grail legend, only if a questing knight goes to the Chapel Perilous, situated in the heart of the waste land, and there asks certain ritual questions about the Grail (i.e. Cup) and the Lance (which were originally male and female fertility symbols respectively). Then the proper asking of the ritual questions can revive the Fisher King and restore fertility to the land. The application of this Grail legend and this fertility myth of the Fisher King to the waste land of Western civilization of the 1920s led to the writing of the poem.

However, Eliot did not tell his story in a straightforward fashion, but rather wove together episodes of brief conversations and suggestive descriptions with subtle and ambiguous symbols drawn from ancient literary works and myths, so that there is much colour and variety in the poem but also frightful obscurity. It is well known that the original manuscript for the poem was about twice as long, and that with the helpful suggestions of Ezra Pound Eliot trimmed it down to its present length. Many scholars and literary critics have since taken much trouble to interpreting the poem, but there can be no reasonable excuse for the excessive obscurity of the work chiefly because the poet tries either to gain his wish-for effect or possibly to display his great learning and ingenuity and profundity of thought, the great eulogies of innumerable critics notwithstanding.

The poem is divided into five sections. The first section deals chiefly with the theme of death, sterility, and meaninglessness of life. April or spring brings new life to the vegetable world, /but in "the waste land",

> "the dead tree gives no shelter, the cricket no relief, And
> the dry stone no sound of water",

but only "fear in a handful of dust". The several interloping passages describe the meaningless life of European aristocrats: Marie and her cousin the arch-duke, the vain waiting of Tristan for Isolde ("Oed' und leer das Meer" — "Desolate and empty the sea"), the hyacinth girl unable to speak or see and becoming neither living nor dead, the crowd that goes over London Bridge being more dead than alive, and the burial of a corpse in Stetson's garden, all point to the same theme of death with no hope of regeneration. The most important episode in this section is certainly the one about Madame Sosostris and her "wicked pack of cards", with "the drowned Phoenician Sailor", "Belladonna, the lady of the Rocks", "the man with three staves", "the Wheel" and "the one-eyed merchant" but without the "hanged Man", for here are given many of the symbols used in the poem. The title of the section, "The Burial of the Dead", suggests the death and burial of the Western world or the waste land.

The second section, entitled "A Game of Chess", emphasizes the meaninglessness of love and lust in the human world, with the high society represented by Cleopatra (as obvious from the first line here which is lifted out of Shakespeare's "Antony and Cleopatra") and the lower world represented by Lil whose husband is returning from demobilization. Again here the theme of death is recurrent throughout:

> I think we are in rats' alley
> Where the dead men lost their bones.

'Are you alive, or not? Is there nothing in your head?' The third section, "The Fire Sermon", deals chiefly with the river. The river of the modern world is contrasted with that in the Elizabethan days. In 16th-century England, the sweet echo from Spenser's "Prothalamion" celebrating his own wedding, "sweet

Thames, run softly, till I end my song", is contrasted with the debris left on the river banks after the feastings and love-makings of the evening before in modern Western cities:

> "empty bottles, sandwich papers,
> Silk handkerchiefs, cardboard boxes, cigarette ends
> Or other testimony of summer nights."

A similar contrast is given of the same river of today and of yesterday:

> "The river sweats
> Oil and tar [referring to today]

is contrasted with

> "Elizabeth and Leicester
> Beating oars
> The stern was formed
> A gilded shell
> Red and gold
> The brisk swell
> Rippled both shores
> Southwest wind
> Carried down stream
> The peal of bells
> White towers" [referring to Elizabethan England]

Especially strikingly sordid is the love scene of a modern-age typist and the carbuncular young man, with their loveless love-making and his abrupt departure. Then the section ends with the repeated words of "burning" to indicate the "fall" of a modern city or of the whole modern civilization, deserted by God ("O Lord thou pluckest me out").

The fourth and shortest section, "Death by Water", more directly and markedly points to the theme of death. Phlebas the Phoenician is made to represent the modern man (when he forgot not only "the cry of gulls, and the deep sea swell" but also "the profit and loss") whose death by water is vividly pictured:

> A current under sea

Picked his bones in whispers. As he rose and fell
He passed the stages of his age and youth
Entering the whirlpool.

Then the section ends on the general warning of death waiting for everybody:

Gentile or Jew
O you who turn to wheel and look to windward
Consider Phlebas, who was once handsome and tall as you.

The fifth and last section finally touches upon the Grail legend. After the first nine lines describing Christ's agony in the Garden of Gethsemane and his trial before Pilate and his crucifixion, there is the reference to the two apostles going on their difficult journey to Emmaus:

Here is no water but only rock
Rock and no water and the sandy road
The road winding above among the mountains
Which are mountains of rock without water
...
Sweat is dry and feet are in the sand
...
Here one can neither stand nor lie nor sit
There is not even silence in the mountains
...
But red sullen faces sneer and snarl
From doors of mudcracked houses

Then "the third who walks always beside you" is supposed to represent the resurrected Christ. But the picture next shifts to the crack-up of the whole Western civilization:

Who are those hooded hordes swarming
Over endless plains, stumbling in cracked earth
Ringed by the flat horizon only
What is the city over the mountains
Cracks and reforms and bursts in the violet air

> Falling towers
> Jerusalem Athens Alexandria
> Vienna London
> Unreal

Then eventually the Perilous Chapel in the Grail legend is at hand:

> In this decayed hole among the mountains
> In the faint moonlight, the grass is singing
> Over the tumbled graves, about the chapel
> There is the empty chapel, only the wind's home.

The chapel may have "no windows" and there are only the "dry bones", but there is a cock "on the rooftree" and its crow "in a flash of lightning" and "Then a damp gust / Bringing rain". "Then spoke the thunder / DA" and the poet shifts over to three Sanskrit words of which the first syllable all happens to be "da": "Datta" meaning "give"; "Dayadhvam" meaning "sympathize"; and "Damyata" meaning "control", and the suggestion is given by the poet that these three words contain the secret for the regeneration of the waste land. So, reverting back to the Fisher King myth, the poet sees hope before him for Western civilization:

> I sat upon the shore
> Fishing, with the arid plain behind me
> Shall I at least set my lands in order?

London Bridge is falling dowm falling down falling down for now "the arid plain" (or the waste land) is "behind" him, and like the Fisher King reviving with his vigour he can at least set his own lands in order, though he may not be able to save the whole declining Western world as the London Bridge is falling down and its fall may not be prevented. He becomes like Arnaut in Dante's "Purgatorio" who was happily waiting for his purgation and he "hid him in the fire which refines him" ("Poi s'ascose nel foco che gli affina"), wishing himself to be like a swallow ("When shall I be like the swallow" — "Quando fiam uti chelidon") and comparing himself to "The Prince of Aquitaine at the ruined tower" (Le Prince d'Aquitaine à la tour abolie") who has twice crossed the river of

Hell (Acheron) victoriously. He feels somewhat confident that he can supply what is needed ("Ile fit you" — "I'll supply you with what you need")as Hieronymo in Thomas Kyd's play "The Spanish Tragedy" in his feigned madness promises to supply the needed play of murder and revenge. Finally the thunder-roll of the three Sanscrit words "Datta, Dayadhvam, Damyata", is again given, to be followed by the repetition of another Sanscrit word "Shantih shantih shantih" which according to the author's note is equivalent to "The Peace that passeth understanding" in English.

Although the main theme in "The Waste Land", accentuating on spiritual crisis in the Western world of modern capitalism and on the urgent need for regeneration, is a well-grounded analysis of modern Europe that argues effectively against any apology for the maintenance of the status quo in the bourgeois West, yet the suggested change coming from an ultra-conservative intellectual like Eliot is inevitably based upon extreme idealism as he introduces the vegetation myths and the Grail legend, which in turn necessarily end in religion. There is satire here and there on the sordid love affairs, but then they usually have to do with the lower classes, like Lil's abortions and her fear of her husband's return, like the typist and her "affair" with a small house agent's clerk, like the episode of "Richmond and Kew / Undid me", and like the suggestions of "The nymphs are departed" "by the waters of Leman". Of course this is only natural with Eliot who in time mixed himself more and more with the aristocratic people and therefore had less and less sympathy for the poor and the low (he had more sympathy for the lower classes when he wrote "Prufrock", "Preludes", "Rhapsody on a Windy Night" and "Morning at the Window", in 1915—17). But the poet's disillusionment toward the postwar Western world is something not to be overlooked or underestimated in any assessment of "The Waste Land" for after all that is the main theme, nor should we forget his satire on the love and lust in the West in the 20th century albeit it is directed chiefly toward the poorer people in "The Waste Land".

The chief charm in "The Waste Land", particularly for the Western reading public, is the language and the style in the poem, besides the extremely involved myth and legend and symbolism. Also the lyricism that comes up everywhere, often quite unexpectedly, is what endears the poem to many readers.

> April is the cruellest month, breeding
> Lilacs out of the dead land, mixing
> Memory and desire, stirring
> Dull roots with spring rain.

These first lines (and more to follow immediately after) derive their charm from the combination of lyrical strain with "hard, dry" images advocated by the Imagists. Sometimes much pathos enters into a passage possessing rhythmical beauty:

> Unreal City,
> Under the brown fog of a winter dawn,
> A crowd flowed over London Bridge, so many,
> I had not thought death had undone so many.

And the repetitious use of almost the same words with different twists of meaning can also produce felicitous meditative effects in a curious way:

> If there were water
> And no rock
> If there were rock
> And also water
> And water
> A spring
> A pool among the rock
> If there were the sound of water only
> Not the cicada
> And dry grass singing
> But sound of water over a rock
> Where the hermit-thrush sings in the pine trees
> Drip drop drip drop drop drop drop
> But there is no water

Once in a while a very simple episode told in a very casual, conversational tone can be very effective, like the bit about Marie in section one:

> Summer surprised us, coming over the Starnbergersee
> With a shower of rain; we stopped in the colonnade,
> And went on in sunlight, into the Hofgarten,
> And drank coffee, and talked for an hour.
> Bin gar keine Russin, stamm' aus Litauen, echt deutsch.
> And when we were children, staying at the arch-duke's,
> My cousin's, he took me out on a sled,
> And I was frightened. He said, Marie,
> Marie, hold on tight. And down we went.
> In the mountains, there you feel free.
> I read, much of the night, and go south in the winter.

This desultory speech, approaching the stream-of-consciousness that sounds so very much like real human speech, here has a peculiar charm of its own. Then the surprise quotation from Wagner's "Tristan und Isolde":

> Frisch weht der Wind
> Der Heimat zu
> Mein irisch Kind
> Wo weilest du?
> ....
> Oed' und leer das Meer.

as it is interwoven with the hyacinth girl episode, renders Section One interesting with all this strange sequence of ideas in curious association with one another. There is no denying the attraction from this inventive coup of modernist writing.

The abundance of humour that follows upon serious passages is another important asset to "The Waste Land". In the significant account of the pack of cards held by Madame Sosostris, the episode winds up unexpectedly with the "famous clairvoyant's" casual remark:

> Thank you. If you see dear Mrs. Equitone,

Tell her I bring the horoscope myself:
One must be so careful these days.

In the episode about Lil and her demobbed husband, the announcement of the closing time for the pub ("HURRY UP PLEASE ITS TIME") is repeated again and again to interrupt the flow of conversation, and then the bidding of farewell by the speakers at the end of the section adopts the farewell speech by the mad Ophelia ("Goodnight Bill. Goodnight Lou. Goodnight May. Good night ....") Here in both cases the effect of gross incongruity is achieved, that may induce a wry smile from the reader. Similarly, the abrupt use of certain well-known lines by some well-known poets, inserted *in medias res,* frequently brings about some sort of comic effect:

> "The Chair she sat in, like a burnished throne," (from Shakespeare's "Antony and Cleopatra")
>
> "Sweet Thames, run softly, till I end my song." (from Spenser's "Prothalamion")
>
> "When lovely woman stoops to folly" (from Goldsmith's "The Vicar of Wakefield")
>
> "Those are pearls that were his eyes," (from Shakespeare's "The Tempest")

while more frequent echoes from Marvell, Milton, Webster, and non-English writers Dante, the Bible, Ovid, Vergil, Baudelaire, Verlaine, and St. Augustine all have their twofold effect of providing literary associations and poetic background on the one hand and of adding to the ambiguity and obscurity of the poem on the other.

The frequent introduction of the supernatural and of superstition must be considered a grave shortcoming, though certain passages of that nature may have their peculiar attractions for some readers, like the episode about Stetson:

> "There I saw one I knew, and stopped him, crying: 'Stetson!
> 'You were who with me in the ships at Mylae!
> 'That corpse you planted last year in your garden,

'Has it begun to sprout? Will it bloom this year?
'Or has the sudden frost disturbed its bed?
'O keep the Dog far hence, that's friend to men,
'Or with his nails he'll dig it up again!
'You! hypocrite lectuer! — mon   semblable, — mon
   frère!'
or "the third who walks always beside you":
   "Who is the third who walks always beside you?
   When I count, there are only you and I together
   But when I look ahead up the white road
   There is always another one walking beside you
   Gliding wrapt in a brown mantle, hooded
   I do not know whether a man or a woman
   — But who is that on the other side of you?"
A vivid picture it is, and fluently told, but still it refers to the
incredible story of the risen Christ beside the two apostles. Though
we may argue here with Hamlet's advice to Horatio:
   "There are more things in heaven and earth, Horatio,
   Than are dreamt of in our philosophy."
yet myths and legends are after all myths and legends, in spite of
the fact that they have become very popular and extensively used
in literary writings since the beginning of the Twentieth Century,
and the fortune-telling Madame Sosostria and her Tarot pack of
cards and her horoscope, the blind soothsayer Tiresias, the Fisher
King and the Hanged Man, and the whole of the Grail legend are
involved with superstition and supernaturalism and therefore
belong to the realm of idealism, not materialism. Yet the tradition
of religion, especially Christian religion, has been a very long one
in Europe and has exerted its extremely broad and lasting influence
upon the minds of the greatest majority of people there, so that
supernatural elements and superstitious beliefs have been taken for
granted for centuries and myths and legends have been regarded by
many as normal and even authentic, and it is under such circumstances that even intellectuals and scientists in the West today often

believe in religion and other quite unscientific phenomena. T. S. Eliot was no exception, and he became even an avowedly orthodox believer in Anglo-Catholicism after 1927 though when he wrote "The Waste Land" (1922) he only seemed to accept the Grail legend.

Symbolism which has been one important characteristic of modernism in 20th-century literature in Europe plays its prominent part also in "The Waste Land". The titles for the five sections of the poems are themselves symbols: "The Burial of the Dead" obviously stands for the disintegration of Western civilization; "A Game of Chess" may indicate the utter meaninglessness of modern Western life, particularly of love as something of importance both in the aristocratic circles and in low life; "The Fire Sermon" suggests the burning (possibly in hell or purgatory) that inevitably befalls both the high and the low; "Death by Water" tells clearly the unavoidable fate of death coming to everybody as it does to the Phoenician sailor Phlebas; while "What the Thunder Said" is symbolic of the possible regeneration for the doomed people in the West if they follow the correct path as pointed out by the Grail legend and obey the three suggestions of "Give" ("Datta"), "Sympathize" ("Dayadhvam") and "Control" ("Damyata"), according to what the thunder said.

Minor symbols are to be found almost everywhere in the poem. The first two of the four parts in the first section symbolize the failure of the Western world to overcome death by regenerating though the vegetable world could revive every spring.

> "you know only
> A heap of broken images, where the sun beats,
> And the dead tree gives no shelter, the cricket no relief,
> And the dry stone no sound of water."

These lines symbolize the failure to regenerate, as also the following lines which more specifically symbolize the individual's perilous state:

> "I could not

Speak, and my eyes failed, I was neither
Living nor dead, and I knew nothing,
Looking into the heart of light, the silence."

The symbolism of the cards ("the drowned Phoenician Sailor", "Belladonna, the Lady of the Rocks", "the man with three staves", "the Wheel", "the one-eyed merchant", and "The Hanged Man")held by Madame Sosostris are obviously based on the myth. Then the crowd flowing over London Bridge symbolizes the numerous people in the British metropolis who are just as well as dead, and Stetson is one of them.

In the second section Cleopatra symbolizes the lady of a high social station while Lil stands for the poor woman whose husband has gone to war. "My nerves are bad tonight" represents the woman leading a miserable existence neither alive nor dead, whereas the passage:

"'What shall we ever do?'
The hot water at ten.
And if it rains, a closed car at four.
And we shall play a game of chess,
Pressing lidless eyes and waiting for a knock upon the
door."

suggests the life of *ennui* led by a loveless, idle couple.

In the third section, the idea of death is suggested in several places:

"But at my back in a cold blast I hear
The rattle of the bones, and chuckle spread from ear to
ear.

....

Musing upon the king my brother's wreck
And on the king my father's death before him.
White bodies naked on the low dry ground
And bones cast in a little low dry garret,
Rattled by the rat's foot only, year to year."

Again here we find symbols of people of different social levels indulging in their lustful love affairs: "the nymphs — and their friends, the loitering heirs of City directors", Sweeney and Mrs Porter, the typist and the small house agent's clerk, Elizabeth and Leicester and the couple meeting at Richmond and Kew, and finally perhaps a suggestion of Dido (with the mention of "To Carthage then I came").

Then in the fifth and last section, the mention of

> Jerusalem Athens Alexandria
> Vienna London

suggests the big cities both ancient and modern, the first three standing for the flourishing Western civilization in Palestine (representing Christianity), in Greece and in Egypt (in the Hellenistic Age), while the two in the second line represent the great cultural centres in 19th-century and early-20th-century Europe.

While there are many other minor symbols throughout the poem, the major ones mentioned above should suffice to show the intentions of the author and the due effects produced. "The Waste Land" is a representative poem of modernism in 20th-century Europe, also in the sense of its prevalent use of symbolism.

"The Waste Land" was a highly controversial poem in the early years after its publication, but now its reputation as a poem of importance is established in the whole Western world just as its author Eliot's fame as a poet of importance is now generally [ac-knowledged. For each reader the poem should be judged according to its deserts, or rather viewed both from its obvious merits and its equally obvious shortcomings.

"The Hollow Man", written in 1925 between "The Waste Land" and "Ash Wednesday", represents the inter-stage between doubt and faith for the poet although the tendency is quite obviously toward the adoption of the Christian faith. However, the dominant theme was still very much the same as that in "The Waste Land".

The two epigraphs, "Mister Kurtz — he dead" and "A Penny for the Old Guy", are two exemplary cases of the "hollow man": Kurtz the once domineering imperialist agent dies finally a miserable, lingering death, while the traitor Guy Fawkes who tried to blow up the parliament buildings in 1605 was burned up on November 5 every year in the form of a stuffed effigy by children who went around begging for pennies to buy fireworks. In the former case the "big" man feared by everybody turns out to be hollow and thoroughly contemptible whereas in the latter case the scarecrow figure of Old Guy is literally hollow because he is stuffed. So here Eliot tries obviously to represent two different types of "hollow man" in the post-war Western world, with their colonies and financial empires collapsing and their material progress in the way of inventions and discoveries leading to war and destruction.

But different from "The Waste Land", the theme of death in "The Hollow Men" is more directly related to religion. The civilized people in the West are not really alive, in Eliot's view, and so they are described to be living in "the dead land", "the cactus land", "this hollow valley", "this broken jaw of our lost kingdom", or "this beach of the tumid river", and terms such as "death's dream kingdom", "death's twilight kingdom", "a fading star", and "dying stars" are mentioned again and again, in order to compare with Dante's Inferno and Purgatorio (as "death's other Kingdom" refers vaguely to Paradiso) except that they are only "the hollow men" or "the stuffed men" and not "lost violent souls". The fifth and last section is the climactic one: here the author first substitutes "the mulberry bush" in the children's rhyme with the ironic "prickly pear" (suggesting possibly the baneful effect of the desirable modern civilization), then he points out the fine and not-so-fine contradictions in modern life of increasing complexity:

> Between the idea
> And the reality
> Between the motion
> And the act
> Falls the Shadow

with a sprinkle from the Lord's Prayer ("For Thine is the Kingdom"), and winds up with a powerful final stanza which is supposed to be

adapted from the words in one of children's games but which may
be variously interpreted as the poet's prediction of the future fate
of Western civilization:

> This is the way the world ends
>
> This is the way the world ends
>
> This is the way the world ends
>
> Not with a bang but with a whimper.

The last line, coming after the cumulative repetitive effect of the
three preceding lines, is especially weighty, with the contrastive use
of "bang" and "whimper". The poet's postwar disillusionment has
reached a new height of irony, but the whole poem leans more than
ever before to an outcry against the spiritual crisis of people without
faith and paves the way for a more open declaration for the sore
need of religion in his poems written after 1927.

"Ash Wednesday" marks the beginning of a new period of
poetic output for T.S. Eliot. Not unlike John Henry Newman's
"Apologia Pro Vita Sua", here Eliot uses poetic language and poetic imagery to explain the different and difficult stages of his spiritual struggle from scepticism, through doubt and conquest of doubt
with the aid of grace, to his final attainment of hope in Anglo-Catholicism. The very complex imageries of the Lady, then the Virgin
(Mary), the Word, the Garden, and the Rose, interspersed with
the words and prayers said at the ritual for Ash Wednesday, have
little attractions for us, but the first of the six sections of the poem
has its undeniable and almost irresistible fascination of delightful
lyricism, as the poet speaks of his newly attained decision to turn
away from the things of the world, of his dissatisfaction with transitory glory on earth, of his awareness of earthly existence being
hopelessly limited by time and space, and then of his wish to forget the hopes and desires between birth and death. The first eight
lines are especially lyrically beautiful:

> Because I do not hope to turn again
>
> Because I do not hope
>
> Because I do not hope to turn

Desiring this man's gift and that man's scope
I no longer strive to strive towards such things
(Why should the aged eagle stretch its wing?)
Why should I mourn
The vanished power of usual reign?

And sadly though almost rhapsodically the poet mourns the temporal and spatial limitations of man and therefore has to turn to
something "upon which to rejoice":

Because I know that time is always time
And place is always and only place
And what is actual is actual only for one time
And only for one place
I rejoice that things are as they are and
I renounce the blessed face
And renounce the voice
Because I cannot hope to turn again
Consequently I rejoice, having to construct something
Upon which to rejoice
And pray to God to have mercy upon us
And I pray that I may forget
These matters that with myself I too much discuss
Too much explain
Because I do not hope to turn again
Let these words answer
For what is done, not to be done again
May the judgement not be too heavy upon us.

Because these wings are no longer wings to fly
But merely vans to beat the air
The air which is now thoroughly small and dry
Smaller and drier than the will
Teach us to care and not to care
Teach us to sit still.

Here the poet's airings of his renunciation of the things of this world

276

and his awareness of the inconsequential nature of human existence are fully revealed in lyrical verse, and because this despair is something more easily comprehensible to us we may feel the agonies of the poet though we may not quite approve of his decided renunciation of life on earth in order to search for religious faith and for God.

"Four Quartets", commonly regarded as the last major work by T.S. Eliot, was the composite title for four separate poems that were written between 1935 and 1942. The word "Quartets" indicated the close affinity of its structure to the musical composition of a "quartet" such as Beethoven's, with five sections to each poem. The four poems are each named after a place of special significance to the poet: "Burnt Norton" (1935) refers to a manor house in Gloucestershire, England, that the poet once visited; "East Coker" (1940) is named after a village in Somersetshire where the Eliot family had lived in the 17th century before migrating to New England; "The Dry Salvages" (1941) are some rocks off the coast of Cape Ann, Massachusetts, where Eliot spent summer holidays as a child; and "Little Gidding" (1942) is the name of a village in Huntingdonshire where Nicholas Ferrar in 1625 set up an Anglican religious community and where the poet paid a visit in 1936. The names of places are emphasized because according to Eliot it is in places that one enters into history and escapes from it and "Four Quartets" is a philosophical poem on time and eternity, on history and the present, on those rare moments that are timeless, and moments of time must be in places.

In "Burnt Norton" the poet speculates, from the point of view of philosophy and religion, on the question of time and eternity. As a devout believer in Christian religion who is endowed with a philosophic bent, Eliot is dissatisfied with time present, time past and time future, or with any time in history, because

"If all time is eternally present
All time is unredeemable."

So he first indulges in the footfalls that "echo in the memory":

>   "Memories of childhood
>   Down the passage which we did not take
>   Toward the door we never opened
>   Into the rose-garden."

But

>   "human kind
>   Cannot bear very much reality.
>   Time past and time future
>   What might have been and what has been
>   Point to one end, which is always present."

So he wants to be

>   "At the still point of the turning world. Neither flesh nor
>   fleshless;
>   Neither from nor towards; at the still point, there the
>   dance is,
>   But neither arrest nor movement. And do not call it fixity,
>   Where past and future are gathered. Neither movement
>   from nor towards,
>   Neither ascent nor decline. Except for the point, the still
>   point,
>   There would be no dance, and there is only the dance.
>   I can only say, *there* we have been; but I cannot say
>   where.
>   And I cannot say, how long, for that is to place in time."

Only in that case can he obtain

>   "The inner freedom from the practical desire,
>   The release from action and suffering, release from the
>   inner
>   And the outer compulsion".

But the complexity of the problem is the conquest of time through
time:

>   "Time past and time future
>   Allow but a little consciousness.
>   To be conscious is not to be in time

> But only in time can the moment in the rose-garden,
> The moment in the arbour where the rain beat,
> The moment in the draughty church at smokefall
> Be remembered; involved with past and future.
> Only through time time is conquered."

So it is necessary to have

> "a place of disaffection
> Time before and time after
> In a dim light".

Eliot's religious faith makes him seek for eternity, out of the present in time:

> "Words move, music moves
> Only in time, but that which is only living
> Can only die. Words, after speech, reach
> Into the silence. Only by the form, the pattern,
> Can words or music reach
> The stillness."

So love is timeless while desire is not:

> "Desire itself is movement
> Not in itself desirable;
> Love is itself unmoving,
> Only the cause and end of movement,
> Timeless, and undesiring
> Except in the aspect of time
> Caught in the form of limitation
> Between un-being and being."

Here, though the philosophical speculation is a bit abstruse, yet the poet's intense yearning for eternity, so adeptly expressed in highly lyrical verse, has certain charms rewarding for the reader.

"East Coker" begins with further speculation on the relation of time to change and constancy. The first thirteen lines make up a beautiful lyric on the perennial changes in the physical world, along with the passage of time:

> "In my beginning is my end. In succession

Houses rise and fall, crumble, are extended,
Are removed, destroyed, restored, or in their place
Is an open field, or a factory, or a by-pass.
Old stone to new building, old timber to new fires,
Old fires to ashes, and ashes to the earth
Which is already flesh, fur and faces,
Bone of man and beast, cornstalk and leaf.
Houses live and die: there is a time for building
And a time for living and for generation
And a time for the wind to break the loosened pane
And to shake the wainscot where the field-mouse trots
And to shake the tattered arras woven with a silent motto."

Then there is another charming imagined picture of the poet's ancestors of long ago who used to live in East Coker, and the employment of certain archaic words adds to the feeling of the passage of time:

"In that open field
If you do not come too close, if you do not come too
close,
On a summer midnight, you can hear the music
Of the weak pipe and the little drum
And see them dancing around the bonfire
The association of man and woman
In daunsinge, signifying matrimonie —
A dignified and commodious sacrament,
Two and two, necessarye coniunction,
Holding eche other by the hand or the arm
Whiche betokeneth concorde. Round and round the fire
Leaping through the flames, or joined in circles,
Rustically solemn or in rustic laughter
Lifting heavy feet in clumsy shoes,
Earth feet, loam feet, lifted in country mirth
Mirth of those long since under earth
Nourishing the corn. Keeping time,

Keeping the rhythm in their dancing
As in their living in the living seasons
The time of the seasons and the constellations
The time of milking and the time of harvest
The time of the coupling of man and woman
And that of beasts. Feet rising and falling.
Eating and drinking. Dung and death."

And there is yet another passage lamenting the inevitable passing away of people and of moments:

"O dark dark dark. They all go into the dark,
The vacant interstellar paces, the vacant into the vacant,
The captains, merchant bankers, eminent men of letters,
The generous patrons of art, the statesmen and the rulers,
Distinguished civil servants, chairmen of many committees,
Industrial lords and petty contractors, all go into the dark,
And dark the Sun and Moon, and the Almanach de Gotha
And the Stock Exchange Gazette, the Directory of Directors,
And cold the sense and lost the motive of action.
And we all go with them, into the silent funeral,
Nobody's funeral, for there is no one to bury."

Here of course the aristocratic temper of the poet surfaced as he only mentioned the great ones (with the only exception of "petty contractors" that contains the deprecatory word "petty"). And then there are other passages of note:

"Or as, when an underground train, in the tube, stops too long between stations
And the conversation rises and slowly fades into silence
And you see behind every face the mental emptiness deepen
Leaving only the growing terror of nothing to talk about."

These are lines that remind one of the youthful Eliot composing "Prufrock". But the sad fact that "East Coker" was written after the beginning of the World War II was recorded here:

> "So here I am, in the middle way, having had twenty years—
> Twenty years largely wasted, the years of *L'entre   deux
>   guerres —*"

Even for the obviously stoic temper of the poet, his religious faith
("the pattern") was maintained, but with a difference:

>   "As we grow older
> "The world becomes stranger, the pattern more com-
>   plicated
> Of dead and living. Not the intense moment
> Isolated, with no before and after,
> But a lifetime burning in every moment
> And not the lifetime of one man only
> But of old stones that cannot be deciphered.
> There is a time for the evening under starlight,
> A time for the evening under lamplight
> (The evening with the photograph album).
> Love is most nearly itself
> When here and now cease to matter."

So he winds up by saying: "In my end is my beginning."

"The Dry Salvages", written during the dark days of World
War II (1941), begins with a special accent on the sea: "The river
is within us, the sea is all about us;" and returns again to the theme
of time, to the past and the future:

> "And under the oppression of the silent fog
> The tolling bell
> Measures time not our time, rung by the unhurried
> Ground swell, a time
> Older than the time of chronometers, older
> Than time counted by anxious worried women
> Lying awake, calculating the future,
> Trying to unweave, unwind, unravel
> And piece together the past and the future,
> And piece together the past and the future,

Between midnight and dawn, when the past is all deception,
The future futureless, before the morning watch
When time stops and time is never ending;"

And the poet turns again to the theme of death and birth and the yearning for eternity:

"There is no end of it, the voiceless wailing,
No end to the withering of withered flowers,
To the movement of pain that is painless and motionless,
To the drift of the sea and the drifting wreckage,
The bone's prayer to Death its God. Only the hardly,
    barely prayable
Prayer of the one Annunciation."

Here the thoughts in "The Waste Land" are reiterated, but the poet's religious faith now provides the solution. Eliot goes on to speak of "moments of happiness", and finds that

"We had the experience but missed the meaning,
And approach to the meaning restores the experience
In a different form, beyond any meaning
We can assign to happiness."

And he adds:

"Now, we come to discover that the moments of agony
...
...   are likewise permanent
With such permanence as time has. We appreciate this
    better
In the agony of others, nearly experienced,
Involving ourselves, than in our own.
For our own past is covered by the currents of action,
But the torment of others remains an experience
Unqualified, unworn by subsequent attrition.
People change, and smile: but the agony abides.
Time the destroyer is time the preserver."

But the poet's final aim is at the timeless:

                "But to apprehend

> The point of intersection of the timeless
> With time, is an occupation for the saint —
> No occupation either, but something given
> And taken, in a lifetime's death in love,
> Ardour and selflessness and self-surrender."

This is what Eliot the religious zealot hopes for, but he adds modestly:

> "For most of us, there is only the unattended
> Moment, the moment in and out of time,
> The distraction fit, lost in a shaft of sunlight,
> The wild thyme unseen, or the winter lightning
> Or the waterfall, or music heard so deeply
> That it is not heard at all, but you are the music
> While the music lasts. These are only hints and guesses,
> Hints followed by guesses; and the rest
> Is prayer, observance, discipline, thought and action.
> The hint half guessed, the gift half understood, is Incarnation."

Here the true believer speaks. But then "the impossible union" of "the past and future" and this "freedom from past and future", according to Eliot,

> "For most of us, this is the aim
> Never here to be realised;
> Who are only undefeated
> Because we have gone on trying."

"Little Gidding", the last and best known of the "Four Quartets", was written in 1942 when the poet served as a fire-watcher during World War II and witnessed the heavy night bombing and fire raids inflicted upon London in the darkest moments of the war. The first section of the poem ends apparently with a comment on the ravages of the war:

> And what the dead had no speech for, when living,
> They can tell you, being dead: the communication
> Of the dead is tongued with fire beyond the language of the

living.

> Here, the intersection of the timeless moment
> Is England and nowhere. Never and always.

Then, after describing the death of air, of earth, of water and fire, in section 2, an imagined conversation in the Dantesque fashion takes place between the poet and a "dead master" as they supposedly encountered each other at dawn after an air-raid "'at this intersection time of meeting nowhere, no before and after / We trod the pavement in a dead patrol."). Like some one in Purgatory the stranger speaks of the past and the future:

> "For last year's words belong to last year's language
> And next year's words await another voice."

And he adds that now "between two worlds"

> "I find words I never thought to speak
> In streets I never thought I should revisit
> When I left my body on a distant shore."

And, resembling some one in Dante's *Inferno* or *Purgario*, the stranger relates his experience "As body and soul begin to fall asunder" and recounts his state of mind thereafter:

> "The conscious impotence of rage
> At human folly, and the laceration
> Of laughter at what ceases to amuse."

and:

> "the rending pain of re-enactment
> Of all that you have done, and been; the shame
> Of motives late revealed, and the awareness
> Of things ill done and done to others' harm
> Which once you took for exercise of virtue."

This apparently imitative exercise modelled after Dante is of considerable interest especially as revelation of Eliot's imaginings of life-after-death.

Eliot in "Little Gidding" recalls his visit once to this village and reminisces the people and the events connected with the struggle there in the mid-17th century between the Puritans and the Anglicans. His comments are:

> "We cannot revive old factions
> We cannot restore old policies
> Or follow an antique drum.
> These men, and those who opposed them
> And those whom they opposed
> Accept the constitution of silence
> And are folded in a single party.
> Whatever we inherit from the fortunate
> We have taken from the defeated
> What they had to leave us — a symbol:
> A symbol perfected in death."

Then after a brief parenthetical discursion to discuss the importance of the use of the right words, the poet ends on an optimistic note:

> "We die with the dying:
> See, they depart, and we go with them.
> We are born with the dead:
> See, they return, and bring us with them.
> The moment of the rose and the moment of the yew-tree
> Are of equal duration. A people without history
> Is not redeemed from time, for history is a pattern
> Of timeless moments. So, while the light fails
> On a winter's afternoon, in a secluded chapel
> History is now and England."

These lines sum up the four poems together: the relation between the dead and the living, between the rose of life and the yew-tree of death, between time and eternity or the timeless, and the conclusion leads to religious faith, with the final aim

> "to apprehend
> The point of intersection of the timeless
> With time."

"Four Quartets" had its strong appeal to the Christian world because of its fervid, philosophic quest after religious faith as

the highest spiritual bliss for all humanity, and the labyrinthian logic of search for the timeless is gratifying while the exquisite lyrical
beauty of verse is delightful and extremely artfully phrased. For
us the lyrical charm becomes the chief attraction of the poem, with
certain fascinating pictures of people and events that have elapsed
with the inevitable passage of time.

Surprisingly enough, some of Eliot's minor poems deserve special mention, "Journey of the Magi" was an almost Browningesque
poem, comparable to "Childe Roland to the Dark Tower Came", but
there is a typical Eliot ending that makes all the difference. Of course,
even in the earlier description of the journey, Eliot's version was
more colourful and picturesque, "the silken girls bringing sherbet"
and "six hands at an open door dicing for pieces of silver" providing
bits of fun and irony that can not be found in the totally sombre picture in Browning's poem. But the references to Birth and Death
in the last nine lines of the Eliot poem bring us back to "Ash Wednesday" and "Four Quartets", for here Eliot the now devout sear-
cher for "death's other kingdom" surfaces, especially when the poem
ends on a typical Eliot line: "I should be glad of another death."
This is a delightful poem, unusual for Eliot with its striking absence
of obscurity but preserving nevertheless the humour and irony in the
earlier Eliot pieces. Such lines as

"Then the camel men cursing and grumbling
And running away, and wanting their liquor and women,
And the night-fires going out, and the lack of shelters,
And the cities hostile and the towns unfriendly
And the villages dirty and charging high prices."

are at once traditional and modern, that is, a curious blending of modern diction "wanting their liquor and women" with the other very
conventional expressions.

"Marina" is another charming little lyric based faintly on the
story of loss and subsequent rediscovery of Marina by her father Pericles in the Shakespearean drama. The miraculous preservation of
Marina from death and other mishaps is used here by Eliot as a sym-

bol of regeneration both physical and spiritual, at a time when the poet was immersed in his thoughts of regeneration. But the charm of the poem lies more in the beautiful rhapsodic, lyrical outpourings of extreme joy and wonderment upon a father's rediscovery of his daughter lost after so many years, more in the great lyrical gift of T. S. Eliot, than in the symbolic significance attached to the story by the author. The first stanza:

> "What seas what shores what gray rocks and what islands
> What water lapping the bow
> And scent of pine and the woodthrush singing through the
>   fog
> What images return
> O my daughter"

and the briefer and slightly altered version in the last stanza:

> "What seas what shores what granite islands towards my
>   timbers
> And woodthrush calling through the fog
> My daughter."

and the striking imageries in the second stanza:

> "Those who sharpen the tooth of the dog," "Those who
> glitter with the glory of the hummingbird," "Those who sit
>   in the sty of contentment", and
> "Those who suffer the ecstasy of the animals",

are the gems that give distinction to the poem. Of course, the only lines that recall the elderly Eliot:

> "This form, this face, this life
> Living to live in a world of time beyond me; let me
> Resign my life for this life, my speech for that unspoken,
> The awakened, lips parted, the hope, the new ships."

are also worthy of note.

"Choruses from 'The Rock'" are more straightforward verses speaking for the Christian Church. Here Eliot deplores the fact that churches are much neglected by the common people and speaks forcefully for the need to build up the church and to have faith in religion,

and while doing so he lashes at the social vices in the bourgeois West.
The voices of the UNEMPLOYED are reproduced:

> "No man has hired us
> With pocketed hands
> And lowered faces
> We stand about in open places
> And shiver in unlit rooms.
> Only the wind moves
> Over empty fields, untilled
> Where the plow rests, at an angle
> To the furrow. In this land
> There shall be one cigarette to two men,
> To two women one half pint of bitter
> Ale. In this land
> No man has hired us.
> Our life is unwelcome, our death
> Unmentioned in 'The Times'."

At another place a similar passage is given, though not entirely with
the author's approval:

> "And some say: 'How can we love our neighbour? For love
> must be made real in act, as desire unites with desired;
> we have only our labour to give and our labour is not
> required.
> We wait on corners, with nothing to bring but the songs
> we can sing which nobody wants to hear sung;
> Waiting to be flung in the end, on a heap less useful than dung.''

Although this last passage is followed by the author's remonstrance
that these people only talk of right relations of men but not of men to
God, yet the above speech tells the truth just the same.

Of course the poet also remonstrates the Western bourgeois
society:

> "When the Stranger says; 'What is the meaning of this city?
> Do you huddle close together because you love each other?'
> What will you answer? 'We all dwell together

　　　　To make money from each other? or 'This is a community?'"
Or again:
　　　　"Men have left God not for other gods, they say, but for no
　　　　　　god;
　　　　And this has never happened before
　　　　That men both deny gods and worship gods, professing
　　　　　　first Reason,
　　　　And then Money, and Power, and what they call Life, or
　　　　　　Race, or Dialectic.
　　　　The Church disowned, the tower overthrown, the bells up-
　　　　　　turned, what have we to do
　　　　But stand with empty hands and palms turned upwards
　　　　In an age which advances progressively backwards?
Here Eliot the anti-Communist reveals himself by mentioning "Di-
alectic" together with "Reason", "Money", "Power", "Life" and
"Race".

　　　The general drift of thought in "The Rock" is no different from
Eliot's later poems professing his religious faith, but here the "sin"
(or is it the "gift") of obscurity is absent, making the poem much easier reading, and much more pleasant in that respect for the common
reader.

　　　The two poems grouped under the title of "Coriolan": "Triumph-
al March" and "Difficulties of a Statesman", are rare specimens among
Eliot's later poetry because in these two poems there is mild satire on
the war machine of Western nations and on a statesman, rare for an
aristocrat like Eliot. "Difficulties of a Statesman" is particularly interesting because here the statesmen are supposed to include "The
Companions of the Bath, the Knights of the British Empire, the Cavaliers, /O Cavaliers! of the Legion of Honour, /The Order of the
Black Eagle (1st and 2nd class), /And the Order of the Rising Sun",
and then the poet goes on to point out, with mock seriousness:
　　　　"The first thing to do is to form the committees:
　　　　The consultative councils, the standing committee, select
　　　　　committees and sub-committees.

One secretary will do for several committees."
The whole poem is a satire on the political machine of any Western country such as Britain, and so it is a rare thing for one who claims to be "royalist in politics".

If T.S. Eliot is first of all a poet, he is also rated very highly as a critic. His two important critical essays are: "Tradition and the Individual Talent" (1919) and "The Metaphysical Poets" (1921).

Two important points of view on literary criticism are raised in "Tradition and the Individual Talent". According to Eliot, "tradition", in literature or poetry, is not simply something handed down from literary predecessors, but is something that has been and is being built up by writers from Homer (as far as the European tradition is concerned) to the present day, so that writers have to learn from literary traditions of the past, are judged more or less with reference to tradition and should each make contributions to the ever-growing and ever-developing tradition. This definition of tradition is on the whole sound:

> "It (i.e. tradition) involves, in the first place, the historical
> sense, which ... involves a perception, not only of the past-
> ness of the past, but of its presence; the historical sense com-
> pels a man to write not merely with his own generation in his
> bones, but with a feeling that the whole of the literature of
> Europe from Homer and within it the whole of the literature
> of his own country has a simultaneous existence and com-
> poses a simultaneous order. This historical sense, which is
> a sense of the timeless as well as of the temporal and of the
> timeless and the temporal together, is what makes a writer
> traditional. And it is at the same time what makes a writ-
> er most acutely conscious of his place in time, of his own
> contemporaneity."

Of course this view fits in well with his position of a classicist in literature, though he admits the necessity of something new as contribution by the new writer so long as the new fits in with the old ("its fitting in is a test of its value"). He points out "art never improves" but "the material of the art is never the same", and that "the mind of Europe ... is a mind which changes, and that this change is a development which abandons nothing *en route,* which does not superannuate either Shakespeare, or Homer" ... and "that this development, refinement perhaps, complication certainly, is not, from the point of view of the artist,any improvement." "The progress of the artist is a continual self-sacrifice, a continual extinction of personality."

The second major dictum in "Tradition and the Individual Talent" is more important and perhaps more erratic. "Honest criticism and sensitive appreciation are directed not upon the poet but upon the poetry," declares Eliot, and he adds:

> "To divert interest from the poet to the poetry is a laudable aim: for it would conduce to a juster estimation of actual poetry, good and bad. There are many people who appreciate the expression of sincere emotion in verse, and there is a smaller number of people who can appreciate technical excellence. But very few know when there is an expression of *significant* emotion, emotion which has its life in the poem and not in the history of the poet. The emotion of art is impersonal. And the poet cannot reach this impersonality without surrendering himself wholly to the work to be done.

And these sayings must have had their share in triggering off the new trend of "New Criticism" which came to replace the so-called German Scholarship or the careful study of the poet's historical background and personal history in relation to the analysis of the poem and which rose to prominence in the Western literary world in the 1940s. As a corrective to an over-emphasis on the poet to the neglect of the poem, New Criticism has served a good turn historically, but it too is necessarily lop-sided, and for this Eliot naturally had his part of the responsibility.

"The Metaphysical Poets" was first published in the *London Times Literary Supplement,* as a book review of an anthology "Metaphysical Lyrics and Poems of the Seventeenth Century: Donne to Butler", selected and edited with an essay by Professor Herbert J. C.

Grierson, in 1921. This essay, as its title clearly indicates, was written to counteract against Samuel Johnson's use of "metaphysical poetry" "as a term of abuse or as the label of a quaint and pleasant taste" and to eulogize "Donne, Crashaw, Vaughan, Herbert and Lord Herbert, Marvel, King, Cowley at his best" as "in the direct current of English poetry", with their "precise use of metaphor, simile, or other conceit", with their "elaboration ... of a figure of speech to the farthest stage to which ingenuity can carry it", with their "characteristic effects ... secured by brief words and sudden contrasts", with their "telescoping of images and multiplied associations", with their "development of sensibility" "which could devour any kind of experience". Eliot admitted that these metaphysical poets had "various faults", "metaphysical or witty, quaint or obscure", but "they were, at best, engaged in the task of trying to find the verbal equivalent for states of mind and feeling" and therefore "they are more mature" and "they wear better" ... Then he went on to explain:

"poets in our civilization, as it exists at present, must be difficult. Our civilization comprehends great variety and complexity, and this variety and complexity, playing upon a refined sensibility, must produce various and complex results. The poet must become more and more comprehensive, more allusive, more indirect, in order to force, to dislocate if necessary, language into his meaning."

Eliot deplored the fact these metaphysical poets were followed by two powerful poets of the 17th century, Milton and Dryden, with whom "a dissociation of sensibility set in, from which we have never recovered because Milton and Dryden were followed by Collins, Gray, Johnson and Goldsmith, then Shelley and Keats, and finally Tennyson and Browning:

"Something ... had happened to the mind of England between the time of Donne or Lord Herbert of Cherbury and the time of Tennyson and Browning; it is the difference between the intellectual poet and the reflexive poet, Tennyson and Browning are poets, and they think; but they do not feel their thought as immediately as the odour of a rose. A thought to Donne was an experience; it modified his sensibility."

Then Eliot referred to a number of French poets who had their influence upon him: Jules Laforgue and Tristan Corbiere, who "are nearer to the 'school of Donne' than any modern English poet" and who "have the same essential quality of transmuting ideas into sensations, of transforming an observation into a state of mind".

In other words, with the later poets, there was the "separation of thought from feeling", while in poets like Donne and Chapman "there is a direct sensuous apprehension of thought, or a recreation of thought into feeling". All these comments of Eliot's on the metaphysical poets are important not only because they have been partly responsible for the increased (and increasing?) influence of these poets and especially of Donne upon 20th-century British and American poetry, but more because the traits of the metaphysical school mentioned in this essay, such as the extensive use of metaphor, simile and other conceits, the elaboration of figures of speech, the development of sensibility, as well as the telescoping of images and multiplied associations, are all present in a greater or less degree in Eliot's own poetry, and with these traits come also different degrees of obscurity in different poems.

As editor of an important journal, *The Criterion*, which ran from 1922 to 1939, Eliot naturally became a rather prolific prosewriter, not only in the field of literary criticism, but also in politics, sociology, economics and theology. His first volume of prose, "The Sacred Wood", which contained the essay "Tradition and the Individual Talent", appeared in 1920. His other prose works, chiefly on criticism, included "Selected Essays" (1932), "On Poetry and Poets" (1957) and "To Criticize the Critic" (1965), as well as his Norton lectures at Harvard which were published as "The Use of Poetry and the Use of Criticism" in 1933. His writings on a variety of topics appeared as "After Strange Gods" (1934), originally lectures delivered at the University of Virginia, and "The Idea of a Christian Society" (1939) and "Notes toward a Definition of Culture" (1948). Many of these essays and lectures show Eliot's conservatism, his advocacy of a hierarchical society, his insistence on élitism, and his acceptance of the authority of the Church of England. Some of his views in "After Strange Gods" are so extremely to the right that he himself later suppressed them. In most of his essays Eliot assumed an authoritative pose that led some readers to compare him with Matthew Arnold of Victorian culture. However, Eliot disapproves strongly of Arnold's attitude toward religion: he speaks of "the effect of Arnold's religious campaign" to be "to divorce religion from thought", that is, religion becomes for Arnold simply "morality touched by emotion". While this is true enough, what is one to say of Eliot's religion; is one to approve wholeheartedly of Eliot's élitist Anglo-Catholicism? Nevertheless, Eliot occupied as important a place in British culture in mid-20th century almost as Matthew Arnold in mid-19th century.

T.S. Eliot was also a playwright, though his fame in the field of drama is less important as compared with his high priesthood in poetry and his authority in literary criticism.

Except for the fragments of his earliest experiment in drama, "Wanna Go Home, Baby?" (first published in 1926—27 and retitled "Sweeny Agonistes" after 1932), T.S. Eliot's plays have all more or less to do with religion. Shortly after he wrote his Choruses for "The Rock" (written as a pageant play in aid of a London church's fund in 1934), he completed a full-length play, "Murder in the Cathedral" (1935), for the annual festival of Canterbury Cathedral. "Sweeny Agonistes" (or "Fragments of an Aristophanic Melodrama") is supposedly based on ancient Greek drama as the word "Aristophanic" clearly indicates. The first fragment, "Fragment of a Prologue", simply tells about two girls who are cutting the cards for fortune-telling and then are visited by four men, and it ends when two of the visitors who are Americans make their different comments on London as "a little too gay for us", "a slick place", "a swell place" and "a fine place to come on a visit". The second fragment, "Fragment of an Agon", opens with Sweeny talking about going to "a cannibal island" where there is the cannibal and there is the missionary, and he declares:

"Well that's life on a crocodile isle.
There's no telephones
There's no gramophones
There's no motor cars
No two-seaters, no six-seaters,
No Citroen, no Rolls-Royce.
Nothing to eat but the fruit as it grows.
Nothing to see but the palm trees one way
And the sea the other way,
Nothing to hear but the sound of the surf.
Nothing to all but three things."

And when he is asked "What things?", he answers:

"Birth, and copulation, and death.
That's all, that's all, that's all, that's all,
Birth, and copulation, and death.
... You'd be bored,
Birth, and copulation, and death.
That's all the facts when you come to brass tacks:
Birth, and copulation, and death.
I've been born, and once is enough.
You don't remember, but I remember,
Once is enough."

And later on when one of the girls asks: "What's that life is?" And Sweeny answers, "Life is death." And later he repeats, "Death is life and life is death." Here we find Eliot's satire on human life in the society he lived in as consisting of nothing but birth and copulation and death while on the other hand we see the poet reiterating his equation about life and death.

"Murder in the Cathedral" is possibly the best known and easiest understood of the five verse dramas, and the most overtly religious in theme. While it was written for performance at the Canterbury Festival in 1935, this poetic drama, based on the story of the martyrdom of Thomas Becket in 1170, was meant by Eliot the fervent Christian poet to propagate his religious faith to the world. Thomas Becket, a tradesman's son from Cheapside, was befriended by Henry II and made Chancellor of the kingdom and then Archbishop of Canterbury, but after he entered the Church he was estranged from the king and left England for a long time. The play begins with the chorus of women at Canterbury and three priests there hearing of the Archbishop's imminent return after seven years' exile and commenting on the possible consequence of the event, mostly with fear and uneasiness. All this is strictly in the tradition of ancient Greek tragedy. Then Becket arrives and is faced with four tempters with their different tempting offers, and he rejects them one by one. In the prose interlude between Part I and Part II is given Thomas' sermon in the Cathedral on Christmas Day, in which he explains why in the Mass of Christmas Day not only is there rejoicing in the birth of Christ but is also enacted his Passion and Death, thus anticipating his own martyrdom soon at hand. In Part II, after a brief chorus of the women and the appearance of the three priests with the banners of St. Stephen, St. John the Apostle and the Holy Innocents, enter the four knights to accuse Becket of being a rebel to the king and the law of the land and they start to attack him, but they are interposed by the returning priests and attendants, Then after Becket refuses to obey the King's command to depart from England, the knights leave with a threat to return soon. The priests drag Becket into the cathedral and bar the door against the knights' return, but the archbishop declares: "The Church shall be open, even to our enemies", and orders the door to be opened. The four knights, somewhat drunk, come back, pronounce Becket traitor and kill him, and then they turn round to the front-stage to try to justify their murder to the audience in long prose passages, the last of the four knights even urging the audience to "render a verdict of Suicide while of Unsound Mind." The play ends with the three priests and the chorus of women wailing the archbishop's death and praising his martyrdom.

"Murder in the Cathedral", by obviously eulogizing Becket's

struggle with the king in order to uphold the Church's authority, points clearly to Eliot's fervid Anglo-Catholicism. The play therefore is not only a vivid portrayal of Thomas Becket the martyr who unwaveringly sacrifices even his own life in serving God, but it very definitely exalts religion above earthly interests and places the power of the Church above temporal authority whether of kings or of any other person or institution. This is obviously the inherent meaning or message of the drama. That there may be yet a deeper level of meaning to be found in the play, that Becket's martyrdom is comparable to the crucifixion and resurrection of Christ, is of course quite possible but remains to be conclusively proved. The vehicle of ancient Greek tragedy was here obviously made use of by Eliot to express his sentiments of a devout Christian.

For us "Murder in the Cathedral" is a powerful play of a heroic figure who can resist all sorts of temptations of earthly pleasures and political power (including his revenge on the king and his domination on behalf of the Pope) and even the glory of martyrdom, who can follow the will of God and obey the order of the Church, and who can even sacrifice his life in defying the unjust commands of the king that are opposed to the instructions of the Pope. Although we may have our own views toward the Christian religion, the heroism of one who can resist temptations on the one hand and defy tyranny on the other is certainly worthy of our respect, and the portraiture of Becket as such a hero is very well given here in the play. The passages in the chorus of women at Canterbury as well as the speeches of Thomas Becket and the three priests and the four tempters also occasionally rises to poetic heights of lyrical beauty, while many lines uttered by the chorus of women picture vividly these labouring people and show the poet's sympathy for them. The first few lines of the chorus in Part I may be quoted here to illustrate the above-mentioned points:

> Here let us stand, close by the cathedral. Here let us wait.
> Are we drawn by danger? Is it the knowledge of safety, that
>   draws our feet
> Towards the cathedral? What danger can be

> For us, the poor, the poor women of Canterbury? What
>   tribulation
> With which we are not already familiar? There is no danger
> For us, and there is no safety in the cathedral. Some pres-
>   age of an act
> Which our eyes are compelled to witness, has forced our feet
>   Towards the cathedral. We are forced to bear witness.

Here we find the loose verse lines employed by Eliot to fit the occasion and the mood of the utterances made by the speakers in the drama, in accordance with his theory of how verse should serve the purpose of the drama, in his essay "Poetry and Drama" (1951).

Eliot wrote four other full-length plays in the last decades of his life: "The Family Reunion (1939), "The Cocktail Party" (1949), "The Confidential Clerk" (1953), and "The Elder Statesman" (1959). They are all verse dramas and all have to do with more or less Christian themes, and curiously enough, except for the first of these, they all achieved popular success as theatrical productions. However, "The Family Reunion" and the three other plays are somewhat different from "Murder in the Cathedral" (and "The Rock") in that they do not deal directly with any religious theme but rather ostensibly with the drawing-room world of polite society. "The Family Reunion", written nearer in point of time to his major religious poems "Ash Wednesday" and "Four Quartets", is more involved with myth and ritual. As a link between Eliot's earlier plays and his three last comedies the play begins with the drawing-room atmosphere but ends definitely on the Christian doctrine of sin and expiation. Containing two parts and six scenes the verse play opens with several members of an English aristocratic family gathering on the Dowager Lady Moncheney's birthday at her country house Wishwood in the north of England as they wait for the return from abroad of the eldest son of the family Harry, Lord Moncheney. Two other sons are coming but they never arrive: on the way John got badly hurt at a car accident and Arthur was forbidden to drive after his over-speeding and subsequent collision into a roundsman's cart. Harry the central figure arrives, but he ruins his mother's plans for him to marry her deceased cousin's daughter Mary and to settle down at the country estate, by announcing that he himself has pushed his wife overboard whereas the previous report received in the family was that she was swept off the deck in a storm in mid-ocean. He is very nervous, feeling himself pursued by "the sleepless hunters" that will not let him sleep, and his servant Downing is called in for investigations by the worried family and then the family physician Dr. Warburton is sent for. Mary, who had been a playmate of Harry's in their younger days and who reminds him of his childhood at Wishwood which had been kept completely unchanged by his mother's orders, however tells him what he needs to change is "something inside" him and then he suddenly sees with his own eyes through the parted curtains the Eumenides (as in Greek tragedy) that previously had only haunted him in his dreams. Harry then is conscious of something wrong in his family and tries to find out about his father from Agatha, his mother's youngest sister. Agatha reveals to him that his father had been in love with her and had at one time planned to murder his mother but Agatha had stopped him because Harry was then already in his mother's womb, and then his father had gone to live abroad. And this suggests to Harry that he too probably only thought of murdering his wife instead of actually pushing her overboard. But Agatha tells Harry that though his thoughts of murder, like his father's, did not become crime to deserve punishment by law, yet this is a matter of sin and expiation, and so Harry decides to leave home immediately and this decision brings death to his mother who has already been very ill and she dies on this her birthday.

Though the theme of "The Family Reunion" is therefore that of sin and expiation that ends with Harry going away to become a missionary in order to atone for the family sins, yet there is a significant undercurrent of which even Eliot himself may not be aware, for the play is an exposé of the skeleton in the cupboard in an English aristocratic family and it gives a vivid picture of the various vices of the idle, hypocritical high society in England as a whole. It matters little whether Harry's pushing his wife overboard is a dream or a fact; it doesn't matter that the plotted murder of Amy by her husband and her sister Agatha is nipped in the bud by Agatha's stricken conscience; what matters is that such thoughts of murder are not uncommon in the so-called polite society and that even when murder is actually committed by a peer or some such dignified personage it can easily be covered up in the name of an unfortunate accident like a terrific storm sweeping people overboard in mid-ocean. Besides this, the author himself even speaks on behalf of some members of the upper society against some others in the bourgeois-aristocratic world, as we find in the conversation of Violet, Gerald and Charles near the beginning of the play:

Violet: England's bad enough, I would never go south,
　　　　Simply to see the vulgarest people —
　　　　You can keep out of their way at home;
　　　　People with money from heaven knows where —
Gerald: Dividends from aeroplane share.
Violet: They bathe all day and they dance all night
　　　　In the absolute minimum of clothes.
Charles: It's the cocktail drinking does the harm:
　　　　There's nothing on earth so bad for the young.

And then the examples of Harry's two brothers John and Arthur, who have been "a great disappointment" to their mother even according to Dr. Warburton, are not untypical cases of younger sons of peers of England, while Amy is another representative figure of domineering old dowagers. Thus "The Family Reunion" is in a sense a satire on an English aristocratic family whose members brought together by the reunion are depicted with all their sins and vices and foibles. Here, in spite of the poet's own conscious effort to the contrary, we are at least reminded of his portrayals of Prufrock and the lady in "The Portrait of a Lady" and similiar figures in his earliest poems.

The theatrical failure of "The Family Reunion" led Eliot to write his three later plays in a different fashion, partly I suppose to cater to the audience in England at the time but more importantly to illustrate his new theory of verse drama set forth in his essay "Poetry and Drama" (1951). "The Cocktail Party" (1950) was a comedy more easily acceptable to the London theatrical world of the twentieth century. The play begins with a cocktail party in the fashionable society in London where idle repartee in the comedy-of-manners fashion is carried on without the presence of the hostess, and Edward Chamberlayne the host has to make excuses for her, by pretending that she has gone to visit an ill aunt. Gradually all except an "Unidentified Guest" take their leave and Edward has to confess that his wife Lavinia has left him, but it is only later that we are informed of Edward's affair with Celia and of Peter once chasing after Lavinia and now in love with her, while two other characters Julia and Alex run in and out of the room with all sorts of obvious excuses. Strangely enough, however, the Unidentified Guest makes Edward declare his desire now to get his wife Lavinia back, and Celia feels herself having made a mistake about Edward. Then the Unidentified Guest turns out to be a psychiatrist and Edward and Lavinia and Celia all arrange appointments with him and wait in his separate consulting rooms. He succeeds eventually in reconciling Edward and Lavinia who decide to make the best of a bad bargain by going back to live together while Celia disillusioned in earthly love is sent by Sir Henry Harcourt-Reilly the psychiatrist to his "sanatorium" which means becoming a missionary to work for heavenly love. The last act of the play finds all the earlier participants except Celia meeting again at another cocktail party at the Chamberlaynes' drawing-room, and the story ends with Edward and Lavinia living happily together in real Christian love (which according to Neo-Platonism would eventually lead to love for God), whereas Celia is reported to have died a martyr while serving the natives of distant Kinkanja, thus achieving truly saintly love in Christian faith. The theme here is again a religious one, touching on Eliot's favorite topic in his later years on love as the highest Christian virtue to strive for, and here we have two kinds of love: earthly love which may be a reflection of love for God and heavenly love which means direct service to Christianity. But the story interest is kept up in a high pitch of excitement throughout the three acts, with the well-managed theatrical devices of surprise and suspense plus the very clever use of "deus ex machina" via the psychiatrist and his two assistants Julia and Alex, and therefore the play achieved success on the stage. However, the character-portrayal here is weak, even the major figures merely serving as puppets in the handling of the plot, and the verse is usually hardly distinguishable from prose despite its suppleness and naturalness in dialogue. Of course, Eliot argues against the charge of unpoetic verse in his later plays, as reported of his own comment about "The Cocktail Party": "I laid down for myself the ascetic rule to avoid poetry which could not stand the test of strict dramatic utility," and he admits that his verse in drama "will not be 'poetry' all the time. It will only be 'poetry' when the dramatic situation has reached such a point of intensity that poetry becomes the natural utterance, because then it is the only language in which the emotions can be expressed at all." Taken as a whole, "The Cocktail Party" is a very ingeniously written play which is engrossing as well as instructive: the dramatic situations are well managed and by guiding the intricate and improper sex relations in high society (including extra-marital amours and intra-marital quarrels involving almost all the major characters Edward and Lavinia and Celia and Peter) onto the righteous paths of happy conjugal love and self-sacrifice for the natives of a distant country, the theme appears to be a worthy one, even though the poet's zeal of a fervent Christian cannot be shared by everyone outside the Christian world.

"The Confidential Clerk", presented at the 1953 Edinburgh Festival and soon after in New York, is almost a farce dealing chiefly with the age-old story of search for parentage. Sir Claude Mulhammer, a London financier, and his wife Lady Elizabeth both have extramarital children, though their legitimate marriage was a childless one. He has an illegitimate daughter, Lucasta Angel, whose parentage is kept secret though he supports her financially, and he knows Colby Simpkins to be his illegitimate son who has been taken care of since childhood by a Mrs. Guzzard and whom now he engages as his confidential clerk to replace the retiring Eggerson. Lady Elizabeth's illegitimate son has been lost long ago and when she returns from her trip to her latest "master" of "mind control" in Switzerland and meets Colby, she takes to him almost instantly and begins to believe him to be her long-lost child. Lucasta likes Colby enormously but is warned in time by Sir Claude and she becomes engaged to a Mr. B. Kaghan, a promising young man in the financial circles in London. A dispute ensues between Sir Claude and Lady Elizabeth over the true parentage of Colby, and Mrs. Guzzard is sent for who is supposed to be Colby's widowed aunt but is actually the nurse employed by Sir Claude to bring up Colby. The upshot is that Colby turns out to be the son of Mrs. Guzzard and a disappointed musician while B. Kaghan is actually Lady Elizabeth's long lost son, and the play ends with marriage for Lucasta and B. Kaghan and with Colby recommended by Eggerson to be organist of a parish church first and a clergyman eventually ... So here again, as in "The Cocktail Party" the major figures go their separate ways: B. Kaghan and Lucasta to be united in love and connubial bliss (earthly love) while Colby is to follow his bent for music and then to take orders (heavenly love). But there is a secondary theme in the drama: the common contradiction between one's vocation and avocation. Sir Claude is interested in pottery and Lady Elizabeth dabbles in occult religions, whereas Colby loves his music and plays the piano and Eggerson finds his joy in his garden. But they all spend their lives in doing other jobs. Of course, the poet tries to minimize the contradiction by explaining that Sir Claude would never have become a good potter nor could Colby ever aspire to be a first-rate pianist. Nevertheless, the discrepancy is there and that is the way of the world, at least according to Eliot.

Perhaps the most interesting thing about this play is its exposé of loose moral behaviour among the lords and the ladies, and the satire lies in the open and unashamed avowal by both Sir Claude and Lady Elizabeth of their extra-marital relations and their illegitimate children, so much so, that Sir Claude at first shows reluctance to acknowledge Colby as his son because knowing his wife to have a "strong maternal instinct" he is afraid she may become jealous of his having two illegitimate children both alive while her only extra-marital son is now lost. In fact, Lady Elizabeth seems to feel so much better when at the end of the play she finds herself to have one son and her husband to have one daughter, with Colby belonging to neither of them. Eliot may not be aware of such strange vying between a husband and a wife for more illegitimate children but such behaviour seems not uncommon in the Western world today, perhaps especially in the aristocratic circles. On the other hand, the religious undertone is definitely there in the play, yet it is much feebler than in "The Family Reunion" or even "The Cocktail Party".

"The Elder Statesman", written after Eliot's happy second marriage, contains a love story with quite a number of lyrical passages. However, the religious theme of sin and expiation again assumes prominence in the play. Lord Claverton had risen from plain Dick Ferry to Mr. Richard Claverton-Ferry after marriage and then to the position of a peer and had had a successful political and financial career as M.P. and chairman of public companies. He has just retired on grounds of poor health, and the doctor arranges for him to go to an expensive convalescent home at Badgley Court. He has a daughter, Monica, whom he is extremely fond of and who is engaged to be married to a promising young lawyer Charles. He has a good-for-nothing son, Michael, who is always getting into some trouble or other. Then the story is unfolded of Lord Claverton's past. His old friend at Oxford, Fred Culverwell, who had learned from Claverton's example to live beyond his means and then served a term of imprisonment for forgery, has now returned to England as a prominent citizen from the Central American state of San Marco where he had grown wealthy in his career of systematic corruption within the law. He has changed his name into Gomez and has come back to associate himself with his old friend Claverton as a prominent man now in England. But for some purpose or other he hints about Claverton's old reckless ways, especially about his once having run over an old man and killed him while driving, without bothering to stop his car. Another reminder of Claverton's past misdemeanor is the appearance of a woman at Badgley court whom he had paid off with a lot of money in order to avoid a breach-of-promise suit but who has since become a well-known revue star and is now quite well off as a widow. Then his son Michael gets dismissed from his job and is taken on by Gomez to go abroad to take up a job in San Marco. All these things awaken in Claverton's conscience the feeling of sin and guilt, for though everything he did in the past was within the law and he cannot now be punished for it, yet he feels the necessity of expiation and so the first thing he does is to confess the whole thing to someone he truly loves, his daughter Monica, and also her lover Charles. When he is forgiven by them, he feels that his son leaving him is also some sacrifice that may serve as expiation, and finally he bids farewell to his daughter Monica and her lover Charles and himself waits for the death which he knows will come shortly. The play ends with a brief love scene between the young lovers Monica and Charles that contains autobiographical echoes of Eliot's own happy life with his second wife.

Though here again is the theme of sin and expiation, with confession and love as the most effective means of expiation, yet in "The Elder Statesman" as in "The Family Reunion" and "The Cocktail Party" the author perhaps quite unconsciously gives an exposé of the prevalence of evil-doings among the people of the upper classes in England. Some of the guilty actions, like pushing one's wife overboard with no one else around, like the plotting of murder by attempting to use many different devices (though never carried out), like ruining a young girl and then paying her off to avoid a lawsuit, like running over and killing an old man without stopping to look, are all rather serious offences some of which are even punishable by law if detected, but in the plays they seem to be simply burdens on one's conscience, or just common sins which will easily be forgiven if one confesses and expiates with love. All this shows definitely Eliot's aristocratic stand, but all this also points on the one hand to the moral degeneracy in the fashionable society in London and on the other to the hypocrisy behind the splendid facade of the Christian doctrines of sin and expiation.

It is interesting that the classical, conservative and Anglo-Catholic poet T.S. Eliot in the last decades of his life spent so much time and energy in the writing of four plays for the modern stage, plays which are comedies or farces meant at least partly to entertain the public, though in each of them there are either religious overtones or to some critics different levels of hidden or not-so-obscure meanings for the edification of the élitist audience. It has also been suggested that each of the four is based more or less upon four ancient Greek plays as sources of inspiration: Aeschylus' "Choephoroi" with the Furies in the Orestes myth as source for "The Family Reunion" (this is a very definite case of borrowing as the Furies appearing in both plays cannot fail to testify); Euripedes' "Alcestis" as source for "The Cocktail Party" (Eliot himself speaks of Sir Henry Harcourt-Reilly the psychiatrist as his modern-day counterpart of Heracles in "Alcestis"); Euripedes' "Ion" (with its story of a misplaced child and of conflicting parental claims on him) as source for "The Confidential Clerk"; and Sophocles' "Oedipus at Colonus" (with its story of an old king expiating his youthful crimes) as source for "The Elder Statesman". Then, of course, these plays being derived partly from ancient Greek drama further show the poet's claim for himself of "classicist in literature".

The emphasis on some deeper or symbolic meaning for each of his plays, far beyond the characters and events presented on the surface, distinguishes Eliot's verse dramas from the ordinary run of dramatic literature not only in England but in all Europe. His fervent Christian beliefs bring into all his plays, including his later comedies and farces, the element of love as the chief saving grace for all people portrayed by him. Whereas heavenly love is to be preferred (e.g. in the cases of Thomas Becket in "Murder in the Cathedral", Harry in "The Family Reunion", Celia in "The Cocktail Party" and Colby in "The Confidential Clerk"), earthly love is also highly valued (e.g. in the cases of Edward and Lavinia Chamberlayne in "The Cocktail

Party", Lucasta and B. Kaghan in "The Confidential Clerk" and Monica and Charles in "The Elder Statesman"), because human love (e.g. in the case of Dante and Beatrice) is supposed to be a reflection of love for God or at least can lead to divine love. And this insertion of a deeper meaning into the surface meaning of a play makes Eliot's dramas, especially his last four verse plays, constitute almost a totally new genre in stage drama, a form of theatrical performance for popular entertainment and at the same time works of ethical meaning for serious thought. So there is the emphatic use of symbols and myth in Eliot's later plays, as also in his later poems.

T.S. Eliot was born and brought up in the United States and his family background in America's mid-West and especially his education received at Harvard left their strong impact upon him not alone in his earlier poetry but also in his more mature works, but his long stay in Britain and his decision to join the Church of England and become a British citizen made it perhaps more proper to consider him a British rather than an American poet, though his reputation and influence both as poet and as critic have made him an important literary figure in the whole English-speaking world.

b. W. H. Auden

Wystan Hugh Auden (1907—1973) was born in York, and was educated at Oxford (1925—28). For a time he was interested in geology and thought of becoming an engineer. He then visited Germany and returned to England to become a provincial schoolmaster (first at Helensburgh, Scotland, and then in Worcester from 1930 to 1935) and later worked for a government film unit. In 1932, he was co-founder of the Group Theater. In the 1930's he was one of a group of modernist poets in England with strong inclinations toward the Left, the group that included also Louis MacNeice and Cecil Day Lewis of Ireland and Stephen Spender. He was an ambulance driver on the republican side during the Spanish Civil War in 1936—38 and he travelled to Iceland and to China. In the 1930s he considered himself a socialist, fell strongly under the influence of Marx and also of

Freud and Nietzsche. He migrated to the United States early in 1939 and became an American citizen in 1946, but embraced the Anglican faith. He once served with Strategic Bombing Survey in the U.S. army in Germany in World War II. He stayed mostly in America both during the war and after, tea ching in a number of American universities (University of Michigan, Swarthmore, Bryn Mawr, Smith College, Bennington College, Barnard College), but was elected Professor of Poetry at Oxford for 1956—60 tenure, giving a few lectures there each year. With the ageing of T. S. Eliot, Auden became for a while the most publicized poet of the English language. In the last years' of his life (i.e., after 1957) he bought a farmhouse in Austria as his summer home, for which he wrote "Thanksgiving for a Habitat" (1958—1964).

Auden had a long poetic career, starting to write in his twentieth year (1927) and continuing for more than half a century, till shortly before his death in 1973. His poetic output falls very definitely into two periods, 1927—1938 and 1939 and after, as he himself indicated clearly in the groupings of his "Collected Shorter Poems" into 4 parts(1927—32; 1933—38; 1939—47; 1948—57).

Auden and his coterie of MacNeice, Spender and Day Lewis were never truly Marxist and revolutionary even in their younger days. They were generally considered possessed of Leftist political views partly because to go Left was quite a common path for younger intellectuals in the 1930s under the influence of the consolidated position of the Soviet Union at the time, and partly because under the influence of Post-World-War-I economic ruin and Oswald Spengler's disillusionment at Western material civilization they did not want to go conservative as did T.S. Eliot but rather decided to turn radical in the choice before them of fascism and socialism. Actually the furthest Auden went to the Left in his poetry of the 1930s was to condemn Hitler and Mussolini and imperialist wars (e.g. "Easily, my dear, you move, easily your head", "In Time of War", "September 1, 1939") and to uphold "the struggle" for Republicanism (in his poem "Spain 1937"). But most of these were either omitted or very much abridged in the author's authorized collected editions, including also three stanzas prominently missing from "In Memory of W. B. Yeats". Of these, "Spain 1937" is naturally the most outstanding, as far as its theme is concerned. The first six stanzas begin with descriptions of the discoveries and inventions and religious faith of "yesterday" (from the Middle Ages through the Renaissance to the Enlightenment and Industrial Revolution), but the 4th, 5th and 6th stanzas end with the significant remark of "But today the struggle". Eight stanzas follow to indicate which of the paths to pursue, and the answer at their end is: "I am your choice, your decision. Yes, I am Spain."

And what follows is a description of the numerous people who have come from all over the world to join in the strug le in Spain, from "remote peninsulas", "sleepy plains", "aberrant fishermen's islands" and "the corrupt heart of the city", and "All presented their lives" to engage in the struggle. Reference is then made to th International Brigade.

Madrid is the heart. Our moments of tenderness blossom
As the ambulance and the sandbag:
Our hours of friendship into a people's army".

Then four stanzas follow to describe the bright prospects of "Tomorrow", with the last two ending emphatically on the words "But today the struggle". Then two stanzas on "today" vividly portraying the threat of death and the sufferings to be endured by those joining in the present struggle. Finally the poem ends on the definite note of pessimism:

"The stars are dead; the animals will not look:
We are left alone with our day, and the time is short and
History to the defeated
May say Alas but cannot help or pardon."

The last two lines are truly, in the author's own words, "rhetorically effective" and are given as an example by the poet himself to explain why a poem with such lines should not be included in his authorized edition of poetry. The two lines are indeed called "wicked doctrine" by the later, more religious-minded Auden because he regarded that "to say this is to equate goodness with success." Here the poet was obviously referring more specifically to the word "pardon", for history can never really "help" the defeated except by justifying their cause and eulogizing them for it. But the poem is otherwise a great poem, particularly showing the fervour and enthusiasm of those fighting for the republican cause in Spain at the time, their great courage as well as their high aspirations. In spite of the poet's authorized omission it is only right and proper for many of us today to include the poem as an important work not only of Auden but also a praiseworthy expression of the heroism of all the brave fighters in the International Brigade in the Spanish Civil War.

Likewise the omission of three stanzas from "In Memory of W.B. Yeats" is a regretful suppression because this actually leaves out the poet's censure of Kipling and Claudel and even "the dogs of Europe" and "intellectual disgrace" of early twentieth-century Europe, though superficially the suggestion is of the pardon that the lapse of time would extend to all those ultra-conservative and reactionary people.

A few other poems of the 1930s also demonstrated clearly Auden's progressive views on the politics of the time. In the 6-line "Epitaph on a Tyrant", the poet condemned the tyrant with his pungent last line: "And when he cried the little children died in the street." In "Refugee Blues" and in the first of his second group of "Twelve Songs" that is entitled "So this city has ten million souls", the hopeless and helpless plight of the expatriate and strongly persecuted Jews in Hitler-dominated Europe is most vividly portrayed through the conversation of the wandering victims to whom all ways of life or even bare existence were closed and denied. In "In Memory of Ernest Toller" Auden shows his comradely mourning to Toller though the latter committed suicide. Then, there were a goodly number of poems condemning wars, though the poet did not make any distinction between just and unjust wars.

Auden's early poems, especially those written in the years 1927—32, were very much under the influence of alliterative verse of the Anglo-Saxon period and also of the short-line poems of John Skelton. Many of the early love lyrics of this period were terse but very musical, written in familiar everyday speech free of sentimentality. In "The Letter", one of the earliest pieces composed in 1927, the poet begins with his sharply-etched reminiscence of his first encounter with the beloved:

> "From the very first coming down
> Into a new valley with a frown
> Because of the sun and a lost way,
> You certainly remain:"

And then his sudden rapport upon the receipt of the letter:

> "But now,
> To interrupt the homely brow,
> Thought warmed to evening through and through
> Your letter comes, speaking as you,
> Speaking of much but not to come."

Several of his early poems contain some very haunting lines. In "Missing", we have:

> "Heroes are buried who
> Did not believe in death,
> And bravery is now,
> Not in the dying breath
> But resisting the temptation
> To skyline operations."

In "No Change of Place", we read:

> "Who will endure
> Heat of day and winter danger,
> Journey from one place to another,
> Nor be content to lie
> Till evening upon headland over bay,
> Between the land and sea
> Or smoking wait till hour of food,
> Leaning on chained-up gate,
> At edge of wood?"

Or in "The Secret Agent", there is the story:
> "Control of the passes was, he saw, the key.
> To this new district, but who would get it?
> He, the trained spy, had walked into the trap
> For a bogus guide, seduced by the old tracks."

Or in "The Watershed", strange orders are given:
> "Beams from your car may cross a bedroom wall,
> They wake no sleeper; you may hear the wind
> Arriving driven from the ignorant sea
> To hurt itself on pane, on bark of elm
> Where sap unbaffled rises, being spring."

Or in "Between Adventure", the last two short stanzas run:
> "On neither side let foot slip over,
> Invading always, exploring never,
> For this is hate and this is fear.
> On narrowness stand, for sunlight is
> Brightest only on surfaces,
> No anger, no traitor, but place."

Behind the odd phrasing and the coining of unwonted expressions and thoughts the defiance of traditional views toward heroism and death, toward inanimate natural phenomena, and the daring spirit of youth are in these poems fully demonstrated and point favourably to the innovative vigour of the youthful poet.

Auden's closeness to nature and his interest in place and time and in the world of animals and plants were particularly prominent and attractive in his early occasional poetry. In "Taller Today", we are struck by such lines as:

> "We remember similar evenings,
> Walking together in a windless orchard
> Where the brook runs over the gravel, far from the glacier."

Many short-lined poems of this early period remind one of Skelton. "The Lunar Beauty" begins with two-accented lines:

> "This lunar beauty
> Has no history

Is complete and early;"
or in "Never Stronger", the last stanza runs thus:

"Never stronger
But younger and younger,
Saying good-bye but coming back, for fear
Is over there,
And the centre of anger
Is out of danger."

or in "This Loved One", there are enchanting lines such as:

"Face that the sun
Is lively on
May stir but here
Is no new year."

The odd rhyming such as "sun" and "on", "fear" and "there", and particularly "beauty" and "history" and "early", is very typical of Auden through the whole historical development of his verse.

A rather eccentric way of asking eccentric questions provides another source of charm for Auden's poetry. In one of the songs from "The Orators" (the earliest volume of Auden's poetry), we have the curiously haunting question:

"'O where are you going?' said reader to rider",

and:

"'O do you imagine', said fearer to farer,
'That dusk will delay on your path to the pass,
Your diligent looking discover the lacking
Your footsteps feel from granite to grass?'"

and:

"'O what was that bird', said horror to hearer,
'Did you see that shape in the twisted trees?
Behind you swiftly the figure comes softly,
The spot on your skin is a shocking disease?'"

And here everywhere, especially in the second stanza quoted above, the use of alliterative device is employed with great skill, and this influence of Anglo-Saxon verse was probably borrowed indirectly from

Gerard Manly Hopkins whose extensive application of alliteration must have had its effect upon the younger English poets of the 1920s and 1930s.

Similarly, on "O what is that Sound", the questions asked are poignant with meaning, leading the querist from his sight of "the scarlet soldiers" getting ready for action to his realization of their coming for him and breaking into his house. The last two stanzas are particularly significant and full of excitement:

> "O where are you going? Stay with me here!
> Were the vows you swore deceiving, deceiving?
> No, I promised to love you, dear,
> But I must be leaving.
> "O it's broken the lock and splintered the door,
> O it's the gate where they're turning, turning;
> Their boots are heavy on the floor
> And their eyes are burning."

Auden also wrote Browningesque poems. An outstanding example is "The Detective Story" in which the omniscient poet sees the happiness of different people, from a tramp to a magnate, and how generally that happiness is lost. The poem ends on an ambiguous remark:

> "But time is always guilty. Someone must pay for
> Our loss of happiness, our happiness itself."

There are a goodly number of love poems in Auden's youth, in the mid-1930's. His first group of "Twelve Songs", written generally in the playful mood, not only vary in metre and rhyme scheme but also range from the completely facetious (e.g. the one on the six crippled beggars) to the despondently pathetic (e.g. "Stop all the clocks, cut off the telephone") and from the dreamily reminiscent and sad (e.g. "O the valley in the summer where I and my John") to the jokingly sceptical (e.g. "Some say that love's a little boy"). They are not great poems surely, but they surely contain distinctive qualities that mark the ingenuity of a budding poet.

In the 1930s Auden also wrote short poems on places he visited

and the writers he read, and invariably he saw in each something new
and modern and different. In "Oxford" he writes of scholars working in their laboratories ("Mineral and creature, so deeply in love
with themselves") and of the various phenomena outside the environs
of the campus ("Outside, some factories, then a whole green country
/Where a cigarette comforts the evil, a hymn the weak/ Where thou-
sands fidget and poke and spend their money"). In "Dover", aside
from a Norman castle and ships and lighthouses and the Old Town
and Georgian houses, the accent is laid on soldiers, "all they are killing is time/ A pauper civilian future". In "The Capital", there is
the contrast between the rich ("Quarter of pleasure where the rich
are always waiting,/ Waiting expensively for miracles to happen",)
and the miserable ("Factories where lives are made for a temporary
use/ Like collars or chairs, rooms where the lonely are battered/ Slowly like pebbles into fortuitous shapes"). In "Brussels in Winter",
there is a similar contrast between "the old, the hungry and the humbled" and those living in "ridges of rich apartments". In "Musée
des Beaux Arts", Auden shows his penetrating appreciation of the
painting of the old masters there:

> "About suffering they were never wrong,
> The old masters",

and:

> "They never forget
> That even the dreadful martyrdom must run its course
> Anyhow in a corner, some untidy spot
> Where the dogs go on with their doggy life, and the torturer's
>   horse
> Scratch its innocent behind on a tree."

In a similar way Auden made scintillating comments on some of the
great writers of the West. So in a sonnet on A. E. Housman, he
wrote:

> "Heart-injured in North London, he became
> The Latin scholar of his generation.
> Deliberately he chose the dry-as-dust,

Kept tears like dirty postcards in a drawer;
Food was his public love, his private lust
Something to do with violence and the poor."
Rimbaud is said to know of "The Nights, the railway-arches, the bad sky", and "the cold had made a poet". His longer poems on Voltaire and Melville are much greater pieces. In "Herman Melville" Auden traced the American novelist's career from his last years backward, and after describing vividly "Moby Dick" with the two succinct lines,

"The maniac hero hunting like a jewel
The rare ambiguous monster that had maimed his sex",
The poet begins to philosophize and sum up the "simple" "truth":
"Evil is unspectacular and always human,
And shares our bed and eats at our own table,
And we are introduced to Goodness every day,
Even in drawing-rooms among a crowd of faults."

"Voltaire at Ferney" is much more powerful. The old man at Ferney was highly eulogized as a great fighter ("the fight/ Against the false and the unfair/Was always worth it."), and his ways of struggle "cajoling, scolding, scheming", were compared to those of a clever child "against the infamous grown-ups" as he was favourably compared to his fellow French Enlighteners Diderot and Rousseau:

"there was much, though, to be done,
And only himself to count upon.
Dear Diderot was dull and did his best;
Rousseau, he'd always known, would blubber and give in."
The best six lines of the poem are most typical of Auden's youthful conversationalism and striking combinations of words and phrases:

"So, like a sentinel, he could not sleep. The night was full
of wrong,
Earthquakes and executions. Soon he would be dead,
And still all over Europe stood the horrible nurses
Itching to boil their children. Only his verses
Perhaps could stop them. He must go on working. Over-
head

The uncomplaining stars composed their lucid song."
Here "earthquakes and executions", "the uncomplaining stars" and
"the horrible nurses/ Itching to boil their children" are typical gems
of expression not infrequently found in Auden's verse. This poem on
Voltaire is perhaps the highest tribute to be paid to the great
French Enlightener and Auden's best political piece next to
"Spain".

In this period Auden also wrote some short poetical pieces on
common individuals. His "Miss Gee" and "Victor" are two of the
best of this genre, comparable in their terseness of expression and their
unsentimental and matter-of-fact tone to such classical specimens
as "Richard Cory" and "Miniver Cheever" of Edwin Arlington Robinson.

But the most important of all Auden's short poems of his early
years is certainly the one entitled "Lullaby" that begins with a most
unexpected and musical love-call:

"Lay your sleeping head, my love,
Human on my faithless arm;"

The second line hearkens all the way back to John Donne's "Go and
Catch a Falling Star" and "For God's sake hold your tongue and
let me love", and finds its echo in the American poet Edna St. Vin-
cent Millay's poem "What Lips my Lips Have Kissed, and Where
and Why." This points very definitely to Auden's modernism, and
Donne's, and to how and why Donne became so popular in early
20th century.

In this poem by Auden, there are a number of other most impressive and memorable lines whose modernity is unmistakable and thoroughly enchanting:

"But in my arms till break of day
Let the living creature die,
Mortal, guilty, but to me
The entirely beautiful."

And

"but from this night

Not a whisper, not a thought,
Not a kiss nor a look be lost."

What is perhaps only next in importance to "Lullaby", among Auden's early poems, is "On this Island". Here the poet describes with much affection and delight "the swaying sound of the sea", "the chalk wall" falling to the foam, the shingle scrambling after the sucking surf, and the ships "far off like floating seeds," and calls on the stranger to look on this island, very much in the spirit of Robert Browning's "Home Thoughts from Abroad" and "Home Thoughts from the Sea".

In the 1930s Auden made two memorable visits to distant and not-too-distant parts of the world, to Iceland and to China, and these trips led to fruitful results in poetic output. Aside from the shorter poem "Journey to Iceland", he wrote a long poem in four parts, "Letter to Lord Byron", begun on his outwardbound voyage to Iceland and concluded on his homeward journey from Iceland. His "Sonnets from China" (also known as "In Time of War") include altogether 27 sonnets in rather irregular rimeschemes.

"Journey to Iceland" gives a stirring account of scenes in remote Iceland and of the poet's impressions of them. Here Auden sees "white wings flicker and flaunt", witnesses

"a glitter
Of glacier, sterile immature mountains intense in the abnormal northern day, and a river's fan-like polyp of sand",

and finds:

"a horse-shoe ravine, an issue of steam from a cleft
in the rock, and the rocks, and waterfalls brushing
the rocks, and among the rocks birds,"

as well as

"A narrow bridge over a torrent,
a small farm under a crag."

However, "North means to all 'Reject'", and

"Europe is absent: this is an island and should be a refuge."

"Letter to Lord Byron" is the only long poem of importance in

Auden's early poetry. While its first part begins with the poet writing on the ship bound for Iceland and its fourth and last part was written on board the ship "Dettifoss" as he had "done with the Icelandic scene" and "heading for England's pleasant pastures green", the themes touched upon in the poem are as diverse as those in Byron's "Don Juan" or "Childe Harold's Pilgrimage." The poet apologizes for his use of the Rime Royal for the "letter" instead of "Ottava Rima" which was Byron's vehicle for "Don Juan", but he needs no apology in the desultoriness of his conversational verse, in his ever-present touches of satire and humour, and in his frequent use of all sorts of odd rhymes double and triple.

The poem begins with the author's apology to Byron for the liberty of writing this "letter", and plunges into wild satirical hits on the popular figures of the modern world (e.g. Gary Cooper, Coughlin, and Dick Sheppard) being persecuted with innumerable fan-mail. Then in a very typical Byronic fashion the poet comments humorously on his own heavy cold:

> "Professor Hous man was I think the first
>   to say in print how very stimulating
>   The little ills by which mankind is cursed,
>   The colds, the aches, the pains are to creating;
>   Indeed one hardly goes too far in stating
>   That many a flawless lyric may be due
>   Not to a lover's broken heart, but 'flu.'"

And the author's reflections on Jane Austen and her novels can reach a height of scintillating literary criticism:

> "You could not shock her more than she shocks me;
>   Beside her Joyce seems innocent as grass.
>   It makes me most uncomfortable to see
>   An English spinster of the middle class
>   Describe the amorous effect of 'brass',
>   Reveal so frankly and with such sobriety
>   The economic basis of society."

In Part II, Auden pretends to introduce to Byron 20th-century England:

> "Huge plate-glass windows, walls absorbing noise,
> Where the smoke nuisance is utterly abated
> And all the furniture is chromium-plated."
> "To start with, on the whole we're better dressed;
> For chic the difference today is small
> Of barmaid from my lady at the Hall.
> It's sad to spoil this democratic vision
> With millions suffering from malnutrition."

And our author even imagines Byron's Don Juan in 20th-century
Britain:

> "Don Juan was a mixer and no doubt
> Would find this century as good as any
> For getting hostesses to ask him out,
> And mistresses that need not cost a penny.
> Indeed our ways to waste time are so many,
> Thanks to technology, a list of these
> Would make a longer book than 'Ulysses'".
> "But if in highbrow circles he would sally
> It's just as well to warn him there's no stain on
> Picasso, all in wrestling, or the Ballet.
> Sibelius is the man. To get a pain on
> Listening to Elgar is a sine qua non.
> A second-hand acquaintance of Pareto's
> Ranks higher than an intimate of Plato's.
> "The vogue for Black Mass and the cult of devils
> Has sunk. The Good, the Beautiful, the True
> Still fluctuate about the lower levels.
> Joyces are firm and there there's nothing new.
> Eliots have hardened just a point or two.
> Hopkins are brisk, thanks to some recent boosts.
> There's been some further weakening in Prousts."

Then, rather facetiously Auden steals a line from one of Wordworth's
sonnets and deplores the present state of decline in Britannia:

"Byron, thou should'st be living at this hour!
　　What would you do, I wonder if you were?
Britannia's lost prestige and cash and power,
　　Her middle classes show some wear and tear,
　　We've learned to bomb each other from the air,
　　I can't imagine what the Duke of Wellington
Would say about the music of Duke Ellington."

This curiously abrupt transition from the highly humorous to the subtly satirical, this effective blending of the highly ludicrous with the slightly pathetic, and this happy combination of brisk haphazard phrasing and dubious double rhyming, all provide us with the "just right" reminiscences of the Byronic verse in "Don Juan". The "tongue-in-cheek" quality that constituted the typical Byronic style is here imitated to perfection.

Part III of the "Letter" deals more extensively with literary criticism. Auden tries to defend Byron, but has to admit adverse comments from George Eliot and T.S. Eliot:

"A 'vulgar genius' so George Eliot said,
Which doesn't matter as George Eliot's dead,
But T.S. Eliot, I'm sad to find,
Damned you with: 'an interesting mind.'"

Wordsworth's sustained popularity in the 20th century is mentioned, apparently for Byron's benefit, and a desultory discussion follows on art and artists, with such terse lines as

"All Cézanne's apples I would give away
For one small Goya or a Daumier".

And:

"Because it's true Art feels a trifle sick,
You mustn't think the old girl's lost her kick,
And those, besides, who feel most like a sewer
Belong to painting not to Literature."

Part IV gives a rambling account of the poet's own life and career, starting from his childhood and going on to his taking up poetry and his "teaching English in a boarding school." And rather tamely the poet ends the "Letter" with his return to England from Iceland:

> "And summer's done.   I sign the usual pledges
> To be a better poet, better man;
> I'll really do it this time if I can."

And facetiously he winds up the last stanza by addressing himself to Byron to whom this verse epistle is supposed to have been addressed

> "I hope this reaches you in your abode,
>   This letter that's already far too long,
> Just like the Prelude or the Great Northern Road;
>   But here I end my conversational song,
>   I hope you don't think mail from strangers wrong.
> As to its length, I tell myself you'll need it,
> You've all eternity in which to read it!"

"Letter to Lord Byron", as an early work by a 30-year-old poet, certainly shows great promise for Auden in his clever manipulation of the technicalities of verse and in his subtle blending of humour and irony, both of which qualities were kept up by him all through the half century of his poetic career.

In 1939, the year in which Auden left England for America and which therefore marked an important change in his midcareer, he wrote three memorable poems in memory of three outstanding European figures who were his friends: W.B. Yeats, Sigmund Freud and Ernst Toller.

"In Memory of W. B. Yeats" was a high tribute paid to the Irish poet by Auden.   Not only was nature ("the dead of winter", "a dark cold day") in sympathy with the decease of the great writer, but his death made him one with the broad mass of his readers and admirers ("Now he is scattered among a hundred cities", "he became his admirers").   Yeats is described as one of the common people ("You were silly like us") but gifted in poetry: "Mad Ireland hurt you into poetry," sums up very adroitly the whole development of Yeats' poetic career. Auden's curious negative comment on time as forgiving in every way and pardoning even those retrograde authors like Kipling and Paul

Claudel as well as "all the dogs of Europe" and "intellectual disgrace" is followed by an optimistic note of rejoicing that Yeats' poetry has its healing power for "human unsuccess" and distress:

> "With the farming of a verse
> Make a vineyard of the curse
> Sing of human unsuccess
> In a rupture of distress.
> "In the deserts of the heart
> Let the healing fountain start,
> In the prison of his days
> Teach the free man how to praise."

This eulogy of Yeats marks the emergence of the new Auden of growing maturity who could face the social evils bravely and find his way somehow out of complete pessimism.

"In Memory of Ernst Toller" was an elegy of one comrade for another, for Auden and Toller were both inclined to the Left in the "maddening" 1930's for the European intellectuals, though the latter plunged more deeply into the struggle and was harder hit in the land of Hitlerite Germany. The early stanzas of the poem pose a number of queries into the why and wherefore of Toller's suicide, and then Auden turns nostalgicly into a brief recollection of their erstwhile common endeavour to set "an example for the young":

> "Dear Ernst, lie shadowless at last among
> The other war-horses who existed till they'd done
> Something that was an example to the young."

Finally, in the last stanzas Auden seeks comfort from his new belief in human destiny and in a hopeful future:

> "We are lived by powers we pretend to understand:
> They arrange our loves; it is they who direct at the end
> The enemy bullet, the sickness, or even our hand.
> "It is their tomorrow hangs over the earth of the living,
> And all that we wish for our friends: but existence is believing;
> We know for whom we mourn and who is grieving."

"In Memory of Sigmund Freud" shows Auden's great respect for the Austrian doctor and psycho-analyst. The poet classifies Freud among "those who were doing us some good" and points out that "still at eighty he wished/To think of our life."With much astuteness the poet makes here and there generalized comments on the doctor:

> "He wasn't clever at all, he merely told
> The unhappy Present to recite the Past",

and

> "If often he was wrong and at times absurd,
>   To us he is no more a person
>   Now but a whole climate of opinion
>   Under whom we conduct our differing lives."

and especially the doctor's great sympathy for the mentally sick:

> "But he would have us remember most of all
> To be enthusiastic over the night
>   Not only for the sense of wonder
>   It alone has to offer, but also
> Because it needs our love."

"New Year Letter", a long poem written for January 1, 1940, was truly a landmark in the development of Auden's poetic career. He had left England for the United States in 1939 and had settled there,and this was his first new year in a new environment and the beginning of his new phase in life. The Second World War had begun in Europe in September of 1939 and though Auden was now far from the scene of war in America, yet it was quite certain that the second major world strife must have shocked him and so made it necessary for him to readjust himself to this new world situation.

The long verse epistle in 3 parts was addressed to a friend Elizabeth with whom the poet shared their common background of being born and brought up in England and of now living in the United States and for whom he had much affection. The first part begins with his reminiscences of the preceding New Year's Eve in Brussels and then he recaptures the events that took place in Europe in that year, 1939.

The unrest in August finally led to the beginning of war in Poland on September 1st, and the poet now in America struggles on against great odds to bring order into his "sense, feeling and intelligence", especially in art, while all over the world there were "vast spiritual disorders" in the last ten years. The second part of the verse epistle brings us again to the New Year's Eve of the "scrambling decade" of 1930s, as the poet once again tries to make the best of everything here and now. Here, however, after mentioning Wordsworth's being once attracted to the French Revolution of sans-culotte and Jacobinism, Auden indulges in a very unfavourable description of the Proletarian Dictatorship in Russia and in a very much distorted picture of Marx. The 3rd part again refers to the death of the Old Year and the poet addresses to his intimate friend Elizabeth and talks of "where to serve and when and how?" He remembers in England certain limestone moors where Eden seems to be, and he contrasts it with "that other world ... of fully alienated land,"

"An earth made common by the means
Of hunger, money, and machines."

There the old civilization is dying ("a day is drawing to a close" and "all the special tasks begun/By the Renaissance have been done"), but all the varieties of the "New Anthropos" that have emerged are not satisfactory and only represent tyranny and violence. And after reviewing what is happening in America and Europe and even "weary Asia", Auden comes to his ideal for the building of "the Just City":

"Where Freedom dwells because it must,
Necessity because it can,
And men confederate in Man."

Auden then wakens up again to the arrival of the new year, and realizes that his ideal is wishful thinking that is still far away:

"But wishes are not horses, this
Annus is not mirabilis;
Day breaks upon the world we know
Of war and wastefulness and woe;"

and:

> "The New Year brings an earth afraid,
> Democracy a ready-made
> And noisy tradesman's slogan, and
> The poor betrayed into the hand
> Of lackeys with ideas, ..."

And finally Auden calls on Elizabeth to go on struggling:

> "We fall down in the dance, we make
> The old ridiculous mistake,
> But always there are such as you
> Forgiving, helping what we do.
> O every day in sleep and labour
> Our life and death are with our neighbour,
> And love illuminates again
> The city and the lion's den,
> The world's great rage, the travel of young men."

Thus the poem ends on the note of Christian forgiveness and helpfulness to each other and love, which has come to be the new faith for Auden beginning from the 1940s.

"For the Time Being", written in 1941-2 but not published till 1944, further revealed the poet's new-gotten faith in Christianity though at that time he was still strongly under the influence of Kierkegaard's Christian Existentialism, which believes that man is responsible for his acts and therefore must make his leap of faith in fear and trembling for this embraced faith may very well be a wrong and corrosive choice. "For the Time Being", with its subtitle "A Christmas Oratorio", is the retelling of the ancient Christian myth of Christ's birth in modern terms. The first of the 9 sections that make up the poem, "Advent", tells of the modern background (the political situation in the modern world and the condition of personal civic virtue) for the advent of Christ is followed by "The Annunciation" in which the birth is formally announced with rejoicings and by "The Temptation of St. Joseph" which gives the unconventional psychological state of Joseph whose wife Mary is to give birth to Christ, the Son of

God. Then "The Summons" declares through the words of the three wise men the poet's acknowledgement of the greatness of Caesar whose seven kingdoms stand for the material well-being and scientific progress of the modern age, and "The Vision of the Shepherds" relates from the viewpoint of the three shepherds the author's complaint about the mass civilization and his aspirations for love in the contemporary world. "At the Manger" narrates the traditional story of the three wise men and three shepherds gathering about the manger where Christ is born, but ends with their common desire for Love, linking it up with Space and Time:

"Space is the whom our loves are needed by,
Time is our choice of How to love and Why."

Perhaps the section entitled "The Meditation of Simeon" gives the most concentrated dose of Auden's "modernist" brand of Christian faith as he speaks through the words of the traditional pious man Simeon his scepticism and his solutions to this scepticism regarding the Fall of Man and the union of the Word with the Flesh. Here the poet talks of "the emancipation of Time from Space", of the Infinite manifesting itself in the Finite, of the relations between the One and the Many and between what is Real and what is only Appearance, and of his other philosophical speculations. "The Massacre of the Innocents" is supposed to be Herod's own apology for his rule in Judea and his objection to the notion of a finite God who has been born, and all in terms of the contemporary world. "The Flight into Egypt", the final section, confirms the poet's Christian faith, speaking of Christ as "The Way", "The Truth", "The Life". "For the Time Being" is an interesting and important work, because it shows Auden's struggle from scepticism to faith in Christianity, and his acceptance of the old Christian myth of Christ's birth in terms of the modern world.

"The Sea and the Mirror", another long poem written and published in the mid-forties, reveals Auden's lyrical gift in his years of maturity. From the subtitle of the poem, "A Commentary on Shakespeare's 'The Tempest'", we may see the poet's personal interpretation of the great drama, which he begins by writing in his "Preface",

> "Which goes to show that the Bard
> Was sober when he wrote
> That this world of fact we love
> Is unsubstantial stuff:
> All the rest is silence
> On the other side of the wall;
> And the silence ripeness,
> And the ripeness all."

Prospero is painted a thoroughly disillusioned man as he addressed Ariel before he frees him and leaves the island to go back to Milan. He no longer wants his dukedom ("I am glad that I did not recover my dukedom till/-I do not want it"), has no use for his books ("Now all these heavy books are no use to me any more, for/Where I go, words carry no weight"), knows what age means ("Age/Knows only too well it has got away with nothing") and what magic means ("The power to enchant/That comes from disillusion"), even blames himself for what he has done to Antonio ("All by myself I tempted Antonio into treason") and to Caliban ("Caliban remains my impervious disgrace"), begs pardon from all, including Alonso, Sebastian, Stepheno and Trinculo, wonders if Ferdinand would keep on loving Miranda and Miranda would remain rapturous over the brave new world ("Will Ferdinand be as fond of a Miranda/Familiar as a stocking? Will a Miranda who is/No longer a silly lovesick little goose,/When Ferdinand and his brave world are her profession,/ Go into raptures over existing at all?") and realizes whether he himself has been drunk all along and is only now "cold sober" ("As if I had been on a drunk since I was born/And suddenly now, and for the first time, am cold sober"). And every one among "the supporting cast" in the play is made to utter his or her own innermost thoughts, all more or less in disillusionment, except for Antonio who in despair will keep his own will as before. Then in the third and last part which was written in prose, "Caliban to the Audience", through the words of Caliban are voiced the poet's comments on Shakespeare's art in relation to real life and here again we find Auden using modern expressions about the modern world. He speaks of Shakespeare as caring not a rap for "the strait-laced Unities" or "sad sour Probability", and eulogizes the bard's "mixed perfected brew" that includes "the magnificant tropes of tragic defiance and despair, the repartee of the high humour, the pun of the very low, cultured drawl and manly illiterate fellow". He mentions Shakespeare's dictum of dramas as "a mirror held up to nature" and questions whether the creation of Ariel and Caliban fits in with the definition. Then Auden suggests that the magic as represented by Ariel finally deserts the ageing Shakespeare who now has to turn to Caliban ("The dark thing you could never abide to be with") and then to leave everything and everybody, to bid farewell to all his created characters high and low. Then, finally, the author concludes by saying that while "Our unfortunate dramatist, there-fore, is placed in the unseemly predicament of having to give all his passion, all his skill, all his time to the task of 'doing' life," the char-acters he creates (including Ariel and Caliban) after their theatrical performances have come to realize they really represent "that Whol-ly Other Life from which we are separated by an essential emphatic gulf of which our contrived fissures of mirror and proscenium arch ... are feebly figurative signs". The last lines of the speech refer to Shakespeare's dramas as "the Perfected Work", and give Auden's rhapsodic eulogy of Shakespeare:

> "Its great coherences stand out through our secular blur
> in all their overwhelmingly righteous obligation; its voice
> speaks through our muffling banks of artificial flowers and
> unflinchingly delivers its authentic molar pardon; its spaces
> greet us with all their grand old prospect of wonder and
> width; the working charm is the full bloom of the unboth-
> ered state; the sounded note is the restored relation."

Auden's last important long poem is "The Age of Anxiety" which came out in 1947 and was called "A Baroque Eclogue" that contains the actions and words of four displaced persons spending one night together in a New York bar. Fitly sub-titled "A Baroque Eclogue" the poem deals with four characters indulging from evening till early next morning in drinks, thoughts and dreams in a bar and later at the apartment of one of them, at their pastoral after-work ease amidst the terrors of war, and written in rather over-exuberant language with numerous haphazard and unexpected expressions in alliterative verse. The Prologue sets the background — that of war— which is revealed through the radio broadcasts (which curiously blends the horrible news of war with smooth propaganda for the sale of bonds for the donage of blood and other advertisements) and through the thoughts of the four characters separately in response yet with the same refrain, "Many have perished; more will." Malin of the Canadian Air Force thinks of their bombing flights: "Death and damage darted at our will". Quant the civilian thinks of "littered lifeless along low coasts" and "in blood-spattered barns bandaged men". Emble the university sophomore enlisted in the Navy thinks of "deaf deeps, dens of unaffection" and of "some in lifebelts/Floated upright till they froze to death." And Rosetta the only woman in the group and a buyer for a big department store thinks of "long hospital trains/Smoothly slide with their sensitized freight/Of mangled men." All these are expertly-managed alliterative lines of peculiar charm. Then the four persons make their separate speeches, commenting on the horrors of war but the almost equal terrors of peace and showing thereby their despair and dissatisfaction with the entire historical development of the human race. Then in Parts Two and Three follow a discussion of "The Seven Ages" of a human being and a dream of "The Seven Stages" in which they wander through different lands together or in pairs. "The Seven Ages" is obviously based on Jaques' "All the world's a stage" passage in Shakespeare's "As You Like It", only here the modern man of the twentieth century is presented instead of the Englishman of the 16th century. The first age of infancy and the second age of childhood are described by the four speakers in turn, involving new experiences in life and contacts with adults. The third age of youth tells chiefly of love of different sorts, and then the fourth age of adulthood shows the partings of ways

as one "finds out/ where his world lies." Then a sort of summing-up
for the fifth age is Quant's passage:

> "We move on

> "As the wheel wills, one revolution
> Registers all things, the rise and fall
> In pays and prices, peregrinations
> Of lies and loves, colossal bangs and
> Their sequential quiets in quick order."

The sixth age is well described by Malin:

> "He looks far from well; he has fattened on
> His public perch; takes pills for vigour
> And sound sleep, and sees in his mirror
> The jawing genius of a jackass age,
> A rich bore."

Malin then winds up the seventh age:

> "He is tired out
> His last illusions have lost patience
> With the human enterprise. The end comes; he
> Joins the majority, the jaw-dropped
> Mildewed mob and is modest at last."

And Quant asks Rosetta to sing the whole story of man from birth
to death:

> "With luscious note
> Smoothly sing the softer data of an
> Unyielding universe, youth, money,
> Liquor and love; delight your shepherds
> For crazed we come and coarsened we go
> Our wobbling way; there's a white silence
> Of antiseptics and instruments
> At both ends, but a babble between
> And a shame surely."

Then come the Seven Stages the four characters pass through.
They start from the same mountainous district towards the same valley, and the tumbledown Mariners' Tavern. Then youth and age se-

parate, left and right from the high heartland to the maritime plains. Next from the rival ports two of them take a plane and the other two go by train and all four arrive together at the city, and they visit the different parts of the city together ("Publishing houses, pawnshops and pay-toilets" and hospitals, "Politics free from fevers, Cancer and constipation", and women's prison, slums, suburbs, tenniscourts, greenhouses and vegetable gardens, and the State Asylum), and they finally come to "the big house" which is described as built by some scoundrel with ill-gotten gains, from Quant:

"A scholarly old scoundrel,
Whose fortune was founded on the follies of others,
Built it for his young bride.
She died in childbed; he died on the gallows,
The property passed to the Crown."

And then from Rosetta who views from the outside:

"I have watched through a window a World that is fallen,
The mating and malice of men and beasts,
The corporate greed of quiet vegetation,
And the homesick little obstinate sobs
Of things thrown into being."

They then pass through a graveyard, on the entrance of which the wooden sign reads:

"Here impulse loses
Its impetus; thus
Far and no farther
Their legs, resolutions
And longings carried
The big, the ambitious,
The beautiful; all
Stopped in mid-stride
At this straggling border
Where wildflowers begin
And wealth ends."

Then they again separate, Malin and Emble westward on bicycles and Quant and Rosetta eastward by boat, until they arrive together at the hermetic gardens, with "Special perspectives for speculation", where there are extraordinary charms of "random rose walks, and rustic bridges", a theatre and lawns and the parterre. They feel "uneasy and unwell" and one by one they plunge into the labyrinthine forest and vanish down solitary paths, until they meet again at the forest's edge. In the last lap of the seventh and last stage of their journey the four are beset with fear and doubt, until Quant speaks last:

"God's in his greenhouse, his geese in the world," and they woke up where they were in a booth at the bar and it is closing time.

The last three of the six sections that make up the poem are much shorter and less significant, as the four are on their way to Rosetta's apartment (Part Four: The Dirge), they arrive and talk and then the party breaks up (Part Five: The Masque), and Quant and Malin go back to their own living quarters (Part Six: The Epilogue). After the two long episodes of "Seven Ages" and "Seven Stages", the four are once again brought back from their world of thoughts and of dreams. The dancing and the lovemaking of Rosetta and Emble make them dream of the millennial Earthly Paradise, in Rosetta's and Emble's speeches:

> "The shops which displayed shining weapons
> And crime-stories carry delicate
> Pastoral poems and porcelain groups.
> "Nor money, magic, nor martial law,
> Hardness of heart not hocus-pocus
> Are needed now on the novel earth."

But in the Epilogue, as Quant and Malin are going back to their normal duties in early dawn, they are again fully aware of the realities facing them and so Malin thinks:

> "Do we learn from the past? The police,
> The dress-designers, etc.
> Who manage the mirrors, say — No.
> A hundred centuries hence
> The gross and aggressive will still

Be putting their trust in a patron
Saint or a family fortress,
The seedy be taking the same
Old treatments for tedium vitae,
Religion, Politics, Love."

And he speaks of "the noble despair of the poets":

"We would rather be ruined than changed,
We would rather die in our dread
Than climb the cross of the moment
And let our illusions die."

But finally Malin's thoughts end curiously on the solemn note of Christian faith:

"His Question disqualifies our quick senses,
His Truth makes our theories historical sins,
It is where we are wounded that is when He speaks
Our creaturely cry, concluding His children
In their mad unbelief to have mercy on them all
As they wait unawares for His World to Come."

"The Age of Anxiety" refers to the modern age, especially the years of anxiety that most people felt during and shortly after the Second World War. The poet describes here not those actively participating in the world strife, at least not those presently engaged in the horrible acts of war, yet the four characters, two of them not directly connected with the fighting and the other two (one in the navy and another in the air force) in their momentary respite from active participation in killing or being killed, feel the war in their bones, and though most of the time they indulge, in the course of an evening till dawn, in idle thoughts and fanciful dreams of the seven ages and seven stages of humanity, their feelings of anxiety over the ugly social realities facing the modern world never for a moment leave them. The poet admits the innumerable unpleasant things that worry everybody, but throughout the poem and especially in the last two sections he seems to feel that love should heal the many woes in the world and that Christian religion will eventually bring the ideal "World to come".

The conclusion is abruptly arrived at but it is conclusion never-theless. Auden, like T.S. Eliot, finally turned to Christianity for consolation and solution for the world's wrongs.

Auden's shorter poems after 1950 show the poet's enthusiasm for nature in his old age. "In Praise of Limestone" reveals his fondness for a limestone landscape, with its "surface fragrance of thyme", its "secret system of caves and conduits", its spurting springs and ravine and cliffs, its hilltop temple, and its wild and formal vineyard. It is not always appreciated by the common herd who may prefer "granite wastes", "clays and gravels" and "the oceanic whisper", but for Auden himself:

"What I hear is the murmur
Of underground streams, what I see is a limestone landscape."
A somewhat longer poem containing seven sections but dealing also with Auden's delight in nature is "Bucolics". In all seven sections the natural phenomena, including winds, woods, mountains, lakes, islands, plains and streams, are eulogized together with gods and heroes, Auden's peculiar touch of light humour blended with serious thoughts is always there. So in "Mountains", there is the curious comment on nature and bourgeois civilization.

"A civil man's a citizen. Am I
To see in the Lake District, then,
Another bourgeois invention like the piano?
Well, I won't. How can I, when
I wish I stood now on a platform at Peurith,
Zurich, or any juncture at which you leave the express
For a local that swerves off soon into a cutting? Soon
Tunnels begin, red farms disappear,
Hedges turns to walls,
Cows become sheep, you smell peat or pinewood, you hear
Your first waterfalls."
In "Islands", we find two short stanzas that resemble Chinese poetry with the poet's reflections on well-known figures of the past:

"His Continental damage done,

　　　　Laid on an island shelf,
　　Napoleon has five years more
　　　　To talk about himself.
　　"How fascinating is that class
　　　　Whose only member is Me!
　　Sappho, Tiberius and I
　　　　Hold forth beside the sea."

In "Streams", the first two quatrains give us an extremely simple yet
high praise of clear water in the streams:

　　　　"Dear water, clear water, playful in all its streams
　　　　As you dash or loiter through life who does not love
　　　　　　to sit beside you, to hear you and see you,
　　　　Pure being, perfect in music and movement?
　　　　"Air is boastful at times, earth slovenly, fire rude,
　　　　but you in your bearing are always immaculate,
　　　　　　the most well-spoken of all the older
　　　　Servants in the household of Mrs. Nature."

Auden is certainly a prominent "nature" poet, to whom various
natural phenomena and reflections of well-known historical figures
in connection with their natural environment called for thoroughly
delectable lines in verse.

Auden's poetry in the last twenty years of his long life shows
his complete calm and resignation. In his "Horae Canonicae",
which contains seven detachable pieces on the ostensibly seven periods
of the day assigned to prayer and worship, actually are represented
the lives of city-dwellers not only from dawn to evening and to the
following cockcrow, but also their whole careers from birth to death
are somehow symbolized. "Prime", stands for the dawn, or the
birth, when "the gates of the body fly open to ... the gates of the mind".
"Terce" describes the rise in the morning of the hangman, the judge,
the poet, the Big Ones, as well as each of us. Especially both serious
and comic are the prayers of "each of us" at the moment:

　　　　"Let me get through this coming day
　　Without a dressing down from a superior,

Being worsted in a repartee,
Or behaving like as ass in front of the girls;
Let something exciting happen,
Let me find a lucky coin on a sidewalk,
Let me hear a new funny story."

In other words, the ways of everyday world for the common folk are here well depicted, alongside with those of the Big Ones "Who can annihilate a city" and therefore "cannot be bothered with this moment". Then the third section, "Sext", tells of different people (a cook, a surgeon, a clerk, a besieging general, a bacteriologist, the prosecutor) who are engaged in their vocation, of monuments and odes to be written to the nameless heroes (including "the first flaker of flints/ Who forgot his dinner" and "The first collector of sea-shells" who remains celibate) and of the crowd that does not see "a boring match, a train wreck, a battleship being launched" and is never distracted by "a barking dog, a smell of fish, a mosquito on a bald head"."Nones" reveals a time of rest when all the terrible things taking place in the morning are forgotten and regular business of the day resumes: "The shops will re-open at four/, The empty blue bus in the empty pick Square/Fill up and depart." "Vespers" represents two types of thinkers or dreamers, an Arcadian and a Utopian, and their conflicting likes and dislikes, hopes and fears. "Compline" refers to the end of the day when everything is to be wound up. "Lauds" is very early the next morning when the small birds sing and the cock crows and all men and women are "in solitude, for company." The sections "Terce" and "Sext" are the most interesting because they give the social realities, with comments, while "Vespers" is meditative and reveals truthfully the different dreamers and their different dreams, distinguishing the good old Arcadians and the more modern Utopians, but both being no more than dreamers.

While satires are few and they are never very strong, especially in Auden's later poetry, a rare instance may be found in which the great ones are taken for a ride, as in "The Managers", The poem begins in its very informal tone and style:

"In the bad old days it was not so bad:
      The top of the ladder
Was an amusing place to sit; success
      Meant quite a lot — leisure
And huge meals, more palaces filled with more
      Objects, books, girls, horses
Than one would ever get round to, and to be
      Carried uphill while seeing
Others work.   To rule was a pleasure when
      One wrote a death-sentence
On the back of the Ace of Spades and played on
      With a new deck."

And the poem winds up by showing no sympathy from the people for
what the great ones have to go through in their rule:
      "No; no one is really sorry for their
            Heavy gait and careworn
      Look, nor would they thank you if you said you were."

But the most outstanding feature of Auden's poetry of his last two
decades was his absorbing interest in history. "T The Great" and
"Makers of History" are mild satires mixed with humour, upon the
"great ones", but different from "The Managers", these two poems
link the "magnates" to history.   "T The Great" deals with some tyrant who is feared by everybody:
      "And fugitives, their horse-hooves drumming,
            Cried: — 'Death is on you. T is coming!"
and who is
      "A synonym in a whole armful
            Of languages for what is harmful."

Then T is replaced by N who is to be replaced by S, and T cannot win
Clio's cup again.

    "Makers of History" is more definitely a humorous and sar-
castic sketch of "Greatness" who may have their "obediences/ Before and after" and who may give "four-letter pep-talks to the
troops/ And polysyllabic reasons to a Senate/ For breaking treaties",

yet he is not loved by Clio, for

"these mere commanders,
Like boys in pimple-time, like girls at awkward ages,
What did they do but wish?"

These references to history and indications of the poet's interest in history are summed up as it were in "Homage to Clio" where her "silence" is emphasized again and again and where Clio the muse of history is favourably compared with Aphrodite and Artemis. But Auden does not think the muse of history is favourably disposed toward the poets. He writes at the end of the poem:

"I dare not ask you if you bless the poets,
For you do not look as if you ever read them
Nor can I see a reason why you should."

A much greater poem is "Memorial for the City". Auden had always his great admiration for ancient Greece and Rome, particularly for the city of Rome in its heyday; and he liked to compare the new cosmopolitan city such as New York City where he spent quite a stretch of his life, with the Fall of the City a theme that haunted him often in his later years. In "Memorial for the City" the poet contrasts "Homer's World" with "the ruins of this Post-Virgilian City"; with the Ancient Greeks earth is magnified while

"gods behave, men die,
Both feel in their own small way",

but in the contemporary world, "Our grief is not Greek" and

"We are to pity
Neither ourselves nor our city;
Whoever the searchlights catch, whatever the loudspeakers blare,
We are not to despair."

And the conclusion here is: "The crime of life is not time." Then follows a lengthy account of what happened after the grandeur that was Rome, in European history, from Pope Gregory and the Emperor to Luther and Mirabeau and Napoleon, from the Cathedral and Law Courts and Police Headquarters to the Grand Hotel and the Emergency Committee. The religious undertone runs through the poem as the 2nd section ends with the line:

"Faithful without faith, they died for the Conscious City"
and at the close of the 3rd section, the poet writes:

"No; that is our hope; that we weep and it does not grieve,
    That for It the wire and the ruins are not the end:
This is the flesh we are but never would believe,
    The flesh we die but it is death to pity;
    This is Adam waiting for His City."

And finally in the 4th and last section the spirit of history, of religion, of Christianity which Auden believes in narrates the great names in history and legend and concludes by transcending the delusions of the Great Metropolis:

"As for Metropolis, that too-great city, her delusions are
    not mine.
Her speeches impress me little, her statistics less; to all who
    dwell on the public side of her mirrors resentments
    and no peace.
At the place of my passion her photographers are gathered
    together; but I shall rise again to hear her judged.

"Memorial of the City" is a tour de force that reveals Auden's view of history, particularly of the historical development in the big metropolises of the world, and his Christian belief inevitably is employed in the summing-up though his mildly satirical and frequently humorous comments on historical and legendary figures and events are often very delightfully and aesthetically expressed in rich language and supple verse.

Toward the last years of his life, two poems are significant for their comment on history. "Moon Landing", written in August 1969 after the first visit of the astronauts on the moon, contains the poet's philosophical reflections on that great technological event. He called it "so huge a phallic triumph" and "a grand gesture", but remarked that

        "from the moment

The first flint was flaked this landing was merely
    a matter of time."
He then made a down-to-earth statement:
    Worth going to see? I can well believe it.
    Worth seeing? Mneh! I once rode through a desert and was
      not charmed."
And somewhat cynically he added:
    "Unsmudged, thank God, my Moon still queens the Hea-
      vens as she ebbs and fulls, a Presence to glop at,"
and he wound up with his quiet meditation:
    "Irreverence
    is a greater oaf than Superstition.
    Our apparatniks will continue making
    the usual squalid mess called History:
    All we can pray for is that artists,
    Chefs and saints may still appear to blithe it."
This was an old man's cynicism, one might say, but the poem is one
of significance.

    "Archaeology", Auden's last completed poem, is comparable
perhaps to Tennyson's "Crossing the Bar" and Robert Browning's
"'Epilogue' to 'Asolando'", in that here the poet was already somehow anticipating his death, with this difference that he was here actually commenting on archaeological finds and therefore looking backward rather than forward. In a way this piece reveals to us the old
stable-minded and outspoken poet at his best. He was extremely
sincere when he wrote:
    "guessing is always
    more fun than knowing,"
and
    "When Norsemen heard thunder,
      did they seriously believe
    Thor was hammering?
    "No, I'd say; I'd swear
    That men have always lounged in myths

as Tall Stories."

But the "coda" that concludes the poem betrays the aged poet's look beyond his grave by making his odd comment on history:

"all
our school text-books lie.
What they call History
is nothing to vaunt of,
being made as it is,
by the criminal in us;
Goodness is timeless."

The very last line here and his reference to the Crucified attest to Auden's Christian fervour.

Auden also collaborated with Christopher Isherwood in the writing of three plays: "The Dog beneath the Skin" (1935), "The Ascent of F6" (1937) and "On the Frontier" (1938), and also of a travel book "Journey to a War" (1939) recording their visit together to China. Of the three plays, "The Ascent of F6" is the best known that marked Auden's leanings to the Left in the 1930s, as it had to do with British colonialism. F6 is the name of a mountain dividing the two parts of Sudoland dominated by two colonial powers Britain and Ostria. To settle the dispute between the two countries over the claim of the ownership of the mountain, the natives suggested that the first white man to reach the summit of F6 would be master of both the Sudolands for a thousand years. The British expeditionary force led by Michael Ransom all but reached the top when they were destroyed by an avalanche. The political symbolism here may be clearly seen, with both authors then enthusiasts of the Left.

W.H. Auden was both a British and an American poet. He earned his fame as poet early in life. Born in 1907, he was already known for his verse in the late 1920s and the 1930s. He had a long poetic career of almost half a century which may easily be divided into 2 periods: from the late twenties to the early forties constituted his youthful period of lyricism and inclination to the Left, and from the late forties to the end of his life when he became meditative and an Anglican Christian. He followed chiefly the Germanic tradition, travelling to Iceland and attracted to the Norse sagas in his early youth and then becoming an admirer of Goethe in the sixties. He distinguished himself first with the use of alliterative verse and Skeltonic short lines, and particularly with his mixing of the solemn and the flippant and with his indulgence in odd collocations of words and in a facile conversational style. He was never really a communist and his only truly Left utterance was "Spain 1937" in which he laid his special emphasis on "today the struggle". Otherwise he was a rebel, even in his love poetry, as he eulogizes "faithless" love in his now famous poem that begins:

> "Lay your sleeping head, my love,
> Human on my faithless arm."

And his somewhat juvenile "Letter to Lord Byron" shows very vividly his youthful fling very much in the same humorous satirical strain that Byron was master of in his "Childe Harold" and "Don Juan".

His departure from England to become naturalized in the United States in the crucial years of World War II formed a natural break in his poetic career as well as in his life. He gradually discarded whatever Leftist leanings he had had prior to 1939 and deserted Marxism for Anglicanism, though some of his radical views, not in politics but in social problems, still remained in his poetry. His mildly satirical touches could still be found here and there, and his typical serio-comical style and his eccentric and unconventional phrasing was with him till his old age. He could still be very bitter and dissatisfied with the ways of the modern world, and uttered such sentiments in his verse with little reserve, but now in his hopes for a better future he eventually turned to love and friendship and thence to Christian religion which last was fortunately never very obtrusive. His elegiac poems on his contemporaries such as Yeats, Toller and Freud show his balanced estimates of these men he admired if not befriended, and his appreciations of great writers of the past are often very keen and astute, in the cases of A.E. Housman, Rimbaud, Melville and especially Voltaire. His poetry after the 1950s centred much on the world of nature and on history, showing his fondness and delight in the beauty of nature and making some very penetrating remarks on the development of history. He always wrote in very easy conversational verse curiously studded with delightful and unusual phrasings. He was the greatest of the younger generation of Leftist poets in the late 1920s and the 1930s, outranking Spender, Day Lewis, Isherwood and even MacNeice, but following the Second World War he became a prominent and popular poet in the whole English-speaking world, with his adaptation of many Americanisms and his absorption of expressions even from the musical stage and the Blues singers.

c. Louis MacNeice, Stephen Spender and C. Day Lewis

Three other poets, Louis MacNeice, Stephen Spender and C. Day Lewis, are usually mentioned together with W.H. Auden, for the reason that they four constituted a group of poets of avant-gardism in the late 1920s and the 1930s. While Auden was unquestionably the most outstanding of the circle, not alone because he had a longer poetic career and greater prestige and influence in the United States as well as in England, but also because his early poetry was more original and scintillating and filled with more haunting phrases than the others. MacNeice was possibly the least committed to the Left though more gifted as a poet than Spender or Day Lewis.

MacNeice (1907—63) was born in Belfast, northern Ireland, of Irish parents, his father being a bishop. He was educated in England at Marlborough College and then at Oxford (1926—30), and, being distinguished in his studies in Classics, he lectured on Classics for ten years at the University of Birmingham (1930—36) and at Bedford College for Women, London (1936—40). He was visiting lecturer in poetry at Cornell University in 1940, before he became feature-writer and producer for the British Broadcasting Corporation (1941—49), and was an outstanding writer of radio plays under the title of "The Dark Tower" (1947). In 1950—51 he was director of the British Institute in Athens. In the last year of his life (1963) he was Clark Lecturer at Cambridge University.

MacNeice's poetry was never strongly aimed at social reform though he was ever interested in political affairs. He contributed to the "New Verse", the most important verse-magazine of the thirties which was founded by Geoffrey Grigson in 1933 and which was not really Leftist but only full of "social reference". MacNeice himself had this to say in 1938 in his essay "Modern Poetry" about his ideals of a poet:

> "I would have a poet able-bodied, fond of talking, a reader of the newspapers, capable of pity and laughter, informed in economics, appreciative of women, involved in personal relationships, actively interested in politics, susceptible to physical impressions."

"Informed in economics" and "actively interested in politics" seemed to be as far as MacNeice was willing to go in the sharing of political views of Auden, Spender and Day Lewis, who themselves were not true Marxists though claiming to follow Marx and, curiously enough, also Freud. This was the spirit of the age and many intellectuals quite naturally toed the line somewhat.

MacNeice translated "The Agamemnon of Aeschylus" (1936) and Goethe's "Faust" in an abridged form (1951), "The Poetry of W.B. Yeats" (1941) and "Varieties of Parable" which included essays on Spenser, Herbert, Becket, etc.

In 1936 he travelled to Iceland with Auden, and the journey was responsible for their joint effort, "Letters from Iceland" (1937). He also wrote a poetic drama "Out of the Picture" (1937) which was strongly influenced by the collaborate plays of Auden and Christopher Isherwood. From 1938 to 1961 he published nine volumes of verse, of which "Autumn Journal" (1939), "Ten Burnt Offerings" (1951) and "Autumn Sequel" (1954) contained long poems. His unfinished autobiography, "The Strings Are False", appeared posthumously in 1965.

The most effective and best known poem of MacNeice's is "Bagpipe Music", most frequently anthologized and rightly. Though the poem is only humorously satirical, yet the irony is that of a revolutionary socialist to whom the enticements of wealth and pleasure and the appeasements of mild reforms and temporary reliefs are far from satisfactory. The background is Scotland, therefore "bagpipe music" which stands for the outward show of mirth to simple-minded Scottish nationalists. On the one hand, the poet condemns the ostentation of the rich and the barbarism of the ruling class in the first two stanzas, culminating in the line about the corpse, "Sold its eyes for souvenirs, sold its blood for whisky", while on the other hand he utters the bitter remarks of the poor and the wretched:

> "All we want is a bank balance and a bit of shirt in a taxi",
>
> "Mrs. Carmichael had her fifth, looked at the job with repulsion,
> Said to the midwife, 'Take it away; I am through with overproduction'."

and

> "It's no go the Government Grants, it's no go the elections,
> Sit on your arse for fifty years and hang your hat on a pension."

The choice of apt words for satirical phrasing and easy-going rhythm in irregular rhymes further add to the force of the irony in the verse.

There is some peculiar charm to be found in MacNeice's early poetry. In "Snow", the poet's reaction to the snow and pink roses separated by the great bay-window was:

> "World is suddener than we fancy it."

and

> "World is crazier and more of it than we think,
> Incorrigibly plural."

and when the author peels a tangerine and spits the pips, he feels

> "The drunkenness of things being various."

Here we have striking ideas in striking phrasing that distinguish MacNeice.

Similarly, in "Sunday Morning", when the poet listens to the playing of music or drives out fast to an outing, he feels he

"can abstract this day and make it to the week of time
A small eternity, a sonnet self-contained in rhyme."

Or in "The Sunlight on the Garden", the author tells of the odd impression he gets from the sunlight on the garden:

"The sunlight on the garden
Hardens and grows cold,
We cannot cage the minute
Within its nets of gold;
We cannot beg for pardon."

The years of World War II had their grim stamp on Mac-Neice's mentality. "Brother Fire" records ironically his personal experience during the London blitz in 1943. He calls the enemy bombers "a dog":

" 'Give the dog a bone' — and so we gave him ours;
Night after night we watch him slaver and crunch away
The beams of human life, the tops of topless towers."

He writes more bitterly in "The Mixer", in which the mixer or wanderer was an unfortunate participant in both the world wars, so though he survived the first one:

"Behind his eyes are shadows of a night
In Flanders but his mind long since refused
To let that time intrude on what came after."

The second war was too much for him:

"So in this second war which is fearful too,
He cannot away with silence but has grown
Almost a cipher."

But the bitterest of his war poems was entitled "Charm", in which the speakers of the poem came to the Thames but "all/ The bridges were down", and as they were forced to take the ferry "there was the ferryman just as Virgil/ And Dante had seen him", and the ferryman said coldly: "If you want to die you will have to pay for it."

Melancholy found its expression in other ways in MacNeice's poems. In "Entirely", the poet suggests that it is impossible for any one to understand life wholly. One learns very little from the great thinkers:

"When we try to eavesdrop on the great
Presence it is rarely
That by a stroke of luck we can appropriate
Even a phrase entirely."

It is equally difficult to be entirely satisfied with love:

"almost hourly
Bell or siren banishes the blue
Eyes of Love entirely."

And the poem concludes by declaring no right path to be chosen for one's life:

"but in brute reality there is no
Road that is right entirely."

MacNeice also shows his gift in making effective character sketches such as we find in a poem entitled "Les Sylphides". Here a short-sighted man takes a girl to a ballet and without the help of eyesight his imaginative powers enable him to enjoy the show and make his evening together with her a big success. And then the poet's irony has its full play in the last two stanzas:

"So they were married — to be the more together —
And found they were never again so much together,
Divided by the morning tea,
By the evening paper,
By children and tradesmen's bills.

"Waking at times in the night she found assurance
In his regular breathing but wondered whether
It was really worth it and where
The river had flowed away
And where were the white flowers."

Here MacNeice was really touching upon a rather universal theme of so many marriages in all time and space.

"Prayer Before Birth" is perhaps almost a misanthropic piece which seems to suggest that it would be better not to be born. Possibly the second stanza of the poem tells the bitterest tale:

"I am not yet born; console me.
I fear that the human race with tall walls wall me,
With strong drugs dope me, with wise lies lure me,
On black racks rack me, in blood-baths roll me."

And the last two lines of the verse run thus:

"Let them not make me a stone and let them not spill me,
Otherwise kill me."

Despite his religious family background, MacNeice abandoned Christianity early. He never was a Marxist, though he claimed Marx's influence and Freud's. He had the Irish wit as well as Irish melancholy, and many of his early poems were meditative and his war poems showed his bitter attitude toward the two wars, especially the second one. He grew especially pessimistic in his last years. As a poet of the avant garde group of the 1920s and 1930s he is only second to Auden in his poetic gift, though both of them could not be compared with either Spender or Day Lewis in their heyday of Leftism in the 1930s.

Stephen Spender was born in London in 1909, son of a prominent Liberal political journalist Harold Spender who was connected with the London newspapers and with the Manchester Guardian and was a biographer of great political figures in Britain "Herbert Henry Asquith" and "David Lloyd George". He attended University College School in London and then University College at Oxford. He was a contemporary of Auden and MacNeice while at Oxford, editing "Oxford Poetry" with MacNeice in 1929 and sharing the Leftist views of Auden, MacNeice and especially C. Day Lewis. He travelled widely in Europe and outside it, and in the 1930s was a regular contributor to "New Verse" and "New Writing". In the mid-1930s, like many other progressive intellectuals of the West Spender went to Spain to fight on the republican side.

In 1938 in his "Trial of a Judge" which he chose to call "A Tragedy in Five Acts", he expressed the anti-totalitarian feelings then in England. However, his fervour in the thirties for a new world of political and economic justice was not purely Marxist, but in his early critical work, "The Destructive Element" (1935), he argued for the combination of Marxist views with those of Freud, a viewpoint not uncommon among Western intellectuals in the period between the two world wars. But in 1946, in his critical book "Poetry since 1939", Spender looked back upon W.H. Auden and the poets of the thirties, and he gave a perhaps accurate description of the group of four poets, Auden, Louis MacNeice, C. Day Lewis and himself:

"In the thirties there was a group of poets who achieved a very wide reputation as a 'school' of modern poetry. They were not in a deliberate sense a literary movement; they were rather a group of friends, contemporaries at the Universities of Oxford and Cambridge, influenced by each other in a personal way.... They had certain ideas in common. They consciously attempted to be modern, choosing in their poems imagery selected from machinery, slums and the social conditions which surrounded them. ... Their poetry emphasized the community, and, overwhelmed as it was by the sense of a command disease, it searched for a communal cure in psychology and leftist politics. ... To a great extent, their poetry, though leftist, expressed the problem of the liberal divided between his individual development and his social conscience."

During the Second World War he served as a fireman in the National Fire Service in London and later became "a small hack of a war-time branch of the Foreign Service" (in the poet's own words). In 1939—41 he worked together with Cyril Connolly, a well-known author, in the editing of "Horizon", and in 1953—67 he was co-editor of a monthly publication "Encounter" to which contributions were made by Virginia Woolf, Christopher Isherwood,

351

Cecil Day Lewis, as well as the English poet Edith Sitwell and the famous Algerian writer Albert Camus. In 1947 Spender was a Counsellor for the Section of Letters, UNESCO. He also taught poetry in the American universities of Cincinnati and California, in 1953 and 1959, respectively. He himself explained his change from intense interest in politics to more personal matters by saying that the war compelled him to turn from outward events to search for "a universal experience through subjective contemplation."

Spender's poems are often confessional, especially so with his early pieces. "My parents kept me from children who were rough" gives minute psychological analysis of the poet as a small boy, when he fears the lithe, strong-sinewed and tough children of the lower classes on the one hand, and yet he is rather conscience-stricken at the unnatural class-barrier that prevents him from being friends with them. The last two-and-a-half lines of the 3rd and last quatrain of the poem reveal very effectively the mental contradictions of the poet:

> "They threw mud
> While I looked the other way, pretending to smile.
> I longed to forgive them, but they never smiled."

Another poem, "What I Expected", shows how Spender's early expectations met with setbacks. While he was

> "Expecting always
> Some brightness to hold in trust,
> Some final innocence
> Exempt from dust,"

what actually happened

> "Was the gradual day
> Weakening the will
> Leaking the brightness away,
> The lack of good to touch,
> The fading of body and soul."

The rise of Fascism in Europe in the 1930s was responsible for some of the most powerful of Spender's poems. In "Perhaps" references are made to Chancellor Dollfuss and the Reichstag Fire, while "Van der Lubbe" is supposed to be the ironic speech of the defiant victim of German fascism before a fake trial. Of the many protests of World War II and especially of 'fascist concentration camps and of the London Blitz (including "Thoughts during an Air Raid", "Air Raid across the Bay at Plymouth", "A Man-made World", "Memento", "Epilogue to a Human Drama", and "Ultima Ratio Regum"), "Ultima Ratio Regum" (a Latin phrase meaning "The Ultimate Argument of Kings" and here referring to cannon) contains a very effectively-worded first stanza:

> "The guns spell money's ultimate reason
> In letters of lead on the Spring hillside.
> But the boy lying dead under the olive trees
> Was too young and too silly
> To have been notable to their important eye.
> He was a better target for a kiss."

whereas the fate of the victims at Belsen and Buchenwald Concentration Camps was most grimly described in "Memento":

> "Their eyes sunk jellied in their holes
> Were held up to the sun like begging bowls
> Their hands like rakes with finger-nails of rust
> Scratched for a little kindness from the dust
> To Many, in its beak, no dove brought answer."

But the subtlest accusation was to be found in "The Double Shame" where the damage caused by the bombings is indirectly related through the objects left over from the burning which took the toll of the owners:

> "Solid and usual objects are ghosts,
> The furniture carries cargoes of memory,
> The staircase has corners which remember
> As fire blows reddest in gusty embers,
> And each empty dress cuts out an image
> In fur and evening and summer and spring
> Of her who was different in each."

Spender's Leftist sympathies were most obvious in his poems describing the sufferings of the poor and the miserable. In the poem "Moving through the silent crowd", which gives an indelible picture of the unemployed workers,

"They lounge at corners of the street
And greet friends with a shrug of shoulder
And turn their empty pockets out,
The cynical gestures of the poor."

In "An Elementary School Classroom in a Slum", the poor school- children's pallid, twisted faces are first described with vividness, then the room with its sour cream walls and a map is depicted, and the miseries of the children are summed up in one very succinct line: "All of their time and space are foggy slum". Then in the last stanza the poet bursts forth with his hopes for the children:

"Unless, governor, teacher, inspector, visitor
This map becomes their window and these windows
That shut upon their lives like catacombs,
Break O break open till they break the town
And show the children to green fields, and make their world
Run azure on gold sands, and let their tongues
Run naked into books, the white and green leaves open
History theirs whose language is the sun."

In another poem, "A Footnote (from Marx's chapter, 'The Working Day')", Spender wrote again on poor children, this time childlabourers, with such striking lines as:

"Stunted spirits in a fog
Wearing pits and mills
Into tapestries of smoke,
You whisper among wheels
Calling to your stripped and sacred mothers
With straps tied round their waists
For dragging trucks along a line."

Spender also wrote with great sympathy on prisoners. In "The

Prisoners", there is an effective stanza on their miserable existence

> "They raise no hands, which rest upon their knees,
> But lean their solid eyes against the night,
> Dimly they feel
> Only the furniture they use in cells."

And then follows a summing-up of the whole lives of these prisoners:

> "Their Time is almost Death. The silted flow
> Of years on years
> Is marked by dawns
> As faint as cracks on mud-flats of despair."

What is even more striking is Spender's lament on the defeated heroes (including Lorca and Fox) of the Spanish Civil War, in "The Fall of a City". This poem has too much of sadness attached to the defeat, with the saving grace coming in the last stanza:

> "But somewhere some word presses
> On the high door of a skull, and in some corner
> Of an irrefrangible eye
> Some old man's memory jumps to a child
> Sparks from the days of energy.
> And the child hoards it like a bitter toy."

These are memorable poems of the Leftist movement among the intellectuals of the West in the 1930s, and Spender headed the list of his group in this Leftism if not anywhere else.

As a poet Spender has a lyrical side to be remembered. "The Landscape near an Aerodrome" gives a vivid picture of the landing of an air-liner:

> "More beautiful and soft than any moth
> With burring furred antennae feeling its huge path
> Through dusk, the air-liner with shut-off engines
> Glides over suburbs and the sleeves set trailing tall
> To point the wind. Gently, broadly, she falls
> Scarcely disturbing charted currents of air."

And then after full descriptions of the travellers and the landscape they observed, the landing is finally accompanied by the tolling of bells, and at the very end of the piece, the poet ironically magnifies the influence of Religion with the huge church that blocks out sunlight,

> "To where, louder than all those batteries
> And charcoaled towers against that dying sky,
> Religion stands, the Church blocking the sun."

Spender also went in for love poetry. In "The Room above the Square", he bewails his lost love in three lyrical stanzas by first reminiscing the original light in the room above the Square and then witnessing the falling of the light and finally climbing along to the high room alone:

> "Now I climb up alone to the high room
> Above the darkened square
> Where among stones and roots, the other
> unshattered lovers are."

The best specimen of Spender's love lyrics is the song, "Stranger, you who hide my love." Comparable to Auden's "Lay your sleeping head, my love", this lyric deals also with inconstancy in love and with arguments on its behalf. The first stanza of the poem is a perfect twentieth-century equivalent of hedonism in love to Herrick's "Gather Ye Rosebuds While Ye May" or even Donne's "Go and Catch a Falling Star". Written nearly three centuries later than either poem named above, Spender's version necessarily is conveyed through more complicated reasoning and suggestive phrasing though lyricism is still present in its abundance:

> "Stranger, you who hide my love
> In the curved cheek of a smile
> And sleep with her upon a tongue
> Of soft lies that beguile,
> Your paradisal ecstasy
> Is justified is justified
> By hunger of all beasts beneath
> The overhanging cloud

> Who to snatch quick pleasure run
> Before their momentary sun
> Be eclipsed by death."

In a way this is more forceful than Auden's lyric, not only because the doubling up of "is justified" shows the author's emphasis but also the mention of "hunger of all beasts ... to snatch quick pleasure" before death produces a more direct image of animalism and accentuates the brevity of human existence. But the crowning glory of the poem lies in its last stanza, which leads one to the dreamland or timeless land:

> "Oh, but supposing that I climb
> Alone to a high room of clouds
> Up a ladder of the time
> And lie upon a bed alone
> And tear a feather from a wing
> And listen to the world below
> And write round my high paper walls
> Anything and everything
> Which I know and do not know."

The oldest of the group of four Leftist poets in the 1930s is Cecil Day Lewis (1904—1972). He was born in Ireland and was educated at Sherborne School and Wadham College, Oxford. He edited "Oxford Poetry" with Auden in 1927, and then taught at schools in Oxford and Helensburgh and then at Cheltenham until 1935. After that he embarked on a writer's career, writing poetry under his own name and using the pseudonym of Nicholas Blake for his numerous detective novels. He was known as a left-wing poet, together with Auden and Spender, and like them he dropped his radical political views during World War II and turned to traditional poetry to express his personal thoughts and feelings. During the war he was employed at the Ministry of Information and was busy with lecturing and broadcasting besides writing. He had a big poetic output besides translating Virgil's *Aeneid*. He was the immediate predecessor of Auden as Professor of Poetry at Oxford in 1951—55, and was made Poet Laureate in 1968. His early volume "The Magnetic Mountain" (1933) was significant at the time of its publication on account of the "social reference" contained in many of the poems therein.

"You that Love England", an outstanding poem in "The Magnetic Mountain", shows Day Lewis persuading his readers to go Left. The 1st, 2nd and 3rd stanzas all end with a line or two of exhortation to seek a new faith. The 1st stanza ends with calling the readers' attention to "the entrance of a new theme?" The 2nd stanza calls them to "seek a new world, a saviour to establish /Lost-lost kinship and restore the blood's fulfilment." The 3rd stanza asks the readers: "Only/Submit to the visiting angel, the strange New healer". Then at the close of the fourth and last stanza, the readers are told to be prepared for revolution:

> "Need fight in the dark no more, you know your enemies.
> You shall be leaders when zero hour is signalled,
> Wielders of power and welders of a new world."

In a simpler poem "Where are the War Poets?" Day Lewis puts everything in a more outright way:

> "They who is folly or mere greed
> Enslaved religion, markets, laws
> Borrow our language now and bid
> Us to speak up in freedom's cause.
> "It is the logic of our times,
> No subject for immortal verse —
> That we who lived by honest dreams
> Defend the bad against the worse."

Though these as poems are not great poetry, yet the stirring spirit of the intellectuals of the 1930s for some radical change is clearly expressed here.

Day Lewis' later verse fell back into the old rut of the Georgian poets of the early years of the century, and so unlike Auden and MacNeice, or even Spender, had hardly anything to redeem itself. Occasionally he could rise to meditative verse as in his sequence of sonnets on childhood, entitled "O Dreams, O Destinations", and still rarer do we find a poem like "Nearing Again the Legendary Isle", in which he satirizes the chorus girls on the stages of the modern West by comparing them ludicrously to the sirens in ancient Greek mythology. The poem is especially poignant with meaning when the ones the modern sirens try to lure are mostly poor labouring folk ("Hunger and sweat have stripped us to the bone") and the chorus girls past their prime ("Voices grow shrill and paint is wearing thin") are also objects of the poet's sympathy rather than scorn. In a sense this is a satire on modern Western civilization, or at least on one aspect of it.

d. Hugh MacDiarmid

Hugh MacDiarmid (1892—1978), pseudonym of Christopher Murray Grieve, was born in the small town of Langholm, Dumfriesshire, Scotland, within a short distance of the English border and the home of the great Border ballads. His father came from a family of mill-workers while his mother was of peasant origin. He was proud of his working-class inheritance and of the Scottish "frontier spirit" and "Border life", as he stated clearly in his autobiographical work "Lucky Poet: A Self-study in Literature and Political Ideas" (1934). His father being a rural postman and the family living in the post-office buildings, he had constant access to the Langholm library upstairs with its 12,000 books. He first attended Langholm Academy and then the University of Edinburgh. During World War I he served with the Royal Army Medical Corps in Salonika, Greece, and then in Italy and France.

As early as his mid-teens he followed the socialist movement of the day and for decades afterwards he continued to participate in the movement as journalist, public speaker and literary critic. Then after his demobilization in 1920, he joined the fight for political and cultural independence for Scotland, serving as editor of "The Scottish Chapbook" (1922—23), "The Scottish Nation" (1923), and "The Northern Review" (1924), and making re-evaluations of modern Scottish literature and culture in his "Contemporary Scottish Studies". Then after making a complete reassessment of Scotland, politically and culturally, in "Albyn, or Scotland and the Future" (1927), he and Cunninghame Graham, Compton Mac-Kenzie and Erskine of Mar founded in 1928 the National Party of Scotland, from which he was expelled four years later when it was taken over by the moderates. In the meantime he also took up the writing of lyrical poetry, and his two early volumes of verse, "Sangschaw" and "Penny Wheep" came out respectively in 1925 and 1926, as well as his long poem and acknowledged masterpiece "A Drunk Man Looks at the Thistle" (1926).

In 1934 the poet joined the Communist Party but was expelled in 1937 for his Nationalist deviation, was reinstated on appeal and then was expelled again in 1938, and later in 1957 he rejoined. However, he always worked for the Communist cause not only to be testified by his three "Hymns" to Lenin but also in his many other poems preaching Marxism. From 1933 to 1942, as a result of his explosive writings and revolutionary activities that offended the ruling class, he retreated with his second wife Valda Trevlyn to a remote island of Whalsay in the Shetlands, where they lived in abject poverty in a small cottage amidst wild nature and in isolation from the outside world. However, while he acquired there peculiar interests in people and objects of nature including herring fishers and stones and the raised beach, he still kept himself aware of the Spanish Civil War and German Fascism in the late 1930s and early 1940s.

In 1942 he took up a war job in a Clydebank munitions factory in Glasgow and then joined the Merchant Service to work on ships in the Clyde estuary. In the 1950s he travelled extensively to the Soviet Union and China and almost every European country and lectured in Canada and the United States. His fame came to him late, as he received the honorary LLD from the University of Edinburgh in 1957 and was Professor of Literature at the Royal Scottish Academy in 1974. He was even awarded a Civil List pension in 1951, but even this in no way diminished his attacks on the governmental authorities or the ruling class as a whole. He has been considered the greatest Scottish poet since Burns.

MacDiarmid's Scottish Nationalism (or patriotism) and his Marxism went hand in hand, in complete accord one with another, just as his role as a revolutionary and that as a poet were ever consistent rather than otherwise. In his early collection of lyrics, "Penny Wheep" (1926), in a poem entitled "Gairmsboile" he already declared his faith in Scotland, particularly in her past and her future:

"For we ha'e faith in Scotland's hidden poo'ers,
The present's theirs, but a' the past and future's oors."

In his long poem-sequence published as early as 1926, "A Drunk Man Looks at the Thistle", MacDiarmid made frequent references to Scotland, with the Drunk Man as symbol of the poet and the thistle as the national emblem of Scotland. While in this long poem MacDiarmid spoke frequently of Burns and other Scottish heroes and writers, William Wallace, John Knox, G.K. Chesterton, Dunbar and of the Scottish battles for independence at Flodden and Bannockburn, on several occasions he also expressed his hopes for Scotland: "the time may be

When Scotland sall find oot its destiny,"

and:

"No Edinburgh Castle or the fields
O'Bannockburn or Flodden
Are dernin' ur' the miskent soul
Scotland sae lang has hod'n."

Yet he is hoping against hope, as it were:

"O Scotland is
The barren fig.
Up, Carles, up
And roond it jig.
Auld Moses took
A dry stick and

Instantly it
Floo'ered in his hand.
Pu' Scotland up,
And who can say
It winna bud
And blossom tae.
A miracle's
Oor only chance:
Up, Carles, up
And let us dance!"

In his next long poem-sequence "To Circumjack Cencrastus" (1930), in a brief poem entitled "Lourd on My Hert", he showed his despair for Scotland:

"Lourd on my hert as winter lies
The state that Scotland's in the day.
Spring to the North has aye come slow
But noo dour winter's like to stay
For guid,
And no' for guid!"

Then in the third and last stanza, some one yells that the dawn is coming, but actually it turns out to be just more snow.

Aside from many allusions and references to his Border antagonism toward English oppression throughout the different periods of his verse, MacDiarmid often thought of the past grandeur of Scotland in contrast with the miserable present as he ended his poem entitled "Hostings of Heroes":

"But in the place of all this
What have we today?
Dingy parades of vermin!
Details of the English army
In clothes the colour of excrement;
....
God! What a crawl of cockroaches!"

And from his younger days to his old age, he ever aspired for true independence and freedom for Scotland. In an early lyric, "Separatism", he wrote:

> "If there's a sword-like sang
> That can cut Scotland clear
> O'a' the warld beside
> Rax me the hit o't here.
> "For there's nae jewel till
> Frae the rest o'earth it's free,
> Wi' the starry separateness
> I'd fain to Scotland gie ...."

In a slightly longer poem, "Unconscious Goal of History", he again expressed his hope:

> "That wi' a new vitality may endower
> My thieveless country: ...
> ...
> Sae that my people frae their living graves
> May loup and play a pairt in History yet
> Wi' sufferin's mair like a Genius's than a slave's"

Again in "Behind the Symbols", he wished:

> "Let the hearts of my people be lifted up
> Once more with the daily sight
> Of an eagle wheeling on majestic vans
> That is our Scottish birthright.
> "Fill their lives again with the noblest form
> At liberty in Europe still —
> The red stag pausing with lifted hoof
> On the sun-assailing hill."

He had such great love for his native country that he sometimes identified himself completely with Scotland. In "Conception", he declared:

> "indeed I could not be myself
> Without this strange, mysterious, awful finding
> Of my people's very life within my own
> — this terrible blinding discovery

Of Scotland in me, and I in Scotland."

Even in his old age, as late as 1966, he showed his genuine affection in a poem "A Change of Weather (Scotland: February 1966)"; while recording the February scene in Scotland with deep feelings, he turned his thoughts inevitably to Scotland in the third stanza:

"Yet thinkin' o' Scotland syne's like lookin'
Into real deep water whaur the depth
Becomes sae great it seems to move and swell
Withoot the slightest ripple, yet somehoo gi'e me
An unco sense o' the sun's stability
And fills me, slowly, wi' a new ardour and elasticity."

And he wrote frequently on the two biggest cities in Scotland, Edinburgh and Glasgow, and bewailed the degeneracy in both. In a very short poem "Edinburgh Toun", he recorded the brutal shooting of the working class by the police there:

"O Edinburgh toun, Edinburgh toun,
Police are setting sleet-boxes roun
To shoot the workin'-classes doun
Under a Chief Constable."

In "Edinburgh", the poet made a more thoroughgoing condemnation of the wicked "capital of Scotland" as

"Dark symbol of a society
Of 'dog eat dog'"

And he mentioned the corrupting forces or "all the darkness of industrialism" in the terrible city:

"So the social corpse, the dead class,
The dead mode of life, the dead religion,
Have an after life as vampires."

However, he still had hopes for Edinburgh:

"So the mighty impetus of creative force
That seeks liberation, that shows even through
The scum of swinish filth of bourgeois society,
The healthy creative force will break through
— even in Edinburgh — and good, human things grow,

Protecting and justifying faith
In regeneration to a free and noble life
When labour shall be a thing
Of honour, valour, and heroism ..."

Yet for the people in Edinburgh the poet showed his great sympathy, so in "Talking with Five Thousand People in Edinburgh" (1945), he deplored, "There is no one really alive in Edinburgh yet", and mentioned their common failings:

"the same unresolved discords,
The same sultry hates, the same murderous impulses
Below the surface of decorous lives, the same
Hopeless struggle against an evil no one dares name".

and also

"the mutual criticisms,
The sneers, the belittlings, the cynical acceptances,
Misunderstandings, indifferences, looking down their
   noses,
Pursing their mouths, giving meaning looks, till I saw
   all these people
As specialists in hates and frustrations, students of help-
   less rages,
Articulators of inarticulate loathings".

He realized that

"the trouble was no one knew where the centre lay
Of the system of discontent in which they were pent,"

that "Edinburgh is no worse than anywhere else", while he again expressed the hope:

"Edinburgh is capable here and now of a human life
As illimitably greater than any it has yet known,
As any human being's is to the lowest order of animal
   existence."

Though in the poem MacDiarmid mentioned the great Scottish communist fighter Maclean, and Marx and "The Red Flag", he made a very elusive remark concerning his belief in Communism:

> "I must be a Bolshevik
> Before the Revolution, but I'll cease to be one quick
> When Communism comes to rule the roost,
> For real literature can exist only where it's produced
> By madmen, hermits, heretics,
> Dreamers, rebels, sceptics."

MacDiarmid also wrote about Glasgow. In "Glasgow, 1960" he merely recorded what he saw in the city after many years of absence, and showed his disgust at the meaningless ways of life there not unsimilar to what he had witnessed before his "long exile". In "In the Slums of Glasgow" the poet instead of writing of the miseries of the slum-dwellers emphasized rather the multiform individuals and ways of life in the slums very much the same as elsewhere, only the shining light of human soul being more easily visible in the slums because

> "Life is more naked there, more distinct from mind,
> Material goods and all the other extraneous things that
> grow
> Hardening over and hiding the sheer life."

But it is in the "Third Hymn to Lenin" that MacDiarmid touched on the essential evils of the capitalism in Glasgow. However, this will be dealt with later.

MacDiarmid regarded himself as a Marxist as early as 1932, and formally joined the Communist Party in 1934. Though his expulsion from the Party on account of his Nationalism may not be well grounded, yet he was certainly not very strict in his belief in Marxism. Most outstanding are his three "Hymns" to Lenin, aside from his numerous references to Lenin and Marx and also Stalin in his poems through the decades. In a well-known poem "The Seamless Garment", published in the same year as "First Hymn to Lenin" (1931), he mentioned Lenin in the same breath as the famous Austrian lyric poet (Rainer Maria Rilke) whose poetry he compared with "A seamless garment o' music and thought". Here Lenin was praised as "at home with" "working class life", and Lenin's "secret" is said to be about "the coordination atween/ Weaver and machine." In "First Hymn to Lenin", MacDiarmid compared Lenin to Christ and pointed out that "You [i.e. Lenin] mark the greatest turnin' point since him [i.e. Christ]". He then compared Lenin to great poets:

> "I glimpse again in you that mightier poo'er
> Than fashes wi' the laurels and the boys
> But kens that it is shared by ilka man
> Since time began."

And then he declared that people now turned to Lenin:

> "For now in the flower and iron of the truth
> To you we turn; and turn in vain nae mair,
> Ilka fool has folly eneuch for sadness
> But at last we are wise and wi' laughter tear
> The veil of being, and are face to face
> Wi' the human race."

In "Second Hymn to Lenin", MacDiarmid again placed Lenin beside poets and writers:

> "Ah, Lenin, you were richt. But I'm a poet
> (And you c'ud make allowances for that!)
> Aimin' at mair than you aimed at
> Tho' yours comes first, I know it."

Here the third line seems to value a poet higher than Lenin, but the fourth line immediately makes the correction by giving first place to Lenin's aims. The whole poem seems to deal with the comparison of Lenin's contribution to that of the poets, and occasionally poetry seemed to take a prior place to politics:

> "Sae here, twist poetry and politics,
> There's nae doot in the en'.
> Poetry includes that and s'ud be
> The greatest poo'er amang men."

And the last two lines of the poem even more definitely suggested superiority of poetry to politics though Lenin's approval is here appealed to:

"Ah Lenin, politics is bairns' play
   To what this maun be!"
However, the true intent of the author in the poem is quite clearly
to ask of poets to acquire "Lenin's vision" in order to give great
power to their poetry; in other words, the writer is here talking
about poetry and in his opinion Lenin's teachings are of first im-
portance to the poets if the latter are to truly exert their great in-
fluence in the world. This is quite obvious if we examine carefully the
four important middle stanzas in the poem:
   "Poetry like politics maun cut
   The cackle and pursue real ends,
   Unerringly as Lenin, and to that
   Its nature better tends,
   "Wi' Lenin's vision equal poet's gift
   And what unparalleled force was there!
   Nocht in a' literature wi' that
   Begins to compare.
   "Nae simple rhymes for silly folk
   But the haill art, as Lenin gied
   Nae Marx-without tears to workin' men
   But the fu' course instead.
   "Organic constructional work,
   Practicality, and work by degrees;
   First things first; and poetry in turn
   'll be built by these."
"Third Hymn of Lenin" begins with a reference to Glasgow, but
quickly turns to a powerful eulogy of Lenin:
   "On days of revolutionary turningpoints you literally
         flourished,
   Became clairvoyant, foresaw the movement of classes,
   And the probable zigzag of the revolution
   As if on your palm;
   Not only an analytical mind but also
   A great constructive, synthesizing mind

Able to build up in thought the new reality
As it must actually come
By force of definite laws eventually,
Taking into consideration, of course,
Conscious interference, the bitter struggle
For the tasks still before the Party, and the class it leads
As well as possible diversions and inevitable actions
Of all other classes, — Such clairvoyance is the result
Of a profound and all-sided knowledge of life
With all its richness of colour, connexions and relations."

This is truly high praise of Lenin, to be found in no other poem by a poet of MacDiarmid's magnitude in twentieth-century Britain.

And the poet goes on to speak of "the logic of your speeches", "like some all-powerful feelers/ Economic, political, ideological", and makes an appeal to Lenin to solve the problems in Glasgow as he solved those in Russia:

"Be with me, Lenin, reincarnate in me here,
Fathom and solve as you did Russia erst
This lesser maze [i.e. Glasgow, or Scotland], you greatest
    proletarian seer!"

Then the author proceeds to give a terrible picture of modern Glasgow, and Scotland:

"The whole of Russia had no Hell like this.
There is no place in all the white man's world
So sunk in the unspeakable abyss.
Only a country whose chief glory is the Kirk,
A country with our fetish of efficiency and thrift,
With endless loving sentiment to mask the facts,
Has such an infernal masterpiece in its gift.
"A horror that might sicken your stomach even,
The peak of the capitalist system and the trough of Hell,
Fit testimonial to our ultra-pious race,
A people greedy, lying, and unconscionable
Beyond compare."

The poet continues to give full descriptions of the slums of Glasgow in contrast with the lives of the ruling class. Finally the poem ends with another song to Lenin:

"Spirit of Lenin, light on this city now!
Light up this city now!"

Lenin was frequently mentioned in MacDiarmid's verse aside from the three "Hymns", but was most highly praised in "Krassivy". Here the poet declared that if you inquired about Lenin of a Russian woman who had been a young girl in 1917,

"Her eyes lighted up and her reply
Was the Russian word which means
Both beautiful and red.
Lenin, she said, was 'Krassivy, Krassivy' "

Finally, "The Skeleton of the Future", a poem written "at Lenin's Tomb", should be mentioned, where the poet spoke of "The eternal lightning of Lenin's bones."

MacDiarmid made several mentions of Marx in his verse, and he declared himself a Marxist, but he revealed his belief in Marxism nowhere more strongly than in the poem, "And, Above all, My Poetry is Marxist". There, after stating that great poets like Wordsworth, Keats, Rimbaud and Milton all "undergo a kind of crisis in their art," the poet made his powerful declaration:

"Fools regret my poetic change — from my 'enchanting
early lyrics' —
But I have found in Marxism all that I need —
...
It only remains to perfect myself in this new mode.
This is the poetry I want — all
I can regard now as poetry at all,
As poetry of today, not of the past,
A Communist poetry that bases itself
On the Resolution of the C.C. of the R.C.P.
In spring 1925: "The Party must vigorously oppose
Thoughtless and contemptuous treatment

Of the old cultural heritage
As well as of the literary specialists ...
It must likewise combat the tendency
Toward a purely hothouse proletarian literature'."

And MacDiarmid remained a Marxist after the "red decade" of 1930s, when a number of other British poets deserted the Marxist cause, as he wrote in "Third Hymn to Lenin":

"Auden, Spender, those bhoyos,
All yellow twicers: not one of them
With a tithe of Carlile's courage and integrity."

MacDiarmid also addressed a poem to Stalin. In "Lamb Dearg Aboo (To Stalin)", he salutes Stalin as he calls into mind this old battle-cry of the Scottish people "Lamb Dearg Aboo" and the several struggles of Scottish Gaels for independence and freedom from "the English, Money, the Church and the Law" from 1645 and 1745 to 1945. He affectionately links Scotland with Stalin by pointing out:

"Ah, Stalin, we Scots who had our first home
In Caucasian Georgia like yourself see how
The processes of history in their working out
Bring East and West together in general human triumph
now —
— Lamb dearg aboo!"

And this Scottish battle cry of "Lamb dearg aboo" means "The Red Hand to Victory."

And because of his strong faith in Communism, MacDiarmid praised highly the Scottish Communist John Maclean(1879—1923) who died for his Communist activities. Besides being mentioned elsewhere in MacDiarmid's verse, two special poems were written on John Maclean. In the longer poem, "John Maclean, (1879—1923). Maclean is called

"One of the few true men in our sordid breed,
A flash of sun in a country all prison-grey,"

and the poet calls

"For vengeance on the murderers of John Maclean,"
and declares that

"Scotland will think yet of the broken body
And unbreakable spirit, Maclean, of you,
And know you were indeed the true tower of its strength."

Then in a shorter poem "Krassivy", John Maclean was mentioned together with Lenin. Here MacDiarmid considered Maclean as "the greatest" name in Scotland, "next to Burns", and he ended the poem by stating:

"John Maclean too was 'krassivy, krassivy',
A description no other Scott has ever deserved."

Though MacDiarmid never was a very strict Marxist, nor did he participate in many revolutionary activities for the socialist or communist cause as he did for Scottish Nationalism, he saw through the cruel oppression and exploitation in the capitalist society and attacked the social evils in his verse. As early as 1926, in his masterpiece "A Drunk Man Looks at the Thistle", he described vividly the General Strike of 1926, praised it and deplored its failure. He first spoke of the ugly reality in Britain:

"Sae ran the thocht that hid ahint
The thistle's ugsome guise,
'I'll brak' the habit o' my life
A worthier to devise.
'My nobler instincts sall nae mair
This contrar shape be gi'en
I sall nae mair consent to live
A life not fit to be seen!"

Then he referred to the outbreak of the General Strike as "a rose"!

"Till a' at aince a rose loupt oot
— I watched it wi' surprise.
"A rose loupt oot and grew, until
It was ten times the size
O' ony rose the thistle afore
Hed heistit to the skies.

372

> "And still it grew till a' the buss
> Was hidden in its flame.
> I never saw sae braw a floo'er
> As yon thrawn stock became.
> "And still it grew until it seemed
> The haill braid earth had turned
> A reid reid rose that in the lift
> Like a ball o' fire burned."

Then the sudden collapse of the General Strike was bewailed:

> "Syne the rose shrivelled suddenly
> As a balloon is burst;
> The thistle was aghaistly stick,
> As gin it had been curst."

The poet's sympathy for the Strike is too obviously revealed here.

MacDiarmid very frequently indulged in satire in attacking capitalist exploitation and social injustice. In "Joy in the Twentieth Century", the first stanza tells of the general joy:

> "Life isn't so bad, life isn't so bad,
> No matter what the pessimists say
> Every now and again the general heart
> Goes up like a lark soaring light and gay."

Then in the second stanza, after mentioning

> "the glad cries
> Of hundreds of thousands of men and their families,"

the poet comes out with the "great tidings":

> "Today the Railwaymen get a twopenny rise!"

Then in the third and final stanza the irony is driven home.

> "It seemed as though the very sun
> Had multiplied itself. A penny had been
> Great tidings; whole twopence is enough
> To dazzle the entire terrestrial scene."

In another short poem "Reflections in an Ironworks", MacDiarmid followed in the tradition of Shelley and Ernest Jones in their poems "To the Men of England" and "The Song of the Lower Classes" respectively by pointing out that the workers of military weapons are producing these weapons for the ruling class to use, as he wrote:

> "You are still only putty that tyranny rolls
> Between its fingers! You makers of bayonets and guns
> For your own destruction! No wonder that those
> Weapons you make turn on you and mangle and murder —
> You fools who equip your otherwise helpless foes!"

MacDiarmid occasionally spoke very sharply against government oppression and on the miseries of the poor. In "Think Not That I Forget", he declared sweepingly:

> "There are buildings in every town where daily
> Unthinkable horrors take place."

He mentioned "cruelty and lust and filth", "Corruption and lawmade crime", and he condemned the crimes of war:

> "All 'gallant soldiers' murdering for pay"

and

> "heroic airmen blithe to give
> Poor tribes Death from the air,"

and he called the readers' attention to the responsibility of the crimes resting chiefly upon the aristocrats:

> "These Yahoos belong to no single class.
> You'll find far more in proportion to numbers
> In palaces and west-end clubs than in the mass."

In another poem "The Glass of Pure Water", MacDiarmid particularly emphasized the miseries of the slum people, "of the poor people of all the world", and called aloud "for the ending of all Government", "Since all Government is a monopoly of violence". He declared with vehemence that:

> "the hellish interests of private property
> In land, machinery, and credit
> Have corrupted and concealed from the sun,

From the gestures of truth, from the voice of God,
Hundreds upon hundreds of millions of men,
Denied the life and liberty to which they were born."
But the poet still entertained hopes for the poor and miserable. In
"The Belly-Grip", he expressed the wish:
"Come let us finish the whole damned farce
Of law and order on murder based,
On the power to coerce and starve and kill,
With all its hypocrisy, cruelty, and waste;
And safe from all human interference give
Every man at least ample means to live."
He hoped that
"Our kings and statesmen in a few years will all dwindle
To nothing, big though they may loom today,"
and he predicted the eventual riddance of Mosley and Lloyd, Mac-
Donald, Baldwin and Thomas, leading politicians in Britain in
the 20th century.

MacDiarmid also satirized against the Christian Church.
Especially in "After Two Thousand Years", he pointed out sarcas-
tically: "The Christians have had two thousand years.
And what have they done? —
Made the bloodiest and beastliest world ever seen
Under the sun."
And then he ridiculed in turn Christian banks, Christian churches
and bishops, with the bitterest irony. MacDiarmid wrote much
about the Civil War in Spain in the 1930s and against Fascism. In
a poem written during the Spanish War, "Fascists, You Have Kill-
ed My Comrades", he started with a strong denunciation:
"Fascists, you have killed my comrades
And their wives and children!
You have killed them!
It were better that you should all rot in your vices,
In the bottomless filth of damnation,
And that they should live!"

Then he added:

> "Take your victory — I fling it to you as a bone
> Is flung to a pack of snarling curs.
>
> Cannibals, blood-suckers, carrion beasts
> That feed on the dead."

Finally, in a "postscript" written two years after the war, he eulogized Spain and the International Brigade:

> "Spain! The International Brigade! At the moment it seems
> As though the pressure of a loving hand had gone,
> ...
> My hands that were full of love
> Are empty again ... for a while,
> For a little while!"

There is another poem by MacDiarmid entitled "The International Brigade" which begins:

> "Honour forever to the International Brigade!
> They are a song in the blood of all true men."

The poet enumerates with much affection the different characteristics of men of different nations that made up the brigade: the Swiss, the Poles, the English, the Bulgarians, the Spanish, the French, the Americans, the Germans and the Italians, and refers to the battle of Guadalajara that "brought face to face/Anti-Fascists Italians fighting" and "Italians sent to Spain/ To fight in a cause completely unknown to them", "to shed their blood/For Spanish generals, bishops, and big landowners." Then he declares:

> "No man worth calling a man can deny
> The wonder and glory of the International Brigade,
> They will live in history forever.
> ...
> The fire of life woke and burnt in these men
> With that clear and passionate flame
> That can only burn in those whose hearts are clean."

A longer poem entitled "Major Road Ahead" was written by Mac-

Diarmid soon after the end of the Spanish Civil War. The poet wrote,
"They are gone." Then:

"They were the people of destiny.
Of destiny, not fate.

...

In the presence of the fact
There is nothing to do
But bow the head.

...

They were people of more than genius or talent,
They were people of electricity.

...

They were faith.
Ardour transfigured by faith,
The unconsciousness of faith,
The madness of faith which multiplies strength
And knows no possible barrier."

After this admission of defeat and this exaltation of the fighters,
the poet sums up the situation and looks ahead:

"It was not logical that the Spanish workers should fight
  one against ten
Against World Fascism. — But so it was,
It was not logical that they should contend
Against superior numbers, superior armaments, superior
  civilisation.
But it was so. And in the end
It will be seen that they have won,
And are consubstantial with all that has ever really lived
And lives forever as part and parcel
Of the very meaning and purpose of life.
An imperishable honour to man;
One of the greatest turning points in human history
When mankind was faced at last with the sign:
                    MAJOR ROAD AHEAD.

The Battle continues.

For the spirit knows no compromise."

Another poem eulogizing the International Brigade is entitled "An English War-Poet". Though the poem primarily deals with an English poet Siegfried Sassoon who took part in the First World War and whose poem "Sherston's Progress" was here criticized by MacDiarmid for the inadequate portrayal of the weakened pacifist George Sherston, yet here the author took the occasion to praise once again The International Brigade as

"men who passionately believed
In the cause for which they fought;"

and he declared at the end of the poem:

"And the war in Spain ...
Will never end till they win it,
Since they fight for Spain and not
Just for Castles in Spain."

These are certainly among the most memorable passages on the glories of The International Brigade in the Spanish Anti-Fascist War, ever written by a European poet of high standing.

Another anti-Fascist poem by MacDiarmid is "In Memoriam Garcia Lorca". The poet first praised the great Spanish poet and spoke of his death:

"Lorca's love of his people, clear in his writings,
Met with a passionate response. His songs and ballads
Were quickly caught up all over revolutionary Spain.
The Fascist henchmen could never forgive
His popularity and devotion to the people.
They shot him and made a bonfire of his books
On Carman Square in Granada.
'Fear not! This debt we shall repay!'
Lorca's poetry, however, can never be silenced.
It will continue to blow as free as the wind
Over the wide spaces of heroic Spain.
Lorca, dead, lives forever.

> The poet has been turned into earth and silence,
> Yet every day he dies and resuscitates in the heart of
>   Spain,
> In the heart of the world, because today the world
> Bleeds and throbs together with the people of Spain."

Then the poem ends with the author's sharp condemnation of the Spanish fascists who killed Lorca:

> "I cannot utter any words but this:
> Murderers! Murderers!"

Though MacDiarmid claimed to be a Marxist, yet he was first of all a poet. There is, however, no discrepancy between his role as Marxist and that as poet, for he followed Marxist teachings not only in his own poetry but also in his theorizings about what a poet should do and what good poetry should aim to be. He not only declared his poetry to be Marxist,in the poem "And, above all, my poetry is Marxist", but in a number of his other poems on the role of poets and poetry he invariably negated the neutral role of art and of poetry and insisted that poetry should deal with burning social problems of the day. In "The Black Guards", MacDiarmid spoke against "the poetry of War and Civil War everywhere/ The poetry of the world-wide Night of the Long Knives", against the Muses seized by "The Black Guards — Finance, Religion, Law, Capitalist Culture", and he advocated what he called "my poetry of World Consciousness."

In "Against Infantilism", MacDiarmid fought against the "bourgeois notions":

> "That art must be neutral, equally indifferent
> To good and evil, knowing no pity, no anger,"

and

> "That human nature cannot be changed".

He also fought against the "decrepit terms"

> "Of realism, romanticism, classicism,
> Naturalism, and all the witless rest
> Of isms, flourishing in the parent mire of scholasticism"

as well as "narcissism", "the primary capitalistic neurosis". He also condemned the Scottish writers who were

> "forced
> Either to distort the content of Scottish life
> In order to make it conform
> To some desperate personal wish- fulfilment
> Or flee from it entirely — into the past,
> Into fantasy, or some other reality-surrogate."

He also criticized severely "the so-called/ Middle class vanguard" with:

> "Its essential moral weakness and above all
> Its intellectual poverty thinly coated
> By a veneer of artistic sophistication",

so that

> "literature and art can be nothing
> For them except day-dreams or 'shots' in the arm".

Against all this terrible reality in the world of art or poetry around him, the author insisted that

> "Art must be related to the central issues of life,
> ......
> A Dundee jute mill, Singer's, Beardmore's,
> The ghost towns, ruined fishing villages, slave camps,
> And all the derelict areas of our countryside."

and declared that

> "The writer not first and foremost concerned with these
> Lacks the centrality that alone can give
> Value to his work — he is a trifler, a traitor,
> To his art and to mankind alike,
> A fool choosing flight and fantasy,
> Not to be pitied, but despised."

Then he pointed out:

> "It is a lying cry to say
> That human nature cannot be changed.
> It can be, and is being, completely."

He spoke emphatically:

> "Outside the revolutionary movement there is no place
> For any writer worth a moment's thought."

So he urged

> "The radicals' enthusiasm
> For social transformation — the revolutionists'
> Advocacy of profoundly-altered social systems."

And he affirmed that

> "There is a vast accumulation
> Of evidence from the sociological sciences,
> Politics, the philosophy of history, to substantiate
> The necessity, the sanity and the wisdom
> Of deep changes in all institutions, customs,
> Habits, values — in short, civilizations.
> Human nature is the last thing we need to worry about."

And the author ends the poem by calling upon Scottish writers that

> "The height and depth of your writings
> Will be measured by the extent to which
> The dialectic of our era find expression
> In the artistic imaginary — how widely, forcefully, clearly
> ...
> The burning contemporary problems are expressed in it,
> The class war, the struggles and ideals
> Of the proletariat bent on changing the world,
> And consequently on changing human nature."

So in the poem entitled "Poetry and Propaganda", MacDiarmid first told the true poet that

> "His place is not with lads and ladies
> And millionaires and learned men
> Enough to prove himself among them,
> And turn his back upon them then
> And join the people among whom
> Alone the Muse's wings have room."

Then he declared that it was impossible to
> "imagine any worthy son
> Addressed in compliment to such
> Or allied to exploitation and social wrong,"

that
> "slavery none can extol today
> Nor chant in favour of charming wage-cuts
> Nor sing of tyranny's bracing sway,"

and that
> "They do not sing of sound finance
> Or praise wage-slavery openly."

And at the end of the poem MacDiarmid equates poetry with propaganda by announcing:
> "In short, any utterance that is not pure
> Propaganda is impure propaganda for sure,"

This is surely a fatal blow at the bourgeois theory that poetry should not be propaganda.

As a poet MacDiarmid had much affection for other poets. First of all, there is John Davidson (1857—1909), a fellow Scottish poet with his "materialistic and rebellious philosophy", for whom a special elegy of affectionate intimacy was written, "Of John Davidson" (1932). A much higher estimate was given to Rilke's poetry which was one of the major themes in "The Seamless Garment" (1931) where Rilke's poetry is compared with "a seamless garment o' music and thought" and Rilke's name is mentioned alongside of Lenin's.

Of the Scottish poets, Burns was referred to again and again in MacDiarmid's verse, always with much affection and respect, especially in his masterpiece "A Drunk Man Looks at the Thistle", where he was referred to as "Rabbie". Of contemporary writers, MacDiarmid showed his closeness to James Joyce and W. B. Yeats, and also to T.S. Eliot, while of the great Russian writers to whom he showed his respect the name of Dostoevski was the most frequently mentioned in MacDiarmid's verse.

MacDiarmid's long years of secluded life at Whalsey in the remote Shetland Islands had their strong impact upon his later poetry, though in his early lyrics he already showed his deep interest in wild nature and his inclination toward philosophizing. One short lyric in his first volume "Sangschaw" (1925), entitled "The Bonnie Broukit Bairn" (words in Scots dialect meaning "The Pretty Neglected Child"), is an innocent, almost childlike song on earth, a planet completely neglected by Mars and Venus and the Moon. "The Watergaw", a dialect word meaning an "indistinct rainbow", is another brief lyric that describes most vividly the poet's wonder-struck sight of a rainbow with its shivering light above the on-set of rain ("A watergaw wi' its chittering licht/ Ayont the on-ding") and his thought ever after of that foolish light and its possible meaning. And the expression of there being no smoke in the lark's house that night ("There was nae reck i' the laverock's hoose/That nicht") to indicate a dark and stormy night, to be followed by "an' nane i' mine" ("and none in mine", to indicate my heart was dark and stormy too), is both picturesque and thought-provoking. A more philosophical early poem "The Eemis Stane" compares the world with an unsteady stone ("eemis stane") swaying in the sky, and the stone calls into the poet's mind "eerie memories" falling like a blizzard ("yowdendrift") so that he could not read the words cut out in the stone even if the moss ("fug") of fame and the lichen ("hazel-raw") of history had not buried ("yirdit") them. In his first volume of verse the poet seemed to be more impressed by the moon than by any other object of nature. "Au Clair de la Lune" contains four lyrics. In the first piece "Prelude to Moon Music", the first stanza deals with the transitoriness of human history:

"Earth's littered wi' larochs [i.e. fragments] O' Empires,
Mackle nations are dust.
Time'll meissle [i.e. crumble] it awa', it seems,
And swell nae must [i.e. bad smell]."

And the second stanza alludes to the music coming from the moon:

"But wheest! [i.e. hush] — whatna music is this,

> While the win's haud [i.e. held] their breath?
> — The Moon has a wunnerfu' finger
>   For the back-lill [i.e. thumb-hole on bagpipe chanter]
>   o' Death!"

The second piece of the series, "Moonstruck", describes the moon seeing the poet and straightway leaping ("loupit") clean on the quick of his heart and giving him a start, and the third and last stanza tells the effect of this upon the poet:

> "An' the roarin' o' oceans noo'
> Is peerieweerie [i.e. dwindled to a thread of sound] to me:
> Thunner's [i.e. thunder's] a tinklin' bell: an' Time
> Whuds [i.e. flits] like a flee [i.e. fly]."

MacDiarmid's sojourn at Whalsey enabled him to meet many country-folk remote from "civilization", who left their vivid impressions upon the poet and consequently were very affectionately described in his verse. In "With the Herring Fishers" and "Off the Coast of Fiedeland", the herring fishers and the poet's fishing expeditions with them are faithfully recorded with much nostalgia and accompanied with philosophical remarks of some depth. Especially in the latter poem, the theme of innocent love between "a workin' lad and a workin' lass" is introduced with strong feelings:

> "An' I'll sail Earth's seas as lang as I maun
> Mixin' my blood wi' the bitterest brine
> If that is the only airt I can win
> At last to mixin' my blood wi' thine."

> "For a workin' lad and a workin' lass
> Can lo'e each ither juist at least as weel
> As Royalty or the wealthiest folk
> Or onybody trained in a public skeel."

A longer poem, "Island Funeral", deals with the simple country people and the remote island environment in a detailed account of a funeral procession in an island village. There is the procession winding "like a little snake"; there is the "grey world" where "sea and sky/ Are colourless as the grey stones"; there are "the men in the stiff material/Of their homespun clothes" walking "with the springing step of the mountaineers", and the women wearing "black shawls,/ And black or crimson shirts"; there is also "a line of tawny seaweed" fringing the bay "between high-water mark and low"; there is the crowd pouring "from the narrow lane/Into the cemetery"; there is the coffin lying "tilted a little sideways/On the dark grey sand flung up from the grave"; there is the little priest reading "the Latin prayers" and the dead woman's son handing a bottle to the priest who then twice "sprinkles the coffin and the grave/ with holy water"; there are "believers and unbelievers" among the mourners; there are four gravediggers filling in the grave "with dark grey sand" and an old man with a yellow beard helping them "in levering a great slab of stone/Until it lies flat upon the grave"; then finally there is the crowd scattering east and west and the four gravediggers "laughing now/With the merriment of clowns". After this rather lengthy, vivid description of the funeral procession and the burial, the poet philosophizes on the deserted state of the island:

"There are fewer and fewer people
    On the island nowadays,
And there are more ruins of old cottages
    And occupied homes."

He recalls that

"Fifty years ago a visitor wrote: 'They are there to stay
And that fact accounts for a great deal.
It is partial explanation of the contentment
On the faces of the island women.
It is a reason for the repose and settledness
Which pervades an island village.
...

There is no restlessness,
Or fret of business
Or anxiety about anything.
It is as if the work was done,
And it was one eternal afternoon'."

But he bewailed the fact that:

> "There is little life left on the island now,
> And soon the last funeral
> Will take place there,
> And in the rowdy chaos of the world
> The sound of this cornet will be heard no more
> — One will listen and one's face will never
> Light up with recognition and appreciation again."

However, the poet claimed:

> "Materialism promises something
> Hardly to be distinguished from eternal life.
> ...
> — The minds or souls of these old islanders —
> Have existed during an eternal time in the past
> And will exist for an eternal time in the future."

And he predicted:

> "The cornet solo of our Gaelic islands
> Will sound out every now and again
> Through all eternity.
> I have heard it and am content for ever."

"Island Funeral" is a nostalgic eulogy of some remote island north of Scotland where the poet once lived with joy.

In another poem of some length "Direadh III", MacDiarmid wrote rhapsodic passages on his visit to Direadh:

> "Here in this simple place of clean rock and crystal water,
> With something of the cold purity of ice in its appearance,
> Inhuman yet friendly,
> Undecorated by nature or by man
> And yet with a subtle and unchanging beauty
> Which seems the antithesis of every form of art,
> Here near the summit of Sgurr Alasdior
> The air is very still and warm.
> The Outer Isles look as though
> They were cut off of black paper

And struck on a brilliant silver background,

....

The western sea and sky undivided by horizon,
So dazzling is the sun
And its glass image in the sea.

...

I lie here like the cool and gracious greenery
Of the water-crowfoot leafage, streaming
In the roping crystalline currents,
And set all about on its upper surface
With flecks of snow blossom that, on closer looking,
Shows a dust of gold."

And in such a setting the poet indulged in philosophical speculations:

"It is easy here to accept the fact

...

The class state, the church,
The old-fashioned family and home,
Private property, rich and poor,
'Human nature' (today meaning mainly
The private-profit motive), their own race,
Their Heaven and their 'immortal soul',
Is all potently evanescent,
Even as we know our fossil chemical accumulations
Of energy in coal, peat, oil, lignite and the rest
Are but ephemeral, a transitory blaze
Even on the small time-scale of civilized man."

And then the sight of "the flight of a bird" suddenly reminds the poet of the far away and the long ago, "to fly away"

"To the distant Adriatic and the cypress-fringed waters
    of Eridanus
Or to the fabulous Hesperides,
Where beside the dark-blue ocean
Grow the celestial apple-trees."

And he added:
> "I again felt the mind of the poet reaching out
> Across the centuries to touch mine.
> Scotland and China and Greece!"

And with his love for Scotland and "the Gaelic genius", he ended the poem by resting his faith on what is eternal:
> "Let what can be shaken, be shaken,
> And the unshakable remain."

This beautiful poem, linking MacDiarmid's panegyric on beauty of nature with his philosophical meditations and patriotic sentiments is certainly one of the best specimens of modern English lyricism.

MacDiarmid also wrote some beautiful poems on wild nature such as he recalled from the memories of his life in Whalsay. In "Mirror Fugue" he gives a delightful picture of the gulls he once saw:
> "While I've seen a wheen gulls
> Seem to equal the croods,
> O' the white waves by joinin'
> Hands wi' the cloods [i.e. clouds],
> Till atween them they've made
>   A complete and clean
> Heavenly facsimile
> O' the hydrosphere
> — Till the shapes in the lift [i.e. sky]
> And the seas' wild smother
> Seemed baith to mak'
> And to mirror each other."

In "The Storm-Cock's Song", the poet compared his song to a storm-cock's:
> "My song today is the storm-cock's song.
> When the cold winds blow and the driving snow
> Hides the tree-tops, only his song rings out
> In the lulls in the storm. So let mine go!"

In the 4-lined poem "On the Ocean Floor", the author sang of

"the lightless depths" that lie beneath the waves and of the
"tiny shells incessantly raining
On the ocean floor as the foraminifera die."
In "Bagpipe Music", MacDiarmid sang ecstatically of the many
flowers and of the bagpipes comparable to them:
"Flowers. A flower-bed like hearing the bagpipe."
and then:
"The bagpipes — they are screaming and they are sorrowful.
There is a wail in their merriment, and cruelty in their
triumph,
They rise and they fall like a weight swung in the air at
the end of a string.
They are like the red blood of those peonies.
And like the melancholy of those blue flowers.
They are like a human voice — no! for the human voice
lies!
They are like human life that flows under the words.
That flower-bed is like the true life that wants to express
itself
And does ... while we human beings lie cramped and
fearful."
But most thoughtful and philosophical and most poetically
beautiful is his speculative poem on stones: "On a Raised Beach". The
poet first compared "the inward gates of a bird" to those of stones:
"The inward gates of a bird are always open.
It does not know how to shut them.
That is the secret of its song,
But whether any man's are ajar is doubtful.
I look at these stones and know little about them,
But I know their gates are open too,
Always open, far longer open, than any bird's can be,
That everyone of them who has had its gates wide open
far longer
Than all birds put together, let alone humanity,

Though through them no man can see,
No man nor anything more recently born than themselves
And that is everything else on earth."
Then he further speculates on the essence of stones:
"We are so easily baffled by appearances
And do not realize that these stones are one with the
stars.
It makes no difference to them whether they are high or
low,
Mountain peak or ocean floor, palace, or pigsty.
There are plenty of ruined buildings in the world but no
ruined stones.
No visitor comes from the stars
But is the same as they are.
He thinks of the indispensability of stones and their longevity of
existence and unchangeability, and their importance to human
beings:
"But the world cannot dispense with stones.
They alone are not redundant.

These stones go through Man, straight to God, if there
is one.
What have they not gone through already?
Empires, civilizations, aeons.

... The moon moves the waters backwards and forwards.
But the stones cannot be lured an inch further
Either on this side of eternity or the other.

......
What happens to us
Is irrelevant to the world's geology
But what happens to the world's geology
Is not irrelevant to us.
We must reconcile ourselves to the stones,

Not the stones to us.

...

These stones have the silence of supreme creative power.
The direct and undisturbed way of working
Which alone leads to greatness.

...

These bare stones bring me straight back to reality.
I grasp one of them and I have in my grip
The beginning and the end of the world,
My own self, and as before I never saw
The empty hand of my brother man,
The humanity no culture has reached, the mob."

The poet even related the stones to the meaning of life and death:

"I lift a stone; it is the meaning of life I clasp
Which is death, for that is the meaning of death;

...

Each of these stones on this raised beach,
    Every stone in the world,
Covers infinite death, beyond the reach
Of the dead it hides;

...

No heavier and colder and quieter then,
No more motionless, do stones lie
    In death than in life to all men."

The poetic flight of fancy is surely most admirable in a poem
like this, and this is a good specimen of meditative verse by a twentieth-century poet.

MacDiarmid's best known poem is "A Drunk Man Looks at
the Thistle", written in Lowland Scots when he was 23 and published separately in 1926. In this long dramatic monologue of a
poem the drunk man was the poet himself and the thistle stands
for Scotland, and so the themes dealt with here are of a great variety, from his expressions of national pride to his criticisms on
certain aspects of Scottish life, from his comment on his own life

and experience in love to his affiliation with his kindred souls, poets like Burns and Dunbar and T.S. Eliot and Shakespeare and different writers from different lands Spengler and Nietzsche, Carlyle and G. K. Chesterton, Melville and Hawthorne, Tolstoi and Dostoevski, especially Burns and Dostoevski, and finally from his desultory remarks on Christianity to his speculations on mysteries of time and death and fate. He bewails the passing of the past glories of Scotland:

> "Sic transit gloria Scotia — a' the floo'ers
> O' the Forest are wede awa!"

He writes yearningly of Burns:

> "Rabbie, wad'st thou wert here — the warld hath need,
> And Scotland mair sae, o' the likes o' thee!"

He recalls affectionately his "bonnie lass" who's gone away:

> "The munelicht's like a lookin'-glass,
> The thistle's like mysel',
> But whaur ye've gane, my bonnie lass,
> Is mair than I can tell."

Then as a drunk man he sees a thistle and compares it to all sorts of fantastic things:

> "Grinnin' gargoyle by a saint,
> Mephistopheles in Heaven,
> Skeleton at a tea-meetin'
> Missin'-link — or creakin'
> Hinge atween the deid and livin."

He comments bitterly on Scotland, on Edinburgh and Glasgow:

> "What are prophets and priests and kings,
> What's ocht to the people o' Scotland?
> ...
> And Edinburgh and Glasgow
> Are like ploomen in a pub."

He sometimes wonders at the thistle and at life and death and God and man:

> "The thistle like a snawstorm drives,

> Or like a flicht o' swallow lifts,
> Or like a swarm o' midges hings,
> A plague o' moths, a starry sky,
> But's naething but a thistle yet,
> And still the puzzle stands unsolved.
>
> Beauty and ugliness alike,
> And life and death and God and man,
> Are aspects o't but nane can tell
> The secret that I'd fain find oot
> O' this bricht hive, this sorry weed,
> The tree that fills the universe,
> Or like a reistit herrin' crines."

Especially toward the last part of the long poem, the poet expresses again and again his patriotic sentiments toward Scotland:

> "Whatever Scotland is to me,
> Be it aye pairt o' a' men see
> O' Earth and o' Eternity.
> Wha winna hide their heids in 't till
> It seems the haill o' space to fill,
> As t'were an unsurmounted hill.
> He canna Scotland see wha yet
> Canna see the Infinite,
> And Scotland in true scale to it."

And he declares the duty of a Scottish poet:

> "A Scottish poet maun assume
> The burden o' his people's doom,
> And dee to brak' their living tomb.
> Mony ha'e tried, but a' ha'e failed,
> Their sacrifice has nocht availed.
> Upon the thistle they're impaled.
> You maun choose but gin ye'd see
> Anither category ye
> Maun tine your nationality."

MacDiarmid is therefore first of all a Scottish poet who loved his native land and his people, but he is also an inspired poet who has love and sympathy for all the down-trodden people in the world and has his great speculative thoughts of affection and understanding for the world of nature, for fishes and fowls and flowers and even stones.

e. Dylan Thomas

Dylan Thomas (1914—1953) was born in Swansea, Wales, and was educated at Swansea School. He worked for a time as a newspaper reporter in Wales. His early verse "The Eighteen Poems" appeared in 1934, followed by "Twenty-five Poems" (1936) and "The Map of Love" (1939), and they attracted much notice, partly because he followed the tradition of Welsh bardic poetry which was written to be sung or recited and of which the charm lay in the chime of rhyme and alliteration, partly because he fell under the influence of "sprung rhythm" of Gerard Manly Hopkins with not only alliteration but also internal rhyming   but chiefly on account of the strange violence of his imagery. He then went to London and still lived largely on journalism, reviewing for newspapers and magazines. During the war he was rejected for the army and worked for B.B.C. and did screen work and even in the post-war years he was reputed as a script writer for screen and radio and as a broadcaster. His bohemianism and fatalistic addiction to alcohol both before and after the war, and his later lecture tours in the U.S.A. (1950—53), where he made effective readings of his own and other poeple's poetry, led to many legends about him, and after his later poems "Deaths and Entrances" appeared in 1946, he was acclaimed a great poet on both sides of the Atlantic, but he died suddenly and prematurely in November 1953 in New York, possibly as a result of his alcoholism. A year after his death, in 1954, his most famous work, the radio play "Under Milk Wood" was first broadcasted by the B.B.C., then staged for a short run and finally published. It was sub-titled "A Play for Voices" and the life of a Welsh small coastal town named Llaregyb was described by different

Voices. The narrative begins with the First Voice and Second Voice about the town on a moonless night in spring, then the Voices of dreaming inhabitants and of the dead are given. With the arrival of morning, blind Captain Cat and the local bard, the Rev. Eli Jenskins of Bethesda House describe the natural beauty of the locality, and then the business of the day and the gossip and memories of the men and women there are related through speeches and songs of a schoolmaster, a domestic servant, a baker, a postman, an undertaker and several other women. The story ends with the end of the Spring day and the sleeptime for the town's inhabitants. The play was most effective on the radio, through hearing, and not so effective in reading.

Dylan Thomas' boyhood must have had its great effect upon him, as a number of his better poems were based on his reminiscences of early childhood, such as "The Hunchback in the Park", "Fern Hill", and "After the Funeral" (subtitled "In Memory of Ann Jones"). "The Hunchback in the Park" is an extremely vivid character sketch of a hunchback that the poet must have remembered from his childhood, and was written in the Welsh bardic tradition, with seemingly impersonal portrayal but with much latent sympathy.

"All night in the unmade park
A solitary mister
Propped between trees and water
From the opening of the garden lock
That lets the trees and water enter
Until the Sunday sombre bell at dark"

This poem has the distinction of the almost total absence of punctuation marks, there being only 2 full-stops in seven stanzas of 6 lines each and no commas at all. This is of course one characteristic of Welsh bardic poetry which also often pays little attention to formal grammar, and thus adds to obscurity in meaning.

"Fern Hill" is a rhapsodic poem on Dylan Thomas's innocent and joyous childhood when he seemed to be extremely free in his enjoyment of nature. Here it's the happy, unconventional and entangled expressions that are particularly delightful, though they are occasionally obscure. So the poem begins with two simple yet thought-provoking lines:

"Now as I was young and easy under the apple boughs
About the lilting house and happy as the grass was green."

Here the house becomes "lilting" and "grass was green" in order to identify everything with happiness. Similarly, "all the sun long", "all the moon long", "happy as the heart is long", "in the moon that is always rising" and "Time held me green and dying", all these expressions have their peculiar charm of suggestiveness and poetic fancy though they are not exactly grammatical or idiomatic.

"After the Funeral", written in memory of Ann Jones who was the poet's aunt, is one of Dylan Thomas's great poems that shows his poignant feelings of affection for the deceased with a realistic record of his childhood reminiscences. Here the poet recalls the details of the burial connected with his aunt Ann Jones and considers himself her bard to sing of her virtues and to compare her real self when alive with the stone statue at her grave. The aunt's figure, humped and with her flesh "meek as milk" and her scrubbed and "sour humbled hands", is very vividly pictured with much affection, showing her to be a poor, simple, withered woman worthy of respect but eulogizing her very highly in such lines as

"Whose hooded, fountain heart once fell in puddles
Round the parched worlds of Wales and drowned each
sun"

and

"that her wood-tongued virtue
Babble like a bellbuoy over the hymning heads,
Bow down the walls of the ferned and foxy woods."

It is a simple poem, but the poet's genuine affection for a simple country woman is overflowingly expressed in the numerous details chosen in connection with her life and her funeral.

Perhaps the chief reason of Dylan Thomas' fame as a poet

lies in the strange violence of his imageries that stem from his fiery passion and rebellious spirit in connection particularly with the problem of life and death. One of his best-known poems is "A Refusal to Mourn the Death, by Fire, of a Child in London". This is a striking "refusal", but the poet tries to justify it by looking at the problem of death in connection with all mankind, by suggesting that unless and until the universal problem of death is solved he shall not "mourn the majesty and burning of the child's death", adding that:

"Deep with the first dead lies London's daughter",
and concluding with:

"After the first death, there is no other."

In verse style, in the first six lines of the poem there are definite echoes of Gerard Manly Hopkins' "sprung rhythm",

"Never until the mankind making
Bird beast and flower
Fathering and all humbling darkness
Tells with silence the last light-breaking
And the still hour
Is come of the sea tumbling in harness."

The use of "darkness" to modify the three phrases "mankind making", "bird beast and flower fathering" and "all humbling" piled on top of one another, as well as the repeated employment of alliteration are a little confusing but the whole thing can be very effective if read aloud properly.

Another powerful poem was one written for the poet's dying father, "Do Not Go Gentle into That Good Night." Here the poet's rebellious spirit that manifests itself in his call on his father to defy death at the last moment is expressed in calm but at the same time violent words, and here for once there's no obscurity in word or meaning. The title "Do Not Go Gentle into That Good Night", repeated five times in the poem, and its accompanying line of violence "Rage, rage against the dying of the light", repeated four times, together suggest very definitely that before death there should be a struggle, whether you be wise man (2nd stanza), good men (3rd stanza), wild men (4th stanza) or grave men (5th stanza), and then in the 6th and last stanza of the poem the poet's father on his dying bed is directly addressed,

"Curse, bless, me now with your fierce tears, I pray.

Do not go gentle into that good night.

Rage, rage against the dying of the light."

This poem is thus another piece on the problem of death which seemed to be forever and very strongly engraved in Dylan Thomas's mind.

But Dylan Thomas's attitude was not always a negative, or pessimistic one, for he understood the biological theory of indestructibility of matter, that things animate and inanimate live and grow and die and turn into some other things, and so death is not necessarily the end of everything and at least that is one of the reasons why he refused to mourn the death of a child by fire. In a poem "This Bread I Break", he traced the bread coming from the oats and the wine coming from grapes, and in "The Force that through the Green Fuse Drives the Flower", he wrote:

"The force that through the green fuse drives the flower

Drives my green age; that blasts the roots of trees

Is my destroyer."

And again:

"The force that drives the water through the rocks

Drives my red blood, that dries the mouthing streams

Turns mine to wax."

Thomas also had a great lyrical gift, which was best seen in his "Poem in October". In this poem celebrating his 30th birthday in October, he reminisces his past and describes the natural scene at his birthday with true feelings and beautiful images. Let's take two passages from this poem:

"My birthday began with the water —

Birds and the birds of the winged trees flying my name

Above the farms and the white horses

398

And I rose
In rainy autumn
And walked abroad in a shower of all my days."
And then the last stanza of the poem:

"And there could I marvel my birthday
Away but the weather turned around. And the tree
Joy of the long dead child sang burning
In the sun.
It was my thirtieth
Year to heaven stood there then in the summer noon
Though the town below lay leaved with October blood.
O my heart's truth
Still be sung
On this high hill in a year's turning."

Thomas very seldom dealt with political themes. "The Hand that Signed the Paper" is a rare exception, in which inhumane pitiless rulers are strongly attacked. They are accused of their ruthless killings:

"The hand that signed the paper felled a city;
···
Doubled the globe of dead and halved a country."

They are held responsible for fevers and famines:

"The hand that signed the treaty bred a fever,
And famine grew, and locusts came."

And finally these rulers are regarded as devoid of pity or sympathy:

"A hand rules pity as a hand rules heaven;
Hands have no tears to flow."

Dylan Thomas may not be a great poet, but he was certainly a promising poet, and if he had not met with premature death, he might have left us a greater volume of first-rate poetry.

f. Robert Graves

Robert von Ranke Graves was born in London in 1895, of

mixed Irish-Scottish-Danish-German parentage, his father being a minor Irish poet and his maternal great-uncle being a German historian. He was educated at Charterhouse and then with the arrival of World War I he joined the Royal Welsh Fusiliers and in the Battle of the Somme in 1916 he was seriously wounded and officially reported to be dead, but he actually survived to read his own obituary in the London *Times*. He then studied at Oxford, took a B. Litt. degree and in 1926 taught for a year as Professor of English Literature at the Egyptian University in Cairo. In 1929 he wrote an autobiographical account of his own life experience up to that time, "Goodbye to All That", and in the same year he settled down in Majorca, the largest of Spain's Balearic Islands in the Mediterranean, until the Spanish Civil War, when he returned to England and lived chiefly in a farmhouse in Devon up till 1947. He first discovered the poetry of a minor American Laura Riding in 1925, and his intimate literary and personal associations with her lasted from 1926 to 1939. With her he ran the Seizin Press and published books, and they collaborated on a critical work "A Survey of Modernist Poetry" (1927). He returned to Majorca after 1947.

Graves began writing poetry early (volumes published in 1916, 1921 and 1923) and was one of "Georgian" poets and also a war poet (about World War I), but in his later successive volumes of "Collected Poems" he left out many of his early poems. He lived chiefly on his writings, but he was known first of all as a writer of historical novels, particularly his two books on imperial Rome, "I Claudius" (1934) and "Claudius the God" (1934), which earned for him several prizes for prose and in which Graves reconstructed historical figures and events with lively details of the Roman court, including its corruption and scandal in the reigns of Emperor Claudius (41—54 A.D.) and of his immediate predecessors. Besides his many other historical works he wrote on classical myths, culminating in his work "The White Goddess" which contained a history of mythology and voiced his critical views on poetry, with the white goddess as the female deity to guide the poets. His fame as poet came late. It was only after the appearance of his "Colle cted Poems" in 1959 that he was recognized as a poet of importance in both England and America. He was Professor of Poetry at Oxford in the years 1961—1966, and was Clark Lecturer at Cambridge University in 1954—55 and lecturer at M.I.T. in the U.S. in 1963, besides receiving a number of awards for his poetry.

Graves is chiefly known today for his poetry on romantic love, but he also distinguishes himself as a metaphysical or meditative poet. In his early verse he was somewhat under the influence of early 16th-century poet John Skelton and of the popular ballads, but almost all the way through his poetic career may be found unmistakable echoes of John Donne and the Cavalier poets of early 17th century. He usually kept up the use of rhymes and metre and thereby resisted the trend of free verse of Modernism.

Graves wrote on romantic love with a difference. There is on the one hand something ironical and mocking that approaches cynicism, and on the other hand there is the down-to-earthness about physical love that is downright risqué. Of the latter kind, the much anthologized "Down, Wanton, Down" refers so directly to the lover's physical desires though such primitive passion is chidden by the poet himself drawing the line between "What is man and what mere beast". A little more covertly is the act of love-making referred to in "The Thieves", where the poet's words of reproach are jokingly given:

"Theft is theft and raid is raid
Though reciprocally made."

But more often than not Graves dealt with the inconstancy of love, not exactly in Donne's light-hearted tradition of the fickleness of women, but much more seriously, somewhat resembling Swinburne's view: "With eyes forgetful/ Weeps that no loves endure". This almost sad thought on love's brevity appeared in a very early poem of Graves', "Love Without Hope" (1920), but was best expressed in "Sick Love", with its title taken from "The Song of Songs" in the *Old Testament*. Here the poet begins with the hedonistic spirit in "be fed with apples while you may", directly echoing Herrick's "Gather Ye Rosebuds", but the picture is gloomier than that in any love lyric by the Cavalier poets of the 17th century when we come to the 4th and last stanza:

"Take your delight in momentariness,
    Walk between dark and dark — a shining space
    With the grave's narrowness, though not its peace."

Similar lines on this theme are numerous with Grave. Take "The Love Story". Here the poet recorded his own experience in boyhood, including his joyousness after he fell in love, but "These were all lies", he then declared, and again came the tragic and almost cynical ending:

"In tears I recomposed the former scene,
    Let the snow lie, watched the moon rise, suffered the
        owls,
    Paid homage to them of unevent."

Again, in a dialogue poem "Dialogue on the Headland", Graves subtly suggested that lovers even in the heyday of their passion were not able to keep their fears and doubts out of their minds. Even after the lover swears the age-old oath of "Though the sea turns to slime", etc., and then substitutes with the modern expression of "Whatever happens", the "she" remains unreassured:

"He: I said: 'Whatever happens' Are you coying?
    She: You'll not forget me — ever, ever, ever?"

The final question-mark here reveals something highly philosophical, the dubious intimacy even between two dearest to each other on the one hand and the unpredictability of human relationships with the change in time — and in space, on the other.

More poignant but no less cynical on the theme of love is "Never Such Love". The poem opens with the almost conventional declarations of love by lovers, tinged with irony:

"Twined together and, as is customary,
    For words of rapture groping, they
    'Never such love', swore, 'ever before was!'"

Contrast with all loves that had failed or staled
Registered their own as love indeed."
And this was followed by a truism, which may be a bit cynical but
too true:

"Better in love to seal the love-sure life,
For truly love was before words were,
And no word given, no word given."
So all lovers are warned not to utter love and least of all to write
it down. Yet Graves still wrote a number of poems celebrating love
in a very serious way, such as the short 7-lined poem "She Tells Her
Love While Half Asleep":

"She tells her love while half asleep
In the dark hours,
With half-words whispered low:
As earth stirs in the winter sleep
And puts out grass and flowers
Despite the snow,
Despite the falling snow."
In love poetry there is some resemblance between Graves and
Auden. Both followed the tradition of Donne and the Cavalier
Poets of the 17th century, on the brevity of love and its inconstancy.
While Auden excelled in lyricism (e.g. "Lay your sleeping head, my
love, / Human on my faithless arm"), Graves went into the question
more philosophically (e.g. "Sick Love", "Never Such Love"), but
both were modernists on this point as they broke away from the
poetic tradition of romantic love in 18th- and 19th-century England
and also differed from Donne and the Cavaliers in that, in accordance with the modern practice and the modern *mores,* they do not
blame or apologize for the acts of inconstancy or hedonism in lovers but take such things as a matter of course and as even highly
justifiable, with their philosophical considerations of human existence in this changing world.
Graves also wrote quite a number of serious poems that are
meditative and philosophical, that are usually ironical and even

cynical. In "Warning to Children", in a mocking way he pointed out to children that their search for truth was fruitless and would inevitably end in meeting with ridiculously repetitious experience. The apparent pointlessness of the repetition of four lines of verse "Blocks of slate ..." three times actually serves as an effective warning to children (and adults too) if and when they try to find out about "the greatness, rareness, muchness,/ Fearness of this precious only/ Endless world". "To Evoke Posterity" contains a much more cynical dissuasion against human efforts to gain fame. It begins by saying, in Graves' inimitably striking phrasing,

"To evoke posterity
    Is to weep on your own grave."

Then the poem goes on with the enumeration of various kinds of punishment dealt out to those who make names for themselves in history.

Graves took part in World War I, but his war poems written during and shortly after the war years have largely been forgotten. A short poem "Dawn Bombardment" recording the firing of coastal guns at the beginning of the war does not eulogize the soldiers from the patriotic point of view as do most of Rupert Brooke's poems, nor does it describe the horrors of war and its destructiveness as in the poems of Wilfred Owen, Isaac Rosenberg or Siegfried Sassoon, but it tells merely of the meditative effect of gunfiring on the mind of the soldier:

"Guns from the sea open against us:
    The smoke rocks bodily in the casement
    And a yell of doom goes up.
    We count and bless each new, heavy concussion —
    Captives awaiting rescue."

But long after the war, Graves also wrote about the still-remembered days of the fighting. In "Recalling War", written twenty years after 1918 and curiously a year before the second world debacle, war was strongly condemned as such and an anticipation of another war imminent was told with much horror and apprehension:

"War was return of earth to ugly earth,
War was foundering of sublimities,
Extinction of each happy art and faith
By which the world had still kept head in air.

And we recall the merry ways of guns —
Nibbling the walls of factory and church
Like a child, pie-crust; felling groves of trees
Like a child, dandelions with a switch!
Machine-guns rattle toy-like from a hill,
Down in a row the brave tin-soldiers fall:
A sight to be recalled in elder days
When learnedly the future we devote
To yet more boastful visions of despair."

The ironic use of such words and expressions as "the merry ways of guns", "the brave tin-soldiers" and "more boastful visions of despair", paints the horrors of war and tells the poet's hatred of it more profoundly than simple narrations or descriptions of actual fighting and the destruction it brought.

A more cool-headed and shrewd comment on war, written in calm recollection, is casually and almost playfully expressed in the delightful lyric "The Cool Web". While the poem as a whole shows the sagacity of an elderly man looking back at the past, the last lines in the two stanzas quoted below reveal the poet's horrors of war in progress and his stoicism toward it in retrospect:

"Children are dumb to say how hot the day is,
How hot the scent is of the summer rose,
How dreadful the black waters of evening sky,
How dreadful the tall soldiers drumming by.
But we have speech, to blunt the angry day,
And speech, to dull the rose's cruel scent,
We spell away the overhanging night,
We spell away the soldiers and the fright,"

Here the poet's cynical attitude toward the war is somewhat veiled, remembered after a distance of decades, as the two phrases "how dreadful" and "spell away" represent the two different emotional states between then and now, but the feeling of disgust is present in both cases.

Though Graves wrote many prose works, particularly historical novels, and earned his fame as well as his living thereby, he is known to have considered these works only performed by his left hand to serve as day-labour in order to provide him with livelihood for the writing of poetry, and certainly he wrte verse all through his life in spite of the unevenness of merit among his voluminous output.

Graves wrote not infrequently on poetry and poets in his verse. He declared his way of writing poetry or at least exhorted other poets the way to write, in "The Devil's Advice to Storytellers". Here "story-tellers" naturally includes prose writers, but presumably the advice is in this case given particularly to poets, being written in verse. The poets are counselled not to aim primarily at an attempt at truthfulness or an appearance of truth, but to just put down persons and things of this world as one sees them and forget about any motive for anything or any moral to convey:

"Assemble, first, all casul bits and scraps
That may shake down into a world perhaps;
People this world, by chance created so,
With random persons whom you do not know —
The teashop sort, or travellers in a train
Seen once, guessed idly at, not seen again;
Let the erratic course they steer surprise
Their own and your own and your readers' eyes;
Sigh then, or frown, but leave (as in despair)
Motive and end and moral in the air;
Nice contradiction between fact and fact
Will make the whole read human and exact."

This is written in a colloquial and informal and slightly humorous style peculiar to Graves and reminiscent of Browning, as indeed this declaration of what poetry should do and what poets should be is not unsimilar to similar theory (and practice) of Robert Browning's (e.g. "How it Strikes a Contemporary", "House"). Graves on the whole lived up to this view in his verse, as he recorded many of the persons and things he sees, sometimes at random, in his poems (e.g. "A Slice of Wedding Cake", "Dialogue on the Headland", "Gulls and Men", "Full Moon", "The Straw", "The Blue Fly", "Friday Night","On Dwelling","The Great Grandmother","Welsh Incident", "Nature's Lineaments", "The Laureate", etc.). But he was very stern as he spoke of his own love poems: in "A Plea to Boys and Girls", he asked youthful readers to "call the man a liar who says I wrote/ All that I wrote in love, for love of art."

Graves wrote more often against critics. In "The Reader Over My Shoulder", he declared half humorously but half angrily against those who criticized or praised him, and claimed proudly that regardless of his judges and patrons he would go his own way in the writing of poetry:

"For you in strutting, you in sycophancy,
Have played too long this other self of me,
Doubling the part of judge and patron
With that of creaking grindstone to my wit.
Know me, have done: I am a proud spirit
And you forever clay. Have done."

Similarly in "The Poets", contrasting critics with "any honest housewife" who has "a nose for fish, an eye for apples" and

ould instantly distinguish from the workers
The lazy liars and the petty thieves",

Graves ridiculed at them ("all unhrifty writers")for their failure ("failure of the usual five" senses) in distinguishing major poets from insignificant ones.

Graves had his positive ideals for poets. In "To Juan at the Winter Solstice", he tried to advise his own son Juan on the poetic career the young man obviously meant to embark. The first stanza is very typical of Graves:

"There is one story and one story only.

> That will prove worth your telling,
> Whether as learned bard or gifted child;
> To it all lines or lesser gauds belong
> That startle with their shining
> Such common stories as they stray into."

Then the last stanza leads up to the poet's credo on the White Goddess, the Triple Goddees who according to mythology once reigned supreme in a matriarchal culture, the nurse to inspire modern poets:

> "Dwell on her graciousness, dwell on her smiling,
> Do not forget what flowers
> The great boar trampled down in ivy time.
> Her brow was creamy as the crested wave,
> Her sea-blue eyes were wild
> But nothing promised that is not performed."

The last line throws the responsibility of success or failure back on to each poet.

There is also a short poem entitled "The White Goddess", originally affixed as an epigraph to the monumental prose work on mythology of the same title mentioned above. Here the poet suggests to all poets to seek out the White Goddess and promises the fruits of the search:

> "But we are gifted, even in November
> Rawest of seasons, with so huge a sense
> Of her nakedly worn magnificence
> We forget cruelty and past betrayal,
> Heedless of where the next bright bolt may fall."

Finally, a word should be said of the abundance of humour and the high degree of originality in language to be found almost everywhere in Graves' poetry. In "Lost Acres" he links up humorously and at the same time meditatively the unexplored regions in one's mind, which may be very pleasant or quite the opposite. In "The Great-grandmother", the poet points out humorously yet very keensightedly how an aged woman may confide to her great-grandchildren her innermost thoughts that she would conceal or only half-disclose to their elders, her own children and grandchildren. In "Nature's Lineaments", natural phenomena ranging from rocks and trees to clouds are humorously compared to different parts of human force, and human feelings are sometimes even attributed to them. Perhaps the most typical is "Lollocks", the title of which was invented by the poet to refer to petty annoyance resulting from sloth and sorrow, and which is applied to little children and "the imbecile aged" and "naughty wives". The following stanza illustrates well the poet's insight into the insignificant yet common things in life brought out with much flow of humour and careful choice of words:

> "The signs of their presence
> Are boils on the neck,
> Dreams of vexation suddenly recalled
> In the middle of the morning,
> Languor after food.
> Men cannot see them,
> Men cannot hear them,
> Do not believe in them —
> But suffer the more,
> Both in neck and belly."

One wonders if such verse is a bit too light and insignificant in spite of the humour it contains and provokes! Of course, one can argue that many other poems of the sort such as "Gulls and Men," "The Straw", "On Dwelling" and "Welsh Incident" do contain weighty thoughts under the seemingly lighthearted surfaces. Graves deserves our attention, but one feels that he can hardly match up to the major poets of the century: Hardy, Hopkins, Yeats, T.S. Eliot, MacDiarmid, Auden, even D.H. Lawrence.

g. Edwin Muir

Edwin Muir (1887—1959) was born on a farm in the remote Orkney Islands off northern Scotland and was educated at Kirkwall Burgh School until he was 14, when his family moved to the industrial city of Glasgow. Their life there was wretched and poverty-stricken and his father, mother and two brothers died one after another. Muir had to educate himself and to work on odd jobs chiefly as a clerk in different commercial and shipbuilding firms. In 1919 he married a novelist and critic Willa Anderson and they moved to London where he worked as a literary journalist and served as assistant to the editor of "The New Age". In 1921 the Muirs moved to Prague and to the south of France before returning to Scotland in 1927. In the meantime they translated Kafka's "The Castle" and "The Trial" and various works by German writers, while he kept on writing and publishing his early volumes of poetry. From 1942 to 1949 Muir served the British Council in Edinburgh, Prague and Rome, and in 1950 he was appointed Warden of Newbattle Abbey College in Midlothian (near Edinburgh), Scotland. Between 1955 and 1958 he was Visiting Professor at universities in the United States and England and the last few years of his life he spent in a small village near Cambridge. Besides his seven volumes of poetry that appeared before his collected poems in 1960, he wrote three novels, an autobiography ("The Story and Fable", 1940, reissued as "Autobiography", 1954) and several books of criticism the last of which, "The Structure of the Novel" (1928), is possibly the best known. He was not widely known as a poet till his volume of poems "One Foot in Eden" (1956) and particularly till his "Collected Poems", published posthumously.

Muir's early years in a rural environment in Orkney far from civilization and his painful adjustments first in Glasgow and then his long stays in continental Europe had their effect upon his poetry. He belonged to no school of poetry, and may be considered in antithesis to modernism. What T. S. Eliot said of him is not far from the truth:

> "There is the sensibility of the remote islander, the boy from
> a primitive offshore community who was then plunged into
> the sordid horror of industrialism in Glasgow, who strug-
> gled to understand the modern world of the metropolis in
> London and finally the realities of Central Europe in
> Prague."

To this perhaps should be added the pervading influence of the Christian belief in the Fall of Man and the penetrating tradition of the ancient myths of Greece and Rome.

We should not consider him as one who idealized the past, but Muir seemed to be always fascinated by the primitive human society and by the closeness to nature that he experienced in his childhood in the remote Orkney islands. His best poems are those that deal with nature and in which his fondness of the natural world in its simplicity is implicitly revealed. "The Wayside Station" is a good example. Here a countryside scene is unfolded before the readers, from morning till dusk, and leisurely descriptions of smoke and clouds, of sea-gulls and the waves, then of the farmstead on the little hill, of the cattle, the ploughboy, the farmer and the lovers and finally of the woods, the bright snare slip and the lonely stream. The last three and half lines about the lonely stream touch eventually upon the important theme of time:

> "The lonely stream
> That rode through darkness leaps the gaps of light,
> Its voice grown loud, and starts its winding journey
> Through the day and time and war and history."

This last line lifts Muir above the station of a poet who is interested in religion and myth but shows his absorption in human existence in history and in the passage of time. Similarly, in a poem entitled "Then", Muir in his very quiet but firm way considered the progress of human history as no more than a record of cruel wars and massacres, no more than blood on the wall:

> "There were no men and women then at all,
> But the flesh lying alone,
> And angry shadows fighting on a wall
> That now and then sent out a groan
> Buried in lime and stone,
> And sweated now and then like tortured wood
> Big drops that looked yet did not look like blood
> And yet as each drop came a shadow faded

411

And left the wall.
There was a lull
Until another in its shadow arrayed it,
Came, fought and left a blood mark on the wall,
And that was all; the blood was all."
This last line is a strong indictment of human civilization as such.

In another poem "The Animals", Muir made use of the creation story in the Christian Bible and tried to point out that with only the animals created by God on the 5th day (this was an obvious erroneous reiteration of creation in the Bible) they ever remained the same and were happy in their innocence as they thought of time and of life and death. On the other hand, Muir tried to describe the simple fight between simple animals, in the poem "Combat". The creatures may be very cruel and engage in very fierce fighting, yet their life-and-death struggle often end in a draw, with "the killing beast that cannot kill" ending in despair.

"The Island" is very obviously a panegyric of the remote Scottish island where Muir spent his early life. Here you have a picture of the peaceful and happy existence of men and animals and plants in a primitive environment. There is something rhapsodic in such lines as:

"Men are made of what is made,
The meat, the drink, the life, the corn,
Laid up by them, in them reborn."

In one of his earliest poems "Horses" (1925), Muir eulogizes the horses that seem terrible, wild and strange yet are actually admirable creatures with "their conquering hooves", "their great hulks", "their bossy sides", their "steaming nostrils", their brilliant eyes and their manes. In a poem 30 years later on obviously the same subject, "The Horses" (1956), the poet contrasts the terrors of war with the horses that arrive late that evening, showing thereby his totally different attitude toward modern civilization that brought war, and toward the horses that had been sold to buy tractors and now had returned.

Muir's belief in the biblical story of the Fall of Man is part of his views on primitive innocence as contrasted with sordid modern civilization. In "Adam's Dream", Muir tried to visualize what Adam dreamed he saw after his Fall with Eve following the taking of the forbidden fruit. The poet imagined the result of the Fall by describing what many men and women (i.e. the human race who were his offspring) do that he could not understand. In "One Foot in Eden", Muir still more vividly idealized what is in Paradise or Eden, in contrast with "the other Land" or the human world after the Fall. Even in "Merlin", the poet tries to ask the enchanter whether man could ever recover his lost innocence and destroy time.

Muir wrote quite a number of poems on old myths, particularly on ancient Greek stories about the Trojan War (i.e., "Troy", "Ballad of Hector in Hades", "The Return") about Priam and Hector and Ulysses, and he tried to tell these old legendary figures in the modern way. These poems sometimes reveal the poet's gift of imagination, of placing mythical people in a different time, but otherwise there is little significance.

Muir was not a great poet and he has become better known in the last quarter of a century chiefly because his ideas about human innocence and his interest in ancient myths and in the Christian doctrine of the Fall of Man aroused the curiosity and therefore admiration of many Western readers in their failure to find themselves out of the morass of modern capitalist civilization that have brought war and spiritual crises. However, as a poet who was disillusioned in the modern West and who wrote on simple nature and time, he deserves our attention.

SECTION VI ENGLISH PROSE FICTION:
1920—1940

a. James Joyce

James Joyce (1882—1941) was born to a declining middle class family in Dublin, Ireland. "A Praiser of his own past", his father was at one time a rather prominent figure but their family finances worsened as James grew up. Like the hero Stephen Dedalus in his autobiographical novel "A Portrait of the Artist as a Young Man", Joyce went to two Jesuit schools in succession, Clongowes Wood College and Belvedere College, at the ages of 6 to 9 and 11 to 16 respectively. In his early youth he was extremely religious but in his last year at Belvedere when he was asked to take orders he rejected the Catholic faith, like Stephen Dedalus. Joyce won several exhibitions carrying monetary awards while in college, but he gradually became a rebel against the philistinism of Dublin. In 1898 he went to study at University College, Dublin, where he went in for modern languages and distinguished himself by writing a review of Ibsen's new play "When We Dead Awaken" which was accepted by the "Fortnightly Review" (April 1900). He graduated in 1902 and became acquainted with the well-known figures of the Irish Literary Renaissance of the time: W.B. Yeats, Lady Gregory, George Moore, J. M. Synge and George Russell ("A.E.") who were then making plans for the Irish Abbey Theatre. As he refused to take part in the Irish nationalist movement while at college, so he was later to be strongly opposed to the Irish literary movement of Yeats, Lady Gregory, et al.

Again like Stephan Dedalus, Joyce eventually chose "silence, and cunning" as his mode of action. After his brief attendance at the Medical College in Dublin which was cut short by the inability to pay the requisite fees and expenses by his family, he left Ireland and went to Paris. There he continued his medical studies while supporting himself as a teacher of English. He was recalled to Dublin by his mother's fatal illness. After a short spell as a schoolteacher, he left Ireland again for the European Continent in 1904 with his girl Nora Joseph Barnacle who was an uneducated peasant girl from Galway in West Ireland but who lived with him until his death in 1941. They first went to Trieste, Italy, teaching English in a Berlitz school, and then moved to Zurich, Switzerland, where they remained till 1920. For twenty years, 1920—1940, Joyce settled in Paris until with the fall of France in December of 1940 he was forced to move again to Zurich. He died in Zurich shortly afterwards, in 1941.

After he moved to Zurich from Trieste in 1914, he got a grant from the Royal Literary Fund and then in 1916 a Civil List Grant. His patrons include Mrs. Harold McCormick (Edith Rockefeller) in 1917—19 and the English feminist and editor Harriet Shaw Weaver in 1917—41.

Joyce's early lyric poems, "Chamber Music", were published in 1907. His second finished book, a collection of 15 stories entitled "Dubliners", appeared in June, 1914. Then in 1916 came out a New York edition (London edition 1917) of his highly autobiographical work, "A Portrait of the Artist as a Young Man", which was earlier serialized in "The Egoist" (February 1914—September 1915) through the efforts of Ezra Pound and of which the original manuscript "Stephen Hero" was posthumously published in 1944. When "Ulysses" first appeared in book form in 1922 (after its earlier serialization in the "Little Review", March 1918—December 1920), it was banned in both Britain and the United States on the charge of obscenity, and only the history-making decision by Judge Woolsey in 1933 lifted the ban first in the United States and then soon after in Britain. Joyce's last book, "Finnegans Wake", was published in 1939.

Joyce is and will be remembered as a novelist, but a passing mention may be made of the "tour de force" in one of his poems, "I hear an army", which was lifted out of his verse in "Chamber Music" and included in Helen Gardner's admirable collection "The Oxford Book of English Verse, 1250—1950" (published in 1972). Here, in this short poem of three quatrains, following the thundering roar of charging charioteers, the last two lines fall into a soft romantic strain:

My heart, have you no wisdom thus to despair?
My love, my love, my love, why have you left me alone?

So he already anticipated in his youthful days the multi-sided genius of the Irish virtuoso that was to be.

"Dubliners" as a collection of short stories was written in the traditional style, yet many of the germs of the minor characters and story-threads in "Ulysses" are already contained in some of these episodic narratives. What is more important, some of the stories are themselves poignant tales of desperate human search for illusory ideals that find fuller expression in Joyce's maturer works. "Araby", the third of the 15 stories, tells the final disappointment of the belated boy visitor at the bazaar for which he cherished so much hope all through the week. In the 9th story, "Counterparts", the hopes of a drinking bout with his friends in the evening for Farrington the good-for-nothing clerk of a small business concern are dashed as all sorts of unpleasant things happen to him both before and during the hours in the bars. "The Dead", the last and the saddest of the stories, reveals the futility of everything and everybody depicted, the two aged sisters Miss Kate and Miss Julia and their big Christmas party, their not-too-young niece Mary Jane and her music lessons, their housemaid Lily with her bitter memories of the young men that tried to get what they can out of her, the habitually drunk Freddy Malins and his silent, adoring mother, Miss Ivors the humorless ideologue of Irish nationalist movement, the good-natured Mr. Browne though he was a Protestant, and above all the jolly good fellow Gabriel Conroy and his sore disappointment at his wife Greta who fell into hopeless gloom when accidentally her dead first love was brought to mind. The accounts of the different inhabitants of Dublin who have failed in their different ways culminate in the thoughts of death awaiting each and every human being in spite of all that he or she tries to do to make something out of life. Though there is the note of resignation at the very end of the story as the hero Gabriel "heard the snow falling faintly through the universe and faintly falling, like the descent of their last end upon all the living and the dead," yet the general impression the reader gets from "The Dead" and all other stories in "Dubliners" is the feeling of pervading gloom over all Dublin, as the author wrote to his publisher about the whole book of "Dubliners": "I chose Dublin for the scene because the city seemed to me to be the centre of paralysis."

"A Portrait of the Artist as a Young Man" is an autobiographical sketch of the author's childhood and early youth. The first event of importance, as seen and recorded by the boy hero Stephen, was the death of Parnell and the conflicting views over politics and religion (or, more specifically, over whether the Irish bishops and priests should preach loyalty to the British rulers or side with Parnell the Irish patriot) at the family Christmas dinner. Then there was the strong impression of Stephen being wrongly punished by Father Nolan, to be followed by the boy's successful appeal to the rector. Next followed a series of commonplace yet vivid scenes in the schoolboy's life: two big caravans carting away most of the furniture in the house and the family moving to a more modest dwelling; his first encounter and attraction toward a girl that came to nothing; his acting the chief part in the Whitsuntide play in his second year at Belvedere; his college essay that bordered dangerously on heresy; his visit to Cork with his father Simon to sell their family property there and to listen to the latter as "a praiser of his own past"; his adolescent experience with a woman of the streets and his remorseful sense of mortal sin long afterwards. A long episode of the youth's religious fervour ensued as he heard sermons at a "retreat" giving details of hell and sin and eternal punishment and then after much hesitation he went to seek for confession at an obscure Dublin church. But soon enough he rejected the offer by the director of the college to join the Jesuit order especially when his family was just then faced with another house removal resulting from their failure to pay their rent. After his entry to the university Stephen became soaked in the philosophy of Aristotle and Aquinas and the dainty songs of the Elizabethans, caring nothing for physical sciences or religion or politics or physical attractions of women but indulging in purely intellectual speculations on beauty and truth, on Aristotle's definitions of pity and terror, on the lyrical, epical and dramatic forms of art. Disillusioned in his ephemeral love for a girl of whom he knew very little but for whom he wrote some very striking lines of verse, and at the same time disgusted thoroughly with his companions and his superiors at college and with his family, Stephen's made his decision at the end of the book, as Joyce also did in his youth, "to go away":

"I will not serve that in which I no longer believe, whether it calls itself my home, my fatherland, or my church: and I will try to express myself in some mode of life or art as freely as I can, using for my defence the only arms I allow myself to use — silence, exile, and cunning."

"A Portrait of the Artist as a Young Man" is autobiographical in the truest sense of the word, for "with this key" Joyce "unlocked his heart". Here Stephen Dedalus, alias James Joyce, tells the world of his physical and mental occurrences from early childhood to maturer youth and by tracing the development particularly of his spiritual make-up he reveals the whys and wherefores of his whole literary career. It may seem strange that all his writings have to do with Dublin and the Irish while he was avowedly disgusted with the drabness and philistinism of the bourgeois Irish society in Dublin, but it may also be explained perhaps that only by his self-imposed exile was he enabled to see at a distance more clearly, more objectively, the things and the people he wrote about. But the thing of first importance is our knowledge of the author himself: his social, political and religious background and his attitude toward it; his actions, words and thoughts plus his sub-conscious mind; his world out-look that does not stay put but is forever changing ... and this is especially so with James Joyce, for in his "Ulysses" as in "A Portrait" it is chiefly the novelist himself acting, speaking and thinking, particularly with the central figure Leopold Bloom and of course also Stephen Dedalus. We cannot truly understand "Ulysses" without knowing about Joyce via "A Portrait", let alone appreciating it.

The title "Ulysses" itself tells us all too clearly that Joyce meant to model his new prose epic of Leopold Bloom, Stephen Dedalus and Marion Tweedy Bloom on the Homeric story of Odysseus (alias Ulysses), Telemachus and Penelope in "Odyssey". The division of the tale also into 18 episodes to correspond to those in the Greek epic is not the essential thing, certainly not any more important then the observance here of the three unities (i.e., time not to exceed 24 hours, place limited to one city, and action centering on one hero, plus his son and wife) as supposed to have been dictated by Aristotle. The chief parallel, if any, between the ancient Greek poem and the modern Irish novel, whether deviced by the author or understood by the reader, is the narration of various activities of a man and his immediate family, more or less in the picaresque tradition, while there are vast differences naturally, with more than two thousand years and hundreds of miles separating the chief figures in their totally different political, social and psychological environments. The old Greek world with its supernatural beings and magic and its slave society is inevitably replaced by early 20th-century Ireland with its colonial and essentialy bourgeois social structure, with the result that the superhuman hero Ulysses of the ancient epic becomes the "little man" Leopold Bloom of the modern novel. Both works are "picaresque", however, for though the heroic exploits of Ulysses have very naturally become the humdrum everyday life of Bloom, yet the incidents that the two major fictional figures meet with one after another may all be considered adventures of a "picaro" of one sort or another (with "picaro" used here to refer to the big man and the little one alike). There is a further point of striking difference between the two narratives, the emphasis on actions first and on speeches next in the older book of verse being supplemented in the modern prose fictional work with at least equal emphasis on the thoughts and even subconscious mind of the characters, as evidenced in the ever-present use of "monologue interieur" or the "stream-of-consciousness" method.

Almost the whole of "Ulysses" is devoted to the narration of one day's life in Dublin the Irish capital (on June 16, 1904) of a Jewish advertisement-canvasser, Leopold Bloom (to whom 14 of the 18 episodes in the novel are devoted), with the first three reserved for Stephen Dedalus and the last epidode for Marion Bloom. Or, perhaps more properly we may consider this novel as chiefly about Dublin and the inhabitants therein, and in that sense the book may even be regarded as an exposé of modern bourgeois Dublin for which the author had the strongest disgust and from which he imposed his self-exile.

The first three episodes in "Ulysses" is about Stephen Dedalus and they constitute in a sense a continuation of "A Portrait of the Artist as a Young Man", though between the last part of the former novel and the beginning of this one there has been a gap of two years (1902—1904) during which time Stephen (Joyce) had left Ireland and then had come back for his mother's fatal illness. The first episode about Stephen Dedalus (corresponding to "Telemachus" in Homer's "Odessey") describes Stephen spending his early morning on June 16, 1904, in a disused Martello tower, overlooking Dublin Bay, with a medical student Malachi Mulligan and an English literary tourist Haines. Very insignificant details are recorded here: Mulligan shaving himself with a razor and reproaching Stephen for refusing to kneel down in prayer upon the request of his dying mother, and Stephen retorting with his repetition of Mulligan's remark about "Dedalus whose mother is beastly dead"; an old milkwoman arriving in time to give them the milk that the three youngsters need for their breakfast at the moment, and the three young men then walking to the sea and Mulligan bathing himself while Haines sits on a rock and smokes; Haines intending to make a collection of Stephen's witty sayings as Mulligan says Stephen "proves by algebra that Hamlet's grandson is Shakespeare's grandfather and that he himself is the ghost of his own father", etc.; but here and there remarks of some weight fall from the lips of Stephen Dedalus:

"I am the servant of two masters, ... an English and an Italian ... The imperial British state ... and the holy Roman catholic and apostolic church .... And a third,... there is who wants me for odd jobs."

and from the Englishman Haines:

An Irishman must think like that, I daresay. We feel in England that we have treated you rather unfairly. It seems history is to blame.

The second episode (corresponding to "Nestor" in Homer's "Odyssey") begins with Stephen conducting a history lesson to his pupils at Mr. Deasy's school, and here the futility of school lessons is very successfully described and the call to go to a hockey game comes as a relief to both the pupils and the teacher. Then the old man Mr. Deasy pays Stephen his salary and asks the latter to get his "literary friends" to publish a letter in some newspaper on the prevention of foot-and-mouth disease in Ireland. The question of the persecution of the Jews is brought up by Mr. Deasy, to be answered by the appearance of Bloom who later in the novel is doomed to persecution by some patriotic Irishman.

The third episode about Stephen (corresponding to "Proteus" in the Homeric epic "Odyssey") first introduces the "stream-of-consciousness" method in full swing. Random thoughts and associated ideas rush into Stephen's mind as he walks on along the strand. He thinks of visiting his maternal uncle Richie Golding, and in his mind's eye and ear he seems to hear his father's contemptuous remarks on the said uncle and to see Richie lying in bed and asking his son Walter to bring malt for Stephen. Then on seeing a pigeon-house on his way, he remembers a French lampoon on the pigeon and that leads him on to thoughts of his Paris days, including his "Latin Quarter" hat and his acquaintance there with an exiled Irish conspirator Kevin Egan who had his various hideouts in "gay Paree". Next Stephen walks near the edge of the sea and looks back at the Martello tower, then he sees the carcass of a dog and then a live dog barking at him, and all this sight and hearing is mixed with the passing thoughts on the objects he saw and heard, until his fear of the dog provokes his memories of brave "pretenders" saving men from drowning, and this last makes him remember the man "that was drowned nine days ago off Maiden's Rock". A man and a woman are next seen with their dog trotting and sniffing, as they wade a little way in the water and then come out and then they pass him, while all these impressions call for his various brief comments in his mind. In the meantime, amidst all the miscellaneous wanderings of his brain, he recalls occasionally the key to the tower, the Englishman Haines, the banknotes in his pocket that he received from Mr. Deasy, and Deasy's letter on the foot-and-mouth disease. This is followed by his metaphysical speculations ensuing from the sight of his shadow that "lay over the rocks as he bent, ending. Why not endless till the farthest star?" The thought of "the good bishop of Cloyne" then leads him on to that of "a woman to her lover clinging", to a "girl I knew in Paris". Then he notices the water full in the Cock Lake and watches the upswinging tide: "Day by day; night by night: lifted, flooded and let fall. Lord, they are weary: and, whispered to, they sigh. Saint Ambrose heard it, sigh of leaves and waves, waiting, awaiting the fullness of their times." Then he imagines the sea also takes away human lives: "A corpse rising saltwhite from the undertow, bobbing landward, a pace a pace a porpoise. There he is. Hook it quick. Sunk though he be beneath the watery floor. We have him. Easy now." And thoughts of the dead man's smell and appearance are accompanied by disconnected whims and reveries — of thunderstorm and Lucifer, of "Lawn Tennyson, gentleman poet" and the author's bad teeth, of a handkerchief and a silent ship as "he turned his face over a shoulder".

These first three episodes are summarized here in great detail, especially the third one, because here we find the typical use of the "stream-of-consciousness" method in the typical Joycean way, not only with the blended juxtaposition of actions-words-and-thoughts of the central character in curious interaction and sometimes with obscure inter-suggestions, but also the ever-present subtle word-play (e.g. "Lawn Tennyson" given above) and literary echoes of well-known lines or phrases of Shakespeare and Swift and Thomas Gray with witty twists (e.g. "a cliff that beetles o'er his base", "Cousin Stephen, you will never be a saint", "Feefawfum. I zmellz de bloodz odz an Iridzman", "the simple pleasures of the poor", "Five fathom five thy father lies", "a seachange this", "My cockle hat and staff and my sandal shoon").

Then we come to the main body of the novel, the fourteen episodes devoted to Leopold Bloom which tell the story of this Irish Jew's day in Dublin. Of the 14, the first three sections are the most lucid, the most interesting and the most vivid and realistic descriptions of Bloom the hero. First there is his marketing for kidney and preparation for his wife's and his own breakfast ("Calypso"). Then the second part relates his visit to the post office to receive a "romantic" letter from a typist Martha that is addressed to his pseudonym "Henry Flower", then his meeting with a Mr. M'Coy who tries to borrow valises for his wife's imaginary concert tour, next his brief attendance in All Hallows Church and his purchase of a soap while ordering a face-lotion for his wife, later his encounter with one Bantam Lyons who borrows his newspaper to see about the races later in the day, and finally his taking a bath in the "Mosque of the baths" ("The Lotus-Eaters" in Homer's "Odessey"). The third episode narrates how he goes in the company of Mr. Power, Martin Cunningham, and Simon Dedalus on a cab to the Glasnevin Cemetery to attend the service and burial of a friend Patrick Dignam ("Hades" in "Odessey"). The fourth section is a little confusing, as the hero makes his visit to the office of the Freeman's Journal and National Press to make arrangements for the publication of an advertisement of Alexander Keyes' "high-class licensed premises", and also to persuade the editor Myles Crawford to say something good about the advertised licensed premises in a column in his evening paper "The Telegraph", while Stephen Dedalus also comes in to ask the editor to publish Mr. Deasy's letter on the foot-and-mouth disease, and then numerous other visitors also enter the office for some purpose or other ("Aeolus" in "Odessey"). In the fifth episode, Bloom crosses the bridge over the Liffey and sees many people and objects of interest that make him reminisce all sorts of things, before he enters a restaurant where the sight of vulgar, carnivorous eaters revolts him and he eventually decides to allay temporarily his hunger by having a cheese sandwich and a glass of Burgundy at a pub called Davy Byrne's ("The Lestrygonions"). Then in the sixth section Bloom gets to the national library to find in a back number of the "Kilkenny People" the design for the advertisement to be published for Keyes' licensed premises, and there a multi-voiced discussion is already going on over Shakespearean lore, more specifically over the personality of Hamlet, with Stephen Dedalus as the main speaker and the well-known poet George Russell ("A.E.") participating ("Scylla and Charybdis." in Homer's

"Odyssey"). Up to this point the story thread centres chiefly on Bloom or partly on Stephen, and it is not difficult to follow the narration. The portraiture of Leopold Bloom becomes fuller and fuller (except in the sixth part where Stephen dominates in the discussion on Shakespeare) as his multifarious activities are unfolded to the reader.

Then in the seventh episode the story broadens and the streets of Dublin (as Bloom and Stephen Dedalus walk past them) are described in eighteen short scenes, including the multifarious activities of persons of all ages and ranks. There are (1) Father Conmee the Jesuit rector of Clongowes Wood College and Corny Kellcher the undertaker; then (2) a stout lady flings a copper coin to a one-legged sailor up Eccles Street; (3) two daughters of Simon Dedalus (Katey and Boody) are at home eating chunks of bread with peasoup; (4) Marion Bloom's latest flame Blazes Boylan buys pears, peaches, tomatoes and strawberries at a fruit stall to be sent to "an invalid" and flirts there with the blond girl by promising to telephone her later on; (5) Stephen Dedalus is in a street watching cars and trams passing by; (6) the shopgirl Miss Dunne wonders if Boylan were in love with Marion to whom the fruits are to be sent and then receives a telephone call from Boylan; (7) Ned Lambert conducts a young clergyman the Reverend Hugh C. Love over the ancient site of the council chamber of Saint Mary's Abbey ("the most historic spot in all Dublin") where Silken Thomas proclaimed himself a rebel in 1534 and the Jews once held their synagogue; (8) The humorous parasite Lenehan describes to Mr. M'Coy an annual dinner given by the mayor Val Dillon and attended by Mrs. Marion Bloom; (9) Mr. Bloom buys two books ("The Awful Disclosures of Maria Monk" and Aristotle's "masterpiece") for his wife Marion at a bookstore and then adds one frankly pornographic work entitled "Sweets of Sin" after reading a few passages from it; (10) Mr. Simon Dedalus meets his daughter Dilly at Dillon's auction room and reluctantly gives her a shilling and two pennies following her repeated entreaties for more; (11) Mr. Kernan, a commercial traveller of the old school, walking in the street, buys gin at a good bargain, and admires his own appearance before the sloping mirror of a hairdresser, as he reminisces about the hanging of Emmet and the burial of Dignam and hurries and barely misses the viceregal cavalcade; (12) Stephen Dedalus in the street buys four books for sixpence at a bookcart and meets his sister Dilly with the purchase of Chardenal's French primer; (13) Father Cowley meets Simon Dedalus in the street and waits for Ben Dollard the musician to say a word to Subsheriff Long John Fanning to arrest two men prowling around his house; (14) Martin Cunningham walks down the street and shows Mr. Power and others the charity list on which Bloom puts down five shillings for the bereaved Mrs. Dignam; (15) Buck Mulligan and Haines eat melanges and scones and butter together and talk about Parnell's brother in the corner of the shop and about Stephen Dedalus talking about Shakespeare; (16) A certain Mr. Farrell walks past Mr. Bloom's dental windows (obviously another Mr. Bloom here who was a dentist); (17) Master Patrick Aloysius Dignam, in mourning for his father, walks in the street with the pound and half of porksteaks bought at Mangan's as he goes back home and reminisces about his father who just died the day before; (18) finally the cavalcade of the viceroy of Ireland passes by the streets of Dublin, and is greeted by Mr. Thomas Kernan, Mr. Simon Dedalus, the Reverend Hugh C. Love, Blazes Boylan, etc. All the eighteen short scenes in this episode ("the Wandering Rocks") are concerned with the streets of Dublin rather than with Bloom though the various people and events in Dublin serve as background for Bloom's story. Here we may also discern the author's purpose of depicting the goings-on at Dublin via the story of Bloom and family as well as vice versa.

The next or the eighth episode concerning Bloom deals chiefly with the Ormond Restaurant where the barmaids Miss Lydia Douce and Miss Mina Kennedy flirt with their customers Mr. Simon Dedalus and Blazes Boylan when Boylan is on his way to Eccles Street to meet Marion Tweedy Bloom. There in the restaurant Leopold Bloom and his maternal uncle Richie Goulding have their dinner, and the musician Ben Dollard together with Simon Dedalus provide musical entertainments at the piano. Bloom under his pseudonym of Henry Flower is writing a letter to Martha while listening to the lovesong from the opera "Martha" and reminiscing of Marion Twedy singing in the old days. Then Boylan comes on his jingling, haunting-car to have a glass of sloe-gin and is off to keep his appointment with Marion Bloom at four o'clock. Bloom eventually leaves the restaurant amidst the rhythm of a marching song(corresponding to "The Sirens" in "Odyssey").

The 9th episode relating to Bloom ("The Cyclops" in "Odyssey") takes place at Barney Kiernan's, one of the famous public-houses in Dublin in the first decade of the 20th century. The leading figure here is a fierce Sinn Feiner, called "the Citizen", who first speaks against the "Irish Independent" founded by Parnell, then argues with Bloom about Wolfe Tone and Robert Emmet and about putting force against force, and finally in his blind fury throws a biscuit-box at Bloom.

Then Bloom comes to this pub chiefly to look for Martin Cunningham in order to arrange for the payment of the insurance of Dignam to the widow, but not finding the man there he decides to go to the court to locate him. Next, the parasite Lenehan says Bloom really is going to the races because he knew the dark horse Throwaway would win the race and so he must have betted on it (this is a joke because earlier when one Bantam Lyons asked Bloom for the newspaper in order to look up the racing column, Bloom said he was just going to *throw* it *away*, and that was later interpreted to mean that Bloom knew beforehand the horse Throwaway would win the race). But Martin Cunningham has arrived at the pub before Bloom returns, and Bloom is asked to pay for the drinks all round because he has won at the races, much to Bloom's confusion.

The tenth episode concerning Bloom relates the hero Bloom sitting in the summer evening on the seaweedy rocks and watching three young girls Gerty MacDowell, Cissy Caffrey and Edy Boardman, as well as Cissy's two curlyheaded twin brothers Tommy and Jacky and also the eleven-month-old Baby Boardman in his pushcar. Gerty the most refined of the three girls is dreaming of her former lover, a handsome boy of her age, Reggie Wylie, but is yearning now for a different man:

> "a manly man with a strong quiet face ... perhaps his hair slightly flecked with grey ... they would be having a beautifully appointed drawingroom with pictures and engravings ..."

Then the ball kicked by one of the twin-boys rolls toward Bloom and he picks it up and throws it toward Cissy, but it rolls and stops right under Gerty's skirt. Gerty kicks at the ball but misses it, and she lifts her skirt just a little for the second kick. But aware of the lonely gentleman (Bloom) with the story of a haunting sorrow written on his face, she feels a warm flush and ventures to look at him who meets her gaze. And he seems to be the man she has dreamed of. Meanwhile with the fall of dusk Gerty's companions are thinking of going home and they run down the strand to see the Mirus Bazaar fireworks over the houses, but Gerty remains, with Bloom watching her as she swings her buckled shoes and transparent stockings. Then Cissy whistles to call her, and Gerty waves her handkerchief and smiles her smile as she walks away. Bloom sits alone for a long time, indulging in a long silent monologue as he seems to smell the perfume scent from the girl's waved handkerchief and then lapses into reminiscences of his love-making with Molly Bloom in the old days. ("Nausicaa" in "Odessey")

In these three episodes 8,9, and 10, we have again three delightful skits about Bloom in a restaurant, in a pub and on the beach.

The next two sections are the least interesting and the most confusing and unsavoury in the whole novel, the eleventh episode (corresponding to "To Oxen of the Sun" in Homer's epic "Odessey") has to do first with the goings-on in the Lying-in Hospital in Holles Street and then with what happens in Burke's public-house. Earlier in the day Bloom had heard from a Mrs. Breen about a Mrs. Purefoy having a "very stiff birth" ("She's three days bad now."), and so after leaving the rocks he goes to the Lying-in Hospital of which the owner is A. Horne and the doctor is O'Hare. (Ironically Joyce employs Late Middle English in the introductory passages in this episode.)

In the common room of the hospital Bloom meets a group of medical students drinking and feasting with Stephen Dedalus and parasite Lenehan in spite of a nurse begging them not to drink because there is a woman upstairs giving birth to a child. They discuss the question of whether to save the mother or the baby in case there be peril in child-birth, and Bloom bewails the fact that his only son Rudy died on the eleventh day of his birth. The youngsters however, exchange lewd but witty words and some even sing lewd songs without minding the sister's pleading for quietness. Then Malachi Mulligan appears and later it is announced that finally an heir has been born. Haines suddenly appears and then disappears, and discussions are carried on regarding births of twins and infant mortality. Then all the visitors, including Stephen Dedalus and Bloom, rush out of the Lying-in Hospital and run toward Burke's pub, hollering in the street on their way. They all order drinks at the pub and Stephen Dedalus drinks a lot. Most of them drink absinthe but Bloom only has a glass of wine. Then the closing time comes and all eleven of them are asked to leave the pub, some going to the bawdyhouse.

The twelfth episode ("Circe" in "Odessey") deals with Bloom's and Stephen Dedalus' adventures in the brothel, Stephen being drunk, Bloom out of his quasi-paternal care for the youth follows him to the nighttown. Amidst the cries of children, the swaying of an idiot, the shrill singing of Cissy Caffrey, the marching of two soldiers and the hoarse voice of a virago, enters Stephen Dedalus, followed by Lynch and welcomed by the bawd. Earlier, after Stephen's departure from the Lying-in Hospital, Bloom had entered the pork butcher's shop and then emerged with a pig's crubeen and a sheep's trotter, he having lost sight of Stephen. Almost overrun by a motorman, Bloom seems to see his father Rudolph, his mother Eileen and his wife Marion, even the druggist Sweeny from whom he bought the soap for Marion earlier in the day. Then he is seized by the bawd, but again he falls into a vision of Gerty MacDowell and Mrs. Breen, the former flirting with him and the latter accusing him of coming to the haunts of sin. And also Uncle Richie Goulding and others enter into his thoughts. Then Bloom reminisces how Stephen jumps in first class with a third class ticket and explains why he follows the youth ("Still, he's the best of that lot .... He'll lose that cash."). He gives the pig's crubeen and the sheep's trotter to a mastiff and is caught in the act by two watchmen for "cruelty to animals". He gives his name to the watchmen as "Dr. Bloom, Leopold, dental surgeon", but the card falls from inside the leather headband of Bloom's hat, with the name of Henry Flower on it, and Martha seems to appear and recognize him as Henry Flower. Challenged by the watchmen who had seen the card of Henry Flower, Bloom gives his profession as "a literary occupation. Author-journalist." And he seems to see Myles Crawford the editor of The Telegraph, Philip Beaufoy the writer of a prize story in "Tit-Bits" that Bloom read once, and Mary Driscoll his erstwhile servant girl whom he had had dishonourable designs on. He seems to be pleading not guilty in the lawcourt and the cross-examination seems to proceed, with J. J. O'Molloy acting as barrister pleading on Bloom's behalf. Then again in his imagination Bloom finds himself accused by several women including Mrs. Barry, Mrs. Bellingham, and the Honourable Mrs. Mervin Talboys (the first for writing an anonymous letter to her, the second for sending her stolen flowers and the third for sending her in double envelope an obscene photograph), etc. Next appear the jurors, with Martin Cunningham as foreman and including Jack Power, Simon Dedalus, John Henry Menton, Miles Crawford and others, and finally the judge, Sir Frederick Falkiner, pronounces a sentence on Bloom of imprisonment and of hanging afterwards. The second watchman appears and points to the pig's feet in Bloom's hand as "the bomb" or "infernal machine with a time fuse". Bloom pleads he'd been to a funeral and the apparition of Paddy Dignam appears, as well as the figure of John O'Connell the caretaker.

Then after all the visions described above, Bloom comes back to reality and meets a young whore, Zoe Higgins. But soon again Bloom seems to be "Leopold! Lord Mayor of Dublin!", and "the world's greatest reformer", greeted by a millionairess, a noblewoman, a bishop, an archbishop and the peers, and he seems to be making a speech: "I stand for the reform of municipal morals and the plain ten commandments. New worlds for old. Union of all, Jew, Moslem and Gentile ..." Soon he is once again attacked and then he is considered as "a finished example of the new womanly man", and Bloom says, "O, I so want to be a mother." Then he is stoned and is burned, and he is again with Zoe Higgins. He follows her into the musicroom where he finds Lynch and another whore Kitty Rocketts, and also Stephen and another whore Florry Talbot.

As Stephen philosophizes, strange figures appear and there is much lewd talk and action, with Bloom participating. Then Bella Cohen the whore-mistress enters, and the fan she holds seems to carry on a conversation with Bloom, then Bella herself and then many other figures appear and talk with Bloom. Then Bella goes to Stephen and he is about to give her all the money he has with him, but Bloom intervenes and pays her only what Stephen should pay her, and he counts the money that's left and promises to take care of it for Stephen, the latter being too far gone in his drinks. Then in Bloom's imagination again miscellaneous people appear, including Lenehan, Blazes Boylan, Marion, the two girls at the Ormond Restaurant Minna Kennedy and Lydia Douce, Mrs. Dignam holding a widow's insurance policy, Martin Cunningham, Lynch, and even Shakespeare (Shakespeare appears immediately after Lynch says, "The mirror up to nature"). Then after much dancing appear Stephen's mother and Buck Mulligan, and soon Stephen rushes out of the brothel, followed by Bloom who has to pay for the lamp broken by Stephen during his flight. After Bloom and Stephen are out in the street, there seems to be a hue and cry after them.

Now in Stephen's mind there seem to appear the soldier Private Carr and Cissy Caffrey and even Lord Tennyson and Edward the Seventh. Then distant voices are heard of "Dublin's burning!", followed by the comments by Father Malachi O'Flynn and the Reverend Mr. Haines Love, The Voice of All the Damned and The Voice of the Blessed as well as the Voice of Adonai, and then Corny Kellecher

430

identifies Bloom and Stephen. Finally two watchmen arrive and drive the gathering crowd away, after Bloom has told them Stephen is Simon Dedalus' son. Corny Kellecher the undertaker goes and Bloom leads and guides Stephen on their way, in the meantime thinking of his long-lost baby son Rudy.

This long section is one of the most objectionable as well as the most obscure of the eighteen episodes of the novel, objectionable because of the lewd talk and the obscene scenes in the brothel, and obscure because the innumerable people and events visualized in the mind of Bloom or of Stephen are given side by side with the few things the two and others actually do and say, and the visualized and the actual are not given separately but merged completely into one story. And the curious word-play and subtle literary echoes (e. g. Stephen's speech: "To have or not to have, that is the question." Lord Tennyson: "Theirs not to reason why.") that crop up here and there often add to humour but sometimes lead to confusion. However, this is another typical instance of the employment of the stream-of-consciousness method in fiction, and it is either condemned or praised by critics in the West partly for that reason.

The thirteenth episode relating to Bloom ("Eumaeus") actually belongs to the third and last "Part" of the book. This episode deals chiefly with Bloom and Stephen on their way to No. 7, Eccles Street, Bloom's home address, after their departure from the night town.

Coming out of the brothel Bloom finds Stephen's mind somewhat unsteady and as the youth wants something to drink Bloom decides to go to the cabman's shelter nearby. There being no conveyance of any kind at this time of the night, the two have to proceed on foot. On the way, a man at the sentrybox of a corporation watchman recognizes and salutes Stephen who returns the salute and enters into a short conversation with him, with Bloom remaining a short distance away. The man turns out to be a former friend of Stephen's father and being down and out asks Stephen to find a job for him and then entreats for some money. Stephen gives him half a crown and the man departs and Bloom rejoins Stephen.

Coming to the cabman's shelter, Bloom orders coffee and a bun for Stephen and they meet a number of stevedores and a sailor named Murphy who begins to tell tall tales of his adventures on the seas, at Stockholm, in Peru, in Trieste, etc. Bloom tries to lead the narrator on to Gibraltar and Europa Point where his wife Marion spent her girlhood, but the sailor says he's tired of "all them rocks on the sea ... and boats and ships", and goes on to other matters, to his son Danny going to sea, to the image at his own chest tattooed in blue Chinese ink. The face of a streetwalker now appears for a moment and is gone. Then Bloom asks Stephen whether he as a good Catholic believes in the soul, and the young man gives a very ambiguous answer: "They tell me on the best authority it is a simple substance and therefore incorruptible." The group then go on to talk about accidents at sea, ships lost in a fog, collisions with icebergs, etc. Soon some one is talking about the natural resources of Ireland and about "all the riches drained out of it by England levying taxes on the poor people", and the fall of England is predicted "despite her power of pelf on account of her crimes". But Bloom is sceptical on this last point. However, Stephen shows his patriotism by saying, "But I suspect ... that Ireland must be important because it belongs to me". Then Bloom reads about the burial of Dignam in "The Telegraph" and about the horse Throwaway at the races. Then some one suggests that "One morning you would open the paper ... and read, *Return of Parnell*". Next, Bloom produces his wife's photo taken when she was young and shows it to Stephen, and later Bloom advises Stephen against wasting his valuable time with profligate women but suggests one day taking a wife "when Miss Right came on the scene." But soon Bloom finds that Stephen hadn't had his dinner that night, so he invites the youth to his home, and they leave the cabman's shelter, with Stephen leaning on the older man. On the way they talk about music and meet a horse pacing by them, until they reach the house. On the whole, this episode is typical of Joyce's almost naturalistic way of jumbling up a whole mass of events and words of a group of persons revolving round the two central figures Bloom and Stephen.

The next episode, Bloom's 14th, or the last-but-one of the whole book (corresponding to "Ithaca" in Homer's "Odessey"), deals chiefly with Bloom in conversation with Stephen Dedalus before and after their arrival at No. 7, Eccles Street. The experimental form of questions and answers is used here to tell the story.

On their way from the cabman's shelter to No. 7, Eccles Street, Bloom and Stephen Dedalus discuss numerous topics: music, literature, Ireland, Dublin, friendship, woman, prostitution, the Roman Catholic Church, etc. On some of these topics they agree and on some others they don't.

On arriving home, Bloom discovers he has forgotten his latchkey, so he enters his house by climbing over the area railings, lights the gas, climbs the stairs, lets Stephen in by the halldoor, and they go down into the kitchen. Bloom kindles the fire, puts a saucepan on it to boil, washes his hands with the lemon-flavoured soap bought the morning before, makes offer to Stephen to wash and is rejected, then the kettle boils and Bloom makes two cups of cocoa. Here we find occasional yet elaborate explanations relating to water supply in Dublin and Bloom's admiration for water.

From his erroneous speculation that Stephen is engaged in mental composition while silently drinking the cocoa, Bloom is led to reminiscences of his contact with literature and music in his early years and then the older man thinks of his relations with the younger in many curious ways. A most interesting catechism is inserted here:

What, reduced to their simplest reciprocal form, were Bloom's thoughts about Stephen's thoughts about Bloom and Bloom's thoughts about Stephen's thoughts about Bloom's thoughts about Stephen?

He thought that he thought that he was a Jew whereas he knew that he knew that he knew that he was not.

Then the answers to follow the respective parentages, baptisms and educational careers of the two if the reticence between them were removed. (This is obviously meant by Joyce to show the great gap between the two men, in fact between any two human beings in general.)

Then Bloom's thoughts of how best to act toward his wife Marion are detailed. Next comes the exchange of views between Bloom and Stephen on the languages and on music. Then Stephen's recitation of a chanted legend of a Jew's daughter being a murderer leads to reactions from Bloom who begins to think of his daughter Millicent in her babyhood and in her adolescence. Finally Bloom returns to Stephen the sum of one pound and seven shillings that he had taken care of on Stephen's behalf during their adventure in the night-town. Finally Stephen takes leave, under the stars, and they shake hands while they hear the chime of the bells in the Church of St. George. As Bloom tries to re-enter the house he finds himself obstructed by the rearranged furniture in the front room effected by Marion Bloom during the preceding day. Then follows a detailed description of the various objects in Bloom's library. Then he sits down, removes his collar, unbuttons his clothes, and then follows his ambitious meditation on his ultimate ambition of "a thatched bungalow-shaped 2-storey dwellinghouse of southerly aspect," to be called "Bloom Cottage. Saint Leopold's Flowerville." Then he maps out for himself "his civic functions and social status among the country families and landed gentry", and the acquisition of vast wealth by rapid means is visualized in detail, through industrial channels and "the independent discovery of a goldseam of inexhaustible ore". Then he looks into the first and second drawers of his writing table and the contents therein are recorded. Especially significant are "a bank passbook issued by the Ulster Bank" and "certificate of possession of £900 Canadian 4% (inscribed) government stock" that indicate Bloom's financial status. Then Bloom imagines the possibility of reverses of fortune that might deprive him of these "supports", and thoughts come to him of poverty, mendicancy, destitution, nadir of misery, and other attendant indignities. Next he speculates on what to do in order to preclude such reverses of fortune, and the suggestion is either "by decease" or "by departure", and since the latter is preferred, he is not so sure whether to depart to some place in Ireland or to go abroad. Finally Bloom recounts all the things that had happened to him during the preceding day. Then after perceiving his wife's clothing he enters the bed, and he finds "the presence of a human form, female, hers, the imprint of a human form, male, not his, some crumbs, some flakes of potted meat, recooked, which he removed". This last makes him think of his possible predecessors as his wife's lovers, the last being Hugh E. (Blazes) Boylan, and he asks what his own sentiments are toward her lovers, whether it be envy, jealousy, abnegation or equanimity, and then what retribution, if any.

This episode ends with a conversation between narrator and listener, the listener being Marion who was actually lying awake and the narrator being Leopold Bloom. The listener asks questions, answered by the narrator, but the last question "Where" is unanswered because Bloom has gone asleep.

This episode illustrates Joyce's experiment in the inclusion of numerous details of actions, words and thoughts, particularly in connection with the personality of each of the three major characters, Leopold Bloom, Marion and Stephen Dedalus, and with the interrelationship between Bloom and Stephen and between Bloom and Marion.

The last of the eighteen episodes in "Ulysses" (corresponding to "Penelope" in the Homeric epic "Odessey") contains the well-known forty unpunctuated pages of Mrs. Marion Bloom's "silent monologue" before she falls asleep. This is possibly the most typical specimen of the stream-of-consciousness of a certain character whose thoughts merge into one another so naturally that no idea ends before the next one begins. This of course is what generally happens in real life, and the association of ideas is arranged with expertly care by the author. The result is these forty pages with no complete sentences make easy reading, the surprising lucidity surpassing ordinary prose passages in most modern novels. The influence of Freud and his psycho-analysis is here also very prominent and unmistakable, particularly as Marion's thoughts border on the subconscions or the unconscious.

Molly starts thinking about her husband's uncustomary request to have his breakfast in bed, and then remembers his efforts once to please a certain Mrs. Riordan who is then described deprecatingly with details. She turns back to comment none too favourably on Poldy (i.e. Bloom) and on an old maid Miss Stack who seems to be "sweet" on him. She suspects Poldy of flirting with other women or even being unfaithful to her, but she seems not to care. She remembers their maid servant Mary who was once asked to eat at their table by Bloom but who steals potatoes and charges high prices for oysters. She then thinks of Boylan and his eyes on her feet, of her girl friend Josie and her husband, of a certain Mrs. Maybrick that poisoned her husband, of Bartell D'Arcy kissing her on the choir stairs, of her earlier lover Gardner and of "that other fool Henry Doyle", of a respectful old gentleman Professor Goodwin, of her throwing a penny to a lame sailor, of the songs she sang on her concert tours, of her hating the mention of politics, of her enjoying the dinner given by the Lord Mayor, of the clothes and the face lotion she would like to buy, of the sound of a distant train reminding her of "Love's Old Sweet Song" that she sang, of her memories of Gibraltar and the heat there in her youth, of the books she used to read such as "The Moonstone" and "Eugene Aram", of a letter she once received from a Mrs. Dwenn who wanted to know the recipe for pisto madrileno, of her wish to have a love letter from Hugh Boylan and of the first love letter she ever received from Mulvey to whom she pretended that she had been engaged to the son of a Spanish nobleman, of herself inheriting the English accent from her father and her eyes and figure from her mother, of remembering Bloom once boasting he could row a boat and then of the two of them nearly got drowned, of wondering what kind of book is "Sweets of Sin" that Bloom had bought for her, of her disapproval of sending her daughter Milly to learn to take photographs, of imagining Milly now old enough for some one to dance attendance on her, of her experience in a box at the Gaiety with a gentleman of fashion staring down at her and Bloom on the other side "talking about Spinoza and his soul that's dead I suppose millions of years ago", of Stephen Dedalus getting all those prizes and of his father Simon

Dedalus "such a criticizer" with "a great big hole in his sock", of the report of Paddy Dignam's funeral in the paper, of her knowing "that French letter" still in Bloom's pocketbook, of Stephen Dedalus being 20 or more and of herself "not too old for him", and finally of the time Bloom proposed marriage to her and she answered yes.

It is true there are quite a few of what one might call smutty passages in these forty pages which are really not necessary though Joyce would probably argue that those are very naturally thoughts to come to the mind of one like Marion Bloom and that therefore it wouldn't be realistic representation to leave them out of the silent monologue. But for most of our readers this feature is highly objectionable.

However, setting the above objection aside, there is much to be said about the novelty of the experiment in this last part of "Ulysses" which aims at a detailed study of the intricate workings of the heroine's conscious and subconscious mind. For this passage is in its inimitable way a realistic psychological record of a rather ordinary woman character in modern fiction, though we cannot entirely endorse Arnold Bennett's overhigh praise: "The long unspoken monologue of Mrs. Bloom which closes the book (forty difficult pages, some twenty-five thousand words without any punctuation at all) might in its utterly convincing realism be an actual document, the magical record of inmost thought by a woman that existed. Talk about understanding 'feminine psychology'! ... I have never read anything to surpass it, and I doubt if I have ever read anything to equal it."

"Ulysses" was condemned as pornographic when it first appeared, and in recent years it has been very highly eulogized in the Western literary world as one of the greatest works of fiction in the 20th century. A fair estimate of the book would be that it is an uneven novel, with its numerous merits and equally numerous shortcomings. In the first place, this is a modern epic in prose, telling the adventures chiefly of a little man in one day in bourgeois Ireland but also of the many-sided activities of the city of Dublin, as far as possible in an objective way and with minimum interference from the author. In the second place, this is an important specimen in English of a modern novel written in the stream-of-consciousness style which aims at revolutionizing the fictional art by emphasizing the depiction of man's inner world of thought above the narration of events or the utterance of speeches. Though in novels psychological study began to have its place in the 18th and 19th centuries in Europe, it is not till the 20th century that under the influence of Freud and his psycho-analysis, thoughts of people are sometimes given precedence to their actions and words and are not just used as explanations of those actions and words. In this adoption of the stream-of-consciousness method Joyce went farther than Virginia Woolf, in his "Ulysses", where he dealt with more characters in a wider scope of their activities than we find in "Mrs. Dalloway" or "To the Lighthouse". In the third place, "Ulysses" has its strong appeal to the intellectuals, with the numerous subtle wordplays and ever-present literary echoes that on the one hand suggest the natural association of ideas going on all the time in Bloom's or Stephen's mind and on the other hand invoke humour or irony in the mind of the reader. In the fourth place, at least half of the book is brilliantly written. Of the eighteen episodes, the more significant include the first three that have to do with Stephen Dedalus, and the three following scenes about Bloom at his home, about his visits to the post office and the church and the bath, and about the burial of Dignam. Next in importance are the 9th and 10th sections that deal respectively with the discussion on Hamlet and the occurrences in the streets of Dublin, the 13th episode that describes Bloom's adventure with the three girls on the rocks near the shore, and the last that gives the unpunctuated monologue of Marion Bloom. These scenes not only produce vivid portraits of a number of minor figures (such as Buck Mulligan, Mr. Deasy, Simon Dedalus, Gertrude MacDowell, John Eglington, Uncle Richie Goulding and Blazes Boylan) and careful etchings of the three major characters Leopold Bloom, Marion Bloom and Stephen Dedalus, but they contain also many scintillating passages of wit and humour and irony (though little satire) as well as brief descriptive skits of interesting interplay between Bloom and his numerous acquaintances.

The first major defect of "Ulysses" lies in the amorality that seems to pervade the whole work. There is no right or wrong, no moral or ethical or social principle held by the author in order to guide the reader along, although occasionally Joyce seems to show just a faint trace of sympathy for Bloom or Stephen or even Marion. But, generally speaking, the impression one gets of the novel is that facts (including words and thoughts) are given as facts in the most matter-of-fact way. I suppose the author's intention is to be a hundred percent objective in his narration and that is to be truly realistic in his way of thinking. And that partly accounts for his numerous passages of straightforward descriptions of sex relations that may well be considered "pornographic".

The second shortcoming is the unevenness of the novel as a work of art. As stated above, there are some episodes that are brilliantly written, but even in these we may find many tame passages that jar with the bright spots before and after. The only five episodes that succeed in maintaining unbroken charm are when Stephen teaches school and talks with Deasy, when Bloom prepares the breakfast and meditates on Marion and Milly and Dignam, when Stephen carries on his heated arguments on Shakespeare, when Bloom and Gertrude MacDowell and her companions spend their late afternoon on the beach, and when Marion thinks and thinks and thinks before she falls asleep. The most unsuccessful episodes are: the conversation between Bloom and Stephen in the early hours of the morning that is curiously presented in the questions-and-answers form, the diffuse descriptions of the goings-on at the Lying-in Hospital, and the overlong representation of illusion and reality in all-too-rapid transition back and forth in the scenes in the night-town. In these chapters the trouble is not so much in the dull contents (though some scenes *are* admittedly dull) as in the clumsy and often unwieldy form that is employed in an experimental way.

The complaint of obscurity is the third major flaw of "Ulysses", especially in the numerous episodic scenes in the office of the Freeman's Journal and National Press and in the eighteen almost entirely unrelated bits in the happenings in the Dublin streets (except for the very loose link provided by the viceregal progress through the Irish capital). Of course obscurity is wellnigh unavoidable in the use of the stream-of-consciousness method, but it must be admitted that the obscurity brought about by the use of such a method in "Ulysses" is certainly much greater than in Virginia Woolf's "Mrs. Dalloway" or "To the Lighthouse". This obscurity is partly due to the author's love of word-play which can sometimes be very brilliant, but more often than not because the identities of the different minor characters generally have to be introduced gradually by their own words and deeds and not outright by the author.

Yet a fourth drawback of the novel is that it hardly contains any clearly-intended satire on the Dublin society or on any of the more important characters in the story, though the author reveals elsewhere his great disgust for the state of affairs in Dublin, Ireland. Joyce even lacks the strong patriotic sentiments of Yeats and other outstanding Irich writers connected with the Irish Abbey Theatre, although he mentions Parnell many times and also other revolutionary Irish leaders like Wolfe Tone. On the other hand he shows his definitely negative attitude toward the Sinn-Feiner known as The Citizen who delivers his harangue in Barney Kiernan's publichouse in the 12th episode.

It is difficult to arrive at a final estimate of Joyce's "Ulysses", after weighing the merits and demerits of the book as analyzed above. Yet at least we can say that it is an important book, because it indicates clearly where the wind is blowing in the field of prose fiction in 20th-century Europe, that in modern novels the exploration of the inner world of human existence has become more important or at least as important as the external events and the spoken words in human society. Besides, Joyce's intention to make this book a 20th-century epic comparable to Homer's "Odessey" is at least partly fulfilled from the artistic point of view. It is an epic because it tells a long and engrossing tale of a typical man (Bloom as Odysseus or Ulysses) and his wife (Marion as Penelope) and his son (in this case Stephen Dedalus is Bloom's "spiritual" son rather than "consubstantial" like Telemachus), and particularly of the hero's numerous adventures. The gap of more than two thousand years between Homer's "Odessey" and Joyce's "Ulysses" naturally made the 20th-century writer deal (1) with a "little man" of an advertisement canvasser rather than a big princely hero, (2) with his wife who is none-too-faithful to him but who has sufficient affections for him in her way and is ever ready to welcome him home even in the small hours of the morning,(3) with the hero's humdrum existence and his very tame adventures in a single town rather than Odysseus' valiant struggles with numerous supernatural forces, (4) with the use of prose rather than verse, and(5) with the employment of the stream-of-consciousness method rather than the traditional narrative pattern that emphasizes external action and pays little attention to the subtle workings of the human mind. Besides, Odysseus or Ulysses in the Homeric epic was actually a very different hero from Achilles in "Iliad" or Aeneas in "Aeneid", more an adventurer (at least in the major portions of the epic) than a military hero reputed in war, and therefore it may well be said that "Odessey" was a deviation from the orthodox epic tradition in European literature and was in a sense the first instance of the picaresque literary tradition in Europe. But because it was written at the primitive stage of human civilization when man still had to struggle hard against natural forces known and unknown, the supernaturals became very naturally what the hero was up against. But in the modern world the adventures the hero Bloom is engaged in have to be different from those Odysseus or Ulysses had to face, they have to be human individuals and institutions as well as the hero's and the heroine's own conscious and subconscious mind. In this sense "Ulysses" is an epic and at the same time a picaresque novel, though the picaresque novels of the past dealt chiefly with external actions and secondarily with spoken words and touched upon the thoughts of the characters only in so far as they had their bearings upon the actions and words and not independently for the illumination of the inner mental world of the characters. So the second major significance of "Ulysses" is that it is a modern epic as well as a modern picaresque novel and starts a thoroughly modern tendency in these two literary *genres*.

In "Ulysses", there are many bright spots that light up the scene like splendent flares of fireworks, sometimes in an episode that does not distinguish itself as a whole with its brilliance. The appearance of the old milk woman in the first episode is a good instance. The description of the poor old woman as a"messenger from the secret morning", her naiveté and her profundity as revealed in her colloquy with the three young men Stephen Dedalus, Mulligan and Haines, and her simple arithmetic in adding up the money owed her for her milk and finally her contentment with the florin she received—all these are delightful pictures of a woman of the people painted very vividly and colourfully, thanks to the author's intention of absolute objectivity in his portrayal of characters.

A similar scene of a felicitous portrait is that picturing Mr. Deasy the schoolmaster in the second episode. Here Deasy with his stern voice restores order among the contending young pupils around him, he pays Stephen and then lectures to the youth on "Money is power" and quotes Shakespeare's "Put but money in thy purse", he calls himself "an old fogey and an old Tory" but claims his loyalty to Ireland and he shows his fervent belief in the ways of the Creator and comments that a woman brought sin into the world, that "I have rebel blood in me too", and finally he tries to do some good to his people by wanting his letter on the foot-and-mouth disease to be published in some newspaper. A few touches here, and there he stands, as if alive.

The fourth episode in which Bloom first appears is perhaps the most variegated part of the whole novel. Here almost all the important threads and some of the unimportant ones in Bloom's daily life are touched upon: the major threads being his relations with his wife Marion, with his daughter Milly, and indirectly with Blazes Boylan, while minor events include (1) his pseudonym Henry Flower and the letters he received from different girls under that name, (2) his relish for the inner organs of beasts and fowls as food, (3) his impending trip to attend the funeral of Paddy Dignam, (4) his fondness for his cat, (5) his reading of the newspaper, (6) his observations on his way to and from the porkbutcher Dlugacz's, (7) his cogitations in passing by the publichouse Larry O'Rourke's, (8) His reactions to an advertisement of vast sandy tracts purchasable from the Turkish Government in the newspaper, (9) his conversation with Marion over the breakfast and the letters received in the morning, (10) his reading of the letter from his 15-year-old daughter Milly, (11) his entrance into the back garden, (12) his reading of an old number of "Tidbits" and his bowel movement, (13) his dream of writing a sketch or a story himself, (14) his wish to find out the time of the funeral and (15) his hearing the church bells. Of these details the very succinct comment on Larry O'Rourke, the intermittent conversation between Bloom and wife plus his musings as he takes up the tray of breakfast to her, and Milly's letter and Bloom's reminiscences of her and of the dead little Rudy are especially treasurable as masterly compositions of psychological depth. Even the short passage about the meaning of the word "metempsychosis" in the book "Ruby: the Pride of the Ring" is enlightening about Marion's impatience with scholarship and Bloom's dubious scepticism with regard to religion and the existence of souls after death.

One of the highlights in the novel as far as students of English literature are concerned is naturally the ninth episode in which Shakespeare and especially "Hamlet" are discussed at length. The discussion was opened, as it were, by John Eglinton when he said:

> Our Young Irish bards have yet to create a figure which the world will set beside Saxon Shakespeare's Hamlet though I admire him, as old Ben did, on this side idolatry.

Soon enough Stephen Dedalus' imagination comes into play:

> The play begins. A player comes on under the shadow, made up in the castoff mail of a court buck, a wellset man with a bass voice. It is the ghost, the king, a king and no king, and the player is Shakespeare who has studied *Hamlet* all the years of his life which were no vanity in order to

play the part of the spectre. He speaks the words to Burbage, the young player who stands before him beyond the rack of cerecloth, calling him by a name:

Hamlet, I am thy father's spirit

bidding him listen. To a son he speaks, the son of his soul, the prince, young Hamlet and to the son of his body, Hamnet Shakespeare, who has died in Stratford that his namesake may live for ever.

Is it possible that that player Shakespeare, a ghost by absence, and in the vesture of buried Denmark, a ghost by death, speaking his words to his own son's name (had Hamnet Shakespeare lived he would have been prince Hamlet's twin) is it possible, I want to know, or probable that he did not draw or foresee the logical conclusion of these premises: you are the dispossessed son: I am the murdered father: your mother is the guilty queen. Ann Shakespeare, born Hathaway?

George Russell, the poet A.E., is said here to object to "this prying into the family life of a great man". Then, following long digressions and interrupted remarks on Ann Hathaway, a question was put to Stephen:

Is it your view, then, that she (i.e. Ann Hathaway) was not faithful to the poet?

To which Stephen made his illuminating remark:

Where there is a reconciliation, there must have been first a sundering.

which he later elaborated:

If you want to know what are the events which cast their shadow over the hell of time of *King Lear, Othello, Hamlet, Troilus and Cressida,* look to see when and how the shadow lifts. What softens the heart of a man, Shipwrecked in storms dire, Tried, like another Ulysses, Pericles, prince of Tyre? ... A child, a girl placed in his arms, Marina.

Marina, a child of storm, Miranda, a wonder, Perdita, that

which was lost. What was lost is given back to him: his daughter's child. "My dearest wife", Pericles says, "was like this maid." Will any man love the daughter if he has not loved the mother?

After mentioning Shakespeare's will in which he left to his wife only his second best bed, Stephen went further to make his autobiographical interpretations of Shakespeare's other plays:

He drew Shylock out of his own long pocket. The son of a maltjobber and moneylender he was himself a cornjobber and moneylender with ten tods of corn hoarded in the famine riots. His borrowers are no doubt those divers of warship mentioned by Chettle Falstaff who reported his uprightness of dealing. He sued a fellowplayer for the price of a few bags of malt and exacted his pound of flesh in interest for every money lent. How else could Aubrey's ostler and callboy get rich quick? All events brought grist to his mill. Shylock chimes with the Jewbaiting that followed the hanging and quartering of the queen's leech Lopez, his Jew's heart being plucked forth while the sheeny was yet alive: *Hamlet* and *Macbeth* with the coming to the throne of a Scotch philosophaster with a turn for witchroasting. The lost Armada is his jest in *Love's Labour Lost*. His pageants, the histories, sail fullbellied on a tide of Mafeking enthusiasm. Warwickshire Jesuits are tried and we have a porter's theory of equivocation. The *Sea Venture* comes home from Bermudas and the play Renan admired is written with Patsy Caliban, our American cousin. The sugared sonnets follow Sidney's. As for fay Elizabeth, otherwise carroty Bess, the gross virgin who inspired *The Merry Wives of Windsor*, let some meinherr from Almany grope his life long for deephid meanings in the depth of the buckbasket.

Elsewhere Stephen adds in the same vein:

As for his family, his mother's name lives in the forest of

Arden. Her death brought from him the scene with Volumnia in *Coriolanus*. His boyson's death is the deathscene of young Arthur in *King John*. Hamlet, the black prince, is Hamnet Shakespeare. Who the girls in *The* Tempest, in *Pericles*, in *Winter's Tale* are we know. Who Cleopatra, fleshpot of Egypt, and Cressida and Venus are we may guess.

He had three brothers, Gilbert, Edmund, Richard. Gilbert ... is nowhere: but an Edmund and a Richard are recorded in the works of sweet William.

... In his trinity of black Wills, the villain Shakebags, Iago, Richard Crookback, Edmund in *King Lear*, two bear the wicked uncles' names. Nay, that last play was written or being written while his brother Edmund lay dying in Southwark.

He has hidden his own name, William, in the plays, a super here, a clown there, as a painter of Italy old set his face in a dark corner of his canvas. He has revealed it in the sonnets where is Will in overplus ... Richard, a whoreson crookback, misbegotten, makes love to a widowed Ann (what's in a name?), woos and wins her, a whoreson merry widow. The note of banishment, banishment from the heart, banishment from home, sounds uninterruptedly from *The Two Gentlemen of Verona* onward till Prospero breaks his staff, buries it certain fathoms in the earth and drowns his book. It doubles itself in the middle of his life, reflects itself in another, repeats itself, protasis, epitasis, catastasis, catastrophe. It repeats itself again when he is near the grave, when his married daughter Susan, chip of the old block, is accused of adultery .... Age has not withered it. Beauty and peace have not done it away. It is in infinite variety everywhere in the world he has created, in *Much Ado about Nothing*, twice in *As You Like It*, in *The Tempest*, in *Hamlet*, in *Measure for Measure*, and in all the other plays which I have not read.

Finally, Stephen agrees with Judge Eglinton that Shakespeare is all in all:

> The boy of act one is the mature man of act five. All in all. In *Cymbeline,* in *Othello* he is bawd and cuckold. He acts and is acted on .... His unremitting intellect is the hornmad Iago ceaselessly willing that the moor in him shall suffer.

And then John Eglinton winds up the discussion:

> When all is said Dumas *fils* (or is it Dumas *Père?*) is right. After God Shakespeare has created most.

After which Stephen (or was it Joyce?) replied;

> For a guinea, you can publish this interview.

Here in this episode there is enough of wit, mental speculation, literary interpretation, humour and irony on Shakespearean scholarship and criticism to bring delight to all who have a fair knowledge of Shakespeare's life and works! Here is Joyce's attempt to explain Shakespeare's transition from comedies through tragedies to tragicomedies in his playwright's career of a quarter of a century, contributing his theory amidst so many other theories. The fact that almost all the way through the discussion the author (or Stephen) seems to have his tongue in his cheek, while trying to link up in earnest what's in the plays with the life of the playwright by citing facts based on genuine scholarly findings or merely ideas ingeniously suggested by certain critics. The height of humour comes with Stephen's prompt answer of "No" to Eglinton's query whether he believes in his own theory. Stephen's answer seems to be the author's too. Both know that they have probably gone too far, though there's no denying that some of the remarks are verifiable if not already verified. At least the whole episode is extremely engrossing, and deserves to be rated highly as a document of Joyce's literary criticism.

"Finnegans Wake" was Joyce's last work, published in 1939. It took him altogether seventeen years to write (sections of it having appeared separately as "Work in Progress") and it was considered by the author himself as his masterpiece. The title of the book was taken from an Irish-American ballad about Tom Finnegan, a hod carrier who fell from a ladder and was apparently dead, but who revived during the wake when every one got drunk and some one spilled some whiskey on him. The main story of the novel, however, evolves round one night of the dreams and nightmares of an innkeeper Humphrey Chimpden Earwicker(abbreviated as H.C.E., standing for "Here Comes Everybody" and identifiable with the great sleeping giant Finn MacCool, supposedly buried under the city of Dublin) of whom Finnegan was a predecessor, and whose wife was Anna Livia Plurabella (standing for Ana Liffey the river that runs through Dublin as well as Ireland, or Eve or Iseult, and abbreviated as ALP). Two other characters of importance are the two sons of HCE and ALP, Shem and Shaun, who represent respectively introvert and extrovert, artist and practical man, creator and popularizer. The theme in the novel is that of death and resurrection, or that of cycles of change in the course of history, based essentially upon the cyclical theory of history as advanced by the Italian philosopher and historian Giovanni Batista Vico (1668—1744), that history passes through four phases: the divine or theocratic, when people were governed by their awe of the supernatural; the aristocratic (as in the days of Homer in ancient Greece); the democratic and individualistic (as in the transition from feudalism to the era of capitalism); and the final stage of chaos, a state of confusion leading human beings back to their reverence for the supernatural. Like W. B. Yeats, Joyce seems to have come to believe in this theory of cyclic pattern of social evolution, feeling that faith in religious myths is due to return to dominance in human society. Of course, this is sheer idealism!

However, the theme is not so important, the dream is not so important, the characters HCE and ALP and Shem and Shawn are not so important, as the language employed or rather manipulated by the author in the novel, language of words and phrases of multi-meanings and various suggestions and especially of puns that produce ambiguities and symbolic significances. All this naturally and in-

448

evitably leads to obscurity and confusion, particularly with the author's great learning and indulgence in his diversified mythical knowledge. Of course, it is once again Joyce himself whose life and thoughts are interwoven into the book, and it is Dublin that is revealed in the novel, but Joyce's idea here, more than even in his "Ulysses", is first of all to represent the whole cosmos via Dublin and to depict all humanity through his inevitable self-revelation, and that is too great an ambition for any writer to attempt to accomplish in any single work, if it is possible at all.

"Finnegans Wake" has been praised by some, but most critics and readers find that the huge efforts needed to decipher the multifarious meanings and suggestions and undertones are frequently not worth the while. The obscurity everywhere is the fatal blow that hinders the understanding and diminishes the pleasure that may be garnered from the reading of the novel. Too much symbolism further harms the realistic narration and the vivid character portraiture that are essential to any literary work. It should be admitted that certain passages in the book may contain great merits, as in the closing pages of the novel where Anna Livia Plurabelle (now totally identified as the river of life) forsakes her husband, sons and daughters and all the past and flows down to meet the sea her father, and where her monologue contains much lyrical beauty of a strange, unearthly type. But elsewhere the heavy-going reading resulting from the necessity to read repeatedly and even to be helped along by ample annotations makes most readers turn back, especially when a thorough comprehension of the book is none too rewarding in the end. Joyce defeats his own purpose.

b. Virginia Woolf

Virginia Woolf, née Stephen, was the daughter of the well-known English essayist, critic and biographer Sir Leslie Stephen. She was born in London in 1882 and was educated at home by private teachers and by her frequent contact with her father's eminent and political friends and with the large collection of books in the family library.

After her father's death in 1904 she and her sister and two brothers settled in Gordon Square, Bloomsbury, which later became the centre of certain writers and painters known as the Bloomsbury Group, of which the chief participants included Lytton Strachey the biographer, J. M. Keynes the economist, Bertrand Russell the philosopher, Desmond MacCarthy the critic, E.M. Forster the novelist, Roger Fry the art critic, as well as Virginia's sister Vanessa Bell an artist and her husband Clive Bell also an artist, and Virginia's husband Leonard Woolf a writer on politics and international affairs. Most of these people achieved their distinction in their varied fields and the Group was considered to hold unorthodox principles and sparkling intellectual conversations. In 1912 she married Leonard Woolf and the two together founded the Hogarth Press in 1917 which published a number of Virginia Woolf's own novels as well as some of T. S. Eliot's poems and Katherine Mansfield's short stories.

As early as her childhood she suffered from periods of nervous depression. Beginning from 1905 she began to write for the *Literary Supplement* of *London Times* and she continued to do so almost to the end of her life. In March 1915 her first novel "The Voyage Out" was published and it brought with it enthusiastic welcome from the public. Her second novel, "Night and Day" (1919), was also written in traditional form. Then, beginning from her next attempt at fiction, "Jacob's Room" (1922), she experimented with her new style of writing. Here the narrative about the central character Jacob Flanders is not presented in a continuous story: after his first appearance as a small boy on the seabeach in Cornwall, he is shown in a series of episodes at Oxford, London, Paris, Greece and other places, and he is portrayed by different people from different social stations who observe his various activities on the Oxford campus, in the British Museum Reading Room, at Versailles, on the Acropolis and elsewhere. The whole effect is a poetic presentation of city and country scenes in which the hero appears.

It was in the 1920s that she had her well-known "quarrel" with some of the established British novelists of the time, including chiefly Arnold Bennett, John Galsworthy and H. G. Wells. She objected strongly to them as "materialists", "because they are concerned not with the spirit but with the body", "that they write of unimportant things; that they spend immense skill and immense industry making the trivial and the transitory appear the true and the enduring." (in "Modern Fiction", 1925). She disapproves of "the form of fiction most in vogue", according to which "the writer is constrained — to provide a plot, to provide comedy, tragedy, love interest, and an air of probability". Then after pointing out with her own theory of a novel:

> "Examine for a moment an ordinary mind on an ordinary day. The mind receives a myriad impressions ... trivial, fantastic, evanescent, or engraved with the sharpness of steel. From all sides they come, an incessant shower of innumerable atoms; and, as they fall, as they shape themselves into the life of Monday or Tuesday, the accent falls differently from of old; the moment of importance came not here but there; so that, if a writer ... could write what he chose, ..., there would be no plot, no comedy, no tragedy, no love interest, or catastrophe in the accepted style .... Life is not a series of gig-lamps symmetrically arranged, life is a luminous halo, a semi-transparent envelope surrounding us from the beginning of consciousness to the end. Is it not the task of the novelist to convey this varying, this unknown and uncircumscribed spirit, whatever aberration or complexity it may display, with as little mixture of the alien and external as possible."

This sounds almost like a manifesto for the "stream of consciousness" type of fiction, and Woolf follows up with her praise of James Joyce as "the most notable" of "several young writers" who

> "attempt to come closer to life, and to preserve more sincerely and exactly what interests and moves them, even if to do so they must discard most of the conventions which are commonly observed by the novelist. Let us record the atoms as

they fall upon the mind in the order in which they fall, let us trace the pattern, however disconnected and incoherent in appearance, which each sight or incident scores upon the consciousness. Let us not take it for granted that life exists more fully in what is commonly thought big than in what is commonly thought small ..... In contrast with those whom we have called materialists, Mr. Joyce is spiritual; he is concerned at all costs to reveal the flickerings of that innermost flame that flashes its messages through the brain, and in order to preserve it he disregards with complete courage whatever seems to him adventitious, whether it be probability, or coherence, or any other of these signposts which for generations have served to support the imagination of a reader when called upon to imagine what he can neither touch nor see."

Of course Virginia Woolf had tried out her technical experiments with fiction in her earlier sketches which were collected and published under the title of "Monday or Tuesday" in 1921, and among these sketches we may already see the extreme richness of the author's imagination in one short piece "The Mark on the Wall" or in another "An Unwritten Novel", in both of which are visible "the flickerings of that innermost flame that flashes its messages through the brain". But beginning from 1925, Woolf finally launched her novels that belonged either definitely or more-or-less to the new style of "stream of consciousness": "Mrs. Dalloway" (1925), "To the Lighthouse" (1927), "Orlando" (1928), "The Waves" (1931), "The Years" (1938) and "Between the Acts" (1941). These novels, aside from their great psychological depths, contain much poetry in them or at least give us the feeling of poetic flow in her prose that is delightfully lyrical.

She was also a literary critic who contributed reviews regularly to the *Literary Supplement* of *London Times,* and these reviews and other essays were collected and published in "The Common Reader" (1925) and "The Second Common Reader" (1932). In these critical essays Woolf is never pompous but writes in an intimate, personal tone.

Woolf was also a feminist. She wrote three essays on three separate requests to which she contributed a guinea each, and these three pieces were collected into one book entitled "Three Guineas". All three had to do with the subject of women: one for a woman's college building fund, another for a society promoting the employment of professional women, while the third to help prevent war and "protect culture, and intellectual liberty". In "Three Guineas" she deplores the lack of opportunities for women to receive higher education in Britain and therefore women have little influence especially in politics, and she also points out the small pay received by most women employed in professional work because few women can enter Cambridge or Oxford and few of them can pass the Civil Service Examination on account of their limited education, and so she refuses to sign a pledge "to protect culture and intellectual liberty " because women are treated as inferior and therefore cannot be expected to have any real influence in protecting culture and intellectual liberty. Her feminism is also shown in some of the chapters in "A Room of One's Own" (1929). In "Shakespeare's Sister" (taken from chapter three), as Woolf comments on the women in Shakespeare's plays and decides that "it would have been impossible, completely and entirely, for any woman to have written the plays of Shakespeare in the age of Shakespeare", she imagines the poet to have had an "extraordinarily gifted sister" and then says that such a sister has no chance at all to use her gift for poetry",

Recurring attacks of mental tension and breakdown troubled her both in her childhood and after her marriage. In fact, it is known that she suffered from mental depression often after finishing a book. In 1941, in the midst of the many London raids in the Second World War, she took her own life by drowning.

"The Voyage Out", Virginia Woolf's first novel written more or less in the traditional way, nevertheless contains a few rather brilliant character-portraits and not a few germs of her later fiction of the psycho-analytical style. The first part of the book is a very light and airy narrative. Mr. and Mrs. Ambrose (Ridley the scholar and Helen his beautiful wife) left London on a ship with its owner her brother-in-law Willoughby and his innocent daughter of twenty-four, Rachel, as well as another scholar Mr. Pepper. Then they stopped at Lisbon to pick up Mr. and Mrs. Dalloway (Richard and Clarissa who were later to become central figures in "Mrs. Dalloway") whom they dropped at another port not far away, and then they sailed on again to some place in South America where Willoughby left them to go up the Amazon River on rubber business and where for some few months the Ambroses and Rachel and Pepper remained at an old villa owned by Willoughby. Even here Virginia Woolf's remarkable gift of vividly portraying her characters with a few strokes of her pen reveals itself first in distinguishing the two queer scholars Pepper and Ridley Ambrose, then in sketching the business man Willoughby who had his factories at Hull and eight ships running between London and Buenos Ayres, who aimed at becoming an M. P. some day and who had his great affection not only for his daughter Rachel but also for his deceased wife Teresa. But Woolf achieved distinction particularly in her brief yet penetrating psychological study of the aunt Helen and the niece Rachel. The Dalloways who only put in their very brief appearances are very definitely satirized as a couple of haughty but very shallow members of the ruling class in England. The novel only truly comes to life when two young men among the English visitors at a hotel nearby, Terence Hewet and St. John Hirst, are introduced together with a host of others, especially when Hirst is shown to be attracted to the aunt Helen while Terence falls in love with Rachel the niece. The tragic love between the latter two, ending in the lengthy illness and then death of Rachel, constitutes the highlight in the book, as the author spends much effort in describing the awakening to love of the Miranda-like Rachel and her prolonged suffering from fever that worries all the others. Here the author seems to disappear from the scene and the characters are allowed to proceed with the story themselves quite freely. In the last quarter of the novel, beginning with the expedition up the river in which only Helen and Rachel, Terence and St. John, and the organizers Mr. and Mrs. Flushing participate, there is more psychological analysis of the four major figures, especially of Rachel and Terence, as their exuberant thoughts run along with the words they exchange and with the few actions of their experience in the new environment. The novel certainly deserves the high praise from the authors friend E. M. Forster who writes of it:

> "It is a strange, tragic, inspired book whose scene is a South America not found on any map and reached by a boat which would not float on any sea, an America whose spiritual boundaries touch Xanadu and Atlantis. ... The closing chapters ... are as poignant as anything in modern fiction."

However, the two most widely read and appreciated of Virginia Woolf's novels belong most definitely to the category of the stream-of-consciousness technique: "Mrs. Dalloway" and "To the Lighthouse".

"Mrs. Dalloway" has greater unity than "To the Lighthouse", in that the story is centred upon the titular heroine. All the characters in the book have to do with her, with the exception of Septimus and Rezia (of course, Septimus' death by suicide is mentioned in connection with the appearance of his doctor Sir William Bradshew at Clarissa's party), so that there can be no doubt that Clarissa Dalloway is the central figure. However, it may be argued that the lighthouse or rather the visit to the lighthouse is the major thread that binds the novel "To the Lighthouse" together and achieves unity there.

In "Mrs. Dalloway" the stream-of-consciousness method is used most deliberately and also most successfully in the first part of the book, from the heroine going out to buy flowers to her hearing a pistol shot and the explosion of a motor car outside the florist shop when Septimus steps onto the scene. In these early scenes the thoughts of Clarissa merge with her actions and words, such as:

> " 'That is all,' she said, looking at the fishmongers'. 'That is all,' she repeated, pausing for a moment at the window of

a glove shop where, before the War, you could buy almost perfect gloves. And her old Uncle William used to say a lady is known by her shoes and her gloves. He had turned on his bed one morning in the middle of the War. He had said, 'I have had enough.' Gloves and shoes; she had a passion for gloves; but her own daughter, her Elizabeth, cared not a straw for either of them".

And when thoughts come they jump from one thing to another, from the present to the past, and recapitulations or flashbacks as in the movies are inevitable, though here the "recherche du temps perdu" is more for its own sake rather than to use it to explain some present action or to anticipate the future. So the disjointed thoughts are given chiefly to produce a fuller portrait of the character. A good instance may also be found in the following passage as the heroine walks on in St. James Park:

"So she would still find herself arguing in St. James's Park, still making out that she had been right — and she had too—not to marry him. For in marriage a little licence, a little independence there must be between people living together day in day out in the same house; which Richard gave her, and she him. (Where was he this morning for instance? Some committee, she never asked what.) But with Peter everything had to be shared; everything gone into. And it was intolerable, and when it came that scene in the little garden by the fountain, she had to break with him or they would have been destroyed, both of them ruined, she was convinced; though she had borne about with her for years like an arrow sticking in her heart the grief, the anguish; and then the horror of the moment when someone told her at the concert that he had married a woman met on the boat going to India! Never should she forget all that! Cold, heartless, a prude, he called her. Never could she understand how he cared. But those Indian women did presumably — silly, pretty, flimsy nincompoops. And she wasted her pity.

For he was quite happy, he assured her — perfectly happy, though he had never done a thing that they talked of; his whole life had been a failure. It made her angry still."
A passage like this is comparable to certain bright spots in Joyce's "Ulysses", though the train of thought here is more continuous than jumping about. A passage like this also seems to justify her accusation of Bennett, Wells and Galsworthy as "materialists" "concerned not with the spirit but with the body", but unfortunately there aren't enough passages of this kind in the novel to sustain the high level of character portraiture we expect to find in this new style of fictional writing.

However the general impression one gets is a thoroughly well-depicted picture of the heroine, not only from all her own actions and words and thoughts but also from the description of her relations with her husband Richard, her daughter Elizabeth, her former lover Peter Walsh, her oldtime friend Sally who has become Lady Rossiter, and other people she knows and has contact with. Mrs. Dalloway is shown with all her defects and foibles, but the satire is a very mild one always and there is sympathy for her throughout the story. By the use of the stream-of-consciousness method the author succeeds in making the heroine conscious of her own weaknesses and imperfections particularly in connection with the big party that she gives in imitation of the noble dame of the bourgeois-aristorcratic society and introduces people of all sorts and idiosyncrasies and that takes up some fifty pages of a none-too-fat book. Especially the scene of the presence of the Prime Minister at the assemblage which seems to add to the lustre of the party and to satisfy the hostess' vanity is filled with irony because the prime minister looks "so ordinary", "all rigged up in gold lace" and withdraws with old Lady Bruton "into a little room", and yet, as "Clarissa escorted her Prime Minister down the room, prancing, sparkling, with the stateliness of her grey hair", "with Sally there and Peter there and Richard very pleased", the hostess herself was aware that "these triumphs ... had a hollowness". And this novel on the whole proves the truth of Virginia Woolf's own dictum in her essay "Modern Fiction" that "Any method is right, every method is right, that expresses what we wish to express, if we are writers," and "Mrs. Dalloway" deserves the same kind of praise which Woolf lavishes on "Ulysses" and "Tristram Shandy" and "Pendennis":

"This method has the merit of bringing us closer to what we were prepared to call life itself; did not the reading of 'Ulysses' suggest how much of life is excluded or ignored, and did it not come with a shock to open 'Tristram Shandy' or even 'Pendennis' and be by them convinced that there are not only other aspects of life, but more important ones into the bargain."

The episodes about Septimus and Rezia constitute almost a separate story within the main framework of one day in Mrs. Dalloway's life and have their own significance. Here we have a soldier who has had his share of the long drawn-out trench warfare, who upon his return from World War I, and while stationed in Italy for a time, gets himself married to a Milanese girl hat-maker, and who is suffering now from some sort of mental derangement that makes him say again and again that he will kill himself. He is in a way persecuted by two very different doctors. Dr. Holmes the general practitioner reassures the man and his wife repeatedly that there is "nothing whatever the matter" with the patient, whereas the great West End physician and specialist on diseases of the mind Sir William Bradshaw considers Septimus to be "very seriously ill", "a case of extreme gravity", of "not having a sense of proportion", and recommends "a long rest in bed" in one of his "homes" "down in the country" where Septimus "would be perfectly looked after". Finally, this poor man trying desperately himself to recover from a nervous breakdown is so "persecuted" by Dr. Holmes and Sir William Bradshaw that he actually is forced more or less to end his life by plunging himself down the large Bloomsbury lodging-house window in order to escape from their power over him. This sub-plot is thus chiefly a satire on the treatment of the mentally sick by doctors high and low, though there is also a faintly suggested blame on the nervous strain resulting from the trench warfare of 1914—1918.

Great credit must also be given to the author for her successful portraiture not alone of the heroine but even of several minor figures dancing around her: Peter Walsh as once her lover who is a "failure" back from India, Richard Dalloway the husband as M.P. with his Committee in the House of Commons, and Sally Seton the old friend who possibly suggests Woolf's fellow-poet V. Sackville-West, even Elizabeth the daughter of seventeen who is very much under the influence of her history tutor Doris Kilman (who is always praying with her and wearing a mackintosh), even old Aunt Helena who used to be so formidable yet kind at Bourton but who now comes to the party, past eighty and ascending staircases slowly with a stick. Somehow these minor figures come to life either with a few glimpses into the past or via some flitting reminiscences of the heroine. In these character-sketches Virginia Woolf is particularly gifted as she wields this new method of hers which has been named by her as the stream of consciousness. Though the fact of her being born to the upper classes necessarily tempers her satire of the bourgeois-aristocratic society with a superabundance of humour that emanates from her understanding and sympathy for those she knew so well, "Mrs. Dalloway" is nevertheless a masterpiece of its kind in the sharp etching of the élite society of England in the early post-World-War-I days. The canvas in the novel is admittedly a much smaller one than Joyce's "Ulysses", yet Mrs. Dalloway the heroine is certainly a more colourful figure even than Leopold Bloom, the two being comparable in that in both cases the novel deals with one day in the central figure's life. The language in Woolf's novel is much more fluid and delightful, sometimes even lyrical, though there is more variety of style in Joyce's book.

"To the Lighthouse" contains little social satire but there is more sympathetic treatment of the major characters, particularly of Mrs. Ramsay who sometimes appears rather sombre and even tragic. The Ramsays with their eight children and four friends (Lily Briscoe the spinster painter, William Bankes the elderly scientist, Charles Tansley the scholarly aspirant of professorship and old Carmichael who eventually distinguishes himself as a poet) live on a small island in the Hebrides off northern Scotland, and their talked-of trip to the lighthouse nearby at the beginning of the novel is not realized till ten years later, toward the end of the book. The stream-of-consciousness method is carried out here as in "Mrs. Dalloway" but not so ostentatiously, though in certain passages the analysis of a major character's inner workings of mind goes deeper and subtler than in the earlier novel. Mrs. Ramsay whose whole life is devoted to her care for her children and to her admiration for her husband nevertheless thinks occasionally of social problems:

> "more profoundly, she ruminated the other problem, of rich and poor, and the things she saw with her own eyes, weekly, daily, here or in London, when she visited this widow, or that struggling wife in person with a bag on her arm, and a notebook and pencil with which she wrote down in columns carefully ruled for the purpose wages and spendings, employment and unemployment, in the hope that thus she would cease to be a private woman whose charity was half a sop to her own indignation, half a relief to her own curiosity, and become what with her untrained mind she greatly admired, an investigator elucidating the social problem."

But Mrs. Ramsay is first of all a mother of a big family, and her thoughts are therefore centred upon her children after all, so the stream of her consciousness runs most deeply in her contemplation of children:

> "Oh, but she never wanted James to grow a day older! or Cam either. These two she would have liked to keep for ever just as they were, demons of wickedness, angels of delight, never to see them grow up into long-legged monsters. Nothing made up for the loss. When she read just now to James, 'and there were numbers of soldiers with kettledrums and trumpets', and his eyes darkened, she thought,

why should they grow up, and lose all that? He was the most gifted, the most sensitive of her children. But all, she thought, were full of promise. Prue, a perfect angel with the others, and sometimes now, at night especially, she took one's breath away with her beauty. Andrew — even her husband admitted that his gift for mathematics was extraordinary. And Nancy and Roger, they were both wild creatures now, scampering about over the country all day long. As for Rose, her mouth was too big, but she had a wonderful gift with her hands. If they had charades, Rose made the dresses; made everything; liked best arranging tables, flowers, anything. She did not like it that Jasper should shoot birds; but it was only a stage; they all went through stages. Why, she asked, pressing her chin on James's head, should they grow up so fast? Why should they go to school? She would have liked always to have had a baby. She was happiest carrying one in her arms. Then people might say she was tyrannical, domineering, masterful, if they chose; she did not mind. And, touching his hair with her lips, she thought, he will never be so happy again, but stopped herself, remembering how it angered her husband that she should say that. Still, it was true. They were happier now than they would ever be again. A tenpenny tea set made Cam happy for days. She heard them stamping and crowing on the floor above her head the moment they woke. They came bustling along the passage. Then the door sprang open and in they came, fresh as roses, staring, wide awake, as if this coming into the dining-room after breakfast, which they did every day of their lives, was a positive event to them, and so on, with one thing after another, all day long, until she went up to say good-night to them, and found them netted in their cots like birds among cherries and raspberries, still making up stories about some little bit of rubbish — something they had heard, something they had picked up in the garden. They had all their little treasures .... And so she went down and said to her husband,   Why must they grow up and lose it all? Never will they be so happy again. And he was angry. Why take such a gloomy view of life? he said. It is not sensible. For it was odd and she believed it to be true; that with all his gloom and desperation he was happier, more hopeful on the whole, than she was. Less exposed to human worries — perhaps that was it. He had always his work to fall back on. Not that she herself was 'pessimistic', as he accused her of being. Only she thought life — and a little strip of time presented itself to her eyes — her fifty years. There it was before her — life. Life , she thought — but she did not finish her thought. She took a look at life, for she had a clear sense of it there, something real, something private, which she shared neither with her children nor with her husband. A sort of transaction went on between them, in which she was on one side, and life was on another, and she was always trying to get the better of it, as it was of her; and sometimes they parleyed (when she sat alone); there were, she remembered, great reconciliation scenes; but for the most part, oddly enough, she must admit that she felt this thing that she called life terrible, hostile, and quick to pounce on you if you gave it a chance. There were the eternal problems: suffering; death; the poor. There was always a woman dying of cancer even here. And yet she had said to all these children, You should go through it all. To eight people she had said relentlessly that (and the bill for the greenhouse would be fifty pounds). For that reason, knowing what was before them — love and ambition and being wretched alone in dreary places — she had often the feeling. Why must they grow up and lose it all? And then she said to herself, brandishing her sword at life. Nonsense. They will be perfectly happy. And here she was, she reflected, feeling life rather sinister again, making Minta marry Paul Rayley; because whatever she might feel about her own transaction, she had had experiences which need not happen to every one (she did not name them to herself); she was driven on, too quickly she knew, almost as if it were an escape for her too, to say that people must marry, people must have children."

This passage is comparable, in a miniature way, with Molly Bloom's meditations in bed at the end of Joyce's "Ulysses", though the other is in the first person singular, unpunctuated and in incomplete sentences. And there are quite a number of similar passages of lengthy meditations recorded of Mrs. Ramsay and Lily Briscoe, of the former's very subtle sort of relationship with her husband and of the latter's observations of the people around her, particularly of Mr. and Mrs. Ramsay and Bankes and Tansley. Then there is a touch of pathos in the second of the three main sections of the novel, "Time Passes", in which is shown how Mrs. Ramsay died suddenly one night, how Andrew died in the War, how Prue died of childbirth and how this house on this island in the Hebrides was deserted for ten years, and in which the scene of the deserted house and the conversations of the caretaker Mrs. McNab and her helper Mrs. Bast make up an elegy of the three dead people and of the inexorable ravages brought about by the passage of time.

The third and last part of the book, "The Lighthouse", deals chiefly with the family's visit finally to the lighthouse that had been put off for ten long years. Only Mr. Ramsay and James and Cam are left to go on the visit, and Lily Briscoe back at work on her painting is now the one to meditate and observe the goings-on around her. But Mrs. Ramsay's spirit is still with them, hovering especially over the cogitations of Lily Briscoe who remembers "the astonishing power that Mrs. Ramsay had over one" and laments that "Mrs. Ramsay has faded and gone … she recedes further and further from us … all her being, even her beauty, became for a moment, dusty and out of date." At about the same time, Mr. Ramsay, in the boat sailing toward the lighthouse with Cam and James, is still the tyrannical figure he used to be and if he should say something quite unreasonable, "James thought, then I shall take a knife and strike him to the heart,"this last being an old symbol of the children's fear and rebellion against his tyranny.

Compared with "Mrs. Dalloway", "To the Lighthouse" showed signs of decline of Virginia Woolf as a great novelist and as a wielder of the stream-of-consciousness method. Only Mrs. Ramsay is a truly well-drawn character but there is too much passivity about her, and the psycho-analysis of the major figures including even that of Mrs. Ramsay herself falls short of the brilliant interweaving of thoughts with actions and words in the earlier novel. And there is almost no social criticism to speak of here as we find a lot of it in the portraiture of Mrs. Dalloway and Peter Walsh and Sally Seton and in the depiction of the heroine's party and of the tragic outcome of Septimus brought about chiefly by the two doctors Holmes and Bradshaw.

"Orlando; A Biography" was a less successful but more experimental and daring work than any of her other novels. It begins with Orlando as a boy of sixteen in an aristocratic family in Elizabethan England who having no opportunities for military ventures turns to the writing of poetry and of a tragedy of horrid crimes. He attends on the queen, then meets and falls in love with a Muscovite princess but retires to his country house after the princess' sudden departure. He goes back to his literary career and later on prevails on Charles II (in late 17th century) to send him to Constantinople as ambassador extraordinary. Upon his return to England he is rewarded with a dukedom and enters into the notorious social gatherings of the time, getting himself mixed up with women of ill repute including Nell Gwyn, Charles II's mistress. He wakes up after a seven-day trance and finds himself to have changed into a woman and a dancer Rosita Pepita. As Lady Orlando she lives through the centuries, from the time of Queen Anne in early 18th century through the Victorian age to early 20th century. She knows Pope and Swift and Addison and later marries a sailor. She finishes and publishes a poem begun in the 16th century and wins a prize. Then she has a baby and in 1928 drives her own car back to her estate in Kent. The book is supposedly inspired by the author's great friendship for the poet Victoria Sackville-West to whom the novel was dedicated. Some critics have suggested the novelist's reference to Sapphism or her interest in the feminine and the masculine within an identical person, but the novel is after all not much more than a curiosity in literary history.

"The Waves" was also an experimental work in fiction in which there is no connected story, but which contains descriptions of nature in a day from dawn to dusk and also interior dialogues of several characters giving glimpses of their lives from childhood to old age. They are shown together in their childhood, then they go their several ways, only to meet again once at a dinner in a French restaurant in London and then later again to share their meals together at Hampton Court. Their lives are uninteresting but different one from another and their attitudes toward nature are also divergent. There are six characters each of whom utters a soliloquy at one moment in their lives (at one moment in the day), prologued with a description of the natural world around them. Then there is a seventh character, Percival, whose departure for India serves as the first reunion for all of them. Of the six major characters, two of them are social outsiders, Louis whose father is a banker in Brisbane and who has an Australian accent while Rhoda is a fatherless orphan, so that both are strangers to the English upper class. Therefore they two are self-conscious from their childhood and react to their alien position in English society. More prominent than the others is Bernard who seems to bring all of them together, and he makes the final soliloquy which serves as the summing-up of the novel. In this novel, Woolf emphasizes the role of nature upon human individuals though each of them usually reacts differently to the same natural scene. Except for the representation of social inequality in the interior dialogues of Louis and Rhoda, the novel is just another experiment in the stream of consciousness method, but lacking in depth as compared with "Mrs. Dalloway" or "To the Lighthouse".

"The Years" is in a sense a historical novel in that it deals with the lives of the Pargiter family in England between 1880 and 1918 and then (skipping the significant year of 1919 which marked the emancipation of women in England with the passage of the bill for women's suffrage) to the "present day". Though the novel contains more political implications than any other work of fiction by Woolf, as there are powerful descriptions of urban poverty and violence and of striking economic disparities within and between the social classes, yet public events are still subordinated to domestic scenes and dinner parties, while historical incidents are only alluded to such as the deaths of Parnell and of King Edward, the Irish Civil War, the women's emancipation movement, the rise of Mussolini, etc., but they are not commented upon, nor are those incidents given their historical significance or their effect upon the characters' lives.

Besides the Pargiters, there are here also two "outsiders" who don't belong to the English upper class: Nicholas Pomjalovsky who is a foreigner and a homosexual and Eleanor who is one of those "daughters of educated men". Eleanor and Nicholas, like Louis and Rhoda in "The Waves", feel strongly their dubious position as aliens to the English "society", and so Eleanor asks Nicholas, "When shall we live adventurously, wholly, not like cripples in a cave?" Three generations of Pargiters are dealt with. At the beginning of the book Abel Pargiter of the first generation makes his clandestine visit to his mistress while his wife Rose lies dying in their huge house. For the next generation there are four Pargiter daughters and three Pargiter sons. One of the daughters Rose has painful memories of "a certain engagement" and later becomes a suffragette. Another daughter Delia as a girl daydreams about the Irish revolutionary Parnell but later gets herself married to a conservative Anglo-Irish landlord. A third daughter Milly marries a rustic gentleman in the south of England and lives contentedly producing his children. The eldest of the four Eleanor neither marries nor rebels and then in her old age regrets not having found herself a companion. The three Pargiter sons follow the three professions commonly chosen by gentlemen's sons, the scholar (Edward, a classical scholar at Oxford), the law (Morris who later makes a prosperous marriage) and the army (Martin who had wished to be an architect). None of the seven children are satisfied with their lives. Two daughters of another and relatively poorer branch of the Pargiter family, Maggie and Sara, are described to have grown up in a shabby apartment, with the former entering into a relatively happy though unconventional marriage with a foreigner and the latter becoming isolated and harmlessly insane. Even lawyer Morris' daughter Peggy who stands for the new woman and becomes a doctor is isolated and embittered and leads what she herself calls a "suppressed life", now that she is thirty-seven and her hair is turning grey. Another youngster, scholar Edward's nephew North, after spending years in the army and on an African sheep farm, returns to London feeling himself out of place and begins to think of marriage as the only way out after a long bachelorhood. So when all these Pargiter people of the second and third generations meet together at Delia Pargiter's elaborate family reunion none of them is really satisfied with life as they feel the strong contradictions between their private and public worlds or between their personal desires and the objective conditions of the society and they react keenly to the artificial boundaries set up between people, or to the petty tyrannies of the household or to the split between the young and the old, though every one of them present is making a good income and is sharing his or her middle-class privileges. Throughout "The Years", Virginia Woolf seems to be tracing the historical development of English society from the optimism of the last decades of the 19th century to the pessimism of the"present day", and there is in it the feeling of decline for England with the passage of the years. However, the book appears scattered and loose in structure, though the author's social criticism is here sharper than in her earlier novels. But, above all, the novelist's intensified feeling of despair and despondency seems definitely to point on the one hand to her intellectual maturity and on the other to the approaching tragic end of her life. The mounting individualism of the writer as a middle class intellectual of the Bloomsbury group, marching head-on against the disintegrating English society on the eve of World War II, inevitably led to her personal destruction when the worldwide debacle finally came.

Virginia Woolf's last novel, "Between the Acts" is certainly the weakest of her later works of fiction. The hosts for the village play are first described, including the old grandpa Oliver and his grandchildren, the mother Isa and Giles "the father of her children", and also Mrs. Swithin the sister of old Oliver, and then they are joined by two visitors, the oversexed Mrs. Manresa and the man who came with her, William Dodge. The play eventually begins on the lawn, with the players drawn largely from the villagers, and the audience arriving, and then Miss La Trobe who is the author as well as the director of the play. The drama contains several episodes drawn chronologically from English history. The highlights are the Elizabethan era and the Victorian age, with intermissions after each of the two episodes, and finally the drama closes with "The Present Time, Ourselves" when the audience are merged with the players to make up "ourselves". At the end, a clergyman emerges to collect from the audience the contributions to the performance for the benefit of the church, and then he looks in vain for the author Miss La Trobe to appear. The dispersing audience are at a loss as to the message of the play and divergent interpretations are offered. Then the novel winds up with the departure of all the audience and players and finally the author, and the hosts only are left on the Pointz Hall.

The story is scattered and the characters are very indistinctly presented. However, the play given in the novel is obviously meant to present the decline of England from the glorious days of the two queens Elizabeth and Victoria to the humdrum and degenerating English society of the twentieth century. If there is any satire at all in the novel, it is to be found near the very end of the play, when the megaphone from somewhere speaks out: "Before we part, ladies and gentlemen, ... let us talk in words of one syllable, without larding, stuffing or cant, ... And calmly consider ourselves ... Some bony. Some fat. ... Liars most of us. Thieves too .... Consider the gun slayers, bomb droppers here or there. They do openly what we do slyly. ... A tyrant, remember, is half a slave. Item the vanity of Mr. H. the writer, scraping in the dunghill for sixpenny fame ....Then there's the amiable condescension of the lady of the manor — the upper class manner. And buying shares in the market to sell 'em .... O we're all the same. ... Look at ourselves, ladies and gentlemen! Then at the wall; and ask how's this wall, the great wall, which we call, perhaps miscall, civilization, to be built by ..., scraps and fragments like ourselves?" This may be regarded as Mrs. Woolf's own cynical comment on the boasted"civilization"of her society,including attacks on different individuals therein. But the ending of the play is a tame one, and so is the ending of the novel. Except for one significant speech by Isa, the hostess of Pointz Hall, somewhere near the end of the play, "O that my life could here have ending", which represents somehow the author's own valedictory anticipatory to her suicide which took place shortly after her completion of "Between the Acts" (as the last entries in her "Diary" testify.)

Virginia Woolf was an important novelist in early twentieth-century England. She was known in her time chiefly for the use of the stream-of-consciousness method in fiction, for her critical battle waged against Bennett, Wells and Galsworthy, for her important role in the Bloomsbury group of prominent intellectuals who exerted so much influence upon British culture in the 1910s, 1920s and 1930s, and for her activities as a feminist both before and after the year 1919 when British women won their rights of suffrage. Since the Second World War of which she was in a sense a victim, her reputation has soared somewhat, especially since the 1960s, and she has been placed among the major writers of English fiction of early 20th century and eulogized for her realistic and critical interpretation of political-social life in Britain particularly in the 1920s and 1930s. Her critical essays in the two series of "The Common Reader",her short stories and her novels especially of her later years (including "Mrs. Dalloway", "To the Lighthouse', "The Waves", "The Years") are now appreciated not only for the beautiful prose style which is frequently poetic, but chiefly for her critical insight, for her realistic presentation of the inner mental worlds of her fictional characters, and for her subtle though occasional satiric thrusts on the personal foibles and social vices of the upper middle classes of England that she knew so well because she herself was one of them.

In the development of the English novel Mrs. Woolf shares honours with James Joyce in perfecting the stream-of-consciousness type of fiction which was begun (but not widely noticed) in England by Dorothy Richardson (1873—1957) with her twelve-volume novel "Pilgrimage" (1915—1938). Resembling Joyce's "Ulysses", Woolf's "Mrs. Dalloway" deals with one day in the principal character's life, while special emphasis is laid on the interior thoughts of the heroine rather than on the exterior happenings. This is a truly modern tendency, which has arrived with the ever growing complexity of human existence as the modern man/woman not only does things and says things, but does a lot of thinking which may or may not have anything to do with his/her actions or speeches. Although the "interior monologue" may be traced back to Flaubert in the 19th century and even to Sterne and Richardson in the 18th, or all the way back to the long soliloquies in Shakespeare, yet except for some few soliloquies in Shakespeare and for certain passages in Sterne, the thoughts of the characters in the older fictional classics are given to explain these people's actions and words and not for the sake alone of presenting the thoughts themselves. Actually, especially true with the modern man/woman in the modern world, thoughts may take up much of his/her time and assume great importance in his/her life, so Joyce's and Mrs. Woolf's attempt to highlight the thoughts in relation to the actions and speeches of their characters is in a sense a worthy effort toward greater realism in depicting modern life. Especially in their merging of the thoughts with the actions and speeches of their characters in the so-called stream-of-consciousness method we find their further groping for a more realistic presentation of life, for in real life one's actions and speeches are very frequently interrupted by one's thoughts, or rather actions, speeches and thoughts follow one another interspersed and interlarded in haphazard fashion in one's conscious existence, with the passage of time serving as a continuous stream. Actually there are moments (and they are not too few with some people) in one's life in which there is a vacuum (i.e. no actions, speeches, or thoughts at all) while time flows on, but at any rate thoughts very frequently fill in the gaps of human consciousness when there are no actions or speeches and while these thoughts may be very trivial, they may also be important, or at least significant for the revelation of the character or personality or major characteristics of a person. Of course, Joyce in "Ulysses" and more especially Woolf in "Mrs. Dalloway" or "To the Lighthouse" often inserts extremely long passages of "interior monologue" that seem to outbalance the actions and speeches of importance, yet at least their over-emphasis on thoughts as an indispensable and important part of human consciousness serves as a modern and healthful corrective to the neglect or total omission of human thoughts in many fictional works of the earlier centuries. However, it is easy to note down the actions and speeches of persons other than the writers themselves, but it is difficult and almost impossible to peep into the inner workings of mind of any one outside the author. So, Joyce's Leopold Bloom's thoughts presented in "Ulysses" must have been largely drawn from Joyce's own thoughts in his adult experience (and Stephen Dadelus' thoughts from Joyce's in his youth), just as Mrs. Dalloway's (and possibly also Mrs. Ramsay's in "To the Lighthouse") thoughts must have derived from Virginia Woolf's own recollections of what she thought on different occasions. This is possible and may more easily lead to success in one novel or in two or three, but beyond that the thoughts of the characters must have been simply imagined by the author and in that case they may not appear real and lifelike as they are not taken directly from real life. This seems to be a necessary limitation for the practitioner of the stream-of-consciousness technique, and restricts the employment of the device by a large number of novelists, especially if they do not belong to the group of thoughtful or highly imaginative people. And, after all, actions and speeches are usually more important than thoughts in the lives of the fictional characters as in real people, except when the characters or the authors are those who indulge in thoughts and fancies, like Uncle Toby and Laurence Sterne, and so though significant thoughts should be represented in fiction, yet in the choice ough of details to be included in their narration the novelists should pounce upon more actions and speeches of the characters rather than their thoughts. However, Joyce and Woolf have certainly made their important contribution to the development of the novel by emphasizing the thoughts of the characters with the introduction of the stream-of-consciousness device.

In comparison with Joyce, Woolf's canvas is a smaller one as her experience was restricted to her own social circle whereas Joyce had more contacts with people in all walks of life (at least in Dublin). On the other hand Woolf in her novels and stories is a subtler and more careful etcher of the intricate workings of her character's minds than Joyce, and her psychological analysis sometimes goes beyond the major characters and includes some minor figures like Septimus and Sally Seton in "Mrs. Dalloway" and Lily Briscoe and Charles Tansley in "To the Lighthouse", while Joyce only concentrates his attention on the principal figures like Leopold Bloom and Marion Bloom and Stephen Dadelus in "Ulysses". And Virginia Woolf writes an enviable prose style that flows limpidly on and on and sometimes bits of her prose passages are truly poetic, and while both Joyce and Woolf have their moments in which they go in for social criticism or even social satire, more often than not they have much sympathy for the characters of their creation, and there is usually plenty of humour to dilute the satire. However, Woolf's satiric thrusts at the vices and foibles, social and personal, that belong to the English upper middle classes, like Joyce's social criticisms on Dublin life, are sometimes very penetrating and at the same time quite subtle, and this is something not to be overlooked in any overall evaluation of Woolf as of Joyce's writings. Virginia Woolf was a staunch feminist all her life. She showed her active participation in the struggle for women's rights, particularly in her "Three Guineas", and she never faltered even after women were granted the rights of suffrage and jobs, but fought on even in her last novels, such as "The Years". But she was a pessimist, with her pessimism growing from the 1920s through the 1930s until the advent of the Second World War when the terrible violence and the destruction wrought during the siege of Britain by German bombers became too much for her to endure. Her suicide and all her bewailings of the decline of Britain from Victorian prosperity and power to Edwardian and Georgian loss of prestige and post-World-War-I depression may be something negative, but they are nevertheless indications of her protest, albeit a mild one, against the capitalist status quo in Britain.

c. E. M. Forster (1879—1970)

Edward Morgan Forster was born in London. His father was an architect and his mother's family was known for its evangelical tradition and its devotion to reform and philanthropy. He himself was not a Christian but could not free himself entirely from the influence of Christianity. His attendance at a public school at Tonbridge was an unhappy one, but he enjoyed much his years at Cambridge University where he formed lasting friendships, and he and his intellectual companions were absorbed to the views of Cambridge philosopher G.E. Moore and founded "Apostles" that stressed the need for true friendship in the hypocritical world. Shortly after the Boer War he started his career as a journalist, and contributed to the Independent Review which was an organ of liberalism in opposition to the aggressive foreign policy of the Conservative Joseph Chamberlain Government. He went to Greece with his friend G. Lowes Dickinson the Greek scholar and spent some time in Italy, and he was much inspired by ancient Greek literature and mythology and Italian Renaissance art. He wrote and published four novels in the first decade of the 20th century. During the First World War he spent much time as a Red Cross worker in Egypt which was responsible for his books "Alexandria: A History and a Guide" (1922) and "Pharos and Pharillion" (1923). In the meantime both in the years before and after the First World War he became associated with a circle of London intellectuals known as the Bloomsbury Group, so called because these people met and formed an informal group in Bloomsbury district, at the homes of Virginia and Leonard Woolf and Vanessa (Virginia's sister) and Clive Bell, where were gathered a number of well-known figures. Many members of the Bloomsbury group were originally followers of G.E. Moore in Cambridge and they showed their distinct antipathy toward the respectable society in England, prided themselves on their intellectual aloofness, advocated liberalism in politics, education and art, fought for freedom for women, for colonial peoples, for the poor, even for homosexuals, and emphasized the importance of harmony between spiritual life and material civilization and the need of mutual understanding in human relationships. Forster had a long and continuous contact with the Bloomsbury Group and was very much under the influence which was discernible in his novels.

Forster paid an extended visit to India in 1912—13 with G. Lowes Dickinson and then another shorter trip there in 1922, and out of his experience in the sub-continent came his most important novel, "A Passage to India". He also wrote another novel "Maurice" that dealt with a homosexual's search for truth and happiness, but it was not published till after his death in 1971. In the 1920s he also wrote some short stories, published in two collections: "The Celestial Omnibus" (1922) and "The Eternal Moment" (1928), and delivered a series of Clark Lectures at Cambridge University in 1927 which were collected and published in the same year under the title of "Aspects of the Novel", and roused much interest as a discursive discussion on the theory of fiction by a novelist.

In the Post-World-War-II years, he received an honorary fellowship at King's College, Cambridge, where he spent most of his time. In 1951 was published a collection of his miscellaneous essays "Two Cheers for Democracy", which contains two parts: Part I was written mainly in the 1930s and entitled "The Second Darkness", while Part II begins with a well-known essay "What I Believe", followed by groups of essays on "Art" and "Places". In the preface, Forster explains the title of the book: "We may still contrive to raise three cheers for democracy, although at present she only deserves two"; and the two cheers democracy deserves are, according to the essay "What I Believe": "one because it admits variety and two because it admits criticism." Earlier in 1936, another collection of essays was published, "Abinger Harvest", with four parts, of which the second part includes essays on Ibsen, T. S. Eliot, Proust, Conrad and others.

"Where Angels Fear to Tread" (1905), the earliest of Forster's novels, is a hit on the narrow-mindedness and hypocrisy of the respectable middle class in England. The Herritons, especially Mrs. Herriton the mother, cannot swallow up the idea of remarriage for the 30-year-old daughter-in-law who is a widow with a nine-year-old daughter. But before they can prevent her, the young woman has already married a dentist's son in Italy. The marriage does not work out well and the wife died in childbirth. Then there is the struggle for the new-born baby whom his Italian father will not give up. The infant is stolen and in an accident he is killed. The Herritons and their conservative views of respectability are censured here and hence the title of the book is taken from the proverb: "Fools rush in where angels fear to tread".

"The Longest Journey" (1907) scores another hit on the English middle class notions of respectability when the public announcement of Stephen as an illegitimate son of the chief character Rickie's mother led to a strong sense of shame to Rickie's wife Agnes who insisted on Stephen being sent abroad. Stephen's refusal to go and Rickie's open quarrel with Agnes over her scheming to banish Stephen indicate the author's disapproval of the narrow-minded views of family honour, especially with Rickie's tragic sacrifice of his own life to save his drunkard half-brother from the rails at a railway crossing. Yet another theme in "The Longest Journey" is satire on the English public schools of the day, which was based chiefly

Forster's his own experience at the boarding school at Tonbridge.

"A Room with a View" (1908) stresses Forster's view of the importance of harmony and understanding in human relationships. The heroine in the novel, Lucy Honeychurch, was brought up in a middle class English family with its conventional standards of "good breeding", and so when she and her elderly cousin Charlotte Bartlett did not get from an Italian Pension in Florence the promised "room with a view" over the Arno River and another guest at the Pension, Mr. Emerson, offered to give them his own room and that of his son that provided a better view, they declined the offer and considered it rather bad form, and they only agreed on the exchange upon a clergyman the Reverend Mr. Beebe's persuasion. Later, Lucy had many occasions meeting the Emersons and seeing the sights with the father and the son George. Once she alone witnessed one Italian in a quarrel stabbed by another and falling dead right in front of her, she fainted away and then upon recovery found herself in the arms of George Emerson who had been there all through the scene. Another time when Lucy on sightseeing was left alone and she fell down a hill slope, and there George Emerson came by and kissed her. She took all this as unforgivable rudeness and effrontery from George and left Florence for Rome immediately with her cousin. Lucy after her return to England was affianced to a man named Cecil Vyse, who disapproved of her numerous social engagements and wanted to restrict her activities, and this went against her desire for independence. In the meantime, the Emersons moved to live in the neighbourhood, and Lucy eventually broke up with Cecil Vyse and married George Meredith. On the one hand in this novel Forster described the passing of the old conventions governing marriage in respectable families, while on the other he apparently tried to illustrate his idea of social harmony as more essential to matters of love and marriage and general human conduct than rigid conventions of the genteel society.

"Howards End" (1910) is the last and the most outstanding of the four early novels of E. M. Forster, and it is the most complicated in plot construction. The story deals chiefly with two families in England, the Wilcoxes who represent the upper class in England with their affected genteelness and hypocritical "good taste" and the Schlegels who stand for petit-bourgeois intellectuals of part-foreign (in Schlegels' case part-German) origin with their freer conduct and more sympathetic inclinations and broader artistic and cultural interests, while occasional though vital events are touched upon that involve a third family of lower social station, the Basts, poor but aspiring to be on an equal footing with their "betters", intellectually and culturally. The Schlegel sisters Margaret and Helen got acquainted with the Wilcoxes during their holiday trips to the European Continent, then suddenly Helen on a visit to Howards End, one of the country homes of the Wilcoxes, wrote her sister Margaret about her falling in love with young Paul Wilcox, and though their innocent flirtation only lasted a few hours, her aunt rushed to Howards End to try to dissuade the girl from what she thought to be an undesirable match. The Schlegels went one evening to a concert to listen to Beethoven's Fifth Symphony, and on departure Helen took by mistake an umbrella belonging to one Leonard Bast, a poor, young, white-collared clerk at an insurance company, and the two sisters got to know him and his wife Jacky who was several years older. Bast then worked in a bank and lost the job with the reduction of the staff there, and when Wilcox didn't offer help to the Basts, the Schlegel sisters were outraged and Helen brought the starving Basts to the wedding of Wilcox's daughter Evie in order to shock them, but it turned out that Wilcox the father and Jacky Bast had been secretly lovers long ago. However, Margaret forgave Wilcox and married him, while Helen went to the Continent of Europe and came back pregnant with Leonard Bast's child. Wilcox's elder son Charles struck down Leonard for his seduction of Helen and Leonard died of heart failure, while Charles was sentenced to three years in prison for manslaughter. Finally, Wilcox left Howards End, and Margaret and Helen lived there with Bast's child.

While the objective effect of the story is the revelation not only of the hypocrisy and egoism but also of moral degeneracy of the upper classes in England who pretended to be genteel and morally irreproachable, yet Forster didn't seem particularly to censure the illegitimate love affairs of Wilcox and Jacky Bast and of Helen Schlegel and Leonard Bast, what he was primarily driving at was the importance of true and complete understanding and love in human relationships, the lack of which was largely responsible for the unhappiness and even the tragedy that took place in the story. So he called strongly for mutual understanding as he made one of the characters exclaim: "Only connect", adding "only connect the prose and the passion, and both will be exalted, and human love will soon be at its height," and his belief was that the sorrows and misfortunes of civilized people came largely from their inability or failure to "connect with bitterness until all men are brothers." To him the differences in class distinctions and in wealth are not so important but cannot be bridged over without the attainment of social harmony. His belief did not come from Christianity or any other religion, but emanated from a petit-bourgeois intellectual's idealistic conviction in the pursuit of love and harmony and understanding in all human relations. He showed thus his dissatisfaction with the existing human society in England and its hypocrisy and conventional respectability, but his suggested solution was no more than a Utopian dream.

"A Passage to India" (1924), Forster's acknowledged masterpiece, was the result of his two trips to India, in 1912—19 and in 1922. It is significant that he went there not in the heyday of British imperialism under Robert Clive and Warren Hastings, nor at the battle of Plassey and during the intermittent Anglo-French wars in India in the 18th century, but shortly before the World War of 1914—1918 and a few years after it when the British Empire was already tottering after the Boer War and it only took another world war to end its imperial rule in the South Asian sub-continent. And it must also be remembered that Forster was an enlightened intellectual who had explicit belief in liberalism and freedom.

The novel is divided into three parts: Mosque, Caves and Temple. The story begins with the arrival in India of Mrs. Moore and her protégé Miss Quested, on a visit to Ronny Heaslop, City Magistrate of Chandrapore, Mrs. Moore's son and Miss Adda Quested's fiancé, and then there was Mrs. Moore's meeting by accident at a mosque with Dr. Aziz of Minto Hospital. Both Mrs. Moore and Miss Quested were eager to meet Indians on an equal footing and they and Dr. Aziz took a liking to each other soon after their acquaintance. Inadvertently Dr. Aziz invited the two women to a visit to his home and they accepted the invitation, but soon he realized that his home was too cramped and too dirty to invite English ladies to and decided to take them to see the Marabar Caves twenty miles away from the city. Of course even in this early section the novelist took good care to give a number of concrete examples of racial prejudice in India: (1) the English sahibs looked down on all Indians except for the Maharajahs and Maharanis in the Indian States and the few biggest landowners in British India, (2) all the English gentlemen and ladies with very few exceptions (e.g. Cyril Fielding, Principal of the Government College) were inclined to be kind and fair and equitable to the Indians only in the first few months of their arrival in India, and (3) in spite of a few gestures of the British rulers' kindness to the natives, the gap between the reigning race and the ruled populace was practically insuperable (e.g. the exclusive Chandradore Club was only open to the British and no Indians were ever to be admitted as guests). The idea of the "White Man's Burden" in British colonialism such as Heasley's remark that "we're out here to do justice and keep the peace", is given by the author with disapproval. Even Fielding who was shown to be most sympathetic and fair-minded, when asked the question, "how is England justified in holding India?", was only "disinclined" to give the only proper answer taught every Englishman in India, and that is, "England holds India for her good." Trying to be fair, Forster also pointed out here the disunity in India, particularly between the Hindus and the Moslems.

Part II, entitled "Caves", describes what happened to Dr. Aziz and his party at the Marabar Caves and the aftermath and finally the trial at the court. Dr. Aziz took all sorts of trouble to prepare for the party's visit to the Caves, but Cyril Fielding was late for the train and at the Caves Mrs. Moore was soon tired after the first cave and stayed behind, and Dr. Aziz had to go on visiting the caves with Miss Quested and a guide. Then suddenly something happened: Mrs. Quested had a hallucination of being insulted by some one in one of the caves, she rushed down alone and was picked up by one Miss Derek's car and went back to Chandrapore. Dr. Aziz failed to find her but met Fielding, and when the party minus Miss Quested returned from the Caves on the train, Dr. Aziz was arrested for having insulted Miss Quested according to the latter's own testimony. While Dr. Aziz's Indian friends arranged to defend him at the approaching court-trial and Fielding was the only Englishman to believe Dr. Aziz innocent, all the English gentlemen and ladies, from the higher-ups (including the Collector Turton, Magistrate Ronny Peasley, the Civil Surgeon Major Callendar) to the District Superintendent of Police Mr. McBride and even Miss Derek who worked for an Indian Maharajah and his Maharani, stood solidly on the side of Miss Quested who however suffered from mental shocks and occasionally doubted her own testimony against Aziz once in her conversation with Ronny and then in her letter to Fielding. Then at the court-trial which was presided over by an Indian Magistrate Mr. Das, Mr. McBride spoke for the prosecution and then witnesses were called one by one to give evidence, but when Miss Quested was called, she was at first rather confident, then soon enough she became a bit hesitant, with "I am not quite sure", and "I cannot be sure", and the next moment she shook her head and declared "I'm afraid I have made a mistake" and "Dr. Aziz never followed me into the cave", and finally came out with "I withdrew everything", and the trial ended with Aziz released from prison. And the author commented very ironically, "Miss Quested had renounced her own people", and only Mr. Fielding who now admired her was there to help her get out of the crowd and into his college campus. She then admitted it was probably the guide who had followed her into the cave and given her such a shock. In the meantime Mrs. Moore who had hurried away from the heat in India and from the court trial died at sea, on her voyage from Bombay to England. Mr. Fielding helped Miss Quested by successfully persuading Aziz to drop charging her of 20,000 rupees as compensation for injury to his reputation, and of course Heaslop broke off his engagement to Miss Quested who now went back to England. Before Fielding went back to England for a short visit, he declared to Miss Quested about India and Indians: "Justice never satisfies them, and that is why the British Empire rests on sand".

Part III, entitled "Temple", chiefly tells of Aziz's new job at the Indian State of Mau where his friend Professor Godbole was now Minister of Education, and then describes the ceremony at the Buddhist temple there. Fielding returned from England and came to Mau with his new brother-in-law Ralph (Fielding married Ralph's sister who was Mrs. Moore's daughter Stella by her second marriage), and Aziz upon their meeting was at first antagonistic toward Fielding (Aziz's remarks: "I wish no Englishman or Englishwoman to be my friend"), but later they became friends again. However, being married Fielding now had to act like an English Sahib in India, and so this meeting was "their last free intercourse". The last few pages of the novel contains some very powerful lines. First about the friendly relations that had existed between Fielding an Englishman and Aziz an Indian:

"All the stupid misunderstanding had been cleared up, but socially they had no meeting-place. He (i.e. Fielding) had thrown in his lot with Anglo-India by marrying a countrywoman, and he was acquiring some of its limitations, and already felt surprised at his own past heroism, would he today defy all his own people for the sake of a stray Indian? (referring to Aziz)" Then in the conversation between the two, when Fielding said that "the British Empire really can't be abolished because it's rude," Aziz retorted, "Very well, and we have no use for you," and then, "Clear out, all you Turtons and Burtons." Then finally, Aziz began to predict: "Until England is in difficulties we keep silent, but in the next European war, — aha, aha! Then is our time," and he added, "India shall be a nation! No foreigners of any sort!" and "Down with the English anyhow. That's certain, clear out, you fellows, double quick, I say. ... we shall drive every blasted Englishman into the sea." This was not just Aziz's, but also Forster's, prophecy, and it came true with the English rulers expelled from India shortly after the end of the Second World War.

There is no question of where the author's sympathy lies in this long narrative dealing with racial inequality between the Anglo-Indians and the Indians in British India, and this is a powerful antidote to the imperialist jingoism of Rudyard Kipling and his like. Of course, many of the Indians are described in the novel as ignorant, superstitious and backward generally, and the disunity between the Moslems and the Hindus and the terrible treatment of Indians of lower caste such as the Untouchables are also touched upon, but many of the better-educated Indians such as Dr. Aziz and his friends are portrayed in a favourable light and the fact of their being rudely and even brutally treated by the British ruling class in India is related with strong and unmistakable censure and indictment. One shortcoming in the novel is the author's obvious attempt to limit the racial persecution and discrimination to only the English sahibs of long standing in India, as distinguished from the recent visitors to the colony from England and also from the educated people in England, such as those at Cambridge University, and in so doing the author seems to put the blame of racial inequality to the colonial system practiced by the British rulers in India. Even Fielding who was for long years a friend of the Indians like Dr. Aziz began to find it impossible for him to remain friendly to his former friends after he married an Englishwoman and had to act the part of an English sahib from then on as a result. However, Forster's sweeping statement here that all English rulers in India had to be brutal toward the Indians was a strong attack on colonialism and his refutations of the imperialist theory of "the White Man's Burden" via Aziz and the other enlightened Indians as well as Fielding and even Mrs. Moore, are also powerful and convincing.

The four major characters in the novel are all very carefully depicted, though each of them stands for a type or a point of view in the struggle between the Indians and the Anglo-Indians. Mrs. Moore and Adela Quested stand for the more enlightened English ladies among the recent arrivals in India, with the elderly woman more sympathetic and weaker in character while the latter also very frail emotionally and physically but more daring in her pursuit of truth. Their common desire to know India and to meet Indians as social equals leads eventually to mishap for both, but the younger woman relapses from her shock and proves to be the truer heroine in the end by admitting the true facts regardless of her own reputation among her compatriots. Aziz stands for the westernized intellectual among the Indians, who knows the true facts of British rule in India and the general British contempt for the native population but who is eager to welcome as his friend any open-minded Englishman or Englishwoman. He is devoted to his dead wife but has his own failings in mixing occasionally with women of evil repute. Cyril Fielding is the Englishman who dares defy the world to declare the innocence of his friend Aziz but who has to follow the way of an English sahib as soon as he marries an Englishwoman and has to maintain his official status in India. All four are in this sense rounded figures who may each have virtues of his or her own, but who have his or her limitations arising out of his or her own class origin and social environment. But the author seems to have his admiration for each of the four, treating them all as well-meaning people who are ready to bring the two races together against all sorts of social and political handicaps.

The story is well told, with much preparation for the major

events of the visit to Marabar Caves and the subsequent court trial. The precipitancy of incident after incident before and during the visit to the Caves is succinctly related, with humour and satire, and then the lengthy preparations for the court trial lead up to the climactic scene of the trial itself, with the theatrical pronouncements of Aziz's innocence coming unexpectedly from Miss Quested. There is something extremely dramatic in the few utterances of the heroine that unmistakably show her character and create the element of surprise in the plot. The last or third part of the novel is a bit weak, but the story has to be wound up, and here is told also the author's conclusive remark that no reconciliation was possible between the British rulers and the subject race and that the only possible solution was the liberation of the Indian people following another world-scale debacle for the British.

Both the theme of "A Passage to India" and the artistic accoutrements of the story are commendable, and here we find Forster for once emerging from the domestic dramas of his earlier years and rising to the height of social criticism in his last major effort at fiction.

A few words must be said about Forster's important essay "What I Believe", written shortly before the beginning of the Second World War in September, 1939. This essay is important because it not only gives us Forster's own views on the human society but also the Bloomsbury doctrine, i.e., the common view of the Bloomsbury Group to which Forster belonged. Here Forster believes in personal relationships but rejects the "Age of Faith" he says he lives in. He denounces force and violence but deplores the fact that they always come to disrupt the human world. He upholds "tolerance, good temper and sympathy" as the things "that matter really", he has "two cheers for democracy because it admits variety and permits criticism". Writing two decades after World War I and a few months before World War II, Forster here laments that "all society rests upon force", and consoles himself that "all the great creative actions, all the decent human relations, occur during the intervals when force has not managed to come to the front. These intervals are what matter. I want them to be as frequent and as lengthy as possible, and I call them 'civilisation'." He speaks against "hero-worship", against "the Great Man", and prefers "different kinds of small men — a much finer achievement." He nevertheless believes in aristocracy, "not an aristocracy of power, based upon rank and influence; but an aristocracy of the sensitive, the considerate and the plucky." And he attacks vehemently those who are in power: "As soon as people have power they go crooked and sometimes dotty as well, because the possession of power lifts them to a region where normal honesty never pays. For instance, the man who is selling newspapers outside the Houses of Parliament can safely leave his papers to go for a drink and his cap beside them; anyone who takes a paper is sure to drop a copper into the cap. But the men who are inside the Houses of Parliament — they cannot trust one another like that, still less can the Government they compose trust other governments. No caps upon the pavement here, but suspicion, treachery and armaments. The more highly public life is organized the lower does its morality sink; the nations of today behave to each other worse than they ever did in the past, they cheat, rob, bully and bluff, make war without notice, and kill as many women and children as possible." This is certainly very devastating criticism on the European scene prior to World War II. However, though Forster was somewhat pessimistic here, he still had his convictions in the future of human society. Though he only believed in abstract moral virtues and in theoretical tenets of liberalism and democracy, at least he showed his courage in defying the terrible crimes perpetuated by the ruling cliques of his time.

d. Katherine Mansfield

Katherine Mansfield (1888—1923), pseudonym of Cathleen Mansfield Beauchamp, was born in Wellington, New Zealand. She was daughter of a wealthy merchant and banker and was educated first at schools in Wellington (1898—1903). She came to England in 1903 and attended Queen's College, London, from 1903—1906. She returned to New Zealand and went to the Royal Academy of Music, Wellington, 1906—1908. She settled in London in 1908, and started to contribute to different periodicals in England, to "The New Age" in 1910—1911, and then to John Middleton Murry's "Rhythm" and "The Blue Review" in 1911—1913. She also served as reviewer for "Westminster Gazette" (1911—1915) and together with Murry and D.H. Lawrence she founded the "Signature" magazine in 1916 and she later contributed to "The Athaneaum" in 1919—1920. In her private life she married one named George Bowden in 1909, was separated from him shortly after in the same year, but she did not gain her divorce till 1918. In the meantime she began to live with John Middleton Murry in 1912, but was only able to marry him till 1918. She was of poor health all her life, later contracted tuberculosis and from 1916 to the last years of her short life she often had to go to south of France or Switzerland every year for her health. The First World War left its mark upon her outlook, so that like other post-war intellectuals of the "Lost Generation" her philosophy grew to be one of pessimism and disillusionment in life and she adopted a passive attitude of non-resistance to social evils.

Her writings consisted chiefly in her 70-odd short stories that appeared in five collections, from 1911 to 1924, and it is as a gifted writer of short stories that she has been known since her lifetime. As early as 1910 appeared in the magazine "The New Age" a series of her satirical stories based chiefly on her own experiences in England, in Belgium and in Bavaria in southern Germany, and these were collected and published under the title of "In a German Pension", her first collection of stories, in 1911. Later, she also wrote stories arising out of her memories of her native country and her family in her childhood and early youth. Her second volume of stories, "Bliss, and Other Stories", came out in 1920, which was followed in 1922 by another collection, "The Garden Party and

Other Stories", which also contained stories with Continental as well as English backgrounds. Two other groups of short stories were published posthumously: "The Doves' Nest and Other Stories" in 1923 and "Something Childish and Other Stories" in 1924. Other books of hers include "The Journal of Katherine Mansfield", both published by The Albatross Modern Continental Library, in 1933 and 1934 respectively, as well as "The Scrapbook of Katherine Mansfield" (Alfred A Knoff), also edited by John Middleton Murry, in 1949.

Possibly the best known and one of the most carefully written of Mansfield's many stories is "The Garden Party", which is also the most typical of her as a short story writer. A very wealthy family is giving a garden party, and the story begins with detailed descriptions of elaborate morning preparations by the mother and daughter of the Sheridan family for the party to be given in the afternoon, including the location for the large tent, whole trays full of pots of pink lilies, and fifteen different kinds of flags to mark out fifteen different kinds of sandwiches and cream cakes. These preparations are made with the help of workmen and flower-venders and house servants, and interposed by the speeches and thoughts of the members of the family, especially the interior monologues of Laura who as the central figure in the story comes out, as if quite unexpectedly, with her thought of blame on "these stupid class distinctions" between the workmen and the upper class to which she and her family belong. Then the news of a workman's death through a fall from his horse is suddenly made known, and Laura with her great sympathy for the poor and the wretched feels quite naturally that their garden party should be called off. But everybody else laughs at her "silly" and "stupid" idea, and the garden party in the afternoon turns out to be a great success. Then after the guests are all gone, the head of the family, Mr. Sheridan, mentions the death of the workman and shows some pity toward the dead man with a wife and half a dozen children, and Mrs. Sheridan suddenly has "one of her brilliant ideas" and suggests putting some of the left-over food from the party in a big basket and taking it to the deceased workman's wife and children. Then follows another lengthy description of Laura taking the basket to the cottage on a smoky and dark street quite nearby, entering timidly into the dead workman's house, seeing first his sister-in-law and then his wife and eventually the dead young man lying stretched out in his bedroom, and finally hurrying back with her cries and vague cogitations on life.

This story is most typical of Katherine Mansfield because in the first place the theme is that of the gap between the two social strata in the western world of poor labouring people and the idle rich, with the author very definitely showing her sympathy for the lower class but at the same time rather calmly acknowledging and accepting the unbridgeable gap in between. In the second place, the interior monologue especially of the central character in the story is very finely textured and emerges everywhere, thus rounding up the character portrait and at the same time rousing the readers' interest in the important psychological make-up of an introspective figure in the modern world. There is thus the striking contradiction between the shallow and insignificant social content of the story on the one hand and the apparent psychological depth of the central figure on the other. But the prose style is delightful, and the choice of diction is always so careful and appropriate.

The longest short story in this collection, "At the Bay", is a scattered naturalistic record of the Burnell family (Stanley and Linda Burnell and their children Kezia, Isabel and Lottie, and his sister Beryl and her mother Mrs. Fairfield) and their neighbours (the Harry Kembles, Jonathan Trout and children, and Mrs. Stubbs and children) spending their very ordinary day (from dawn till night) near the beach. Bits of dialogues and some descriptions of scenes plus a limited account of interior monologues of different characters enliven up the story, but there are no striking themes nor outstanding character portraits to give the reader any lasting impression.

"Bliss" is another very popular story that is typical of another aspect of Mansfield. Here the detailed description of a young matron of thirty, Bertha Young, feeling happy and satisfied with every-thing, with her life of luxury and upperclass refinement, with her dinner and entertainments at home, with her nice child and her adoring husband, and then comes a surprise ending, when her "bliss" is literally dashed to pieces when the woman guest whom her husband seems to dislike turns out actually to be adored by him and who seems to be arranging for a clandestine rendezvous with him the next day. Here the surprise ending is only a matter of tech-nique that is meant to attract the common run of readers, but the very fine points of the heroine's feeling of "bliss" portrayed in such minuteness and with such poignance all the way up to the last page show the author's successful psychological analysis of an upper-class English woman with all her superficial attractions and put-on refinement. If we have a mind to, we may see the spiritual inaneness in this woman of idleness in the soulless civilized Western society of early 20th century, but of course the author would never dream of such a thing, as she draws the central character Bertha Young with much fondness and sympathy, only occasionally showing a bit of a smile at the heroine's ignorance of the real outside world and at her vain joys in her comfortable and affluent existence. In other words, humour rather than satire is the dominant mood in the story, with just a tint of sentimentalizing Mansfield occasionally indulges in.

More sentimental is another well-known and finely-written story, "A Cup of Tea". Again this is a very simple story. The heroine Rosemary Fell is a happily married woman of a really rich family who in her shopping for expensive antiques meets a young, battered girl asking her for the price of a cup of tea and takes her home to be her guest, but who finding her husband impressed by the prettiness of the girl very abruptly sends her away. The ap-parent theme is again a rich and happy woman's inherent jealousy, but actually the author is asking a more fundamental question about the heroine's idea of happiness in spite of her outward life of luxury and ease. Again we have a surprise ending, and again the true significance of the piece is the vivid portrayal of an apparently happy woman among the idle rich, which may serve as an exposé if not a satire of the high society in London though the author never for a moment intended it.

A rare story with the central character coming from the really poor folk is "Life of Ma Parker". Ma Parker started out her life at sixteen as kitchen-maid in London, then as "help" to a doctor's house, and then she married a baker and gave birth to thirteen children of whom seven were buried before her husband died of consumption. She had to struggle hard to bring up the remaining six children of whom one daughter "went wrong" and took one of her sisters with her, while two of the boys emigrated and the third son went to India with the army. The youngest daughter Ethel married a good-for-nothing waiter who died of ulcers the year the little grandson Lennie was born, and the old woman and Ethel had to bring up the sickly boy Lennie who followed his granny about everywhere but who also died of TB eventually. The story ends with Ma Parker wanting to cry and having nowhere to go. She couldn't go back to Ethel, she couldn't remain and cry at the gentleman's flat where she was then working, she couldn't even sit on some steps because then a policeman would speak to her. So "Ma Parker stood, looking up and down. The icy wind blew out her apron into a balloon. And now it began to rain. There was nowhere." Such a tragic ending to the story produces more pathos than does a picture of a dying woman. Though the author makes no comment here, her accusation of the society where such wretched people exist is definitely indicated.

Similar to "The Life of Ma Parker" is "The-Child-Who-Was-Tired", which was a sort of an adaptation or almost a translation of the Russian writer Tchekhov's story entitled "Sleephead", though here the victim of oppression and exploitation is a child rather than an old woman. This girl who appears to be dead-tired and sleepy all through the story is treated very cruelly by her employer family and is made to endure all sorts of hardships in her state of hopeless fatigue. The ending, not unlike that of Ma Parker, is the child falling on to the floor, "walking along a white road with tall black *trees* on either side, a little road that led to nowhere, and where nobody walked at all — nobody at all." The ending which seems endless spells out the same fate for this child as for Ma Parker — a life of misery that will drag on and on, with no relief or respite in sight.

Katherine Mansfield seems to be particularly interested in child psychology, much of which was apparently based on her own early experience back in New Zealand and therefore was especially vivid and penetrating. "The Little Girl" tells of a little girl so afraid of her father who is always so stern and often whips her, and then she finally understands him and is reconciled to him when he treats her so thoughtfully, one night as they are left alone at their home and she has a terrible nightmare. The details not so much of ordinary actions as of childish thoughts revolving within her brain give us a most humane and sympathetic portrait of the little girl throughout the short narrative. One story about children touches directly on the class barriers in the Western society is "The Doll's House" where the daughters of a washer-woman are literally segregated from the rest of the children in the local school, so much so, that they are forbidden to see the Doll's House at the home of the Burnells where all the other school children are invited.

Though most of her stories deal with the middle class and upper middle class life in England and in New Zealand, and even the dreams and aspirations of the poorer people in her stories are for the attainment of life and culture of the wealthy and at least the affluent, yet frequently in spite of her original intentions the pictures unfolded before the reader may very well be taken to serve as excellent exposé if not subtle satire of the ways of the hypocritical rich people in the Western society of the twentieth century. So "Marriage à la Mode" is almost unquestionably a satirical sketch of a rich woman who has forsaken the simple ways of her businessman husband and has assumed a new way of life by mixing with some aristocratic-minded friends and adopting the hypocritical pose of a circle of highbrow ladies and gentlemen. Even in a story like "The Tiredness of Rosabel", where the poor girl is hungry and tired out at the end of her day's work and going back alone to her dull room up four flights of stairs, what she has been dreaming all the way back and then after her arrival in her room is about the fairylandish life of the very rich in which she is taken to shopping and lunch and a ball and then is engaged and married to the very rich and cultured Harry. Here the wishful thinking on the part of the poor work-a-day girl is simply "the desire of the moth for the star" and does not suggest in the least any debunking of the idle life of the wealthy. Here lies the limitation of the author born to a wealthy family herself and never having to face poverty or destitution at any stage of her short life.

Somewhere in between the two stories immediately mentioned above, may be placed a piece like "The Daughters of the Late Colonel", in which the two middle-aged spinsters seem to be completely lost in their memories of their newly-deceased father of a colonel and which seems to suggest that they are quite confused over what they should do in their lives thereafter. The tragi-comic tale in which the death of the father seems to have brought the life of the two daughters to a complete standstill is a curious mixture of abundant humour and mild satire sprinkled over with a touch of sentimentality. Here we see all too clearly both the forte and the defect of a typical Katherine Mansfield story.

In her best stories, Mansfield made expertly use of the device of interior monologue which suggests the stream-of-consciousness way of story-telling highlighted by Virginia Woolf and particularly by James Joyce.

e. Aldous Huxley

Aldous Huxley (1894—1963) was born of the famous Huxley family of illustrious scientists and scholars, with the great biologist Thomas Henry Huxley as his grandfather and Dr. Thomas Arnold of Rugby as his maternal great grandfather and the novelist Mrs. Humphrey Ward as his aunt. He was educated at Eton and Oxford and then worked as a literary journalist and dramatic critic. He started to write stories, and then novels, and in his early novels he was much under the influence of Thomas Love Peacock of the 19th century as he developed the technique of what might be called conversation-pieces in which the story threads are loosely woven together while the emphasis is placed on the conversations of eccentric characters. He moved among the contemporary circle of writers and artists and other intellectuals and so most of the characters in his early novels ("Crome Yellow", 1921; "Antic Hay", 1923; "Those Barren Leaves", 1925; and "Point Counter Point", 1928) are taken from middle class intellectuals and other upper class people of the 1920s in Britain who were generally obsessed by Post-World-War-I disillusionment and pessimism and held antagonistic attitudes toward both the fascists and the communists.

In the 1930s he wrote his mock-utopian book entitled ironically "Brave New World" (1932), and then "Eyeless in Gaza" (1936), a confusing novel with its innumerable flashbacks in the shape of an adult's Proustian reminiscences of his childhood and youth. Then followed, "Ends and Means" (1937), dealing with the philosophy of non-violence or pacifism and non-attachment, and later "After Many a Summer" (1939), written after his settlement in America and concerned with an American millionaire and various persons around him. In his old age Huxley turned to the Christian religion and to mysticism which manifested themselves in his novels of the 1940s and 1950s. Of his works the two outstanding books seem to be "Point Counter Point" and "Brave New World", for which he will probably be remembered.

"Point Counter Point", unquestionably Aldous Huxley's masterpiece, is a penetrating satire on the upper middle class and middle-class world in Britain in the years between the two world wars, though for various reasons the book's popularity has been steadily on the wane in the few decades since World War II, one obvious reason possibly being the current loss of interest in the social reality in England of the 1920s.

The title is taken from the musical term of "counter point" and clearly indicates that the story is not about one hero or heroine but is made up of many threads blended into a harmonious melody. First published in 1928, shortly after Oswald Spengler's trenchant though pessimistic book "The Decline of the West" (Der Untergang des Abendlandes", 1918—23, English translation, 1926—29), Huxley's novel gives an all-round exposé of the curiously mixed society in London in the Post-World-War-I years with an assembled portraits of members from minor aristocracy (Lord Edward Tantamount) and owners of big business (Sidney Quarles) to all kinds of intellectuals and political figures. Six families stand out prominently above the others. There is the Bidlake family headed by John Bidlake the well-known painter (probably suggesting the real painter Augustus John) with his three wives and flanked by his son Walter and his daughter Elinor who was married to Philip Quarles. There is the Quarles family that includes Sidney Quarles and his wife Rachel and their son Philip. There is the Tantamount family including chiefly Lord Edward Tantamount and his wife Lady Tantamount and his daughter Lucy. There is the family of a peasant painter Mark Rampion (possibly drawn from D. H. Lawrence) and his wife Mary. There is the family of General Knowles and Mrs. Knowles and above all her son Maurice Spandrell. Then there is Denis Burlap (resembling John Middleton Murry in some ways) and his wife Susan and his platonic relationship with Beatrice Gilray. Besides the prominent figures belonging to the above-said six families, there are the two outstanding political figures of Everard Webley (definitely suggesting the then leader of the fascists in Britain Oswald Mosley) and Illidge (possibly alluding to some member of the Communist Party in Britain).

The general picture of the English upper society described in the novel is that of moral degeneracy and loss of hope for social and political well-being and there is the prevalent sexual promiscuity among most of the respected, dignified men and women of that society. Particularly notorious among the latter are the aristocratic "siren" Lucy Tantamount and her frivolous lover Walter Bidlake, Denis Burlap the editor of magazines with his hypocritical attempts at forming all sorts of "platonic" affiliations with women, Sidney Quarles the pompous old business man who keeps mistresses in London, and the good-for-nothing Maurice Spandrell who indulges in and is fed up with debauchery and fornication and who finally ends in murder and then self-destruction. There are also some very carefully drawn portraits of eccentric and ridiculous characters of different degrees of cynicism, such as the aged painter John Bidlake who has enjoyed his fame of a great artist and has had his fling in his frivolous relations with women high and low, Philip Quarles the unimpassioned and unsuccessful writer of fiction who has no love for his own wife Elinor but who likes to flirt occasionally with highbrow women, and the peasant-born painter Mark Rampion who with his wife of aristocratic birth Mary tries to live a simple life in an industrialized world and who criticizes everybody and everything in the capitalist society with his intellectual pose of a cynic. Rampion, supposedly a caricature of D.H. Lawrence, is almost the only major character in the novel whom the author does not openly ridicule or satirize.

One of the highlights in the book has to do with Everard Webley, very definitely an ironic replica of Oswald Mosley, who is shown as at once the absolutist leader of the British fascists (alias the British Freemen) and the humble lover running after the neglected wife of an Elinor Quarles. His pathetic death under Spandrell's blow in front of Elinor's little house and the way Spandrell with the help of the scared Illidge wraps up his corpse to be dumped into the car are both ludicrous and satirical, and are passages fit to serve as the climactic point in the loosely-put-together novel. However, Aldous Huxley, somewhat like Rampion, hits out both at the extreme right and at the extreme left, and so he creates the ridiculous portrait also of Illidge to represent the British Communists, Illidge who was born of a factory-worker's family, who is now an assistant at Lord Edward Tantamount's biology laboratory, who as a member of the Communist Party gets himself involved in the Hyde Park riot following Webley's address to the British Freemen there, and who finally is present and scared stiff at the sight of the murdered Webley. That Illidge is as much of a caricature to be ridiculed as Webley is obviously what Huxley was driving at, and Rampion's words once addressed to Philip may very well be taken to stand for the author's view on the matter:

"But it's so silly, all this political squabbling, ... so utterly silly. Bolsheviks and Fascists; Radicals and Conservatives; Communists and British Freemen — what the devil are they all fighting about? I'll tell you. They're fighting to decide whether we shall go to hell by communist express train or capitalist racing motor car, by individualist bus or collectivist tram running on the rails of state control. The destination's the same in every case. They're all of them bound for hell, all headed for the same psychological impasse and the social collapse that results from psychological collapse."

This is surely the most hopeless shortcoming of a bourgeois intellectual like Aldous Huxley, in spite of the general satirical exposé of the capitalist world between the two wars presented so vividly in the novel. Here the author's mood was very much like that in Spengler's "The Decline of the West", the pessimism of upper class intellectuals in capitalist Europe who lost their spiritual beliefs in God and Christianity and all the moral scruples bound up with religion but who finding no way out of the impasse for the material progress that led to war and destruction and spiritual emptiness and cynicism, was yet unwilling to relinquish their desire for extreme individualism in the face of Fascism and at the same time was biased under false propaganda and therefore sceptical of what socialism and communism could bring to them. Brought up in an environment of affluence, Huxley had no sympathy for the poor working people whom he always spoke of with contempt in the novel. Hence, "Point Counter Point" is after all a work of decadence by a decadent writer, although the picture on the whole is a savage attack on the decadent society in England in the 1920s and the book is in that respect a faithful though somewhat exaggerated sociological document of the upper class society of Aldous Huxley's time.

"Brave New World" was written more or less in the tradition of Samuel Butler's "Erewhon" and "Erewhon Revisited", or even of Swift's "Gulliver's Travels", rather than in that of Plato's "Republic" or Thomas More's "Utopia" or even Morris's "News from Nowhere". It was more a satire or an ironic warning on the foreseeable doom of an over-mechanized civilization, than any serious augury or anticipation of a millennium. Especially in the first few chapters of the book the over-emphasis on mechanization in the modern Western world is thoroughly satirized with the preposterous suggestions of the new human race being mass-produced and incubated in test-tubes in laboratories, of human embryos being developed and hereditarily "mind-conditioned" by "sleep-teaching" into different "castes" of Alphas and Betas (i.e., the keener and more intellectual groups) and Gammas, Deltas and Epsilons (i.e., the more sluggish groups), of the new human children not being taught any history or knowledge of the past (including home, family, father and mother, monogamy, romance, etc.), and of the new human beings being told that every one belongs to every one else and that promiscuity is something taken for granted or even compulsory. Then a very thin thread of story is developed between the girl Lenina and the boys Bernard Marx and Henry Foster, and Lenina and Bernard spend their weekend at the New Mexican Reservation where they meet the aboriginal Indians who still live the way of the savages in human history. Then the greater part of the book has to do with Linda the Mexican Indian woman and her son the savage John whose ways of life arouse great curiosity and uproar among the new human beings and whose knowledge of human society in the past and of Shakespeare is placed in juxtaposition and contrast with the state of affairs of the new human race in the year 632 A.F. (after Ford, instead of A.D., or after Christ). The author seems to leave it to the reader to judge which world (A.F. or A.D.) is the better one, though he is apparently inclined to prefer the good old human world, or even the aboriginal state of human savages. "Brave New World" shows clearly Huxley's thorough disgust and disillusionment with the materialistic modern Western society on the one hand while on the other his imaginings of a future mechanized world appears equally unsatisfactory to him, and he vaguely indicates the good old Rousseauistic formula of "Return to Nature" or return to the old state of "the noble savage". Hence ''Brave New World of Shakespeare's Miranda''.

Huxley represents another case of Post-World-War-I pessimism, and another case of ambiguous literary fame for writers of the interwar years in the Post-World-War-II critical circles of the West. The decline today of his reputation as a brilliant novelist in the 1920s is sometimes accounted for by the lack of interest today in the careful analysis and portrayal of the intellectual and cultural élite in Britain of the twenties. However, even as a "period piece", a novel like "Point Counter Point" deserves to survive as a vivid, realistic representation of the bohemian and intellectual London society in the 1920s and a subtle though mild satire on that society into the bargain. "Brave New World" is at least a pseudo-utopian or mock-utopian work that satirizes over-mechanization in the modern Western world to the neglect of spiritual advancement, and it serves as a link between earlier books of a similar nature and Orwell's "1984" and "The Animal Farm" of the 1940s.

f. Lewis Grassic Gibbon

Besides Hugh MacDiarmid the poet in Scotland, the most outstanding progressive Scottish writer was Lewis Grassic Gibbon who wrote more than a dozen books in his rather brief life either under his real or assumed name but whose chief claim to fame in the historical development of English literature rests or should rest almost solely on his great trilogy of fiction "A Scots Quair", consisting of

"Sunset Song" (1932), "Cloud Howe" (1933) and "Grey Granite" (1934).

Lewis Grassic Gibbon (1901—1935), pseudonym of James Leslie Mitchell, was born in a Scottish peasant's family on a farm in Kincardinshire in the Highlands, in a land of hills and the sea. At 15 he went to an academy, Mackle Academy, Stonehaven, and distinguished himself there in the writing of essays. He left it after a year and found work as a reporter on the "Aberdeen Journal", and then later he moved to Glasgow to work for the "Scottish Farmer", another magazine. At 20 he fell ill and returned to his home for a while to help in the fields. Shortly after that he joined the army on account of his desire for travel, and for eight years he worked as a clerk in the army and later in the Royal Air Force and had the opportunity to go to the Middle East where he examined the great reliques of antiquity and mused on the origins of human society. There he met an archaeologist who later took him to Central America where he studied the remains of the Maya civilization and gathered enough material to write a book on it later. "Hanno, or The Future of Explorations" was published in 1928. By 1928 he left the army and for the seven remaining years before his death in 1935, he wrote no less than 16 books. He tried to sell his short stories and articles to the wrong magazines until H.G. Wells noticed him and put him on the right track. A collection of short stories, called "Calends of Cairo" was published in 1931, while two novels, "Stained Radiance" and "The Thirteenth Disciple" appeared respectively in 1930 and 1931. His masterpiece: "A Scots Quair" was published in 1946 in a single volume. Another book, "Niger: The Life of Mungo Park" (1934), was also published under his pseudonym, while yet another work "The Conquest of the Maya" (1934) was issued under his own name. Early in 1935 he underwent an operation on a duodenal ulcer from which he did not rally.

"A Scots Quair" simply means a Scottish book ("Quair" being the Scottish word for "quire", meaning a set of papers or a volume), but this trilogy is quite a monumental work in the sense that the three books cover the life of three generations from Chris' father to her son, and deal with a panoramic view of three different social environments in Scotland, village (Kinraddie), provincial town (Segget) and industrial city (Duncairn). Chris Guthrie the heroine, a woman from a peasant's family, runs through the three books and forms the logical link as the years roll by, from before the First World War down to the General Strike of the late 1920s and after. She grew up from a young girl to ripe womanhood as she experienced marriage and remarriage and the death of both the first and second husbands (Tavendale the peasant and Colquohoun the clergyman) and then her life with her son Ewan and her third marriage (with Ogilvie the unemployed foreman at a sawmill) until she finally returned to the farm where she had lived as a little girl. As social fiction, this series of three novels traces the different stages in the awakening of the Scottish people to active struggle in the social and political arena, beginning with social protests among the peasants and ending with the struggles of the working class with the capitalists and the bourgeois government.

"Sunset Song" begins with the years before the war of 1914—18. Chris, a crofter's daughter, at first lives with her father John Guthrie, her mother and a big family of brothers and sisters. When she ends her college education, her mother poisons herself and her twin babies rather than go through another pregnancy. Chris' brutal father becomes paralyzed, and she nurses him until his death. Then she marries Ewan Tavendale, a foreman at a neighbouring farm, with whom she has a son, Ewan, and they live happily until the First World War when the elder Ewan is recruited into the army. At the training camp he becomes an obscene drunkard. Later Chris learns that he is shot as a deserter at the Western Front. She then marries the new minister, Colquohoun, who has strong social convictions and much sympathy for the poor and the workers and who supports the trade unionism which the post-war ferment brings to Kinraddie. The novel is filled with details of deaths during the war and of the expropriations of the last of the peasantry in Scotland, following the invasion of the countryside by capitalist agriculture. "Cloud Howe" shows the further invasion of the land by capitalist forces, in the spinning mills of the town of Segget. The General Strike of 1926 is depicted here, with reference particularly to its effect upon Segget where the conflicts are brought to a high pitch of excitement at the time, and the collapse of the strike leads to the spiritual collapse of Colquohoun who has been outspoken on behalf of the unemployed and the needy and thus regarded as a radical. Then with the economic crisis of 1929 the mills are closed and the Means Test is brought in, and Colquohoun who has already withdrawn into an inner world of brooding and mysticism, dies after a passionate sermon. In the meantime, Chris begins to have unorthodox religious views, while her son Ewan at first has an interest in archaeology. In "Grey Grantte", Chris and her son by her first marriage, Ewan, move from the provincial town to live in the industrial town of Duncairn. She runs a boarding house and he abandons his study of prehistory and works in the steel works. After being beaten up by the police during a strike, Ewan becomes a Communist. He rejects the girl he loves after finding that under pressure from the authorities of the school where she teaches she has dropped party activities. He goes on organizing a hunger march of the unemployed to London. Chris, who has married for the third time, finds that the marriage (with a former peasant) means nothing to her, and he leaves her and emigrates to Canada. She then returns to farm the land at her family's original farmstead.

In "Sunset Song", besides Chris the heroine who sees all the people and all the events passing by her, the figures of her father John Guthrie and her first husband Ewan Tavendale, both hard-working, poor but proud peasants, are very effectively drawn. Though a very rough and rather selfish person, John Guthrie is shown to love the land and love his work and have the energy and determination to support a big family with his indefatigable labour. Ewan Tavendale is a much more cheerful and unselfish lad but the imperialist war of 1914—18 breaks out and in the atmosphere of crazy fervour for enlisting and fighting for the supposedly patriotic cause he joins the army. When he comes back to his home on leave, he becomes tainted with all the foul ways he has learned in the bitter days of battle, and Chris finds it impossible to live with him any longer, but he goes back to the war and as he somehow realizes his mistake of joining and fighting for the ruling class who alone profit from the war and he starts to run away from the battlefront, he is arrested and condemned as a deserter and immediately shot to death. Chris's reaction to the occasion of his death and her fond remembrance of him ever after point to the author's bitter condemnation of the imperialist war for butchering an innocent man like Tavendale. And war profiteering is also vividly described in this first volume. Also in "Sunset Song" there are some very colourful scenes of Scottish life among the peasants, e.g. Chris' first wedding as well as beautiful pictures of nature and the seasons in the countryside.

In "Cloud Howe" the political events play a more important part in the lives of the major characters. The Reverend Robert Colquohoun who has already appeared in the first volume and has married Chris becomes the central figure in the second book, and the spiritual struggle of the clergyman, from his attempt to harmonize his religion with his sympathy for the workers and from his eagerness for a change, through his more or less active participation in the workers' movement, down to his growing spiritual crisis after the failure of the strike and finally to his disillusionment in Christianity and his last sermon and then his death, is depicted with much care and sympathy. The conflict between capital and labour, as represented by the landlord capitalist Mowat on the one hand and the weavers on the other, is a fine picture of realistic social strife, and the climactic events of the Armistice Day march and of the strike are set against the background of the General Strike of 1926, the economic crisis of 1929 and the betrayal of the Labour Government headed by Ramsay MacDonald, that lead eventually to the steady increase in unemployment and the final closing down of the factory. The figure of Mowat, with his pretensions to aristocratic ways, his life of luxury and dissipation and his final embarrassmetn and financial disaster, is satirized, while the weavers are all sympathetically described, as the latter suffer from hunger and cold and are turned out of their miserable homes because they cannot pay their rent, but they still retain their triumphant spirit of revolt against the capitalist as well as their good humour and enthusiasm even in their lives of poverty.

In "Grey Granite" the political conflict is further brought to the fore-stage in the narration. The young Ewan Tavendale, Chris' son, now emerges as the central figure, and the spiritual development of the lad, from his original interest in archaeology and aloofness from his fellow workers in the foundry, through his participation in the strike and his arrest and imprisonment, down to his joining the Communist Party and finally his leading the march of the workers to London, is traced with ample details and striking transitions.

The character of Chris Guthrie whose life from childhood to ripe old age of retirement runs through the trilogy as the major thread of story is naturally the most carefully portrayed image of a Scottish peasant woman who is ever close to nature and close to the people and who loves labour and hates hypocrisy and tyranny and is courageous enough to stand up against any act of injustice. Much of the story is told by her or seen through her eyes, and her feelings and thoughts are fully revealed along with the march of events. Gibbon is a writer from the labouring folk and "A Scots Quair" a unique work of fiction.

g. Lewis Jones

Lewis Jones the Welsh writer (1897—1939) is almost completely unknown to the outside world, but he wrote two novels about the miners in South Wales in the late 1930s. He was born of a miner's family in South Wales, and in his youth he was a miner himself, then for many years he worked in a trade union and in a communist organization in his native mining district. In the years of the Civil

War in Spain, he took an active part in raising funds to help in the anti-fascist fighting in Spain and died suddenly as a result of his strenuous work. During his leisure Jones wrote two novels which told a continuous story of somewhat autobiographical contents and were published shortly before his death, "Cwmardy" in 1937 and "We Live. The Story of a Welsh Mining Valley" in 1939.

The two novels deal with the life of the miners in Cwmardy in South Wales and with their struggle with the capitalists, and Len Roberts is the hero throughout the story. The first novel begins from the 1890s and takes us down to immediately after the First World War while the second novel picks up the thread of the story and goes on to the middle 1930s, to the years of the Spanish Civil War. "Cwmardy" starts off with Len Roberts as a little boy, and the story is partly about his father, the big, strong miner Jim Roberts, and his mother Shane and his sister Mary who dies miserably after being seduced by the son of a foreman. The background of the mining district is given, together with Ben the Barber and Dai Cannon the worker who preach sermons. But the central thread of the story is about Len who first goes to school and then leaves it to work with his father in the pit of the mines. Then follows a vivid account of an explosion in the mines, and of the inquest that follows, and of the death of another victim who meets with an accident in the mines, and dies, also because of the lack of safety measures to protect the miners at work. The climax of the book comes with the description of the historical event of the ten-month strike of the Welsh miners in 1910—1911, and with the development of the strike is told the growth of Len Roberts from an inexperienced young miner to a strong and capable fighter for the workers' rights. Here are also given pictures of the oppressors including Lord Cwmardy as the capitalist-owner of the mines and Mr. Hicks and Mr. Higgins as his managers as well as full portraits of Ezra Jones the leader of the miners and his daughter Mary. Ezra Jones takes part in the workers' movement on account of his personal misfortune and the tragic death of his wife, so he does not have too much sympathy for the workers, and he slips gradually from firm leadership to a weak-kneed attitude toward the capitalists and a readiness to compromise at the height of the strike. Len Roberts takes a more prominent part in the workers' movement as the strike goes on, and he fights against Ezra's growing opportunism, together with Ezra's daughter Mary who has done much for the strike and who is now in love with Len. Then the wily capitalists and their managers try first with tricks to break the strike and later call in the police and even the regular troops to suppress the workers, but the strikers are firm under the leadership of Len and they win the strike eventually. Then the second major event in the novel is the outbreak of the First World War. The capitalists make use of the war not only to protect their interests against those of the foreign capitalists but also to suppress the workers. The miners are first of all called up to serve in the army, under the pretext of patriotism, and then when prices go up during the war and the capitalists profit from it, the requests of the miners to raise their wages are refused, again under the slogan of making sacrifices for the country. Jim goes to the war, but Len remains behind because he is physically disqualified and he keeps on working in the interest of the miners. He and Mary organize lectures to teach the miners about Marxism and that meets with strong opposition from the capitalists and they two have to argue also with Ezra, against the latter's opportunistic thinking. Then the novel ends with the Armistice and with the lesson learned by Len and Mary from the war.

"We Live", the sequel to "Cwmardy," treats of the events between 1924 and 1936. The highlights in this novel are the General Strike in 1926 and the agitation to go and help the republicans in the civil war in Spain in the middle 1930s. In the General Strike episodes there are both the exposé of Ezra Jones's opportunist theories and practices and the attack on the treachery of the Labour Party leaders and higher trade union officials who were chiefly responsible for the collapse of the strike. Mary Jones is now married to Len Roberts and the couple not only lead the miners in their fight against the capitalists but they struggle and then break with Mary's father Ezra. And when the strike finally ends, the workers are described to be firmly united and furious toward the small group of traitors who have sold out the interests of the masses to the government. Then, toward the end of the book, we are told how the miners are excited by the news of the civil war breaking out in Spain and how Len Roberts goes with a number of his fellow workers to participate in the war there and finally dies in action. This is particularly interesting as reflecting the wave of protest against fascism then sweeping over England, with many workers and progressive intellectuals joining in the fighting in Spain.

Although these two novels "Cwmardy" and "We Live" are not widely known in Britain, apparently on account of the limited number of copies published, yet they contain a most vivid account of the Welsh miners at work and during their struggle, set against the historical background of the first four decades of the 20th century. Four major historical events are colourfully described: the ten-month strike of Welsh miners in 1910—1911, the First World War, the General Strike of 1926 and the civil war between the fascists and the republicans in Spain in the middle 1930s, and in each case is highlighted the struggle between the capitalists, the reformist Labour Party and other opportunists on the one hand and the workers on the other. And these two novels also succeed in creating vivid characters in Len Roberts and his father Jim Roberts and Mary Jones and her father Ezra Jones. Len Roberts may be weak and inexperienced at first but becomes stronger and firmer with the experience of each struggle. From his first admiration for Ezra to his final break with him, from his first interest in Mary to his final comradely companionship with her, we may see the natural development of Len's character. Though Big Jim seems simple enough and has many weak points, yet he displays his courage and selflessness in being ever ready to help his fellow workers in time of trouble. Ezra Jones's character is revealed to us, from his first signs of weakness and compromise to his final act of treachery, and such a development is well explained by his dominant personal motive in joining in the strikers' movement in the first place. Mary's great affection for her father at first, her gradual suspicion of him and then her final break with him are very carefully unfolded before us, with full analysis of her inward struggle between her love for him and her duty toward the workers and their cause. Her relations with Len, showing a new kind of love which is based on comradeship for a common cause, are also worth pointing out. Even some of the minor characters are vivid enough including Ben the barber, Dai Cannon the worker-and-preacher, and Shane the mother of Len Roberts.

Though "The Ragged Trousered Philanthropists" give a fuller description of the life of the workers, in "Cwmardy" and "We Live" we have a vivid treatment of the intense class struggle between the workers and the capitalists (and also the opportunists) and there are also some finely-etched character portraits among the workers.

Unfortunately Lewis Jones died early, shortly after the writing of the two novels.

h. Richard Aldington

Richard Aldington (1892—1962) was born in a lawyer's family. He studied for a while in London University but pecuniary difficulties forced him to start making his own living as a reporter on athletics for a London newspaper. Before the First World War he came into contact with the group of poets known as the "Imagists", and beginning from 1914 his imagist poetry began to appear. In 1916 he joined the army and the life at the front had its strong impressions on him which were later reflected in almost all his writings. After his return from the war he worked for the Literary Supplement of London "Times". From 1919 to 1929 he did much work in translation, chiefly from the French, and published several volumes of his own poetry. The following decade of 1929—1939 was the period of the flowering of his literary talent, during which time he published no less than seven novels beginning with his best known work "The Death of a Hero" (1929) and including "The Colonel's Daughter" (1931), "All Men Are Enemies" (1933), "Women Must Work" (1934) and "Very Heaven" (1937). In this period he also wrote and published two books of short stories "Roads to Glory" (1930) and "Soft Answers" (1932), and two long poems "A Dream in the Luxembourg" (1930) and "Crystal World" (1937). Then, on the eve of the Second World War, he left England to settle down in America and after that he wrote another novel "Rejected Guest" (1939) and an autobiographical "Life for Life's Sake, A Book of Reminiscences" (1940) and two biographies "The Duke" (about the Duke of Wellington, 1943) and "Lawrence of Arabia, A Biographical Enquiry" (1956).

One of the leading poets among the Imagists, Aldington in his poetry aimed at aestheticism and formalism. However, he is best known for his novels, especially for his "Death of A Hero". In this novel while the first part is a satire on the egoism and hypocrisy in a bourgeois family (with the sarcastic descriptions of "dear papa" and "dear mama") which somewhat resembles that in Samuel Butler's "The Way of All Flesh", the bulk of the novel is a ruthless condemnation of imperialist war which thoroughly disillusioned the hero George Winterbourne and finally killed him just as it ruined the author spiritually. The story of the life of George Winterbourne as unfolded in the novel is a realistic picture of the post-war generation in England, often called "the lost generation", that suffered terribly from the spiritual damages received from the war. In the novel there is also much satire on artistic and literary figures in England at the time, including Upjohn the un-original painter, Shobbe who runs a literary review, Bobbe who poses as a "left" intellectual and Tubbe as the Tory and Anglo-Catholic (this last character being actually a satire on T.S. Eliot).

"The Colonel's Daughter" also deals with the damages of the war which killed so many young men, including the sweetheart of the country girl who was the heroine of the novel, but it gives a more extensive picture of the different characters in a small village ranging from an aristocrat who practically owns all the land around the village to a chauvinistic colonel. "All Men Are Enemies" is more like a sequel to "The Death of A Hero", describing here also the life experience of an intellectual who has had a painful experience in the war, but here the whole tone is more sad and the entire atmosphere is filled with pessimism. However, there is more social significance in this novel for here the author blames the social system in England and considers the ruling class as responsible for the miseries of the people, and at the end of the book the hero Antony after having gone through the vicissitudes of life arrives at the philosophic conclusion of despising the bourgeoisie, the merchant, money and the world of hypocrisy and of believing that socialism is something that will come quite inevitably.

i. A. J. Cronin

Archibald Joseph Cronin (born in 1896) was at first a medical doctor and his profession provided him with plenty of contact with the labouring people. He began to write fiction in the 1930s and only after he achieved considerable success in the literary field that he gave up his medical practice and devoted himself to a writer's career. His first novel, "The Hatter's Castle" (1931), contains a vivid portrait of a proud and selfish man of wealth who tyrannizes over his own household and displays his complacency and egoism in his dealings with others. Then came "The Stars Look Down" (1935) and "The Citadel" (1937), two novels that established his reputation as a novelist.

The theme in "The Stars Look Down" is the struggle between the miners and their employers, with a story lasting almost 20 years (from early 1920s to late 1930s), and including vivid descriptions of the miserable existence of the workers, of a strike lasting three months and of the tragic collapse of a coal pit resulting in the death of many miners. These scenes of suffering and death of the miners, contrasted with the life of ease and luxury of the capitalists, produce effective satire on the glaring social inequality in the bourgeois world. The two major characters are representative figures of two confronting classes: David Fenwick the miner and Richard Parlass the owner of the mines. The former grows from his early youth of immaturity to a firm determinate fighter and then an M. P. and ends with confidence in his struggle even after losing to a capitalist named Gowlan in a parliamentary election campaign and having to return to work in the mine, while the latter tenaciously pursues his own profit and neglects the safety measures at the pit and thus is actually responsible for the death of many miners when the pit collapses. The novelist also reveals the internecine struggle among the capitalists themselves when Gowlan the upstart member of the society becomes the owner of the mines which the young Arthur Parlass, son of old Parlass, has lost. On the whole, the novel is a sympathetic study of the conflict between the workers and the capitalists, siding with the former while satirizing the latter.

The scond and better known novel by Cronin is "The Citadel". The story here has to do with the life experience of a medical doctor and includes naturally much of the author's own adventures in life. A young physician Andrew Hanson at the beginning of the novel was moved by what he saw of the poverty and miseries of the miners who lived near him, and he felt that science should be used to serve the human race. He then moved to London in order to have a better chance for his medical career. At first he felt disgusted over the practice of other medical doctors in the English capital using improper means to get more clients, but gradually he fell under the influence of his vicious environment and began to work eagerly for his own name and for profit out of his profession and he gave up his former ways of rendering service to the society without stooping to material interests. Toward the end of the novel, however, Manson met with an incident of great spiritual disturbance and, conscience-stricken, he decided to give up his desire for wealth and reputation and to return to his earlier way of thinking, to make his science serve the people.

The Second World War marked a definite decline in Cronin's

creative power as he began to be more and more segregated from the common people until he left England to live in America and Switzerland in the 1940s and his later works lacked social significance.

j. George Orwell

George Orwell (pseudonym of Eric Blair, 1903—1950) was born in Bengal, India, where his father worked for the Civil Service. The family moved back to England in 1907 and in 1917 Orwell as a scholarship boy entered Eton where he contributed regularly to the various college magazines. He left Eton in 1921 and from 1922 to 1928 he joined the Indian Imperial Police in Burma. Part of his experience of these years was later reflected in his first novel, "Burmese Days" (1934). He was fed up with his role in imperial officialdom and he resigned from his post at the Burmese police and went to Paris in 1928 to live among the very poor people there and to learn at first hand about the life of the unemployed and of tramps and menial workers. He returned to England in 1929 and took up work first as a private tutor and later as a schoolteacher (1932). "Down and Out in Paris and London" was published in 1933. Due to his poor health, he soon gave up teaching and worked as a part-time assistant in a bookshop at Hampstead, London, until 1935. For a time he was commissioned by a left-wing publisher, Victor Gollancz, to make a personal survey of the depressed areas of northern England, and he not only lived among the unemployed workers there but with the most depressed among them. The result of his investigation was reported in "The Road to Wigan Pier" (published in 1937). Then in 1936 he went to Spain to fight in the Spanish Civil War on the republican side, not with the International Brigade but with P.O.U.M., a dissident Communist group with anarchist affiliations. He was wounded by a bullet through the neck and escaped from Spain with the secret police behind him. However, he was thoroughly disillusioned with the events there and an analysis of the fighting up to the failure was recorded in "Homage to Catalonia" (1938). Returning to England he earned his living by reviewing novels for the "New English Weekly", until 1940. In the thirties, besides the above-mentioned books he also published a number of essays and three novels: "A Clergyman's Daughter" (1935), which describes a girl escaping from her tyrannical father to dwell among tramps, prostitutes and hoodlums of nocturnal London, "Keep the Aspidistra Flying" (1936) which narrates the plight of an idealistic hero rebelling against the prevailing money-ethic, and "Coming Up for Air" (1939) which tells of a middle-aged insurance agent going back for a holiday to the village of his early childhood. During the Second World War he was a member of the Home Guard and worked for the BBC Eastern Service from 1940 to 1943. In 1943 he became literary editor of "Tribune" and contributed a regular page of political and literary commentary, "As I Please". From 1945 he became a regular contributor to the "Observer" and went as a special correspondent for the paper to France and Germany. Later he became a regular contributor to the "Manchester Evening News". He suffered from tuberculosis and was in and out of hospital from 1947 until his death in 1950, in London. His name became widely known with the publication, in 1945, of "Animal Farm", which turned out to be a best seller. "Nineteen Eighty-Four" attained a similar success and aroused much interest also as a film and on the television.

Of his early novels, "Burmese Days" is particularly interesting because it is significantly comparable to E.M. Forster's important work "A Passage to India" which appeared about ten years before. The theme is also that of racial discrimination in Britain's colony in the Orient (this time, however, it's Burma instead of India), and the story is also about one Englishman (Flory instead of Fielding in Forster's novel) standing alone against his colleagues in defence of his Indian friend, about an English girl fresh from England and about the strong atmosphere of racial prejudice in an administrative centre of English colonial officials. What is more, one gets the impression that Flory stands for Orwell just as Fielding stands for Forster, and so it is quite obvious that "Burmese Days" was an expression of Orwell's revulsion against the oppression and persecution of the natives in the colonial empire of Britain.

The two books that brought the author to the limelight of the bourgeois Western world are "Animal Farm" and "Nineteen Eighty-Four". "Animal Farm", which has a sub-title "A Fairy Story", tells first of the revolt of a group of various animals on a farm against their human master Mr. Jones and then of the pigs with their leader Napoleon assuming domination and tyranny over all other animals. The narrative proceeds from the earlier declaration of "All animals are equal" and goes on gradually to the tyrannization of the pigs over all "the lower animals" and to the glorification of the pig-leader Napoleon who "is always right" and to whom is given "the credit for every successful achievement and every stroke of good fortune". The whole book was supposed to be a bitter attack on fascism, but actually it was maliciously aimed at the rumoured practices in the Soviet Union and at Stalin. It is quite obvious that his earlier schooling at the aristocratic public school of Eton and his once rejected imperial training in India and with the Burmese police came back with a revenge, after he renounced imperialism in his mid-career and seemed to work for the leftist camp for quite a number of years.

"1984" was an anti-utopian book somewhat in the tradition of Aldous Huxley's "Brave New World", but here instead of portraying the hopelessness of a future world of true progress and prosperity Orwell wrote a bitter and venomous satire on the Soviet Union and on Stalin. The central character in the novel, Winston Smith, is working in the Ministry of Truth (which is supposed to stand for the ministry of propaganda and which is maliciously described as a centre where truths are distorted and falsities are manufactured) in London, the chief city in one of the three fascist states in the world, Oceania. The whole picture is that of a human society where there is nothing but tyranny and suspicion and mental as well as physical torture for most of the people, and Smith and his girl Julia are trapped into joining an underground organization against the Inner

Party and its leader Big Brother and then are persecuted and arrested and treated very brutally. This is an even more thinly disguised attack on what the author imagined to be the state of affairs in the Soviet Union under Stalin. Written in the heyday of the cold war between the Western world and the Soviet Union, this novel naturally earned its popularity.

George Orwell who in his youth was for some years an apparently staunch supporter of the leftist movement which was dominant among the intellectuals in Europe in the late 1920s and early 1930s, obviously fell under the influence of the sudden swing to the right that came in 1939 when many avant garde writers blindly regarded Stalin's strategic non-aggression pact with Hitler as the joining of the forces of communism with German fascism and they even tried to equate the former with the latter. Then the wave of the cold war following Churchill's Fulton speech of 1947 spurred Orwell further on to his anti-communist writings. While Orwell was in a sense a representative figure of the unsteady pendulum-motion leftward and then rightward of many European intellectuals from the post-World-War-I years to the post-World-War-II period, his two notorious anti-communist books "Animal Farm" and "Nineteen Eighty-Four", written supposedly against fascism of all sorts, exerted their malignant effect against socialism and communism in the English-speaking world.

k. Evelyn Waugh

Evelyn Waugh (1903—1966) was born in Hampstead and educated at Lancing and Oxford. He was second son of Arthur Waugh, publisher and literary critic, and brother of Alec Waugh, a writer of popular novels. He studied modern history at first, then studied art, taught schools in London (1924), worked for some time for the "Daily Express", and mixed with high society. He wrote critical biography "Dante Gabriel Rossetti" in 1927, and in 1928 published his first novel, "Decline and Fall", which immediately established his fame as a novelist. His second novel of repute was "Vile Bodies" which came out in 1930, the year the author joined the Roman Catholic Church, and in 1935 he completed his biography of the Elizabethan Jesuit martyr Edmund Campion which was awarded the Hawthornden Prize in 1936. In the 1930s his other novels "Black Mischief" (1932), "A Handful of Dust" (1934) and "Scoop" followed, and in these years he travelled extensively in most parts of Europe, the Near East, Africa and tropical America. In 1939 when the Second World War began, he was commissioned in the Royal Marines and later was transferred to the Royal Horse Guards, serving in the Middle East and in Yugoslavia. In 1942 he published "Put Out More Flags" and in 1945 "Brideshead Revisited", followed by "When the Going was Good", "The Loved One" and "Helena", the last being a historical novel. Then appeared his trilogy of war novels, entitled "The Sword of Honour", which began with the first volume, "Men at Arms" (1952), that won the James Tait Black Prize, and the second and third volumes, "Officers and Gentlemen" and "Unconditional Surrender", appeared respectively in 1955 and 1961.

"Decline and Fall" is an uproarious farce, a much exaggerated comedy, and a penetrating exposé of middle class and upper middle class English life, though, as claimed by the author, "everything is drawn, without malice, from the vaguest of imaginations", and "it is meant to be funny". The "prelude" of the novel tells how Paul Pennyfeather, the hero, becomes an innocent victim of an annual college debauchery at Oxford and is dismissed as a theological student for indecent behaviour. The rest of the book is a picaresque tale of Pennyfeather's adventures. First he is a teacher at a small, out-of-the-way boarding school called Llanabba Castle in North Wales (in Part I); then he serves as the tutor of the only son of an extremely wealthy widow Mrs. Margot Beste-Chetwynde in her country house called "King's Thursday" in Hampshire, England, and later as her lover and husband-to-be (in Part II); and then again, he becomes a convict for undertaking white slave traffic and is a prisoner serving his sentence in Blackstone jail until he is mysteriously ordered to be sent to a sanatorium for an appendicitis operation and is reported to have died on the operating table, but he is actually smuggled abroad to Margot's villa in the Greek Island of Corfu and thence to be returned to England to take up once again the study of theology at Oxford (in Part III). Here there is almost satire everywhere, from the rotten school in Wales with all its ridiculous inmates, to the equally rotten but more flippant social life in the household of the mysteriously rich widow of an earl, and then to the fantastic goings-on in an unorthodoxly-run prison under its ambitious experiment-minded governor of a sociology professor. While some of the episodes are so incredidable and so totally void of probability (e.g. the repeated story of deaths and resurrections of Captain Grimes the schoolteacher with a wooden leg, the strange behaviour of the little haughty drunk of a boy Peter who later inherites an earldom, and the thoroughly ludicrous adventures of Paul Pennyfeather in prison), a few truly satirical portraits emerge in the sketches of Dr. Fagan the schoolmaster, of Professor Silenus the architect, of the Labour Minister of Transportation Sir Humphrey Maltravers, and above all, of Margot Beste-Chetwynde who as a great and charming society lady amasses much wealth out of white slavery traffic and gets away with it by shifting the punishment of the crime very trickily and almost imperceptibly onto the innocent Pennyfeather her prospective husband. The matter-of-fact interviews of the girls enlisted to prostitution, by this impeccable lady of high society, provide bitter sarcasm on the hypocritical bourgeois world than even to be found in Shaw's "Mrs. Warren's Profession". It is perhaps surprising that such a distinguished writer of the élitism as Evelyn Waugh was capable of satirizing in such downright candid fashion the social life he was so familiar with. Of course, in the "author's note" that prefixes the novel, Waugh did utter emphatically "I have never met any one at all like any of the characters."

"Vile Bodies", published shortly after "Decline and Fall", added much to Waugh's fame as a promising novelist. It was written more or less in the same fashion as its predecessor, being a heavily-spiced satire on English upper-class world of the 20th century. This time the theme is more a concentrated dose of the dark side of high society in London, the title "Vile Bodies" referring particularly to all sorts of "parties" or social gatherings: "masked parties, savage parties, Victorian parties, Greek parties, Wild West parties, Russian parties, Circus parties, parties where one had to dress as somebody else, almost naked parties in St. John's Wood, parties in flats and studios and houses and ships and hotels and night clubs, in windmills and swimming baths, tea parties at school where one ate muffins and meringues and tinned crab, parties at Oxford where one drank brown sherry and smoked Turkish cigarettes, dull dances in London and comic dances in Scotland and disgusting dances in Paris — all that succession and repetition of massed humanity. ... Those vile bodies."

With "parties" or social gatherings as the centre of attraction, the novel necessarily deals with numerous figures of some importance in the narrative, with not one or two heroes or heroines towering above the rest. Here the Prime Ministers (Mr. Outrage and Sir James Brown), Archbishop of Canterbury, Home Secretary and many titled Lords and Ladies appear in their ridiculous or ludicrous lights, together with their "Younger Generation" and other members of the upper class circles in Britain, most of whom are frivolous and indulgent in drinking debaucheries and more especially in spreading gossip and scandal almost all the time. The story begins with all these aristocratic people suffering from seasickness on a bad English Channel crossing, then with the strange fate of some of them at the hands of the Customs officials, then with an incredible gathering of an old assortment of guests at the parlour of the modernistic Shepherd's Hotel owned by a woman of aristocratic pretensions, then with the activities of two Lords (a marquess and an earl) vying in writing society gossip columns for the newspapers and in reporting directly from two parties they attended, one at a Savage Party and another at the home of the incumbent Prime Minister Sir John Brown. There are also descriptions of a party at an airship, of the reported death by accident at a West-End hotel, of the performance of an American Revivalist Mrs. Ape and her "Bright Young People" with wings at the town house of Viscountess Metroland, of a shooting of a film on Colonel Blount's estate about the career of the great religious reformer John Wesley, of the excitement and mishaps at a motor race, and of an uproarious party of the "Younger Generation" in the ward-room of a nursery home where a badly wounded young woman of fashion at the races was supposed to be recuperating. All these scenes in themselves are laughter-provoking and full of frivolity as well as revolting and satirical. Especially sharp and biting are the episodes relating to the society column in the London newspapers and the notorious scandal-mongering and the consequent libel actions against the reporters, and while on the whole these passages lead to much humour as well as satire, occasionally the devastating reports on certain social events result in the suicide of reporter from among the impoverished aristocracy and in the eventual ousting of a prime minister from his office. But the general temper of the book is a hilariously comic one, as one social party after another (the "vile bodies") and their participants chiefly from the high society of aristocracy and decadent intellectuals are ridiculed for their various foibles and indulgences and crimes.

Though lacking in unity of plot as compared with "Decline and Fall" and weaker in character portrayal than the later novels such as "Brideshead Revisited", "Vile Bodies" nevertheless distinguishes itself by containing much more pungent satire on upper class life in England, especially in London, than most of Waugh's other works of fiction. And the facile language adds to the charm of the book. The chief shortcoming is the over-abundance of humour throughout, through the employment of obvious exaggeration everywhere, andt hat certainly dilutes the satire considerably, with the suggestion of improbability for the persons and events described in the novel. Perhaps Waugh knew too well the high society, the object of his satire, and so quite inevitably, almost naturally, his sympathy for some of the ridiculed and debunked people seeps out of the text somewhat in spite of the author's original intentions.

"Brideshead Revisited" was first of all a Catholic novel, in which Waugh as a devout Catholic tried to portray chiefly the several members of a Catholic family of English aristocrats in order to illustrate the theme of "the operation of divine grace on a group of diverse but closely connected characters," in the author's own words in his preface to the 1959 revised edition of the book. Told in the first person singular, the narrator Charles Ryder first describes his associations with a younger son of the Marquis of Marchmain, Lord Sebastian Flyte, at Oxford, where they had many scenes of debauchery together and Sebastian was already an addict to alcohol. Then the other members of the Marchmains are introduced: (1) the Marquis who disclaimed Catholicism and lived abroad at Venice for years with a mistress, (2) his wife Lady Marchmain who had such high religious fervour that most other members of the family found it difficult to endure living together with her, (3) their eldest son the Earl of Brideshead who was conceited and full of affectation but a very strict Catholic, (4) their elder daughter Julia who was haughty and wayward and reluctant to conform to the rigorous discipline of the Catholic Church, (5) her fiancé and later husband Rex Mottram who was a pushing politician ready even to be converted to Catholicism in order to marry Julia, (6) the youngest daughter of the family Cordelia whose precocity enabled her to know and participate in many important happenings in the family and (7) last but not least, Charles Ryder the narrator who was Sebastian's best pal and then became friend of the family and eventually Julia's lover and who was supposed to piece together the many episodes in the separate threads of the story. It is worthy of note that Waugh the author succeeded so well in painting the many vivid portraits of all the major characters mentioned above and in linking up the disconnected parts of the tale to present a fascinating picture of an aristocratic family in England to whom Catholicism was not only a faith but also an obsession. I suppose this is a faithful picture of people who are born and brought up in the atmosphere of the Catholic church so that they feel the religion not only in their heads but also in their hearts, and therefore they act accordingly in the end: even Sebastian who rebels all along goes finally to a monastery; even the Marquis of Marchmain who for many years broke with religion eventually returns to receive the last sacrament just before dying; even Julia who consistently defies the stiff restrictions of the Catholic Church returns at last to the faith and gives up marrying Ryder after her divorce from Rex. These instances show that Catholicism has gotten into the blood of these apparently rebellious people so that they eventually are obliged to submit to it, and this is of course the view held by the author who was a staunch believer. However, this does not constitute a merit for the novel, but the real saving grace for the book is the subtle satirical effect, perhaps quite contrary to the author's intentions, of the degeneracy and hypocrisy of these aristocrats who commit all sorts of sins — keeping a mistress, taking a lover, indulging ever in drinking bouts — and yet who still hope to win divine grace by performing all the rites of the Catholic Church. And according to the common belief of almost all who join the Catholic Church, it does seem possible for one to sin and even to commit crimes and yet to be forgiven simply by going to confessions and particularly by receiving the last sacraments before dying. This hypocrisy inherent in the Catholic Church is itself a matter for satire, which is all the way latent in the novel though the author is possibly not even aware of it simply because he was himself a Catholic and therefore took for granted all those practices of the Catholic faith. Of course, the fact that Waugh was himself so familiar with the sort of high life among the Catholics in England makes it quite impossible for him to detect the hypocrisy inherent in the Catholic Church, and so his accounts of the lives of the members of the Marchmain family are rendered with so much sympathy and understanding that the readers are easily led to overlook the dark side of the picture. However, for the more discerning reader the descriptions of the dissolute existence of the Marchmains provide all too definitely an exposé of the degeneracy and hypocrisy of the aristocratic and wealthy Catholics in 20th-century England.

Though "Brideshead Revisited" deals with the story of diverse members of the Marchmain family in different historical periods, yet the device of the narrator serving also as one of the active participants in the story enables the author effectively to tell only the highlights of the tale in separate episodes and yet to link them up into a continuous narrative. And Evelyn Waugh in this novel succeeds in telling a most engrossing tale in his usual fluid and readable style.

1. J. B. Priestley

J.B. Priestley(John Boynton Priestley, 1894—)was born in Bradford, Yorkshire, and was educated at Yorkshire and Oxford. He joined the first world war and was three times wounded. He was a prolific writer and contributed to periodicals in London and other places in England. He was as much a novelist as a playwright, and he also wrote much prose. Of his novels, "The Good Companions" (1929) is certainly the best known and most widely read, and next to it, "Angel Pavement" (1930). Of his dramas, "Dangerous Corner" (1932) was probably the play that first brought him success on the stage. In the later Thirties he wrote two other "time plays": "Time and the Conways" (1937) and "I Have Been Here Before" (1937). In the 1940s, he wrote a number of other plays, including "The Linden Tree" (1947) and "The Inspector Calls" (1945).

"The Good Companions" tells a popular story of the adventures of a travelling concert party in the English provinces. It begins with three separate episodes in the lives of three major characters in the novel: Jess Oakroyd who is an elderly carpenter in the small town of Bruddersford in northern England, Inigo Jollifant who is a young teacher at the Washbury Manor School near the North Sea and Elizabeth Trant who is an unmarried woman of thirty-seven and an heiress of less than 200 pounds a year upon her father the colonel's death. But change of fortunes comes to all three of them: Oakroyd is unreasonably dismissed from his job, and vexed by his son and wife at home takes the road to go south; Jollifant also loses his teaching job because he has offended the wife of the headmaster and leaves school to seek for adventures elsewhere; and Miss Elizabeth Trant has bought a car from her nephew and goes on a holiday tour by herself to the cathedral cities in England. Then by sheer chance all three of them after encountering their individual adventures run into a concert party by the name of Dinky Doos which is just then falling to pieces, and the three of them provide the company with just the help the party needs, Miss Trant to finance it, Inigo Jollifant to contribute to it his talent of composing popular tunes and of serving as pianist and Oakroyd to give it all the carpentry needed for making stage sets and other set-ups, and they then decide to restart the travelling troupe and renaming it "The Good Companions" and the show is once more on the go. Then the concert company moves from one town to another and meets with mishaps and good fortunes, failures and triumphs, and the bulk of the novel deals with the adventures of all the different members of the troupe on the road. Then finally the company breaks up and as the different members go their different ways, so the three major figures who have been the guiding spirit of the company now meet their varied fortunes: Miss Trant to be married to an old-time sweetheart of hers who is a Scottish doctor named McFarlane; Inigo Jollifant to go together with a young musical comedienne of the company named Sessie Dean and both to work for good pay in a musical comedy; while Oakroyd to return home to be reconciled to his dying wife and then to migrate to Canada to live with his daughter Lily and her family. So this is a typical picaresque novel with a whole series of adventures and a happy ending for the major characters in it.

"The Good Companions" tells an engrossing tale which may be lacking in unity but is nevertheless full of fun and good humour. It is written in the traditional way and contains some tall tales and quite a number of superfluous and tiring details, while the emphasis is laid almost entirely on the incidents that happen to the various persons and the conversations that lead to uproarious laughter or occasionally to sadness, and comparatively little attention is paid to the psychological make-up of the numerous characters as individuals, including even the major characters. In that sense, this is truly a bestselling romance that appeals to the general reading public rather than to the intellectuals and the élite and is therefore quite contrary to the new temper of the modern novel written by D.H. Lawrence and James Joyce and Virginia Woolf. Indeed, the materialism that Mrs. Woolf accuses Bennett, Wells and Galsworthy of may be more correctly aimed at Priestley here, for in a book like "The Good Companions" the "spiritual" side is almost totally neglected. But the author seems to take great delight himself in telling a very exciting and complicated story and the chief saving grace of the novel is the abundance of humour as Priestley laughs and smiles and feels high or low in close communion with the characters he has created and with his readers. Of course most of the characters in the novel are simple and warm-hearted and they come from the common people, and in spite of their different shortcomings they deserve our sympathy.

"Angel Pavement" tells quite a different story from that of "The Good Companions". It deals with the lower middle class employees and their employers in a small business firm selling veneers and inlays in London, and narrates how they were at first almost faced with financial ruin, how then their trade revived with the arrival of a Mr. Golspie from the Baltic, and how finally the disappearance of Golspie once again brought disaster to the whole firm and all those connected with it. In other words, this is the tale of an unscrupulous adventurer Golspie and of all the staff and workers in a small shop, told in an atmosphere of mystery and described with numerous details of the personal relationships of the many characters at the shop and in their homes. It is a realistic sketch of one poor section of London and the author relates everything with his inimitable humour. All the characters except Golspie are treated with much sympathy, but Golspie is exposed at the end to be a treacherous adventurer who thinks only of his own personal gains and never hesitates to place many innocent people in jeopardy as soon as his private interest is endangered. Here again Priestley writes in the old-fashioned way of narration, resembling the naturalistic style of Arnold Bennett's. But there is hardly any satire or social criticism to be found in this rather sluggish novel.

Priestley's plays are also known for the abundance of humour in them, but at least some of them touch on more philosophical problems than do his novels.

"Dangerous Corner" (1932), the play that first brought him fame as a dramatist, begins with a group of upper middle class people of modern England gathered for a drawing-room conversation after dinner when one of them speaks of the danger in telling the truth and another responds by saying "life's got a lot of dangerous corners", and then follows a whole series of truth-telling that involves many unpleasant incidents of forgery, robbery, bribery and disloyalty between spouses in the different families they belong to and finally the host of the house even shoots himself. But suddenly there is a brief blackout on the stage and the characters all resume their original poses at the beginning of the play and carry on the conversation as before, yet this time nobody mentions any of the dangerous corners of life and they have their normal round of fun and dance, and the play ends happily, for the dangerous corner has been safely passed. This clever stage trick which is partly responsible for the popular success of the play, contains nevertheless an interesting philosophical idea that many human affairs happen by chance and not by necessity, but at the same time it leads to the author's subtle satire on the externally dignified members of the modern British society who may behave like upright ladies and gentlemen but who actually have many skeletons in their cupboards, i.e. who in their thoughts and deeds have committed many evils. Unfortunately the play wins its popularity chiefly on account of its theatricality and its idealistic suggestion of the rule of chance in human affairs, and not so much for the exposé of the concealed crimes and misdeeds of the upper classes behind the facade of their refinement and wealth.

"An Inspector Calls", modelled somewhat after the Russian writer Gogol's "The Inspector-General" and first produced in the Soviet Union upon the author's visit there, follows in its plot construction a pattern similar to that in "Dangerous Corner".

Here an unknown inspector makes an unexpected call upon a well-to-do English family, and upon his visit are brought to light one after another many despicable and even criminal deeds of despotism and egotism and moral degradation committed by practically every member of that family. The satire on the immoral and even scandalous behaviour of seemingly upright and respected individuals of the upper layers of English society is unmistakably there, and the irony that most of these offences and misdemeanors have been hidden there untouched all the time until the call of the inspector stirs them all up is very grim and biting. However, here as in "Dangerous Corner", Priestley manages to infuse much humour into his satire and irony and thus alleviates somewhat the effect of the bitterness or disgust and makes the readers and the audience somehow sympathize with those hypocrites who lead their double existence of a respectful exterior and a contemptible interior until they are unfortunately exposed to view. I suppose the characters in his plays as in his novels are people the author not only knew but was quite familiar with, and he was too much of a bonny good fellow not to condone them and make light of their failings.

After the Second World War Priestley turned more and more to the right politically. At his best, he was a minor novelist and dramatist, who enjoyed much popularity from the late 1920s to the mid-fifties.

m. Graham Greene

Graham Greene (1904—) was born at Berkhampstead and received his education at the school there (where his father was headmaster). Then he went to Oxford and he joined "The Times" as sub-editor in 1926—30 and as movie critic in 1937—40. He was literary editor for "The Spectator" in London in 1940—41, and then served in the Foreign Office in London in 1941—44. He was director of Publishers Eyre and Spottiswoode in 1944—48 and of The Bodley Head in 1958—68. He began his career as a novelist with "Babbling April" in 1926 but did not gain recognition till his fourth novel, "Stamboul Train" (1932) which he called an "entertainment" to distinguish it from serious works of fiction. The major event in his life was his conversion to Roman Catholicism in 1927, which had its strong and lasting effect upon many of his novels. He established his fame as an important novelist with "Brighton Rock" (1938), which was followed by "The Power and the Glory" (1940),"The Heart of the Matter" (1948), "The End of the Affair" (1954), "The Quiet American" (1955), "Our Man in Havana" (1958), "A Burnt-out Case" (1961), "The Comedians" (1966), "The Honorary Consul" (1973), "The Human Factor" (1978) and "Doctor Fischer of Geneva or The Bomb Party" (1980). Greene also wrote some successful plays ("The Living Room", 1953; "The Potting Shed", 1957; "The Complaisant Lover", 1959) and films based on the plays. He travelled extensively and many of the foreign lands (Mexico, West Africa, Vietnam, Cuba, Belgian Congo, Haiti) he visited were described in his novels.

"Brighton Rock" deals with a story of gang warfare and racketeering in the seaside resort of Brighton. The three major characters in the novel are Pinkie (the 17-year-old leader of the gang), Rose (a young waitress in a cafe), and Ida Arnold (a middle-aged woman interested in solving a murder case), and the book is actually a murder mystery. Pinkie and his gang managed to murder, very mysteriously, a man named Fred Hale who was responsible for the death of the former leader of the gang, but while Hale was being strangled he somehow died of heart failure, and the coroner declared the death to have come from natural causes. Ida Arnold strongly suspected that it must have been murder, and she tried hard and steadfastly to verify her suspicion. In the meantime Pinkie knew that owing to carelessness there was an unfortunate clue to the murder left in a restaurant and as he tried to cover it up he found that Rose the waitress there was already aware of it. To prevent the girl from revealing what she knew, he even tried to marry her, and he did have the marriage ceremony performed by a lawyer employed by the gang but it was a terrible sin for Catholics (Pinkie and Rose were both Catholics) to be married outside the church. Pinkie was unscrupulously brutal to the extent of murdering one of his gang simply for fear of betrayal and he even threatened to kill the said lawyer if the latter should reveal the second murder. But knowing some one (actually it was Ida Arnold)to be trying to persuade Rose to desert him, Pinkie succeeded in making Rose agree to commit suicide with him together. But Rose at the last moment threw away the pistol instead of shooting herself just as Ida Arnold arrived on the scene with a policeman, and then Pinkie, hindered from throwing a bottle of vitriol at his pursuers, was himself blinded by the deadly chemical and he finally killed himself by jumping down a cliff. The novel ends strangely with Rose confessing everything to an old Catholic priest who merely told her to "hope and pray", and then said, "You can't conceive, my child, nor can I or any one the ... appalling ... strangeness of the mercy of God". Perhaps this last sentence was Greene's "message" in this novel, which expressed his orthodox Catholic faith.

It is difficult to interpret a novel like this which has earned for Greene such great and lasting popularity. At first glance one would suggest that here the author was merely following or catering to the popular modern Western taste for violence and horror, for murder and brutality, for a complicated and intriguing solution to a murder case, for a peep into the underworld of gangsterism and racketeering. That possibly is true, but that doesn't provide a satisfactory evaluation of the novel or an explanation of the book's popularity not only with the general reading public but also with the more serious critical world of the West. To us perhaps the novel is noteworthy because it gives a rather thoroughgoing exposé of the terrible criminal actions of gangsters and racketeers in modern Western cities: the gangsters who work together and swear loyalty to one another and yet who would kill one another ruthlessly as soon as there are any signs or suspicions of betrayal (witness the relations between Pinkie the gang-leader and his followers and also between Fred Hale and his aids) and then the apparent refined aristocracy of a big gangster-leader and his relations with the small gangster group (witness the relations between Colleoni and Pinkie). Colleoni doesn't appear much in the story yet his assumed dignity is very definitely a satirical caricature of the big leaders of big gangs and rackets in all big cities of the Western world, while Pinkie is a much fuller portrait of a small-time gangster whose most unscrupulous treachery and consistent brutality are painted in the blackest colours together with his occasional thoughts of sin and guilt as a Roman Catholic. Here one sees the conflict or inner contradiction of a believer of the Catholic Church who commits crime after crime and knows all the time that he is sinning and acting against the dogmas of the Church and yet keeps on with his nefarious deeds. This is especially interesting to us who are born and bred in an environment devoid of the all-pervading influence of the Christian Church, particularly of Roman Catholicism, because there the religious ideas are even latent in the innermost consciousness of most people born to the faith and cannot be eradicated whether they are true believers or not. And this also shows that a novel like this reflects the true psychological reality of many human beings brought up in a strong religious environment like that of the Roman Catholic Church and that in that sense "Brighton Rock" is a faithful representation of one section of British social life, that of the underworld of violence and criminality.

However, when the old Catholic priest says to the innocent Rose near the end of the novel, that "the Church does not demand that we believe any soul is cut off from mercy", and that "a Catholic is more capable of evil than anyone, I think perhaps — because we believe in Him — we are more in touch with the devil than other people," one suspects that it is Graham Greene the Roman Catholic writer who is here speaking, and while the second idea is sheer superstition, the first view is something that is actually preached in the Catholic Church and therefore it must be regarded as a realistic touch. More importantly, these two sentences quoted above appear not only in this novel but the philosophical content embodied in them pervades many other fictional works of Graham Greene, so that there is often in Greene's novels the careful portrayal of Catholic sinners or even criminals who persist in doing what they know to be sinful and evil but who may still hope to be forgiven by God according to the Catholic dogmas and who therefore still win a certain amount of sympathy from the author. Yet another thing to be noted here is that to these Catholic perpetrators of sins or crimes in Graham Greene's fiction the spiritual contradiction lies generally between good and evil rather than that between right and wrong as in the case of ordinary non-religious people. The foremost mental preoccupation with religion, with sin and repentance, with absolution or damnation, with God and the redemption of the soul, placed in curious juxtaposition with the evil thoughts of murder, debauchery, treachery and all the other nefarious deeds, produces intricate psychological workings in the major characters and leads to deep pathos and intense irony, and this unique blending of religious faith with persistent sinning and criminality adds much to the complexity in character-portrayal and to the suspense in story-telling and therefore is a great asset to the art of narration for the novelist.

"The Power and the Glory" is a maturer and subtler work of art than "Brighton Rock", although it is also a Catholic novel written according to the same religious logic and telling almost as exciting a story. Here the hero is a "whisky priest" in one of the provinces in Mexico where once the Catholic clergymen were not only legally prohibited from performing their duties but were openly pursued as criminals to be shot. All the priests had left the province but two, and one of them had capitulated by being formally married to a wife and thus bringing contempt to himself and the Church. But this "Whisky priest" would not give up his God-serving profession, though he had many weaknesses and committed many mortal sins, such as drinking brandy and whisky and even having a daughter by an innocent woman, yet he felt he could still perform with efficacy the God-given functions of a priest like receiving confessions, performing masses and administering sacraments to believers. So while he knew he was hunted together with a Yankee robber and homicide by the police and pursued after from village to village, he still preached mass and carried out the Consecration of the Host to the villagers surreptitiously in the darkness before dawn because they had asked him with much eagerness to have the religious rites performed to them. He was more than once almost identified and caught by the police, but he barely escaped. And then after much suffering he finally succeeded in crossing the border to another province where the clergy would be safe, and then he was enticed back by a wily man who brought him back across the border ostensibly to save the soul of a dying man but who did that actually to betray him in order to claim a reward from the police. The priest suspected the betrayal but came back nevertheless because to perform the religious rite of extreme unction to a dying man was his priestly duty, and though he knew himself to be a bad priest, still he was a priest and must do his duty. This harrowing tale of the priest-hero, tortured by self-mortification over his innumerable sins and trudging wearily on his way under the threat of capture and death, is on the one hand an exciting story of narrow escapes and unpredictable prospects and on the other the careful psychological study of a highly introspective character, but from the author's point of view, it is above all an illustration of the Catholic Church's triumph over all sorts of sinners who may have committed mortal sins yet who are ever repentant and at crucial moments are willing to sacrifice even their lives in order to work for the Church to save human souls. It is strange to find a man like Graham Greene to have such staunch faith of a Catholic, but it is on account of this that his Catholic novels have proved to be so popular in England and elsewhere though quite a large number of the readers appreciate more the artistic merits of his novels rather than their religious subject matter.

Grahma Greene is one of the outstanding novelists living in England today. He is chiefly known for his Catholic novels, which are both illustrations of the Catholic faith in conflict with human sins, and subtle portrayals of unique figures in the criminal world of the modern West. We have little use for the religious faith of the author or of the many Catholic believers in the world, but the artistic achievement in vivid story-telling and in the psychological study of characters in these stirring novels should not be overlooked. Of course, in writing hair-raising tales in the detective-story style Greene was obviously catering also to the popular taste for violence and horror among the general reading public of the West today. Greene will turn out more stories in the future and so it is not the right time to make an overall estimate of his career as a novelist as yet.

n. Jack Lindsay

Jack Lindsay was born in 1900 in Melbourne, Australia, of an artist's family, and had his education at Queensland University, specializing in ancient languages of Greek and Latin and already beginning to write some poetry. He went to England in 1926, and, meeting with the General Strike shortly after his arrival in London, he joined in the workers' movement. Later he became a member of the Communist Party of Great Britain. In the first year after his arrival in England he organized a publishing house for literary writings in which he was simultaneously manager, translator, illustrator, proofreader and typesetter. The venture soon ended in failure and for almost three years after 1930 Lindsay experienced serious financial difficulties, living in a remote region in Cornwall and associating with the life of the poor peasants, fishermen and miners there.

Lindsay began his literary career as soon as he arrived in England, with the publication of his translation of Aristophanes' comedy "Lesistrata". In 1928 he started a magazine "The London Aphrodite", in which were published articles attacking theories of the German philosopher Oswald Spengler and of the English novelist D.H. Lawrence as well as the poetry of T.S. Eliot.

In the 1930s Lindsay's creative output was many-sided as well as voluminous, chiefly in the field of historical fiction, with "Rome for Sale" (1933), "Ceasar Is Dead" (1934), "Runaway" (1935), "Adam of a New World" (1936), "To Arms" (1938) and "1649, a Novel of a Year" (1938), but also in poetry, with "Who Are the English" (1936), "On Guard for Spain" (1937) and "England, My England" (1939), and also a book of critical biography, "John Bunyan, The Maker of Myths" (1937). In his historical novels Lindsay tried to find the struggle between the progressive and reactionary forces in history not alone in political and economic fields but also in the social and cultural world such as the struggle shown in "Adam of a New World" between the progressive scientific and philosophic thought and the religious dogmas of the Catholic Church. "1649, a Novel of a Year", the most important of the lot, relates the struggle of the bourgeois revolution in England at its height, in the year of 1649, and in the book the author gives very vivid pictures of the conflicting forces not just including the Royalists or the Cavaliers and the Parliamentarians but also the distinct groups within the Parliamentary camp: the more revolutionary groups the Levellers and the Diggers as well as the Roundheads (or the Independents) and the Presbyterians. "On Guard for Spain" is Lindsay's contribution to the anti-fascist campaign against Franco in Spain. In his poetic pamphlet "Who Are the Englishmen?" Lindsay pointed out that the true representatives of the English people are the workers, and he wrote about the glorious revolutionary tradition of the English people from John Ball and the peasants' uprising of 1381 to the Luddites and the ‚Chartists. In another poetic pamphlet "England, My England", Lindsay contrasted the attitude of the workers toward their native country with that of the wealthy capitalists and pointed out that to different persons the expression of "my England" has a different meaning altogether. "John Bunyan" is the first of Lindsay's literary biographies of well-known progressive English writers of the past and in it he tries to emphasize the democratic Puritan writer as one who voiced the increasing discontent among the poor people in England in the second half of the 17th century.

During the years of the Second World War Lindsay wrote his war-poems "In Action" (1942) and "Second Front" (1944) and war-novels "We Shall Return" (1941) and "Beyond Terror" (1943), also "Hello, Stranger" (about the work of women in industry during the war years, published in 1945), all of which are full of intense anti-fascist feelings. Then after the end of the war Lindsay was again engaged in four distinct forms of writing: poetry, fiction, literary biography and literary criticism, and miscellaneous prose. Of the last genre may be mentioned "A World Ahead" (1950), a book recording his visit to the Soviet Union in 1949, and "Rumanian Summer" (1952), a work written jointly with Maurice Cornford about the history of the Rumanian people's struggle for liberation from foreign domination and about Rumania after liberation.

Lindsay's works on literary history and literary criticism after 1945 include: "Charles Dickens" (1949),and "George Meredith: His Life and Work" (1955);his numerous critical essays such as "The Progressive Tradition in Our 19th Century Literature", "On Some of the Problems concerning Socialist Realism", "The British Scene: What is Happening to Our Culture?", and "The Paris Commune and English Literature", and above all, "After the 'Thirties': The Novel in Britain and Its Future" (1956), a rather comprehensive work dealing with the development of the English novel from the 1920s through the 1930s to the post-war period and with certain artistic and technical problems in fictional writing. Lindsay was editor of the journal "Arena" (in 1950—51), a bi-monthly organ of the progressive literary movement at the time, and after that he was one of the editors of the "Marxist Quarterly".

Besides his works on historical fiction of which "Men of Forty-Eight" and "The Great Oak", dealing respectively with the revolutionary events in 1848 (both the revolution in France and the Chartist Movement in England) and in 1549 (Kett's Rising in England) are the more prominent ones. Lindsay turned to the writing of life in contemporary Britain, with his series of "Novels of the British Way",which include "The Betrayed Spring" (1952), "Rising Tide" (1954), "The Moment of Choice" (1955) and "A Local Habitation" (1957). In these novels Lindsay tried to reflect the social reality in England after the Second World War and to point out certain important social problems of the day and to suggest possible solutions. Of the four, while "The Moment of Choice" deals chiefly with the peace movement in 1950 and "A Local Habitation" with the housing problem in post-war years, "The Betrayed Spring" and "Rising Tide" are more important. The theme in "The Betrayed Spring" is the betrayal of the trust of the people by the Labour Party in the winter of 1946—47 and the novel contains in it apparently four parallel threads of story only loosely linked up in action one with another and taking place in four different localities in England about four distinct groups of people. Actually, the four separate threads of story in the novel are not chosen at random but they constitute a composite whole, for together they give a rather comprehensive picture of the chief manifestations of class struggle going on in 1946—47: with the London thread narrating the strike on the docks and in the hotels and the lives of the workers and their families in the English capital; with the Lancashire episodes describing the workers in the coal-mines there and the nationalization of coal and then the fuel crisis; with the Yorkshire sections revealing the conditions in the light industry, in the textile mill in particular, chiefly from the angle of the capitalists but also touching on the minor skirmishes between them and the workers; and then with the Tyneside chapters concerned with a trade-union official who betrays the members of his union in his pursuit after personal position and material gains; and finally with the short "End-piece" in which two major characters in two of the story threads, the two ex-soldiers from the Second World War Dick Baxter the Lancashire miner and Harry Manson the Communist student of the London School of Economics meet in London talking about the national situation in the "betrayed spring"of 1947 and gathering news about another ex-soldier Kit Swinton the son of a Yorkshire textile mill-owner and receiving a letter from the sister of the fourth ex-soldier (killed in the war) Jean Kackenzie, wife of a Tyneside trade-union official Will Emery. While the "End-piece" and the occasional references to the relationship of the four ex-soldiers of a common army unit seem to provide the feeble external link between the four separate threads; these threads have yet a strange inner unity in that the characters in them are all representative persons and groups of persons among the workers and the capitalists engaged in the fierce class struggle under the regime of the Labour Government, the "betrayers" of the working class.

"Rising Tide", the second of the "Novels of the British Way", is in a way a continuation of one of the four major threads in "Betrayed Spring", the first novel of the series, for it deals with the London dockers and with two major characters both of whom have already appeared in the earlier novel, Jeff Burrows the docker and Phil Tremaine the daughter of a docker. The major event in "Rising Tide" is the big strike of the London dockers in the summer of 1949 in support of the Canadian seamen's strike which is traced from before the strike down to the end of it. This novel contains successful portrayals of the two major figures Jeff and Phil who are described as very inexperienced at the beginning of the novel but who grow steadily as the strike goes on and the struggle deepens and who become well-steeled fighters in the conflict, able to engage in battle themselves and also to help others join in the fight.

SECTION VII   LITERARY CRITICISM IN
ENGLAND: 1920—1940

a. A General View

Literary criticism in Europe began with the theory of literature and art as works of imitation of nature, as preached by Plato and by Aristotle, with differences, in ancient Greece and persisting through the ancient Romans down to the Neo-Classicists in Western Europe in the 18th century, but as early as the time of Horace and then the age of Sir Philip Sidney, the theory of literature as aiming to please (or delight) and to teach (or instruct) became the dominant trend, with minor disputes over whether to please in order to teach or merely, chiefly to delight. With the arrival of the romanticism in Europe in the late 18th and early 19th century, the importance of self-expression for the poets and the emphasis on the spontaneity of feelings replaced largely the theory of imitation of nature or of delighting in order to instruct, though Shelley and Keats in their critical utterances still advocated the high teaching mission of poets. In the later stage of the 19th century there was on the one hand Matthew Arnold insisting on the "high seriousness" of poetry, while on the other there emerged a group of aesthetes including Pater and Wilde who advocated strongly art for art's sake.

In England in the 20th century, many important writers in the other genres than literary criticism, such as Yeats and T. S. Eliot in poetry and Virginia Woolf and D. H. Lawrence in prose fiction, as well as professional critics such as I. A. Richards, F. R. Leavis and poet-critic William Empson, expressed their divergent views on literary criticism. Yeats, who was chiefly celebrated as a poet and a playwright, nevertheless fell under the influence of the French symbolists through Arthur Symons in the 1890s and then of the early experiments of T. S. Eliot and Ezra Pound, and he voiced his approval of aestheticism and symbolism and illustrated it in his own verse. T. S. Eliot, while emphasizing the consideration of all literature as indivisible from the literary tradition of his own country and of all the other related countries, yet insisted that "Honest criticism and sensitive appreciation are directed not upon the poet but upon the poetry", without forgetting "the importance of the relation of the poem to other poems by other authors, "or" the relation of the poem to its author". And some of these ideas of Eliot's led, through such other critics as Richards and Empson, eventually to the school of New Criticism that prevailed especially in the United States in the middle decades of the present century. Related to T. S. Eliot were the critical views of Ezra Pound and his associates T. E. Hulme (1883—1917) and F. S. Flint, which voiced the ideas of the poetic movement known as Imagism around 1910.

Pound as the most active founder of Imagism wrote later in an essay entitled "A Retrospect" (from "The Literary Essays of Ezra Pound", 1954) recalled the origin of the movement and explained its meaning: "In the spring or early summer of 1912, H.D., Richard Aldington and myself ... agreed upon the three following principles: 1. Direct treatment of the 'thing' whether subjective or objective. 2. To use absolutely no word that does not contribute to the presentation. 3. As regarding rhythm: to compare in the sequence of the musical phrase, not in the sequence of a metronome." Then he called attention to the fact: "The first use of the word 'Imagiste' was in my note to T.E. Hulme's five poems, printed at the end of my 'Ripostes' in the autumn of 1912," and he further explained: "An 'Image' is that which presents an intellectual and emotional complex in an instant of time." And after "A few dont's", and his brief discussion on European poets from Dante and Shakespeare to Swinburne and Yeats and "vers libre", Pound finally wound up by saying: "Only emotion endures". But T.E. Hulme who died in World War I in 1917 became an almost legendary figure after his death as the key thinker of Imagism in England with his important influence upon T.S. Eliot as well as Ezra Pound. His essay "Romanticism and Classicism" (probably written in 1913 or 1914 and collected in a volume of his essays entitled "Speculations" in 1924) has sometimes been considered almost as a sort of manifesto for Imagism. He first declared that "after a hundred years of romanticism, we are in for a classical revival" and that "the particular weapon of this new classical spirit, when it works in verse, will be fancy," and then after a lengthy discussion on the distinctions and also contrasts between romanticism and classicism, he came to certain very definite notions: that "beauty may be in small dry things", that "the great aim is accurate, precise and definite description", that "a period of dry, hard, classical verse is coming", that "the particular verse we are going to get will be cheerful, dry, and sophisticated", that "plain speech is essentially inaccurate" and that "it is only by new metaphors, that is, by fancy, that it can be made precise".

In the early decades of the present century the confrontation of Virginia Woolf (and E. M. Forster) and D. H. Lawrence with the old novelists of an older tradition including Arnold Bennett, H. G. Wells and John Galsworthy was another striking event in the field of literary criticism. Bennett, Wells and Galsworthy in their different ways followed the traditional ways of fiction-writing of the 19th century, and Mrs. Woolf attacked them by accusing them of being "materialists". Whether or how far that epithet fitted them is much less important than the fact that here the writer of a new school of novelists showed her dissatisfaction and even disgust with the by then already somewhat outdated emphasis on meticulous, naturalistic descriptions of external details of life, to the neglect of "the innermost flame which flashes its messages through the brain" (Woolf's words). She considered Bennett, Wells and Galsworthy as "materialists" who "write of unimportant things" and "spend immense skill and immense industry making the trivial and the transitory appear the true and the enduring" while she praised James Joyce as "spiritual" and eulogized Conrad and Hardy and Tchekov. On the other hand, the traditional theories of literary criticism were attacked by D. H. Lawrence, himself a novelist of no small influence. Lawrence declared in his essay on John Galsworthy,

> "Literary criticism can be no more than a reasoned account of the feeling produced upon the critic by the book he is criticizing. Criticism can never be a science: it is, in the first place, much too personal, and in the second, it is concerned with values which science ignores. The touchstone is emotion, not reason. We judge a work by its effect on our sincere and vital emotion, and nothing else."

Besides this stress on emotion, Lawrence placed his emphasis on morality and the relationship between one human being and another as the important contents of a novel. In his essay "Morality and the Novel" he first pointed out, "The business of art is to reveal the relation between man and his circumambient universe, at the living moment," then he added: "And morality is that delicate, for ever trembling and changing *balance* between me and my circumambient universe, which precedes and accompanies a true relatedness", and finally he wound up by declaring: "The great relationship, for humanity, will always be the relation between man and woman," "and the relation between man and woman will change for ever, and will for ever be the new central clue to human life." Of course, this last is certainly a somewhat biassed view, one typical of D.H. Lawrence and is supported by his novels.

E.M. Forster as a minor novelist and a minor critic made his contributions to literary criticism chiefly in his informal book on the art of the novel: "Aspects of the Novel" (1927). He belongs to the quie conversational type of English criticism with its stress on the illumination of rather commonsense utterances such as the distinction between flat and round characters in fiction and the demarcation line between story and plot in a novel, etc. Especially interesting is his attempt to negate the importance of the use of a certain effective narrative method in fiction-writing when he says: "For me the whole question of method resolves itself not into formulae but into the power of the writer to bounce the reader into accepting what he says."

Finally, it is essential to touch on literary criticism in 20th-century England that was based more or less on Marxist principles of dialectic materialism and historical materialism. The two outstanding critics of this group, Christopher Caudwell and Ralph Fox, both of whom flourished in the 1930s, will be dealt with separately. A general survey of Marxist literary criticism and of its minor critics will be briefly given here.

Marxist literary criticism in Britain may be said to originate with the establishment of the Communist Party of Great Britain in 1921 and the founding of the periodicals "Labour Monthly" (1921) and "The Workers' Weekly" (1923) which later became the "Daily Worker" in 1930. Then "Modern Quarterly" appeared in 1938 which in the course of time was renamed "Marxist Quarterly" and "Marxism Today". Besides, in 1933 was started the revolutionary magazine "Storm" but it was short-lived, and in 1934 was launched the "Left Review" of which Ralph Fox was an editor and T. A. Jackson, Alick West, Sommerfield, Jack Lindsay, Montagu Slader, Edgell Rickwood, Naomi Mitchison were among the contributors. In the 1930s, important works of Marxist literary criticism were written by Ralph Fox in his "The Novel and the People" (1937) and by Christopher Caudwell in his "Illusion and Reality" (1937), also by O'Casey in his "The Flying Wasp" (1937) and by T.A. Jackson (1873—1955) in his "Charles Dickens: The Progress of a Radical" (1937).

Alec West's "Crisis and Criticism" (1937) was written to engage in battle with the critical theories of such critics as T. S. Eliot and I.

A. Richards. West tried to represent the true significance of literary heritage of great classical writers, and, objecting to the tendency of the day to consider art as mystical indications of the artist, he emphasized the importance of making literature truly reflect social reality and struggle for the establishment of a socialist society.

O'Casey in his "The Flying Wasp" (1937) attacked the British theatre of the day and criticized severely the contemporary English drama which had no serious thought content but merely tried to please the audience with theatrical tricks. He suggested the restoration and development of good classical traditions of European drama and particularly spoke in behalf of Shakespeare against certain modern critics who tried to misinterpret Shakespeare. O'Casey's "The Green Crow" (1956) criticized the tendency of many contemporary writers to indulge in sheer subjectivity and separate themselves from social reality. O'Casey pointed out that writers should enter into the life of the people and listen to everything, observe everything and then think about everything. He praised Shaw for his great contributions to English drama in dealing always with burning questions of the day and he called on the writers to create heroic characters out of members of the working class.

T. A. Jackson in his "Charles Dickens: The Progress of a Radical" battled against certain critics' distorted evaluation of Dickens. He considered Dickens a courageous critic of Victorian society as against the view of Dickens as a singer and eulogizer of Victorian England or as an old-fashioned and hopelessly sentimental writer. In the book Jackson made a thorough study of the great 19th-century novelist, first tracing the general development of the writer and his views on social problems together with his historical background and then discussing the novels separately and in detail and finally coming to an analysis of Dickens' outlook as a whole. He particularly emphasized the great novels of the later period of Dickens' literary career, such as "Bleak House", "Hard Times", "Little Dorrit", "A Tale of Two Cities", "Great Expectations" and "Our Mutual Friends", works which delved more deeply into the social conflicts of the day and which have therefore been attacked and neglected by not a few critics since the novelist's time. In the critical comments on certain of the novels Jackson may have uttered rather debatable things, but on the whole the book is a powerful answer to the biassed criticism with regard to Dickens.

After the flowering of Marxist literary criticism in the late 1930s and a comparative lull in the war years, critics like West and Jackson and Lindsay and O'Casey wrote more and maturer critical works after the end of the Second World War. T. A. Jackson collected his essays on great English writers of the past and their works that had appeared separately in the London "Daily Worker", and published them in book form in 1950 under the title of "Old Friends to Keep". The essays are not long and are written in simple language and with very plain comments, but they are useful in reintroducing to the general reading public the glorious tradition of progressive literature of the past centuries from Bunyan and Defoe and Swift down to the 19th century writers like Thackeray and Charlotte Brontë. Jack Lindsay continued his essay on "John Bunyan" written in the 1930s by writing "After the 'Thirties', The Novel in Britain and Its Future" (1956), in which he tried to make a thorough and comprehensive study of the English fiction of the 20th century from where Ralph Fox had left off in "The Novel and the People" to the 1950s. Lindsay has also written two other critical works, "Charles Dickens" and "George Meredith". Alick West had exchanged blows with T.S. Eliot in the 1950s when he in an essay entitled "Abuse of Poetry and Abuse of Criticism" sharply criticized the latter for attempting to lead the reading public away from objective reality and away from reason. In the postwar years West has written more critical works, including his scintillating book on G.B. Shaw, "A Good Man Fallen Among Fabians" (1950), in which he tried to give a Marxist evaluation of the great Irish dramatist in answer to distorted interpretations of the Fabian writer by some critics. Though sometimes in the book West enters into abstractions from which it is difficult to emerge, this critical essay is generally sound in emphasizing Shaw's role in attacking ruthlessly the capitalist society and in advocating socialism though it is Fabian socialism most of the time. In 1958 West wrote another critical work, "Mountains in the Sunlight".

Among the other outstanding critical works based on the principles of Marxism that have appeared since the Second World War are George Thompson's "Marxism and Poetry" (1940) and Arnold Kettle's "An Introduction to the English Novels" (in two volumes, 1951—1953). The latter work is particularly significant as a comprehensive study of the major novelists and their major novels from the 18th century down to the present day, a much more ambitious task than Jackson's "Old Friends to Keep" and Ralph Fox's "The Novel and the People" because here detailed examinations of the great novels with Marxist literary principles are attempted. Although Kettle seems in some cases (as in that of Jane Austen) to be still too much under the influence of the literary criticism of the past century to be able to free himself entirely from traditional bias, he has succeeded generally in employing the method of historical materialism in his analysis, ever emphasizing the social background of the novelist and the novel and examining each writer and each work of fiction from the class viewpoint.

b. I. A. Richards

The really prominent literary critics of early 20th-century England who were just critics and not at the same time poets or novelists are I. A. Richards and F. R. Leavis.

Ivor Armstrong Richards (1893—1981), educated at Cambridge, held teaching appointments there and, then in China at Beijing and later for many years at Harvard. His chief books on criticism are "The Principles of Literary Criticism" (1924), "Science and Poetry" (1926) and "Practical Criticism" (1929) which made him a distinguished figure in 20th-century criticism in England. Then, together with C. K. Ogden, he started a new system of "Basic English" which was supposed to be a much simplified English language with a vocabulary of only 850 words, and textbooks were written and used in experiments for a number of years in different parts of the world. However, his three critical works written in the 1920s have had their lasting influence upon later English and American critics, particularly those known under the appellation of New Criticism.

In a way Richards' critical theory stemmed from the classical critical dogmas of Matthew Arnold, with his emphasis on the "values" recorded in the arts which is comparable to "the high seriousness" of Arnoldian claim for literature. Of course Richards as a 20th-century intellectual added to his "values" the importance of "communication" for the artist, so he says, in "The Principles of Literary Criticism": "The two pillars upon which a theory of criticism must rest are an account of value and an account of communication." But he adds that "the artist is not as a rule consciously concerned with communication, but with getting the work ... right, apparently regardless of its communicative efficacy", and so "to make the work 'embody', accord with, and represent the precise experience upon which its value depends is his major preoccupation." He even admits: "Much that goes to produce a poem is, of course, unconscious. Very likely the unconscious processes are more important than the conscious," and besides, "nearly all speculations as to what went on in the artist's mind are unverifiable, even more unverifiable than the similar speculations as to the dreamer's mind." Then Richards affirms above everything else the importance of the values latent in the arts: "The arts are our storehouse of recorded values. ... Both in the genesis of a work of art, in one creative moment, and in its aspect as a vehicle of communication, reasons can be found for giving to the arts a very important place in the theory of experience. ... But subtle or recondite experiences are for most men incommunicable and indescribable. ... In the arts we find the record in the only form in which these things can be recorded of the experiences which have seemed worth having to the most sensitive and discriminating persons .... The arts, if rightly approached, supply the best data available for deciding what experiences are more valuable than others." These ideas are hardly disputable, the only question that remains seems to be what these "values" really mean and what they actually stand for — and in this sense it may be equated with the similarly ambiguous call for "high seriousness" of the old Arnoldian logic.

Richards distinguishes "the scientific use of language" from "the emotive use of language", and that "for emotive purposes logical arrangement is not necessary". He then points out "the chief uses of the word 'Truth' in Criticism": (1) "the scientific sense" which "is one very little involved by any of the arts", and (2) "the most usual other sense"'is that of acceptability ("internal acceptibility" or" 'convincingness'"), "in this sense ... 'Truth' is equivalent to 'internal necessity' or rightness", and Richards tries to illustrate this with his interpretation or explanation of Keats' highly ambiguous dictum of "Beauty is Truth, and truth beauty", by paraphrasing it as "'What the Imagination seizes as Beauty must be Truth,' said Keats." And finally Truth in a third sense is given by Richards: "Truth may be equivalent to Sincerity".

Richards as a teacher at Cambridge in the 1920s regularly asked his students to comment freely on the short, unidentified poems distributed to them and then lectured on the poems and on the students' written comments, and the documentation of this experiment of his was largely responsible for his book "Practical Criticism", in which he tried to delve to the very bottom pit of literary criticism by trying to explain how to find out the meaning of a book or a poem one is to comment on. So he points out first the difficulties in reading any poem:

> "The *original* difficulty of all reading, the problem of *making out the meaning,* is our obvious starting-point. The answers to those apparently simple questions: 'What is a meaning?' 'What are we doing when we endeavour to make it out?' 'What is it we are making out?' are the master-keys to all the problems of criticism."

He goes on to explain: "The all-important fact for the study of literature — or any other mode of communication — is that there are several kinds of meaning. ... The Total Meaning we are engaged with is, almost always, a blend, a combination of several contributory meanings of different types. Language — and pre-eminently language as it is used in poetry — has not one but several tasks to perform simultaneously." Then he proceeds to suggest his "division into four types of function, four kinds of meaning" for any poem or other literary work. He calls them (1) Sense (something said by the author), (2) Feeling (the author's feelings towards the something said), (3) Tone (the author's attitude to his listener) and (4) Intention (the author's intention or aim, conscious or unconscious). Whether "meaning" should be divided into those four kinds or in some other way is much less important than Richards' insistence on the ambiguity of meaning for any work of art, than the unmistakable suggestions arising therefrom that "the total meaning" of a work of art is frequently extremely complex and therefore allows of various interpretations by various readers or listeners, that this complexity of meaning yet allows of analysis and ought to be analyzed in some way or other, and that the comprehension of the meaning in any artistic work is the first and fundamental requirement for any attempt at criticism that is at all of any value. Thus these ideas of Richards' lead very naturally to such an influential work of criticism as "Seven Types of Ambiguity" (1930) by William Empson and eventually to the close analysis of poetry and the objective, formalistic principles and methods used by the American New Critics including such prominent figures as Cleanth Brooks, John Crowe Ransom, Allan Tate and Robert Penn Warren.

c. F. R. Leavis

Frank Raymond Leavis (1895—1978), born in Cambridge, and educated at Cambridge University, was a don there almost all the time until his retirement. Another important activity of his was the founding and editing in Cambridge of the quarterly critical review entitled "Scrutiny" from 1932 to 1953, to be followed by the reprint of all the papers therein in twenty volumes in 1963, with the author's essay affixed to them, "A Retrospect." His fame as a critic grew with the years after the beginning of his career at Cambridge in the 1930s and vied with that of I.A. Richards. However, he did little of theorizing on literary criticism, but spent most of his energy, aside from teaching, on the careful examination of writers and their works. He re-evaluated the English poetic tradition in "New Bearings in English Poetry" (1930) and "Reevaluation: Tradition and Development in English Poetry" (1936). He was much under the influence of T. S. Eliot and set the modern order of precedence in the historical tradition of English poetry from Shakespeare and the Metaphysical Poets down to Pope, Blake, Hopkins and Eliot. He was better known for his historical treatment of English prose fiction in "The Great Tradition" (1948), in which he applied his practice of close textual analysis beyond the domain of poetry into the field of fiction. In this respect he was following the ways of I.A. Richards and William Empson. But he specially admired D.H.Lawrence whose novels as well as critical concepts he both exalted ("D. H. Lawrence", 1930; "D. H. Lawrence: Novelist", 1955). From Eliot and from Lawrence he derived his élitism in literary criticism, preaching intellectual aristocracy against popular taste. Even in his early book "Mass Civilization and Minority Culture" (1930) he declared that "culture has always been in minority keeping", and throughout his career he maintained his "necessary attitude of intransigence" not only toward the middlebrow intellectuals and the Establishment of the mind as represented by the Sunday papers, the British Council, the "Guardian", the "Times Literary Supplement", the Third Programme "intellectuals", and the *entourage* of the "New Statesman", but also the flair for showmanship among the academies, the coterie culture among the English literary societies and artistic circles and the whole alliance of brisk vulgarization between even the universities and the world of press, magazine and radio. Not infrequently he went to the far extreme, and made enemies for himself with the multitude of intellectuals even, not to say with the common reader. His dream of "a live, humane social order" led him to overmuch fondness for and clinging to the past and to his disgust for most aspects of modern life including its technological advances, and accounted for his provincial neglect of foreign literature and his impatience for the wide, subtle plurality of modern multi-national culture. His attack on C. P. Snow in his

Richmond Lecture, "Two Cultures? The Significance of C. P. Snow" (Cambridge, 1962), which was aimed at Snow's Rede Lecture of 1959: "The Two Cultures and the Scientific Revolution" and which led to much controversy and public discussion, showed very clearly both Leavis' puritannical defence of what he considered to be élitist culture and his overmuch disgust with modern development in popular culture in the wake of scientific progress.

Leavis in his long years in Cambridge helped to set the tone for literary preferences from the 1930s down to the 1960s, and in his critical comments on the big writers of the past, whether on poets like Pope and Dryden, Blake and Hopkins and T.S. Eliot or on novelists like Jane Austen and George Eliot, Henry James and Conrad and Lawrence, there are many gems of mature judgment. Of course Leavis went too far to consider Lawrence as the "greatest English writer of the twentieth century" and to defend Lawrence against almost any defect in "Women in Love", and just as he idolized Lawrence, he failed to see the achievements of such outstanding writers as Joyce and Melville. Some of Leavis' critical dictums on certain English poets and novelists have now been accepted as commonplaces, and his contribution to the moulding of public opinion in that direction cannot be overlooked.

d. Christopher Caudwell

Christopher Caudwell, pseudonym of Christopher St. John Sprigg(1907—1937), was an eminent English literary critic in the 1930s. Born in Putney, he was educated at the Benedictine School at Ealing, left school at sixteen and a half and worked for three years as a reporter on the "Yorkshire Observer". Then he returned to London and joined a firm of aeronautical publishers, first as editor and later as a director. He invented an infinitely variable gear, the designs for which were published in the "Automobile Engineer" and attracted a good deal of attention from experts. Before he was 25, he published five textbooks on aeronautics, seven detective novels, and some poems and short stories, all under his own real name. In 1935 under the pen name of Christopher Caudwell, he published his first serious novel, "This My Hand". At the end of 1934 he had come across some of the Marxist classics and in the summer of 1935 he became immersed in the works of Marx, Engels and Lenin. Shortly after that, he finished the first draft of his chief critical work, "Illusion and Reality". Then in December that year he took lodgings in Poplar and later joined the Poplar Branch of the Communist Party. A few months later, he went to Paris to get a first-hand experience of the Popular Front and he came back to England with renewed energy and enthusiasm. He re-wrote "Illusion and Reality", completed the essays published subsequently as "Studies in a Dying Culture", and began "The Crisis in Physics". He also was busy in the Party activities speaking at open-air meetings and selling the "Daily Worker". The Civil War had broken out in Spain, and the Poplar Branch threw itself into the campaign, with Gaudwell as one of the leading spirits. By November of 1936 they had raised enough money to buy an ambulance, and Caudwell was chosen to drive it across France to Spain. After handing it over to the Spanish Covernment, he joined, as did also Ralph Fox, the International Br igade, and, again like Fox, he was killed in action in 1937. "Illusion and Reality", which had been in the press when he left for Spain, was published shortly after his death, in 1937. "Poems" and "The Crisis in Physics" came out in 1939, and "Further Studies in a Dying Culture" appeared in 1949.

"Illusion and Reality: A Study of the Sources of Poetry" contains an Introduction and 12 chapters which may be grouped into four major parts: (1) the discussion of poetry in general, beginning from the earliest origins of it to its modern period (Chapters 1, 2 & 3), (2) a discussion of modern English poetry, from the Renaissance to the 20th century (Chapter 4, 5, & 6), (3) an examination into the elements that make up poetry, including a critical examination of psychoanalysis of Freud and his followers Jung and Adler, a study of the language used in poetry and of the psychical self of the poet, and the relation of poetry to other related arts (Chapters 7, 8, 9, 10 & 11), and (4) a forward look at the future of poetry (Chapter 12).

In the Introduction to the book, Caudwell declares his use of the method of historical materialism. He goes back to the primitive society for the birth of poetry when poetry was "heightened languages" and "characteristically song" and "combined with dance, titual, and music, becomes the great switchboard of the instinctive energy of the tribe". Then after the death of mythology he comes to the development of modern poetry which is capitalist poetry. He says the bourgeoisie has the illusion of freedom which is reflected in bourgeois poetry. He points out:"Capitalist economy ... is the economy of a sham individualism and a hollow freedom for the majority .... Seen from the viewpoint of the bourgeois, bourgeois society is a free society where freedom is due to its individualism, to its completely free market and its absence of direct social relations, of which absence the free market is the cause and expression. But to the rest of society bourgeois society is a coercive society whose individualism and free market is the method of coercion."

Then Caudwell relates the different stages of the bourgeois illusion of freedom: "The working out of the truth (the growth and increasing prosperity of capitalism), next as a gradually revealed lie (the decline and final crisis of capitalism) and finally as its passage into its opposite, freedom as the life-won consciousness of social necessity (the proletarian revolution), is a colossal movement of men, materials emotions and ideas, it is a whole history of toiling, learning, suffering and boring men."

Next, Caudwell discusses the historical development of English poetry from the period of primitive accumulation down to the 20th century,and he divides English into different historical periods:"Primitive Accumulation, 1550—1600; The Transition, 1600—1625; The Bourgeois Revolt, 1625—1650; The Counter-Puritan Reaction, 1650—1688; The Era of Mercantilism, and Manufacture, 1688—1750; The Industrial Revolution and the 'Anti-Jacobin' Reaction, 1750—1825; The Decline of British Capitalism, 1825—1900; The Epoch of Imperialism, 1900—1930; The Final Capitalistic Crisis 1930—''

In the last chapter of the book, "The Future of Poetry", Caudwell refers to three Oxford poets C. Day Lewis, Stephen Spender and W. H. Auden as belonging to the group of bourgeois writers seeking for alliance with the proletariat.

In "Illusion and Reality" Caudwell exposes the bourgeois lie about freedom in the bourgeois society and therefore also freedom for bourgeois art and poetry. He tries to examine the development of English poetry with the principles of historical materialism and succeeds in making some excellent comments on some of the English poets, especially Milton and Pope and certain minor poets of the 17th century.

In the first of his two volumes of "Studies in a Dying Culture", Caudwell discusses two outstanding British authors, G.B. Shaw and H. G. Wells, admitting the contributions of Shaw and Wells but exposing Shaw's Fabianism and his idealistic "life-force" theory and Wells' utopian socialism. He explains the exact position of the great Irish dramatist: "His knowledge of Marx enabled him to attack destructively all bourgeois institutions. But he was never able to solve the problem of 'tainted money' that comes up in his work repeatedly — in 'Widowers' Houses', 'Major Barbara', 'Mrs. Warren's Profession'." — With Shaw "always it is patched up. He seems to suggest that we must accept things as they are until the system is changed. But no immediate steps besides talking are ever to be taken to change the system."

In Caudwell's essay on T. E. Lawrence, after shattering the myth of the heroism of Lawrence in helping the Arabs free themselves from Turkish rule during the First World War, the author makes a significant reference to the rise of the Red Army and of the Communist Party of China.

"In China, too, a race of simple and peasant people, of millions captive to poverty and insolence have been stirred to action by the name of liberty. It is not a story of one hero, but of an army of heroes, performing exploits believed impossible, not aided by bourgeois gold, but repelling again and again attacks financed by bourgeois gold, armed by bourgeois powers, and directed by bourgeois experts. This national rising led by the Red Army of China, and growing constantly in life and influence, is also inspired by the name of liberty, but it is not bourgeois liberty. Bourgeois liberty in the shape of Japanese imperialism, British banking, and American trade, united with the bourgeois Kuomintang Government to crush it. The Red Army is a Communist Army, and wherever it moves it established village soviets. Its leaders and its rank and file have read the words of Marx, Lenin and Stalin …. Chinese nationalism, baffled and outraged for so long, finds its last ardent victorious issue in Communism." That this prediction of Caudwell's written in the middle 1930s, even before the beginning of the Sino-Japanese War of 1937—1945, could have spoken with so much assurance of the "last ardent victorious issue of Communism" in China, not so much shows his keen foresight as reveals his deep-rooted enthusiasm and confidence in the cause of socialism and communism everywhere in the world.

"Further Studies in a Dying Culture" is less important than either "Illusion and Reality" or "Studies in a Dying Culture". However, in one of the five essays in the collection in his "Study in Bourgeois History", Caudwell closely followed the Marxist theory of historical materialism and spoke of all humanity as the creators of history: "Marx was the first who was able to show that history was really made by men — not by man in the abstract as a developing animal, not by outstanding men as sporadic forces, but constantly by the whole group of individuals existing in society." Then, in another essay, in his "Study in Bourgeois Religion", Caudwell made commentaries on Marx's comments on religion and traced the development of religion from the primitive society down to the present day, emphasizing the relation of religion to class struggle in different historical epochs. Especially interesting is the reference to imperialism and fascism as the final development of religion in the 20th century, after a review of all the primitive religions in all six continents through all the forms of Christianity. This new religion of bourgeois decadence is imperialism, the patriotism of the monopoly stage of capitalism, Caudwell writes, "This Sham patriotism, born during the jingo period of British Imperialism and in the Prussian State, reached a new height during the 1914—18 War, and has received its final expression in Fascism." Here the author tries to point out how religion has been used by the ruling classes as a weapon against the oppressed and exploited people.

e. Ralph Fox

Ralph Fox (1900—1937) was born of a well-to-do family in Halifax, Yorkshire, and was educated at Oxford University. He made his first visit to the Soviet Union in 1920 and as early as in 1921—1922, when he was still a college student, he was already connected with the magazine "Plebs" established by the left-wing socialists of the day and wrote for it. In 1925 he joined the Communist Party of Great Britain and started his activities as party worker, journalist and literary critic, contributing to "Daily Worker", "Weekly Worker", "The Communist Review" and "Labour Monthly" articles on the burning questions in British politics and literary life. In the late 1920s he came to China and took part in the revolutionary movement of our people. Then he went to the Soviet Union again and spent a few years in Moscow, working in the Institute of Marx-Engels-Lenin there and writing a number of theoretical and journalistic works, including a biography of Lenin ("Lenin: A Biography," 1933), which gives a vivid account of the history of revolutionary struggle of the Bolshevik Party. His trips to Mongolia, to the Volga River region and Central Asia in the Soviet Union, and to Portugal were responsible for the writing of "Genghis Khan" (1936), "Storming Heaven" (1928), a novel "People of the Steppes" (1925), and "Portugal Now" (1937). As a political theorist, Fox made several contributions to the study of contemporary world politics: "The Colonial Policy of British Imperialism" (1933), "Marx and Engels on the Irish Question" (1933), "The Class Struggle in Britain in the Epoch of Imperialism" (two volumes, 1934), "Communism and Changing Civilization" (1935) and "France Faces the Future" (1926). As a literary critic, Fox wrote an important article on an historical novel by a Flemish writer Charles de Coster, "Tyl Ulenspiegel: Legend of Revolt" (1928), another on the

French writer Henri Barbusse (1935), a speech on Maxim Gorky (at a memorial meeting in honour of Gorky in London, June, 1936), and his most important critical work "The Novel and the People" (1937). A versatile writer, Fox also wrote a romantic comedy in three acts, "Captain Youth" (1922). Toward the end of 1936, many progressive intellectuals all over the world went to Spain to fight against the fascist troops under Franco. Fox also went there. He fought in the Anglo-Irish battalion of the International Brigade and died in action in January, 1937.

While Fox wrote two noteworthy anti-fascist treatises "France Faces the Future" and "Portugal Now", he distinguished himself particularly in the field of literary criticism. In "Tyl Ulenspiegel: Legend of Revolt" he rapturously praised the war of liberation of the Flemish people against their Spanish oppressors in the early Renaissance and pointed out that great works of art always express the fullness of the people's life and that the genuine artist draws on the accumulated wisdom of his people, their creative effort and their indomitable will to uphold national independence and liberty. In his article on Henri Barbusse, Fox shows that the life and work of Barbusse, the great French writer and fighter, are inseparable from the life and work of his people. He points out that Barbusse fought for the resurrection of national traditions in art and directed his critical and theoretical writings against those who advocated the "art for art's sake" theory and disparaged the Classics, and that the French writer's activities in this field more intimately associated with his work as one of the inspirers and recognized leaders of antifascist intellectuals the world over.

The most ambitious book written by Fox is "The Novel and the People". This long "essay", as Fox called it, may be conveniently divided into three parts. In the Introduction (Section 1 of the 12 in the book) the writer first mentions the "limited aim" of the book, "to examine the present position of the English novel and to see what is its future" and then he proceeds to discuss the decay of the novel in England, in early 20th century, and to combat the view that Marxism, because it is a 'materialist' philosophy, is hostile to artistic expression. Then, in Sections 2 and 3, Fox refutes the protest of the literary journalist of the day that "materialism and imagination cannot go to bed together", by saying that "all imaginative creation is a reflection of the real world in which the creator lives". He retorts to the distorted view that Marxism considers works of art as "merely a reflection of economic needs and economic processes", and he explains how according to Marxism the characters in the novels are not just social types who represent different classes or social stations in life but they also have personal characteristics distinguishing them from one another.

The second part of the work (Sections 4 to 8) deals with Fox's brief review of the historical development of the English and also the European novel. He traces the early germ of the novel in Chaucer and Boccaccio and Malory and Lyly's "Euphues" and Sidney's "Arcadia" to "the real founders, Rabelais and Cervantes, then to Defoe, Fielding, Smollett, Richardson and Sterne, and also Rousseau in the 18th century, next to Scott, Jane Austen and Dickens, Thackeray, the Brontë sisters, Hardy and Butler in 19th-century England, and to Balzac, Flaubert and the Goncourt brothers in 19th-century France, and finally to the 20th-century novelists, D. H. Lawrence, H. G. Wells, Aldous Huxley, and James Joyce in England and Marcel Proust in France, under the influence of Nietzsche and Bergson and Freud and Spengler. His theory here that novel rises with the rise of capitalism and declines with the decline of capitalism is a highly controversial one that leads naturally to the over-high praise of the 17th and 18th century novelists as compared with the giants of the Victorian age, and to the need of literature today to restore its great tradition of Cervantes and Rabelais.

The third and last part of "The Novel and the People" (Sections 9 to 12) deals with the author's view of the future of the novel. He gives as excellent examples of well-portrayed revolutionary heroes Zachariah Coleman, Mark Rutherford's printer hero of the "Revolution in Tanner's Lane", and Tyl Ulenspiegel the Flemish beggar hero in the Flemish writer Charles de Coster's historical novel "Tyl Ulenspiegel: Legend of Revolt", and suggested as the possible choice for a revolutionary novel of today the figure of the Bulgarian Communist Dimitrov who courageously fought and frustrated the German Nazi plot of the Reichstag fire engineered in the interests of the Hitlerite fascists. In the final sections of the treatise Fox turns to the language employed and to the fullest use of national cultural heritage. He says, "The revolutionary both accepts all that is vital and hopeful in the heritage of the past, and rejects nothing in the present which can be used to build the future."

Though there are defects and disputable points in "The Novel and the People", the book gives a comprehensive review of the historical development of English and European prose fiction.